POLICY FORMULATION
AND ADMINISTRATION

POLICY FORMULATION

AND ADMINISTRATION

A Casebook of

Top-Management Problems

in Business

By GEORGE ALBERT SMITH, Jr., A.B., D.C.S.

PROFESSOR OF BUSINESS ADMINISTRATION

GRADUATE SCHOOL OF BUSINESS ADMINISTRATION

HARVARD UNIVERSITY

and C. ROLAND CHRISTENSEN, A.B., D.C.S.

PROFESSOR OF BUSINESS ADMINISTRATION

GRADUATE SCHOOL OF BUSINESS ADMINISTRATION

HARVARD UNIVERSITY

FOURTH EDITION

1962

RICHARD D. IRWIN, INC.
HOMEWOOD, ILLINOIS

FOURTH EDITION
First Printing, August, 1962
Second Printing, September, 1963
Third Printing, June, 1964
Fourth Printing, June, 1965
Fifth Printing, May, 1966

Library of Congress Catalogue No. 62–18177

Acknowledgments

THIS NEW EDITION of *Policy Formulation and Administration* is being brought out because of the continued growth and evident interest in the use of the earlier editions; also because of some changes and additions in both concepts and materials which we consider to be desirable. We do not, however, feel that the basic processes of formulating or administering policy have "changed" since the last edition. Nor do we believe we have discovered any radically new improved method of training students to be or to become willing, wise, responsible decision makers, or effective leaders of firms, or departments of firms. Consequently, the pedagogical presumptions of this edition differ somewhat, but not greatly, from those in the predecessor editions.

We feel deeply indebted to the users of the earlier versions who have sent us helpful suggestions, and have given us encouragement in other ways. We could not, of course, incorporate them all, but they have had a considerable influence on our planning of this new volume.

Many colleagues—past and present—have, over a long period of time, worked as members of the various teaching groups which year after year have offered Business Policy in the second year of the MBA program at the Harvard Business School. All these co-workers have made substantial contributions to the course, and to our thinking. It would not be possible to identify them all, so we are not attempting to. Nonetheless, we do acknowledge with genuine gratitude their stimulation and their help. Whatever any of them sees in this book as concepts or as modifications of concepts traceable to him, we hope he will regard it as a practical expression of our appreciation. We are particularly grateful to those currently connected with the course. Their support of the notion of getting out this new edition has encouraged us to produce it; and they have contributed many ideas, and some of the materials.

We ourselves wrote or directed the writing of many of the cases; and we have re-edited and sought to improve others. And still other cases included, as originally written or revised, represent the work of several of our present or former colleagues and assistants at Harvard. Of these, the following are still here: M. T. Gragg, W. D. Guth, E. A.

Helfert, P. R. Lawrence, E. P. Learned, D. C. D. Rogers, A. R. Saitow, and A. R. Towl. The others, now elsewhere, are: C. A. Anderson, J. F. Archer, J. Barker, G. S. Gamble, W. C. Green, E. R. Hanson, J. M. Kinard, E. L. Morris, J. Priedeman, D. R. Schoen, and D. Thain. If this list of names seems unduly long in relation to the total number of cases, its length results largely from the fact that, in some instances, two or three persons have at subsequent times revised cases already written by the original author. We have named them all, as each has made some contribution.

Deserving of our thanks, certainly, are Dean S. F. Teele and Associate Dean R. H. Hassler who have encouraged us and have given us time and organizational assistance to help with the work.

High on the list, also, of those to be thanked are the officers of the business firms who gave us their permission and their time to study their problems, their personalities, their outlooks, their methods of planning and operating, and the plans themselves. We also express our gratitude for their permission to write the cases, to use them ourselves, and to make them available to others. These contributions to business knowledge and to business education are of inestimable value.

We further thank the President and Fellows of Harvard College which hold the copyright on most of these teaching materials for their permission to publish them in this book. And we likewise thank the Director and the Trustees of the Management Development Institute of Lausanne, Switzerland, for its permission to include two cases written there.

For secretarial and editorial help, as well as for many valuable suggestions, we are deeply indebted to Mavis Hibbs Atamian, Mabel T. Gragg, and Priscilla Winslow. Their interest in this effort, which has been very high, has been matched by their efficiency, their patience with us, and their unflagging diligence.

GEORGE ALBERT SMITH, JR.
C. ROLAND CHRISTENSEN

Harvard University
May, 1962

Table of Contents

vii

Introduction

THIS NEW EDITION of *Policy Formulation and Administration* is made up of 35 cases selected from a large number presently or formerly used at the Harvard Graduate School of Business Administration and at the Management Development Institute of Lausanne, Switzerland. Most of these derive from a Harvard course known as Business Policy, which, for many years, has been a required subject for all second-year men in the school's two-year program leading to the degree of Master in Business Administration. Six are from a fairly new and closely related second-year elective course known as Business, Society, and the Individual.

In the first year of the Harvard two-year program as there are no elective courses, all students take the same subjects: Administrative Practices; Control; Finance; The Manager and the American Economy; Marketing; Production; and a special course in case analysis and report writing called Written Analysis of Cases.

This we mention because in the Harvard program, all students, before they begin the second year, have had similar training in fields covering the basic activities and functions of business. They have been introduced to the problems of administrators in business organizations: problems of leading, following, and otherwise participating in group action, of supervising other people, and of fitting their particular businesses into the needs of society. Moreover, since most of the first-year training has been carried on by study and classroom discussion of business cases, our second-year students have acquired considerable facility in dealing with specific business situations. They have had practice in discovering and analyzing problems and opportunities and in working out practical plans for dealing with the problems, in seeking to realize the opportunities they discover, and in assessing the risks that must be taken.

We point this out by way of explaining that, in collecting and writing the cases in this book for our own use, we acted on rather definite presumptions about the educational training and the state of development of the students who would use them. We believe it has been an

advantage to us in second-year teaching to have men whose training in
the first year has been fairly uniform, broad, and, we believe, realistic
in our kind of a society.

The Business Policy course at Harvard has been recentlv described in
the following words:

. . . It covers the fields of policy-making and administration, building upon
and integrating the work of the first year. The viewpoint is primarily at the
level of top management, where company-wide objectives are set and departmental policies and activities are coordinated.

The course emphasizes major specific functions of top management, such as
keeping alert and informed; sizing up the company's situation in the light of
general conditions, and of conditions within the company itself; determining
goals and objectives; in devising plans to achieve them; in organizing the administrative personnel to carry out the plans; guiding and maintaining the administrative organization; continually reappraising and, when necessary, altering
objectives, policies, and organization on the basis of new developments. Moreover, they must, all the while, keep in mind the goals, hopes, and expectations
of society, also the mission which our society—by tradition and by law, both
undergoing continual change—expects our business system to perform.

During the course the student deals with the problems of a large number
of companies in widely diversified industries. He thereby acquires an understanding of the nature of such problems and of the responsibilities of company
managements, including directors. He also develops his own ability to deal
realistically with matters involving policy formulation and requiring administrative skill.

One major objective of the course is to develop the habit of thinking from
this over-all point of view, in order that the student, both early and later in his
business career, and regardless of the management level in which he is located,
may guide his own and his department's activities in such a way as to make the
most effective contribution to the business as a whole, and, no less, to assure
himself that the firm is making a positive contribution to society.

The six cases in this volume in the section titled "The Business
Leader and Public Responsibility," from the related course, Business,
Society, and the Individual, are in form and purpose virtually the same
as the cases from the basic policy course. They differ only in that they
are somewhat more specialized, their emphasis being on the problems
of top management in working out conflicts of interests, and/or putting
into reasonable and workable focus the economic and the noneconomic
factors in managerial matters. The inclusion of a number of such cases
in the required policy course at Harvard is in prospect. Hence, another
reason for their inclusion in this book.

We also point out that this volume includes cases from international companies and/or involving international business problems. This is an innovation, and very much in keeping with the times.

It should be clear that these cases were not prepared for any early introductory course in business. Hence, they are best used by reasonably advanced persons, who, in school or in business educational programs, or by actual experience, have acquired considerable familiarity with the principal activities of business, with the methods and tools used by executives, and with the fundamental problems faced by all administrators responsible for taking action in our complex society.

Nonetheless, these and similar cases have been used successfully in other graduate and undergraduate programs by students with quite varied educational backgrounds. In such instances the cases have probably been most effective in courses for seniors and graduate students. Moreover, they have also been used with notable success in management programs for business executives at Harvard and other universities, as well as in in-company programs.

THE NATURE AND PURPOSE OF TOP MANAGEMENT CASES

Each of the cases presented in this book describes an actual company as of the time the case was written. To preserve confidences, fictitious names have been used in some instances, and sometimes the geographical locations have been changed. In no instance has the industry been altered. Almost always the case contains information about the industry and its competitive conditions; some historical background about the company itself; some financial and statistical data; information about the company's products, its production and marketing methods and facilities, its organization plan, and its executive personnel.

These cases are not like law school cases in either nature or purpose. A law school case is a court decision, usually a decision by an appellate court. Being an official judgment, the decision is a part of the law. It is to be learned and heeded as precedent.

Our cases present situations about which something is yet to be decided, or redecided. They more nearly resemble medical school cases—patients to be examined by advanced students under the watchful eye of the doctor-instructor. The student makes his examination, interprets the data into a diagnosis, prescribes treatment, and gives treatment. And he is left largely on his own, so long as the teaching doctor considers him to be on the right track.

In one sense, our cases are reports; in another sense, they are not. They *do* report facts, and in some instances they also report opinions of people within the companies. But they do *not* evaluate the facts or opinions; nor do they specifically state problems or necessarily suggest solutions. They are essentially raw materials for student use. Alone or in small groups, during preparation and later under the teacher's guidance in the classroom, students discover and analyze problems and opportunities and work out practical plans for dealing with them, as the officers of the firm do in the actual situation.

It should be emphasized that these cases are not intended to be "examples" and they should not be studied or taught as such. In no instance was a particular company selected because we believed it to be the "best" or the "worst" in its industry, nor because we thought it was "average" or "typical." Obviously, some of these firms had been well managed; others not so well. Some were in very good condition; others in critical condition. But, in each case, in the actual situation, the person or persons responsible for the particular venture were obliged to recognize and deal with the problems as they were. The problems may be desperate emergencies calling for drastic action. They may be basic policy decisions of long-range significance, even though not requiring emergency handling. Or they may be the somewhat less dramatic, but nonetheless important, problems of routine administration, keeping things going on an even keel from day to day.

It has been our experience and the experience of many other teachers that, by using cases such as these, a teacher and his students can together create "ways of thinking," "ways of feeling," and "ways of doing" which accelerate tremendously both intellectual growth and emotional development. The discussions of these cases, in the students' rooms and in the classroom, can be made to approximate to an amazing degree the kinds of discussions that the officers of the companies have in their own offices and committee rooms.

An important by-product of case study and discussion is the accumulation of much information about business affairs. The main, though more elusive, products, however, are: insight, intellectual power, judgment, imagination, practical common sense, leadership ability, responsibility, and self-confidence.

THE QUESTIONS OR PROBLEMS IN THE CASES AND THEIR SOLUTIONS

At the top level, an executive does not have any "all-wise" adviser to inform him what problem or problems he should be watching or working on at a particular time. That he must decide himself. And he has no reference book to look into, no infallible aid to give him *the* solution. He must, nevertheless, find *some* solution, some *workable* solution. This he does by the use of experience, the exercise of his judgment, usually after discussion and consultation with others. And neither before a decision is made, nor after, can he be absolutely sure he has taken the *right* action. For there is no *absolute right* in the area of important business decisions. There are, for the most part, only opinion and judgment.

The administrator must be willing and able to work in such a climate, which is often uncomfortable. He must accept the responsibility for reaching decisions on the basis of limited facts and in the face of many unknowns. Almost always, some of his associates or other parties involved will disagree with him. He should take their disagreement and their views into account. Finally, however, he himself must analyze, decide, plan, and act. His is the usually lonesome situation of the exerciser of ultimate responsibility. Moreover, he must work under time pressures and with less evidence than he would like to have. He must work with people who, like himself, are imperfect. He inevitably will make some mistakes. If he is experienced and mature, he will expect this, and will allow for it. But he will hope to reach wise decisions most of the time. If he does, he is a successful business leader.

This clearly suggests that the cases do not include any "official" or "demonstrably correct" answers. We do not have, nor do our associates have, "official" questions or "approved" solutions. It is part of the student's task as it is part of an executive's task to discover questions and to distinguish the important from the unimportant. In some instances, neither we nor our colleagues would agree exactly as to what "the most fundamental problems or opportunities" are; and in still more instances we do not agree on the "best possible course of action." If we did, we would question the reality of our cases and perhaps also the quality and integrity of our own views. Complicated business situations such as are presented here are episodes taken out of contemporary business life. Since we are all different people, we will (and should) attach to these problems at least somewhat differing interpretations and envision somewhat differing or substantially differing solutions or courses of action.

We, the authors, do have our own ideas about each of the cases we are offering; so do our associates. In some instances, we hold our views with strong conviction. In others, we are much less sure of what we think. And we change our views from time to time. So we certainly do not feel that we *know* what should be done in each of the situations presented.

Moreover, we hope that our fellow teachers who use these cases will not be disposed to force their views on their students. We think that as instructors, we all perform our function best if we train the student to make independent decisions and to develop and defend his own views. Therefore we should not, in our opinion, except rarely, give "lectures" about these cases. We should conduct "discussions" in which the students have the major role. And when "discussion" is the kernel of the teaching-learning method, our function as class leader is not to ensure that the discussion follows an exact pre-planned pattern. We should, rather, give the students the experience of freely expressing and supporting their views. We should probe for weak spots in their reasoning, and in their presentation; guide them back to basic issues if they stray into bypaths; help them to think clearly, realistically, and creatively; help to keep things in perspective; and require the students to express themselves effectively. We think this is best achieved if we work mainly with their ideas rather than with our own.

REASONS FOR INCLUDING OLD CASES WITH UP-TO-DATE ONES

We deem it desirable for students to study cases drawn from several time periods. Actually, it would not be possible to gather, write, experiment with, and publish 35 brand-new cases. These processes require

Termination Year	Number of Cases
1937	1
1943	1
1946	4
1947	1
1949	1
1950	1
1951	2
1952	1
1953	5
1956	4
1957	5
1958	1
1959	3
1960	1
1961	4

time. But even if we had an unlimited number of skilled case gatherers and could compress the time needed to establish the teaching value of each case, we still would include in our selection a number of "old" cases, covering various stages in economic cycles. In this book there are cases whose terminating dates range from 1937 to 1961. They cover periods of depression, recovery, conversion to war, conversion to peace, conversion to defense mobilization, recession, and prosperity. The student will, as he goes through these widely varying situations, if he is astute, discover which kinds of problems are closely related to the current state of general business conditions and which kinds are timeless in their nature. He will see to what extent it is true that "change" is a principal characteristic of the environment in which the businessman lives and works.

The list on page xiv shows the distribution of the 35 cases by year of termination.

RANGE OF INDUSTRIES REPRESENTED

The cases are drawn from over 30 different industries. The industries and services represented are: aircraft, automobiles, biscuits, candy, cement, ceramics, consulting, drugs, electrical controls, electronics, emergency breathing equipment, farm machinery, foods, foundry, grocery, hardware, heavy machinery and machined parts and subassemblies, ladies' bags and belts, lead and zinc, leather, office equipment, oil, oil equipment, pharmaceuticals, plastics, rivets, soap, steel tubing, and tires and other rubber products. It is not intended that these cases make the student become or try to become expert in any of the fields. By thoughtful study and discussion of the cases he can, however, gain a "general feel" of each industry represented and be able to discuss intelligently the problems of the companies in the several areas.

The inclusion of many industries, rather than concentration upon a few (with more cases per industry), offers some very real advantages. It gives the student a wider perspective and increased flexibility in his thinking. And it gives him the chance to learn that the basic tasks of business administrators are surprisingly alike from industry to industry, even though there are wide variations in the particular problems.

Another pedagogical method which has much to be said for it but which differs from the one we are here following assumes a different sort of gain for the student. Its schema is to use fewer companies, with several cases on each company. This method has the advantage of getting more deeply into any one firm; it has the disadvantage of putting limits on the number of industries whose administrative problems a student can study and with which he can work. Such a method is used in *Problems of General Management,* recently published by C. Roland Christensen, a co-author of this book, together with two of our colleagues, Edmund P. Learned and Kenneth R. Andrews.[1] In some few programs, both books are used with selections from each. Where this

---

[1] Homewood, Ill.: Richard D. Irwin, Inc., 1961.

is done, it is the hope that a class may gain from the theoretical benefits of each method.

SIGNIFICANCE OF THE OUTLINE HEADINGS UNDER WHICH THE CASES ARE GROUPED

It would not, in our opinion, be an irreparable loss if we had no headings, no outline of topics. An apprentice working under and with experienced businessmen does not usually have any "topical outline" from which to learn. By watching, studying, asking, thinking, imagining, co-operating, and taking action himself over a fairly long period of time, he comes to know how to perform the many functions of a manager. He grows into an executive by experience. He may, as he progresses, formulate some generalizations to describe the work of administrators. Or he may not. The important thing is that he learns how to *perform* his functions, not just how to classify them. Nevertheless, it is probable that he will attain competence more quickly if he thinks of the total job in terms of its component parts, each conceived and articulated in some useful terminology. And we think he could, in turn, probably train others more readily with such helps.

Certainly in a course of study of this kind there are good reasons for developing a speaking acquaintance, as well as a working acquaintance, with the basic elements that make up the processes of administration. We therefore have arranged the cases in this book under seven simple headings representing important attitudes and stages in the administrative task:

I. The Perspective of Top Management.
II. Sizing Up Situations, Formulating Policies, Discovering Opportunities, Assessing Risks, and Planning Programs of Action.
III. Organizing Administrative Personnel and Putting Plans into Action.
IV. Control.
V. Follow-Up and Reappraisal.
VI. Day-to-Day Administrative Problems.
VII. The Business Leader and Public Responsibility.

The cases included under the first heading, "The Perspective of Top Management," are introductory in their intent. Discussions of these cases are expected to open to the students a top-management point of view and to serve as an introduction to the basic concepts which will be developed with more thoroughness in the subsequent cases. The student is given a sense of the atmosphere or environment in which top-level business executives work. He is helped to visualize the men and the positions in "top management" (including directors), whether in a large company or a small one. Executives become actual people, not boxes in an organization chart drawn on a piece of paper. And, as people, they are seen to have the range of normal human frailties as well as strengths. The student finds that the manager deals with, and works through, other people. He discovers that an administrator's life includes much routine work, as well as many nonroutine matters; that new problems and new opportunities constantly appear and old ones both reappear and disappear; that "change" and the "unexpected" must in fact be expected. He also begins to see what is meant by "sizing up a situation," by "developing programs," by "planning," and by "taking action."

The student begins to understand the nature and origin of policies, to see that policy formulation is not necessarily a formal process, although at times it may be. He sees how the true leader puts an imprint on his firm. He finds that in some situations policies are adopted by vote or edict but that in more instances, perhaps, policies grow into being by unplanned action, by custom or precedent, and only then are stated and adopted officially. He finds also that policies may be in use and well understood without ever having been reduced to specific statement or adoption. And he discovers that there are instances in which there is a discrepancy between a *"stated"* policy and an *"actually practiced"* policy. The practices followed by the members of an organization may differ from the announcements and wishes of the top management. They may differ from what the management thinks is being done. In this regard, the student will observe that policy formulation is not the sole prerogative of the heads of companies; rather, much policy making is done (and should be) at fairly low levels in organizations. A wise administrator, however, is aware of such "in-the-ranks" policy making and gives it his conscious approval or deals with it otherwise.

From the introductory cases the student acquires increased familiarity with the nature of leadership, and also with the nature of authority. He becomes aware of the great difference between "formal authority" and "effective authority." Effective authority cannot be conferred from above; it must be earned and awarded from below.

So much for the implications and possibilities of the first topical heading. Before discussing the next four sections, an observation about heading VI, "Day-to-Day Administrative Problems." This section includes cases which allow the student to see, at close range, the members of top management organizations working together on their routine administrative problems, as well as on questions of company objectives and major policy changes. Some of the case material included in this section, for example, consists of detailed reports of management conferences. In these cases the administrative processes described in the following paragraphs are in full play. The method of case construction for this section varies somewhat from that for other sections in order to permit a more intimate inside look at company operations.

The second, third, fourth, and fifth headings encompass at least nine fundamental concepts and steps in the process of administration: (1) sizing up situations; (2) formulating policies; (3) discovering opportunities; (4) assessing risks; (5) planning programs of action; (6) organizing administrative personnel; (7) putting plans into action; (8) controlling parts of and all of vital situations, or, said another way, keeping informed; and (9) following up and reappraising previous thinking and actions in the light of unfolding events. The final section (Part VII) emphasizes the social responsibilities of the business leader.

The reasoning behind the general outline headings and their sequence derives from two sets of facts: (1) the administrator, in his world of activity, *tends* to follow such a sequence of steps and (2) there are, furthermore, very real pedagogical reasons for emphasizing certain aspects of the administrator's work in a progressive sequence and in a cumulative manner.

To do what we refer to as "sizing up a situation," a chief executive, alone or together with the members of his management organization, usually has to take the following steps: gather information; assess the significance of what he learns; sort the important from the unimportant; trace symptoms back to basic causes; and select out the main thing or things toward which he is to devote more intensive attention. These steps in combination constitute a "sizing up of the situation" or "an analysis of the company's position." The doctor calls it "making a diagnosis"; the military man calls it "making an estimate of the situation." We hold no strong brief for any of these phrases. The point is that the business executive has to do the kinds of examining, analyzing, and deciding that are connoted by these phrases.

Next, having decided what the nature of his problem or problems or opportunities really are, the executive must formulate understandable and explainable goals, and must devise a program or programs of action. This includes: setting both long-range and short-range objectives; formulating basic policies and operating plans; and weaving these together into an over-all program. During this process, the executive must be extremely careful that in his thinking he has not skipped lightly over the intermediate steps that must be taken to move the company from where it actually is to where he would like it to be. He must take into account the limitations and strengths of employees, of the company's finances, of competitors, of the total situation. He must give careful weight to the time factors involved. He must ask himself such questions as: "How long will this or that take?" "In what order should various parts of the program be started?" "Can Part B be begun before Part A is finished?" In working out the basic purposes, policies and plans, he (with his associates) determines the character of the company.

All these planning activities call for the use of foresight, imagination, and vision—the creative characteristics. They must be fed by confidence, enthusiasm, and the will to take calculated risks. Yet they must be tempered and held in line by judgment and common sense. Above all, the plans must be geared to the present or potential abilities of people —people now in the company or obtainable from somewhere else. The planning must include determinations of *who* will do what—and we mean *specifically who,* not just *somebody.*

After a size-up has been made, the opportunities identified, and the general and specific programming has been done, the administrator takes the next extremely important step of actually launching the program, of putting the plans into effect. The emphasis changes from *thinking* to *acting.* People must start *making* the decisions and *performing* the functions that were planned for them. The chief executive changes from playwright, to casting director, to producer.

The heads of business organizations work with and through other people. This statement seems trite, perhaps, but its implications are so often overlooked that it warrants frequent repetition and consideration. The keenest analyses and the most brilliant plans of the administrator will come to naught unless the people on whose efforts he must depend work together effectively along the lines planned. When someone is starting a new business, he must find, train, and develop into a working team the key people needed. With a going concern in which substantial changes in objectives and operations are to be undertaken, the chief officer (with the help of others, usually) may have to find some new person or persons with special abilities; and he also may have to retrain, to some extent, persons in the existing management group. Of course, many new plans do not require new people or retraining. But in any case, the chief officer must see that he has, insofar as he can obtain them, assistants who are capable, collectively, of carrying out the company's program.

This leads us to the next consideration, the importance of keeping track of things. Since the chief officer is responsible for *what actually happens,* he needs to watch actual performances and actual results closely and promptly so that he can guide the organization toward the predetermined goals, if that still seems wise in the light of developments, or away from those goals if this is indicated. He needs to have coming to him, from inside the company and from outside, a flow of information—often called a "system of controls." Such information is as important as military intelligence to a general. The system probably includes regular and occasional accounting and statistical reports, other written reports, oral reports, and information from industrial and general news sources. A very important part of this control process is informal person-to-person discussion, by means of which the responsible officer can find out not only "what is happening" but also "how does this man or that man feel about what is happening?" That may well indicate what is likely to happen next.

It is worthy of emphasis that control information should be much more than historical data. Rather, it must also include live, "still-happening" data, so that in the light of unfolding events a timely, usable basis is provided for reappraising the wisdom of the original analyses, the plans, and the effectiveness of the organization's actions.

When the chief executive makes this essential reappraisal—takes another look at his original objectives and reviews progress to date—he may find that the expected results *are* being achieved. When this is true, it is probable (although not absolutely certain) that the original size-up and program were of good quality and that the organization is efficient. It is always possible, of course, that still better results might have been achieved by different decisions and different actions. Very often—indeed, more often than not—the reappraisal reveals that the expected results are *not* being achieved. Then the executive is put on notice that there were weaknesses or breakdowns in one or more areas: size-up, planning, selecting and training people, or performance, for instance. If the control information is adequate, it will help him discover *where* the actual or potential trouble lies and will thus indicate where corrective or, preferably, preventive steps should be taken.

We stated earlier that an administrator *tends* to perform his functions in the order just suggested. And that *is* the tendency; but he does not, in practice, usually finish one step before he starts the next. More likely he jumps back and forth somewhat (often, too much) between analysis, planning, and making organizational moves. Furthermore, in our discussion of these elemental parts of the administrative process, we have perhaps implied that the executive discovers and solves one problem at a time. Manifestly, his life is not that simple. Quite the contrary. He deals with many problems concurrently, each at a different stage of development. This crisscrossing of problems and stages of problems to be dealt with at any given time increases the difficulties of management by a sort of geometric progression. A competent administrator must have special talent for dealing with dynamic, complex situations.

And the reason for including a section on public or social responsibilities is of somewhat self-evident purpose. We wish, however, to emphasize that in the world of 1962 our private enterprise system—probably more than ever before—is on trial, in the eyes of both our friends and our enemies, and its survival, we believe, will depend on the willingness and the wisdom of the head of the firm to operate a profitable venture—profitable in a very broad sense—for the investor, for the worker, for the customer, for the supplier, for the community, and for the country. And this is not easy to do, for men of intelligence and good will can easily disagree on what is fair, reasonable, possible, and in the public welfare.

It is the mission of our economy to help our society attain its goals. And the business leader—in a business-oriented society such as ours—has a difficult, but unavoidable responsibility here. Financial profits are essential (they are essential even in Russia), but they are not enough. Our freedoms of action in our economy presume a great amount of self-restraint. We are one of the few last nations in which it is believed human beings can exercise it adequately. If we fail, so does our type of society. Hence, this section of cases.

Now let us return to the matter of our "outline of cases" and look at it this time from the standpoint of its pedagogical value. We have already suggested that learning to be a good administrator is a slow job and that it primarily is a matter of developing capacities rather than accumulating information. Clearly, people do not develop capacities at the same rate or in the same order. Nor do any two persons learn exactly the same things from the same discussion of a particular case. So we would urge anyone using these cases *not* to expect any particular case on any given day to develop a specific ability or degree of ability. It is better to let the learning process proceed by cumulative effect without attempting minute direction.

Students and instructors probably will find it natural and easy to change emphasis as they progress from the earlier cases to the later ones. At first the development of sound analyses will require, and will deserve, a great deal of the preparation time and the class time. During this initial period the students and the instructors probably will minimize the amount of time spent on matters of planning, taking action, and follow-up. Later, after the members of a class have increased their facility at making reliable size-ups, they will devote less preparation and class discussion time to the size-up and relatively more to the other matters.

By the time a class approaches the cases near the end of the outline, it will be fairly clear, I believe, that "reappraisal" is essentially the same as "appraisal." And it will be apparent, furthermore, that the route of travel from size-up, through planning, organizing, putting plans into action, control, and to reappraisal is not a straight line, starting at one place and ending at another. The route is much more like a circle. Even in dealing with one problem the administrator goes around the circle many times. And, as we have said, he is busy with many circles. And his job is never really finished. As soon as he has his company more or less on top of a certain situation, something usually will have happened, inside the company or outside, that makes it necessary for him (with his associates) to deal with that same situation again, or with a new one. Society will have changed; technology will have changed. He must adjust to it.

THE ORDER IN WHICH THE CASES MAY BE STUDIED

It is most certainly not necessary to study these cases in the order of their places in this book. To be sure, we have arranged them in this order because we believe that, if they are studied in about this sequence, the student's progress will be facilitated. But anyone should feel free to take them up in some different order; we would expect other teachers in the light of their own experiences and particular educational situations to make changes as they see fit, both in the order of presentation and in the outline itself.

Actually, many of these cases could be taught in almost any sequence. In our course we have used some of them early in some years and later in other years. We have, in fact, sometimes used a particular case early and then used it again later with the same class in the same year. Quite clearly, the emphasis changes, the thoroughness changes, and the quality of the discussion is improved as the students grow in ability, regardless of which case is being used.

PREPARING A CASE FOR CLASS

The question of how students should prepare a case for class has been put to us many times by our own students and also by people studying and teaching these cases elsewhere. Actually, the question is often put: "What is the *best* way to prepare a case?" That one we cannot answer, inasmuch as we do not think there is any *best* way. There are perhaps many good, useful ways. Each of us must develop the one (or ones) that serve him best. Moreover, we must change our approach somewhat to deal with each new situation. And each case is a new situation. So there is no formula, no basic pattern, that we can pass on. We can, at most, make a few observations, and they should be considered as having no stamp of authority.

We recommend, with the qualifications just stated, the following to the student: We suggest you first read the case through to get a general impression of what it is about, how it comes out, and what kinds of information it contains. We think there is a real advantage in doing this first reading as much as a day or two before the time when you must do your thorough and final preparation. There is value in getting the general situation into your mind in time to mull it over, both consciously and subconsciously, for a while. That is true of any important problem one has to deal with—in school, in business, anywhere. But, back to case preparation.

For the second reading, we suggest you take the time to proceed slowly and carefully, studying the tables and other exhibits and making some notes as you go. Perhaps some headings will occur to you under which you want to summarize what you believe are especially pertinent facts. The headings, of course, will vary from case to case. Moreover, what at first looks like a basic fact or issue may come to seem less important than something else as you work longer.

While going through these first two stages, we usually ask ourselves something like the following questions: "Does this company seem generally to be doing well, or not doing well?" "Is it making or losing money?" "Is its current financial situation strong or weak?" "Does it seem to be faring better or worse than competitors?" Next, perhaps: "On what basis must any one company compete with the others in this particular industry?" "At what kinds of things does it have to be especially competent in order to succeed?" And then: "Does this company seem to be competent at those particular kinds of things?" If another company is getting along better, we try to decide why. "How is the whole industry doing?" "Is it growing and expanding?" "Or is it static or declining?"

"Have the officers of this company selected appropriate and achievable objectives?" "Are they good for society?" "Do the separate objectives fit together into one general program that makes sense and which, if carried out, would lead to success?" "Are they, in fact, carrying out the program?" "What, in the very nature of things, are the important functions in this situation?" "Does this company have sufficiently capable people in the key positions?" "Do they work together effectively?" "Does the nominal leader of the company really lead it" "What do his record, or his plans, or his statements seem to indicate about his basic ability?"

Many other such questions may be asked, all of them helping us make our size-up of the company and its situation.

If we conclude that the company is doing well, that the management has sound plans and is made up of people with the kinds of ability needed for the present and the future, we presumably would advise the officers to continue in the present course, watching as they go along for any new developments.

If, however, we find signs of trouble and trace the trouble to fundamental causes, we should end up with a reasonably compact statement of what basic issues or situations must be dealt with in order to get the company out of difficulty or to avert impending trouble.

Here we must devise a program of action of some kind. We must explore and decide what we would like to see done. But we must be realistic and take into account all the limiting factors of the actual situation. We must, in effect, plan a bridge (one that in reality could be built) to carry the company from where it is to where we think it should go.

The questions we have cited are only suggestions. You will think of others, and the sequence in which you put them to yourself is up to you. Perhaps, however, when you feel you are about at the end of your preparation, it will be well to ask: "Have I worked this thing through to the point where, if I really had a chance to talk to the person or persons responsible for this company, I could (1) talk intelligently with them about their company and their job in managing it; (2) show them why the main issues I have distilled out as a result of my analysis are really of first importance; and (3) give them a co-ordinated program of action that would be practical and would have a reasonable chance to succeed?"

We urge students to discuss the cases with one another while preparing them. Men in business discuss their problems with other key people. But be sure you do your own independent work and independent thinking. Don't be too stubborn to recognize a better idea than your own, but be sure you really understand it, and accept it, before you treat it as your own.

One more observation. Not infrequently, students express the wish for more information than is in the case; they feel they can't make a decision without more facts. Don't hide behind that bogy. For one thing, businessmen never have all the facts they would like to have. And, as far as the cases are concerned, they all contain enough information so that you can decide and recommend something sensible. Be sure you learn how to use, and do use, all the information you have.

OUTSIDE READING

Our reference here to outside reading is not necessary in relation to specific cases. These cases can, and at our school and at many other places do, make up the subject matter of a complete course. An instructor may wish to ask his students to read, during the course, a small number of books in such fields as: directors and their functions; executive action; or executive training. Such readings may add background for what can be developed in case discussions. But such reading is not necessary to full use of the cases.

The individual instructor will know better than we whether some particular outside readings will help his particular students. This is, we think, quite a personal matter, depending on the disposition and methods of the instructor and on the backgrounds and interests of the students themselves.

Taking a somewhat longer-range view of background reading, we would point out, however, that we have for many years urged our students, while they are in school and during the rest of their lives as well, to read widely and thoughtfully. This we suggest to all of you who study policy formulation and administration.

Read with discrimination as many books and magazine articles as you conveniently can in the areas of administration and leadership. There is a growing amount of good literature in these fields, and we believe it will increase in both quantity and quality as we all learn more about these subjects. Whatever you do read, do not regard it as necessarily authoritative or final, however. Read to stimulate your own thinking. Endeavor to keep aware of what is happening in our own society and in other societies. Be open-minded but decide for yourself what is good and profitable, and have your own reasons for your conclusions. See how you can use what you read and what you conclude about it in your own situations. Let the sole objective be not that you aim to *know* more; rather that you aim to be able to *achieve* more as an effective and useful leader. Having said that, let us add—and this is not a contradiction—that the acquisition of knowledge itself can help make of life a fuller and a richer experience.

Read biographies and autobiographies of men and women who were or are themselves leaders in many fields. Read many kinds of history, with special attention to the people who were in the forefront of movements. Read a good daily paper and/or weekly news magazine in order to keep in touch with the world today. Furthermore, when reading such news, look at events through the eyes of the persons who head businesses, educational institutions, government agencies, churches, or other kinds of organizations, noting what kinds of decisions they make and what actions they have to take. This will make you appreciate, perhaps more than you do now, what the responsibilities of prominent leaders really are. You might also sometimes ask yourselves what you would do if you were in their positions.

We strongly suggest reading in many fields other than business, inasmuch as business is only one aspect—though a very important one—of our complicated civilization, all the parts of which influence and are influenced by one another. A business leader will be the more effective and more useful to society the better he understands human nature and the more fully he is acquainted with past and present movements in the arts, the sciences, and the humanities in our civilization and in other civilizations.

Clearly, such suggested readings as these are lifelong assignments and are not calculated to make easier the discussion of a particular case on a particular day in the classroom, although they may help sooner than one might suppose. Over a period of time, of course, such habits of reading can open up great sources of pleasure and also great sources of help, which, when combined with our own interpretations of our own experiences, can further our growth and development as human beings, our usefulness as citizens, and our capacity for service as administrators. If we do so grow and develop, we will be better able to deal wisely with the many "case problems" that will actually confront us in the several areas for which we have, or will have, responsibility—in business itself and elsewhere in life.

PART I

The Perspective of Top Management

Wayland Company

"I GUESS I'm a fugitive from big business. After 20 years working for large companies, I was fed up with the frustrations, tension, and uncertainties caused by the internal politics in the vice-presidential class and decided to go in business for myself," Mr. Edward H. Cole, president of the Wayland Company, Wayland, Massachusetts, said in November, 1955.

I thought it might be nicer to build something for myself rather than to keep on trying to push things through committees. You know, there is an awful lot of featherbedding at the top of a large company. Still, it must take a really determined man to be the president of a large company; he must have stepped on many companies or people along the line. Originally, I never wanted to have a business of my own, but now I find it great fun to run a small company. You can get a great kick out of beating some of the big people and staying profitable. The real problem seems to be to keep a small company small. If you begin getting too many fingers in the pie, it slows down action, and the advantage of a small business is the ability to act quickly and be flexible. If you take that ability away, you have lost a good bit of the immediate advantage of smallness. In our three years of operation we have managed to stay small while growing, but we have not been profitable. We need at least another $20,000 invested in the business before we will break even. My cousin, the treasurer, and I thought we had enough money to get this business started profitably, but now we are in trouble.

Balance sheets and income statements for 1953 to 1955 are shown in Exhibits 1 and 2. Exhibit 2-A is prepared from Exhibits 1 and 2.

The Wayland Company was incorporated in Massachusetts in October, 1952, by Mr. Cole and a cousin in order to acquire the assets of the proprietorship of Mr. Ronald N. Furman, the inventor of a Self-contained breathing apparatus. Mr. Furman had developed the unit in 1951 while a consultant to the Burgin Machine Works; upon leaving this position, it was agreed that he and Burgin each would have one-half of any patent rights which might be granted on the unit. In 1952 Burgin had made a verbal agreement to produce the units and Mr. Furman to sell them. Wayland paid $4,000 for Mr. Furman's interest in the pending patents and the assets of his proprietorship. Both Mr.

Exhibit 1

WAYLAND COMPANY

Comparative Balance Sheet for Fiscal Years Ending October 31, 1953–55*

	1953 $	1953 %	1954 $	1954 %	1955 $	1955 %
Assets						
Current Assets:						
Cash	$ 4,256	11.82	$ 1,103	3.57	$ 3,445	9.02
Accounts Receivable	5,150	14.31	6,231	20.17	9,332	24.42
Merchandise Inventory	12,145	33.74	10,760	34.84	13,637	35.69
Supplies	834	2.32	1,108	3.59	1,108	2.90
Total Current Assets	$22,385	62.19	$19,202	62.17	$27,522	72.03
Fixed Assets:						
Tools and Equipment	$ 1,844	5.12	$ 2,117	6.85	$ 1,918	5.02
Automobile	2,697	7.49	2,457	7.96	1,701	4.45
Office Equipment	1,547	4.30	1,469	4.76	1,543	4.04
Improvements	290	0.81	310	1.00	272	0.71
Total Fixed Assets	$ 6,378	17.72	$ 6,353	20.57	$ 5,434	14.22
Other Assets:						
Patents and Licenses	$ 3,764	10.45	$ 3,529	11.43	$ 3,294	8.62
Incorporation Expense	1,000	2.78	1,000	3.24	1,000	2.62
Prepaid Rent	500	1.39	500	1.62	500	1.31
Utility Deposits	75	0.21	75	0.24	75	0.19
Prepaid Insurance and Interest	1,097	3.05	225	0.73	386	1.01
Prepaid Royalties and Commissions	794	2.21	....	....	....	....
Total Other Assets	$ 7,230	20.09	$ 5,329	17.26	$ 5,255	13.75
Total Assets	$35,993	100.00	$30,884	100.00	$38,211	100.00
Liabilities						
Current Liabilities:						
Notes Payable—Bank	....	....	$ 5,000	16.19	$ 9,250	24.21
Notes Payable—Finance Co.	....	....	1,098	3.56	275	0.72
Notes Payable—Burgin Machine Works	$ 2,271	6.31	....	....	....	....
Accounts Payable—Trade	5,252	14.60	6,379	20.65	15,426	40.37
Employees' Stock Reserve Acct.	540	1.50	....	....	....	....
Employees' Withheld Taxes	363	1.01	161	0.52	117	0.31
Accrued Liabilities:						
Expenses	....	....	....	....	753	1.97
Royalties	....	....	381	1.23	1,107	2.90
Interest	....	....	....	....	345	0.90
Payroll Taxes	103	0.29	24	0.08	37	0.10
Municipal and State Taxes	4	0.00	203	0.66	9	0.02
Total Current Liabilities	$ 8,533	23.71	$13,246	42.89	$27,319	71.50
Other Liabilities:						
Notes Payable—Bank	$ 1,120	3.11	....	....	....	....
Notes Payable—Finance Co.	....	....	$ 275	0.89	....	....
Notes Payable—Officers	5,000	13.89	12,339	39.95	$ 5,819†	15.22
Total Liabilities	$14,653	40.71	$25,860	83.73	$33,138	86.72
Capital Stock	$41,500	115.30	$43,640	141.30	$51,840	135.67
Earned Surplus (Deficit)	(20,160)	(56.01)	(38,616)	(125.03)	(46,767)	(122.39)
Total Net Worth	$21,340	59.29	$ 5,024	16.27	$ 5,073	13.28
Total Liabilities and Net Worth	$35,993	100.00	$30,884	100.00	$38,211	100.00

* Balance sheet for start of business, November 1, 1952, not available.
† Maturing December 1, 1956.
Source: Auditor's report; percentages prepared by Harvard Business School staff.

Furman and the Burgin Machine Works were to receive a 3% royalty on the manufacturer's selling price of the Self-contained units; however, Mr. Furman sold his royalty rights to an individual employed by the Wayland Company early in 1954.

Under a written agreement with the Burgin Machine Works, Wayland had exclusive sales rights on the unit, while Burgin retained exclusive manufacturing rights. For the first six months Wayland was to pay Burgin on the tenth of the month following collection of the accounts receivable. In May, 1953, Wayland bought out Burgin's interest by paying $16,000 for the parts inventory, fixtures, and tools. "They could not produce as was required, and we were not satisfied with the quality of the products," Mr. Cole explained. Management later felt that $16,000 was an inflated cost. Wayland moved into rented quarters of 1,600 square feet and began to assemble the units itself, although it continued to buy all the parts.

In 1955 the organization consisted of six people: Mr. Cole, president; Miss Helen D. Cole, secretary and treasurer; Mr. Richard M. Tucker, design engineer; Mr. Paul A. Fuller, assistant to Mr. Cole; Mr. Herbert L. Carson, production manager; and Mrs. Audrey Bradley, secretary and senior employee.

PRODUCT LINE

The Wayland Company manufactured breathing equipment. The two principal products were the Pocketaire Self-contained breathing apparatus and the Pocketaire Portable oxygen unit. Both products are illustrated in the company advertisements shown in Exhibit 3. Self-contained units, which were used principally by firemen in rescue work, consisted of two cylinders containing oxygen, a regulator delivering a constant flow of oxygen, an air bag, a mask assembly, and a harness for attaching the apparatus to the body. Of the two cylinders, one supplied oxygen for the period of a rescue; when that tank was exhausted, the operator switched to the other cylinder that supplied five minutes of oxygen for escape. The interchangeable work cylinders came in three sizes: 5 minutes, 15 minutes, and 25 minutes, making the respective weights of the total unit $4\frac{1}{2}$ pounds, $6\frac{1}{2}$ pounds, and 9 pounds, and the prices $98.50, $118, and $126, respectively. The company also sold an industrial unit designed for use under safety suits. This unit had only one 15-minute cylinder; it weighed $4\frac{3}{4}$ pounds and cost $98.50. The $5.25 carrying case and the $4.50 goggles were optional equipment and not included in any of the

Exhibit 2

WAYLAND COMPANY

Comparative Statements of Profit or Loss for Fiscal Years Ending October 31, 1953–55

	1953 $	1953 %	1954 $	1954 %	1955 $	1955 %	1956 $	1956 %	1957 $	1957 %
Net sales	$22,188	100.00	$38,170	100.00	$59,036	100.00				
Cost of goods sold:										
Beginning inventory	......	......	12,145	31.82	10,760	18.22				
Purchases	23,613	106.42	11,935	31.27	26,896	45.56				
Outside contracting	448	2.02	2,249	5.89	2,194	3.72				
Less: Ending inventory	(12,145)	(54.74)	(10,760)	(28.19)	(13,637)	(23.10)				
Total	$11,916	53.70	$15,569	40.79	$26,213	44.40				
Gross profit before factory overhead	$10,272	46.30	$22,601	59.21	$32,823	55.60				
Factory overhead:										
Salaries	$ 2,066	9.31	$ 4,931	12.92	$ 5,694	9.65				
Insurance	......	......	......	......	363	0.61				
Rent, light, heat, telephone	1,740	7.85	1,475	3.87	846	1.43				
Depreciation—machinery, tools, and patents	1,269	5.72	299	0.78	541	0.92				
General (including repairs)	147	0.66	62	0.16	......	......				
Taxes on equipment and payroll	......	......	309	0.81	315	0.53				
Total	$ 5,222	23.54	$ 7,076	18.54	$ 7,759	13.14				
Gross profit on sales	$ 5,050	22.76	$15,525	40.67	$25,064	42.46				

Selling expenses:

Salaries	$ 4,200	18.93	$12,028	31.51	$ 7,150	12.11
Royalties and commissions	2,230	10.05	3,203	8.39	2,246	3.81
Discounts allowed	……	……	664	1.74	1,095	1.86
Advertising	4,648	20.95	2,211	5.79	6,136	10.39
Auto and depreciation	1,695	7.64	1,531	4.01	……	……
Promotion and traveling	4,973	22.41	4,419	11.58	7,913	13.40
Taxes	……	……	375	0.98	241	0.41
Utilities	……	……	1,450	3.80	946	1.60
Insurance	……	……	1,103	2.89	211	0.36
Total	$17,746	79.98	$26,984	70.69	$25,938	43.94

General and administrative expenses:

Salaries	$ 4,320	19.47	$ 2,215	5.80	$ 1,262	2.14
Payroll and property taxes	479	2.16	172	0.45	132	0.23
Office expenses	430	1.94	947	2.48	1,465	2.48
Legal and accounting	1,764	7.95	1,197	3.14	1,075	1.82
Insurance	821	3.70	1,130	2.96	255	0.43
Depreciation	172	0.78	176	0.46	216	0.37
Interest	……	……	247	0.65	839	1.42
Donations	12	0.05	……	……	……	……
Utilities	……	……	737	1.93	2,033	3.44
Total	$ 7,998	36.05	$ 6,821	17.87	$ 7,277	12.33
Net loss	($20,694)	(93.26)	($18,279)	(47.89)	($ 8,151)	(13.81)
Add: Discounts received	34	0.15	8	0.02	……	……
Services rendered	500	2.25	……	……	……	……
Less: Loss on sale of automobile	……	……	185	0.48	……	……
Net loss for year	($20,160)	(90.86)	($18,456)	(48.35)	($ 8,151)	(13.81)

Source: Auditor's report; percentages prepared by Harvard Business School staff.

Exhibit 2-A

WAYLAND COMPANY

Selected Balance Sheet and Operating Ratios

		October 31, 1953	October 31, 1954	October 31, 1955
(R)	Current ratio.........................	2.62	1.45	1.01
($)	Net working capital...................	$13,852	$5,956	$203
(R)	Acid test ratio........................	1.20	0.64	0.51
(%)	Current assets to total assets...........	62.19	62.17	72.03
(%)	Total fixed assets to total assets........	17.72	20.57	14.22
(R)	Net worth to debt.....................	1.46	0.19	0.15
(%)	Net worth to total assets...............	59.29	16.27	13.28
(Days)	Receivables turnover*...................	83.56	58.77	56.91
(Days)	Inventory turnover†....................	....	264.80	167.53
(%)	Total assets to net sales.................	162.22	80.91	64.72
(%)	Fixed assets to net sales................	28.75	16.64	9.20
(%)	Operation profit to net worth..........	(96.97)	(363.83)	(160.67)
(%)	Net profit to net worth................	(94.47)	(367.36)	(160.67)

* Accounts receivable × 360/net sales.
† Average inventory × 360/cost of goods sold.
Source: Prepared from Exhibits 1 and 2 by Harvard Business School staff.

above manufacturer's suggested retail prices, to which management believed distributors adhered. Since all oxygen sold in the United States was medically pure, users could refill Pocketaire oxygen cylinders from any large-size standard cylinder in which the pressure was at least 1,800 pounds by using a recharging adapter sold by Wayland for $17.

The Portable oxygen unit was developed in 1953 in co-operation with Linde Air Products Company, a division of the Union Carbide and Carbon Corporation, and other manufacturers of oxygen gas. The 17-pound unit was packed either in a leatherette case designed to resemble a suitcase or in a hard-wearing fiber utility case and consisted of two small, standard medical oxygen cylinders with standard medical valves, a regulator, and disposable plastic face masks. The outfit, which supplied an hour of oxygen, cost $89.50 complete; the regulator alone sold for $34.50, and an adapter, which permitted using the regulator on large standard cylinders, cost $7. Principal purchasers were doctors and people with breathing difficulties who should have supplementary oxygen on hand in case of emergency.

Management believed the principal features of both lines of equipment were lightness, compactness, convenience, and low cost. Exhibit 4 shows pictures and gives descriptions of competing products. Management believed equipment competing with the Self-contained unit was either too heavy, too complicated, or took too long to put on before getting into the fire. A city fire department chief and the head of the city fire school, where the Self-contained unit was tested in 1952, wrote:

"We like Pocketaire because it goes on the firemen instead of on the trucks." A testimonial from the technical adviser of a city civil defense unit read as follows:

It has been interesting to note that in smoky fires, when unprotected men have been knocked out or reduced to copious tears, men wearing Pocketaire, without goggles, have experienced little or no lachrymation and no aftereffects.

Exhibit 3

WAYLAND COMPANY

Copies of Advertisements Showing Wayland Products

Your masks made possible seven rescues and a number of reconnaissance and ventilation tasks in heavy smoke and sulphur dioxide. The average citizen, to judge from his actions at Christmas and New Year, places small value on human

Exhibit 3—Continued

WAYLAND COMPANY

Copies of Advertisements Showing Wayland Products

Pocketaire
Breathing Equipment

Model 1510-S   Weight 4¾ Lbs.   Life 15 Minutes

The Model 1510-S Pocketaire is ideally suited for use in Safety Suits, as a smoke mask on aircraft, or wherever a small, light, self-contained breathing apparatus is necessary for work that can be completed in fifteen minutes or less. Because the usual Pocketaire escape cylinder is without access in safety suits, and is unnecessary for fire fighting in confined areas such as in aircraft, it is not incorporated in the Model 1510-S in favor of lighter weight, smaller bulk, and lower cost.

Used with the modern, lightweight fire suit illustrated above, Pocketaire fits conveniently under the hood, with the cylinder slipped into a simple loop of fibreglass cloth. No suit alterations are necessary.

The wearer can clear the breathing bag at any time by flattening with external pressure through the hood, which discharges all rebreathed air out of the mask exhalation valve. The bag may then be immediately re-inflated with fresh, cool oxygen by pressing the recharging button on the end of the regulator. This button is easily operated through the hood with the gloved hand as illustrated. The recharging button is therefore protection against accidental deflation of the breathing bag due to unintentional external pressure.

Product of the Wayland Company, Wayland, Massachusetts

Exhibit 3—Continued

WAYLAND COMPANY

Copies of Advertisements Showing Wayland Products

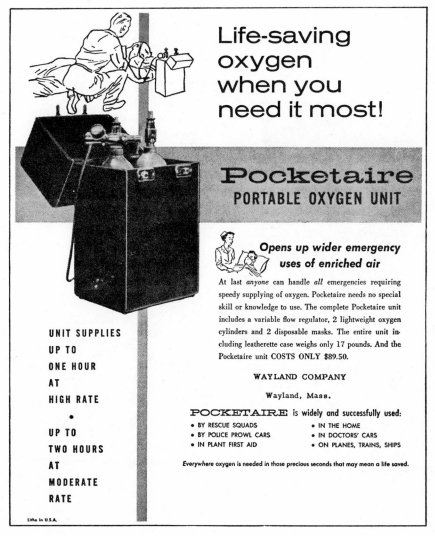

life. Lawyers, judges, and juries seem to value life at $7,500. Seven lives at $7,500, a total of $52,500, is a handsome return for the price of two masks. . . . Civil Defense bought three masks in 1953 and six in 1954. It intends to purchase six more within the next few weeks.

Mr. Tucker, design engineer, said the major criticisms of the Self-contained unit made by the potential customers were that: (1) it did

Exhibit 3—Continued

WAYLAND COMPANY

Copies of Advertisements Showing Wayland Products

not have the approval of the Bureau of Mines, which is the only government body approving mine safety equipment; (2) there was a build-up of carbon dioxide (CO_2) in the rebreathing bag under excessive work loads; and (3) the mask did not cover all the face.

The Bureau of Mines, in Schedule 13-C, set up minimum time limits for breathing equipment of one-half hour for escape purposes and one hour for all other uses. Commented Mr. Cole:

> In other words, our units may be used for escape from a mine but not to enter for rescue. In designing Pocketaire, it was our belief we could not produce the correct unit for which there was a vital need in the fire service for first-in men—a unit which would be light, compact, and easily carried as routine equipment for first entry of all fires—if we took into consideration the requirements of Schedule 13-C.

He pointed out that Pocketaire advertisements were accepted by the National Fire Protection Association's *Fireman Magazine;* Oklahoma A. & M.'s publication, *Protective Breathing Equipment;* and *Best's Safety Directory.* Both Mr. Fuller and Mr. Tucker agreed, however, that "The Bureau of Mines is still our big bugaboo, because their approval of products has been so well exploited by other suppliers."

Mr. Tucker said the problem of CO_2 build-up was really complicated. Some CO_2 stimulates breathing, but with hard exertion one breathes more deeply and some CO_2 accumulates in the rebreathing bag; however, the wearer can clear the bag by flattening it and then immediately reinflate it with oxygen by pressing a button on the front of the regulator. It would be possible, Mr. Tucker thought, to add a canister of chemicals, but this would complicate the unit and require replacement. Company experiments showed the largest unit would supply oxygen for 27 minutes of hard work, and management had found no reports showing that CO_2 build-up had ever caused more than a severe headache. Mr. Tucker commented, "I think this matter of CO_2 build-up raises an important question: Are you using breathing equipment to beef up the men and send them into places they normally wouldn't go or are you using breathing equipment to protect the men?"

Some equipment competing with the Self-contained unit used chemicals instead of oxygen cylinders. Mr. Tucker pointed out that any one chemical combination was not effective against all gases. The user of a chemical unit had either to predict that a certain gas in a limited quantity would be released in a fire, or, at the outbreak of a fire, to ascertain exactly what gases were released and then attach the proper canister. He felt that while such predictions were possible in industry or in mines such was not the case in ordinary fire fighting.

Because Pocketaire's all-nasal mask protected the lachrymal tear duct in the nose, management said eye protection was unnecessary unless there was a gas present which directly attacked the eyes, such as sulphur dioxide, or the skin, such as a heavy concentration of ammonia, chlorine, and some aldehydes. They recognized that the goggles were not overly satisfactory but pointed out that men can see better and feel temperature increases quicker with goggles and some men suffer from claustrophobia in a full-face mask.

Several manufacturers produced units similar to the Portable oxygen unit, but Mr. Fuller, assistant to Mr. Cole, said these were usually much heavier, less compact, and more expensive. He said that surgical supply houses sometimes reported that doctors made objections to Pocketaire, such as, "I don't want that unknown brand—I'll take the other one made by a manufacturer who makes other equipment I use. Sure it's more expensive than Wayland's, but it's a lot more substantial and complete." Mr. Fuller thought, however, that a light neat-looking unit

Exhibit 4

WAYLAND COMPANY

Examples of Products Competing with the Self-contained Unit

Mr. Cole commented on competitive equipment as follows: Wayland Self-contained units were inhalators that delivered a constant flow of oxygen. They competed mostly with Demand-type units, in which the user's breathing regulated the flow of gas. Because they were costly and complicated, the use of Rebreathing units was limited to mines. The Self-generating units were used in mines and, to some extent, in industry, but the canisters were costly and not effective against all gases. The Demand-type equipment made by the Scott Aviation Corporation and the Mine Safety Appliances Company (MSA) required larger cylinders than ours because they did not use a rebreathing bag. The Scott Air-Pak and some MSA units used air, not oxygen. Mr. Cole pointed out that many people believed it was safer to use air units in petroleum vapors and other explosive gases; however, he emphasized that atmospheric temperature, not oxygen content, was the key to spontaneous combustion.

The brief descriptions and photographs of the products shown were furnished and approved by the manufacturers.

Mr. Cole made the following comments about competitive equipment: The Oxygen Equipment Manufacturing Company (OEM) inhalator was most similar to and competitive with the Wayland Portable unit, but 25 minutes was too short a time. Portable resuscitators provided automatic breathing for a victim through alternating positive and negative oxygen pressures; such units were popular with police and rescue squads, despite their weight and cost, because

Exhibit 4—Continued

WAYLAND COMPANY

Examples of Products Competing with the Self-Contained Unit

REBREATHING TYPE

MSA ONE-HOUR OXYGEN BREATHING AP-PARATUS: This Rebreathing unit permits the most efficient utilization of O_2 supply. The wearer's breathing regulates the O_2 supply from the relatively small cylinder. Chemicals in the $1 replaceable canister remove CO_2 from the exhaled breath, and the O_2 remaining is reused. Unit weighs 18 pounds and costs $250.

DEMAND TYPE

SCOTT AIR-PAK (illustrated): Uses pure compressed air, not oxygen. Nonrebreathing type, delivers fresh air on each inhalation through a demand regulator to the mask in any quantity and at any rate required by the user. It has Bureau of Mines approval, minimum air duration of 30 minutes at extreme exertion, weighs 30 pounds, and costs $229. Smaller 15-minute, 19½-pound unit costs $184.50. Recharging equipment sells for approximately $225. MSA makes three sizes of Demand-type apparatus, using either air or oxygen: the $149.50, 11-pound SLING MASK designed for 8–10-minute jobs or escapes; the $169.50, 18-pound CUB MASK with a 15–20-minute supply; and the $214.50, 30-pound AIR or O_2 Mask which has Bureau of Mines approval for its 30-minute duration at hard work.

SELF-GENERATING TYPE

CHEMOX: Instead of cylinders and valves, this MSA unit uses a $6.60 replaceable chemical canister which evolves oxygen as needed and removes carbon dioxide. The unit has Bureau of Mines approval, lasts a minimum of 45 minutes at hard work, weighs 13½ pounds, and costs $165.

Exhibit 4—Continued

WAYLAND COMPANY

Examples of Products Competing with the Portable Unit

resuscitation had been found more effective than manual artificial respiration. If O_2 was not piped into the rooms, hospitals generally used units similar to the McKesson one, although nurses sometimes complained about pushing around the large cylinders.

The brief descriptions and photographs of the products were approved and furnished by the manufacturers.

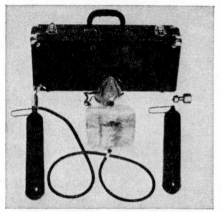

OEM PORTABLE UNIT: Two special cylinders supply 25 minutes of oxygen through a reusable mask. Packed in a case, it weighs 8 pounds, costs $54.50, including recharging adapter.

EMERSON RESUSCITATOR: Unit performs three functions: resuscitation; inhalation; and aspiration, which is the removal of fluid obstructions from the throat. Utility Model shown weighs 33 pounds, can provide nearly 1.5 hours of resuscitation, and sells for $410. A "Featherweight" $253 model weighs, with one tank, only 18 pounds. By admixing air with the O_2, it can resuscitate for 50 minutes.

McKESSON EMERGENCY OXYGEN AND RESUSCITATION UNIT: By squeezing the rebreathing bag and forcing air into the patient, unit may be used as a resuscitator. Depending whether standard E or D cylinders are used, oxygen is supplied for approximately 80 minutes, or 25 minutes; weight is 22 pounds, or 17½ pounds; height is 30 inches or 20 inches; and cost is $77.80 or $74.20. The regulator alone sells for about $35.

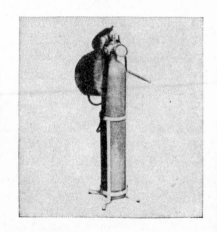

would appeal for personal use to people with breathing difficulties.

In 1955 Wayland became the distributor for municipalities and industry of the Kreiselman Bellows Resuscitator, which was made by Ohio Chemical and Surgical Equipment Company, Madison, Wisconsin, and sold for $65. The resuscitator consisted of a face mask, a valve, and a small bellows and was used to revive a trapped or otherwise immovable victim where heavy equipment could not be brought into action.

SALES

Management believed that the potential market for the Self-contained apparatus was very large but had found the information available from sources such as the National Fire Protection Association, insurance companies, and publications such as *Fire Engineering, Occupational Hazards, National Safety News* very sketchy. "The main problem in the sales area is that neither we, nor, as far as we know, the people like Linde and Ohio Chemical we work with, nor our competitors have any real market information; we all work by guess," Mr. Cole said.

The *Reader's Digest* estimated in 1953 that 6,000 firemen were injured or killed each year from smoke or gas poisoning.[1] Mr. Cole had been unable to find actual statistics but pointed out that with 20,000 fire departments and 700,000 paid or volunteer firemen in the United States, "We have a long way to go before we give protection to even the key men." One competitor claimed to have sold over 18,000 units to fire departments and industry since World War II. In industry such equipment is used for hazardous areas, plant fire protection, tank cleaning, sewage inspections, and so forth. "Ever-increasing awards and workmen compensation claims are enforcing an expanding market," Mr. Cole said. He quoted an editor of a technical journal as saying, "It is a waste of time to try and get statistics on the number of present units in use, because the market has not been touched."

Mr. Cole also foresaw a wide market for the Portable oxygen unit. He believed there were some five million persons in the United States who suffered from breathing difficulties caused by heart condition, asthma, and other allergies and that many of these people could get relief by the administration of oxygen during their periods of distress. This estimate was made by the medical department of a national company that checked the record of its employees needing oxygen equip-

---

[1] August, 1953, p. 33.

ment during the past four or five years. The proportion was then extrapolated to give some indication of the United States market. Commented Mr. Cole, "The figure is impressive, although I don't know if we've really delved into it too much. Of course, it doesn't mean that all five million people necessarily need our unit, that they could afford it, or that doctors recommend our unit. It does indicate, however, that we have a large market and perhaps can sell a thousand units a month." Mr. Cole felt that the availability of oxygen was important to such people and the more portable the unit the freer the life such a person might live. He also thought the unit might be sold to doctors, particularly to those country general practitioners who would save time if they had an emergency unit available in their cars. Units could be used by hospitals, rescue squads, beach life guards, and in police prowl cars and hospital first-aid stations.

Wayland sold its products to three types of distributors: fire equipment distributors, safety supply houses, and surgical supply houses. The first two outlets sold the Self-contained units and most of the Portable units; surgical supply houses sold only Portable units. To qualify as a distributor, a firm had to carry and demonstrate Wayland products. Discounts to all types of distributors on all products were 30% off list price on complete units and replacement parts. Terms were 1%, 10 days, net, 30 days. For a year a national manufacturer had had exclusive national distribution rights to the medical supply field of the Portable unit and received a discount of 45%; however, Wayland was disappointed with the sales volume and terminated the agreement.

The international distributor that handled Wayland's export sales received a chain discount of 30% and 20%, making the margin 44%, but it paid for all advertising and promotion.

Mr. Cole and Mr. Fuller said that distributors, especially those in the New England area, made very little effort to sell Wayland products. One surgical supply distributor commented, "Ed Cole comes in here and talks to the boys, and then they pick up the Portable unit and sell a couple more of them but then they drop it, because it isn't an everyday item that everybody wants." Another said, "Sure, I guess the doctors could use it, and a couple of the boys tried to sell it, but let's face it they make lousy money when they call on doctors so they go where the volume is, the hospitals, and the hospitals can't see using those small cylinders." Mr. Fuller then tried unsuccessfully to get the distributor to sell regulators to the hospitals. A third surgical distributor explained his refusal to sell Pocketaire: "I never heard of Wayland before, but it looks like a good product. Still, I guess I'm old fashioned but I'd just as soon some other distributor makes the fast buck introducing it. When the others are interested, you come back and see me." Mr. Fuller thought he would make a sale on his next visit.

Fire equipment distributors and safety supply houses, while generally smaller and less well established than surgical supply houses, made more effort, Mr. Cole thought, to sell Wayland products and were faster paying. According to Mr. Fuller, many fire equipment distributors occupied small inaccessible offices, offered no terms or discounts, but relied solely on long-time friendship with the fire chiefs for getting sales. Some firms became Wayland distributors by answering Wayland advertisements or direct mailings and sending in several initial orders. Under these circumstances, Mr. Cole sometimes had to decide whether or not to grant a new distributorship in the territory of an old but inactive distributor. He had found it unwise to rely only on credit ratings in selecting distributors, because small and seemingly financially shaky firms often generated the most volume. Wayland billed the ultimate consumer directly if it was worried about receiving payment. Mr. Cole said one small unpromising firm bought a demonstrator and later returned it; months afterwards the same firm ordered four units and eight months later bought ten. Mr. Fuller believed this example illustrated the time lag that often existed between demonstration and sale. "I once demonstrated a unit, heard nothing for two years, and then got an order for eight units," he said.

Wayland kept records of distributors by state, city, type of business, sales of each unit, and total sales. Exhibit 5 shows a summary of sales by state together with selected data related to the markets for both products. The following table of sales to Pennsylvania is an example of Wayland sales data, minus the city identification:

Distributor	Self-contained	Portable Unit	Total Sales
Fire equipment distributor, selling to both industry and municipalities............	$ 653.29	$ 634.46	$1,287.75
Surgical supply house....................		125.30	125.30
Fire equipment distributor...............	443.00	110.60	553.60
Surgical supply house....................		125.30	125.30
Safety supply house.....................		62.65	62.65
Multistate scientific organization.........	1,836.24		1,836.24
Fire equipment distributor...............	71.45	140.44	211.89
Fire equipment distributor...............	1,186.92		1,186.92
Fire equipment distributor...............		117.02	117.02
Total sales.......................	$4,290.90	$1,315.77	$5,506.67

Exhibit 5

WAYLAND COMPANY

Market Data and Sales by States
November 1, 1954, to October 31, 1955

State	Population	All Physicians	Physicians in General Practice	Hospitals	Firehouses	Firemen*	Wayland Distributors	Wayland Sales	Average Sales per Outlet
Alabama...	3,033,000	2,321	807	118	218	1,257	1	$ 200.20	$ 200.20
California .	13,032,000	20,763	5,764	442	686	11,218	8	3,756.50	469.56
Colorado ..	1,549,000	2,385	565	103	158	968	1	210.29	210.29
Conn......	2,241,000	3,777	1,055	73	292	2,762	10	4,384.93	438.49
D.C.......	853,000	2,483	503	30	1	1,098	1	79.82	79.82
Georgia ...	3,621,000	3,391	1,048	158	204	1,918	2	2,122.75	1,061.38
Illinois....	9,361,000	12,529	4,271	365	961	6,400	6	1,494.28	249.05
Indiana....	4,330,000	4,420	1,726	142	553	3,341	1	160.82	160.82
Iowa......	2,692,000	2,829	1,068	117	928	1,149	2	2,162.14	1,081.07
Kentucky..	3,005,000	2,638	1,060	126	279	1,247	1	105.68	105.68
Mass......	5,016,000	8,715	2,445	228	364	9,739	7	3,777.31	539.62
Michigan..	7,236,000	7,900	2,082	272	781	5,126	1	117.91	117.91
Miss.......	2,111,000	1,562	732	110	147	619	1	1,118.25	1,118.25
Nebraska ..	1,381,000	1,581	630	116	486	713	1	62.65	62.65
New Jersey.	5,420,000	6,737	2,151	163	428	5,477	7	2,452.77	350.40
New York.	16,124,000	31,146	8,890	525	1,693	18,437	21	11,715.00	557.86
N.C.......	4,285,000	3,913	1,270	189	232	1,542	1	364.67	364.67
Ohio......	8,966,000	10,873	3,376	263	1,088	6,912	5	1,226.94	245.39
Oklahoma.	2,168,000	2,226	771	129	248	1,383	1	192.84	192.84
Oregon....	1,669,000	2,098	719	79	362	1,318	1	133.53	133.53
Penn.......	11,159,000	14,727	4,497	353	2,011	6,300	9	5,506.67	611.85
R.I........	845,000	1,036	303	25	104	1,186	2	540.33	270.17
Texas.....	8,563,000	8,750	2,650	567	592	5,829	1	297.37	297.37
Vermont...	378,000	563	183	28	170	189	1	126.00	126.00
Virginia...	3,579,000	3,652	1,324	129	337	1,518	1	94.33	94.33
Wash......	2,570,000	3,238	953	140	481	2,129	4	2,029.02	507.26
Wisconsin .	3,694,000	3,926	1,398	223	587	2,845	2	2,304.79	1,152.40
Canada....	14,009,429	17,076	7,754	1,120	2,223	n.a.	1	5,129.13	5,129.13
Other Exp..	....	....	....	....	....	....	1	980.31	980.31

Totals..............	101	$52,779.38	$ 522.57
Office Direct Sales....		6,256.71
Total Sales..........		$59,036.09

* Full-time equivalent employment of state and local governments, October, 1955; breakdown of volunteer firemen not available.

NOTE: Paid fire departments usually keep all equipment, including fire suits, on the trucks; volunteer fire departments usually have the firemen keep their own equipment in their cars and bring it to the fire.

Source: Sales from company records; Population, Bureau of the Census, *Current Population Reports;* Firehouses, from survey by the National Fire Protection Association; Physicians and Hospitals, from *American Medical Directory,* 19th Edition, published by the American Medical Association; Firemen, Bureau of the Census, *State Distribution of Public Employment.*

Mr. Cole explained that an initial order for a demonstrator made a man a distributor, a fact which helped depress the average sales per outlet. Mr. Cole intended Wayland advertising to generate leads for distributors to follow up rather than to induce orders itself for company products, which he felt must be demonstrated. During 1955 the company advertised in *Fire Engineering, Occupational Hazards, Law and Order, National Safety News, Journal of the American Medical Association,* and *Best's Safety Directory.* Wayland had had several publicity articles published, including one which, Mr. Cole said, was in 63% of all U.S. newspapers using Associated Press service. It "not only created interest but was responsible for a large boost in actual sales." To increase sales volume, Mr. Cole said it would be necessary to have an $8,000 to $10,000 advertising program planned by a publicity agent. He pointed out that there were currently no channels to reach effec-tively the biggest market for the Portable unit, those people with breath-ing difficulties; the public rarely entered surgical supply houses, some of which required prescriptions to buy O_2 units. Therefore he wanted a publicity firm to plan articles which the medical profession would consider ethical, whether doctors or the lay public read them. Mr. Cole wished to run a series of 13 advertisements, one-sixth of a page, in *Business Week,* which would cost about $500 apiece.

Mr. Cole hoped Wayland eventually could afford to supplement its advertising with four salaried salesmen. In 1955 the company had five salesmen besides Mr. Cole and Mr. Fuller: one full-time man, who had the Metropolitan New York, Long Island, and New Jersey area and received 25% on direct sales and an 8½% override on distributor sales; and four part-time men, who got a 30% discount on all sales and passed on 20% to the distributors. As an experiment, Mr. Cole had hired three medical students to sell Portable units directly to doctors. "In short, I think we've got to do the selling, because the firms cer-tainly aren't going to do it for us," Mr. Cole said.

The Wayland Company had found it difficult to get distributors be-cause of the entrenched position of established manufacturers. In 1955 Wayland announced it had entered suit against a competitor for $250,-000 in triple damages, or a total of $750,000. It charged that company with spreading false, misleading statements in regard to Pocketaire equipment, unlawful contracts and combinations with some dealers and distributors to restrain trade, thereby tending to bring about a monopoly on the sale of artificial breathing devices. It further charged that com-pany's method of doing business precluded certain dealers and dis-tributors from selling the products of the Wayland Company.

In 1955 Wayland was engaged in internal discussion on the level of its products' prices. Originally, the company had deliberately priced one of the three models of the Self-contained unit below $100, because it believed municipalities generally required fire chiefs to get approval on all purchases over $100. Mr. Cole recognized that his company's prices were lower than his competitors' but was opposed to raising them:

> I think it would be a tragedy to raise prices at the time I feel sales are beginning to grab hold. We've doubled our sales of the Self-contained units. It is the first real feeling we've had that we're getting hold of the market, and I'd hate right now to throw a monkey wrench in it anywhere along the line. I would rather see Pocketaire accepted and stronger and then raise the prices. As for the Portable unit, we've just made an arrangement with Sears, Roebuck & Company to have it placed in their catalog, and so it would be embarrassing to both of us if we raised the prices now.

Others in the company disagreed with Mr. Cole. Mr. Carson and Mr. Tucker were in favor of a price rise, while Mr. Fuller was uncertain. Mr. Carson said, "Only one unit is under $100, and with the case or goggles the price automatically goes over $100. One or two fire chiefs have to order under $100, so they merely order it without one cylinder and order extras such as goggles, recharger, or case later." Mr. Tucker added:

> I don't think price is that important. You see, I'm a backwoods boy from Ohio. If we did $60,000 in sales and lost $6,000 last year, I suggest we charge 10% more. To me it is just that simple. If we sell at that price, we make a profit; if not, we're out of business. Therefore let's try it and see what happens. I don't see any other alternative, and I can't see how talking week after week about prices does any good at all.

PRODUCTION

Wayland products were assembled in a 1,200-square-foot room by Messrs. Tucker, Fuller, and Carson. All parts were bought; typical assembly operations were gluing together the parts of the face mask and bag, welding the parts of the regulator and adjusting it, and packing the finished product for shipment.

Mr. Carson, production manager, described his job as follows:

> My biggest interest is to make sure things are right when they are shipped out of here. I'd rather be here than in the field selling to be sure everything is thoroughly tested. After all, I am a volunteer fireman, too, and maybe I'll have to wear this equipment some day. I do everything from floor sweeping to assembling. On Saturdays I come in here to clean the floor because no one else seems to be interested in doing it. I had a man come in to quote on that job sometime ago but he wanted $12 a week; I didn't think we could afford that. Sometimes my wife and I come in at night to get things ready for the next morning. I think my future lies with this company, but I was trained as a mortician and still pay $10 a year dues so I can always have a mortician's job in the future.

Mr. Tucker spent about one-third of his time keeping the perpetual inventory cards on parts and finished units and running the cost control system he had devised. He said he did not get bids on all of the parts: "I know about what the prices ought to be and I have a little machine shop near by which makes most of our parts so that it is a waste of time getting quotes."

In 1954 Mr. Tucker built up cost sheets for each of the different Wayland products. He added up the cost of parts, using the original prices from the perpetual inventory cards. He said this system raised a difficulty because of an initial order of $62 worth of parts; $32 might be for the original tools so additional orders would cost $30. He was uncertain what price should be transferred to the product cost sheet.

Ed Cole and I argue about this all the time. I want to keep this as though I am buying tools all the time, because I want to be able to change my source of supply and be flexible in our methods of construction. Therefore I could get a second supply of any part or change an item $\frac{1}{16}$ of an inch without showing any change in the product cost list. . . . As I have often said, I feel we are not charging enough for our products. I think we need more money for research and development, and since Ed turns everything into a percentage-of-sales basis the higher I price the goods the more he will have to sell them for. So if direct arguing fails, I can give my cost not dishonestly, but toward the high side, and help with my own argument. What do you think I should do?

Mr. Cole commented:

Dick Tucker's not fooling me; I've tried for two years without success to explain how I use percentages for budgeting. Anyway, I don't like surprises, especially on the annual statements. Dick's overpricing of raw material provides a margin of safety in my calculations—a margin that wouldn't begin to allow for the time and money we've given this business for nothing.

Exhibit 6 shows Mr. Tucker's product cost estimates for selected periods, 1954 to 1955.

Two other figures were added to the list of parts costs in compiling a product cost list. Mr. Tucker added 10% of total parts cost to cover spoilage, shrinkage, and freight-in. For a few months during 1954 he and the other two assemblers kept daily time charts from which he compiled standard times for each job. Then he divided these times by an arbitrary 70% efficiency factor and multiplied by an arbitrary rate, $3 an hour, to get a total labor cost for each product.

Actually, this is all an addition of lies. These costs can't mean much. For example, over the period of the last six months we had such sales as to justify one man for 24 hours a week. . . . I think these figures (in Exhibit 6) are interesting and useful to see if our costs are going up or down, but I think

Exhibit 6

WAYLAND COMPANY

Mr. Tucker's Product Cost Estimates

	Jan., 1954	Dec., 1954	Nov., 1955
1. Portable Unit (without cylinders):			
Total parts	$15.73	$13.51	$13.65
10% allowance	1.57	1.35	1.37
Labor	3.00	3.00	3.00
Total manufactured cost	$20.30	$17.86	$18.02
2. 4½-Pound Self-contained Unit:			
Total parts	22.54	24.41	26.12
10% allowance	2.25	2.45	2.61
Labor	6.00	6.00	6.00
Total manufactured cost	$30.79	$32.86	$34.73
3. 6½-Pound Self-contained Unit:			
Total parts	26.77	28.92	31.72
10% allowance	2.61	2.90	3.17
Labor	6.00	6.00	6.00
Total manufactured cost	$35.38	$37.82	$40.89
4. 9-Pound Self-contained Unit:			
Total parts	27.44	30.06	32.76
10% allowance	2.74	3.00	3.28
Labor	6.00	6.00	6.00
Total manufactured cost	$36.18	$39.06	$42.04
5. 4¾-Pound Industrial Self-contained Unit:			
Total parts	22.78	24.07	26.08
10% allowance	2.28	2.41	2.61
Labor	6.00	6.00	6.00
Total manufactured cost	$31.06	$32.48	$34.69

Source: Company records.

trying to extrapolate them into profit or loss statements is a waste of time, although Ed Cole likes to do it.

In the fall of 1954 Mr. Carson took over the inventory control system, but three months later Mr. Tucker relieved him. Mr. Carson afterwards was at a loss to explain this move: "Running the system came easily to me." Mr. Tucker explained, "I like to keep track of the parts myself since I'm constantly improving the products."

Mr. Cole, who noted that he had been used to complicated control systems in the large companies in which he had worked, said he had carried most of the control information in his head but now he wanted more accurate costs for budgeting purposes. At a breakeven point he figured his costs as a per cent of net sales would run as follows: purchased materials, 37%; direct costs and factory overhead, 13%; selling costs, 10%; advertising, 10%; general and administration, 12%; royalties, 4%; and profit, 14%.

Mr. Cole was not sure at what sales figure these percentages would be made but thought it might be in the neighborhood of $100,000 to $250,000 of sales.

FINANCE

"My cousin and I have invested money in the company, loaned money to the company, guaranteed loans to the company, but now the company needs more money," Mr. Cole said. "We need $5,000 to $10,000 in the immediate future and another $40,000 to $50,000 later on."

Mr. Cole had investigated four ways of obtaining new money: (*a*) He talked to the banks, the regional Small Business Administration, and a local development corporation, and he came to the conclusion that credit, as far as Wayland was concerned, was frozen. He said at times he even thought of moving the company to another state because of the local banking situation. (*b*) He asked the banks about the possibilities of a loan against a big order from a large and reputable company but was told he could only get a loan on the accounts receivable. (*c*) He checked through a Boston finance company to investigate the possibilities of a factoring arrangement and found that such an arrangement could be made when accounts receivable ran about $30,000. (*d*) He found that trying to sell blocks of stock through underwriters was financially unfeasible for his size of issue.

Mr. Cole wanted to sell stock at par, $10, to such people as would not interfere with his management. He said he did not want to sell the stock to another company because he wanted to keep management control. "We're trying to develop a business, not milk it, and we don't want anyone else to come in and milk it either. The question is, can we get this capital and at the same time keep control?" Originally, he was wary of selling small blocks of stock because he didn't want to be bothered by the small stockholders, but he had discovered that his fears were unfounded. According to Mr. Cole, selling small amounts of stock locally posed some difficulties: "I need to sell the stock but it takes a lot of time, and for the company's growth I must spend that time on sales. I've lived most of my life in Europe and I don't know many people in this area. I don't belong to the clubs, I don't go to the cocktail parties and mix, so, frankly, I am considered an outsider."

In 1955 there were outstanding 5,289 shares of Wayland common stock, of which 4,419 shares, or 83.5%, were held by company personnel. Most of the other stockholders were friends or acquaintances of Wayland management and had bought stock after hearing of the company's problems. Mr. Cole did not believe in soliciting friends. "Getting your friends to buy stock is a fast way to lose friends; however, if they come and ask to become stockholders, that's all right." The stockholders and their holdings were as follows:[2]

Name	Number of Shares	%
Mr. AB	20	0.4
Mr. BC	100	1.9
Mr. BC and company	200	3.8
Mr. CD	100	1.9
Mr. DE	200	3.8
Mr. EF	200	3.8
Mr. FG	50	0.9
Mr. Edward H. Cole	1,503	28.4
Miss Helen D. Cole	1,505	28.4
Mr. Richard M. Tucker	369	7.0
Mr. Paul A. Fuller	1,005	19.0
Mr. Herbert L. Carson	30	0.6
Mrs. Audrey Bradley	5	0.1
Lawyers	2	....
Total	5,289	100.0%

ORGANIZATION

Employees described Wayland as a close-knit organization; everyone knew everyone else's salary. They each felt they reported directly to Mr. Cole, for whom all expressed great admiration. Mr. Fuller thought that Mr. Tucker should be in charge of production with Fuller and Mr. Carson reporting to him but added that he, Fuller, would report to Mr. Cole on sales matters. Descriptions of company personnel are given in Exhibit 7.

Employees described Mr. Cole as polite, but strong when he had to be, a very patient explainer, and an executive who "works like a dog in trying to see all of the angles." Mr. Cole said of himself:

Somebody has to say yes or no around here, and that is me. . . . I want to spend most of my time on sales but, in fact, I do whatever seems to be necessary. . . . To run a company, I think, takes a good second-class mind and a singleness of purpose; if you have a first-class mind, you go mad, if no singleness of purpose you don't have the drive. I don't like driving others but I like to stimulate them into action. I think my value to the company is that I've had broad experience and a fair amount of training in marketing; I pick good salesmen. I think people like to work for me, at least they say they do. I think my most important quality—be it temperament or luck—is that I am resilient and I bounce and I am determined. If I can find a door or way out of the box we are in, I'll go through it; if not, I will just go through the darn wall.

[2] Five shares per employee were distributed in December, 1954, in lieu of annual vacations.

Employees agreed that Mr. Cole had no mechanical ability, or was "ham-handed," as one employee put it. One person felt the president sometimes oversold a client. Another said that Mr. Cole sometimes spent too long trying to decide between two alternative courses of action. "If it's that hard to decide, it couldn't matter *much* which alternative he picked. Still, some of the mistakes he has made within the last three

Exhibit 7

WAYLAND COMPANY
Descriptions of Company Personnel

Edward H. Cole* Age: 54
Position: President Salary: $75/week
Background:
 After finishing Yale Sheffield in 1924, became liaison officer in Germany, France, and England and finally managing director of the English interests of Lehn & Fink Products Corporation. In 1937 joined Jergens Woodbury Sales Corporation as eastern sales manager. After six years with the Royal Air Force, worked first for G. Frank Sweet, Inc., advertising agency, and then became vice-president of Pierce's Proprietaries in Buffalo.

Helen D. Cole* Age: Over 40
Position: Treasurer and Secretary Salary: $40/week
Background:
 A.B., University of Vermont, 1932. Worked for the Black Rock Bank and during World War II was in the accounting department of McGuire Industries. Joined Wayland as a part-time employee in 1952.

Richard M. Tucker* Age: 40
Position: Design Engineer Salary: $120/week
Background:
 B.S. in Engineering, Massachusetts Institute of Technology, 1942. After a year in industry, worked in M.I.T. Radiation Laboratory until it was dissolved in 1945. From 1945–47 ran a radio repair shop, and from 1947–50 taught high school physics. After two years with Aero Medical Research Unit of Yale Medical School, joined Burgin Machine Works from which he came to Wayland in 1953.

Paul A. Fuller* Age: 26
Position: Assistant to Mr. Cole Salary: $75/week
Background:
 Graduated from the Kent School in 1947, worked two years as a salesman for Bridgeport Hardware, and then attended the University of Bridgeport for a year before going into the Army. From 1951–52 was a salesman for Johnny Seesaw Ski Equipment. Joined Wayland in 1952.

---

* These people, with the lawyer, are on the board of directors.
Source: Interviews with company personnel.

Exhibit 7—Continued

WAYLAND COMPANY

Descriptions of Company Personnel

Herbert L. Carson   Age: 33
Position: Production Manager   Salary: $70/week
Background:
   Graduated from N.H. Junior College in 1942 and entered the Navy.
In 1945 attended the American Academy of Embalming and, following
a year of apprenticeship, managed a funeral home for five years. Worked
for Burgin Machine Works prior to joining Wayland early in 1953.

Audrey Bradley   Age: Over 30
Position: Secretary   Salary: $23/week
Background:
   Widow with two children receiving social security benefits which
prevent her working full time. When benefits expire in 1964, hopes to
have a full-time job with Wayland.

---

years have shaken his confidence a bit; I don't think he's gambling anymore." Commented Mr. Cole, "I think I know my own flat sides; I don't
broadcast them."

Mr. Richard M. Tucker was the design engineer and also the highest
paid person in the company (see Exhibit 7). Mr. Tucker said of himself:

Sometimes I'm worth $100 an hour because I happen to know something
that improves our product; sometimes I'm worth $5 an hour; sometimes I'm
worth 50 cents an hour; sometimes I'm worth nothing at all. I have to wear
many hats—I'm not only the engineer but I also have to work on production,
do the purchasing, and keep the cost system going. I like working in a small
company; in fact, I think I'd go crazy if I had to go back to a big one. I don't
want to be a school teacher again. I had enough of trying to teach a bunch of
auto mechanics. I'm the kind of guy who can work at triple speed for three
days and then collapse. With my engineering background and the work I have
done in physiology, both before coming here and after, I think I know about
as much about breathing equipment as anyone; however, I need someone out
here to talk to who has a technical background such as mine. As to my future
here, I don't have any particular ambition to be president, although I think I
could do the job; I want to run a research and development department.

Fellow employees expressed great admiration for Mr. Tucker's technical ability, mind, and knowledge of his field but had doubts about
his administrative ability. Mr. Carson said:

We think we have to have a top-notch engineer like Dick to make improvements and invent new products, but, unfortunately, he has to do many jobs

for which we could hire a girl. Perhaps it would be better if he just stuck to one problem at a time, although I realize they all have to be done.

Mr. Paul A. Fuller, son of a long-time friend of Mr. Cole, divided his time between sales and production work. In October, 1955, he was in charge of Wayland exhibits for the Chicago safety show. Mr. Fuller said:

> I'm interested in capital appreciation; that's why I invested $10,000 in this company and took out a loan to finance it. When I was looking for a job, all the companies that I talked to told me about the pension I'd have when I was 65 if I didn't make mistakes. . . . As to my future here, I will run the company some day unless someone else comes in that is more qualified to do the job. I think I am capable of taking over the company tomorrow; you have to be tough to run a company, and, unlike some of the men here, I could fire half of the employees tomorrow if it was necessary for the company's growth. In fact, I'd do it at the drop of a hat.

Others in the company said Mr. Fuller had a good mind, a fertile imagination, and much ambition; he had suggested many ideas for new products or improvements. With his young wife, he had rebuilt an old cabin into a house, a job which included digging a cellar, adding rooms, and installing heating. Mr. Tucker considered this a pretty good example of Mr. Fuller's being "uninhibited" and willing to try anything. One person described Mr. Fuller as a strong starter and a weak finisher: "He starts off knowing all the answers but soon finds he doesn't, gets bogged down, and starts on something else. Now he's asking questions far more quickly than he ever did before." Miss Cole commented, "Paul's enthusiastic, liable to jump to conclusions, and inclined to make decisions himself when Ed's away without awaiting his return; later he realizes that he should have waited." Most employees agreed that Mr. Fuller would some day run the Wayland Company.

FUTURE PLANS

Mr. Cole talked about the future as follows:

> I feel that if this company fails there's only one person that is responsible, and that is me; if we succeed, everyone has had a hand in the success. I think if we can get over the present hurdles of finance and marketing problems, which will take a couple of years, there's a real future for the people here. We need financing, we must find some new products or find new markets for our present products, and we must develop a marketing organization. I'll put whatever financing we get into working capital rather than into bricks and mortar. In other words, I'd rather work on the marketing end than expand our production facilities. I'm sure the Wayland Company has a great future.

Stacey Tile Company

THE STACEY TILE COMPANY suffered losses each year after 1928; its sales declined from $997,835 in 1926 to $1,867 in 1934, and increased to only $43,948 in 1935. On August 1, 1936, P. B. Gilbert obtained control of the company. Mr. Gilbert was experienced in tile manufacture; he had started in 1920 with one of the large tile companies, had served as foreman, factory superintendent, and general manager, and in 1926 had been made president of that company. He resigned from this position in 1935 because he could obtain no more than a small proprietary interest in the company and wanted to enter business for himself. When he assumed control of the Stacey company, he intended to have it operating efficiently by the following spring in order that he might take advantage of the substantial increase in tile sales which he forecast would take place not later than the summer of 1937.

The company, located in New Brunswick, New Jersey, had manufactured floor and wall tile for more than 25 years under the ownership and personal supervision of Mr. Kilmer. After Mr. Kilmer's death in 1931, his widow and his son-in-law, Mr. Pearson, attempted to manage the company. In 1934 they mortgaged its fixed assets to obtain a loan of $60,750 from the Reconstruction Finance Corporation. Because of sustained losses, however, they were threatened with foreclosure proceedings in the spring of 1936. Mr. Gilbert heard of the situation and carefully investigated the company. After finding the officials of the Reconstruction Finance Corporation willing to co-operate with him, he made the following agreement with Mrs. Kilmer: In return for 80% of the company's common stock and an option to buy the remainder, he would personally supervise the company's operations and arrange to give Mrs. Kilmer title to her home which had been held in the name of the company.

Mr. Gilbert's investigation of the company revealed that it had manufactured chiefly floor tile. Virtually all floor tile is made without a glazed surface, whereas most wall tile is glazed. Mr. Gilbert found that the company had the necessary equipment to glaze only one-fourth of its potential tile production. Most of the company's glazing capacity had

30

been acquired in 1928 and had not been used after 1931. Mr. Gilbert also found that the company, then operating at 2% of its capacity, had 20 people in its employ: 15 factory workers, 2 foremen, a plant super-

Exhibit 1

STACEY TILE COMPANY

Selected Balance Sheets

Assets	July 31, 1936	Dec. 31, 1936	March 31, 1937
Current Assets:			
Cash.............................	$ 10,228	$ 715	$ 954
Accounts Receivable...............	2,773	10,865	42,762
Notes Receivable..................	573	471	471
Inventories.......................	6,033	55,183	49,456
Total Current Assets............	$ 19,607	$ 67,234	$ 93,643
Fixed Assets:			
Real Estate.......................	173,468	55,315	55,315
Buildings.........................	68,682	68,682	68,682
Machinery........................	95,106	99,171	99,171
Kilns.............................	39,638	39,638	39,638
Factory Fixtures..................	12,189	12,189	12,189
Automobiles......................	804	804	804
Office Equipment.................	1,307	1,359	1,359
Deferred Assets...................	1,499	207	272
Total Assets.................	$412,300	$344,599	$371,073

Liabilities			
Current Liabilities:			
Accounts Payable.................	$ 2,143	$ 36,749	$ 51,549
Accrued Expenses.................	14,189	19,700	21,819
Notes Payable *..................	.....	72,600	80,600
Total Current Liabilities	$ 16,332	$129,049	$153,968
RFC Mortgage.....................	60,750	60,300	60,300
Reserve for Depreciation..........	92,134	92,134	92,134
Capital:			
Capital Stock	200,000	100,000	100,000
Surplus...........................	43,084		
Deficit...........................	.....	36,884	35,329
Total Liabilities....	$412,300	$344,599	$371,073

* The notes were payable to P. B. Gilbert.

intendent, a bookkeeper, and a stenographer. All the employees had been with the company for 10 years or more. Mr. Gilbert considered much of the company's equipment obsolete and the layout of its plant inefficient. No fans had been installed, and the air was heavy with dust raised by conveyors moving over the factory's wooden floor. The company's balance sheet for July 31, 1936, is included in Exhibit 1.

After his investigation, Mr. Gilbert decided that with repairs and replacements the company could be operated profitably because of its favorable location. In this regard he stated:

Tile buyers have demanded prompt deliveries since the advent of colored tile in 1924. By the use of trucks, the Stacey Company can give 24-hour delivery service to customers within a radius of 300 miles of New Brunswick, an area which includes the market for 60% of the wall and floor tile sold in the United States. In addition, northern New Jersey has been the center of the tile manufacturing industry in the East for a number of generations and little difficulty should be encountered in obtaining capable factory workers. Lastly, the company can purchase raw materials as cheaply as any of its competitors.

At that time, Mr. Gilbert also decided that if he did take over the company, he would confine its activities almost exclusively to the manufacture of wall tile. He explained his decision as follows:

I forecast that a shortage of wall tile will begin by 1938, if not during the summer of 1937. Indications are that building activity will increase substantially, and the price of wall tile will reflect the increase more than the price of floor tile. The floor tile industry is made up of companies also manufacturing wall tile, and of a large number of small operators. The latter group enter and leave competition with price fluctuations and, therefore, set a relatively low peak for floor tile prices. The wall tile industry, on the other hand, is less easy to enter on a shoe string because the manufacture of wall tile requires the use of more equipment, a better-trained working force, and more skillful management. In 1927, tile dealers were held up for as long as two or three months in obtaining wall tile deliveries, and since then, the industry's capacity has been decreased at least 40% by the sale of plants to pottery manufacturers. These plants were sold with the understanding that they would not be used for manufacturing tile.

I realize that by choosing to concentrate on wall tile I am complicating the task of conditioning the Stacey Company, but I believe that my 16 years' experience in the industry will make it possible for me to accomplish a great deal in a relatively short time. Furthermore, I think that during the first year, at least, I can fill in by making some floor tile.

Before Mr. Gilbert definitely made up his mind to take over the Stacey company, he determined in detail what would have to be done in order to have the company operating efficiently by the following spring. His resources were limited, and it was necessary for him to minimize expenditures when making his plans.

Mr. Gilbert hoped that by effective supervision, by careful training of factory workers, and by thoroughly cleaning out the plant, the company could manufacture a large percentage of the highest grade wall tile. Tile is sold in three grades: standard, second, and special. According to figures released by the National Tile Manufacturers' Association, 50% of the wall tile and 80% of the floor tile sold from 1928 through 1935 were of standard grade. Exhibit 2 presents the prices of standard-grade floor and wall tile for the years 1923 through 1936, and of second-grade floor and wall tile for the two years, 1935 and 1936. The differences in price between seconds and specials had been approximately the same as those between standards and seconds.

Exhibit 2

AVERAGE PRICES OF FLOOR AND WALL TILE (INCLUDING TRIM)
IN CENTS PER SQUARE FOOT
(*1923–36*)

YEAR	FLOOR TILE		WHITE WALL TILE		ALL OTHER GLAZED TILE (BLACK AND COLORED)	
	Standards	Seconds	Standards	Seconds	Standards	Seconds
1923	25	..	48	..	77	..
1924	24	..	42	..	76	..
1925	24	..	41	..	75	..
1926	25	..	40	..	78	..
1928	23	..	28	..	61	..
1929	25	..	28	..	49	..
1930	25	..	26	..	38	..
1931	21	..	25	..	31	..
1932	19	..	22	..	25	..
1933	16	..	21	..	27	..
1934	23	..	23	..	30	..
1935	23	18	23	20	32	24
1936	24	18	27	24	36	28

Source: National Tile Manufacturers' Association.

Mr. Gilbert thought that it would be necessary to use two salesmen at the outset to sell the company's tile, one in New York City and the other in cities as far south as Washington, D.C. The salesmen would establish relationships with tile contractors and wholesalers. Mr. Gilbert considered it important that the company obtain the patronage of successful contractors. He explained this by saying:

With the development of colored tile, wholesalers gained in importance. At that time they started to buy tile in relatively large quantities and to keep a stock of the various colors and shapes. In fact, manufacturers encouraged them to assume that function by offering quantity discounts. After 1930 the position of wholesalers was strengthened further because many unemployed tile setters, operating independently, bought tile from them whenever they obtained repair or small installation jobs. It is my belief that many of these tile setters, or pushcart dealers, as they are called, will remain in business for themselves even though established contractors try to attract them by raising wages. But in spite of the fact that wholesalers may retain their present share of the business, I would much prefer to deal with contractors. The wholesalers are constantly exerting pressure for larger discounts, and many of them buy second-grade tile expecting to receive a large percentage of standard-grade tile at no extra cost to them. As long as these conditions exist and the Stacey Company is so located that it can keep contractors satisfied with its service, it seems to me desirable to get as much business as possible direct from contractors.

The chief use of wall tile is for bathroom walls, although it is also used in subways, in hotels, and in office buildings. Floor tile, on the other hand, is extensively used in the corridors of office buildings as well as in many bathrooms. To the lay observer, the difference between standard and second-grade tile is not readily apparent. Even though second-grade tile does not meet United States Government specifications, it is purchased for many houses, apartments, and office buildings. After 1930, manufacturers of glass, linoleum, and cork advertised extensively to secure recognition for their products as substitutes for tile. Nevertheless, Mr. Gilbert thought that, inasmuch as glass was twice as expensive as tile, and much more fragile, its potential market was not large. He added that he did not fear competition from the lower-cost substitutes, linoleum and cork, because they were less durable and appealed to a lower-income group than did tile.

Mr. Gilbert was of the opinion that he would have to give little attention to the sales end of the business, and would be able to spend almost all his time in the factory until it was able to sustain itself.

The early processes in the manufacture of both floor and wall tile are similar. Water and several types of clay are mixed in a "sliphouse" according to carefully prepared formulas, a different formula being used for floor tile than for wall tile. The mixture is filtered and the residue ground fine. It then goes in powdered form to the pressroom, where it is stamped by dies into tile shapes and placed in containers called "saggers." Saggers are of a rough clay composition and are about the size of shoe boxes. The tile is then ready to be baked in a kiln. Either of two types of kilns can be used: a periodic kiln or a tunnel kiln. The former has to be cooled to permit workers to empty and refill it, whereas the latter is kept fired and saggers stacked on conveyors pass through it. After being removed from a kiln, floor tile is ready to be mounted on sheets of paper either in plain style or to produce some design. From 64 to 144 tile pieces are pasted on each sheet one foot square. The tile is graded as it is mounted.

Wall tile, on the other hand, is ready to be glazed after baking, and in that stage it is called "bisque." Inasmuch as bisque is white and can be glazed in any color, it is not uncommon for companies to maintain an inventory of bisque, particularly in pieces for edges and corners, and glaze it only as specific orders are received from customers. The process of glazing takes three days. It consists of spraying one surface of the tile with a prepared solution, and reburning the tile in a kiln. After this second firing the tile is sorted, graded, and packed. Some of the difficulties inherent in glazing are: (1) the coefficient of expansion of the glaze must equal that of the tile body in order that the glaze may not crack (craze) or peel (shiver) after it has been baked; (2) before and during firing the adhesive characteristics of liquid glaze make it vulnerable to factory dirt or chips from saggers; (3) because of increased handling, glazed tile is more likely to be damaged than unglazed tile; (4) between runs of different color glazes, glaze spraying machines have to be thoroughly cleansed or glazes will be discolored.

The Stacey company's kiln capacity on July 31, 1936, is shown in Exhibit 3.

Exhibit 3

STACEY TILE COMPANY

Kiln Capacity—July 31, 1936
Square Feet per Week

First firing or bisque kilns:
11 periodic kilns 132,000

Second firing or glazing kilns:
8 periodic kilns 9,600
1 tunnel kiln 35,000   44,600

Mr. Gilbert found that the tunnel kiln was in good condition, but most of the periodic kilns needed to be repaired. Even so, he thought he could use the five bisque kilns which required the least repair, and not operate the periodic glazing kilns during the first year. Mr. Gilbert considered it possible to obtain good used machines to replace the obsolete machines which the company had. Because of the expense involved, he eliminated the possibility of installing fans, cementing the floor, and scraping and painting the factory building. He figured that such improvements could be made later.

In Mr. Gilbert's estimation, it was essential that the company have a competent factory superintendent and six capable foremen in order to have its factory workers trained properly. He had no men in mind for the positions of foremen, but believed that he could retain the company's factory superintendent, Mr. Hanley, because he appeared eager to co-operate and was well versed in the technique of tile manufacturing.

The company had used outmoded formulas for its tile body. Mr. Gilbert was familiar with body formulas, but realized that the introduction of new ones would necessitate the casting and machining of a complete set of dies. Nevertheless, he decided that such an expenditure would be desirable since he planned to make high-quality tile. He thought it would be advisable, however, to hire a ceramic engineer to develop glazes.

Mr. Gilbert planned that by the first week in September he could have the factory cleaned out, dies made, machines installed, and foremen and some factory workers hired. Furthermore, he thought that the company could deliver at least black and white tile by October 1, and could then start test runs on colored glazes. By November, he expected to have a labor force of 200. Although that number of workers would be in excess of his needs, he believed it would be a saving in the long run to have them trained in advance. Most of the work in a tile factory is done by women who can be classified as semiskilled workers.

Mr. Gilbert decided that $30,000 would be sufficient to repair the plant as has been outlined, and that an additional $30,000 for working capital would enable him to operate. He stated that he could buy raw materials on a hand-to-mouth basis and avoid accumulating inventories by selling what tile he made. Moreover, he thought that little money would be tied up in receivables because tile buyers usually took advantage of the 2% discount allowed them for remitting within 15 days. The National Tile Manufacturers' Association had developed a credit system with a collection agency whereby tile wholesalers and dealers were given an "A" rating provided they paid their bills within 30 days, and a "C" rating if they did not. A company selling tile to a customer with a "C" rating paid a premium to the collection agency of 10% of the sale. This plan had been effective and slow payments were virtually eliminated.

Mr. Gilbert assumed control of the Stacey company on August 1, 1936, and loaned the company $60,000 on its unsecured note. A few days later, he hired a salesman to sell tile in New York City. For this position he obtained the services of Mr. Allen who had been selling tile in that city for 10 years. Mr. Gilbert thought highly of him and was confident that he could work effectively with relatively little guidance. Mr. Pearson was retained to fill the other sales position. A former

purchasing agent of a Middle Western tile company was hired to perform such functions as purchasing, scheduling of production, and talking to small buyers who visited the plant. The company's bookkeeper
and its stenographer were kept to take care of the remaining office
duties.

Mr. Hanley remained as factory superintendent. He began hiring factory workers and directing them in the task of cleaning up the factory.
Four carloads of machinery were purchased from a tile company in
Ohio which was being liquidated; and the Stacey company's presses,
glaze sprayers, conveyors, and pulverizer were discarded. Mr. Gilbert
undertook to hire the foremen himself. He retained the two who had
been with the company and placed them in charge of the day and night
shifts in the pressroom. Mr. Gilbert interviewed many applicants for the
remaining four positions, finally choosing three men—an experienced
machinist and die maker for the machine shop, a sliphouse foreman, and
a sorting-room foreman. The last-mentioned had had 22 years' experience in the tile industry, 10 of which had been as a factory superintendent. For the position of glazing foreman, Mr. Gilbert hired one of
his former employees. The nucleus of the company's organization was
established by the first of September when its last member was added,
a young ceramic engineer.

After a week's delay occasioned by the need for replacing the company's sagger press which broke down, the factory equipment was ready
for test runs. Mr. Hanley, however, had encountered difficulty in hiring
and retaining workers for the factory. He found that very few of the
applicants had had experience in wall-tile production, and most of them
were not accustomed to the exacting work it required. He stated that
many other companies in the surrounding area had already expanded
their production and that the best tile workers were employed. Mr.
Gilbert decided it would be too costly to offer wages which would attract workers from competitors, and he told Mr. Hanley to hire the most
promising applicants with little regard to their experience. By the following January, he had employed a total of 400 persons to retain a
force of 185.

In the middle of October the company produced its first standard-
grade tile. Mr. Gilbert had instructed his sorting-room foreman to set
strict grading specifications for his workers because it would teach them
good habits during their training period and would help to create a company reputation for quality. In November, test runs on colored tile were

begun. Seven months later, formulas had been developed for twenty-four colors of wall tile and eight colors of floor tile.

During this early period Mr. Gilbert spent most of his time in the factory helping the foremen improve the efficiency of their departments. For example, he noted that the company's three kiln operators worked five or six hours overtime each day, and he asked Mr. Hanley for an explanation. Mr. Hanley stated that the three men had been with the company for years and the schedule by which they fired kilns demanded overtime work. He added that he had tried to induce them to change their schedule, but they had refused. Mr. Gilbert had Mr. Hanley dismiss one of the men and change the firing schedule the next day. A similar situation arose in the sliphouse, where nine of the company's former employees worked in three shifts of three men each. When Mr. Gilbert established a standard of performance for them, they rebelled. By replacing two of the shifts with new men, it was found that the standard was easily attainable.

After the middle of November, Mr. Gilbert's typical working day was as follows. He arrived at his office at 8 o'clock in the morning and spent his first hour and a half walking through the factory making suggestions to foremen. He then went to his office to read and answer his mail. Following that, he returned to the factory to see if his suggestions had been put into effect and to continue his search for further possible improvements. He usually talked to Mr. Allen on the telephone for at least 20 minutes before taking one-half hour off for luncheon. Returning to his office, he conferred with his bookkeeper in regard to unpaid receivables and the payment of bills. He had found it necessary to devote at least one hour each day to conferences with customers. He made one trip through the factory in the afternoon and talked to Mr. Hanley for at least two hours before leaving for the day. With Mr. Hanley he reviewed the foremen's daily reports and discussed in detail plans for the next day. In addition to this usual routine, Mr. Gilbert signed all checks, talked to Reconstruction Finance Corporation officials occasionally, made a trip to New York City once every 10 days to see Mr. Allen's customers, conferred at length with Mr. Pearson on Saturday mornings, and planned expenditures by drawing up monthly budgets in rough form. Four or five evenings a week he worked at home. During one evening, for example, he jotted down twenty-two ideas for possible methods of reducing production costs, increasing the company's wall-tile capacity, and improving the quality of its products. Most of the previous evening's ideas were tested the following day. As a conse-quence, the capacity of the company's tunnel kiln was increased from 35,000 to 47,000 square feet of wall tile a week.

The company's sales in December showed a decided drop from Octo-ber and November. Both Mr. Gilbert and Mr. Allen had had the grippe and, as a result, a week's time had been lost. Because of the unsatisfac-tory showing that month, and the expenditure of $8,000 more for ma-chinery and equipment than he had originally planned, Mr. Gilbert had to loan the company $12,600 in December and an additional $8,000 in January. The added investment virtually exhausted his savings.

The company's weekly expenses in January and February, as segre-gated by Mr. Gilbert, were as shown in Exhibit 4. Although the wage

Exhibit 4

STACEY TILE COMPANY

Weekly Expenses—January and February, 1937

Wages	$3,200	
Freight-in	750	
Miscellaneous	500	
Total not postponable		$4,450
Supplies and materials	$1,500	
Coal and oil	420	
Packages	200	
Miscellaneous	200	
Total postponable		2,320
Total		$6,770

expense had remained constant, the other expenses had varied some-what with changes in volume.

To make certain that a sufficient amount of cash would be on hand each week to pay the expenses which were not postponable, a sales agreement was made in January with a wholesaler in New York City. The terms of the agreement were that the company would give the wholesaler's orders preference in delivery over any others for one year and, in return, the wholesaler would buy a minimum of $3,500 of tile a week from the Stacey company. Although most of the company's postponable expenses had been accumulating up to January, Mr. Gil-bert was able to keep his creditors satisfied with partial payments and promises to remit in full as soon as he could.

The company's losses tended to decrease each month until March; in that month it made a profit of $2,500. No depreciation had been charged but, since the previous August, $25,000 of the $38,000 spent on machinery and kiln repairs had been treated as an operating expense of the period. The company's monthly sales from October to March are shown in Exhibit 5. Approximately 75% of the sales had been in New York City and about 65% had been to wholesalers. The size of contractors' orders had ranged from 40 to 1,500 square feet each and had averaged 400 square feet. The size of wholesalers' orders, on the other hand, had ranged from 1,000 to 3,600 square feet each and had averaged 2,000 square feet. During the month of February, the company received an average price of 19½ cents per square foot for its wall tile.

The company had improved the quality of its tile so that, by April, runs of colored, white, and black tile, in both flat and trim shapes, had

Exhibit 5

STACEY TILE COMPANY

Monthly Sales—October, 1936, to February, 1937

	Total	Square Feet of Floor Tile	Square Feet of Wall Tile
October...............	$24,041	21,246	90,388
November..............	17,149	23,342	54,269
December.............	9,432	8,346	33,888
January................	27,251	12,281	107,447
February........	30,102	(Not available)	
March................	37,024	'' ''	

been completed with at least 50% of each run being of standard grade and 35% in other commercial grades. Mr. Gilbert believed that the chief difficulties still confronting the company in further increasing the quality of its wall tile were threefold: (1) the presence of dirt and dust in the factory; (2) improper inspection and handling of tile in the pressroom because of the difficulty experienced in training workers in that department; and (3) sagger chips sticking to the glaze because of careless handling and adjusting of the glazing machines. This last difficulty was particularly noticeable when the glazing foreman was absent for a week.

The company kept no departmental or job cost records. Nevertheless, Mr. Gilbert attempted to recognize wherein costs should and could be reduced by using his previous experience as a standard. Moreover, by a similar system of visual control, but with the assistance of the purchasing agent, he scheduled production and attempted to avoid the accumulation of inventories. Mr. Gilbert hoped that by late summer,

Exhibit 6

RESIDENTIAL BUILDING CONTRACTS AWARDED IN LOWER NEW YORK STATE,
EASTERN PENNSYLVANIA, DISTRICT OF COLUMBIA AND THE FOLLOWING
STATES: NEW JERSEY, MARYLAND, DELAWARE, VIRGINIA*

(Thousands of Dollars)

	1930	1931	1932	1933	1934	1935	1936	1937
January	26,582	26,163	13,305	5,073	5,986	8,549	15,454	36,862
February	28,905	45,771	10,270	6,988	4,018	6,228	12,215	25,516
March	35,006	49,791	16,293	6,343	13,250	12,961	19,997	29,411
April	41,295	46,123	10,232	7,477	7,697	18,065	22,825	.....
May	42,271	45,141	9,233	9,138	8,538	17,596	25,412	.....
June	33,693	35,673	8,538	10,056	13,263	17,400	24,043	.....
July	32,756	29,424	7,856	8,502	7,584	19,091	26,635	.....
August	27,695	24,697	8,429	7,838	5,920	15,367	32,611	.....
September	48,378	25,785	9,416	6,742	6,108	14,761	25,046	.....
October	55,024	31,126	9,409	8,111	10,228	18,850	29,652	.....
November	41,109	20,783	5,670	8,155	8,213	15,679	26,525	.....
December	38,899	15,508	5,708	13,641	6,035	15,570	23,900	.....

* Contracts for the following are included: apartments, dormitories, hotels, dwellings, two-family houses, housing developments, and Home Owners' Loan Corporation improvements.
Source: Dodge Statistical Research Service.

1937, he might be in a position to hire three men: a cost accountant, a man to schedule production, and a plant manager.

On April 21, 1937, Mr. Gilbert sent the following letter to one of the company's directors:

SUBJECT: *Stacey Tile Company—Tunnel Kiln*

I would be neglecting our opportunities and interests if I did not point out and strongly urge action on the following:

With an outlay involving approximately $40,000 we can utilize full factory capacity and increase our sales to $1,000,000 whereas now they will probably remain at about $500,000.

An additional Tunnel Kiln; a twin to the one we now have will do this.

The tile industry is definitely on the upswing because of greatly increased building construction and substantial price increases for our product. I am becoming more and more perplexed as to accepting additional orders. Every day we have had visits and phone calls from customers wanting their deliveries hurried or assured. Today we have orders amounting to $200,000 and our present manufacturing capacity will not permit sales of more than $45,000 monthly.

Immediate action is necessary for us to obtain the greatly increased profits which can be ours during the balance of 1937 and through 1938. From the date of our decision one hundred days is required to construct the kiln.

Our present capacity should net us a profit of $50,000 for 1937. By adding the new tunnel kiln and only obtaining its benefit for 5 months of this year, our profit should be $85,000. In 1938 our sales should be close to one million dollars and our profit $150,000 for the year.

I am relying on expanded sales and profits to give us the working capital necessary to accomplish the above results.

Again, I must say, I endorse this action without any reservations.

P. B. GILBERT

Mr. Gilbert hoped to be able to finance the construction of the tunnel kiln through the Reconstruction Finance Corporation, through a construction company—as he had done earlier in installing sprinklers—or by means of his personally endorsed note. He estimated that with $40,-000 he could cement the floors and paint the factory, as well as pay for the construction of the kiln.

Exhibit 1 reproduces company balance sheets for December 31, 1936, and March 31, 1937, as well as for July 31, 1936. Building contracts awarded by months from January, 1930 to April, 1937 are shown in Exhibit 6.

HMH Publishing Company, Inc.

"I WOULDN'T TRADE PLACES with anyone else in the world. I have everything I've ever wanted—money, success in business, success in the arts. What I've done anybody else can do if he's willing to display a little of the initiative and derring-do that made the country great in the first place, instead of settling for job security, conformity, togetherness, anonymity, and slow death," remarked Hugh M. Hefner, 35-year-old president of HMH Publishing Company, Inc., in July, 1961.

HMH revenue had grown from $268,000 in 1954 to $8 million for the 11 months ending May, 1961.[1] Over the same period, after-tax earnings had increased from a deficit of $23,000 in 1954 to a profit of $313,000 (see Exhibits 1 and 2).

In July, 1961, Mr. Hefner was concerned with furthering the company's growth and development. He planned to achieve this by: (1) the introduction of a new magazine, *Show Business Illustrated;* and (2) an increase in the number of *owned* and *operated* Playboy Key Clubs, the first of which had been in business for 16 months. Because of the uniqueness of each of these activities, relatively little published information was available to Mr. Hefner for analysis; however, he foresaw no difficulties in adding these additional activities.

HMH Publishing was started in 1953 in Chicago by Mr. Hefner to publish *Playboy,* a monthly magazine. In 1961 he explained that *Playboy* was created as an outlet for his own creative ability which had been stifled during his career as copywriter for *Esquire* magazine, and later as a circulation manager for *Children's Activities.*

The first issue of *Playboy* was published in December, 1954. Mr. Hefner contracted with Art Paul, then a free-lance artist, to provide the necessary art and photo work for the issue. Mr. Paul was paid in common stock of HMH Publishing. Other services for that first issue were obtained in similar fashion. In 1961 Mr. Paul was art director of *Playboy.* Mr. Hefner owned 80% of the outstanding common stock in the company, while a few key employees owned the remaining 20%.

The increasing growth in revenue from *Playboy* financed several

---

[1] Exclusive of sales and earnings of International Playboy Clubs, Inc.

Exhibit 1. HMH PUBLISHING COMPANY, INC.

Comparative Balance Sheets 1954–61

(Dollars in Thousands)

Assets	11 M/E 5/31/61	6 M/E* 6/30/60	12 M/E 12/31/59	12/31/58	12/31/57	12/31/56	12/31/55	12/31/54
Current Assets:								
Cash	$ 60	$ 103	$ 112	$ 192	$ 105	$ 33	$ 70	$15
Receivables	934	717	888	709	482	401	187	20
Inventories	715	511	389	264	211	214	44	33
Other		14	1					
Total Current Assets	$1,709	$1,345	$1,390	$1,165	$ 798	$ 648	$301	$68
Investment	†							
Fixed Assets (Net) (Primarily Real Estate)	1,096	882	837	371	385	306	40	7
Other Assets:								
Deferred Subscription Promotions‡	129	100	133	148	134			
Less: Applicable Federal Taxes	67	52	69	77	52			
	$ 62	$ 48	$ 64	$ 71	$ 82			
Other Assets§	207	94	94	57	46	100	29	4
Total Other Assets	$ 269	$ 142	$ 158	$ 128	$ 128	$ 100	$ 29	$ 4
Total Assets	$3,074	$2,369	$2,385	$1,664	$1,311	$1,054	$370	$79

Liabilities	11 M/E 5/31/61	6 M/E* 6/30/60	12 M/E 12/31/59	12/31/58	12/31/57	12/31/56	12/31/55	12/31/54
Current Liabilities:								
Bank Notes	$ 100	$ 50				$ 100		$ 3
Taxes (F.I.T., Payroll and Excise)	284	95	34	66	20	36	$ 6	45
Other	667	720	808	450	535	428	98	
Total Current Liabilities	$1,051	$ 865	$ 842	$ 516	$ 555	$ 564	$104	$48
Land Contract Payable	244	255	259	825	553	380		
Unearned Subscriptions	1,139	879	982	77	52	14	204	40
Deferred Taxes	48	91	95					
Preferred Stock				15	15	14		1
Common Stock	7	7	7	231	136	82	18	13
Surplus	585	272	200				44	(23)
Net Worth	$ 592	$ 279	$ 207	$ 246	$ 151	$ 96	$ 62	$(9)
Total Liabilities	$3,074	$2,369	$2,385	$1,664	$1,311	$1,054	$370	$79

* Company changed to fiscal year ending June 30.
† 25% interest in International Playboy Clubs, Inc. $400 cost; approximate book value $75,000.
‡ Under a 1957 ruling by the I.R.S., the company was allowed to write off this expense over the months in which the income was taken into consideration.
§ Composed of advances to authors and artists.

Source: Company records.

HMH Publishing Company, Inc.

Ratio Analysis

	5/31/61	6/30/60	12/31/59	12/31/58	12/31/57	12/31/56	12/31/55	12/31/54
Current ratio (R)	1.6	1.6	1.7	2.3	1.4	1.1	2.9	1.4
Net working capital ($)	$658,016	$480,138	$547,609	$649,002	$243,427	$83,930	$196,733	$20,264
Acid test (R)	0.9	1.0	1.2	1.7	1.1	0.8	2.5	0.7
Net worth to debt (R)	0.23	0.13	0.09	0.17	0.13	0.10	0.20	(0.09)
Receivables turnover* (days)	38.7	40.5	57.6	60.3	48.4	46.4	59.8	26.9
Inventory turnover† (days)	32.7	32.0	24.8	23.5	23.7	17.0	18.2	NA
Net sales to fixed assets (R)	7.26	7.23	6.65	11.40	9.35	10.01	28.60	38.40
Gross operating profit to net worth (%)	300.3	234.6	395.5	241.6	236.9	391.4	596.9	Loss
Net profit to net worth (%)	53.0	25.9	10.0	38.5	20.1	62.5	110.5	Loss
Cash (days)	2.7	6.2	7.8	17.1	10.7	4.0	23.0	18.4
Other payables (days)	30	43	54	40	55	51	33	55

* Accounts receivable × 360/net sales.
† Average inventory × 360/cost goods sold.
Source: Prepared from Exhibits 1 and 2 by Harvard Business School staff.

Exhibit 2

HMH PUBLISHING COMPANY, INC.

Comparative Income Statements

(Dollars in Thousands)

Sales	%	11 M/E 5/31/61	%	6 M/E* 6/30/60	%	12 M/E 12/31/59
Magazine (net)	60.0	$4,779	67.8	$2,158	68.8	$3,820
Advertising space—gross	36.0	2,873	30.0	954	26.8	1,490
By-products	1.7	133	1.3	43	1.5	82
Trump division		. . .	. . .	. . .	. . .	. . .
Calendar sales	2.3	182	0.9	30	2.9	160
Miscellaneous		. . .		. . .		. . .
Total	100.0	$7,967	100.0	$3,185	100.0	$5,552
Cost of goods sold:†						
Magazine	73.4	$3,506	76.9	$1,659	81.2	$3,103
Advertising sales	84.5	2,428	86.6	827	95.8	1,428
By-products	90.2	120	100.0	43	97.6	80
Trump division		. . .		. . .		. . .
Calendar	74.2	135	3.3	1	76.8	123
Total	77.7	$6,189	79.4	$2,530	85.3	$4,734
Gross profit	22.3	$1,778	20.6	$ 655	14.7	$ 818
(Less) G & A	12.3	982	11.9	377	8.9	495
Net operating profit	10.0	$ 796	8.7	$ 278	5.8	$ 323
Other income (net)	0.0	2	0.1	1	(0.0)	(1)
Operating profit before taxes and unusual items	10.0	$ 798	8.8	$ 279	5.8	$ 322
Profit sharing		. . .		. . .	1.1	62
Federal taxes	5.1	410	4.5	143	2.4	131
Net profit normal operation	4.9	$ 388	4.3	$ 136	2.3	$ 129
Less: Loss on TV	(2.0)	(156)	(4.1)	(132)	(3.4)	(191)
Loss on Jazz Festival		. . .		. . .	(0.6)	(32)
Tax reduction due to loss	1.0	81	2.1	68	2.1	115
	(1.0)	$ (75)	(2.0)	$ (64)	(1.9)	$ (108)
Net profit	3.9	$ 313	2.3	$ 72	0.4	$ 21
Gross profit:‡						
Magazine	71.6	$1,273	76.2	$ 499	87.7	$ 717
Advertising	25.0	445	19.5	128	7.6	62
By-products	0.7	13	(0.1)	(1)	0.2	2
Trump division		. . .		. . .		. . .
Calendar sales	2.7	47	4.4	29	4.5	37
Total	100.0	$1,778	100.0	$ 655	100.0	$ 818
Promotion expenditures				261		588

* Company changed from calendar to fiscal year.
† As a percentage of respective sales (magazine cost as percentage of magazine sales).
‡ As a percentage of total gross profit.

Source: Company records. Percentages prepared by Harvard Business School staff.

%	12/31/58	%	12/31/57	%	12/31/56	%	12/31/55	%	12/31/54
77.1	$3,265	79.3	$2,840	91.4	$2,842	98.3	$1,107	100.0	$ 268
17.3	732	14.1	507	4.2	131	0.9	10		NA
1.6	66	1.7	61	2.1	64				
		1.4	50	2.3	71				
4.0	168	3.5	125		. . .				
						0.8	9	0.0	0
100.0	$4,231	100.0	$3,583	100.0	$3,108	100.0	$1,126	100.0	$ 268
81.0	$2,644	82.4	$2,342	76.8	$2,183				
110.9	812	134.3	681	287.8	377				
86.4	57	91.8	56	68.8	44		NA		NA
	. . .		140.0	70	178.9	127				
73.8	124	60.8	76		. . .				
86.0	$3,637	90.0	$3,225	87.9	$2,731	66.9	$ 754	92.2	$ 247
14.0	$ 594	10.0	$ 358	12.1	$ 377	33.1	$ 372	7.8	$ 21
9.7	410	8.2	295	9.1	282	28.9	325	17.5	47
4.3	$ 184		$ 63		$ 95	4.2	$ 47	(9.7)	$ (26)
0.1	3	(0.3)	(10)	0.6	19	1.9	22	1.1	3
4.4	$ 187	1.5	$ 53	3.6	$ 114	6.1	$ 69	(8.6)	$ (23)
	. . .		. . .		. . .		. . .		. . .
2.2	93	0.7	23	1.7	54	0.0	0	0.0	0
2.2	$ 94	0.8	$ 30	1.9	$ 60	6.1	$ 69	(8.6)	$ (23)
2.2	$ 94	0.8	$ 30	1.9	$ 60	6.1	$ 69		$ (23)
104.6	$ 621	139.4	$ 499	174.5	$ 658				
(13.5)	(80)	(48.6)	(174)	(65.2)	(246)				
1.5	9	1.4	5	5.5	21		NA		NA
	. . .		(5.6)	(20)	(14.8)	(56)				
7.4	44	13.4	48		. . .		. . .			
100.0	$ 594	100.0	$ 358	100.0	$ 377				
	523		433		255		49		1

other enterprises; four were major parts of HMH operations in July, 1961: (1) *Playboy* by-products, the first of which was the *Playboy Annual,* were started in November, 1954; (2) a taped TV show, "Playboy Penthouse," was first produced in September, 1959; (3) International Playboy Clubs, Inc., was organized in October, 1959; and (4) *Show Business Illustrated* was announced in May, 1961.

Other more peripheral HMH ventures included a discontinued magazine and jazz festival, a currently operating travel agency, and a proposed movie.

In 1956 a Trump Division was organized in New York to publish *Trump,* a monthly magazine satire on radio and TV programs. The key people on the staff of *Trump* previously had been associated with Mad comics, the first magazine of this type. *Trump* was discontinued in 1957 because, as one HMH executive said, ". . . of a lack of effective control over the New York operation."

The Playboy Jazz Festival, held in Chicago in the summer of 1959, was produced by Victor Lownes III, promotion director of HMH. The company suffered a small financial loss on the project after donating the first night's proceeds of $50,000 to the Chicago Urban League.

Playboy Tours, a travel organization, was formed in 1960 to conduct guided tours through Europe, Jamaica, Hawaii, and Mexico. The purpose was to prove to the travel industry that *Playboy* was an effective advertising medium for travel ads. In 1961, the tours were running at about 25% of anticipated volume. Advertising revenue from the travel industry was $22,000 for the first five months of 1961 compared to $10,000 for the similar period in 1960.

Arrangements for "The Playboy Story," a movie on the life of Hugh Hefner, were pending in the spring of 1961 between HMH Publishing and Tony Curtis, the Hollywood actor.

The rest of the case will include both industry and company data: first a note on the publishing industry, followed by a description of *Playboy* and an analysis of competition; next in order, discussions of the Playboy by-products; the HMH television show; a note on the restaurant industry followed by a description of Playboy Key Clubs; and last, a description of *Show Business Illustrated.* The case ends with Mr. Hefner's comments on his plans for the company.

PUBLISHING INDUSTRY

Making generalizations about the magazine publishing industry is difficult. A variety of sizes, types, and classes of periodicals[2] are published, based on varying concepts of publishing. The extremes range

---

[2] The terms "periodical" and "magazine" are used interchangeably.

from mass magazines such as *Life* and *Reader's Digest,* which appeal to a broad cross section of the magazine market, to class magazines such as trade magazines, which are directed toward a small, well-defined segment of the magazine market. There are magazines circulated through newsstands, and magazines sold only by subscription. Some periodicals do not solicit advertising revenue; others rely heavily on this source of income. Finally, there are infinitely varied combinations of all the above.

In 1961 a number of recent trends were evident in the magazine industry.

1. According to the *Census of Manufactures,* gross receipts of the periodical publishing industry had risen steadily between 1947–58:

Periodical Receipts
(Dollars in Millions)

Census Year	Total	Subscriptions and Sales	Advertising	Advertising Per Cent of Total
1958	$1,545	$551	$988	64.0%
1954	1,394	530	863	62.0
1947	1,019	407	612	60.0

2. Again according to the *Census of Manufactures,* the number of periodicals declined from 4,610 in 1947 to 3,427 in 1954 and rose to 4,455 in 1958. The only available figures showed monthlies declined from 2,253 to 1,604 and semimonthlies from 233 to 148 during 1947–54.

3. According to a 1961 *Business Week* survey, television and rising costs were combining to decimate the general magazine field. (An excerpt from this survey to convey an impression of the industry in 1961 is given in Appendix A.)

4. According to a survey conducted for the Magazine Publishers Association, Inc., magazines with the same percentage of advertising revenue as *Playboy* were fortunate to break even in 1959 and 1960 (see Exhibit 3).

5. Again according to *Business Week,* the future held in store: (*a*) increased competition in the class audience field, (*b*) greater use of regional editions, (*c*) more merchandising services, and (*d*) rapid changes in magazine content and appearance.

PLAYBOY MAGAZINE

"What is a playboy?" the magazine asked rhetorically in 1956. It continued, "Is he simply a wastrel, a ne'er-do-well, a fashionable bum?

Exhibit 3. HMH PUBLISHING COMPANY, INC.

Percentage Comparison of Costs of Magazine Publishing, 1957–60

	1960 Industry	1960 HMH (6 months)	1959 Industry	1959 HMH	1958 Industry	1958 HMH	1957 Industry	1957 HMH
Income:								
Advertising	3	26	32	25	2	16	3	13
Subscriptions (earned)	64	20	62	20	} 98	17	88	16
Newsstand	5	54	6	55		67	12	71
Total	100	100	100	100	100	100	100‡	100
Costs:								
Paper	19	21	19	21	29	21	18	24
Printing	17	21	17	23	40	26	24	29
Distribution	5	5	6	5	1	6	6	7
Circulation promotion	20	5	19	5	14	7	10	5
Circulation fulfillment	8	3	8	3	..	3	15	3
Advertising	9	5	9	5	..	5	2	5
Editorial	10	12	10	12	19	12	5	13
Accounting	..		..		..		4	
Administrative	10	13	8	10	10	11	..	9
Total costs	100	85	99	84	118	91	83	86
Profit	0	15	1	16	(18)	9	17*	14* / 5†

Comparison of Selected Costs

	1960 Industry	1960 HMH (6 months)	1959 Industry	1959 HMH	1958 Industry	1958 HMH	1957 Industry	1957 HMH
Circulation costs per reader ($)	$1.62	$0.24	$0.95	$0.47	$0.18	$0.45	$0.38	$0.33
Advertising department								
Income per page ($)	6,580	5,330	3,475	3,960	3,723	3,530	3,553	2,940
Cost per ad page ($)	1,072	1,050	636	880	684	1,210	595	1,040
Ad costs per ad income (%)	16.4	19.8	18.3	22.2	18.3	34.4	16.8	35.4
Revenue per copy sold:								
Advertising	$0.11	$0.13	$0.10	$0.11	$....	$0.06	$....	$0.05
Subscription	0.13	0.10	0.14	0.09	0.13	0.07	0.11	0.06
Newsstand	0.03	0.26	0.03	0.26	....	0.26	0.02	0.26
	$0.27	$0.49	$0.27	$0.46	$0.13	$0.39	$0.13	$0.37

* Profit before administrative costs.   † Profit after administrative costs.

‡ Figures developed for each item individually; therefore, columns may not add to totals.

NOTE: Comparable magazine classes shift as from those with advertising income "up to 20% of total" in 1957–58 to those with advertising income "between 20%–40% of total" in 1959–60.

Far from it: he can be a sharp-minded young business executive, a worker in the arts, a university professor, an architect or engineer. He can be many things, provided he possesses a certain *point of view*. He must see life not as a vale of tears, but as a happy time; he must take joy in his work, without regarding it as the end and all of living; he must be an alert man, an aware man, a man of taste, a man sensitive to pleasure, a man who—without acquiring the stigma of the voluptuary or dilettante—can live life to the hilt. This is the sort of man we mean when we use the word playboy."[3]

Another explanation for the appeal of *Playboy* was offered by the Reverend Roy Larson in an article entitled, "The Lowdown on the Upbeats," published in *Motive*,[4] April, 1960:

. . . My own personal explanation for its popularity goes like this: *Playboy* has a strong, almost irresistible appeal for the self-conscious young man who is struggling to establish his own identity, to define his own personality, to work out his style of life. Caught up in a reaction against "blah," he does not want to be just another person, but wants to show, by his manners, his personal taste in music, food, drink, and apparel, that he is someone who is distinctive.

But he is unsure of himself. He doesn't know his "way around." He is deathly afraid of being ludicrous. He doesn't want to goof. He doesn't want to do anything which would indicate that he's a hick, a square, or a clod. And so he needs impersonal guidance and direction and help.

Where does he get it? From *Playboy*, of course . . .

Playboy magazine was published monthly in three regional editions —East, Midwest, and West—and had experienced continual growth in circulation sales and advertising revenue since 1954. In 1954, the magazine had a monthly circulation of 113,000. There was no revenue from advertising space sales. In 1961 monthly circulation was 1.2 million while advertising space sales accounted for 36% of total revenue (see Exhibits 2 and 4).

Advertising sales was under the direction of Mr. Eldon Sellers, executive vice-president of HMH, and Mr. Howard Lederer, advertising director. Ads were solicited by a staff of 20 salesmen located in offices in New York, Chicago, Los Angeles, and San Francisco, and by two publishers' representatives located in Miami, Florida, and Atlanta, Georgia. A schedule of advertising rates is presented in Exhibit 4. Advertising pages usually constituted about 30% of the pages in the magazine.

The content of the magazine was divided into four parts: fiction,

---

[3] The average *Playboy* reader was 29.6 years old, and had an income of $8,150. In addition 41.3% had an executive/professional business title or position.

[4] Magazine of the Methodist student movement.

Exhibit 4

HMH PUBLISHING COMPANY, INC.

Selected Circulation Figures and Advertising Rates

	Date Established	January, 1953	January, 1954	January, 1955	January, 1956	January, 1957	January, 1958	January, 1959	January, 1960	August, 1961
CIRCULATION*										
Dude	1956	......	......	......	......	......	......	......	......	266,024
Gent	1956	......	......	......	......	......	......	......	......	318,364
Escapade	1953	......	......	......	......	......	......	257,612	328,908	313,924
Esquire	1933	819,679	800,920	787,295	747,274	778,190	824,215	812,531	848,034	875,053
Playboy	1953	......	......	113,565	227,605	687,593	788,350	858,656	940,767	1,144,077
Rogue	1959	......	......	......	......	......	......	......	200,000	260,901
Life	1936	5,339,565	5,536,418	5,615,075	5,655,473	5,714,310	5,851,168	6,041,778	6,107,885	6,764,686
ONE TIME BLACK AND WHITE PAGE RATES*										
Dude and Gent										$3,000
Escapade								$1,400	$1,400	1,400
Esquire		$4,850	$4,850	$4,850	$5,190	$5,600	$6,000	6,150	6,150	6,500
Playboy				650	2,100	3,850	3,850	3,850	5,100	7,100
Rogue									700	700
Life		19,200	19,200	20,350	21,775	23,080	26,275	29,375	29,875	31,150
COST PER PAGE PER 1,000 CIRCULATION †										
Dude and Gent										
Escapade									$4.26	$4.46
Esquire			$10.01	$6.16	$6.99	$7.20	$7.28	$7.57	7.25	7.43
Playboy				5.74	5.25	5.50	4.88	4.48	5.74	6.21
Rogue										2.68
Life			6.46	3.62	3.60	4.04	4.38	4.35	4.77	4.50

* No other data available.

† These costs have been "reduced by the common denominator of cost per thousand copy pages. . . . The number of thousand copy pages is determined by taking the average press run for a given period (usually a year) and multiplying it by the total number of pages run in the period and dividing by 1,000."

Source: *Standard Rate & Data Service,* January issues.

nonfiction, cartoons, and photography. In the June, 1961, issue, fiction occupied 10% of the pages; nonfiction 20%; cartoons and photography, 30%; and miscellaneous, 7%. Fictional material was submitted to the magazine by professional authors through their agents. This source accounted for 99% of the fiction used by the magazine. The remaining 1% came from a "slush pile" of manuscripts submitted directly by amateur writers. About 500 manuscripts per week came to the slush pile while 100 per week came from authors' agents. Each and every manuscript was read by a staff member.

Nonfiction material was classified as informative, such as a series on sports cars; or individual viewpoint articles, such as an article by J. Paul Getty[5] or other known personalities. Informative articles were contracted for with authors who agreed to write a definite number of articles per year. Individual viewpoint material originated either with an outside author who sold it to the magazine, or else with the magazine which contracted with an author to write the feature.

Playboy maintained a standard rate schedule for material used in the magazine regardless of the prominence of the author. The lead article or story in each issue was worth a minimum of $3,000. Authors of other articles and stories used in an issue were paid $1,500; $600 was the standard rate for a short short or one-page feature. Any member of the *Playboy* staff who submitted a story or article that was accepted for publication received the appropriate payment.

The great majority of all cartoons used in the magazine also originated outside the regular staff. Cartoons could be submitted by any individual or else contracted for on a yearly basis with professional cartoonists. All cartoons submitted to the magazine were screened by two associate editors. Those that passed the initial screening were reviewed by the entire editorial staff which made the final selections.

The photography and art work were under the direction of Art Paul, art director of *Playboy* magazine. He would determine what was needed in the way of supporting material for each issue. Art work and/or sketches, which usually accompanied the fictional material, were handled by Mr. Paul and his department.

The "Miss Playmate of the Month" section was a special feature included in every issue of *Playboy*. Photographers from all over the country were invited to submit film strips of prospective Playmates. These photos were reviewed by each editor. The selection of each Playmate

---

[5] Mr. Getty, reported to be the richest man in the world, was business and financial consulting editor for *Playboy* magazine.

was by majority vote of the editorial staff, with final approval coming from Mr. Hefner.

Final approval of the material on each page of the magazine rested with Mr. Hefner.

The production, or actual printing of the magazine, was done by Hall Printing Company of Chicago. This part of the process was under the supervision of Mr. John Mastro,[6] production manager, who was responsible to Mr. Hefner. After the contents of the magazine had been selected, edited, arranged by pages, and approved by Mr. Hefner, the magazine went to Mr. Mastro. He purchased the paper and other supplies, supervised the preparation of the printing plates, scheduled production, and supervised the printing of the magazine.

Mr. Hefner demanded that no expense be spared to make the magazine technically perfect. The first few copies off the press were examined by Mr. Mastro with a magnifying glass to check for printing quality, color separation, and other mechanical details of the printing process. These initial copies also had to be approved by Mr. Hefner. It was not unusual for him to delay final printing two or three days until the quality of the printing met with his approval.

Playboy magazine was distributed in two ways. The Independent News Company distributed 80% of each press run to magazine wholesalers throughout the country who, in turn, would resell to individual retailers. All copies of the magazine were sold on consignment. Independent paid 58% of retail; the wholesaler paid 64%; and the retailer, 80%.

The other channel of distribution was subscription sales. Mailing labels were produced from nameplates prepared and kept up to date by HMH's subscription department. These labels were sent to an outside firm that wrapped each copy of the magazine in a plain brown wrapper, affixed the label, and handled the mailing.

Mr. Hefner spoke of three policies he maintained in publishing *Playboy*. The first was a policy of no reduced rates for subscription sales. A one-year subscription to the magazine was $6; the same price as 12 issues at the newsstand price of 50¢. In September, 1960, when the newsstand price was increased to 60¢, the annual subscription rate remained at $6. He commented, ". . . We . . . believe that our advertisers are entitled to an interested audience, an audience that reads the magazine because it wants to, not because it was bribed into buying. . . ."

---

[6] Mr. Mastro's prior experience had been in the printing industry.

The second policy centered around the sale of advertising space in the magazine. The advertising acceptance committee (composed of Mr. Hefner; Mr. Victor Lownes, promotion director; Mr. Sellers, executive vice-president; and Mr. Spectorsky, associate publisher) screened all prospective advertisements to be sure that they were in keeping with the concept of the magazine. Mr. Hefner continued:

> . . . *Playboy* has the toughest ad policy of any magazine in America with the possible exception of *The New Yorker*. It is one way we have of separating ourselves clearly from the cheap girlie magazines, without ever having to read a line of editorial comment. . . .
>
> What makes an ad unacceptable in our eyes? Well, a wide variety of things —a viewpoint that seems in conflict with the concept of the magazine, ads of questionable taste, ads of questionable value, ads that sell too hard, or are un- attractive or that do not complement the *Playboy* reader—his intelligence, education, income level, taste, etc. . . . For example, we will not accept any ads for weight reducing aids, earn money in your spare time, or the like. . . .

The third policy concerned publication of another magazine similar to *Playboy*. Mr. Lownes summed up this issue as follows:

> . . . Every day we come across articles, stories, cartoons, etc. that just aren't good enough to be published in *Playboy*. Why not publish another magazine using this rejected material? We ruled out that idea for two reasons. First, by definition, the second magazine would not be as good as *Playboy*. There was no way to prevent this inferior magazine from becoming identified with us. We want the prestige of good magazines. Second, it would make decision-making too complicated. We would have to juggle stories, cartoons, etc., between the two magazines. For instance, if the circulation of one was lagging, we would have to take from the other in an attempt to increase sales. This would down- grade both magazines. . . .

COMPETITION

Executives at HMH believed their competition came from two sources. The first was *Esquire* magazine. *Esquire* was published by Es- quire, Inc., which also published *Coronet*[7] and *Gentleman's Quarterly*. In addition, Esquire, Inc., operated radio station WQXI in Atlanta, Georgia, and Wide-Lite Corp., a manufacturer of floodlights. In 1961 Esquire, Inc., suffered an operating loss of $46,000 on sales of $23 mil- lion. Esquire, Inc., had a net worth of $5.6 million.

In defining the *Esquire* reader, Harold Hayes, articles editor for *Esquire,* said:

---

[7] Publication of *Coronet* was discontinued in July, 1961.

. . . He's mature. Whatever his field, he has arrived professionally—or he's on his way. He's a sophisticate in the classic sense: knowledgeable, selective, interested in *everything* in the world around him—or else he wouldn't be interested in *Esquire*.

He's a businessman . . . and a busy man. And *Esquire* is ready to meet his most challenging demands. . . .

Our circulation department tells me that so far, our editorial concept is clicking . . . we're getting the sort of man we really want . . . men such as Josh Logan . . . Mac Kreindler . . . Frank Stanton . . . Otto Preminger . . . Senators Jacob Javits and Barry Goldwater . . . John Crosby . . . Conrad Hilton . . . and J. S. Inskip . . . all of whom happen to be *Esquire* subscribers."[8]

Esquire drew its features from two sources. One was its own staff of eight professional columnists; the second was free-lance professional writers, many of whom were very well-known while others were comparative newcomers to the literary field. Publicity departments of both *Playboy* and *Esquire* could cite many of the same well-known contributors.

Mr. Hefner recalled, ". . . that for years *Esquire* had been all alone as the magazine for the young literate urban male. In the early 1950's, however, I felt that *Esquire* had abandoned this market in favor of the more affluent business and professional man. That's where *Playboy* came in. Now *Playboy* is firmly entrenched as the guide for the young urban male. We have far outstripped *Esquire* in circulation."

The second source of competition for *Playboy* came from the ". . . increasing number of cheap girlie magazines trying to imitate *Playboy*. There must be about 50 of them on the market now, all of them trying to hang on to *Playboy's* coattails. These imitators have not made it up to now, and they never will. We're just too far ahead for anyone else ever to catch up."

The content of these other magazines ranged from those composed almost entirely of girls in various stages of undress to formats similar to that used by *Playboy*. As far as could be determined, no research had been conducted by these magazines in an attempt to define their readers. Recent issues of many of these magazines contained little or no advertising. Further, articles by established writers did not appear in them as regularly as in *Playboy* and *Esquire*.

Mr. Hefner concluded his remarks on the competitive situation by adding: ". . . We have given the young city guy a real identification with the magazine by giving him what he wants. I've always edited on

---

[8] In a 1960 study of *Esquire* subscribers, the average subscriber was 40.8 years old and had an annual income of $14,196. In addition, 61.3% had an executive/professional business title or position.

the assumption that my tastes are pretty much like those of our readers. As I develop, so will the magazine. . . ."

Exhibit 4 presents a comparison of *Playboy, Esquire,* and four other magazines in the men's general interest field. *Life* is included as an example of a mass appeal magazine. These magazines are compared on circulation figures, the cost (to advertisers) per page per 1,000 circulation, and one time, one page, black and white advertising rates.

PLAYBOY BY-PRODUCTS

Playboy by-products were commercial products differentiated only by the *Playboy* rabbit trademark (see Figure 1). These by-products were manufactured by outside suppliers licensed by HMH Publishing.

The first by-product, the *Playboy Annual,* was a collection of cartoons, stories, and articles from the first 12 issues of *Playboy* magazines.

Figure 1

Since that time over 25 by-products had been licensed by HMH. These included tie pins, cuff links, jazz records, shirts, and ties.

There were two outlets for the by-products. The first was through International Playboy Clubs, Inc. HMH would sell to International at 50% off the retail price. International in turn would sell to the individual clubs at 40% off retail. The second outlet was mail orders. HMH maintained a complete mail-order department to fill individual customer requests for by-products.

For the 11 months ending May, 1961, by-products sales were $133,-000 with a gross profit of $13,000. Mr. Victor Lownes, commenting on this activity, said:

> . . . do you know of anyone else, besides Walt Disney and *Playboy,* who can sell products distinguished by their commercial trademark? . . . We get almost 100 requests per week from people with ideas guaranteed to make a million if we would allow use of the *Playboy* rabbit. But we are in the magazine business, not the by-products business. Besides, we don't want to be in competition with any of our advertisers. For that reason we are pretty careful as to just what articles we put our rabbit on. . . .

TELEVISION

HMH produced its own television show "Playboy Penthouse" with Mr. Hefner as M.C. The show was sold by two independent distributors to individual TV stations at prices varying between $300–$700. In July, 1961, 20 out of 580 TV stations in the U.S. carried the show. As shown in Exhibit 2, the 37 hours of programing completed during 1959–60 had produced a net loss of $496,000. Mr. Hefner planned to continue to produce new shows and sell past ones as reruns.

THE RESTAURANT INDUSTRY

The term "restaurant" includes the full spectrum of types and classes of eating places. Types of chain restaurants vary from the corner delicatessen up through variety, drug, and department store chains with restaurants, and ending with Howard Johnson's 608 units coast to coast. Classes of restaurants range from the simple decor of the local sweet shoppe to the elaborate appointments of the finest night and supper clubs.

The 1958 *Census of Manufactures* reported that $11 billion was spent for food and beverage outside the home in 230,000 restaurants. It also added that 310 restaurants with annual sales of $1 million and over, representing 0.13% of total restaurants, accounted for 4.34% of total industry sales.

Cities in which Playboy Key Clubs were either planned or already in operation, along with the relative ranking of these cities according to 1958 restaurant sales, were as follows:

Rank	City	Number of Establishments	Total Restaurant Sales (000)	Revenue per Establishment
1............	New York City†	15,062	$1,347,000	$89,400
2............	Los Angeles†	9,246	672,000	72,700
3............	Chicago*	7,283	563,000	77,300
6............	Boston	2,943	246,000	83,600
7............	Detroit	4,140	234,000	56,500
13............	Miami*	1,396	125,000	89,500
26............	New Orleans†	1,001	67,000	67,000

* In operation.
† Under construction.
Source: 1958 *Census of Manufactures*. Company executives noted clubs in operation or under construction.

PLAYBOY KEY CLUBS

Ownership of International Playboy Clubs, Inc., was divided equally between Mr. Hefner; Mr. Victor Lownes, promotion director of HMH; Mr. Arnold Morton, Chicago restaurant owner; and HMH Publishing. International was set up to franchise and supervise the operation of Playboy Key Clubs (see Exhibit 5).

Exhibit 5

HMH PUBLISHING COMPANY, INC.

Balance Sheet of International Playboy Clubs, Inc., and Chicago Playboy Club for the 10 Months Ending June 30, 1961

(Dollars in Thousands)

	International June 30, 1961		Chicago Club June 30, 1961
Current Assets		Current Assets	
Cash	$ 29	Cash	$ 50
Accounts Receivable (Net)*	442	Accounts Receivable	198
Advances to New York Club	199	Inventories	15
Inventories	72	Other	19
Other	73	Total Current Assets	$282
Total Current Assets	$ 815	Fixed Assets (Net)	291
Investments		Total Assets	$573
In New York Club	100		
In Los Angeles Club	94	Current Liabilities	
Fixed Assets (Net)	27	Accounts Payable	$ 57
Other Assets	4	Taxes	79
Total Assets	$1,040	Other	54
		Total Current Liabilities	$190
Current Liabilities		Long-term debt	
Accounts Payable	$ 47	Taxes	$136
Loans Payable	250	Other	42
Due Local Clubs†	89	Total Long-Term Debt	$178
Other	37	Capital	
Total Current Liabilities	$ 423	Stock	$ 10
Long-Term Debt		Surplus	195
Taxes	291	Net Worth	$205
Commissions to HMH	30	Total Liabilities	$573
Other	6		
Total Long-Term Debt	$ 327		
Capital			
Common Stock	2		
Surplus	288		
Net Worth	$ 290		
Total Liabilities	$1,040		

* Only 2% of these receivables were 90 days past due.
† Chicago, Florida, St. Louis, New Orleans.

During its first year of operation, International made agreements in seven cities—Miami,[9] New Orleans, St. Louis, Boston, Baltimore, Detroit, and Pittsburgh—to permit franchised operation of a Playboy club. In June, 1961, executives at International decided that no additional franchises would be given, and that all clubs would henceforth be owned and operated by International (except for the seven cities al-

[9] International repurchased the Miami Franchise in September, 1961, for $600,000. The seven franchises were originally sold for $10,000 a piece.

Income Statement for International Playboy Clubs, Inc.,
for the 10 Months Ending June 30, 1961
(Dollars in Thousands)

	International *June 30, 1961*
Income	
Key fees*..	$622
Commissions on receivables..............................	209
Sale of franchise and franchise services...................	92
Miscellaneous..	2
Total income.................................	$925
Direct costs...	235
Operating profit.......................................	$690
General and administrative..............................	$184
HMH commissions......................................	25
Profit before taxes.....................................	$481
Net profit...	$235

* Income from key fees was deferred over a 5-year period.
Source: Company records.

ready franchised). In reviewing the reasons for this change in policy, Arnold Morton, vice-president of International, said:

> . . . We decided that the clubs were too profitable to give away under a franchise agreement. In addition, since International had to "OK" the design and construction of the club, order silverware, dishes, decorations and other supplies, in fact, have all of the headaches associated with ownership, we might just as well have the profits, too. Besides, it is extremely difficult to maintain control over a franchisee when he is in Miami or New Orleans or even London. . . .

International, as the parent, required the individual clubs—owned or franchised—to operate under set rules. Each club was to use the same forms and procedures for keeping records and ordering supplies, and maintain the same policies regarding prices, service, and standards of quality in their products. In addition, International acted as a factor for each of the clubs. It would purchase the receivables of a club for 90% in cash; the remaining 10% was the fee charged by International for services rendered. Finally, International retained the authority to decide which stage acts would appear at what clubs, and when.

The first club opened in Chicago in February, 1960. It was owned by International, although operated as a separate corporation. The Chicago club was the testing ground for many of the procedures and much of the physical layout used by the other clubs (see Exhibits 5 and 6 for financial data).

The second club, a licensee, opened in Miami in May, 1961. In July, 1961, additional clubs were under construction in New Orleans, New

Exhibit 6

HMH PUBLISHING COMPANY, INC.

Selected Data on the Restaurant Industry

A. Percentage comparison between urban restaurants and Chicago Playboy Club:

	Industry Urban Restaurants Serving Food and Beverage		Chicago Playboy Club 10 months ending June 30, 1961	
	1959 %	1958 %	%	$000
Sales				
Food..............................	77.25	77.57	13.50	168
Beverages.........................	22.75	22.43	86.50	1,079
Total.........................	100.00%	100.00%	100.00%	1,247
Cost of sales				
Food..............................	37.05	37.72	81.50	136
Beverage.........................	30.83	31.18	18.50	199
Total.........................	35.64%	36.25%	27.10%	335
Gross profit.........................	64.36	63.75	72.90	912
Other income......................	1.03	0.82	4.60	57
Total income..................	65.39%	64.57%	77.50%	969
Controllable expenses				
Payroll...........................	32.58	33.04	23.20	290
Employee benefits.................	4.90	4.48	1.70	21
Direct operating expense............	6.01	5.84	4.05	51
Music and entertainment*...........	0.29	0.31	0.24	3
Advertising and promotion..........	2.24	2.09	2.73	34
Utilities..........................	2.01	2.07	1.28	16
Administration and general.........	2.62	2.78	3.95	49
Repairs and maintenance............	1.72	1 90	1.73	22
Fee to International................	...	...	14.50	181
Total.........................	52.37%	52.51%	53.38%	667
Profit before occupation costs...........	13.02	12.06	24.12	302
Occupation costs†..................	5.66	5.84	4.95	65
Profit before depreciation.............	7.36	6.22	19.17	237
Depreciation.......................	1.88	2.00	3.45	45
Profit before taxes....................	5.48	4.22	15.72	192
Add net profit from sales of keys.......	...	...	12.5	157

* It was the practice in the industry to offset entertainment costs against cover-charge income.
† Chicago club leased the building for 10 years at an annual rate of 5% of gross receipts or a minimum of $20,000 per year.

Sources: Horwath & Horwath. Company records.

B. Selected data comparing restaurants with assets of $250,000–$1,000,000 and the Chicago Playboy Club:

	Restaurants of Assets Size $250,000–$1,000,000	Chicago Playboy Club
% Fixed assets.........................	80.34	50.7*
% Current assets........................	19.66	49.3
Current ratio...........................	0.68	1.48
Net worth/debt........................	0.70	0.56
Sales/receivables......................	45.96	6.32
% Profit/net worth....................	6.99	94.0
Sales/total assets......................	2.20	2.18

* Percentages prepared by case writer from Exhibits 5 and 6.
Sources: Robert Morris & Associates, 1961. Company records

Exhibit 6—Continued

C. Selected operating percentages of The Chicago "Golliwog Club":

The Chicago "Golliwog Club," an 88-person capacity cocktail lounge, staffed with costumed waitresses, was opened by the Sheraton Corporation in May, 1961. Annual statements, projected on the basis of two months' operation, showed the following results:

Cost of food/food sales	31.0%
Cost of beverage/beverage sales	31.8
Total cost goods sold	31.7
Beverage sales/total sales	94.5
Payroll and benefit/sales	27.2

Source: Sheraton Corporation.

York,[10] and Los Angeles. The latter two were to be owned by International.

Playboy Key Clubs were night clubs with admission limited to holders of a Playboy key. Membership keys could be obtained after payment of a lifetime membership fee of $50 for a resident key (for persons residing within 75 miles of an operating club) or $25 for a nonresident key (for persons residing outside the 75-mile radius). A key admitted the holder to any Playboy club in operation and extended credit privileges. As of June, 1961, there were 51,000 members. An unannounced $10-annual-account-service fee was considered as a future possibility.

Club managers were experienced restaurant personnel. Each club was under the general supervision of a club manager and an assistant. The club managers were responsible to Tony Roma, operations manager at International.[11]

Playboy Key Clubs were built on four or five levels, depending upon available space. Each level contained a bar. In addition, the second level had a buffet table; the third level, called the library, offered only a floor show, while the fourth level, called the penthouse, had a different floor show, and facilities for a steak dinner. Club patrons were free to circulate among the four levels at will.

The pricing policy was unique for an operation of this kind. Each drink was $1.50, regardless of ingredients; a steak dinner was $1.50; the buffet was $1.50. The only additional charges were cover charges of $1.50 and $2.50 in the library and penthouse respectively. Tipping was encouraged since it provided the sole source of income for the costumed waitresses.

---

[10] The total cost of the New York club was $2.8 million. This cost was broken down as follows:

Land and building	$ 700,000
Building renovation	1,500,000
Furniture and fixtures	600,000

[11] Mr. Roma's prior experience had been with restaurants and country clubs.

A given operation in the restaurant industry, such as the Playboy Key Club, might be variously defined as a restaurant, night club, cocktail lounge, or private club. For example, a Playboy Key Club had a greater proportion of beverage sales than most comparable restaurants, lower entertainment costs than many night clubs, and a greater proportion of food sales than most cocktail lounges.

Executives at HMH felt that the Playboy club was unique in the industry. A typical comment was as follows:

. . . The [Playboy] club is not like a conventional restaurant. In any other restaurant you sit down in one room and you stay put for the entire evening. At the club there are four different levels. Each time a customer walks into a new room it's like walking in all over again and he starts drinking again. The whole club is designed for simplicity and convenience. There is something for all types of customers—for the guy who comes for the entire evening to the guy who just wants a quick drink or bite to eat. There is something doing at all hours of the day, not like other restaurants where they do the biggest part of their business during mealtimes. . . .

No other restaurant has the same ratio of food to beverage that we do. Our business is 25% food and 75% beverage, while the standard for the industry is 25% liquor, 75% food [see Exhibit 6]. When we get the rest of the clubs in operation, we'll be the largest wholesale purchaser of liquor in the country.

No attempt had been made to determine what relation, if any, existed between *Playboy* readers and Playboy club members.

SHOW BUSINESS ILLUSTRATED

In May, 1961, Mr. Hefner announced the introduction of a new magazine to be published semimonthly, *Show Business Illustrated.* ". . . *SBI* will be dedicated to a full coverage of the entertainment arts in the dual role of reporter and critic of current events in radio, TV, movies, records, etc."

To staff the new magazine, Mr. Hefner hired editors, artists, and writers from leading periodicals throughout the country. Mr. Frank Gibney, author of *The Operators* and other books, formerly with *Life, Time,* and *Newsweek,* was made editorial director of *SBI.*

SBI was to be divided into four main parts: (1) The first would be a "news and reviews" section. This would contain brief notes of recent goings-on as well as short critiques of present performances in all elements of the entertainment world. These would be written by "stringers," critics and writers on a retainer to the magazine, as well as by members of the *SBI* staff. (2) The second section would be a "listings and ratings" section. As the name implies this would contain a current listing of movies, plays, TV programs, records, and concerts, and an evaluation of each of these. (3) The third section would be composed of nonfiction stories or articles of current interest to *SBI* readers. The great majority would come from authors' agents with a very few originating with unknown writers. (4) The fourth part would be the photographic material accompanying most of the features and stories. There also would be a liberal sprinkling of comedy and humor.

The prime purpose of the *SBI* staff was to procure, edit, and rewrite manuscripts, and design the layout for each issue of the magazine. Mr. Hefner worked daily with Mr. Frank Gibney, and Mr. A. C. Spectorsky,[12] associate publisher of HMH.

The first edition of *SBI* was scheduled to go on sale August 23, 1961. The newsstand price was set at 50¢, making *SBI* the most expensive semimonthly on the newsstand.[13] A special introductory subscription offer of 12 issues for $4 was available for a limited time. The regular subscription price was 25 issues for $8.50.

In commenting on the introduction of *SBI,* Mr. Lownes, promotion director of HMH, said, ". . . I maintain that *SBI* will very soon become a weekly. One of the real purposes of *SBI* is to keep its readers up to date on current events. This is almost impossible to do in a monthly. Maybe we can do it with a semimonthly, but I really think that to do the job right it will ultimately have to become a weekly. . . ."

FINANCE

Throughout its history, HMH had relied on internally generated funds to finance its activities. Deferred items, such as taxes and subscription income, were also a source of funds (see Exhibit 7). A public offering of 15% ownership in International was planned for the winter of 1962.

FUTURE PLANS

Mr. Hefner commented,

. . . Right now we are concerned with immediate problems. Each day that goes by without a new club in operation costs us money, a lot of money. Now that we are no longer going to operate the clubs under franchise, we are looking for ways to raise the money we need to open up new clubs. The money we get from the stock will be a drop in the bucket compared to what we need. The new magazine, *SBI,* has a lot of problems that must be straightened out before it is

---

[12] Author of *The Exurbanites.*
[13] Mr. Hefner offered a circulation guarantee of 350,000 readers to advertisers.

Exhibit 7

HMH Publishing Company, Inc.

Source and Application of Funds

(Dollars in Thousands)

	1954–55	1955–56	1956–57	1957–58	1958–59	(6 months) 1959–60	1960–61	Total
Source								
Working capital		113			101	68		282
Depreciation	5	14	42	51	65	65	132	374
Other assets						16		16
Profits	69	60	30	94	21	72	314	660
Unearned subscriptions	163	176	173	273	156		260	1,201
Land contract*					259			259
Federal taxes		14	38	25	18			95
Common stock	4		24					28
	241	377	307	443	620	221	706	2,915
Application								
Working capital	177		159	406			178	920
Fixed assets†	38	280	120	37	530	110	346	1,461
Other assets	25	71	28		30		128	282
Unearned subscriptions						103		103
Land contract*						4	11	15
Federal taxes						4	43	47
Preferred stock	1							1
Common stock		26			60			86
	241	377	307	443	620	221	706	2,915

* Purchase of Mr. Hefner's home.
† Primarily real estate.
Source: Prepared by case writer from Exhibits 1 and 2 and company records.

running as smoothly as *Playboy*. The new staff is not yet used to our way of doing things. The new movie that Tony Curtis is going to do will require some of my time.

Finally, there are a lot of inefficiencies and waste going on at HMH. We have been so busy growing that not much attention has been devoted to organization. I work best when I'm in the mood. Although I don't usually get to the office until 2 P.M. in the afternoon, I work well into the night. At least one night a week I'll go right through to dawn. That way I gain an extra day. The other people work just as hard. Even though they put in the time, the work still doesn't seem to get done. For instance, we had a promotional mailing of almost a million pieces planned for the key clubs. At the last minute we discovered that someone had forgotten to provide the envelopes. I see a lot of employees with nothing to do, and others overburdened with work. Our management group is overworked. One of our big problems will be hiring capable people to come in and lighten the load.

But even with all these plans, *Playboy* will always be most important. Not because it was my first success, but because *Playboy* provides the concept on which all the other activities are based. The magazine is the idea that underlies them all. . . .

APPENDIX A

Excerpts from *The Mass Media,* A Special Report*

For magazines, television all too quickly became an evil eye hypnotizing the mass audience as no other medium ever has done. At least partly through starvation inflicted by TV's greedy appetite for advertising dollars, Publishing Row is strewn with the bodies of dead magazines—*Woman's Home Companion, Collier's, Better Living,* and others.

Before television, it was the big, slick general magazines that were the glamorous stars on the mass media scene. The biggest era of the slick general magazines began 25 years ago when Henry Luce launched *Life,* quickly followed by Gardner Cowles with *Look.* This year's 25th anniversary hardly finds the industry in a mood for celebration. Just five years ago, general magazines reached a peak when they set advertising linage records. But today publishers are haunted by the fear that, unless they can somehow exorcise TV's hex, several mass magazines that seem like household institutions will have to fold.

Television has undercut the general magazines in much of their editorial function: excitement, entertainment, and the illustrating of news and information. More important, it has siphoned off advertising.

In fact, magazines are still trying to equal the record for total advertising pages that was set in 1956.

In a Bind. Up to now the mass magazines have chosen to fight TV with numbers—total readers against total viewers. They have pulled out all stops in efforts to fatten their circulation, but this has now trapped them in two vicious cost squeezes.

The costs of attracting and holding the marginal readers, through special

---

* Reprinted with permission from *Business Week Magazine* May 17, 1961.

prices and promotion campaigns, have ballooned out of all proportion to the prices that magazines can charge their readers.

So, too, have the costs of producing and delivering magazines for these expensive additional readers. Costs such as paper, postage, and many forms of labor go up in almost direct relation to circulation as magazines scratch for new readers to justify higher ad rates. Second-class postage rates alone have risen 88% in eight years.

Publishers' profit statements tell the story. Last year, from total revenues of $248.6 million, Curtis Publishing Co. squeezed out net income of only $1.08 million—not enough to cover dividends on preferred stock. In the six months ended December 31, earnings of Meredith Publishing Company (*Better Homes & Gardens*) dropped 72% below the comparable 1959 period.

This isn't merely a recession problem. *Time, Inc.*, in 1956 netted a peak 6% on income and has shown a consistent decline since then. Last year its net on revenues of $287 million amounted to only 3.2%.

Counterattack. General magazines are deep in a restudy of their fundamental function in an era of audience fragmentation and of challenge from TV. Some are crossing over to the other side by buying TV and radio stations as a diversification move. Others are considering deep-rooted changes in magazines.

In the next few years you will see:

A shift in emphasis from mass audience to class audience.

More regional editions that offer flexibility in both advertising and editorial content, even at the sacrifice of the national image that has been carefully built up.

More merchandising services—posters, coupons, and other gimmicks—to make sure the advertiser's dollars work hard at the local market place.

Drastic changes in the content and appearance of magazines.

PATTERN FOR SUCCESS

In seeking new formulas, publishers keep their eye on three magazines that have scored notable successes in the past few years: the biweekly *Look* and two monthlies, *McCall's* and *Reader's Digest.* These publications were impressive exceptions to the dour picture in 1960, and their first quarter of 1961 gave them still further gains in total revenue: 15% for *Look,* 22% for *Reader's Digest,* 36% for *McCall's.*

These magazines have some things in common: they stress the features that most distinguish them from standard TV fare; they pay handsomely for material from first-rate writers; they offer very personal, even intimate, advice to their readers; they use color lavishly.

Perhaps most important, none of them is a weekly; they don't have to clear away each issue in just seven days to make way for a new one, and they don't have to compete with TV, radio, and newspapers for each week's news.

James Forsythe

JAMES FORSYTHE[1] had achieved wide reputation for unusual skill in helping customers to work out difficult financial problems. Many companies sought his services as a director. In 1926 and 1927 Mr. Forsythe had attended the Middle Western alma mater of his father and then transferred to the school of commerce at the state university, where he received a B.S. degree in 1929. He then accepted a position in the credit department of the Merchants National Bank in Providence. In 1934, he was made assistant cashier and loan officer.

The whole policy of the Merchants National Bank became more aggressive when Steven Taylor was elected president in 1934. His election followed the death of William Saunders, who had been president of the Merchants National Bank for thirty years. Mr. Taylor had formerly been president of the United Machinery Company, with headquarters in Providence. As a businessman, Mr. Taylor believed that the credit policy of the commercial banks lacked imagination. He was soon impressed with the constructive attitude of Mr. Forsythe and promoted him to vice-president in charge of the loan department.

Mr. Forsythe and Mr. Taylor had long discussions about building the reputation of the Merchants National Bank among growing enterprises in the Providence area. As one step in this direction, Mr. Taylor was able to interest several leading merchants and manufacturers in becoming directors of the Merchants National Bank. He also encouraged Mr. Forsythe to accept directorships when he could be of real service.

FRANKLIN LEATHER COMPANY

In 1936 Thomas Franklin came into the bank and talked to Mr. Forsythe about the financial condition of his business and the possibility of retirement. Thomas Franklin was president and majority stockholder of the Franklin Leather Company. The company had the highest credit rating and, except for occasional seasonal needs, did not call for bank credit. The Merchants National Bank had worked with Mr. Franklin

---

[1] Vice-president, Merchants National Bank of Providence; director of Franklin Leather Company; and director of Pine Tree Rivet Company.

in the critical period of inventory deflation in 1921. Mr. Forsythe also had worked with Mr. Franklin in financing accounts receivable in 1932. Although there had been no recent need for credit, Mr. Franklin had, from time to time, confided in Mr. Forsythe his entire financial and family situation. These contacts had led Mr. Franklin to name the Merchants National Bank as coexecutor in his will.

Mr. Franklin had frequently expressed the feeling that his son, Merritt, was going to develop some real business ability, but he recognized that it would be a good many years before he could take over full management. Merritt was the Franklin's only child. In 1936, he was a senior at Dartmouth. He stood well scholastically and was generally popular as a varsity halfback. The strenuous years of the depression had brought Mr. Franklin to the conclusion that he ought to retire and make some interim provision for continuing the enterprise until his son had developed adequate experience.

As a result of the discussion with Mr. Forsythe, Mr. Franklin brought in Mr. Raymond Kelly as executive vice-president. Mr. Kelly was fifty years old and had spent his entire career in the leather business. In 1932 two banks had put Mr. Kelly in as president of a small competitor of the Franklin Leather Company. By 1936 it was generally recognized that the situation in this small company was practically hopeless, in spite of improvements shown under Mr. Kelly's leadership. This company was engaged in a line of specialties for which demand had shifted.

Mr. Franklin died suddenly in January, 1937. As executor, the Merchants National Bank, and Mr. Franklin's attorney, John Williams, of Williams, Thompson and Rogers, received a majority of the Franklin Leather Company stock in trust for Mr. Franklin's son, Merritt Franklin. The pertinent terms of Thomas Franklin's will were:

I have heretofore received through James Adams Franklin, now deceased, shares of the capital stock of the Franklin Leather Company which, along with shares otherwise acquired by me, put me in voting control of that company. Consistent with his wishes, it has been my effort to use that control to expand and perpetuate the reputation and business of that company upon the principal of ownership-management by maintaining quality of product and uniform fair dealing and by enlisting the intelligent and interested abilities and co-operation of its employees through fitting recognition and remuneration. It is my desire that these policies be continued. It is my earnest hope that my son may be fitted and may desire to succeed me in the ownership of voting control. To this end, having already given him some shares of stock, I direct that before they shall sell or dispose otherwise of any or all of the shares of common capital stock in the Franklin Leather Company at any time held by them, my Executors or

Trustees shall first afford my son, Merritt Franklin, such opportunity as to them shall seem reasonable to acquire the voting control for himself or for his nominee for his account and benefit at such price or prices as to them respectively shall seem to be fair and reasonable and to represent the then intrinsic value thereof, unaffected by the fact that voting control of said company may be involved in such sale to him or to his nominee; and upon such terms as to times and manner of payment and as to security for any part of the purchase price not paid in cash as to my said Executors or Trustees shall seem meet, without liability upon them for anything which they may do herein in good faith. If my said son shall fail to so acquire said stock it is my wish that, all other considerations affecting my estate or the trusts hereby created being fairly equal in their judgment, my Executors or Trustees give preference to the acquisition thereof by someone fitted in their untrammeled judgment to best serve the successful operations of said company and the interests of its employees. No purchaser of said stock shall at any time be required to make inquiry as to whether any or all of the things hereinabove provided to be done by my Executors or Trustees have in fact been done by them, but on the contrary the execution and delivery by them respectively of any undertakings with respect thereto or of the certificates for such shares and of appropriate instruments of transfer thereof shall be valid and binding upon all parties according to the purpose and intent thereof.

The executors called a special meeting of stockholders to e'ect a board of directors. The trust department asked Mr. Taylor to free Mr. Forsythe so that he might serve on the board of directors of the Franklin Leather Company to represent the bank. The executors also elected to the board John Williams, Raymond Kelly, and four other directors who held small amounts of stock and were employed by the company. The board, in turn, created an executive committee composed of Mr. Forsythe, Mr. Williams, and Mr. Kelly. Mr. Kelly was elected president.

Mr. Forsythe and Mr. Williams immediately had a long and thorough discussion with Mr. Kelly. Mr. Franklin had told of the plans for Merritt when he asked Mr. Kelly to take the position of executive vice-president. The three men agreed that Merritt could not qualify for the job of president for some years. They frankly considered the problems that might face Mr. Kelly when the time came to turn control over to Merritt. In all probability Mr. Kelly would not be able to or want to retire from active business at that time. Much depended upon how soon Merritt Franklin might prove his ability. Mr. Forsythe thought that, even after Merritt became president, it might be well to retain Mr. Kelly's experience by electing him chairman of the board, at a modest salary, or by continuing him as a consultant. The executive committee and Mr. Kelly came to an understanding that he should be free to continue to supervise his own enterprise, the Raymond Kelly Company, Incorporated.

This arrangement had been agreed to by Mr. Franklin when he first hired Mr. Kelly.

The Raymond Kelly Company, Incorporated, was engaged in buying and selling hides. Mr. Kelly had agents in India, Argentina, and other parts of South America. The Franklin Leather Company also had agents in South America. Up to 1941, there was an ample supply, and so competition in purchasing was limited to a few prime grades. The secret of Mr. Kelly's success lay in his knowledge of the buyers and all other key men in the trade, according to Mr. Forsythe.

Mr. Kelly came to the Franklin Leather Company on the basis of a salary plus a bonus based on profits before federal taxes; his compensation averaged about $30,000 a year.

Mr. Forsythe and the staff of the Franklin Leather Company all realized that Mr. Kelly's greatest contribution was his broad acquaintance with the trade rather than his direct supervision of operations. Mr. Kelly usually came into the Franklin Leather Company office in the morning. He talked with the key men about any problems that were brought to him and went over a daily statistical report of operations and financial position. He kept in touch with the agents of the Franklin Leather Company in South America, as well as with agents of Raymond Kelly Company, Incorporated. Mr. Kelly spent several weeks each year traveling at home and abroad in the interests of both companies. On occasion, for example, when it became necessary to decide on moving the plant or installing new boilers, Mr. Kelly laid everything else aside and made a thorough study of the alternatives.

When war broke out in 1939, and particularly after the United States entered the war in 1941, the business of Raymond Kelly Company, Incorporated, became almost dormant under various governmental restrictions. This gave Mr. Kelly time to spend in Washington clearing the red tape necessary for the Franklin Leather Company to stay in business.

After Mr. Franklin's death, Mr. Forsythe had several long talks with Merritt Franklin about his personal adjustments and the future of the business. Merritt felt that now, more than ever, he ought to stay on the job he had taken in the tannery after graduation. Mr. Forsythe had been urging him to take an advanced course in business administration. He understood the terms of the will. And, in his mind, it was clearly necessary to earn the respect and following of the organization "the hard way."

Before his death, Mr. Franklin had discussed with Mr. Forsythe a number of personnel problems growing out of family relationships. The business had been in the Franklin family for three generations. Several branches of the family held small stock interests, and Mr. Franklin had given positions to members of the various families. On the whole, there had been what Mr. Franklin termed a "strong sense of family loyalty."

Soon after Mr. Franklin's death, James Livingstone complained bitterly to Mr. Forsythe about not being made president. Mr. Livingstone was Mr. Franklin's brother-in-law. He held the position of vice-president although his duties were limited to management of one minor specialty department. He felt that at least he should be put in charge of production. Mr. Forsythe said right to his face: "As long as I have anything to do with the company, I will not put you in charge of the plant." He went on to tell Mr. Livingstone that it was up to him as senior member of the family to maintain the loyalty that had always characterized the company. Mr. Livingstone apparently accepted Mr. Forsythe's analysis of his position in the company, and the staff continued to work well with Mr. Kelly.

In the summer of 1937, Mr. Kelly outlined for the executive committee the policies and plans of organization which he had developed to continue Mr. Franklin's general ideas. The occasion for the memorandum was a trip abroad to clear up the import-export business of the Raymond Kelly Company, Incorporated. Mr. Kelly anticipated that during this trip he would also be able to develop outlets for Franklin Leather. The memorandum submitted to the executive committee follows:

OPERATING POLICY—JULY AND AUGUST

Due to my necessitated absence for a period of approximately from July 10 to September 10, I have determined upon the following operating policy to pertain for the company during that time:

The executive conduct of the business will be in charge of a steering committee consisting of Smith, Francis, Jones and Brown for all matters pertaining to general operating policies. The above committee, when functioning in respect to White department, will include Livingstone and Nelson as consultants on cost and raw stock respectively.

The steering committee is to meet in the main executive office daily to discuss the situation of the company generally, and individually as the respective responsibilities lie, namely:

> Smith—All merchandising of the Franklin lines
> Francis—Finance and cost
> Jones—Production and labor
> Brown—General consultant on all matters

Smith will merchandise both the "Franklin Kid" lines of Blacks and Whites, in co-operation and collaboration with the representatives and agents of the company.

Francis will conduct all financial transactions relating to credits, new borrowing and cost. (Arrangements for emergency borrowing will have been made before I leave with the banks with whom the company does business.)

Jones will have charge of the production, and, in consultation with *Smith* and *Nelson,* periodically check on the salability and quality of the production.

Brown will consult generally on all matters pertaining to the business.

Livingstone will consult with the general steering committee on all matters pertaining to raw stock operations after collaboration with *Jones,* and make specific recommendations in respect to the purchases, which will be carried out by *Francis,* since it would be more proper to have an officer of the company do the actual negotiating with our suppliers.

It has been our policy for the past six months' operations to carry an approximate forward-rawstock position of ninety days on the basis of full production. We have concluded that, due to the general slowing up in demand witnessed the past six weeks, it may be necessary by the first of August to cut production somewhat, and, consequently, from July 1 onward our forward position on raw stock will be limited day coverage basis. All raw stock is to be financed to the fullest extent against domestic Letters of Credit, on account of the relative advantage in interest rates, and we will conserve our cash for current requirements.

An analysis of our raw stock position to date reveals that the high-priced skins have been now almost entirely put into process, and booked orders against the majority of these skins will permit of their being worked with small loss, if any. Our coverage of raw stock, other than Brazils, we consider conservatively on the market. Our coverage of Brazils, which is our main coverage and which amounts to approximately 500,000 skins, averages, on the basis price, 71.05 cents per pound, which we know to be conservatively within the raw stock cost of our competitors.

We have approximately 34,000 dozen booked for future delivery and feel justified, our inventory position considered, in accumulating at least up to 3,000 dozen to the increase of the past six months, which amounts to 7,000 dozen, being a total of 10,000 dozen, which would even then leave our finished inventory in an abnormally low position, particularly considering that we are entering our best season for Black Kid.

The nine months' formula, considered in the trade as representing a normal position, indicates that in so far as our Black production is concerned, and irrespective of our orders on hand, it is in a very conservative, snug position, being 7.84 months' supply as against the normal nine months'.

The nine months' formula on our White position is somewhat out of line because of the still unsettled definite operating policy of this department plus the fact that, having concluded that Chinas were the safest and most profitable skin to work, we purchased requirements for next season's operations during this season. Such purchases are a necessity when operating in this market and, consequently, put our position considerably out of line in comparison with our Black position. The nine months' formula on Blacks, however, is not applicable to our White schedule on account of the seasonal character of the business. In respect to our position on Whites, however, raw stock on hand and under contract is conservatively in line with market and could be disposed of with little loss, if any, should we later decide to discontinue the operation of this department.

The arrangement which was extended with *Bevan* for an additional six months' trial period, to terminate on May 31, 1937, was extended one month on account of conditions, but terminated and settlement made on the basis agreed upon as of June 30, 1937. Henceforth the White Kid production will be merchandised by *Smith* in conjunction with the "Franklin Kid" line of Blacks.

The White Kid assorting department will be taken over on approximately July 1 by Mr. *Wilson*, a thoroughly experienced and qualified assorting room foreman and merchandiser, whose function it will be to regularize the uniformity of quality and standardization of grades to a competitive and profitable extent.

We will continue to soak what we consider to be the practical minimum of Whites, 100 dozen per day, on a type of skin, North Chinas, which is the safest to work in respect to profitable merchandising, until we determine upon a definite policy after the survey of the entire White Kid situation has been completed. We are in the slow months now for White Kid demand, which will give us opportunity to go into the question of suitability of raw stock, quality, cost, operating policy, etc., in order that we may be set for the next White selling period. During this slow period we are endeavoring to perfect the quality of our suede production and if this, as anticipated, proves to be entirely competitive, the policy of production and coverage will be determined upon along a conservative basis, utilizing what part of our present White coverage is suitable, plus additional coverage suitable to suede production.

We have entered into a one-year renewal with Walczak, as our European sales supervisor, along more restricted lines, however, whereby all his actions are subject to confirmation by the home office, and whereby his salary has been reduced from $200 to $100 per month, certain countries eliminated and the commission reduced from 2.2% to 2%. It is my purpose during my stay in Europe this summer to make an investigation and survey of our export situation, which will form the basis for determining the best policy in the interest of the company to pursue, following the termination of Mr. Walczak's agreement.

Our cash position as of the date of meeting is:

In bank	$232,113.87
Outstanding accounts receivable	180,075.08
A total current position of	$412,188.95

We do not contemplate the necessity for new money until possibly the month of August, when it should be for a temporary period and will be prompted by the rather protracted seasonal easing in demand which we are currently witnessing.

I have arranged with the office so that they will be enabled to contact me by cable or telephone at any time during my absence should it prove necessary to discuss any matters of policy in which it might be considered that I would be helpful.

The general plan of organization outlined by Mr. Kelly contained no major changes in personnel or in the policies followed by Mr. Franklin, and few questions came to the executive committee (Mr. Forsythe and Mr. Williams) in Mr. Kelly's absence. Mr. Forsythe had developed some "feel" for the leather business from his previous study of Mr. Franklin's problems. He had observed from earlier work with Mr. Franklin that, in order to make a success in the leather business, it was necessary to combine "right prices" with "right skins"; to make a good run in the tan; and to develop personal contacts in the trade. Although without previous knowledge of the leather business, Mr. Williams was an able corporate counsel with broad experience.

The executive committee did consider the suede department with some concern during Mr. Kelly's absence. Mr. Forsythe talked to Merrit Franklin about the losses in this department. Merritt Franklin shared the skepticism of the committee and expressed his doubt that the company had a man really competent to develop this specialty. Although Mr. Kelly was still enthusiastic about the possibilities of suede when he returned from Europe, he finally acknowledged the wisdom of concentrating effort on the well-known and profitable items in the Franklin line.

After he returned from his trip abroad in 1937, Mr. Kelly suggested that the Franklin Leather Company enter into a contract with the Raymond Kelly Company, Incorporated, for exporting leather and importing hides. Mr. Forsythe took what he considered to be a normal view of this problem of conflicting interests. In view of the necessity of keeping Mr. Kelly interested in the Franklin Leather Company and also maintaining his other contacts, Mr. Forsythe and Mr. Williams, as a majority of the executive committee, approved the contract as long as offers were at prevailing market prices. Merritt Franklin understood and approved the situation. After this plan was accepted by the executive committee, Mr. Kelly prepared a formal contract which was examined by the committee and later executed.

Both men had respect for Mr. Kelly's skill in the business, but they realized that in some issues they had to come to an independent judgment. This they considered to be the hazard of countenancing Mr. Kelly's dual position as president of Franklin Leather Company and proprietor of the Raymond Kelly Company, Incorporated. Mr. Forsythe felt that this relation called for more alertness on the part of the directors than he felt responsible for on other boards.

The executive committee meetings were held as occasion demanded, at first once or twice a week. They became less frequent as relations clarified. Board meetings were held when they were needed for declaration of dividends or authorization of contracts. The Franklin Leather

Company paid Mr. Forsythe and Mr. Williams each $1,000 a year. Mr. Forsythe turned this sum over to the bank.

In 1941, Mr. Williams and Mr. Forsythe had about concluded that Merritt Franklin was ready to take over the management and to use his trust income for the purchase of the controlling stock. His induction into the Army interrupted their plans. When Merritt had graduated from Dartmouth in 1936, he went into the tannery as a tanner's helper. This was the hottest, dirtiest, and heaviest work in the company. The old-timers had known Merritt from childhood and were proud of the way he took hold. He had shown an understanding of the business, had discharged minor supervisory responsibilities, and had used his income moderately. Mr. Forsythe believed that Merritt's wartime experience as a technical sergeant at a far Pacific base had further seasoned him.

During the years since the death of Mr. Franklin in 1937, Mr. Kelly and the other executives had discussed all major problems with Merritt Franklin. Actually, Mr. Kelly had made no changes in the key personnel. The younger men, who had been brought in by Mr. Kelly as understudies, had all been selected with the approval of Merritt Franklin. Many of these younger men had been taken on to conduct research for substitutes for tanning materials unavailable during the war. Merritt Franklin came in to see Mr. Forsythe from time to time to discuss operations in the business and general progress of management. According to Mr. Forsythe, everyone in the company knew Merritt and no one would think of doing anything without his knowledge.

The production manager, Mr. Jones, had worked up through forty years in the company. He supervised most of the 250 employees and watched the flow of work. Technical supervision of the actual tanning processes was a highly personal skill according to Mr. Forsythe. Fortunately, the Franklin Leather Company had an excellent head tanner in Mr. Milovitch. His skill in treating varying skins with the proper time and mixture in the tan was critically important in producing uniformly high quality leather. This uniformity had built Franklin Leather's reputation. Although Merritt Franklin was not a skilled tanner, Mr. Forsythe had confidence that he knew enough to pick the right man for the job should the need arise. Mr. Jones and Mr. Milovitch had discussed all major changes with Merritt Franklin since his father's death.

Mr. Smith was a "back-slapping," "poker-playing" sales manager of forty-five who knew everyone in the trade by nickname. The leather business was an "old-line" proposition in which Mr. Smith and his two

Exhibit 1

FRANKLIN LEATHER COMPANY

(*Manufacturers of Glazed Kid*)

	Balance Sheet		Net Change in Balances	
	11/30/35	5/31/45	Dr.	Cr.
Assets				
Cash	$ 75,958.28	$ 377,026.24	$ 301,067.96	....
Accounts Receivable	270,493.82	330,495.01	60,001.19	....
Merchandise—Finished	322,725.44	107,573.94	....	$ 215,151.50
Merchandise—Unfinished	247,534.03	169,413.44	....	78,120.59
Raw Material	237,978.08	257,654.88	19,676.80	....
Material and Supplies	12,221.56	46,384.27	34,162.71	....
Government Holdings	....	318,182.13	318,182.13	....
Total Active Assets	$1,166,911.21	$1,606,729.91	....	....
Land	144,919.50	149,649.50	4,730.00	....
Buildings	450,374.82	462,178.08	11,803.26	....
Machinery and Equipment	257,267.56	330,877.48	73,609.92	....
Prepaid Expenses	7,533.56	18,660.71	11,127.15	....
Cash Value of Life Insurance	145,824.26	73,137.33	....	72,686.93
Notes Receivable—Officers and Employees	4,454.00	26,878.50	22,424.50	....
Other Assets	24,392.63	55,449.20	31,056.57	....
Total Noncurrent Assets	$1,034,766.33	$1,116,830.80	....	....
Total	$2,201,677.54	$2,723,560.71	....	....
Liabilities				
Open Accounts	$ 49,753.55	$ 50,623.41	....	869.86
Accruals	45,843.41	31,843.01	14,000.40	....
Letters of Credit, Drafts, and Other Liabilities	434,166.36	90,036.52	344,129.84	....
Total Quick Debt	$ 529,763.32	$ 172,502.94	....	....
Mortgages or Liens—Real Estate	33,000.00	....	33,000.00	....
Ground Rent	198,000.00	....	198,000.00	....
Total Debt	$ 760,763.32	$ 172,502.94	....	....
Contingent	(300,889.85)	....	....	....
Capital Stock—Preferred	330,000.00	330,000.00	....	....
Capital Stock—Common	330,000.00	330,000.00	....	....
Surplus and Profits	398,777.36	$1,355,432.68	....	956,655.32
Reserves Depreciation	382,136.86	535,625.09	....	153,488.23
Total	$2,201,677.54	$2,723,560.71	$1,476,972.43	$1,476,972.43

salesmen had grown up with their Franklin Leather Company customers and friends.

Mr. Smith and the salesmen called on representatives of the large shoe companies with whom they were individually best acquainted. Mr. Kelly also made calls from time to time when special questions of price arose. The salesmen consummated sales on the basis of price and quality subject to inspection on arrival. Since there were so many variations in skins and tanning runs, the personal reputation of the salesmen over the years had a controlling influence in relations with customers. According to Mr. Forsythe, the price had to be right, but intangible relations determined sales. (During World War II, the government, in effect, took all skins and allocated them to tanners at a fixed price. The government also set ceilings on tanned skins.) Mr. Smith and Mr. Kelly took Merritt Franklin with them on calls and introduced him to all the major customers.

Exhibit 2

FRANKLIN LEATHER COMPANY

Operating Data

	11 Months Ending 11/30/35	6 Months Ending 5/3/45
Sales	$2,257,219.13	$1,873,720.00
Annual profits (before taxes 1945)	159,117.71	329,527.64
Other income	51,230.48	....
Annual dividends	46,200.00	54,752.50
Other outgo	....	....
Net to surplus	164,148.18	274,775.14
Total active assets	1,166,911.21	1,606,729.92
Total quick liabilities	529,763.32	172,502.94
Working capital	637,147.89	1,434,226.98
Other net assets (excluding intangibles)	1,026,769.33	567,730.70
Total	$1,663,917.21	$2,001,967.68
Less fixed liabilities	231,000.00	....
Less other reserves	382,136.85	....
Net worth (tangible)	$1,050,780.36	$2,001,967.68

After Merritt Franklin's discharge from the Army late in 1945, Mr. Kelly took him on a trip to South America to meet the buying agents. Before the war, Merritt had worked in the inspection and receiving department long enough to become familiar with grades and price differentials.

Mr. Forsythe and Mr. Williams had conferred frequently to appraise Merritt Franklin's ability in terms of his father's will. They were agreed, by the time of his discharge from the Army, that Merritt had proved he was not a "ne'er-do-well." He got along well with the organization and didn't squander his money. He knew the main problems in production and sales. About the only thing they weren't sure of was his judgment of price trends and buying ahead. Mr. Forsythe felt that Mr. Kelly knew a good thing when he saw it and would be glad to stay on as a consultant on buying or as chairman of the board. Mr. Forsythe and

Mr. Williams also were both willing to remain on the board if asked by Merritt Franklin.

Financial statements for the period just prior to Mr. Franklin's death and for 1945 are shown in Exhibits 1 and 2.

PFEIFER OIL COMPANY

Mr. Forsythe had been instrumental in working out arrangements to finance the Pfeifer Oil Company expansion before and during World War II. The Merchants National Bank had been the only bank connection during the years in which the Pfeifer Oil Company had become one of the largest independent distributors of oil and gasoline in the Providence area. Sales amounted to about $8,000,000 a year, although net worth was only $750,000. Capital was practically all invested in fixed assets. At the peak of expansion, Mr. Forsythe was invited to become a director of the company.

Mr. Robert W. Perkins was president of the Pfeifer Oil Company, and its dominant stockholder. He gave independent oil-burner dealers a commission on contracts they secured for fuel oil to be delivered by the Pfeifer Oil Company. Mr. Perkins also had developed a comprehensive oil-burner service which he made available to associated independent oil-burner dealers. This service included a direct emergency telephone connection with offices of the oil-burner dealers. This telephone arrangement automatically connected the Pfeifer Oil Company's service department with the customer calling any of the subscribing oil-burner dealers. Mr. Perkins also had arranged an accounting and billing service which took care of billing the service customers for the oil-burner dealers.

The Pfeifer Oil Company had made a practice of never giving data to credit agencies because of the intense competitive situation. Mr. Forsythe believed that this policy accounted for some of the rumors about the condition of the company that arose from time to time. He had made independent studies, satisfying himself that the rumors were unfounded.

Even the Pfeifer Oil Company's own certified public accountants found it difficult to get clear, unemotional pictures of the Pfeifer Oil Company. Mr. Perkins just did not care about technicalities, and he was the "whole show." Mr. Forsythe had learned over the years that everybody else in the organization did what they were told to do; but, owing to the ability of Mr. Perkins, it was a highly efficient organization. The auditors stated in their certificate that trade acceptances, discounted by the Merchants National Bank, did not represent actual deliveries. However, Mr. Forsythe found upon personal investigation that the acceptances were properly secured by warehouse receipts of an independent warehouse company (controlled by Pfeifer Oil Company) delivered to the Pfeifer Oil Company customers for stocks held for their account in the only available storage facilities.

Mr. Forsythe was convinced that Mr. Perkins knew his way around in the oil business and was not dismayed by large competitors or any traditions and formalities. He illustrated this point by a suit that Mr. Perkins profitably prosecuted against one of the major companies for failing to fulfill contracts for delivery to the Pfeifer Oil Company.

Tension in the local fuel oil trade reached a climax during the heating season of 1942–43. Mr. Perkins had seen tankers being sunk and started early in the spring to build up stocks to take care of his industrial and domestic customers during the winter. He talked over his program with Mr. Forsythe, and the two of them worked out a credit formula. On this basis, the Merchants National Bank at one point had loaned the Pfeifer Oil Company more than $3,215,000.

It was during this critical period when the loan was at its peak and conditions in the industry were unsettled that Mr. Perkins approached Mr. Forsythe about becoming a director of the Pfeifer Oil Company. Advances on the oil represented inflated values arising from costs of wartime transportation, and no one knew what kind of government subsidies could be negotiated by representatives of the industry. Mr. Perkins said that he understood the concern that the Merchants National Bank might feel about the large credit extended to the Pfeifer Oil Company and that he would be very happy to have Mr. Forsythe on his board.

Mr. Perkins already had secured some outstanding businessmen as directors. He was acknowledged, even by his competitors, to be an unusually able and aggressive merchant, and he had an enviable reputation with hundreds of retail customers. Mr. Perkins' board included Mr. Murdock, president of a local steel company that made domestic oil tanks. Another member of the board was a large truck dealer with whom the Pfeifer Oil Company had made arrangements for fleet maintenance. Mr. Perkins also had secured as a director one of the vice-presidents of the Lone Star Petroleum Company, which assured the Pfeifer Oil Company of a major part of its oil requirements.

Mr. Forsythe discussed the invitation with Mr. Steven Taylor, president of the Merchants National Bank. Mr. Forsythe explained that he already had all of the data that he felt necessary to justify the credit extended to the Pfeifer Oil Company. Furthermore, he had always had complete access to any additional information that he wished. In fact, he had been in daily, if not almost hourly, contact during some of the periods of greatest stress.

Mr. Taylor and Mr. Forsythe also discussed the possible reaction of the Merchants National Bank board if Mr. Forsythe were to become a director of the Pfeifer Oil Company. Some of the directors were directly or indirectly interested in the oil business.

Finally, Mr. Forsythe and Mr. Taylor concluded that the bank had no security to gain by having an officer go on the board of the Pfeifer Oil Company. Furthermore, the trade position of the Pfeifer Oil Company might be jeopardized in this period of crisis if the name of a bank officer were to be listed among the directors. Mr. Forsythe felt that he would have additional difficulty in answering credit inquiries about the Pfeifer Oil Company if he had to explain why he had gone on to the board at this time.

In explaining his refusal to go on the board of the Pfeifer Oil Company, Mr. Forsythe commented to Mr. Perkins that under other circumstances it would have been of real interest. As it was, Mr. Perkins welcomed his opinion about liquidating inventories and other business problems. As a result of these discussions with Mr. Forsythe, Mr. Perkins had completely liquidated the abnormally large stock by June, 1944. Also he cut receivables down to normal proportions by June, 1945.

THE PINE TREE RIVET COMPANY

Mr. James Forsythe met Mr. John Knoll at a university alumni association banquet in New York in 1936. Mr. Knoll found Mr. Forsythe's aggressive attitude toward credit policy most congenial. He arranged to continue their discussion in Mr. Forsythe's office a few days later when he planned to be in Providence.

Mr. Knoll was graduated from West Point in 1912. He later took some advanced engineering courses and in 1917 completed a special course in business administration at Mr. Forsythe's alma mater. During World War I, he served as a colonel in the Quartermaster Corps, located in Washington. After the war he went to Boston and there became a successful insurance consultant and acquired a comfortable fortune.

Throughout his career in Boston, Mr. Knoll maintained his interest in business management. He frequently expressed to his friends his desire to own and manage a small business. In contacts with his insurance customers, he kept alert to the possibility of finding some business that he might take over.

In 1933, Mr. Knoll bought the Union Manufacturing Company in Brockton, Massachusetts, for $1,200 at auction. He found a capable local manager, and early in 1936 sold his interest for $35,000. The successful outcome of the venture convinced Mr. Knoll that he ought to go into business for himself, and he closed out his insurance practice.

When Mr. Knoll came down to Mr. Forsythe's office, he went over some of the business prospects and problems of the Pine Tree Rivet Company of Providence. The business was owned by George Lewis. Mr. Knoll's attention had been called to the Pine Tree Rivet Company by Edward Kendall, a New York investment broker. Mr. Kendall had planned to register the company with the Securities Exchange Commission and distribute the stock publicly. Mr. Knoll characterized Mr. Kendall as a pretty fast operator. He had spent $20,000 on preliminary surveys and arrangements but could not get a statement in satisfactory shape for the Securities Exchange Commission. After some months of these fruitless negotiations, Mr. Knoll had about decided to go ahead without Mr. Kendall and his associates. He thought he could buy Mr. Lewis' majority stock interest and hold it for himself.

George Lewis was an inventor. He had developed a unique automatic rivet-setting machine, as well as processes for making tubular rivets. Mr. Lewis, however, had a number of other inventions in mind which he was developing in a separate plant in Connecticut. These took the center of his attention, although he still attempted to manage the Pine Tree Rivet Company. Later Mr. Forsythe learned that Mr. Lewis had had some good people under him but that they had no real opportunity to take initiative. The sales manager, Mr. Edmunds, later showed excellent judgment in pricing and setting sales territories for the six salesmen. Most of the 150 employees were under the direct supervision of a foreman reporting to Mr. Lewis.

The company had frozen loans of $30,000 in one Providence bank and had $47,000 in commercial paper spread among fifteen smaller banks in New England.

Mr. Forsythe worked with Mr. Knoll on a plan to refinance the credit arrangements of the Pine Tree Rivet Company. During the discussions Mr. Forsythe learned more of Mr. Knoll's philosophy and methods. His respect increased and in spite of the "shoe-string" appearance of the figures, Mr. Forsythe made the following recommendation to the loan committee of the Merchants National Bank:

PINE TREE RIVET COMPANY

Recommendation

Loan $77,000 to be used to take up loans of old management held by sixteen banks.

Reasons for Recommendation

1. Company in quite comfortable working capital position.
2. At rate at which it is going, probably will pay down regularly and expect to redeem obligation by June 30, 1937. Apparently no necessity for additional loans or capital.
3. Prospects for immediate future extremely bright.
4. Management strong, aggressive, and well qualified to handle company's operations. Active head owns majority interest. Will be resident manager contrasted to previous absentee management and control.
5. By handling this credit now we can secure a fair-sized and valuable account. Cash balances are substantial.
6. Logical move at this time; account now at (   ) but management new to Providence, friendly to this bank, is desirous of doing business here. Management has no personal connections at (   ) at present time.

Business

Two main phases of business: manufacture and sale of tubular rivets; and manufacture and sale of rivet-setting machines. Tubular rivets are manufactured from brass, copper, steel, and aluminum. For rivet-setting machines, sold to heavy users, rough castings are made by other concerns, then assembled with patented parts designed and manufactured by the Pine Tree Rivet Company. Other products include wide variety metal stampings and "spots" for use on furniture, suitcases, golf bags, hand bags, and trunks.

Market for Products

Market for industrial rivets is widespread. Partial list of uses follows:

knife handles	fuses	radios
ball bearings	screens	beds
spark plugs	wheels	tools
brake linings	brooms	sewing machines
trunks & locks	metal boxes	electric instruments
leather products	furniture	measuring instruments
switches	bags	brushes
		overalls

In order to round out use of present stamping equipment, machines may be used for wide variety of stamped articles, not taken advantage of by old management. There are a number of allied lines which may be added without any appreciable capital investment. Company not dependent upon any one outlet for its products. Currently about 30% of the output goes into the automobile industry. This is a problem, however, which the present management expects to investigate and develop for the purpose of obtaining an even more diversified distribution of its products in the industrial field.

Management

President, active manager, and owner of majority control is John Knoll. About forty-five years old, married, three children. Mr. Knoll is well qualified by education, training, and experience to handle company's affairs. Excellent record as successful businessman.

George Lewis, former president, is associated with the company under a six-year contract at $6,000 per year. He has no executive powers whatsoever, but confines his activity to experimental and development work. Will supervise changing of present method of making rivets now being used at Pine Tree Rivet Company to new improved method. Mr. Lewis has no authority to commit the company in any way regarding purchasing, financing, or selling. It was largely due to his lack of ability along these lines that put the company in difficulty.

Financial Condition

Ample working capital; good current earnings record. (Memo continued with detailed description of accounts on financial statement.)

General

New management, John Knoll, known to our bank, and a personal friend of our Mr. Forsythe. Mr. Knoll came to Mr. Forsythe for advice in formulating his plans to buy out old interest and for aid in carrying them through. Mr. Forsythe had been in somewhat intimate contact with the new setup and operations for several months. Mr. Knoll seemed to like our methods and was friendly to us.

January 11, 1937   JAMES FORSYTHE

Mr. Knoll had determined that he wanted to surround himself with a board of directors who could supplement his experience. He asked Mr. Forsythe to become a director and to help him put into effect the financial rearrangements that Mr. Forsythe had outlined.

In talking to Mr. Steven Taylor, president of the Merchants National Bank, about the invitation, Mr. Forsythe concluded that almost anyone would be flattered to serve on the Pine Tree Rivet Company board. Mr. Knoll was a sound aggressive businessman, the other directors were honest citizens, and there was an interesting problem to be worked out. Furthermore, a director could be sort of a shield to ward off the other bankers as Mr. Knoll became better known in Providence. "Accounts can be weaned away."

The small stockholders who had been interested in the company by

Mr. Lewis and by Mr. Kendall's investment house were represented on the board, in a sense, by John Sumner, Esquire, of New York. He had been attorney in the unfruitful registration episode. Mr. Forsythe considered Mr. Sumner to be a very able corporate lawyer and a satisfactory representative for the minority stock owners. Mr. Knoll was always careful to see that these minority stock owners were carefully considered. There were about 200 of them.

Another director, Mr. Robert Larsen, owned a sizable minority interest. He had been a brigadier general in World War I and subsequently settled in Boston. He had been an insurance associate of Mr. Knoll and a close personal friend. He was also a man of substantial means.

Mr. M. J. Goldman was personal attorney for Mr. Larsen and had impressed Mr. Forsythe with his counsel on corporate law.

Robert Wilson also was a close friend of Mr. Knoll and vice-president of the Boston National Bank and Trust Company. Mr. Wilson had wide business connections and a critical point of view toward expansion.

Mr. Knoll confided in Mr. Forsythe that he also felt the need for counsel on manufacturing, production, and labor relations. He did not need the kind of technical advice on plant layout that one would expect to get from an industrial engineering firm. He felt a need for someone who understood his general objectives and could raise questions of policy on a high level. The kind of question that Mr. Knoll was concerned with had to do with scrapping all of their header machines for a new, higher output style. He felt that he needed to know the facts to consider, and also the timing. In due course, Mr. Forsythe was able to put Mr. Knoll in contact with Mr. Henry Patterson, hardware manufacturer and wholesale dealer in Providence. Mr. Patterson was glad to serve on the board because of the contacts with the other directors. His judgment was valued by Mr. Knoll because of his wide experience with somewhat similar, although not competing, companies.

Procedure in working with the directors varied from question to question. Ordinarily, Mr. Knoll would call on the directors about the specific problems on which that director might have some contribution to make. Mr. Forsythe illustrated this by commenting on frequent calls from Mr. Knoll about extending credit to customers, or about financing of equipment. Mr. Forsythe also knew that in regard to the scrapping of the header machines alternatives had been thrashed out thoroughly with Mr. Patterson. After the question had been clarified, however, Mr Knoll presented the issues at a meeting of the full board.

Board meetings were perfunctory. Mr. Forsythe emphasized that the main work of the directors was in conferring with Mr. Knoll. Meetings were held sometimes in New York. In the opinion of Mr. Forsythe, this was primarily an occasion for a "night in the big city." Directors' fees in the Pine Tree Rivet Company were $20 a meeting. However, since most of their service was in informal consultation, the annual compensation was nominal. Mr. Forsythe felt that this was one reason for favoring an annual retainer fee for directors. The minutes of meetings covered only the motions required by law or by other corporate formalities. Copies of the minutes were sent to all directors after the meeting. Mr. Forsythe had accumulated so many analyses of the Pine Tree Rivet Company that he did not keep the minutes in his credit files.

Mr. Forsythe studied reports received by the directors in the Pine Tree Rivet Company by first having his assistant summarize the facts in a standard form. This short-form credit analysis was one of Mr. Forsythe's early contributions to the loan department of the Merchants National Bank. Mr. Forsythe used the graphic portrayal of the flow of funds to keep Mr. Knoll from freezing working capital in plant expansion.

The form reproduced as Exhibit 3 (pp. 87–88) showed the situation early in 1945 when the Pine Tree Rivet Company board had decided to ask the Merchants National Bank for a $150,000 line of credit. Mr. Forsythe had a special cumulative binder for the single sheets on which the data were presented.

Mr. Forsythe also found his graphic flow of funds statement was useful in keeping the board from declaring dividends on the basis of an apparently large bank account. Mr. Larsen had urged the directors to declare a dividend in 1943. The Pine Tree Rivet Company sent a printed report to its stockholders annually. This included a letter from the president discussing sales, contract renegotiation proceedings, expansion, and other activities of the year. The financial statements certified by public accountants at the end of 1943 showed an increase of $125,000 in cash. Mr. Larsen felt that he and the other small stockholders were entitled to some of this cash.

The whole issue was thrashed out at great length among the directors. Mr. Forsythe pointed out that, although they had money in the bank, there was going to be need for cash in the period of readjustment after the war. He added that their dividend policy had always been irregular. Mr. Forsythe concluded that the only safe policy was to clear up their commitments and save their cash.

Mr. Knoll agreed to this point of view. He argued that he had never made any commitments to the small stockholders and that they had bought with their eyes wide open to the risks.

In 1944, Mr. Knoll called on Mr. Forsythe to discuss the purchase of an additional rivet company in Bridgeport. Mr. Forsythe told Mr. Knoll that he would be glad to make a credit analysis of the other company. He was emphatic, however, that as a director, he would object to the acquisition. He told Mr. Knoll: "You have only so much managerial ability. If you buy this company, you will be spreading yourself too thin." Mr. Knoll ultimately agreed with Mr. Forsythe.

Soon after this decision, Mr. Knoll was approached by a large manufacturer who offered to buy the Pine Tree Rivet Company at a substan-

Exhibit 3

PINE TREE RIVET COMPANY

Providence—Manufacturers of Rivets and Riveting Equipment For Approval Line $150,000 Unsecured

LOANS

	High	Low	Balances
1942...........	$ 80,000	....	$69,200
1943...........	125,000	....	41,600
1944...........	80,000	....	39,100
1945...........	(Off since 10/1/44)		3,500 (2 mos.)

Account opened 2/3/37. Present management, headed by majority stockholder, John Knoll, acquired control 12/6/36. Since that time the company had made steady progress through excellent earnings, and its financial picture is well balanced. In rounding out its line and improving its manufacturing, there has been a considerable investment in machinery and equipment. However, no material conversion problems are anticipated as the company is manufacturing the same products and selling to the same customers as in normal years.

Starting with $77,000 loaned in 1937, we have advanced varying amounts from time to time, reaching a peak of $125,000 in 1943. Our experience has been entirely satisfactory and Line is recommended.

R. BRADLEY, *Asst.*

JAMES FORSYTHE, *Vice-President*

CHANGES: 12/31/43—12/31/44 (1 YEAR) (00's OMITTED)

	C.A.	C.&A.	C.L.	W.C.	C.R.	T.L.	N.W.	Sales	Profits
44..........	256.0	95.4	86.7	169.3	2.95	118.9	393.8	1,266.8	25.2
43..........	349.1	192.7	195.4	153.7	1.79	228.3	373.8	1,328.5	34.1
Change.......	−93.1	−97.3	−108.7	+15.6	...	−109.4	+20.0	−61.7	−8.9

	Year Ending 12/31/43	Per Cent	Year Ending 12/31/44	Per Cent
Net Sales.	1,328.5	100.00	1,266.8	100.00
Cost of Sales.	1,047.4	78.84	1,016.4	80.23
Gross Profit.	281.1	21.16	250.4	19.77
Operating Expenses.	177.7	13.38	207.6	16.39
Operating Profit.	103.4	7.78	42.8	3.38
Other Income.	6.4	0.48	9.6	0.76
	109.8	8.26	52.4	4.14
Other Deductions.	10.7	0.80	7.1	0.56
Profit before Taxes.	99.1	7.46	45.3	3.58
Reserve for Income Taxes. .	65.0	4.89	20.1	1.59
Net Profit.	34.1	2.57	25.2	1.99

Use of Funds		Source of Funds	
		Current Net Profits.	25.2
Dividends.	13.8	Prior years refunds, etc.	7.9
Total Decrease.	13.8	Total Increase.	33.1

Resulted in an Increase in Net Worth of. 19.3

DISTRIBUTED AS FOLLOWS:

DEFERRED INCOME   4.9

FIXED AND NONCURRENT ACCOUNTS

Plant and Equipment. . . . .+	25.0	Prepaid Expenses. . . . .−	1.5
Cash Value of Life Insurance. . .+	2.4	Advance Purchase of Machinery+	3.5
Mortgages Payable. . . . .−	0.7	Machines Out of Plant on Lease−	1.3
		Patents, Formulas, etc. . . . .−	2.5
		Reserved for Depreciation. . . . . .+	20.5
Total Increase.	28.1	Total Decrease.	29.3
		Net Decrease.	1.2

WORKING CAPITAL

Finished Merchandise. . . . .+	12.8	Cash. . . . . −	55.1
Work in Process. . . . .+	2.7	Accounts Receivable. . . . .−	42.2
Bank Debt. . . . . −	70.0	Raw Material. . . . .−	11.3
Due Smaller War Plants Corp. . .−	3.3	Accounts Payable. . . . .+	12.4
Accrued Miscellaneous Taxes. . .−	8.2	Accrued Payables. . . . .+	4.6
Miscellaneous Accounts Pay-			
able. . . . .−	2.5	Employees' Deductions. . . . .+	5.0
Reserve: for Income Taxes. . . . .−	46.7		
Total Increase.	146.2	Total Decrease.	130.6
Net Increase.	15.6		
	20.5		20.5

Exhibit 4

PINE TREE RIVET COMPANY
Manufacturers of Rivets and Riveting Equipment

| | Balance Sheet | | Net Change in Balances | |
Assets	12/31/35	12/31/44	Dr.	Cr.
Cash	$ 51,915.20	$ 32,118.82	....	$ 19,796.38
Accounts Receivable—Net	33,484.32	63,270.80	$ 29,786.48	....
Merchandise—Finished	85,766.18	49,385.61	....	36,380.57
Merchandise—Unfinished	....	44,067.07	44,067.07	....
Raw Material	....	67,174.02	67,174.02	....
Total Active Assets	$171,165.70	$256,016.32	....	....
Land, Buildings, Equipment, etc.	438,466.58	573,224.78	134,758.20	....
Prepaid Expenses	2,556.80	4,716.67	2,159.87	....
Other Assets	78,632.73	68,276.08	....	10,356.65
Deficit	148,259.90	....	....	148,259.90
Total Noncurrent Assets	$519,656.11	$646,217.53	....	....
Total	$839,081.71	$902,233.85	....	....
Liabilities				
Notes Payable	$ 83,573.27	....	$83,573.27	....
Open Accounts	6,593.77	$ 33,337.89	....	26,744.12
Accruals	3,630.80	18,315.04	....	14,684.24
Reserve for Taxes	3,410.50	20,147.93	....	16,737.43
Miscellaneous Taxes	....	6,838.82	....	6,838.82
Defense Bond Deductions and Taxes	....	8,066.91	....	8,066.91
Total Quick Debt	$ 97,208.34	$ 86,706.59	....	....
Mortgages or Liens—Real Estate, First	55,000.00	32,175.00	22,825.00	....
Second Mortgage	110,000.00	....	110,000.00	....
Notes Payable Stockholders, Due 2/28/41	18,839.65	....	18,839.65	....
Total Debt	$281,047.99	$118,881.59	....	....
Wage Certificates Exchanged for Preferred Stock	3,725.62	....	3,725.62	....
Capital Stock—Preferred	19,690.00	....	19,690.00	....
Capital Stock—Common	278,414.33	275,116.60	3,297.73	....
Surplus and Profits—Capital	....	24,852.76	....	24,852.76
Surplus and Profits—Earned	....	116,860.25	....	116,860.25
Reserve—Depreciation	256,203.77	366,522.65	....	110,318.88
Total	$839,081.71	$902,233.85	$539,896.91	$539,896.91

tial profit to Mr. Knoll. Again he came down to the Merchants National Bank and had a long discussion with Mr. Forsythe. Mr. Forsythe acknowledged that, so far as the bank was concerned, he would like to see Mr. Knoll continue the management, since their account was attractive. The prospective purchaser had its principal banking connections in Boston. However, Mr. Forsythe pointed out that Mr. Knoll had no one to succeed him. His son was a graduate of West Point and wanted to go into aviation. Because the original plans to sell the stock publicly had not materialized, Mr. Knoll's entire fortune was invested in the

Exhibit 5

PINE TREE RIVET COMPANY

Operating Data

	PERIODS ENDING	
	12/31/35	12/31/44
Sales..................................	$434,623.70	$1,266,823.42
Annual profits (before taxes).............		45,324.27
(after taxes).............	15,536.65	25,176.34
Other income..........................	....	7,853.31
Annual dividends......................	....	13,755.83
Net to surplus.........................	15,536.65	19,273.82
Total active assets.....................	171,165.70	256,016.32
Total quick liabilities..................	97,208.34	86,706.59
Working capital.......................	73,957.36	169,309.73
Other net assets (excluding intangibles)...	186,624.78	256,680.39
Total..............................	$260,582.14	$ 425,990.12
Less fixed liabilities....................	183,839.65	32,175.00
Net worth (tangible)...............	$ 76,742.49	$ 393,815.12

Exhibit 6

PINE TREE RIVET COMPANY

Record of Borrowings from Merchants National Bank

(In Dollars; 000 Omitted)

	1937	1938	1939	1940	1941	1942	1943	1944	1945
January....................	..	25	50	50	50	35	..	80	..
February...................	77	25	50	50	50	35	60	80	..
March.....................	35	25	50	50	50	80	70	80	..
April......................	35	25	50	50	50	80	70	80	..
May.......................	35	25	50	50	50	..	70	80	..
June.......................	30	25	50	50	50	30	125	80	..
July.......................	30	50	50	50	50	..	100	80	..
August.....................	30	50	50	50	50	30	100	80	..
September..................	30	50	50	50	40	..	100	..	..
October....................	30	50	50	50	40	..	100	..	30
November..................	30	50	50	50	40	..	100	..	..
December..................	25	50	50	50	35	..	80	..	..

plant. Mr. Forsythe observed that if Mr. Knoll were to die, the Pine Tree Rivet Company would go on the auction block and his estate would not get much out of it. The Pine Tree Rivet Company was a "natural" supplement to the line of the prospective purchaser and the price was quite attractive. Mr. Forsythe concluded, "John, you'd better sell the damn plant."

Financial statements for the period before Mr. Forsythe became a director and the latest period before sale of the company are shown in Exhibits 3, 4, 5, and 6. The exhibits also include a monthly record of borrowings by the Pine Tree Rivet Company from the Merchants National Bank throughout the time of Mr. Knoll's management.

Commenting to Mr. Steven Taylor, president of the Merchants National Bank, on the advice given to Mr. Knoll, Mr. Forsythe observed, "Steve, I hate to see that account go, but John Knoll is a good industrialist. Wherever he goes we'll at least have our foot in the door." To which Mr. Taylor added, "Jim, we've got to live by developing new risks—not by hanging on to old connections."

HARTFORD CASUALTY COMPANY

One evening in the summer of 1945, on the Merchants Limited from New York back to Providence, Mr. Forsythe sat down in the lounge car beside an old friend, Ted Gorham. Mr. Gorham was treasurer of the Economy Shoe Store Company. The company operated a chain of moderate-priced shoe stores along the North Atlantic seaboard with headquarters in Providence.

Just before they separated, Mr. Gorham suggested: "Say, Jim, why don't you try to get an account from the Hartford Casualty Company? I ran into Jack Stone, their president, in New York this week end, and he is mad as a wet hen at the Providence Trust Bank. He can't get over the fact that they sent us to the Fire, Marine, and Casualty Company of Boston for our blanket liability policy. Jack said that he had a big account at the Providence Trust and felt he ought to get some reciprocity."

Following up this tip, Mr. Forsythe made occasion to see John Stone, president of the Hartford Casualty Company, in Hartford, Connecticut. Mr. Stone was exceedingly cordial and explained his interest in the aggressive policies of the Merchants National Bank of Providence. Mr. Stone was convinced that there was a real community of interest in the business opportunities for banks and insurance companies.

A few days later, Mr. Stone called on Mr. Forsythe in Providence, and the two men had lunch with Steven Taylor, president of the Merchants National Bank.

During the lunch, Mr. Stone said that he had been thinking a great deal of the recent discussion with Mr. Forsythe. He had discussed his qualifications with members of the Hartford Casualty Company executive committee. Members of the committee agreed with Mr. Stone that

Mr. Forsythe would be a valuable addition to the board of the Hartford Casualty Company.

"We would be glad to give you a $100,000 reserve account," explained Mr. Stone, "but primarily what we need is an aggressive director from the Providence area. The Hartford Casualty Company is a relatively new company in the field, but we are expanding rapidly. We believe that able younger executives, like Mr. Forsythe, can perform a mutual service for us and for their other business contacts by throwing business our way. I am making this frank statement of what I expect of directors because I like to have all of the cards on the table."

In the discussion that followed, Mr. Forsythe learned the board was made up of thirty directors from almost as many different cities in the Middle Atlantic and New England states. The board met quarterly at the home office in Hartford. Mr. Stone emphasized the interest that the directors took in the concentrated program of these meetings. Executives of the company arranged a condensed review of industrial developments in the area covered by the company. One of the executives usually had an illustrated talk prepared on the service rendered by the Hartford Casualty Company to customers. Mr. Stone assured Mr. Forsythe that the executive committee took care of all "formalities"; so the board lost no time in bothering with operations of the company.

After Mr. Stone left, Mr. Forsythe and Mr. Taylor reviewed his proposal.

"It looks to me, Jim," commented Mr. Taylor, "like the executive committee really runs the Hartford Casualty Company, and I have an idea that Mr. Stone keeps even the committee pretty much under his thumb."

Mr. Forsythe agreed that it was obvious that the directors, meeting only once a quarter, could not do anything about the management of the company.

"I doubt if we can get the account without going on the board, Steve, but I don't relish being a dummy director."

"I am sure you are right," replied Mr. Taylor, "and I am afraid we would get into trouble with Mr. Stone's ideas of reciprocity. Remember, we have a lot of other insurance business on our books and some insurance men on our board. I have been on the board of the New England Mutual Fire Insurance Company for twenty years, but the whole setup is different. I would never request one of our customers to take out insurance in the New England Mutual, but I do think it is appropriate to tell the boys where a piece of business may be available."

PART II

Sizing Up Situations, Formulating Policies, Discovering Opportunities, Assessing Risks and Planning Programs of Action

Colony Trucking Company

In 1957 Colony Trucking Company operated the largest transportation system of all motor "common" carriers domiciled in the New England states. In terms of revenues, it ranked second in the area in 1956 with an income close to $8 million (Exhibit 1). As of November, 1957, the company had 970 full-time employees, and assets just under $2 million (Exhibit 2).

Colony offered regular transportation services between the metropolitan areas of Boston, Springfield, Pawtucket, Newark, New York City, and New Haven; and between most of the cities and towns in Vermont, New Hampshire, and southern Maine. To service this area the company operated 23 terminals of which 13 were in Vermont and Maine, 6 in Massachusetts and New Hampshire, and one each in New York, Connecticut, Rhode Island, and New Jersey (Exhibit 3).

COMMON, CONTRACT, AND PRIVATE CARRIERS

As a common carrier, Colony offered its services to all shippers on an equal basis. In this respect it differed from "contract" carriers which were hired on an individual contract basis and which usually served only a few shippers. Both these types of "for hire" carriers in turn could be distinguished from "private" carriers which hauled only for the company to which the carrier belonged.

Of these three categories of trucking firms, private carriers operated by far the largest number of trucks, approximately 83% of the U.S. total in 1956. Since these carriers did not operate their trucks for revenue, the freight they hauled did not add to the industry's dollar volume, though it did add to the industry's ton-miles. Common carriers accounted for 93% of total 1953 industry revenue from intercity shipments, while contract carriers accounted for the remainder. All contract and common carriers together accounted for 33% of the total intercity ton-miles hauled by trucks in 1955.

For-hire carriers were further classified by commodities hauled. A "general commodity" carrier hauled all commodities except those it

Exhibit 1. Colony Trucking Company

Comparative Income Statements

Periods Ending December 31, 1948–56 and September 30, 1957

(Dollars in Thousands)

	1948	1949	1950	1951	1952	1953	1954	1955	1956	1957 January 1 to September 30
Net freight revenue	$2,197	$2,712	$3,387	$3,678	$4,886	$5,959	$6,607	$6,905	$8,143	$6,936
Operating expenses:										
Equipment maintenance and garage	367	509	621	573	829	1,042	910	1,000	959	736
Transportation	951	1,152	1,295	1,443	2,023	2,300	2,608	2,711*	3,730*	3,410*
Terminal	249	339	533	618	796	1,049	1,276	1,365	1,632	1,282
Traffic (sales, rating, and advertising)	48	59	86	100	136	167	212	204	238	169
Insurance and safety	139	163	182	207	268	359	360	431	490	331
Administrative and general	215	244	333	372	472	570	687	736	796	621
Total operating expenses	$1,970	$2,466	$3,050	$3,313	$4,524	$5,487	$6,053	$6,447	$7,845	$6,549
Profit before provision for depreciation	227	246	337	365	362	472	554	458	298	387
Less: Provision for depreciation	142	143	168	239	277	349	370	333	261	144
Operating profit	$ 85	$103	$169	$126	$ 85	$123	$184	$125	$ 37	$243
Add:										
Miscellaneous and extraordinary income credits		17	10	5	3	3	1	30	24	1
Gain on disposition of equipment	7†		5	6	67	83	17	14	175	41
Total other income	$ 7	$ 17	$ 15	$ 11	$ 70	$ 86	$ 18	$ 44	$199	$ 42
Total operating profit and other income	92	120	184	137	155	209	202	169	236	285
Less: Other charges:										
Interest paid	17	12	14	22	25	25	36	32	21	8
Provision for bad debts	5	6	2	7	6	4	10	4	6	4
Donations	3	5	8	5	6	9	5	6	3	1
Officers' life insurance premiums	2	8	8	7	7	11	6	6	6	4
Miscellaneous charges	5†	5†				5		2	9	9
Total other charges	$ 27	$ 36	$ 32	$ 41	$ 44	$ 54	$ 57	$ 50	$ 45	$ 26
Reserve for estimated expenses							68‡			
Profit before federal income taxes	65	84	152	96	111	155	77	119	191	259
Provision for income taxes	24	35	74	45	37	58	34	47	50	120
Net profit	$ 41	$ 49	$ 78	$ 51	$ 74	$ 97	$ 43	$ 72	$141	$139

* In 1955 equipment rental fees and purchased transportation costs amounted to $207 thousand; in 1956, to $907 thousand; in the first nine months of 1957, to $844 thousand.

† Loss on sale of equipment.

‡ Reserve for estimated expenses attributable to the year's operations but not properly chargeable to expense accounts. This procedure was allowable under provisions of the 1954 Internal Revenue Code which were subsequently changed.

Exhibit 1a. COLONY TRUCKING COMPANY

Comparative Income Statements

Periods Ending December 31, 1948–56 and September 30, 1957

(As % of Net Freight Revenue)

	1948	1949	1950	1951	1952	1953	1954	1955	1956	1957 January 1 to September 30
Net freight revenue	100.0	100.0	100.0	100.0	100.0	100.0	100.0	100.0	100.0	100.0
Operating expenses:										
Equipment maintenance and garage	16.7	18.7	18.4	15.6	16.9	17.5	13.8	14.5	11.8	10.6
Transportation	43.3	42.5	38.2	39.3	41.4	38.6	39.5	39.3*	45.8*	49.2*
Terminal	11.4	12.5	15.7	16.8	16.3	17.6	19.3	19.8	20.0	18.5
Traffic (sales, rating, and advertising)	2.2	2.2	2.5	2.7	2.8	2.8	3.2	3.0	2.9	2.4
Insurance and safety	6.3	6.0	5.4	5.6	5.5	6.0	5.4	6.2	6.0	4.8
Administrative and general	9.8	9.0	9.8	10.1	9.7	9.6	10.4	10.6	9.8	8.9
Total operating expenses	89.7	90.9	90.0	90.1	92.6	92.1	91.6	93.4	96.3	94.4
Profit before provision for depreciation	10.3	9.1	10.0	9.9	7.4	7.9	8.4	6.6	3.7	5.6
Less: Provision for depreciation	6.4	5.3	5.0	6.5	5.7	5.9	5.6	4.8	3.2	2.1
Operating profit	3.9	3.8	5.0	3.4	1.7	2.0	2.8	1.8	0.5	3.5
Add:										
Miscellaneous and extraordinary income credit		0.6	0.3	0.1	0.1	0.1	0.0	0.4	0.3	0.0
Gain on disposition of equipment	0.3		0.1	0.2	1.4	1.4	0.3	0.2	2.1	0.6
Total other income	0.3	0.6	0.4	0.3	1.5	1.5	0.3	0.6	2.4	0.6
Total operating profit and other income	4.2	4.4	5.4	3.7	3.2	3.5	3.1	2.4	2.9	4.1
Less: Other charges:										
Interest paid	0.8	0.4	0.4	0.6	0.5	0.4	0.5	0.5	0.3	0.1
Provision for bad debts	0.2	0.2	0.1	0.2	0.1	0.1	0.2	0.0	0.1	0.1
Donations	0.1	0.2	0.2	0.1	0.1	0.1	0.1	0.1	0.0	0.0
Officers' life insurance premiums	0.1	0.3	0.2	0.2	0.2	0.2	0.1	0.1	0.1	0.1
Miscellaneous charges	…	0.2†	…	…	…	0.1	…	0.0	0.1	0.1
Total other charges	1.2	1.3	0.9	1.1	0.9	0.9	0.9	0.7	0.6	0.4
Reserve for estimated expenses							1.0‡			
Profit before federal income taxes	3.0	3.1	4.5	2.6	2.3	2.6	1.2	1.7	2.3	3.7
Provision for income taxes	1.1	1.3	2.2	1.2	0.8	1.0	0.5	0.7	0.6	1.7
Net profit	1.9	1.8	2.3	1.4	1.5	1.6	0.7	1.0	1.7	2.0

* In 1955 equipment rental fees and purchased transportation costs amounted to $207 thousand; in 1956, to $907 thousand; in the first nine months of 1957, to $844 thousand.
† Loss on sale of equipment.
‡ Reserve for estimated expenses attributable to the year's operations but not properly chargeable to expense accounts. This procedure was allowable under provisions of the 1954 Internal Revenue Code which were subsequently changed.

Source: Prepared from Exhibit 2 by the Harvard Business School staff.

Exhibit 2

COLONY TRUCKING COMPANY

Comparative Balance Sheets as of December 31, 1948–56 and September 30, 1957, and Selected Ratios

(Dollars in Thousands)

Assets	1948	1949	1950	1951	1952	1953	1954	1955	1956	September 30, 1957
Current:										
Cash in Bank and on Hand	$ 45	$ 44	$ 98	$ 70	$ 15	$ 131	$ 347	$ 207	$ 143	$ 428
Receivables (Net)	197	210	284	382	322	571	595	465	451	677
Materials and Supplies	23	18	24	37	48	104	89	70	117	108
Guarantee Deposits	15	13	18	18	28	18	18	18	49	48
Cash Surrender Value of Officers' Life Insurance	6	10	16	24	33	44	55	66	76	86
Prepaid Items (Taxes, Insurance, Insurance Premiums, etc.)	18	39	50	88	148	136	108	64	84	83
Total Current Assets	$ 304	$ 334	$ 490	$ 520	$ 594	$1,004	$1,212	$ 890	$ 920	$1,430
Fixed Assets:										
Cost	1,001	1,086	1,421	1,810	2,202	2,489	2,599	2,645	2,193	1,906
Reserve for Depreciation	556	578	695	888	1,058	1,253	1,583	1,875	1,594	1,406
Net	$ 445	$ 508	$ 726	$ 922	$1,144	$1,236	$1,016	$ 770	$ 599	$ 500
Other Assets					...	21	27	2	28	29
Total Assets	749	842	1,216	1,442	1,738	2,261	2,255	1,662	1,547	1,959
Liabilities and Net Worth										
Liabilities:										
Current:										
Notes Payable on Revenue Equipment	$ 182	$ 103	$ 151	$ 256	$ 320	$ 292	$ 322	$ 264	$ 14	$ 9
Notes Payable—Unsecured	12	2	...	...	8	14	40*	75*	...	136*
Accounts Payable	124	168	213	239	278	630	551	394	498	467
City, State, and Federal Taxes Accrued	71	79	133	122	160	219	220	133	151	276
Accrued Items:										
Payroll	24	24	50	36	50	48	106	68	91	102
Claims and Other	33	35	33	7	31	99	127	56	33	78
Total Current Liabilities	$ 446	$ 411	$ 580	$ 660	$ 847	$1,302	$1,366	$ 990	$ 787	$1,068

Long Term:

Notes Payable on Revenue Equipment....	100	187	314	409	441	418	310	71	18	10
Total Liabilities.............	$ 546	$ 598	$ 894	$1,069	$1,288	$1,720	$1,676	$1,061	$ 805	$1,078

Net Worth:

Common Stock—1,500 Shares, $100 Par Value..	150	150	150	150	150	150	150	150	150	150
Retained Earnings..........	53	94	172	223	300	391	429	451	592	731
Total Net Worth.......	$ 203	$ 244	$ 322	$ 373	$ 450	$ 541	$ 579	$ 601	$ 742	$ 881
Total Liabilities and Net Worth......	$ 749	$ 842	$1,216	$1,442	$1,738	$2,261	$2,255	$1,662	$1,547	$1,959

* Borrowed from Colony Trucking Company Pension Trust Fund. Under existing income tax laws, pension trust payments were considered expenses even though fund reserves were borrowed by the company on an interest-free basis.

Working capital..........	$ (142)	$ (77)	$ (90)	$ (140)	$ (253)	$ (298)	$ (154)	$ (100)	$ 133	$ 362
Current ratio...........	0.7:1	0.8:1	0.8:1	0.8:1	0.7:1	0.8:1	0.9:1	0.9:1	1.2:1	1.3:1
Fixed assets to total assets..........	59.4	60.3	59.7	63.9	65.8	54.7	45.1	46.3	38.7	25.5
% earned on net worth after taxes..........	20.2	20.1	24.2	13.7	16.4	17.9	7.4	12.0	19.0	15.8

Source: Company records.

Exhibit 3

COLONY TRUCKING COMPANY

Territory Serviced and Approximate Locations of Terminals

Dots represent locations of Colony terminals.
Shaded area roughly approximates the territories serviced by the company.
Source: Company records (outline sketched from American Automobile Association Highway Map).

specifically designated as excluded from its service. "Special commodity" carriers limited their services to enumerated commodities.

STATE AND FEDERAL REGULATION

Colony, in common with other truckers, operated in an industry that
was extensively regulated by both the states and the federal government. State regulation aimed primarily at achieving orderly traffic flow,
and was significant mainly in the areas of speed limits, driving practices, and size and weight limits for equipment. Variations among the
states' requirements have long posed a problem for interstate shippers,
whose equipment must conform to the most stringent regulations of
any state through which it is to pass. For example, even though a carrier hauled a load mostly through states which had legal weight limits
of 40,000 pounds or more, he could carry only 20,000 pounds if he
had to enter a state with that legal limit, unless, of course, he wished
to reload before reaching the state boundary.

Federal regulation affected all carriers engaged in interstate transportation and was administered by the Interstate Commerce Commission (ICC). It covered (1) rates, (2) rights to operate over traffic routes, (3) mergers, acquisitions, and consolidations, (4) stock issues in excess of $1 million, (5) insurance coverage, and (6) safety aspects including qualifications and maximum hours of service of employees, equipment safety, parts and accessories, and maintenance of equipment for all interstate motor carriers. Safety reports on each carrier were kept by the commission and were used to help determine the carrier's "fitness" to be granted the operating rights for which it might apply. Private carriers not competing commercially for freight movements were excluded from federal economic regulation but were still subject to the safety regulations.

Rate Regulation. Local rate bureaus, organized and operated under ICC supervision, provided the machinery through which rates were set or changed. Rates charged by common carriers might be of two types: (1) "class" rates to which commodities were assigned on the basis of such factors as density, susceptibility to damage, ease of loading, and ability of shippers to pay; and (2) "commodity" rates, which applied to the movement of a specific commodity between two designated points and were usually lower than the class rate that would otherwise apply. Requests for commodity rates most often came from carriers who wanted particular freight movements but could not take them away from competing forms of transportation without offering rates lower than the class rates. On a per-ton and/or per-mile basis, both class and commodity rates tended to vary inversely with size of load and length of haul.

Proposals for rate establishment or change were made by carriers to the local rate bureau, where they were subject to hearings at which shippers and other freight carriers often appeared to argue for or against them. A carrier proposing to lower his rates usually met opposition from other carriers who, if they did not follow suit, would stand to lose some of their traffic. Proposals for rate increases were often opposed by shippers whose transportation costs would be increased by the change. After the public hearings, the bureau decided whether or not it would approve a carrier's proposal or recommend a counterproposal. Although it had not been authoritatively adopted as a general policy, rate bureaus attempted to maintain class rate schedules which would allow the local carriers an operating profit close to 7% of operating revenues. (Since these rates were determined largely on the basis of average costs of all carriers in an area, however, there was considerable variability in profit performance.)

If the carrier was not satisfied with the bureau's decision, it could elect to give notice of independent action, after which the proposed rate was published for that individual carrier. This rate was then subject to further contest before the ICC, which had the regulatory power to approve or deny the rate or to set a different one.

Some of the tests used by the commission and its bureaus to judge the reasonableness of rate proposals were: the rates must be reasonably compensatory to the carrier so they will not "burden" other forms of transportation; they must be no lower than necessary to meet competition; and they must not be so high as to allow an unreasonable amount of profit. In order to quote a commodity rate, carriers usually had to prove before the regulatory agency that such factors as ease of loading and the frequency and stability of shipment that were associated with each movement made it economically justifiable to assign a commodity rate.

Rate regulation by the ICC varied between contract and common carriers. For the former it was limited to setting minimum rates, while for the latter the full and exact schedule of rates was regulated. In 1955 the ICC's power to set specific rates for common carriers (both truck and rail) was called in question by a special committee appointed by the President to examine existing federal transportation policy. In essence this committee charged that existing regulation was preventing adequate competition between the various means of transportation and that regulated carriers were losing out to unregulated carriers. One of the committee's major suggestions was to limit the ICC to setting maximum and minimum rates for common carriers rather than specific rates.

In supporting this change the railroads argued that existing ICC policy, which called for testing the effect of all rate proposals on the ability of other forms of transportation to compete, in effect allocated a portion of the total freight business to each type of carrier, and thus prevented real competition. In opposing the change, truckers argued that it would result in a return to the destructive competition which caused federal regulation in the first place. No legislation was passed.

Operating Rights. Under provisions of the Motor Carrier Act of 1935, which was aimed at curbing the extensive and sometimes violent competition existing in the early years of motor transport, common and contract carriers were required to obtain rights to operate over specific routes. Carriers in business before passage of the act were automatically granted rights to operate over their previously established routes under a so-called "grandfather clause." When applying for additional routes, contract carriers had to prove before the ICC that the addition of their services was "in the public interest," but common carriers had to prove such addition was "required by public convenience and necessity." Applications were frequently contested by competing truckers and other carriers serving the area.

While contract carriers generally were successful in proving a case for their applications, as the industry expanded it became increasingly difficult for common carriers to prove that their service over an applied-for route was required. As a result, by 1957 it was difficult for new firms to enter the common carrier business and for existing firms to extend their operations without purchasing or merging with companies already possessing the necessary rights.

COMPANY HISTORY

Robert Danson, president, age 59, founded Colony in 1921 by hauling milk from farms around Barton, Vermont. In the following year, George Danson, executive vice-president, age 51, joined his brother and immediately began to solicit new accounts. His efforts were successful, and by the end of 1927 the company had enough business to warrant operating a fleet of eight trucks. Headquarters had been removed from Barton to Barre, Vermont, where a large meat-packing customer was located.

In 1928 the brothers began delivering Barre products to a large retailer in Boston. They were unable, however, to obtain enough freight to fill their trucks for the return trips, and the major portion of their revenue resulted from freight hauled southward. In the early 1930's, the company was nearly bankrupted when a competing fleet owner operating primarily from Boston to Vermont began soliciting return business at rates reflecting only out-of-pocket costs.

In 1934 George Danson moved to Boston and aggressively solicited new accounts. He immediately rented terminal space in Cambridge, Massachusetts, and within a year freed Colony from overdue debts and increased its fleet from 12 to 18 trucks. The company's major operational base was moved to Cambridge, along with some of the management offices. By 1935, the major portion of Colony's revenue came from trips starting northward.

In an effort to use equipment more efficiently, George Danson began to concentrate on obtaining freight moving from northern New England to Boston. Before World War II, 11 new terminals were added. Through the acquisition in 1937 of a small company with operating rights in southern Maine and a terminal in Portland, the company acquired a triangular transportation network, which significantly increased its flexibility in equipment scheduling.

In 1946 George Danson began what he described as "our ten years of significant expansion." During the first four of these years the expansion was accomplished by extending operations to all previously unserviced points within the system. In 1950 Colony purchased the operating rights of a defunct company to routes connecting Boston and Springfield, Massachusetts, with New York City. This purchase was not approved by the ICC until 1955. According to George Danson, motor carriers operating in the New York area contested it extensively, charging that Colony was "too aggressive" a competitor. "The rights were purchased for $75,000," stated George, "and it cost us just about that much to go through the legal process." The company was allowed, however, to service the routes during the litigation and, by the time final approval was obtained, had increased the number of truckloads carried by approximately 1,000% over the level achieved by the former owner.

After 1955 the company made several acquisitions of rights allowing it to extent its service to Newark, New Jersey; Pawtucket, Rhode Island; and New Haven, Connecticut. The 10-year period of "significant expansion" ended when Colony opened a terminal in New Haven in June, 1956.

TERMINAL OPERATIONS

All the company's 23 terminals performed pickup and delivery service. At each terminal, local freight was loaded on or unloaded from trucks making line-hauls, that is, trips between terminals. The company attempted to have freight picked up and delivered within a two-day period when the distance from the origin and destination terminals could be driven in one night. Since the company served a large number and variety of shippers, realization of this objective required extensive control over terminal operations and equipment scheduling.

Scheduling and Control. Line-haul equipment was scheduled by a central dispatch department located in the Cambridge terminal. Local pickup and delivery operations were scheduled by persons at each terminal. In Cambridge, local dispatch operations were performed from an office with the aid of radio broadcast equipment used to communicate instructions to drivers while away from the terminal. At the smaller terminals this function was usually performed by the terminal manager along with such other functions as rating bills of lading, supervising freight handlers and drivers, and maintaining the terminal's office.

Formal equipment scheduling and control procedures had been devised for the central dispatch department and the larger terminals. Executives found, however, that in spite of these procedures a need still existed for making a large number of on-the-spot scheduling decisions based purely on judgment. Although some of the company's experienced dispatchers were described as "worth their weight in gold," company executives thought that better procedures should be devised though they were not certain how to do so.

Terminal Facilities. Most of the company's terminals amounted to little more than a loading dock and a minimum of office equipment. The most extensively equipped of the terminals occupied exclusively by Colony, the one in Cambridge, had been built in 1947. Freight was moved about the terminal by means of an overhead "drag-line" which could be operated continuously in conjunction with easily connected and disconnected pallets mounted on wheels.

A relatively large volume of freight was necessary to justify investment in specialized dispatching and materials handling equipment. The huge New York and New Haven terminals, which were shared by Colony with other carriers, had been built by the municipal port authorities with the most modern equipment available. Most other terminals in the company's system, however, were not considered large enough to warrant the investment.

Colony executives estimated that the size and facilities of all terminals other than the one located in Cambridge were adequate to handle volumes up to 25% greater than those handled in 1956. Terminal capacity, of course, depended not only on size but also on the efficiency of equipment scheduling. Executives believed that the Cambridge terminal, however, had reached its capacity and occasionally was so overloaded with backlogs of freight that efficient loading and unloading could not take place.

Terminal Balance. Colony terminals located in the northern part of its system were typically smaller than those located in the southern part. This fact reflected the relative concentration of industry in the area served by the company. Since there was a natural tendency for the flow of freight northward to exceed that southward, the company faced a continual problem in achieving a reasonable balance of shipments to and from its individual terminals. (See Exhibit 4 for terminal statistics.)

Exhibit 4

COLONY TRUCKING COMPANY

In and Out Tonnage by Terminal, 1955 and 1956

(In Thousands)

TERMINAL LOCATION	1955 TONNAGE		1956 TONNAGE	
	In	Out	In	Out
Bennington, Vt....................	4.8	4.1	4.1	4.5
Bellows Falls, Vt.................	10.8	15.8	13.6	14.6
Barre, Vt........................	8.7	6.8	9.1	8.7
Bangor, Maine....................	15.7	13.0	17.9	14.1
Burlington, Vt...................	17.8	13.7	19.8	13.8
Berlin, N.H......................	1.5	2.7	2.1	2.2
Cambridge, Mass..................	97.6	100.5	91.4	111.3
Gardner, Mass....................	10.5	6.8	13.1	21.9
Lewiston, Maine..................	12.1	18.2	12.4	20.1
Manchester, N.H.................	10.0	4.9	11.9	6.5
Newport, Vt......................	3.6	5.1	4.0	3.2
New York, N.Y...................	57.6	70.6	60.5	55.1
Newark, N.J.*....................	...	...	14.4	32.4
New Haven, Conn.†...............	...	...	2.5	1.1
Pawtucket, R.I...................	7.8	5.5	11.1	6.8
Portsmouth, N.H.................	10.7	3.7	12.3	4.7
Portland, Maine..................	27.6	17.7	36.1	20.9
Rutland, Vt......................	9.8	6.0	11.9	8.4
Springfield, Mass................	22.9	16.1	29.1	24.8
St. Johnsbury, Vt................	11.9	22.8	12.7	19.8
Waterville, Maine................	8.0	10.0	8.7	10.4
Wells River, Vt..................	9.0	15.0	10.8	13.7
White River, Vt.................	7.8	6.8	8.9	4.3

* Opened in February, 1956.
† Opened in June, 1956.
Source: Company records.

At the beginning of 1957 a management consulting firm hired by Colony recommended the establishment of monthly terminal profit and loss statements which were designed to indicate the extent of unbalanced terminal conditions. The company immediately began preparing them and found that several of the small terminals consistently showed losses. Colony executives were not satisfied, however, with the methods adopted for allocating costs and revenues to each terminal, believing that they understated the value of the unprofitable terminals to the total system. Colony's controller was attempting to devise more equitable methods but had not made any recommendations by the end of the year.

SALES

Sales Force and Advertising.   The company's sales force consisted of 24 regular salesmen and four "national account" salesmen who concentrated their efforts on the larger shippers located in the company's area. These salesmen called on companies within their territories in an attempt to secure promises from responsibl? executives to use Colony's service. The salesmen distributed promotional brochures. The only additional advertising consisted of quarter-page spreads in the yellow pages of local telephone directories.

Regular salesmen were paid salaries averaging about $5,000 per year; national account men were paid salaries ranging from $6,500 to $7,500. Colony executives were in the process of devising an incentive system for salesmen's compensation but were not able to agree as to the basis on which it was to be computed. Statistics reflecting the change in terminal in-and-out tonnage had been recommended as a basis, but this method was not adopted. Executives explained that since the company could not determine which shipments were related to salesmen's activities and which were not, the over-all statistics would not truly reflect a salesman's worth. Salesmen did not take signed orders, and the company did not prepare analyses of its markets.

Company executives considered prompt settlement of shortage and damage claims to be of prime importance in holding customers and creating a favorable reputation among shippers. The company promptly paid the claims submitted by large customers but usually investigated those of smaller customers before settling them.

Interline Shipments.   About 44% of the company's 1956 revenue resulted from interline shipments, that is, shipments originated and/or terminated by other carriers. The relative importance of interline business had grown steadily in the years since 1950 when it amounted to 35% of the company's total. Although most rates charged to shippers under interline agreements were equal to regular class rates, Colony executives thought that the company was at a disadvantage in competing on an interline basis for freight movements which other carriers could handle singly from origin to destination. Transferring freight from one carrier to another increased the possibility of damage and/or delivery delay.

Rate Participation. Colony normally participated in the class rate schedules that were developed by the New England Motor Rate Bureau. In making applications for commodity rates, the company usually would not recommend a rate below 85% of the otherwise applicable class rate. Executives thought this was the lowest the company could go without "getting into trouble with other carriers." Also, the company did not request commodity rates in an effort to "take" business from other truckers since this might lead, they thought, to destructive retaliation. "We will cut rates down to the level of rail rates to get certain types of shipments, though," indicated the company's rate officer.

Colony executives said that they always opposed applications by competing firms for rights to operate over routes serviced by Colony and for reductions in service rates. Approval of either type of application was bound to decrease the company's revenue, they thought.

EQUIPMENT

In October, 1957, the company operated 158 straight trucks, 207 tractors, and 356 trailers. About 50% of the tractors and trailers were used in line-haul operations. The remainder, always the oldest units, were used in conjunction with the company's straight trucks for local pickup and delivery operations. Company executives indicated that part of the Cambridge terminal's overload problem resulted from not having a sufficient number of line-haul units available at the "proper time."

Within the state-imposed weight and size limits, Colony, like other truckers, attempted to obtain equipment with maximum load capacity, since "running cost," for example, fuel and drivers' wages, varied little on a per-mile basis. Manufacturers' improvement in equipment design since 1944 had been significant. In 1944 trailers 35 feet long and weighing 13,700 pounds had a capacity of 1,870 cubic feet. Some 40-foot aluminum trailers produced in 1956 weighing only 7,900 pounds had a capacity of 2,900 cubic feet. Price increases accompanied the improvements in trailer design. In 1944 the average trailer was priced at about $2,000; in 1956, at about $10,000.

Since 1952 legal weight limits in most of the New England states had been increased from 40,000 to 60,000 pounds, making much of Colony's old equipment virtually obsolete. Largely as a result, the company began a major equipment rehabilitation program in early 1956. About 200 old trailers and 35 old tractors were sold, and about 300 new trailers and 75 new tractors were added.

Company executives believed that it would be a wise policy for a company with a stable-sized fleet to replace its equipment every five years. "Since we have continually expanded our operations," stated George Danson, "it has been necessary in the past for us to continue to use our old equipment longer than we perhaps would have otherwise." Prior to 1956 the company had kept its trucks and tractors for close to 10 years and its trailers for about five years.

Repair. Major repair and service work was performed at large garages located in the Barre and Cambridge terminals. Colony also maintained several light-service shops in strategic locations throughout its system. Executives recognized that there was considerable duplication of supervision and inventory costs because of the separate locations of its two major garages but thought that facilities at either location were not adequate to handle all the work.

According to company executives, many competing carriers spent relatively less than Colony on the maintenance of their equipment. Company executives indicated that they rarely questioned sums spent on maintaining equipment condition and looks.

Safety. Since 1945 the company had maintained formal driver-training programs, safety incentive systems, and periodic equipment inspections directed toward decreasing accidents. These measures had succeeded in steadily reducing the company's accident rate per driver from 1.98 in 1946 to about 0.81 in 1957. As a result of this record, the company had been recognized by the various regulatory agencies as a responsible carrier and had been granted lower insurance rates than many competing carriers.

COSTS AND PROFIT

In the period 1948–56, Colony's percentage operating profit (Exhibit 3) compared with that of all Class I carriers[1] as follows:

Year	1948	1949	1950	1951	1952	1953	1954	1955	1956
Colony	3.9	3.8	5.0	3.4	1.7	2.0	2.8	1.8	0.5
Class I Carriers	6.5	5.1	6.6	4.6	4.4	3.9	3.2	4.2	3.5

In 1955 and 1956, company and Class I carrier revenues were divided percentagewise between expenses and operating profit as follows:

[1] From 1950 through 1956, Class I carriers were defined as those having annual gross revenues of $200,000 or more. Before 1950 the lower limit was $100,000; in 1957 it became $1 million.

	1955		1956	
	Colony	*Class I Carriers*	*Colony*	*Class I Carriers*
Net freight revenue............	100.0%	100.0%	100.0%	100.0%
Operating expense:				
Equipment, maintenance,				
garage....................	14.5	10.1	11.8	10.5
Transportation..............	39.3	55.0	45.8	55.8
Terminal...................	19.8	12.9	20.0	11.9
Traffic.....................	3.0	3.0	2.9	2.9
Insurance and safety.........	6.2	4.5	6.0	4.4
Administration and general...	10.6	6.6	9.8	7.7
Depreciation................	4.8	3.7	3.2	4.3
Total..................	98.2	95.8	99.5	97.5
Operating profit..............	1.8	4.2	0.5	3.5

Labor Costs. A major factor tending to lower the operating profits (or conversely to increase the operating ratio) of many carriers was the rising cost of labor. Wages represented, according to George Danson, "the largest single element" in Colony's cost. For all Class I intercity carriers handling general commodities, according to the ICC, wages in 1956 accounted for 53.8% of total revenues. Wage increases in the trucking industry were higher than for industry as a whole: between 1944 and 1956 the average yearly pay of employees engaged in trucking and warehouse operations increased from $2,374 to $5,065, or 113%, as compared with a general increase from $2,196 to $4,042, or 84%.

Colony's wage rates for both union and nonunion employees varied according to location. Drivers working out of New York were paid $2.52 per hour, for example, while drivers out of Boston were paid $2.17 per hour. Vermont was the area with the lowest wage and salary structure. Wage rates for members of the Teamsters' Union were negotiated yearly by statewide carriers' associations and associations of the union locals. George Danson himself was involved in most of these negotiations either directly or as a behind-the-scenes "consultant" for the mangement groups. He was regarded as a leader in the industry and knew many of the labor leaders personally.

Like other truckers, Colony was plagued by the fact that wage increases could not be promptly reflected in rate increases. Before raising their rates, carriers had to go through the formal regulatory procedure, usually including hearings, which often took several months. By the time rate relief was granted, the carriers sometimes found themselves facing another wage increase. This problem had been particularly acute for Colony in early 1957, since negotiations in Massachusetts had resulted in a relatively large rise in labor costs. Since it was difficult if not impossible to anticipate the extent of cost increases, Colony usually did not submit applications for rate increases in advance.

Cost per Ton-Mile. In the trucking industry, costs per ton-mile tend to vary inversely with (1) length of haul and (2) weight of load. Costs per ton-mile varied inversely with length of haul principally because the longer hauls provided more mileage over which to spread terminal loading and unloading and other overhead costs, and because truckers tended to carry heavier loads on the longer hauls. Between 1948 and 1956 industry average terminal costs increased from $1.89 to $3.58 per ton.

In 1954 Colony's cost per ton-mile was approximately $0.112 which compared with an average of $0.095 for other Class I companies domiciled in New England. Ton-miles hauled by Colony in 1954 amounted to 57.3 million.

As compared with other New England and U.S. Class I carriers, Colony's record on average length of haul, average load in tons, and average revenue per intercity ton was as follows:

	1950	1951	1952	1953	1954	1955	1956
LENGTH OF HAUL IN MILES							
Colony...............	116	168	185	186	195	193	207
N.E. average.........	133	131	NA	135	132	132	135
U.S. average..........	235	237	240	242	233	235	230
AVERAGE LOAD IN TONS							
Colony...............	4.76	6.96	7.46	8.26	7.36	7.78	9.48
N.E. average..........	7.5	7.5	NA	7.61	7.61	7.82	8.00
U.S. average..........	9.0	9.12	8.94	9.01	9.11	9.26	9.58
AVERAGE REVENUE PER INTERCITY TON IN DOLLARS							
Colony...............	14.58	14.68	16.47	17.22	19.81	18.86	19.18
N.E. average..........	NA	10.00	9.36	NA	11.43	11.25	11.96
U.S. average.........	10.91	11.24	12.26	12.61	12.33	12.49	12.62

NA = not available.

FINANCE

For financing terminal buildings and equipment, the Danson brothers employed different methods. All but six of the terminal buildings were owned by the Dansons through legally independent real estate investment firms, and all the owned buildings were mortgaged. According to company executives, the rents charged to Colony by the Dansons' firms were determined largely on the basis of estimated market value. The six terminals not owned by the Dansons were leased from other investors.

About 75% of the cost of equipment was paid for with funds borrowed either from banks or equipment manufacturers. In recent years the latter had been relied on most heavily.

Prior to 1956 Colony had purchased all its own equipment. Early in 1956, however, the Dansons organized a separate firm to finance about 75% of the equipment added during the year. This was leased to Colony at rates based on depreciation charges plus a small fee for administrative handling of the transaction. The rates were generally 5% to 10% lower than those of other equipment-leasing firms which included substantial financing charges.

While discussing Colony's financial position, George Danson stated, "At present, I don't have as much money as I need to do everything I want, but our financial structure is adequate for our present level of operations."

For the industry as a whole the financing of motor-carrier equipment and terminals presented two major problems: lack of credit sources and unfavorable terms in the purchase of equipment. Banks frequently would lend only under terms that many motor carriers felt were too stringent. While commenting on this problem in early 1957, an industry spokesman pointed out that small firms have had to finance by "piecemeal methods, on a one-truck or one-terminal basis." Equipment was often purchased under vendor-credit arrangements. Recently, several firms had begun to lease their equipment from manufacturers or separately organized leasing companies. Various means of financing terminal facilities had been developed, including renting of space by a motor carrier to other motor carriers, co-operative association of motor carriers, with each sharing the investment, and privately owned terminal companies which operate on the basis of leases with carrier tenants.

Public Financing. By 1957 the number of highway carriers publicly financed had increased to 26 from a prewar total of one. In commenting on this trend, *Barrons* noted that Wall Street's interest was not confined to carriers that were already large as of the date of issue. For example, when their stock was first offered, several firms had gross revenues under $20 million and at least one had less than $10 million. According to *Barrons:*

These moves, and others like them, point up one of the latest and most interesting twists in transportation—the rough and tumble trucking business is coming of age financially. . . . In short, a spree of empire building, reminiscent of the railroads in their heyday, may well be in the making for the truckers.

OWNERSHIP AND MANAGEMENT

Stock ownership in the company was split 40% each to Robert and to George Danson and 20% to Charles, the youngest of the three brothers. The company relied heavily on profits as a source of funds to finance its expansion, and no dividends on its stock had been declared since the date of incorporation (Exhibit 5). Both Robert and George

Exhibit 5

COLONY TRUCKING COMPANY

Source and Application of Funds, 1948–56

(Dollars in Thousands)

	Application	Source
Increase in current assets............	$1,126	
Purchases of equipment.............	905	
Increase in other assets.............	29	
Reduction of short-term notes payable on revenue equipment......	173	
Increase in unsecured notes payable...		$ 124
Increase in other current liabilities...		671
Retirement of long-term notes payable on revenue equipment.......	90	
Increase in retained earnings........		678
Depreciation charged..............		850
	$2,323	$2,323

Source: Prepared from Exhibit 2 by the Harvard Business School staff.

Danson drew yearly salaries of $52,000. Charles, who had been active in the management of the company since 1938, was paid $32,000.

George Danson was regarded by most company executives as the "real president" of Colony, although Robert held the title. George's office was located in the Cambridge terminal where executives in charge of operations and personnel also had offices. Robert's office was located in Barre, Vermont, where the company's accounting operations were performed. Communication between offices was conducted by telephone and truck-mail. No regularly scheduled meetings of the executive group were held.

Charles, age 36, was formally assigned responsibility for co-ordinating line-haul operations, equipment maintenance, major equipment purchases, and general purchasing. In describing his activities, Charles stated, "Most of my decisions are made in conjunction with my brother, George. Nothing goes on that he doesn't get into somehow. Actually, most of my activity consists of fact-finding and fault-finding. I spend a lot of time raising hell about something going on out in the terminal such as improper loading of freight."

Almost all Colony executives had been exclusively in the trucking business since starting their business careers. Many started as truck drivers and worked their way up through the ranks to their present positions. None had earned college degrees. Most of them were in their forties or fifties.

According to George Danson, a major organizational problem existed in home office-terminal relationships. One home office executive described his experience in dealing with terminal managers as follows:

There is a general feeling around here that the terminal managers cannot be replaced, and it's true we don't have the people to replace them. This presents some real problems in getting the managers to follow instructions sent out from the home office. Mistakes resulting from failure to follow instructions got so bad that I finally decided to put a coupon on the bottom of my instructions which the managers are to clip off and send back to me. Then I file them so that I will have them when a manager uses the excuse that he never received the instruction.

Colony's board of directors consisted of the three Danson brothers, the company's vice-president and general manager, and its controller.

COMPETITION

In 1954 there were 1,176 general commodity carriers and 3,805 other than general commodity carriers holding certificates or permits to operate in New England. The federally regulated highway carriers domiciled in New England numbered 2,202, of which less than 10% were Class I carriers. In addition, 65 firms domiciled elsewhere operated in New England, including the largest firm in the industry.

In competing with the railroads, New England truckers, both private and for-hire, in 1954 accounted for an estimated 50% of total rail-highway ton-miles for intercity transport, as compared with a national average of 28%. Indexes of intercity truck tonnage for Class I carriers, however, indicated that the New England trucking business was expanding less than the national average:

Indexes of Intercity Class I Tonnage (1957-1949 = 100)

	1949	1951	1954	1956
New England..	99	126	134	153
United States	107	148	154	183

For-hire truckers, such as Colony, competed not only with nontruck transport but also with private truckers. Indexes of intercity ton-miles for the various classes of motor carriers indicated that, on a nationwide basis, the latter was the fastest growing group:

Indexes of Intercity Ton-Miles, Trucks (1947-57 = 100)

	1949	1951	1954	1956
Regulated Common and contract carriers	109	164	164	188
Private and nonregulated carriers	111	163	201	241
Total—all trucks	110	164	187	221

The largest common carrier domiciled in New England had 1954 revenues from intercity operations of $9.5 million. The largest carrier operating in New England—and also the largest in the United States—was Associated Transport, Inc., with 1956 revenues of $99.1 million. For this company, operating costs as a percentage of operating revenue were 97.1% in 1954, 100.4% in 1955, and 99.1% in 1956 in spite of a $3.1 million increase in gross revenue during the latter year. In his 1956 annual report, Associated's president attributed low profits to rising costs and stated that emphasis would shift in 1957 from increasing sales to cutting costs.

On the other hand, some large carriers had lower than average operating ratios. For example, 1956 statistics for five large publicly held firms were as follows:

COMPANY	1956	
	Gross Revenues (In Millions)	Operating Ratio
U.S. Truck Lines	40.7	93.6
Pacific Intermountain Express	52.3	95.6
McLean Trucking	21.4	92.1
Interstate Motor Freight	30.2	96.0
Denver-Chicago Trucking	26.2	92.0

A comparison of 102 carriers domiciled in New England with 65 carriers domiciled elsewhere but operating in the New England region showed that the latter typically carried heavier loads and had much longer hauls: In spite of the fact that freight capacity of the trucks most commonly used in New England in 1954 ranged from 12 to 15 tons, 50% of the 102 New England carriers in 1954 had an average load of less than 8 tons, while only 13% had an average load of 12 tons and over. In contrast, only 25% of the 65 outside firms averaged under 8 tons per load, while 40% averaged at least 12 tons. Similarly on length of haul, 75% of the 102 New England firms averaged no more than 200 miles, while only 17% of the outside carriers had so short an average. And only 6% of the New England carriers averaged over 300 miles as compared with 54% of the outside carriers.

In referring to competitors from outside the region, George Danson indicated that the company had "felt the effects" when in 1955 several large carriers formerly operating only in the South and Southwest extended their regular service into the New England area.

INDUSTRY TRENDS AND OUTLOOK

In the years from 1946–56, according to *Business Week,* an estimated 8,000 mergers and acquisitions had taken place in the U.S. trucking industry. Reportedly, many of these transactions involved the aging founders of small, privately owned firms seeking protection from inheritance taxes. Also, many small carriers were reportedly finding their financial problems too difficult to face alone and were looking to merger or sale as the best possible solution. Moreover, according to one executive, "The merger climate is favorable down in Washington . . . The resistance is less. More of the expanding truck lines have decided that it is an unnecessary waste of time and money to oppose a competitor's merger application."

Outlook. As to whether the trucking industry will continue to expand at the expense of the railroads, there was some difference of opinion. A spokesman for one of the large motor carriers predicted that truckers would obtain increasingly large shares of the transportation market on the assumption that the nation's output would tend to be composed of more and more highly fabricated products. Being more valuable per pound and per cubic foot, such products would be better able to afford the generally more costly but more rapid and flexible service of motor carriers. Another source, on the other hand, predicted that the industry's future rate of growth will be slower than that of the general economy and of industrial production. This prediction was based on the fact that ton-mile carriage by regulated truckers had remained approximately level in the years from 1951 to 1955.

In the future, it was expected by several sources that there would be increased co-ordination between the various means of transportation. "Piggy-backing," the movement of loaded motor carrier trailers on railroad flatcars, had already achieved significance by 1957. Within the previous year or so, several airline companies had signed agreements with truckers which resulted in regular air-surface transportation systems. Similar agreements had been made between truckers and waterway carriers. The movement toward co-ordination was being sponsored by several of the Interstate Commerce Commissioners who hoped it would result in a more efficient national transportation system.

BIBLIOGRAPHY OF SOURCES FOR INDUSTRY DATA

AMERICAN TRUCKING ASSOCIATIONS. *American Trucking Trends,* 1950–53, 1955–59 editions.

Barrons, April 2, 1956, pp. 3 ff.

Business Week, June 22, 1957, pp. 168 ff.

Commercial and Financial Chronicle, October 18, 1956, pp. 184 ff.

MOODY'S *Transportation Manual,* 1957–58 editions.

NEW ENGLAND GOVERNORS' COMMITTEE ON PUBLIC TRANSPORTATION. *Motor Freight Transport for New England,* Report No. 5, October, 1956.

Railway Age, April 2, 1956, pp. 40 ff.; April 22, 1957, pp. 43 ff.

TAFF, CHARLES A. *Commercial Motor Transportation.* Homewood, Ill.: Richard D. Irwin, Inc., 1955.

Superb Biscuits, Inc.

CRACKERS AND COOKIES bearing the Superb name appeared on the shelves of about 80% of all retail food stores in the four-state area of Illinois, Michigan, Indiana, and Ohio. Superb Biscuits, Inc., of Chicago produced and distributed a wide line ranging from simple, square salt crackers to filled chocolate-coated cookies sold in foil-wrapped assortments. More than 80 different items and package sizes were available, and company sales reached $7.6 million in 1956. (For financial statements, see Exhibits 1 and 2.)

COMPETITIVE SITUATION

Superb encountered competition of two types. Most important were the "Big Three"—National Biscuit Company, Sunshine Biscuits, Inc., and United Biscuit Company—with combined sales of almost $700 million in 1956 (see Exhibits 3 and 4). According to Superb's estimates, National Biscuit reached 90% of all outlets and had about 40% of the market, while Sunshine sold to about 70% of the outlets and held about 25% of the market. Superb was believed to run a good third in its own territory, with about 22% of total sales.

Competition also came from about six medium-sized or small companies, either local or regional in character, operating in part or all of Superb's territory. Several dozen such firms were scattered throughout the United States.

Product lines of the big companies were essentially the same as Superb's, although they put more emphasis on crackers and on offering a wider variety of items. The smaller companies generally specialized in high-priced fancy cookies, custom recipes, or accessories like ice cream cones.

In contrast to Superb and most other smaller companies, the three large firms were to some extent both horizontally and vertically integrated. Together they had acquired almost 50 small baking or supply companies during the last 30 years, which were either operated as divisions or supplied large portions of the parent companies' flour and packaging requirements. Furthermore, two of the large firms had divi-

118

Exhibit 1

SUPERB BISCUITS, INC.

Income Statement, Years Ending December 31
(Thousands of Dollars)

	1956	1955	1954	1953	1952	1951	1950	1949	1948	1947	1946	1945
Net sales	$7,555	$7,001	$7,156	$7,508	$6,829	$6,374	$5,311	$4,841	$4,676	$4,933	$3,825	$3,704
Cost of goods sold	5,182	4,800	5,002	5,229	4,763	4,516	3,647	3,321	3,398	3,471	2,519	2,434
Gross profit	$2,373	$2,201	$2,154	$2,279	$2,066	$1,858	$1,664	$1,520	$1,278	$1,462	$1,306	$1,270
Selling, delivery, and administration	2,199	2,029	1,990	2,036	1,814	1,672	1,469	1,389	1,289	1,148	946	899
Operating profit	$ 174	$ 172	$ 164	$ 243	$ 252	$ 186	$ 195	$ 131	$ [11]	$ 314	$ 360	$ 371
Other income	23	29	10	10	4	17	14	15	13	4	9	[11]
Total income	$ 197	$ 201	$ 174	$ 253	$ 256	$ 203	$ 209	$ 146	$ 2	$ 318	$ 369	$ 360
Interest expense	11	5	10	20	22	13	16	22	21	7	8	19
Income before income tax	$ 186	$ 196	$ 164	$ 233	$ 234	$ 190	$ 193	$ 124	$ [19]	$ 311	$ 361	$ 341
Federal income tax	91	95	82	119	121	95	73	47	[5]	119	140	246
Net profit	$ 95	$ 101	$ 82	$ 114	$ 113	$ 95	$ 120	$ 77	$ [14]	$ 192	$ 221	$ 95
Preferred dividends	$ 40	$ 41	$ 42	$ 42	$ 43	......	......	......	......	$ 43	$ 21	......
Percentage Analysis												
Net sales	100.0%	100.0%	100.0%	100.0%	100.0%	100.0%	100.0%	100.0%	100.0%	100.0%	100.0%	100.0%
Cost of goods sold	68.6	68.5	69.9	69.6	69.7	70.9	68.7	68.6	72.7	70.4	65.9	65.7
Gross profit	31.4%	31.5%	30.1%	30.4%	30.3%	29.1%	31.3%	31.4%	27.3%	29.6%	34.1%	34.3%
Selling, delivery, and administration	29.1	29.0	27.8	27.1	26.6	26.2	27.6	28.7	27.5	23.3	24.7	24.3
Operating profit	2.3%	2.5%	2.3%	3.3%	3.7%	2.9%	3.7%	2.7%	[0.2]%	6.3%	9.4%	10.0%
Other income	0.3	0.4	0.1	0.1	0.0	0.3	0.2	0.3	0.3	0.1	0.2	0.3
Total income	2.6%	2.9%	2.4%	3.4%	3.7%	3.2%	3.9%	3.0%	0.1%	6.4%	9.6%	9.7%
Interest expense	0.1	0.1	0.1	0.3	0.3	0.2	0.3	0.4	0.5	0.1	0.2	0.5
Income before income tax	2.5%	2.8%	2.3%	3.1%	3.4%	3.0%	3.6%	2.6%	[0.4]%	6.3%	9.4%	9.2%
Federal income tax	1.2	1.4	1.1	1.6	1.8	1.5	1.4	1.0	0.1	2.4	3.6	6.6
Net profit	1.3%	1.4%	1.2%	1.5%	1.6%	1.5%	2.2%	1.6%	[0.3]%	3.9%	5.8%	2.6%
Preferred dividends	0.5%	0.6%	0.6%	0.6%	0.6%	......	......	......	......	0.9%	0.6%	......

Bracketed figures are negative.
Source: Company records.

Exhibit 2

SUPERB BISCUITS, INC.

Balance Sheets, December 31

(Thousands of Dollars)

	1956	1955	1954	1953	1952	1951	1950	1949	1948	1947	1946	1945
Assets												
Cash	$ 189	$ 160	$ 188	$ 134	$ 199	$ 120	$ 123	$ 93	$ 98	$ 149	$ 180	$ 268
Receivables—Net	274	241	234	281	273	256	192	182	156	155	175	105
Inventories	983	753	608	572	449	518	375	326	317	332	306	205
Investments—Restricted	.....	.....	.....	119	109	100	92	82	74	64	56	52
Total Current Assets	$1,446	$1,154	$1,030	$1,106	$1,030	$ 994	$ 782	$ 683	$ 645	$ 700	$ 717	$ 630
Land, Building, and Machinery	$1,487	$1,432	$1,327	$1,229	$1,141	$1,085	$ 995	$ 947	$ 926	$ 892	$ 473	$ 454
Reserve for Depreciation	710	636	574	495	463	410	379	351	302	259	236	254
Net Property	$ 777	$ 796	$ 753	$ 734	$ 678	$ 675	$ 616	$ 596	$ 624	$ 633	$ 237	$ 200
Prepayments	80	75	53	41	34	76	42	26	42	28	53	25
Goodwill	.....	.....	.....	.....	.....	.....	*	450	450	450	450	450
Organization Expense	.....	.....	.....	.....	.....	.....	.....			.....	88	88
Total Assets	$2,303	$2,025	$1,836	$1,881	$1,742	$1,745	$1,440	$1,755	$1,761	$1,811	$1,545	$1,393
Liabilities												
Notes Payable	$ 570†	$ 150	$ 75	$ 113	$ 38	$ 19	$ 22	$ 22	$ 11	$ 75	$ 30	$ 30
Accounts Payable	206	235	205	175	173	238	139	124	232	158	104	89
Accruals	209	217	229	188	156	146	119	82	82	73	98	68
Federal Income Taxes	64	223	178	241	245	238	264	278	241	268	288	351
Total Current Liabilities	$1,049	$ 825	$ 687	$ 717	$ 612	$ 641	$ 544	$ 506	$ 566	$ 574	$ 520	$ 538
Notes Payable—Long Term	.....	.....	.....	$ 281	$ 319	$ 356	$ 244	$ 266	$ 289	$ 300	$ 150	$ 180

Cumulative Preferred Stock ($0.50 Dividend Rate)	$ 428	$ 428	$ 428	$ 428	$ 428	$ 427	$ 428	$ 428	$ 428	$ 419	$ 419	$ 419
Common Stock	122	122	122	122	122	122	122	122	122	122	122	122
Earned Surplus	125	325	387	356	433	103	198	269	340	610	669	723
Total Stock and Surplus	$ 675	$ 875	$ 937	$ 906	$ 983	$ 652	$ 748	$ 819	$ 890	$1,151	$1,210	$1,264
Less: Reacquired Preferred Stock								8	7	2	10	10
Net Stock and Surplus	$ 675	$ 875	$ 937	$ 906	$ 983	$ 652	$ 748	$ 811	$ 883	$1,149	$1,200	$1,254
Total Liabilities	$1,393	$1,545	$1,811	$1,761	$1,755	$1,440	$1,745	$1,742	$1,881	$1,836	$2,025	$2,303
Net Current Assets (Thousands of Dollars)	$ 92	$ 197	$ 126	$ 79	$ 177	$ 238	$ 353	$ 418	$ 389	$ 343	$ 329	$ 397
Current Ratio	117:1	138:1	122:1	114:1	135:1	144:1	155:1	168:1	154:1	150:1	140:1	138:1
Number of Shares—Preferred (1,000)	43	43	43	43	43	43	43	42	42	42	41	41
Earned per Share—Preferred	$ 2.24	$ 5.18	$ 4.49	$	$ 1.79	$ 2.81	$ 2.23	$ 2.70	$ 2.72	$ 1.98	$ 2.47	$ 2.26
Dividends per Share—Preferred	$	$ 0.50	$ 1.00	$	$	$	$	$ 1.00	$ 1.00	$ 1.00	$ 1.00	$ 1.00
Arrearages per Share—Preferred	$ 2.75	$ 2.75	$ 2.25	$ 2.75	$ 3.25	$ 3.75	$ 4.25	$ 3.75	$ 3.25	$ 2.75	$ 2.25	$ 1.75
Total Arrearages (Thousands of Dollars)	$ 118	$ 118	$ 96	$ 118	$ 139	$ 160	$ 182	$ 158	$ 136	$ 115	$ 92	$ 71
Number of Shares—Common (1,000)	122	122	122	122	122	122	122	122	122	122	122	122
Earned per Share—Common	$ 0.61	$ 1.63	$ 1.39	$[0.29]	$ 0.45	$ 0.81	$ 0.60	$ 0.75	$ 0.76	$ 0.51	$ 0.66	$ 0.44
Net Tangible Assets per Share—Common						$ 0.53	$ 1.13	$ 1.89	$ 2.67	$ 5.02	$ 5.70	$ 6.31
Per Cent Return on Net Worth (after Tax)	14.1%	25.3%	20.3%	[1.6%]	7.8%	18.4%	12.5%	13.9%	12.9%	7.2%	8.4%	7.5%

*Goodwill was written off against earned surplus—now carried at $1.
†Short-term funds of $500,000 for seasonal inventory needs included.
Bracketed figures are negative.
Source: Company records.

sions making bread, fresh cakes, cake mixes, dried fruits, potato chips, or similar foods.

Most crackers and a few sweet cookies were standardized high-volume products that carried a low margin and required large-scale automatic production to return a profit to the producer. Most sweet cookies, on the other hand, were specialized products or assortments commanding better prices at lower volumes. Their manufacture called for special machinery or hand operations, while shorter runs necessitated frequent changeovers, especially in single-plant companies. An industry spokesman indicated that the large companies favored the high-volume items that were better suited to their automatic production lines.

There was little differentiation among the high-volume products offered by various makers, except for package design. Significant price differences appeared only during special promotions. Specialties, on the other hand, were claimed to be new and different. Superb officials said new products had to be introduced periodically in order to "show new faces in the market." The large companies were active in this respect, and one of them was reported to have introduced about ten new items over a six-month period. If a new product proved highly successful, however, competitors would probably develop similar items, and it would eventually become standard for the industry. Round cocktail crackers and fig bars, for example, had started out as specialties of two companies. On the other hand, according to Superb officials, many specialties showed a tendency to be "fads" that "went flat" after 90 days or so.

It was customary among the large- and medium-size companies, including Superb, to employ a sales force charged with order-taking in the food stores, and with arranging fresh stock on the shelves or in special displays featuring price reductions or new products. In most stores the salesmen checked stocks and replenished merchandise entirely on their own responsibility. In these cases they had developed a relationship with the store managers, who trusted them to keep the right amounts of salable products on hand. The men also exchanged stale, unsalable packages and rotated the stocks according to age dates on the cartons.

These services were considered important to keep the goodwill of the store and its customers. Industry spokesmen indicated that volume in a given store depended a great deal on the personality and aggressiveness of the biscuit salesman, and they considered it unlikely that independent

Exhibit 3

SUPERB BISCUITS, INC.

Per Cent Changes in Sales and Profits
Three Large Biscuit Companies* and Superb Biscuits, Inc.

	THREE LARGE COMPANIES*				SUPERB BISCUITS, INC.			
Year	Sales (Millions)	% Change from Past Year	Net Profit (Millions)	% Change from Past Year	Sales (Millions)	% Change from Past Year	Net Profit (Millions)	% Change from Past Year
1956..	$698.1	+9.8%	$31.1	+11.9%	$7.6	+8.6%	$0.095	−6.0%
1955..	635.9	+3.8	27.7	....	7.0	−2.8	0.101	+21.9
1954..	612.8	+2.6	27.7	−2.1	7.2	−4.0	0.082	−28.1
1953..	597.4	+4.8	28.3	+1.4	7.5	+10.3	0.114	+0.9
1952..	570.2	+2.5	27.9	+3.7	6.8	+6.2	0.113	+18.9
1951..	556.1	+13.5	26.9	−19.7	6.4	+20.8	0.095	−20.8
1950..	489.9	+2.0	33.5	−3.7	5.3	+10.4	0.120	+57.9
1949..	480.1	−1.3	34.8	+32.3	4.8	+2.1	0.077	− } (negative basis)
1948..	486.5	+10.9	26.3	+4.4	4.7	−4.1	[0.014]	−
1947..	438.5	+22.6	25.2	−5.3	4.9	+28.9	0.192	−13.1
1946..	357.4	+8.4	26.6	+26.0	3.8	+2.7	0.221	+132.6
1945..	329.6	....	21.1	....	3.7	....	0.095	....

* National Biscuit Company, United Biscuit Company, Sunshine Biscuit Company, Inc.
Bracketed figures are negative.
Source: Compiled by Harvard Business School Research staff from Moody's company records.

brokers or jobbers would give similar attention to service. Supermarkets and larger stores generally assigned fixed shelf space to each of the important firms in the area and rotated special promotion privileges among them. Nevertheless, the relationship of the salesman to the store personnel influenced any preferential treatment the company might receive.

Two of the Big Three carried on national advertising programs, using magazines, radio, and television. Smaller companies had to rely more heavily on advertising allowances to retailers, store promotions, and limited local radio, television, and billboard displays. Expenditures proportional to those of the large competitors were considered by Superb officials to be less than proportionately effective.

HISTORY AND ORGANIZATION

Superb Biscuits, Inc., was founded at the turn of the century; it thrived for 25 years, expanding its product line through new items. The depression, however, hit the company hard, and after experiencing severe losses, Superb changed hands in 1936. The new majority stockholder was Earl T. Kingsbury, father of the current president, Richard F. Kingsbury. Although the plant was equipped with modern machinery, the previous management had allowed the quality of the product to slide

Exhibit 4

SUPERB BISCUITS, INC.

Per Cent Return on Net Worth over Twelve Years
Typical Industry Performances and Superb Biscuits, Inc.

COMPANY	PER CENT RETURN											
	1956	1955	1954	1953	1952	1951	1950	1949	1948	1947	1946	1945
National Biscuit Company	11.5%	10.7%	11.9%	11.5%	11.6%	10.8%	14.2%	15.3%	10.7%	12.4%	10.2%	15.9%
United Biscuit Company	8.2	8.1	4.2	9.8	11.2	12.3	14.7	17.2	26.7	32.4	37.4	15.7
Sunshine Biscuits, Inc.	12.5	12.0	12.2	12.8	12.8	14.3	17.9	20.6	20.4	15.4	24.0	11.2
Average of six large and medium companies (weighted average)	10.7	10.1	10.3	11.0	11.3	11.1	14.3	15.4	12.8	13.6	14.2	14.9
Superb Biscuits, Inc.	7.5	8.4	7.2	12.9	13.9	12.5	18.4	7.8	[1.6]	20.3	25.3	14.1

Relative Volume of Three Largest Biscuit Companies
(Selected Years; Millions of Dollars)

COMPANY	1956		1954		1951		1948		1945	
	Sales	%	Sales	%	Sales	%	Sales	%	Sales	%
National Biscuit Company	$410.4	59.0%	$376.4	61.5%	$329.9	59.5%	$296.2	61.0%	$205.0	62.2%
United Biscuit Company	137.1	19.7	117.2	19.4	107.2	19.1	87.7	17.9	50.6	15.4
Sunshine Biscuits, Inc.	150.6	21.3	119.2	19.1	119.0	21.4	102.6	21.1	74.0	22.4
Total	$698.1	100.0%	$612.8	100.0%	$556.1	100.0%	$486.5	100.0%	$329.6	100.0%

NOTE: Comparability is limited by the fact that the large companies have diversified or integrated their operations to some extent. For instance, NBC produces 80% of its own flour requirements and 50% of packaging supplies. NBC also produces bread and cake in the East. Similarly, Sunshine Biscuit and United Biscuit are engaged in comparable fields.

Bracketed figures are negative.

Source: Prepared by Harvard Business School Research staff.

when reverses set in, and Earl Kingsbury was faced with the task of upgrading standards and recovering the acceptance of Superb biscuits in the trade. He believed that poor sales service and lack of freshness control had created considerable ill will.

Bringing with him a number of new executives, Earl Kingsbury attempted to reorient the company to his philosophy of giving high quality for the lowest possible price. Working against heavy financial odds, he effected changes in the production and sales departments, and sales and profits increased. Mr. Kingsbury was characterized by company officials as a shrewd financial operator whose frugality and determination were the main driving forces behind Superb's recovery. They said he had assumed close personal direction of the business and continually made decisions on both details and policy. His door was always open to subordinates, with whom his contacts were many and varied. Many who had worked under Mr. Kingsbury spoke of him as "wonderful" and "smart." When his health deteriorated seriously in 1954, Mr. Kingsbury was forced to resign all duties, and his son Richard, then 26, was elected president. Richard Kingsbury had served under his father for two years in production and traffic.

The company was organized into four departments—sales, production, finance, and legal and personnel. Each was headed by a vice-president (see Exhibit 5). The president met monthly with this group of officers. The board of directors consisted of the president and four members representing some 300 stockholders; the Kingsbury family held a majority of the shares. These board members were the company's banker, an investment broker, and vice-presidents of two suppliers. Meetings were held regularly every month, usually after the officers' meeting, and the board maintained a close interest in operating results and major capital expenditures.

SALES AND PROMOTION

The company's sales organization, under James V. Cannon, vice-president, aimed at three different markets. The first was composed of food stores in the company's four-state home territory. These were called on by 110 salesmen supervised by 10 district managers. Deliveries were made by company trucks, either from the plant or from eight scattered warehouses. William R. Stewart, territorial sales manager, personally administered the large chain store accounts where formal authorization by central buying offices was required for sale of products in the stores. This market accounted for about 60% of sales.

Exhibit 5

SUPERB BISCUITS, INC.
Organization Chart

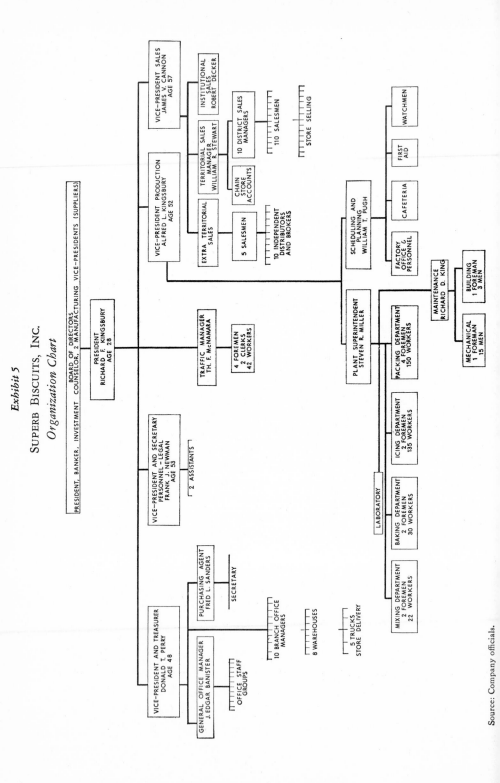

BOARD OF DIRECTORS
PRESIDENT, BANKER, INVESTMENT COUNSELOR, 2 MANUFACTURING VICE-PRESIDENTS (SUPPLIERS)

PRESIDENT
RICHARD F. KINGSBURY
AGE 28

VICE-PRESIDENT AND TREASURER
DONALD T. PERRY
AGE 48

VICE-PRESIDENT AND SECRETARY
PERSONNEL–LEGAL
FRANK J. NEWMAN
AGE 53

VICE-PRESIDENT PRODUCTION
ALFRED L. KINGSBURY
AGE 52

VICE-PRESIDENT SALES
JAMES V. CANNON
AGE 57

GENERAL OFFICE MANAGER
J. EDGAR BANISTER

PURCHASING AGENT
FRED L. SANDERS

2 ASSISTANTS

TRAFFIC MANAGER
TH. F. McNAMARA

INSTITUTIONAL SALES
ROBERT DECKER

TERRITORIAL SALES MANAGER
WILLIAM R. STEWART

OFFICE STAFF GROUPS

SECRETARY

4 FOREMEN
2 CLERKS
42 WORKERS

EXTRA TERRITORIAL SALES

CHAIN STORE ACCOUNTS

10 DISTRICT SALES MANAGERS

10 BRANCH OFFICE MANAGERS

5 SALESMEN

10 INDEPENDENT DISTRIBUTORS AND BROKERS

110 SALESMEN

8 WAREHOUSES

STORE SELLING

5 TRUCKS
STORE DELIVERY

LABORATORY

PLANT SUPERINTENDENT
STEVEN R. MILLER

SCHEDULING AND PLANNING
WILLIAM T. PUGH

MIXING DEPARTMENT
2 FOREMEN
22 WORKERS

BAKING DEPARTMENT
2 FOREMEN
30 WORKERS

ICING DEPARTMENT
2 FOREMEN
135 WORKERS

PACKING DEPARTMENT
4 FOREMEN
150 WORKERS

FACTORY OFFICE & PERSONNEL

CAFETERIA

FIRST AID

WATCHMEN

MAINTENANCE
RICHARD D. KING

MECHANICAL
1 FOREMAN
15 MEN

BUILDING
1 FOREMAN
3 MEN

Source: Company officials.

The second market, accounting for about 15% to 20% of Superb's volume, was outside the home territory in scattered centers of population like Milwaukee, Kansas City, and even Washington, D.C. Five company salesmen, working directly under Mr. Cannon, called on the ten independent distributors who served these areas.

The third market consisted of various private and governmental institutions to which special types of biscuits were supplied on a contract basis. Competition was keen in this field, and bids were negotiated individually. While the first two markets showed only moderate seasonal fluctuations, the third required its heaviest volume during the first four months of the year. Institutional sales were managed by Robert Decker, who had 21 years of service with Superb.

Mr. Cannon had joined the company in 1936 after spending 14 years in the sales department of Scott Paper Company. A relative of Earl Kingsbury, he started as a Superb route salesman and rose to his present position after serving as district manager and territorial sales manager for a number of years.

Mr. Cannon commented that he believed one of the company's bigger problems was the high cost of distribution for the home territory. "Bill Stewart and I wonder about the merits of the present system, which is the most expensive form of selling," he said. He indicated that costs in the home territory totaled about 35% of sales in 1956. This figure included sales salaries and commissions, trade discounts, advertising, delivery, and sales administration expenses, all allocated on the basis of dollar volume. In the large cities outside the territory, where limited advertising was carried on, total costs averaged about 31.5% of sales, while sales costs on institutional business averaged about 20% of net sales. Mr. Cannon said that while institutional accounts were the most desirable in terms of selling costs, their seasonal character and competitive nature prevented the company from taking on a higher volume. In general, Mr. Cannon foresaw even higher selling costs for all types of accounts. He mentioned, for example, that drivers' wages were bounding upward along with rail rates.

In the home territory, company salesmen averaged about 175 accounts each, on which they called weekly. It was estimated that one-fourth of these stores purchased as little as $5 to $10 per month. On an average, it required at least one hour per month to service even the smallest account. Salesmen received a base salary of about $300 per month, plus graduated percentage bonuses for sales in excess of the quotas set with their co-operation by Mr. Stewart. Salesmen generally exceeded their

base quotas, and yearly contests were held for the best salesman. The
men kept detailed records of calls made, new accounts opened, and
sales volume by accounts. From this information, weekly summaries
were prepared for the district managers and the home office. All salesmen worked from route books and timetables prepared by the district
managers. Turnover among salesmen was low, according to Mr. Stewart.

The president commented that he felt the need for increased volume
on present routes. He believed that his big competitors had an advantage in terms of selling costs. He estimated that their volume per
salesman was from one and one-half to two times that of Superb, owing
to larger territories or wider product lines. Furthermore, he estimated
that Superb's delivery costs per sales dollar ran about 20% higher than
competitors' costs, and sales administration about 10% higher. Advertising and promotional costs he considered about equal percentagewise (see Exhibit 6).

Mr. Cannon was weighing the pros and cons of changing from direct
selling in the home territory to independent distributors, as used in the
extraterritorial market. These middlemen, located in the large cities,
generally received a flat 25% discount off list price. Mr. Cannon stated
that they had been very successful in selling Superb products and he
was considering adding several more to the present ten to enlarge the
field. He stated that selling through these channels was "hard selling"
but "good selling," explaining that distributors generally asked for
"special deals" in terms of price concessions or free goods (e.g., one
carton free for every dozen), but at the same time they assumed all
risks and the company was not forced to stand behind them with a
guarantee to take back unsalable stock. "Selling direct through salesmen
is almost like selling on consignment," he said, "while distributors have
no recourse. But then, distributors take on only 'good sellers'—which in
a way is an advantage. Why clutter a store with slow-selling items?"
Mr. Cannon stated that the company's rate of returned goods was not
quite 2% of net sales. He added that selling through distributors required strong men "able to say no" to the many demands for special
favors. Furthermore, he said, the company would be subjected to greater
price pressures, since distributors generally carried more than one brand
of biscuits and would tend to push the brand most profitable to them.

Another change weighed by Mr. Cannon was modification of salesmen's compensation. He said, "We are considering the possibility of
putting our men on straight commission, which would also cover their
expenses. At the moment we have two or three of our district managers

Exhibit 6

SUPERB BISCUITS, INC.

Comparative Breakdown of Sales Dollar
Superb versus Large Companies (Estimates)

	Superb	Estimate for Biscuit Operations of Large Competitors
Gross sales	110.0%	110.0%
Trade commissions	8.0%	8.0%
Returned merchandise	2.0	2.0
	10.0%	10.0%
Net sales	100.0%	100.0%
Raw materials and supplies	52.8%	50.0%*
Direct labor	9.3	9.5
Manufacturing overhead	6.5	7.5
	68.6%	67.0%
Gross margin	31.4%	33.0%
Selling expenses:		
Advertising and promotion	2.8%	3.0%
Sales salaries and commissions	5.8	4.6
Other	1.1	0.8
	9.7%	8.4%
Delivery, warehousing	3.3%	2.3%
Freight	5.1	4.5
General and administrative	10.7	11.2
Interest	0.1	0.1
	19.2%	18.1%
Total expenses	28.9%	26.5%
Net income (before taxes)	2.5%	6.5%
Federal income taxes	1.2	3.2
Net income	1.3%	3.3%

* Lower, according to Superb officers, because of vertical integration.
Source: Company records and estimates of company officers.

stewing over the problem. If they think it is a good idea, we shall tell the other managers, and in turn have them sell it to the salesmen."

Mr. Kingsbury thought the company might well be forced to change its distribution system in the long run. He stated that National Biscuit and some small firms had experimented with a split arrangement, putting salaried men in charge of large chain accounts, while paying the salesmen who covered independent stores on straight commission. "Under such a system," he said, "we would be better set for the eventual transition in food marketing to complete predominance of the large supermarket."

Mr. Kingsbury visualized, as a long-term possibility, the institution of direct delivery of biscuits to chain warehouses, eliminating the individual store deliveries made at present. The few remaining small independent stores would be served by driver-salesmen carrying the necessary stocks in their trucks. This would reduce the number of men required to one-third or less, he said.

Mr. Cannon indicated that the company's resources were insufficient for the extensive market research carried on by its large competitors. The company used an outside firm to supply monthly reports on relative market shares. "Everyone is in research," he said, "but when you are small you must sell hard instead, get more outlets, and keep them well stocked." He said that Superb had to rely on its sales force to bring back information about competitive developments. The district managers held regular monthly meetings with their men, and occasionally all salesmen and sales personnel were brought together to discuss advertising or promotional problems. During 1956 there had been four such meetings, a considerable increase over previous years.

New product and promotional ideas at times greatly stimulated sales according to Mr. Cannon. For example, during 1955 Superb had introduced three products aimed at different nationality groups, using authentic recipes; sales had jumped as much as 35% to 50% in outlying centers of population where these groups were heavily represented. Mr. Cannon believed that such specialties helped to promote regular sales by making the Superb name better known. Promotional ideas of the present year included handing out sample cookies, with an advertising message attached, in the elementary schools of Kansas City. The expense of the samples was borne by the distributor. "We must make little things pay," commented Mr. Cannon, and stated that he was glad the company had begun moving toward such new product ideas and promotions.

Advertising had undergone changes and was still being modified. Before 1936 the company had spent up to 10% of net sales on advertising, especially when sales began to slip. Earl Kingsbury had drastically cut expenditures to an average of $100,000 to $115,000 per year, including co-operative advertising for the home territory which amounted to about 40% of the total. In the recent past, most of the budget was spent on billboards (35%) and on some radio spots (25%). Magazine advertising was negligible. In 1956 the company initiated spots on local television and signed up for another billboard campaign (30% of budget) during the summer. Furthermore, the advertising agency was asked to come up with a suitable slogan tying the product line to reasons for consumer preference for Superb biscuits. The 1957 advertising budget was set at almost $250,000, an increase of about 24% over past years.

Richard Kingsbury believed that during his father's management the lines of authority in the sales department had become blurred because district managers were allowed to carry their problems directly to the president. "This custom resulted in nobody knowing who was to tell what to whom," he said, adding that it was not until five years ago that the sales vice-president had begun to spend most of his time in the central office. Prior to that time he had been mainly occupied with extraterritorial sales. Mr. Kingsbury commented that, except for approving the size of the advertising budget, he made it a point not to interfere in the sales department. He wanted to foster the rebuilding of authority for the department head. He believed that morale and turnover among sales personnel had improved greatly in the last five years, especially because there were no longer numerous hirings and firings.

PRODUCTION

Increased efficiency and better mechanization were the main problems that concerned the vice-president of production, Alfred Kingsbury, an uncle of Richard Kingsbury. He believed that it was vital for the company to increase production without increasing labor costs. "We have not been able to pass on increased costs to the consumer—competitors have not been able to do this either. Automation is the ultimate answer, and we are compelled to go into it, but in the intermediate period we must buy better and produce better. If I could schedule longer runs, for instance, I could double our tonnage output, but our sales force needs variety," he said.

Alfred Kingsbury was made a vice-president when Earl Kingsbury took over the company. He had been a sales representative with another biscuit company and had run food stores before that. Reporting to him were Steven R. Miller, plant superintendent, and William T. Pugh, head of scheduling. Mr. Miller, a chemist and former head of the laboratory, was placed in his present position early in 1956 by Richard Kingsbury, who explained that he had fired two men formerly serving as joint superintendents because they were unwilling to delegate authority and accept new ideas. Mr. Miller, aged 30, was in charge of production, efficiency control, the laboratory, and maintenance. Mr. Pugh, a man of 18 years' experience in the biscuit industry, was in charge of scheduling, hiring of production workers, and related personnel services.

The plant, together with the offices, was located in a four-story building in a suburban area and was served by a spur track of the Rock Island Railroad. The ground floor was used for warehousing and shipping, while the second and third floors contained offices and manufacturing area. The fourth floor was rented to another firm. Major items of equipment were four 200-foot continuous band ovens, a battery of dough mixers that handled about 400,000 pounds of flour and shortening per week, several kneading machines, packaging lines serving the ovens, and three icing, sandwiching, and coating lines. Most of the equipment had been of very advanced design at the time of installation and had been kept in good condition, according to Mr. Kingsbury. Several conveyor arrangements allowed continuous product flow.

Production operations were divided into four sections, mixing, baking, icing, and packing. The plant worked in two shifts, and the work force totaled close to 400 men and women. Labor relations were peaceful, and all workers were unionized. Both Mr. Kingsbury and Mr. Miller indicated that they made sure to consult with union representatives before making any change in operations that affected the workers, and they thought this policy was one of the foundations of labor peace. "We have to build the strength of the union for our own good," said Mr. Miller, who indicated that union stewards attended the monthly meetings of foremen and production management.

Mr. Miller was considered by Alfred Kingsbury to be aggressive, smart, and progressing well in his new job. Mr. Miller said he made it a point to rebuild the authority of his foremen who had been undermined by his predecessors. He indicated that he allowed them more freedom to make operating decisions and required workers to see their foremen first before bringing complaints to him. At the same time he was concerned with quality and efficiency. "Every Friday I get together with my foremen and discuss what we mean by quality—I prefer to call it constancy —and analyze systematically how to do better in it. I also look for savings; just recently we cut expenses $400 per month by using paper towels instead of cloth to clean machinery." To avoid costly stoppages of the continuous production lines, Mr. Miller insisted on extensive preventive maintenance.

Mr. Miller shared the president's concern about introducing better machinery, and kept a file of new developments. He had joined Richard Kingsbury on an extended trip to machinery suppliers in the United States and Europe, and had assisted in selecting several new packaging machines.

Scheduling was described as complicated owing to the large variety of products offered. Both Alfred Kingsbury and Mr. Pugh spent most of their time working out the daily and weekly programs for the four sections. A minimum run of two hours was required for any one product, and the problem was to dovetail inventories and current requirements of the eight warehouses and the extraterritorial markets.

New product development had historically been concentrated in the production area, where one specialist was spending his full time on trying out new recipes. Several years ago a committee had been formed which consisted of Messrs. Alfred Kingsbury, Cannon, Perry (vice-president and treasurer), Stewart, as well as the new products specialist, and the company's part-time art director. According to the president, the committee produced little and met very infrequently until about a year ago when it was realized that more new products were needed. Since that time six new items had been developed and approved, and the committee now met three times per month. Of the six items which had been introduced through in-store promotions, only two showed continued success, two were "slowly dying," after a three-month life, while two never "went off the ground," he said. One of the successful items was a medium-priced assortment, while the other was a new form of cookie. Mr. Kingsbury believed that there were "too many thumbs" in the new product field and said that he was still looking for the best possible method of "hatching ideas" and accelerating their utilization. He said the majority of new ideas actually came from jobbers and distributors, while a few original ideas had emerged from production personnel. "There are not too many ideas that are completely new in this field," he said, and told of an instance where a new cookie had been developed by mistake when a worker used the "wrong" spices.

Alfred Kingsbury stated that new products had to meet high turnover requirements in addition to being different. "In the recent past all biscuit companies have lost five to ten items each due to stores wanting products with faster turnover. More and more items are competing for the available shelf space in a market." He believed that the industry would have to stimulate the basic demand for biscuits if it wanted to grow further.

FINANCE AND CONTROL

Donald T. Perry, vice-president and treasurer, had spent his entire career in varying positions in the biscuit industry. Previously plant manager for a medium-size biscuit manufacturer, he had joined Superb as assistant to the president in 1936, and was appointed vice-president soon thereafter.

Mr. Perry was in charge of finance and purchasing. The general office manager, Mr. Banister, supervised the office and accounting staffs. The company employed a product-cost system that traced labor and materials costs for each product, based on the daily runs through the four production departments. At least four times per year the average costs for each product were compiled and compared to current sales prices, and the gross margin was determined to see whether the product was profitable. Costs, except labor costs, were not recorded by department, but were allocated on the basis of weight of the finished product. Other data collected included average weight of output, barrels produced per hour, percentage yield from raw materials, and cost of finishes. Small variations in coatings, for instance, could prove very costly, according to Mr. Perry. Richard Kingsbury indicated that he favored several changes in the accounting area, particularly an attempt to establish basic standards of output on which to base a "more realistic" allocation of burden. He also wanted a more detailed breakdown of departmental expenses and reorganization of the company's monthly financial reports.

Inventories were taken weekly in each warehouse, and the central office maintained close control over the ordering procedures which were based on four-week moving averages. Owing to the semiperishable nature of the products, no more than one week's inventory of finished goods was kept on hand. Similarly, raw materials were kept down to four weeks' supply at the most. The company's spoilage experience was less than one-fourth of 1% of sales, according to Mr. Perry.

The treasurer considered his most serious problem to be "how to balance the budget." He worried over increased costs due to a rise from wage negotiations which were to start in the spring of 1957. Costs of raw materials and freight showed an upward trend. "There is no end to increases," he said, "and the Middle East troubles have sent commodities way up." He said that the biscuit industry had made general price advances in early 1957, but that this had been just enough to offset some of the cost increases of 1956, leaving no room for the expected 1957 rise. "Price advances are generally made uniformly by the whole industry with the large companies taking the lead," he said, "and only occasional reductions on single products are made individually."

Mr. Perry believed that the company was too small to do any hedging in the commodity markets, which he considered a special field in itself, not even tackled by the large companies. Superb generally bought flour requirements for about 120 days ahead, under standard millers' contracts, and once in a while ventured to buy six months' supply. The latter action involved a risk of paying storage charges to millers should the company be unable to take delivery within the stated period; thus the advantage of lower prices might be eliminated. The purchasing agent, Mr. Sanders, who had 35 years' experience in procurement, believed that Superb paid essentially the same prices for its raw materials as the large competitors, owing to the fact that the large companies generally bought on the plant level rather than centrally.

Quarterly budgets were tentatively prepared, focused mainly on the cash flow required to meet seasonal swings. The president commented that since about one year formal budgeting procedures had "all but gone out of the window," because of the difficulties of forecasting demand and costs.

Every year, to meet seasonal needs, Mr. Perry borrowed several hundred thousand dollars in short-term funds on a line of credit. Superb was still saddled with arrears of $71,000 on its preferred stock, but the president hoped to be able to pay this off within the next year and then start paying dividends on the common.

Proposals made by the production department or the president for expenditures on new machinery were analyzed by Mr. Perry. On the basis of his calculations, Mr. Richard Kingsbury decided on the merits of the purchase and defended it before the board, which passed on every expenditure over $2,000. The board gave its approval on almost all projects presented by him, he said. Richard Kingsbury spent most of his time on finding new ways to mechanize the processes of manufacture.

In the past, many special machines had been developed and built by Superb, but this had become increasingly difficult in recent years, said Mr. Perry. In the early years, Earl Kingsbury had economized greatly and held back on capital expenditures where possible. Up to 1956 Superb had relied solely on internally generated funds for capital outlays and had not considered outside money. The president now felt it was high time the company started looking for long-term loans to finance more machinery.

Mr. Perry also assisted in setting product prices based on cost data, but he said the company had little leeway in pricing standard products where prices tended to be industry-wide. "We must find more specialties on which we can put a price tag of our own," said Mr. Perry, "but still most of the volume is done with a limited number of standard varieties that you must have in order to be competitive. If we withdrew these low-margin products, the customer in the store might not pick up the specialty items either, and our display space would be cut. Moreover, our factory would have greatly reduced volume which would shift burden costs onto other products."

PERSONNEL AND LEGAL

Frank J. Newman, vice-president and secretary, was in charge of the legal affairs of the company and also directed personnel policies. He hired all personnel except production workers. A lawyer by training, Mr. Newman left private practice in 1936 to join Earl Kingsbury first as counsel, later as secretary and clerk; he was made vice-president in 1954. Mr. Newman obtained leases for district warehouses, appraised distributors' contracts, and gave advice on provisions of the Pure Food and Drug Act. Furthermore, he negotiated union contracts with the teamsters' and bakery workers' locals.

Mr. Newman also prepared the agenda for officers', directors', and stockholders' meetings. He said that about a year ago the officers' meetings had "petered out," and Richard Kingsbury had temporarily stopped them altogether. About six months later they were resumed and had been kept up regularly to date. Mr. Newman said that in these meetings the officers considered "matters of over-all policy," which included items like group insurance coverage, the problems of uniform package design, and the volume of institutional sales desirable.

TRAFFIC

Superb maintained a shipping and receiving department under Mr. Thomas McNamara, who had spent 20 years with the Great Northern Railroad before joining the company in 1936. Mr. McNamara supervised the compilation of truck and rail loads of finished products and determined the best possible routing. He worked closely with the sales department.

ORGANIZATIONAL DEVELOPMENTS

Before becoming president, Richard Kingsbury had worked in two functional departments looking for improvements. His interest in efficiency had led to substantial labor savings in shipping. He said it had been easier to convince the teamsters' union of the need for changes than some of the foremen, and he believed that resistance to new ideas had been fostered by the centralized control of his father. Mr. Kingsbury described the two plant superintendents he had fired as unco-operative, hardheaded, antilabor, and as standing in the way of improvements. He said he had eliminated three additional foremen showing similar attitudes. Mr. Kingsbury felt he now had the right man in the superintendent's position, one who could lead the foremen and look for better manufacturing methods.

Soon after becoming president, Richard Kingsbury had issued a directive that prohibited on-the-spot firing by foremen. He said his father had never agreed to this change while he was in control, but Richard Kingsbury believed the exercise of firing authority was inconsistent with good supervision. The directive stated that written requests for the release of a worker should be sent by the foreman to Mr. Newman and be approved by Alfred Kingsbury and Mr. Miller.

Mr. Kingsbury stated that his own youthful age had been a "small powderkeg" at the time of his father's resignation. "There was not much doubt in the minds of the directors about the succession," he said, "but the other executives did not share that certainty as they had little contact with the board. It became a question of whether I was taking over in name or in fact, and at least two of the officers had aspirations. Many lingering animosities came into the open at that time, and I finally had to stop the officers' meetings in early 1956 because nothing could be accomplished in them."

"Co-ordination was lacking between the departments," he continued, "and I stuck my neck out to cut bottlenecks. But the people involved had to cool down first, and I did not resume the meetings for about half a year."

Richard Kingsbury commented on the current meetings as follows: "We are now operating with the vice-presidents as heads of functional line departments. Actually we never act as a management group. The only real co-operative efforts occur if two department heads have an overlapping problem like priority schedules of production. But other matters are treated separately and will likely continue to be treated as such. For instance, advertising policy is handled solely as a sales problem. Actually, the vice-presidents have been used to operating this way since my father's time. There was even terrific interdepartmental animosity; each department tried to push the other around," he said. Mr. Kingsbury explained that there had been so-called "policy meetings" under Earl Kingsbury, but although ideas were debated collectively, Earl Kingsbury personally set policies.

"It is my prerogative to set policies which are self-governing, as contrasted with day-to-day affairs. I mainly concern myself with interdepartmental matters, or with weaknesses in any one department. For instance, I felt I had to take action in the production area—but I take action only if initial suggestions do not bring results," he explained.

In speaking of interdepartmental co-operation, Mr. Cannon said that until recently co-ordination between his department and the factory had not always been the best. During 1956, however, William Stewart had the idea of forming a production planning group to consist of Mr. Cannon, Alfred Kingsbury, the heads of scheduling and sales service, and himself. The group began by working on the problem of slack periods caused by seasonal demand for certain high-volume products, especially institutional biscuits. An attempt was made to forecast such fluctuations and schedule appropriate substitute products to keep the factory operating at capacity. Similarly, the group helped to schedule production on products for which demand was especially heavy. Mr. Cannon stated he felt this group had helped both his department and the production area.

Richard Kingsbury also thought the group was a good idea, as it taught certain sales personnel "the physical facts of life about the factory." He said that salesmen tended to push certain items too hard, thinking they could have more supplies immediately. This resulted in temporary but embarrassing shortages, during which the home territory was generally neglected in favor of outside areas. "This was quite contrary to the natural emphasis required—I still believe that our home territory is our mainstay," he said. "On the other hand," he added, "the factory was tempted to produce items that best fitted its production schedules."

The older executives commented that Richard Kingsbury showed great insight and capabilities, especially for his age. They said his interest in new machinery foreshadowed promising developments. Mr. Perry remarked: "Richard can do a lot of things with people who of themselves would not think of changing their old ways. By being in a position of authority he can spark new thought and urge its acceptance." Alfred Kingsbury said that no major steps were taken either by the president or by the officers without mutual consultation. "Dick is naturally more dependent on the department heads because his experience is shorter. He would not think of doing something without bringing it up with one or all of us. Likewise, we talk to him about our problems and listen to his views."

THE FUTURE

Mr. Kingsbury visualized a need for stricter cost controls and a more unified sales promotion. "I consider our present product line a hodgepodge in terms of appearance," he said, and indicated that, as one step toward improving package design and uniformity, Superb had asked its paper and cardboard suppliers to analyze current packages and suggest changes. This practice was common among small biscuit companies that were unable to afford large sums for professional designers.

The question of product diversification had arisen several times during the past three years. The idea of going into cereals and cake mixes had been discarded owing to the difficulties envisioned in competing with nationally advertised brands. Mr. Kingsbury stated that he and some of his officers felt the company should expand its line "if and when the right opportunity comes." New products might be added either through subcontracting of production or through utilizing the present plant. Mr. Kingsbury felt that the potential of the present sales force might be more fully realized with additional compatible products.

Danford Rubber Company

BETWEEN 1929 AND 1940, the Danford Rubber Company had seven profitable years and five unprofitable years. There was a net loss of $89,-000 for this period. From 1941 through 1947, there were net profits every year, the total being $1,730,000. Operations during the first eight

Exhibit 1

DANFORD RUBBER COMPANY

Comparative Balance Sheet, Fiscal Years Ending September 30, 1935 to 1947; First 8 Months 1948 Fiscal Year

(In Thousands)

Assets	1935	1936	1937	1938	1939	1940	1941
Current Assets:							
Cash..............................$	84	$ 54	$ 70	$ 109	$ 114	$ 104	$ 115
Accounts and Notes Receivable (less							
Reserves)......................	443	545	538	810	977	641	996
Inventory†.......................	306	343	535	370	396	451	402
Tax Refunds......................	....	....	....	....	....	....	....
Total Current Assets............$	833	$ 942	$1,143	$1,289	$1,487	$1,196	$1,513
Other Assets........................	32	29	26	12	4	17	3
Property, Plant, and Equipment (less							
Reserves)........................	341	305	348	330	363	423	391
Deferred Charges...................	13	13	13	8	12	11	11
Total Assets.................$	1,219	$1,289	$1,530	$1,639	$1,866	$1,647	$1,918
Liabilities and Capital							
Current Liabilities...................$	82	$ 146	$ 359	$ 414	$ 453	$ 341	$ 492
Reserve............................	....	....	6	....	42	35	48
Total Liabilities.................$	82	$ 146	$ 365	$ 414	$ 495	$ 376	$ 540
Capital:							
Preferred Stock 7% Cumulative (Par							
$50)...........................	527	527	527	527	527	527	527
Funded Debt, 4% Convertible Debentures Due April 15, 1958, less Sinking Fund Payment...............	....	....	....	....	....	....	....
Common Stock (No Par)...........	243	243	243	243	243	243	243
Surplus:							
Capital............................	325	325	325	325	325	325	325
Earned............................	42	48	70	130	276	176	283
Total Liabilities and Capital....$	1,219	$1,289	$1,530	$1,639	$1,866	$1,647	$1,918

† Lower of cost or market.
‡ Plant includes $214,182 in emergency facilities; plant evaluation reduced by reserves of $642,000 (depreciation) and $214,000 (amortization).
§ Sales warranties, $80,000; tax contingencies, $150,000; reserve for price decline, $103,000.
Source: Company annual reports.

months of the 1948 fiscal year, however, had resulted in a deficit of $97,000 (see Exhibits 1 and 2).

The 1948 loss had occurred, Mr. Forrester, president of the company, stated, because of an early spring industry-wide tire and tube sales slump which caused profit difficulties for dealers as well as manufacturers. This slump was the second postwar evidence that the industry was returning to its traditional pattern of severe competition. Postwar price competition first developed during the early months of 1947. "The tire industry has been in a fight for existence since 1921," Mr. Forrester stated. "In 1921 there were approximately 225 companies manufacturing tires in the United States; in 1948 there were fewer than 30."

Exhibit 1—Continued

DANFORD RUBBER COMPANY

Fiscal Years Ending September 30, 1935 to 1947;
First 8 Months 1948 Fiscal Year

(In Thousands)

Assets	1942	1943	1944	1945	1946	1947	May 31, 1948
Current Assets:							
Cash	$ 922	$ 535	$ 456	$ 276	$1,200	$ 173	$ 45
Accounts and Notes Receivable (less							
Reserves)	589	858	1,103	1,236	1,394	$1,566	801
Inventory†	476	843	826	1,141	1,408	1,436	1,616
Tax Refunds	....	....	....	84	34	....	....
Total Current Assets	$1,987	$2,236	$2,385	$2,737	$4,036	$3,175	$2,462
Other Assets	17	43	89	....	....	....	....
Property, Plant, and Equipment (less							
Reserves)	388	405	619	573	1,172	2,027‡	2,049
Deferred Charges	20	19	20	25	84	81	11
Total Assets	$2,412	$2,703	$3,113	$3,335	$5,292	$5,283	$4,522
Liabilities and Capital							
Current Liabilities	$ 770	$ 960	$1,278	$1,379	$1,802	$1,748	$1,243
Reserve	134	208	246	246	334	333§	279
Total Liabilities	$ 904	$1,168	$1,524	$1,625	$2,136	$2,081	$1,522
Capital:							
Preferred Stock 7% Cumulative (Par							
$50)	527	527	527	527	....	....	....
Funded Debt, 4% Convertible Debentures Due April 15, 1958, less Sinking Fund Payment	....	....	....	....	1,627	1,522	1,416
Common Stock (No Par)	243	243	243	243	243	243	243
Surplus:							
Capital	325	325	325	325	325	325	325
Earned	413	440	494	615	961	1,112	1,016
Total Liabilities and Capital	$2,412	$2,703	$3,113	$3,335	$5,292	$5,283	$4,522

Danford Rubber Company, one of the smaller companies still in operation in 1948, was primarily a manufacturer of quality tires and tubes for passenger cars and trucks. Danford tires were not sold to the auto-

Exhibit 2

DANFORD RUBBER COMPANY

Consolidated Income Statement, Fiscal Years Ending September 30, 1935 to 1947; First 8 Months 1948 Fiscal Year

(In Thousands)

	1935		1936		1937		1938		1939		1940		1941		First 8 Months Fiscal Year 1948	
Net sales	$1,478	100%	$2,044	100%	$2,699	100%	$3,342	100%	$4,542	100%	$3,462	100%	$4,637	100%	$5,261	100%
Cost of sales	1,304	88	1,747	86	2,269	84	2,662	80	3,701	82	3,083	89	4,005	86	4,869	92
Gross profit	$ 174	12%	$ 297	14%	$ 430	16%	$ 680	20%	$ 841	18%	$ 379	11%	$ 632	14%	$ 392	8%
Selling, general, and administrative expense	196	13	246	12	312	11	445	13	560	12	453	13	482	11	515	10
Profit from operations	($ 22)	(1%)	$ 51	2%	$ 118	5%	$ 235	7%	$ 281	6%	($ 74)	(2%)	$ 150	3%	($ 123)	(2%)
Other income	5	0	23†	1	32‡	1	5	0	5	0	14	0	6	0	8	
Other deductions	42	3	49	2	54	2	74	2	15	2	2	0	6	0	39	
Provision for postwar contingencies	...		...		...		...		...		...		...		...	
Net profit before taxes	($ 59)	(4%)	$ 25	1%	$ 96	4%	$ 166	5%	$ 271	6%	($ 62)	(2%)	$ 150	3%	($ 154)	
Income taxes	...		3	0	20	1	33	1	55	1	...		43	1	...	
Net profit after taxes	($ 59)	(4%)	$ 22	1%	$ 76	3%	$ 133	4%	$ 216	5%	($ 62)	(2%)	$ 107	2%	($ 97)	

	1942		1943		1944		1945		1946		1947	
Net sales	$4,803	100%	$7,181	100%	$7,631	100%	$10,592	100%	$12,511	100%	$11,895	100%
Cost of sales	3,770	78	6,006	84	6,413	84	8,900	84	10,554	84	10,687	90
Gross profit	$1,033	22%	$1,175	16%	$1,218	16%	$1,692	16%	$1,957	16%	$ 1,208	10%
Selling, general, and administrative expense	461	10	510	7	552	7	732	7	832	7	758	6
Profit from operations	$ 572	12%	$ 665	9%	$ 666	9%	$ 960	9%	$1,125	9%	$ 450	4%
Other income	4	0	1	0	7	0	13	0	4	0	12	0
Other deductions	...		...		6	0	17	0	57	0	84	1
Provision for postwar contingencies	60	1	36	0	38	1	18	1	0		0	
Net profit before taxes	$ 516	11%	$ 630	9%	$ 629	8%	$ 938	8%	$1,072	9%	$ 378	3%
Income taxes	346	7	436	6	442	6	671	6	509	4	137	1
Net profit after taxes	$ 170	4%	$ 194	3%	$ 187	2%	$ 267	2%	$ 563	5%	$ 241	2%

Parentheses indicate red figure.
† Sale of land, $17,000.
‡ Sale of land, $25,000.
§ Depreciation divided between cost of sales and selling, general, and administrative expense.
NOTE: Tax credit of $57,000 realized in first eight-month period of 1948.
Source: Company records.

mobile industry for new car use but rather were sold in the replacement market. The company also manufactured car batteries, camelback (tire recapping and retreading material), rubber shoe soling, and minor rubber automotive products. These items, sold to independent retailers under the brand name "Danford," were marketed in competition with the products of such industry leaders as Firestone and U.S. Rubber, besides General, Lee, Pharis, Gates, and other tire manufacturers.

Danford Rubber Company was located in Logan, an industrial town of 50,000 population, fifty miles from New York City.

THE INDUSTRY

In 1948 the tire industry included twenty-three companies, of which eleven were located in the Ohio area and seven along the eastern coast. Tire manufacturers could be divided into three groups: (1) the Big Four—Firestone, Goodyear, Goodrich, and U.S. Rubber (1947 sales volume range $410 to $670 million); (2) the General Tire and Rubber Company (1947 sales volume, $126 million); and (3) the so-called "independents" (1947 sales volume range $5 to $40 million). General Tire and Rubber occupied a special position in the tire industry. Formerly a small independent tire manufacturer, General had grown rapidly, until, in 1948, it was the fifth largest unit in the industry. General Tire and Rubber manufactured tires for the replacement market as well as other nonrubber products.

The Big Four sold their branded tires and tubes (1) to the original equipment market (automobile manufacturers), and (2) to the replacement market through 1,600 retail company stores, as well as through "associated retail stores" and independent retail tire dealers. They also manufactured and sold private brand tires to large mail-order companies, department stores, chain automotive product stores, and large oil companies. The Big Four handled complete lines of tires, including both standard tires (4-ply, 100 level—1948 retail price, $15.95 plus tax) and premium tires (extra-value tires—1948 retail price about $35.00). They also manufactured a wide range of products, which included plastics and chemicals.

Independent tire manufacturers concentrated on the replacement market, selling their branded tires normally through independent retail tire dealers, although some had developed mail-order house private brand manufacturing contracts, as well as sales through smaller gasoline station chains. Most independents manufactured some standard tires but concentrated their efforts chiefly on premium tires which were of more durable construction than standard tires and which had some exclusive sales feature, such as nylon cord or heat vents.

In an effort to attract loyal dealers, most independent manufacturers offered their tire dealers advantages which they did not believe larger manufacturers offered: (1) an exclusive sales franchise for an area; (2) the right to make immediate adjustments for faulty tires rather than wait for supervisory inspection; (3) the right to offer two sales warranties on their tires—the standard guarantee offered by all tire companies against faulty material and workmanship, and an additional "road hazard" warranty which insured the tire buyer for a stated period against loss from bruises and blow-outs.

Exhibit 3

DISTRIBUTION OF REPLACEMENT TIRE SALES FOR SELECTED
YEARS, 1922–46
(Percentage of Total Replacement Sales)

Year	Mail-Order and Chain Stores	Oil Companies	Company-Owned Stores	Factory Direct	Independent Dealers
1946	17.0%	19.1%	9.4%	1.5%	51.8%
1941	24.1	15.5	8.8	2.4	48.2
1939	24.0	15.5	7.8	1.0	50.6
1936	17.5	15.8	11.2	0.9	53.5
1932	17.0	6.9	9.3	0.9	65.1
1929	18.9	1.0	4.1	1.0	74.2
1927	9.4	*	0.5	1.0	88.6
1922	1.8	*	*	*	98.0

* Less than 0.1%.

Source: "Tires and Rubber," Standard & Poor's *Industry Surveys*, March 19, 1948, Section 2, p. T3-7. Compiled from estimates of Professor W. W. Leigh of the University of Akron.

Only a limited amount of tire marketing information was available to tire manufacturers. Some companies believed that tires were purchased by the consumer on the basis of brand preference, price appeal, dealer-customer relationships, or special design features. No public trade information, however, was available as to the relative importance of each of these factors or their interrelationship. In 1948, some of the largest tire companies were securing select groups of large retail units with sales of $100,000 and over. Major oil companies were stressing the expansion of gas station tire sales, giving their private brands very wide distribution. Exhibit 3 lists information on distribution channel trends, one important long-run trend being the percentage decline in tires handled by independent dealers.

EARLY COMPANY OPERATIONS

The character and nature of the Danford company reflected the personalities of its two presidents: Mr. Edward Kirk, who founded the firm in 1914, and Mr. Steven Forrester, his successor. Mr. Kirk was described by Mr. Forrester as a man of strong will and determination. He had organized the Danford company rather than remain with a large tire manufacturer "where individual management ideas had limited chance for expression." Mr. Kirk brought with him one of his sales associates, Mr. Forrester. Mr. Forrester stated that he had joined the new firm because he, too, did not like "the regimentation and strict control which large rubber companies forced on their executives." In taking the new job, Mr. Forrester accepted a reduction in annual salary from $7,000 to $2,000.

The Danford company had first specialized in treating crude rubber. This venture had not proved to be profitable, however, and the company turned to the manufacture of automobile tires. During the next thirty years, the bases on which Danford tires were to be sold, and the areas in which sales were to be made, changed from time to time.

Mr. Kirk's original tire sales plan was to serve a regional market at prices 10% under those charged by the larger manufacturers. Severe price competition soon forced abandonment of this program. Next he adopted a sales and pricing program which conformed more closely to what other firms in the industry were doing: (1) build a complete line of tires; (2) distribute these tires nationally; (3) price tires competitively; and (4) promote a brand name through local and national advertising. Danford operated with this basic program until 1931. Profits were realized in most years until 1925 and losses in most years from 1925 through 1930.

OPERATIONS—1931–41

By 1931 a combination of ever-increasing competition, disturbed raw material markets, and depressed business conditions had left Danford in a serious position. Mr. Forrester, who at that time assumed active direction of the company, stated: "We had to fight or die. I decided to switch from national distribution to regional; that is, to a sales territory which could be handled by overnight truck hauls from the factory." With this move the company discontinued national advertising, reduced its sales force from 70 to 9 men, and eliminated 7 branch offices and 27 warehouses. The number of dealers was reduced from 1,200 to 300. Intensive work by the remaining sales force during the next few years, however, substantially increased the number of dealerships in the Northeastern and Middle Atlantic areas. During his first year, Mr. Forrester also completed a voluntary financial reorganization of the firm. Profits were realized from 1931 through 1934.

In a continuing effort to meet competitive developments during the thirties, Mr. Forrester stressed three major objectives: (1) to produce adaptations of Danford tires and tubes which would differentiate them from competitors' products; (2) to diversify Danford's product line; and (3) to strengthen company-dealer relationships.

In the early thirties Mr. Forrester designed a nonchafe inner tube which, he believed, reduced the number of tube failures from rim abrasions. In 1935 he introduced a "Super-Strength" tire which had a 25% stronger carcass, an 11% heavier tread, and a deeper nonskid design than standard tires. These innovations and others were introduced, Mr. Forrester stated, to give the Danford dealers "something new to talk about, something different from our competitors." The company believed this program would enable its dealers to dodge direct price competition from competitive standard-design tires and tubes. Danford itself manufactured standard-type tires and tubes but placed sales emphasis on its distinctive products. The most successful of these adaptations had been the Super-Strength tire; 90% of Danford passenger car tire sales during this period were of Super-Strength type. "Our distinctive feature tires are priced 25% above standard competitive products, but they are below the $30.00 premium tire bracket."

In an effort to avoid the competitive and cyclical aspects in depending solely on tire and tube sales, as well as to use excess plant capacity, Mr. Forrester added the following items to the company's product line during the thirties: (1) storage batteries, 1933; (2) camelback and repair materials, 1935; (3) minor rubber automotive products, 1937; and (4) rubber shoe sole slabs, 1938.

Mr. Forrester believed strongly in the importance of dealer good will. He spent a great deal of time during the thirties traveling and becoming acquainted with each dealer and his territory. He also used these trips as a means of securing dealer and consumer suggestions for possible product improvements. Dealers were urged to visit the plant and become acquainted with company officials. As another integral part of this plan, Mr. Forrester insisted that all company-dealer relations be on an informal basis. Dealers were not to be subjected to close supervision. Danford officers, therefore, did not issue instructions in regard to dealer sales operations or store layout. If a dealer asked for help, however, a company salesman would make suggestions.

In a further effort to increase volume, the company enlarged its sales territory in 1936 to include most of the eastern seaboard.

OPERATIONS—1942–46

During the war, sales expanded from $4 million in 1941, the previous peacetime volume record, to a peak of $12 million in 1946. Gross profits were high during this period, but net profits after tax deductions were small. The company's wartime products were essentially the same as its peacetime products. However, synthetic rubber, rather than natural rubber, was largely substituted. The use of synthetic rubber purchased from the government brought a degree of stability into raw-material prices which neither the industry nor Danford had previously experienced.

In 1948 Mr. Forrester, in discussing the company's history, said: "We haven't been too successful, but we are still here."

EXECUTIVE ORGANIZATION, 1948 (See Exhibit 4, below)

Exhibit 4

DANFORD RUBBER COMPANY

Executive Organization Chart*

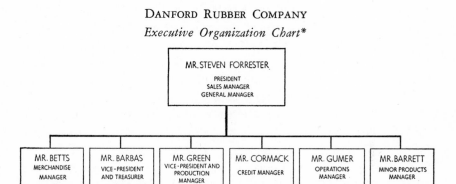

* As prepared by Mr. Forrester.

Described by his executives as the "spark of our organization," Mr. Steven Forrester, sixty-six, was president, sales manager, and general manager. He was responsible for handling all major top-management problems, as well as for making many operating decisions. Mr. Forrester's primary and continuing interest, however, lay in sales, and he spent most of his time on sales problems. He believed two of his most important executive responsibilities were the selection and, if necessary, discharge of salesmen and the discovery of new ideas to differentiate Danford products from those of competitors.

Mr. Forrester had been seriously ill several times in recent years but continued to do his regular work except that he had to give up his former practice of making frequent visits to various departments within the plant, as well as extensive field trips.

Informality was a tradition in the Danford executive organization. All personal relationships between executives were on a first-name basis. Whenever problems required the attention of several men, Mr. Forrester would call a special meeting, but there was no organized committee system. At such meetings Mr. Forrester might have supervisory employees, as well as executives, to counsel him on the problem. "Titles don't make any difference around here."

Each member of the Danford executive group had been hired by Mr. Forrester. With the exception of Mr. Barbas and Mr. Green, they had all had sales experience. "Sometime in the next four or five years I will have to start bringing new, younger men into our group," stated Mr. Forrester. In 1948, all Danford executives were paid over $10,000 a year.

Mr. Betts, fifty-eight, joined Danford in 1932. He had two very successful years as a salesman after which he assisted Mr. Forrester with sales problems. In 1948 Mr. Betts was in charge of pricing and dealer co-operative advertising. Mr. Betts visited large Danford accounts several times a year to help maintain good dealer *esprit de corps,* as well as to secure information about trade conditions. He also handled inquiries regarding salesmen's or dealers' territory limits and special competitive problems. His work was primarily in the tire, tube, and camelback product lines.

Mr. Gumer, fifty-five, had been with Danford twenty-seven years, first as a salesman, then as manager of the storage battery division, next as an assistant to Mr. Forrester, and, since 1942, as operations manager. He outlined his functions as follows: (1) to control inventory turnover; (2) to determine a factory production quota each week; (3) to see that orders were shipped promptly; and (4) to do "a bit of everything." Mr. Gumer spent most of his time working with new orders and shipments, personally checking each incoming order. He said he did not lean heavily on records but rather relied on his memory.

Mr. Barbas, fifty-five, a certified public accountant, had first been employed by Danford from 1925 until 1930. He left to enter the public accounting field in 1931. In 1942 he rejoined Danford and was appointed treasurer.

Mr. Green was in his late fifties. He had been employed by Danford as a factory superintendent for many years before World War II. Previously he had been with the production department of the Goodyear company. During World War II, Mr. Green had left Danford to organize a company of his own. He returned to Danford in 1947 as vice-president of production.

Mr. Cormack, fifty-eight, formerly sales manager of the company's Chicago branch office, had been appointed credit manager in 1925. He checked all new requests for credit.

Mr. Barrett, who was also in his late fifties, joined Danford in 1939. He had formerly managed his own storage battery company.

COMPETITIVE SITUATION—1948

"The competitive situation in 1948 appears to be even more critical than during the thirties," Mr. Forrester observed, "when we had ruthless competition stimulated by productive overcapacity, inventory speculation, and mail-order competition." In 1948, retail competition was marked by three major developments: (1) price cuts either directly by reducing list price or absorbing federal excise taxes or indirectly by excessive trade-in allowances; (2) stimulation of sales through promotional campaigns, such as buying tires for credit with only one dollar down payment required; and (3) introduction of new types of quality tires, such as the low-pressure, super balloon tire, as well as re-entry of second and third grade tires (price range, $10 to $14) which had originally appeared during the thirties.

INDUSTRY CHANGES

Some important developments in the rubber industry had occurred since 1939: (1) The capacity of the industry to produce tires, it was estimated, had increased 35% over prewar. ". . . the industry now has facilities to produce at the highest rate of its history. With excess capacity, each manufacturer has the problem of maintaining his units of production in order not to have a picture of increased costs resulting from operating at too low a capacity. . . ."[1] (2) Total cost increases to all tire manufacturers, for both labor and nonrubber raw materials during this period, had been substantial; 1948 retail tire prices, however, were essentially the same as those in 1941. (3) During the war, facilities capable of producing 1,000,000 long tons of synthetic rubber annually were built. The government had controlled synthetic rubber prices and had thereby effected considerable stability in the pricing of rubber. Under the provisions of the Rubber Act of 1948, government

[1] *Journal of Marketing,* Vol. XII, No. 4 (April, 1948), p. 467.

participation in the synthetic program in regard to price and use was to be continued until June 30, 1950. The same act dissolved the compulsory wartime patent pool under which the research results of all tire companies had been pooled. (4) Along with the expansion in the use of synthetics came a tremendous increase in money and personnel devoted to research and development by tire manufacturers. Goodrich, for instance, erected a $65 million research center in 1947. Eight smaller companies (not including Danford) organized the Copolymer Corporation to do research in synthetic rubber in co-operation with government organizations. In February, 1948, Copolymer announced the development of ultipara, a synthetic which, it was stated, excelled natural rubber for tread use by as much as 30%. (5) During the thirties a majority of tire manufacturers began to diversify into product areas where profit margins were higher than in tires. Many small companies began to manufacture allied rubber products, as did the Big Four. The latter, however, also expanded into plastics and other chemical products. This trend was accentuated during the war and in the immediate postwar period. In 1946, tire sales as a proportion of total company sales for the Big Four were: Goodyear, 73%; Firestone, 62%; U.S. Rubber, 55%; and Goodrich, 45%.[2] Danford sales in 1947 by product line were: tires, 63%; tubes, 10%; shoe slabs, 5%; camelback, 5%; batteries, 8%; and minor rubber products, 9%. (6) The postwar return of competition in some cases had reduced profit margins of some independent tire dealers by one-third.[3] This development had spurred a movement begun during the thirties, whereby the big tire manufacturers attempted to aid independent dealers handling their tires by offering services, such as sales training, store or station layout plans, and budgetary operating controls. The Goodyear company in 1947 and 1948 spent $1 million on a dealer training program. Some of the small manufacturers, too, were attempting to strengthen their dealers by devices, such as the use of sales training films and increased national and regional advertising campaigns.

As a result of a Supreme Court ban on the basing-point system, the steel and cement industries had adopted in 1948 an f.o.b. mill system of pricing and had discontinued the practice of absorbing freight costs. The former practice assured uniform prices to all customers regardless of distance from such mills. The effect of this court decision on the tire industry's practice of absorbing freight charges was not known.

---

[2] *Fortune*, June, 1947 (copyrighted by Time, Inc.), p. 161.
[3] *Super Service Tire Review,* Vol. XLVIII, No. 4 (April, 1948), p. 27.

DEALER ORGANIZATION (See Exhibits 5 and 6)

Exhibit 5

DANFORD RUBBER COMPANY

Dealer Purchases from Danford for the First 8 Months of 1948*—
Selected Towns and States

STATE AND CITY	TOTAL NUMBER OF ACCOUNTS	NUMBER OF ACCOUNTS BY SIZE OF SALES					POPULATION (1940)	RETAIL OUTLETS 1939	
		$500 or Less	$500 to $4,000	$4,000 to $10,000	$10,000 to $20,000	Over $20,000		Automotive	Filling stations
Connecticut:									
Bridgeport.....	6	5	...	...	...	1($20,000)	147,121	68	177
Hartford.......	9	7	1	1	...	......	166,267	64	208
Hazardville....	1	...	...	1	...	......	1,500	...	...
New Britain...	3	2	1	...	...	......	68,685	25	70
Stamford......	6	3	2	...	1	......	61,215	30	87
Delaware:									
Dover.........	1	...	1	...	...	......	5,517	15	9
Wilmington....	1	...	1	...	...	......	112,504	38	111
Massachusetts:									
Boston........	4	1	1	1	...	1($36,000)	770,816	186	531
Cambridge.....	2	2	...	...	...	......	110,879	30	88
Chelsea........	4	2	2	...	...	......	41,259	12	26
Pittsfield.......	4	4	...	...	...	......	49,684	30	71
New Jersey:									
Bayonne.......	2	...	2	...	...	......	79,198	20	51
Jersey City.....	1	1	...	...	...	......	301,173	47	178
Newark.......	4	3	...	...	1	......	429,760	87	321
New York:									
Buffalo........	4	3	1	...	...	......	575,901	160	609
New York City.	28	18	4	5	1	......	7,454,995	1,166	2,706
Rochester......	4	4	...	...	...	......	324,975	157	434
Schenectady....	5	2	3	...	...	......	87,549	42	129
Syracuse.......	1	...	1	...	...	......	205,967	82	262
Pennsylvania:									
Allentown.....	3	1	1	...	1	......	96,904	37	123
Erie...........	1	1	...	...	...	......	116,955	40	163
Philadelphia...	5	2	1	1	1	......	1,931,334	350	1,201
Pittsburgh.....	4	4	...	...	...	......	671,659	139	450

* Compiled from accounts receivable cards of the Danford company.

Source: Sales figures from company records; population figures from Rand McNally's, 1947; retail outlet data taken from U.S. Census of Trade, *Retail Trade, 1939.*

Asked the number of Danford dealers and their respective sales volume Mr. Betts said he could not obtain such information without surveying the company's accounts receivable cards. He estimated that Danford had 1,500 accounts: 600 tire and tube, 200 battery, 200 minor rubber products, 150 shoe sole, 150 export (primarily tires and tubes), and 200 accounts which ordered various products infrequently. An "account" was any dealer who was billed directly. Some of these dealers resold to subdealers in their areas; hence it was not possible to develop a complete customer list. With regard to sales volume, Mr. Betts stated that the dealers selling tires, tubes, and batteries accounted for most of the volume. The minor rubber products accounts with the exception of a number of wholesalers were not large.

Danford dealers were independent merchants. Twenty per cent of them were tire-store operators who sold tires and automotive supplies but

Exhibit 6

DANFORD RUBBER COMPANY

Dealer Accounts by Selected States, 1948

States	No. of Accounts	States	No. of Accounts
California.............	15	Maine...............	20
Connecticut...........	104	Maryland............	28
Delaware.............	3	Massachusetts........	101
Florida..............	29	Michigan............	39
Georgia..............	72	New Jersey...........	50
Illinois..............	10	New York...........	158
Indiana..............	108	South Carolina.......	41
Kentucky............	101	Tennessee............	43

Source: Compiled from company accounts receivable cards.

who did not handle gasoline or do tire repairing. The rest were garages, independently owned gasoline stations, retail stores, and tire-rebuilding firms, most of which carried nationally known gasoline lines. Mr. Betts said that Danford had a low dealer turnover rate, which he attributed to excellent manufacturer-dealer relationships. "Some of our dealers have been with us for thirty years." In May, 1948, the company added thirty new accounts; the over-all number of accounts, however, had remained fairly constant during the previous ten years.

Dealer purchases from Danford ranged from $300 to $70,000 a year. Mr. Betts stated that he would like to have tire and battery accounts maintain a minimum yearly retail sale of $20,000 but that such accounts could not always be obtained. "If a dealer's tire volume warrants, he is given an exclusive territory franchise." Mr. Betts noted that Danford dealers had further advantages in that they were: (1) permitted to make tire adjustments; (2) allowed to return slow-moving merchandise; (3) given protection against any reduction in inventory value through price declines; and (4) not subjected to strict supervision.

Most Danford accounts also carried tires manufactured by one of the large tire companies. Mr. Betts said this procedure had been encouraged, since it gave the dealer a tire on which he could cut prices and which would carry the burden of competition. "If our dealer can get the prospective tire buyer into his shop by advertising a Big Four tire at reduced prices, then we hope he can swing the potential customer over to buy a Danford tire." Some Danford dealers had diversified their product lines by taking on items, such as electrical appliances. Although Mr. Betts did not have information as to the extent of this diversification, he did not believe it a wise move. Some Danford accounts secured fleet tire sales and others did not. "That is a matter for them to decide," Mr. Betts said. "Truck tire sales and fleet sales are much tougher to make than individual passenger tire sales."

Mr. Forrester believed that Danford dealers secured most of their tire business on the basis of good dealer-customer relationships, and he did not think that sales made on that basis could be increased by close company supervision over the retail dealer. Danford furnished its dealers with metal tire stands, advertising clocks, window trim, and posters. It did not do any national advertising but would reimburse a dealer for 50% of the cost of local advertisements. "In addition to visits by salesmen," Mr. Forrester continued, "our most direct relationship with the retail dealer is maintained through our trade bulletins. These bulletins, which are sent out three or four times a week to all dealers and salesmen, contain general industry notes and information on competition trends, ideas for advising customers on extending the life of their Danford tires, and promotional plans which had worked for individual Danford dealers." There was no check to see that these bulletins were used by the dealers.

"In any town, four or five outlets usually do 90% of the tire business," stated Mr. Betts, "but it is difficult to sign up those dealers." He believed there were two essentials for dealer success: (1) acceptance in the trading area, and (2) physical setup and location. Danford salesmen, who selected all new retail dealers, were given the responsibility of checking to see that potential accounts met these two qualifications. Once a prospective account was submitted to the home office, it was again checked by Mr. Cormack for credit reliability and by Mr. Betts for the type of tire sales operation. Danford did not insist on any specific capital requirements for new dealers but required an acceptable Dun & Bradstreet rating. Mr. Betts checked the sales operating policy of new accounts, if they were in the New England and Middle Atlantic areas, to see that the dealer's operations were not basically of a wholesaling nature. He wanted, in these areas, dealers who sold directly to consumers only.

SALES FORCE

In their respective territories the company's seven salesmen (1948) sold all Danford products with the exception of shoe soling. That was handled by a New York broker. The salesmen, who had been selected by Mr. Forrester, were paid on a straight commission basis (except during the period 1942–46), and Mr. Betts believed that the least success-

Exhibit 7

DANFORD RUBBER COMPANY

Mr. Forrester's Letters to Salesmen—May, 1948

Date		Subject
May	2	Test Truck Tire Report
	8	Report of Tire Adjustments
	9	Competition from Other Premium Tires
	9	New Method of Letting Salesmen Know Orders Shipped
	10	Fan Belt Sales Have Dropped
	15	Good Ad Used by a Danford Dealer
	21	Battery Sales (Need to Be Pushed)
	26	Dealer Complaints
	26	Sales of Radiator Hose Down
	29	Sales of Self-Sealing Tubes Down—"What's the Matter?"
	29	New-Type Truck Tires

Source: Company records.

ful grossed $700 a month. "Our salesmen turnover is very low," Mr. Betts continued. "One of our men has been with us for thirty years."

"Our basic sales objectives are different from the big boys," he stated. "Our men try to get around to an account every four or five weeks; the big boys call on them every week. We have one man for the state of Connecticut; they have a salesman for each county. Our accounts basically have to sell tires by themselves. When our salesman calls on a dealer, he first listens for complaints about our tires and service. He then talks to the dealer about local competitive problems and tries to give him suggestions on ways of meeting it. But we don't try to tell the dealer how to run his outfit."

"We are not interested in reports," Mr. Betts noted. "We just want results." Danford salesmen did not submit any regular formal reports.

Each man did, however, send in a daily letter reporting his travel plans and any interesting competitive news to Mr. Betts. Using this source of information, as well as "trade" sources, Mr. Betts and Mr. Forrester made up the previously described bulletins which were sent to both dealers and salesmen. In addition, Mr. Forrester sent out letters directly to his salesmen (see Exhibit 7). "These letters and our bulletins are our principal source of control over the sales force," he stated. In one of his recent bulletins, Mr. Forrester had quoted a letter from an established salesman. The salesman had written, "I recently went over a map of my territory and find there are fourteen good-sized towns in which we do not have representatives. This is really the first time I have taken time out to study closely a map of the territory I cover to make an effort to analyze what the situation is. If we don't have fourteen new accounts in the office within the next thirty to sixty days, it won't be my fault." Mr. Forrester's postscript stated, "That's the kind of enthusiasm that can't fail."

Mr. Forrester, in August, 1948, was receiving two monthly sales reports, both of which he had initiated early in 1948. One consisted of a series of 2 × 5-inch cards which listed sales by salesmen by product. In addition, he received a report which listed each salesman's sales as a percentage of total company sales. Danford did not maintain (1948) records of sales by city or state, although such a report had been compiled in 1941. This report was dropped because it was not used by Mr. Forrester or Mr. Betts.

Mr. Forrester appraised his salesmen as follows:

Salesman	*Comment*
Mr. Crandall:	Extremely good man. Calls on all accounts and keeps plugging. He has the smallest territory of any salesman, but I regard him as one of the best.
Mr. Basken:	Average. He doesn't plug all products—his camelback sales are low.
Mr. Paul:	On the ball selling tires, but we can't get him interested in selling other products.
Mr. Barker: (discharged in June, 1948; replaced by Mr. Snyder)	I discharged him in June. He just didn't get out and sell. We should have fired him before the war, but we decided to carry our sales force as it was. He had been with the company for years, was a nice guy, but just didn't have the stuff. Besides, we discovered he had another job selling boxes on the side.

Mr. Kramer:	Weak salesman. Has been with the company ten years. I have thought of dismissing him because his attitude isn't good. When Mr. Betts asked him why he didn't put more drive into his sales, Mr. Kramer replied, "Because if I can stick with this four or five more years, I can retire."
Mr. Burgard:	Our best man.
Mr. Wunderlee:	Good man. His sales dropped from March through May because he was recuperating from an auto accident.
Mr. Snyder:	A good man.

NEW DISTRIBUTION PLAN

"Effective sales effort means success today," Mr. Forrester stressed. "Raw materials can be purchased (1948) at about the same price by

Exhibit 8

REPLACEMENT RUBBER TIRES: MANUFACTURERS' AVERAGE* COSTS PER TIRE

Synthetic Rubber Tire, August, 1943

	COST PER TIRE			PERCENTAGE OF TOTAL COST		
	10 Manu-facturers†	4 Large Manu-facturers	Total 14 Manu-facturers	10 Manu-facturers†	4 Large Manu-facturers	Total 14 Manu-facturers
Size 600–16 4-ply passenger-car tire:						
1. Direct material	$4.348	$4.048	$4.262	50.3	44.3	48.5
2. Direct labor	0.996	0.867	0.959	11.5	9.5	10.9
3. Net waste	0.145	0.168	0.152	1.7	1.8	1.7
4. Factory overhead	1.605	1.629	1.612	18.5	17.8	18.3
5. Total factory cost	$7.094	$6.712	$6.985	82.0	73.4	79.4
6. Warehouse and shipping expense	0.092	0.224	0.130	1.1	2.4	1.5
7. Transportation	0.265	0.395	0.302	3.1	4.3	3.4
8. Adjustments‡	0.260	0.231	0.252	3.0	2.5	2.9
9. Selling, general, and administrative expense	0.938	1.587	1.123	10.8	17.4	12.8
10. Total cost	$8.649	$9.149	$8.792	100.0	100.0	100.0

* Unweighted arithmetic average.
† These are the so-called "independents."
‡ Allowance for defective tires sold by trade.

Source: *Survey of Rubber Tire and Tube Manufacturers*, U.S. Office of Temporary Controls, OPA Economic Data Series, No. 10 (May, 1947), p. 5.

any company. As for manufacturing a tire, tires are like doughnuts—just stuff with a hole in the middle. Differences in labor output are not so much in machines used as in the willingness of employees to work. Our production costs are higher than the Big Four [see Exhibit 8]. We overcome that disadvantage, however, by more efficient distribution, through the elimination of wholesalers and middlemen, which the Big Four use, and by securing 25% higher prices for our extra-value products than the big boys do for their standard products."

Mr. Forrester planned to use the same basic program which he had evolved in the thirties to meet the competitive conditions facing Danford in the late forties. "Our primary continuing emphasis will be to stress the importance of friendly manufacturer-dealer relationships."

Since 1936, Danford had been attempting, without much success, to secure accounts outside New England and the Middle Atlantic region. Mr. Betts stated that the company had been handicapped because it did not have any branch warehouses. "If our dealer in Dallas wanted a certain type of tire, he either had to wait four days for us to send him one or had to carry a larger stock than he would have if he handled a tire manufactured by a company with a Dallas branch warehouse." In order to expand sales, Mr. Forrester planned to select large and strong accounts in areas outside a day's truck haul from Logan and designate them as wholesaler-distributors. These wholesaler-distributors were encouraged to secure a large number of subdealers. The subdealers would secure Danford products from inventories maintained by the wholesaler-distributors.

Wholesaler-distributors purchased tires from Danford in carload lots, which entitled them to a 2½% discount. In addition, they were given a 3% salesman's commission on all tires which they sold "to themselves," as well as to their subdealers, and a 2½% warehousing credit. Danford extended the same privileges to wholesaler-distributors that it did to regular accounts; i.e., return of slow-moving stock, and protection of inventory against price declines. Mr. Betts, who was responsible for supervision of these outlets, attempted to visit each wholesaler-distributor several times a year; in addition, they received all trade bulletins issued by the company.

"By extending this procedure until we have seminational distribution, we can keep our salesmen busy on the East Coast and use wholesaler-distributors for outlying areas," Mr. Forrester stated. "Our salesmen still have a large undeveloped potential within overnight truck haul of the plant." After a year and a half, Danford had outlets in Wisconsin, West Virginia, Ohio, Georgia, Florida, Kentucky, Arkansas, Virginia, Oklahoma, Kansas, Indiana, and Minnesota. During July and August of 1948, Mr. Forrester had extended the wholesaler-distributor plan to Long Island, and Poughkeepsie, New York, and to one city in Massachusetts. "The Long Island market was very difficult to break into, and we did not have distribution there; our salesman suggested that we sign up the wholesaler-distributor. We split the salesman's normal commission, giving him 2% and the new wholesaler-distributor 3%. We immediately got an order for 600 tires from that firm. In Poughkeepsie, we had a small dealer there already. He will still handle our tires but won't have an exclusive." Mr. Forrester stated that, whereas he did not want to use this arrangement in areas covered by salesmen, it might have to be used to meet competition.

From September, 1947, until May, 1948, wholesaler-distributor sales grew to something more than 20% of total factory sales and then leveled off at about that figure. Not all of this represented new business, however, since some of the accounts had been handled previously by the home office. Mr. Forrester believed that this new plan had been successful. "My estimate is that we will need a sales volume of about $700,000 a month to break even."

SALES

The combined sales of eight rubber firms (Firestone, Goodrich, U.S. Rubber, and five independent companies of which Danford was the smallest) declined 3.7% for the first quarter of 1948 over the similar 1947 period. With the exception of Goodyear, whose sales increased during this period, the remaining members of the Big Four experienced only a slight decline in sales volume; i.e., Firestone, 3.2%. Danford sales dropped 40%. In general, the smaller independent companies made the poorest relative showing, and the larger independents experienced less drastic declines. Dayton Rubber, whose sales dropped 28%, and Lee Rubber and Tire, whose sales dropped 14%, were both firms which had diversified into the mechanical rubber field (conveyor belting), where profit margins were higher than those of the tire industry.

As has been stated, Mr. Forrester was having trouble with his health. During the early part of 1948 he had been forced to relinquish active direction of Danford for several months. In his absence, Mr. Barbas, Mr. Betts, and Mr. Green co-operated in managing the company. Upon Mr. Forrester's return to work in May, he immediately saw the seriousness of the monthly sales declines from $760,000 in January to $450,-000 in May. "I took immediate action, started a sales promotional campaign featuring credits to dealers, so that they could increase customer trade-in allowances. We inaugurated the program by calling all our salesmen together for our first 1948 sales conference and by briefing our dealers with promotional literature. Our June sales jumped to $685,000. We should have started that program sixty days earlier. In addition to the credit which we allowed during this promotion, our dealers further reduced their margins and added to this credit to give the tire buyer a real bargain." Mr. Forrester believed that the 1948 Danford sales drop had resulted in part from the general slump in replacement sales but thought it had been aggravated in Danford's case by two further factors: (1) dealer inventories were too high and (2) Danford dealers did not have the new super balloon tires for which considerable consumer demand had been built up by some competitors.

TRANSPORTATION

Mr. Gumer stated that Danford transportation costs had increased sharply from a prewar 2% of net sales to approximately 5% in 1948. "Freight rates alone have jumped about 50% since the end of the war. We ship by carload lots to the South and Middle West since L.C.L. costs would be prohibitive." Shipments to the Pacific Coast were made by boat. "Larger companies," he explained, "are able to lessen the burden of higher freight rates by locating production units in various sections of the country." Danford sold its products on a delivered price basis and absorbed freight charges on all shipments. If customers ordered in excess of 20,000 pounds of merchandise, Danford gave a 2½% discount.

MINOR PRODUCTS

Mr. Barrett was in charge of sales of minor rubber automotive products and batteries; he also supervised battery manufacturing. These products were sold by Danford salesmen directly to retail dealers and to thirteen automotive product wholesalers. No exclusive sales franchises were given, and a dealer could sell these products without carrying Danford tires and tubes as many did. Mr. Barrett personally prepared any advertising material needed and made up price lists as required; he also visited Danford salesmen and Danford retailers who carried his division's products.

Mr. Barrett stated that Danford batteries were as good as, but not any better than, those produced by competitors. Since it was difficult to secure product differentiation on the basis of quality, competition came primarily in the form of service guarantees. "We give a fifteen-month guarantee on our battery," he stated, "which is equal to or longer than guarantees given by our competitors. Furthermore, we stress good dealer-customer relationships as a prime factor in securing battery sales. I do not try to tell our outlets how to sell these products." Mr. Barrett stated that price competition, even during the thirties, had not been great. He attributed this to the price leadership of the larger firms in the industry which specialized in battery manufacture. "We have a disadvantage in that we have to pay our battery workers tire union wages, which are about 10% above the average wage paid by a battery manufacturer." Danford battery prices were approximately the same as competitors'.

Competition in the rubber automotive products field was keen. Most tire manufacturers made these products so that their dealers could carry a more complete line of products. Pricing was competitive, and there was little product quality differentiation among various brands.

Sales of both Danford automotive rubber products and batteries had slumped drastically in the first half of 1948. Danford battery sales to wholesalers and retailers in 1947 had reached a peak of $150,000 a month; 1948 battery sales had declined in consecutive months until in June of 1948 less than $1,000 worth of batteries was sold to retail or wholesale firms.

In explaining this slump to Mr. Forrester in a conference on July 20, 1948, Mr. Barrett said that the sales recession was an industry-wide condition. "The industry in 1947 produced at the rate of 24 million batteries a year and sold them at the rate of 17 million a year." Mr. Forrester immediately phoned a large Danford battery account to secure further information. In that account's territory, the dealer reported that the Goodrich company, to boost sales, had increased its service guarantee from fifteen months to eighteen–twenty months and decreased its battery prices so that they were lower than Danford's. In order to meet these competitive developments, Mr. Forrester planned to work up a trade-in allowance promotional plan similar to the one used in May for tires.

In early 1948 Danford began to manufacture rubber floor tile. Mr. Forrester had selected this product because of the large current demand for the product and because the manufacture of floor tile utilized the company's existing production equipment. With the exception of batteries, all previously selected Danford minor products had utilized the basic manufacturing facilities of the Danford plant, and all could be sold through Danford salesmen. Rubber floor tiling, however, was to be sold by Mr. Barrett to building supply firms, department stores, and building contractors. Prewar competition had been severe with larger companies in the field such as Hood Rubber and Armstrong Cork. Danford tile orders in June, 1948, were above the limited capacity of the tile production unit, and more finishing machinery would be required to expand capacity above the current volume.

Sales of camelback, under the direction of Mr. Betts, were considered satisfactory. The sale of Danford shoe slabbing, on the other hand, was not. Although sales volume had been maintained, competition had forced the company's New York sales broker to reduce the prices of Danford slabs. "Our slab production costs are higher than the rest of the industry," Mr. Barrett explained. "One factor is that we pay our shoe slab men tire union wages, which are about 10% higher than those of our competitors who specialize in rubber shoe soles." Mr. Forrester stated that if production costs could not be reduced, Danford might have to withdraw from that field.

PRODUCTION

The Danford plant, located on the outskirts of Logan, consisted of ten brick buildings with floor space of 268,000 square feet (June, 1948). Manufacturing facilities had been expanded in 1941 and again in 1945–46. A five-story addition to the main tire fabrication building had been completed in 1946, as well as an office building and power plant. These buildings had been purchased, partially completed, from the Defense Plant Corporation. As a result of this expansion, plant capacity to produce tires had increased from 1,000 tires a day in 1941 to 2,400 a day in 1946. Tire production in May, 1948, averaged 1,000 tires a day. "At capacity tire operations," Mr Green stated, "we would still use only 70% to 80% of the floor space available in the new building."

There were only limited savings to be obtained from the large-scale manufacture of tires, Mr. Green stated. Increased tire production for a company was achieved through the addition of standard tire building machines, rather than from significant changes in type of production equipment used or processes employed.

Approximately 50% of the Danford machinery and equipment on a cost basis had been acquired since September, 1940. Mr. Green stated that Danford's production equipment was in excellent repair and that in some operations, i.e., tire curing, the company had the latest and most efficient equipment yet produced. Danford was installing a new machine which, Mr. Green estimated, would effect substantial labor savings in the tube department.

Mr. Green commented that an inherent disadvantage of a small company was the fact that limited financial resources prevented rapid replacement of machinery. Machinery development in the tire curing and tire building fields was especially rapid. "Within the past two years automatic tire building machinery has improved so that production per machine has increased from 130 tires per day to 170, but Danford has not obtained any." For one reason, the new Danford super balloon could not be built on semiautomatic tire building equipment because of its special features. "It is almost a custom-made tire," Mr. Green stated. "We cannot easily boost production to meet current demand. We didn't have that difficulty with the Super Strength tire, which we could build on semiautomatic machines."

"One reason for our high production costs," Mr. Green continued, "is our plant arrangement. Our milling and compounding operations are in one plant, and operations which use the semiprocessed stock are in other buildings. You can't conveyorize rubber stock, which means we have a great deal of expensive interplant transportation."

The production supervisory staff consisted of nine foremen, twelve assistant foremen, a production scheduling group, tire designers, and two time-study men. "We don't really have a methods department," Mr. Green stated. "When our time-study man comes across better methods for doing a job, he makes suggestions and retimes the job. We originally had three men in the time-study group, but we dropped one man as part of an economy drive in 1947. The two remaining men are overloaded; one sets rates while the other concentrates on time-study work."

The assistant foremen, most of whom were older men formerly employed as tire builders, served as inspectors for their respective departments. They were also responsible for employee training, although Mr. Green said little of that was needed. "We use the same basic work force, and when we rehire, the men are already familiar with our procedures."

Danford employed 400 men in July, 1948; peak wartime employment had been 1,000. Mr. Green planned to hire an additional 150 men in August and September to meet the increased demands for Danford super balloon and Super Strength tires.

Danford workers were represented by the United Rubber Workers of America, CIO. Before World War II, Danford wage schedules had been approximately 10% under those of the Big Four. Mr. Green said that in 1941 the average industry hourly wage was 77 cents; in 1948, it was $1.40, and Danford's was $1.47. Mr. Green stated that some Danford piece rates were 40% above those of a Baltimore competitor; yet the take-home pay of workers in both plants was approximately equal. He attributed these higher piece rates to (1) the failure of Danford to reduce piece rates as more efficient machinery was acquired and (2) hard bargaining on the part of the union.

Danford had never experienced a serious work stoppage, and worker turnover was low. Mr. Green believed, however, that management-worker relations were not satisfactory. "We purchased a machine to replace a man on a five-man tube line, and the union objected to taking the man off. Another man worked but six minutes out of sixty. We wanted to take him off, and the union objected again. Finally, I said I would pay the remaining three men the money for the six minutes which the other man worked; the union accepted. The wage increase for the remaining three men amounted to 45 cents a day per man."

Mr. Green stated that the company had put up suggestion boxes for several months to give plant employees a chance to make suggestions for improving work processes. No suggestions were received.

In attempting to reduce shoe slab manufacturing costs, Mr. Green had told the union that wages would have to be reduced 25%. After numerous conferences with Mr. Forrester, the union accepted a 22% wage reduction. In turn the company agreed to continue shoe slab production and to spend $1,000 improving the layout of the slab department. Mr. Green believed that this could enable the slab room employees to regain part of their wages cut through increased production.

RESEARCH AND DEVELOPMENT

The development section of the production department was primarily concerned with quality control. Mr. Jeans, the chemist in charge of the section, also supplied Mr. Green and Mr. Forrester with information on technical developments in the synthetic rubber field. The company further secured technical advice from large chemical firms from which Danford purchased materials.

Mr. Forrester supplied all ideas for new products. These ideas were translated into engineering designs by tire designers. Danford did not have any regular product testing program, although tires were given tests by various company dealers and officials on their cars.

PURCHASING, ACCOUNTING, AND FINANCE

Mr. Barbas, treasurer of the company, purchased all materials used by Danford and also supervised accounting and financial operations.

Mr. Barbas purchased, on an average, one million pounds of crude rubber per month through a New York City broker, as well as substantial quantities of cotton fabric and chemicals. Mr. Barbas stated that he kept himself informed about raw-material market conditions by reading all available current literature on the subject. Government operations in the synthetic rubber field had stabilized crude prices sufficiently to prevent a repetition of the price swings that occurred during the thirties (price range—3 cents to $1.21 a pound). In 1947, crude prices had ranged only from 13 cents to 25½ cents a pound. In 1948 Mr. Barbas was following a "rule of thumb" in rubber purchases. If crude prices were over 20 cents a pound, he decreased commitments; if under 20 cents a pound, he increased future buying from six weeks to three or four months. "This policy has been very successful to date," he stated.

Danford employed a standard cost system which was controlled on a departmental basis. Actual costs were determined; each department was credited with standard costs; and variances were obtained. Standard costs were adjusted quarterly. They were based on (1) materials at weighted actual cost, (2) direct labor, and (3) overhead, as a percentage of direct labor based on the yearly budget. Standard costs were adjusted more than four times a year if necessary. In July, 1948, Mr. Barbas stated that unabsorbed burden, resulting from reduced manufacturing operations, was very high.

In April, 1946, Danford issued $1,627,000 of 4% convertible debentures due April 15, 1958. The indenture provided for a sinking fund beginning in April, 1947, sufficient to retire two-thirds of the debentures prior to maturity. Danford stockholders subscribed for $800,-000 of the issue, and the balance was sold to the general public by an underwriting firm. Danford paid common stock dividends from 1942 to 1947, inclusive; no dividends had been paid from 1936 to 1941. Stock ownership of Danford was widely scattered with no stockholder owning more than 1% of the stock.

Funds secured from the bond issue were to be used to purchase from the government, and to complete the construction of, an office building, tire plant, and power unit and to purchase new production equipment ($800,000). Funds were also to be used to retire the issue of 7% preferred stock ($527,000) and to add to the company's working capital. The $800,000 allocated for buildings and equipment proved to be inadequate, however, and Danford expended an additional $300,000 on these projects. "Consequently," Mr. Barbas stated, "our working capital position is very tight."

To help meet this cash shortage, Danford had reduced its 2% discount period, so that a customer received this 2% only if he paid between the first and fifteenth of the month after shipment was made. "This has speeded up collection of accounts receivable," Mr. Cormack stated. "I believe Goodyear still allows a 2% discount for sixty days." Danford had not had a major credit loss since 1933.

BOARD OF DIRECTORS

The Danford board of directors consisted of Mr. Forrester, Mr. Cormack, Mr. Barbas, Mr. Mark (company counsel), Mr. Reynolds (a representative of an underwriters firm), and Mr. Fairfield. Mr. Fairfield was chairman of the board of a large textile manufacturing firm.

Mr. Forrester considered his board of limited value. "It could perform a real service if it could secure possible sales connections for Danford with other large firms. During the 1948 sales slump, the only advice of nonemployee members of the board was to push our salesmen harder. I didn't think that was a sound observation."

REPORTS

Mr. Forrester received the following reports: (1) a weekly production report listing totals by products manufactured; (2) a weekly factory inspection report, as well as a monthly summary; (3) a weekly summary of orders received; (4) a monthly profit and loss statement showing profit by product lines; (5) a monthly balance sheet; (6) a monthly maintenance costs report; and (7) a monthly report showing each salesman's sales as a percentage of total company sales, as well as a series of 2 × 5-inch cards listing sales by salesman by product. Mr. Forrester received most of these reports at the end of each month. "My philosophy is that people can make up reports to show just about anything they want to."

NEW SUPER BALLOON TIRES

In 1947 the Goodyear company produced a 4-ply, low-pressure, super balloon tire which afforded greater riding comfort than could be secured by using standard tires. This tire innovation was originally introduced by the Chrysler Corporation on new cars equipped with special "wide tire rims." In June of 1948 Danford was beginning to step up production

Exhibit 9

ALL RUBBER TIRES AND TUBES: COMBINED DEPARTMENTAL
OPERATING STATEMENT

Annually, 1942 and 1945

(In Thousands)

	13 MANUFACTURERS*				4 LARGE MANUFACTURERS†			
	1942‡		1945		1942		1945	
		% of Net Sales		% of Net Sales		% of Net Sales		% of Net Sales
Gross sales..............	§	...	$208,230	...	§	...	$789,529	...
Less: Deductions, allow- ances, discounts, etc...	§	...	33,569	...	§	...	92,639	...
Net sales.............	$ 74,910	100.0	$174,661	100.0	$333,719	100.0	$696,890	100.0
Cost of goods sold........	59,938	80.0	145,479	83.3	269,316	80.0	569,252	81.7
Gross profit..............	$ 14,972	20.0	$ 29,182	16.7	$ 64,403	19.3	$127,638	18.3
Operating expenses:								
Advertising and publicity	$ 949	1.3	$ 3,450	2.0	$ 6,879	2.1	$ 13,058	1.9
Other selling expense....	5,125	6.8	6,507	3.7	21,666	6.5	31,508	4.5
General and administra- tive expense..........	2,149	2.9	4,442	2.5	6,854	2.0	11,552	1.7
Other operating expense‖.	742	1.0	1,534	0.9	10,421	3.1	4,971	0.7
Total...............	$ 8,965	12.0	$ 15,933	9.1	$ 45,820	13.7	$ 61,089	8.8
Net operating profit.......	$ 6,007	8.0	$ 13,249	7.6	$ 18,583	5.6	$ 66,549	9.5

* These 13 manufacturers, the so-called "independents," produced approximately 19% of all rubber tires and tubes in 1945.
† These manufacturers produced approximately 76% of all tires and tubes in 1945.
‡ Only 11 companies reported in 1942.
§ Not available.
‖ In most cases includes warehouse, shipping, freight, etc.

Source: *Survey of Rubber Tire and Tube Manufacturers*, U.S. Office of Temporary Controls, OPA Economic Data Series, No. 10 (May, 1947), pp. 2–3.

of Danford super balloon tires. "We couldn't get into production before because of shortages of the super balloon tire molds and because we had to wait and see if the idea would meet with popular acceptance." Use of the super balloon type of tire was spreading rapidly in 1948, both through original equipment sales and by sales to the replacement market. Although the Big Four, as well as the largest of the independent manufacturers, were producing super balloon tires in 1948, a substantial number of the medium- and smaller-sized independent manufacturers did not yet have them in production.

The Danford super balloon tire had an extra feature, which Mr. Forrester believed would place it in a premium class. This feature provided extra strength and extra safety to the body or "carcass" of the tire. Danford super balloon tires were priced approximately 15% above competitive super balloon tires.

Demand for super balloon tires was so great in 1948 most manufacturers were rationing them to their dealers. Mr. Forrester stated that the expanded sales of super balloon tires, plus increased sales of other Danford tires, promised to put operations for August, 1948, in the black. "I have hopes that we will just about break even this year."

Castengo Steel Company

IN JANUARY, 1946, the Castengo Steel Company, located in Castengo, New Jersey, was resuming civilian business following several years of concentrated wartime production. Castengo's president, Mr. Stevens, believed that sufficient markets in peacetime industry could again be found to insure profitable operations. The chairman of the board of directors, Mr. Farris, while optimistic, was more skeptical of the company's ability to cope with the many problems he envisioned for the postwar period.

The company's product, cold-drawn, seamless steel tubing, had had a number of wartime uses, the principal one being used by manufacturers of airframes and by a few other companies specified by the Army and the Navy.

The Castengo company manufactured seamless steel tubing in its plant at Castengo and sold it throughout the United States. For the most part, it used manufacturers' agents as its sales representatives. The company's tubing ranged from 3 inches to $\frac{1}{16}$ of an inch in diameter in a wide variety of wall thicknesses. It was made from numerous steel alloys to meet special metallurgical requirements.

Castengo had always used manufacturers' agents to reach most of its market. Before the war about one-half of agents' sales were made to steel dealers or supply houses, which in turn sold to small users of tubing. The other half of agents' sales were made direct to tube users, including, among others, companies in the automobile, machine-tool, motor, and refrigeration industries which used tubing in their products; and companies in the chemical, beverage, and food-processing industries which used tubing as equipment for their processes. Small and varying amounts of sales had, in the prewar period, been made by company executives direct to tube users. Castengo's sales were considered in the steel industry as small orders. They were of a size with which the big steel companies generally had not wished to bother. In January, 1946, most of Castengo's output was again going to steel dealers (via the manufacturers' agents), presumably for the purpose of building up dealers' stocks.

Mr. Stevens had been president of the Castengo company since 1941, when his father-in-law and predecessor, Mr. Dalrymple, founder and a large company stockholder, had died. Mr. Stevens had been with the Castengo company since 1935 and had held positions as personnel manager, production manager, and vice-president. For much of this time, however, he had in effect worked as his father-in-law's assistant. Prior to 1935 Mr. Stevens had been a bond salesman for an investment firm.

Mr. Farris, board chairman, represented the interests of a large banker, Mr. Grandi, one of the company's principal financial backers since its formation in 1927. Mr. Farris had been educated in engineering and in business administration and had been first employed by Mr. Grandi as a personal financial assistant. He was made a Castengo board member in 1941 after the death of Mr. Grandi's earlier representative and was appointed chairman of the board in 1942. Until early 1944 Mr. Farris had spent about half of his time at Castengo working on company problems. Thereafter he assumed other important war work with another company which took much of his time. By January, 1946, he was able to spend only a few days a month at the Castengo plant although he remained in close touch with its affairs.

Directly responsible to Mr. Stevens were the following: Mr. George, vice-president and head of the purchasing department; Mr. Purcell, works manager; Mr. Corning, sales manager; Mr. Andrews, treasurer; and Mr. Boyle, metallurgist. In January, 1946, the company had approximately 400 employees; this was 200 more than the prewar number and 250 less than peak wartime employment.

Seamless steel tubing is manufactured in three major steps: (1) piercing and rolling; (2) cold-drawing, and (3) annealing.

The piercing operation is described as follows:

The principal processes for producing seamless tubes are the piercing processes. One end of a cylindrical billet, having a diameter and length sufficient to produce the required size and length of tube, is center-punched. The billet is then placed in a furnace where it is heated to a forging temperature of about 2,000°F. preparatory to piercing. The piercing operation may be done in either one of two ways, known as the Mannesmann process and the Stiefel process. [The Castengo company employed the Mannesmann process.] [A Mannesmann mill] consists of two rolls whose axes are set askew. A mandrel or piercing point attached to a water cooled rod is inserted between the rolls from the delivery end of the machine so that the axis of the mandrel is in line with the point of intersection of the axes of the two rolls. The heated billet, centered end first, is pushed into the revolving rolls. The rolls rotate the billet and pull it slowly forward. The distortion of the metal produces a crack at the center. The piercing point enlarges this crack, thus producing a very thick walled tube.

After each operation the piercing point is removed from the bar, water cooled, and made ready for another billet. [Exhibit 1 shows a diagrammatic representation of the setup of the rolls in the Mannesmann mill.] . . .

After a billet has been pierced, the next operation in the production of seamless tubes is to reduce the thickness and the inside diameter by reeling. In this process, the material is passed between skew rolls and over a mandrel, as shown in Exhibit 2. After this the tubes are sized and straightened in the same

Exhibit 1	Exhibit 2
CASTENGO STEEL CO.	CASTENGO STEEL CO.
Mannesmann mill piercing a solid billet	*Reeling machine*

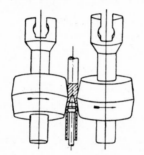 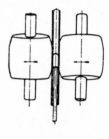

manner as is welded pipe. Usually tubes produced by the piercing process are finished when they come from the straightening rolls. In some cases, where an especially good surface is required, they are given a cold-drawing finish.[1]

Cold-drawing and heat-treating (annealing) are described as follows:

The cold-drawing process as applied to the finishing of seamless tubes is used to produce tubing of smaller diameter and with lighter walls than can be made by hot finishing. It is also applied to shape tubing to forms other than round, or to secure a smooth, bright, scale-free finish on its surface, or to increase its strength and stiffness. Tubes smaller than 10¾ inches in diameter can be finished by cold-drawing.

The process of drawing tubes consists of pulling the tube through a ring-shaped die or collar as shown in Exhibit 3, in which the amount of reduction in a single draw is greatly exaggerated. A mandrel is inserted through the tube to give the proper internal diameter. By this method, the material is elongated and made to flow through the space between the mandrel and the die, thus decreasing both the inner and outer diameters. The amount that the tube can be

---

[1] Wm. Howard Clapp and Donald Sherman Clark, *Engineering Materials and Processes* (Scranton, Pa.: International Textbook Company, 1938), pp. 285–90. Reprinted by permission of the publisher and copyright holder.

Exhibit 3

CASTENGO STEEL CO.

Cold-drawing a seamless steel tube

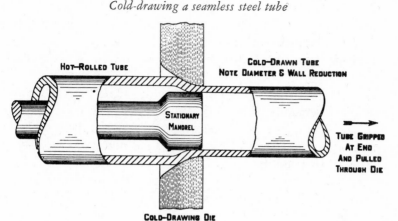

reduced in diameter in one draw will depend upon the ductility of the material. The plastic cold working of this process increases the hardness of the material and makes it less ductile. Where a considerable reduction in diameter is required, it is necessary to anneal the tubing between successive draws.

Before the tube is sent to the cold-drawing bench, one end must be pointed in swaging dies under a power hammer. The pointed end permits the tube to be started through the die and provides a surface to be grasped by the tongs of the draw bench. The drawing operation is carried out on a heavily constructed draw bench. The pointed tube is pushed into the die. The mandrel on the end of a long rod is shoved into the open end of the tube and held in position by a stop at the open end of the tube. The draw carriage, holding the tongs, is run up to the die and the tongs are closed on the pointed end of the tube. The tong hook is then engaged in the traveling chain, [and] the tong carriage . . . moves away from the die, pulling the tube through the die. This process may be repeated with intermediate annealing until the tube has reached the proper dimensions.

The tube must be perfectly free from scale and other defects prior to the drawing operation. This is assured by pickling in an acid, followed by thorough washing in water. During the drawing process, the tube is well lubricated with a mixture of tallow and flour. Tubes with an inner diameter of less than ½ inch are drawn without the use of mandrels.

After the cold-drawing operation, the tubes are straightened, threaded, and tested. It is interesting to note that tubing used in small hypodermic needles is produced by the process outlined above.[2]

By these processes the company manufactured seamless steel tubing and had a capacity for producing 35 to 40 million feet per year, or, in terms of tonnage, 15 to 18 thousand tons.

---

[2] *Ibid.,* pp. 303–5.

Seamless steel tubing was produced by several major steel companies, such as the National Tube Company and Tubular Alloy Steel Corporation, subsidiaries of United States Steel Corporation; Youngstown Sheet and Tube Company; Jones and Laughlin Steel Company; and Babcock and Wilcox Company. In addition, there were about a dozen smaller independents, including Castengo, which specialized in seamless steel tubing.

During the war the tube industry expanded rapidly, largely to meet the increased demands of the airframe industry. The large steel companies built new plants to produce nothing but seamless tubes (see Appendix A). The largest of these plants did not attain capacity production until the summer of 1944; its output was about 75% of the combined prewar output of the 12 independent manufacturers. The war also provided impetus for expanding industrial capacity for electric welded tubing, a competitive product.

Steel tubing may be made by the resistance welding of the edges of steel strip rolled up to form a tube. A single machine will take the flat strip, shape and weld it at a rate of 60 to 150 feet per minute. . . . No other process of tube manufacture can compete with this on the basis of cost. This process is at present confined to relatively thin-walled tubes.[3] [See Appendix B.]

For airframes and other structural uses, welded tubing was considered equivalent to seamless tubing. Limitations of welded tubing, however, were: (1) It could not be manufactured to the close tolerances of seamless; (2) wall thicknesses and tube diameters were limited; and (3) composition was restricted to relatively few alloys. Seamless tubing, on the other hand, could be drawn from a wide range of alloys to virtually any specifications within very small tolerances. In spite of the increased use of welded tubing, company officials believed that because of the many advantages of seamless tubing, it would continue to be the standard for the steel industry.

Mr. Purcell, works manager, was brought to the company in August, 1945, from another independent seamless tube company where he had been assistant production manager. He was the fourth works manager the company had had in as many years. While Mr. Dalrymple was living, he acted as works manager and handled production problems himself. After Mr. Dalrymple's death, the former plant engineer, Mr. Greyforth, was made works manager. Mr. Greyforth had been with the company since its formation and had been the direct supervisor of plant

---

[3] Lionel S. Marks, *Mechanical Engineers Handbook* (4th ed.) (New York: McGraw-Hill Book Co., 1941), p. 1780.

operations under Mr. Dalrymple. Although not a trained engineer, Mr. Greyforth had virtually lived with seamless tube manufacturing operations all his life and was considered an expert on shop practices. After Mr. Greyforth became works manager, several disagreements developed between him and Mr. Stevens. The directors were aware of this but told Mr. Stevens that they did not want drastic action taken in regard to Mr. Greyforth. Nevertheless Mr. Stevens discharged him in 1943. Mr. Greyforth was replaced by Mr. Lee, a rancher whom Mr. Stevens had met on a vacation trip and persuaded to return with him. Mr. Lee worked well with people but had had no previous industrial experience and found the position of works manager a considerable strain. His health began to fail and he resigned from the company in the summer of 1945, returning to his ranch in the Southwest.

Under the new works manager, Mr. Purcell, were three production departments, a scheduling department and a personnel department. The three production departments were *hot mill, cold-draw,* and *heat-treating.* Solid steel billets were pierced and rolled in the hot mill. The tubes then went to the cold-draw department where they were drawn to the desired diameter and wall thickness. Depending on the size of the tube, several "passes" were usually required through the draw benches. Between passes and upon completion of drawing, the tubes required annealing in the heat-treating department. A wide variety of metallurgical and strength characteristics could be given tubes by variations in the original composition of the billets and subsequent heat treatments.

One foreman supervised the hot mill and another the cold-draw and heat-treating departments. After finishing the hot mill, tubes never returned to that department. Tubes were constantly being transferred between the cold-draw and heat-treating departments, however, which made it desirable that these departments be under a single foreman.

Mr. Farris said the plant's draw benches, piercing mills, and heat-treating ovens were used very intensively during the war years. Production was increased by operating equipment on a three-shift basis, with the result that much of the equipment was considerably worn. In October, 1945, the board of directors appropriated $400,000 for the purchase of new mill equipment during the ensuing year. The new equipment was to replace worn equipment on which maintenance charges had become excessive. Company officials believed that this expenditure was necessary and would prove economical. It was not expected that the company's capacity would be significantly altered by the new equipment.

The first equipment purchase, made in the fall of 1945, was a new piercing mill costing $150,000. This mill replaced a mill over 15 years old which had become so worn that it was not only expensive but also difficult to keep in operation. Steel shells already pierced could be purchased from the large steel companies. Mr. Farris explained, however, that Castengo's ability to produce a variety of tubing on short notice would be seriously impaired if it were necessary to rely upon the large companies to deliver shells for each order. With adequate piercing facilities, the company could stock a variety of steel billets and thus be able to manufacture quickly almost any type of tube directly from material on hand.

The scheduling department scheduled orders through the plant and determined production processes for each order. The three men in the scheduling department had been with the company for many years and were thoroughly familiar with all shop practices and procedures. Much of the work of this department was done informally between the head of the department and the foreman of the cold-draw and heat-treating departments. Mr. Farris pointed out that the plant was small enough so that the head of scheduling could walk out into the plant any time and visually appraise the work situation, thereby making it unnecessary to have a formal control system. Furthermore, the scheduling people were familiar with shop routines and worked closely with the two foremen, so that elaborate records of operations required to produce tubes of various specifications were not essential. Mr. Farris said that during 1942 and 1943 he had encouraged the systematizing and formalizing of scheduling department procedures. Equipment such as cardex files and production control boards were provided to assist in this project. No significant change in procedures had taken place, however. The scheduling department personnel as well as the plant foremen had developed their informal procedures under the previous works manager and plant engineer, Mr. Greyforth. Mr. Greyforth, while he maintained no records of operations, was intimately familiar with every operation and each order being processed. It was said that he could put his finger on any order in the plant, and he did much of the planning and scheduling work on the shop floor. Long-standing company practices had developed in this manner, and they had changed only slightly.

According to Mr. Farris, the personnel manager's chief job was to hire employees. The company had been unionized under the Steel Workers Organizing Committee in 1938, and all major personnel matters thereafter had been handled by the union directly with the president. During the war years, when the number of employees increased from 200 to 650, there was constant pressure for additional workers. Castengo was a small town in an agricultural community and the local labor market was soon exhausted. Various plans were used with only partial success to induce southern white, colored, and Nisei workers to come to the Castengo company. Even with the decline of operations from a three-shift to a two-shift basis in 1945, it was difficult to maintain an adequate work force and Mr. Farris believed that for some time the personnel manager would be fully occupied employing labor to meet company needs.

Mr. Farris said that during the war years wages had increased 10% to 15%, and in addition he believed employee productivity had declined. Mr. Farris thought the company had had a small but distinct advantage before it was unionized, in that its labor costs were lower than those prevailing in the larger unionized plants. After 1938, wages were increased, but until the war period he believed the company continued to have a small wage advantage because of relatively high labor efficiency. This advantage had been lost, he believed, by 1946.

The metallurgist, Mr. Boyle, was well trained and experienced in his field. He held a Ph.D. degree in metallurgy from a well-known university and had been employed by a large automobile manufacturer prior to 1939 when Mr. Stevens (then vice-president) hired him. Mr. Boyle's first job was to analyze incoming steel and finished tubes to make sure that metallurgical specifications were met. Within a few months Mr. Boyle had organized this analytical job so that tests were run by a girl with no previous technical training. He needed only to review the results. Partly on his own initiative, Mr. Boyle then began to investigate shop practices. He frequently observed processes which, after laboratory investigation, he believed should be changed in order to improve the finished product. These improvements generally related to the heat-treatment process by which the required physical properties of the metal were obtained. Once Mr. Boyle had determined what he believed to be the proper heat-treating process to obtain a given specification, he would go onto the floor of the plant and tell the workers how it was to be done. Mr. Boyle's suggestions were usually at variance with long-standing practices and therefore were not often accepted. On other occasions his suggestions were not followed because pressure to put work through with minimum delay would not permit the special handling he thought necessary.

Several months after Mr. Stevens became president, Mr. Farris observed friction between Mr. Stevens and Mr. Boyle. Mr. Farris guessed the friction arose because Mr. Stevens, being nontechnical by background and interest, had tended to support the standard shop practices rather than Mr. Boyle's more technical recommendations concerning production operations. Eventually Mr. Stevens tried to discharge Mr. Boyle, but Mr. Farris, acting under the authority of the board of directors, was able to forestall the action.

In addition to his plant work, Mr. Boyle worked on customers' problems. These problems usually concerned situations where the company's tubes had not met fully the requirements as intended, and Mr. Boyle attempted to solve such problems. This work was never undertaken except at the request of a tube customer.

As was stated earlier, in January, 1946, virtually all Castengo tubes were sold through manufacturers' agents. The company had 13 agents located in principal cities throughout the United States. These agents had exclusive sales rights within their areas and were paid a 5% commission on all sales made within their territories. These agents typically represented several manufacturers of noncompeting lines. For example, one of the agents carried a large line of paints in addition to Castengo tubes. It was estimated that before the war approximately one-half of the agents' sales were made to steel dealers or supply firms which stocked steel products for sale to small users. Other sales through agents were made direct to tube users whose requirements, according to Mr. Farris, were too large to be handled promptly by the supply firms and too small to interest the tube departments of the large steel companies. Mr. Farris pointed out that many industrial concerns operated with small inventories and required frequent deliveries. He said that Castengo had obtained considerable business from such concerns because it was able to give delivery of quality specification tubing on a few days' notice. Such orders ranged from 10,000 to 100,000 feet of tubing, although the typical size of orders was close to 10,000 feet.

Mr. Farris said that in the past the large steel companies were not interested in orders of the size usually received by Castengo. He believed the major producers were inclined not to accept orders except in terms of a million feet or more for tubing of the size manufactured by Castengo. He explained that these companies were geared to the manufacture and sale of tubing in large tonnages and were not organized to handle promptly small orders. Furthermore, because of their interest in tonnage as an outlet for steel, these companies concentrated in the production of tubing of 2 inches in diameter and larger. In fact, one of the major producers normally would not accept orders for tubing of less than ½-inch diameter except in very large lots of 3 or 4 million feet.

Mr. Farris said there were probably no great economies to large-scale production of seamless tubing, inasmuch as the production units were piercing mills and draw benches of which Castengo's were essentially the same as those of the large companies. The latter simply had more units of equipment than Castengo.

Mr. Farris suggested that the large companies might give more emphasis to small orders and prompt deliveries in the postwar than in the prewar period. They could easily produce the tubing, and he thought that perhaps their large recent investments in tube mills might lead them to be more aggressive in this market. On the other hand, Mr. Farris was aware that in the past the large steel companies had tended to avoid severe competitive practices that would result in complete dominance of the industry by a few huge firms. They had taken this attitude because of the legal implications of monopolistic control of the industry. He believed that the smaller companies had been allowed to exist under this "umbrella" partially as a concession to a "healthy" industry. Mr. Farris, however, was unable to decide which of these tendencies would finally motivate the big companies in the future. Other Castengo executives were less concerned on this point than he, however, believing that they would be able to retain their outlets on the basis of their previous experience and production record.

In the past, Castengo had sold tubing direct to Cold, Inc., a large and growing manufacturer of refrigeration and air-conditioning equipment. Relations with Cold, Inc., had been established by Mr. Dalrymple during the depression of the 1930's when he renewed an acquaintanceship with the chief executive of that firm. During the middle and late 1930's, sales to Cold, Inc., constituted a substantial portion of Castengo's business. Their tubing requirements declined during the war, but Castengo maintained its connection by furnishing a substantial quantity of tubing for Cold, Inc., even though it was done at a small loss because of price ceilings. Since the end of the war, however, Castengo had been unsuccessful in obtaining any significant portion of Cold's tubing business. According to Mr. Farris, Cold, Inc., had agreed to place its total steel requirements, including tubing, with one of the large steel companies in order to obtain steel sheets required in its manufacturing process. By that means, Cold, Inc., was able to obtain sheet steel which otherwise would have been difficult to obtain.

Several of Castengo's executives, including Mr. Stevens, did not consider the loss of Cold's business important. They pointed out that in order to keep that business, many small, extra services had been required, such as drawing tubing at a loss during the war period. They added that they considered the company was perhaps as well off not to be so largely dependent upon a single customer. Mr. Farris, however, did not entirely concur with these views. He regretted the loss of Cold's business, since he considered it advisable and important to have such direct customers as insurance against possible future loss of business.

A small portion of the company's prewar business could be termed "specialty" business, in which emphasis was placed on deliveries of special specification tubing on short notice. This special business also required meeting close specifications, which in turn depended on careful metallurgical work and closely controlled heat-treating. Sales of specialty tubing had in the past been handled by the company's executives. Mr. Farris said that in 1945 one outstanding example of obtaining specialty business had occurred. One of the board members was associated with an engineering concern engaged in constructing a plant manufacturing phenol, a highly corrosive chemical. The chemical firm for which the plant was being constructed had for many years used in the manufacture of phenol an expensive, special-alloy tubing costing about $900 per ton. The Castengo board member, believing that the Castengo company might be able to supply tubing to meet the chemical plant's needs, turned the problem over to Castengo. Mr. Boyle developed a tube which the company manufactured and sold to the chemical company for $300 a ton, including a very satisfactory profit. Mr. Farris pointed out that costs were high in this type of manufacturing because of special handling required during the entire process. Nevertheless, this instance had been very profitable for both the chemical company and Castengo, and Mr. Farris believed that there might be a real opportunity for the company in this type of business.

The sales manager, Mr. Corning, had been with the company for a number of years and had been assistant to the company's two previous sales managers. When the original sales manager, who had been Mr. Dalrymple's right-hand man, died in 1941, a new sales manager was brought into the company from the industry's trade association. This man, although he was thoroughly familiar with the industry and its customers and showed promise of being a valuable addition to the company's management, left after two years when it became apparent that he and Mr. Stevens were unable to work together effectively. Mr. Stevens then appointed Mr. Corning sales manager. As assistant to the previous sales managers, Mr. Corning had functioned primarily as their office man. He had done little actual sales work. According to Mr. Farris, Mr. Corning was not a typical sort of sales manager in the steel industry, in which sales personnel are characterized as being very aggressive. He was quiet and conservative. He had accumulated a broad practical knowledge of tubular products, but he was in no sense a technical man. Mr. Farris considered him competent at obtaining and analyzing price, cost, and sales data and remarked that his outstanding quality was honesty. While he had been sales manager, he had never made a commitment concerning delivery or other matters which the company was unable to meet. Mr. Corning spent much of his time traveling throughout the country visiting the company's manufacturing agents and encouraging the sale of Castengo tubes. Since Castengo had no salesmen other than Mr. Corning, practically all relations with the company's sales outlets were handled by him. Mr. Corning's organization consisted only of several clerks in his office who handled price and delivery inquiries in his absence.

The company's treasurer, Mr. Andrews, had been with Castengo since its formation. Mr. Farris found him able and accurate in compiling historical financial data of the company's operations, but Mr. Andrews had little interest in current cost or control information. During 1943 a consulting firm was employed to study the company's operations and develop a standard cost system. The system was installed, but Mr. Farris said that revisions had not been made to keep it in conformity with production procedures, with the result that it was soon out of date and quite useless. He added that the system had never been used as a means of comparing operating costs with standards. Mr. Farris concluded from Mr. Andrews' views on cost and control information that he thought such efforts were beyond his realm of responsibility. He apparently realized the importance of such information, but he seemed to think it was not his job to try to educate Mr. Stevens.

Material purchasing was handled by Mr. George, vice-president. Mr. George was related to Mr. Stevens by marriage. Mr. Dalrymple brought him to the company in 1933 after the latter's real-estate business had become unprofitable. After Mr. Dalrymple's death, Mr. Stevens promoted Mr. George to the position of vice-president. According to Mr. Farris, Mr. George had done a satisfactory job of procurement during the war years when priorities and allocations complicated that job. Mr. Farris did not believe, however, that Mr. George's responsibilities would be increased in the future. Because of his lack of technical background, Mr. George was unable to participate in the procurement of plant machinery and equipment. Although related, Mr. George and Mr. Stevens did not work well together, and frequent difficulties arose between them.

Castengo's board, limited by the company's bylaws to seven directors, met once a month in Newark, N.J. It was composed of Mr. Farris, Mr. Stevens, Mr. George, and four men from outside the company. Two of the four outside directors, Dr. Barnes and Mr. Marston, were original members of the board and had served continuously since the company's formation. Another outside director, Mr. Stone, was also an original member of the board, although his service had been interrupted. The final member, Mr. Wentworth, came on the board in 1941 at Mr. Farris' request. The following is a brief statement concerning each outside director:

Dr. Barnes was a retired doctor who was one of the original investors in the company and a friend of Mr. Dalrymple. Dr. Barnes resided in the West and for several years had not attended board meetings. Because of his inability to attend board meetings, he had offered his resignation to Mr. Farris, effective whenever the latter found someone to replace him.

Mr. Marston, a partner of a Newark law firm, was also a friend of Mr. Dalrymple and an original investor in the company. He regularly attended board meetings and expressed interest in and gave advice on company matters. According to Mr. Farris, however, Mr. Marston would rarely take a firm stand on a company problem; he would give his opinion but would readily accede to the views of the majority.

Mr. Stone, also a friend of Mr. Dalrymple and an original investor, had resigned from the company's board in 1937 because of the pressure of other business. He was a member of several other boards of directors and, for the most part, functioned as a trustee representing his family's financial interests, which were substantial. At Mr. Farris' request and encouragement, Mr. Stone rejoined Castengo's board in 1941. Mr. Farris said that Mr. Stone was a "strong" director and, when he attended meetings, was very helpful by his contributions and by the firm stands he took on various issues. Mr. Stone traveled considerably, however, so was able to attend only two or three meetings a year.

Mr. Wentworth, head of a Newark accounting firm, was the most recent addition to the board, having become a member late in 1941. At that time Mr. Farris was anxious to have a board member qualified to give advice on taxes, price negotiations, and other accounting matters

related to government business, and he succeeded in obtaining the services of Mr. Wentworth for that purpose. Mr. Wentworth was the only
director who received any substantial compensation for his services as
a board member. Mr. Farris said that Mr. Wentworth had devoted
considerable time and attention to company matters relating to price
renegotiation, and his services had been invaluable. His contributions,
however, were largely limited to assistance with financial and accounting problems.

Mr. Grandi, Dr. Barnes, and Mr. Stevens each held approximately
10% of Castengo's stock. Mr. Stone and Mr. Marston each held about
half that amount, while Mr. George and Mr. Wentworth owned very
nominal amounts. The balance of the stock was held by approximately
200 investors, none of whom evidenced any real interest in the company's affairs.

Mr. Farris had spent varying amounts of time with the company since
1941. In the fall of 1942 he became concerned over Mr. Stevens' actions toward executive personnel; the discharge of Mr. Greyforth; and
his difficulties with Mr. Boyle in particular. He was successful in convincing the other board members that a survey of the company's management problems should be made, and a consulting firm was retained
for that purpose. The report submitted to the board recommended the
formation of an executive committee to confer with and assist Mr.
Stevens on important problems. It seemed to the board impractical to
form a committee, so Mr. Farris was elected chairman of the board to
carry out the consultant's recommendations. In so doing, the board
formally gave Mr. Farris authority over several matters, among which
were the formulation of company policies for consideration by the
board of directors, defining responsibilities of executive personnel and
control over salaries exceeding $3,000 per year. Mr. Farris said that he
attempted always to work through Mr. Stevens on matters pertaining
to other company executives rather than to take direct steps himself,
though his authority to do so was clear.

Soon after becoming chairman, Mr. Farris formed an operations committee in an attempt to strengthen the company's top management. All
department executives were included in this group, which met bi-
monthly. It was his hope that these meetings would develop greater
mutual understanding of various executives' problems and thereby contribute to smoother, more co-ordinated company operations. One problem that was often the subject of discussion concerned shop practices in
which Mr. Boyle was interested. But because he was virtually alone in
his discussion of manufacturing processes in scientific or engineering

terms, little progress was made in this area. Soon after Mr. Farris was forced to stop attending meetings of the operations committee because of his other wartime responsibilities, Mr. Stevens disbanded it so that executives could spend more time on their assigned jobs and less on what he considered unproductive talk.

In early 1946 Mr. Farris was not sure what action should be taken with regard to the company. In his opinion, the type and volume of the company's business during recent years had concealed managerial deficiencies on the part of the principal operating executives. Other members of the board, however, did not fully share his views concerning the company's management and some of his apprehensions for the future. They intimated that so long as the company's financial condition was satisfactory and profits were regularly forthcoming, there was little reason for them to take any unusual interest or action regarding the company's affairs. Mr. Farris said that he had enjoyed many of his experiences as director and chairman of the board and had learned a great deal, but he believed his real interests and abilities for a career lay along other lines. He knew that Mr. Grandi agreed with him.

Among Mr. Grandi's investments, the Castengo company did not bulk large; yet it had turned out well. In early 1946 the company's stock sold over-the-counter was selling at approximately twice its book value. Mr. Farris had no idea what point of view Mr. Grandi's executors would take toward the company if Mr. Grandi were to die, but he doubted whether they would be as actively interested in the company as Mr. Grandi had been. Neither he nor Mr. Grandi believed that the decisions as to the disposition of the investment should be left until after Mr. Grandi's death. Many of the company's small stockholders, Mr. Grandi believed, maintained their investment in the company, at least in part, because they knew it had his backing, a backing which was highly valued in all financial circles. He knew that Mr. Grandi felt a real responsibility to the small shareholders, most of whom were in no position to form an accurate opinion about the company's prospects or to take action relative thereto. Having worked closely with Mr. Grandi for several years, Mr. Farris knew that any suggestions he might make to Mr. Grandi would be accepted and carried into effect without review or even serious questioning. On matters of this sort, Mr. Grandi habitually followed the recommendations of the subordinate to whom he entrusted responsibility. Mr. Farris was therefore fully conscious of his sole and direct responsibility for any recommendations he might make.

Exhibits 4 and 5 are the company's financial statements through December, 1945. Exhibit 6 presents industry statistics regarding the pro-

Exhibit 4

CASTENGO STEEL COMPANY

Balance Sheet as of December 31, 1928–45

(Thousands Omitted)

Assets	1928	1929	1930	1932	1934	1936	1938	1940	1941	1942	1943	1944	1945
Current Assets:													
Cash and U.S. Bonds	$123	$104	$64	$61	$194	$141	$151	$207	$530	$1,425	$597	$796	$668
Accounts Receivable—Net	95	33	43	30	83	144	82	204	288	440	416	268	389
Inventories	125	124	66	62	92	147	114	270	286	417	463	256	285
Total Current Assets	$343	$261	$173	$153	$369	$432	$347	$681	$1,104	$2,282	$1,476	$1,320	$1,342
Other Assets, Including Postwar Tax Refunds	$6	$40	$26	$9	$22	$19	$16	$10	$9	$8	$109	$131	$43
Fixed Assets:													
Land, Buildings and Equipment—Net	$339	$365	$446	$369	$385	$475	$511	$553	$544	$545	$447	$425	$535
Emergency Facilities—Net										71	108	70	
Dies, Patents and Licenses	82	75	70	51	40	56	40	113	147	178	134	94	69
Total Fixed Assets	$421	$440	$516	$420	$425	$531	$551	$666	$691	$794	$689	$589	$604
Total Assets	$770	$741	$715	$582	$816	$982	$914	$1,357	$1,804	$3,084	$2,274	$2,040	$1,989
Liabilities													
Current Liabilities:													
Accounts Payable	$21	$25	$15	$15	$29	$44	$27	$57	$70	$126	$378	$117	$168
Accruals	13	6	6	5	33	53	16	38	56	107	76	121	73
Taxes			3		18	33	8	169	452	1,332	352	323	192
Other Current Liabilities					13			87	104	4			2
Total Current Liabilities	$34	$31	$24	$20	$93	$130	$51	$351	$682	$1,569	$806	$561	$435
Reserves							$8	$3	$4	$278	$137	$105	$107
Capital Stock	$657	$690	$690	$600	$608	$608	$608	$685	$685	$685	$685	$685	$685
Beginning Earned Surplus					79	200	306	325	318	433	552	646	689
Net Profit for Year				38*	117	147	59*	237	268	246	221	147	150
Less Dividends					77	103		167	153	127	127	104	77
Adjustment					4*			77*					
Surplus End of Year	79	20	1	38*	115	244	247	318	433	552	646	689	762
Total Liabilities and Net Worth	$770	$741	$715	$582	$816	$982	$914	$1,357	$1,804	$3,084	$2,274	$2,040	$1,989

* Red figure.

Exhibit 5

CASTENGO STEEL COMPANY

Operating Statements Years Ending December 31, 1929–45

(Thousands Omitted)

	1929	1930	1932	1934	1936	1938	1940	1941	1942	1943	1944	1945
Net Sales			$430	$1,014	$1,548	$953	$2,360	$2,873	$5,274	$5,385	$4,550	$4,039
Less: Cost of Sales												
Material							531	603			1,217	
Labor							338	366			504	
Burden							708	822			1,788	
Total Cost of Sales							$1,577	$1,791			$3,509	
Less: Scrap Sales							23	30			47	
Net Cost of Sales			329	646	1,063	768	1,554	1,761	2,880	3,913	3,462	3,261
Gross Profit on Sales	$30	$85	$101	$368	$485	$185	$806	$1,112	$2,394	$1,472	$1,088	$778
Less: Selling Expenses	52 }	65 }	87 }	165 }	101	79	164	199	244	294	268	267
General and Administrative Expenses					107	79	116	139	229	266	260	217
Profit from Operations	$22*	$20	$14	$203	$277	$27	$526	$774	$1,921	$912	$560	$294
Plus: Other Income	14	8					7	7	13	22	18	46
Less: Other Deductions			8	13	29	17	52	56	96	10	7	3
Depreciation	28	38	44	55	69	69	†	†	†	†	†	†
Taxes				18	32		157	404	1,320	677	406	187
Provision for Additional Compensation							87	53				
Reserves for Postwar and Other Contingencies									272	26	18	
Total Deductions	$28	$38	$52	$86	$130	$86	$296	$513	$1,688	$713	$431	$190
Net Profit or Loss	$36*	$10*	$38*	$117	$147	$59*	$237	$268	$246	$221	$147	$150

* Red figure.
† Included in cost of sales.

Exhibit 6

PRODUCTION OF SEAMLESS STEEL PIPE AND TUBES IN THE
UNITED STATES

(Net Tons)

Years	Hot-Finished*	Cold-Drawn	Total
1937	1,821,514	146,198	1,967,712
1938	1,203,306	73,715	1,277,021
1939	1,611,559	123,652	1,735,211
1940	1,781,638	178,705	1,960,343
1941	2,252,961	282,214	2,535,175
1942	2,166,892	362,521	2,529,413
1943	2,483,655	407,469	2,891,124
1944	2,674,762	446,515	3,121,277

* Does not include hot-finished tubes subsequently cold-drawn.

PRODUCTION OF ELECTRIC-WELD
PIPE AND TUBES IN THE
UNITED STATES

(Net Tons)

Years	Electric-Weld
1937	450,925
1938	269,186
1939	467,861
1940	554,215
1941	805,250
1942	688,096
1943	1,220,664
1944	1,071,991

Source: *Annual Statistical Report,* American
Iron and Steel Institute (1944), p. 49.

duction of seamless and welded tubing from 1937 through 1944. Exhibit 7 is an organization chart of the company as of January, 1946. Appendices A, B, and C are statements from published literature con-

Exhibit 7

CASTENGO STEEL COMPANY
Organization Chart—January, 1946

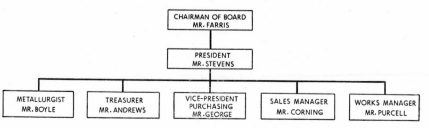

cerning seamless and welded steel tubing and plastic tubing. Appendix D describes briefly some methods by which steel products are marketed.

APPENDIX A

U.S. STEEL OPENS NEW GARY PLANT[1]

Tubular Alloy Steel Corp., Gary, Indiana, a recently established subsidiary of the U.S. Steel Corporation, formally opened its plant April 5 (1944) with more than 200 visitors. . . .

The plant, which began partial operation in January, 1943, is one of the largest in the nation devoted exclusively to the manufacture of alloy and stainless steel tubing.

Demand for seamless tubing, especially cold-drawn, is tremendous, and in a sense the success of the war effort depends upon it. Approximately 300 different vital war items require tubing. Although cutbacks are occurring in some war manufacturing, such curtailments are not in the seamless tube field. Every tube plant in the country is running at capacity.

Plant property covers some 330 acres. . . . The tube producing area alone comprises 665,000 square feet.

Hot finished tubing is produced in a size range of 1¼" O.D. × 10 gage to 8⅝" O.D. × 1½" wall. Tube reduced or cold-drawn tubes are made in sizes ranging from ¼" O.D. × 20 gage to 8" O.D. × 1" wall.

Much of the plant's production is for aeronautical purposes, while the remainder is for Army and Navy ordnance.

APPENDIX B

PRODUCES OVER 19,000 MILES OF ELECTRIC WELDED TUBING[2]

Since the completion of the electric resistance welding tubing plant for the Defense Plant Corporation at Alliance, Ohio, and its operation by the Babcock and Wilcox Tube Company, well over 100,000,000 feet of carbon steel pressure and mechanical tubing has been produced. In designing the plant, provision was made for eliminating the usual variables that plague the tube welding, such as the strip thickness and width. Two electric weld mills are housed in the 665 × 100 foot Main bay. No. 1 mill produces tubes ranging from ¾" to 2½" in diameter, in gages from 0.049 to 0.165 inches and at speeds ranging from 50 to 200 feet per minute. The No. 2 mill is designed to produce tubes ranging from 2" to 4" in diameter, in 0.065 to 0.259 inches at speeds from 30 to 120 feet per minute. Both mills and their accessory equipment have a capacity of about 4,000 tons of tubing a month depending upon the kinds and sizes made.

ELECTRIC WELD PIPE AND TUBING IN RAPID PRODUCTION GAIN DURING WAR[3]

Electric weld pipe and tubing production in 1943 not only increased 153% over 1939 output, but also raised its percentage of total output from 12.4 in

[1] *Steel,* April 17, 1944, p. 64.

[2] *Steel,* October 19, 1945, p. 114.

[3] *The Iron Age,* April 27, 1944, p. 98.

1939 to 20.3 in 1943. Much of this growth in trend of electric weld pipe and tubing has been ascribed to war needs but producers of this type of product are insistent that the gain will by no means be lost when the next so-called "normal" period materializes. . . .

An analysis of the figures . . . does not indicate that the primary position of seamless pipe and tubing is in danger of being toppled. There is ample proof, however, that electric weld pipe and tubing production not only has gained considerably, but will, in all probability, under certain conditions, present competition with seamless for new business.

APPENDIX C

INDESTRUCTIBLE PIPING[4]

One of the significant replacements of metal by plastics in recent times is in the field of conduit tubes and pipes. During the last four or five years, the use of cellulose acetate butyrate for beverage dispensing, syrup processing, vinegar manufacturing, and distilled water industrial piping has steadily increased. Brewers have subjected the plastics to rigid tests; it has passed with flying colors. North Penn Co., for example, reports "satisfactory results" in beer and soft drink dispensing. This firm should know; starting from scratch in the distribution of plastics pipes and tubing about 1941, it has since sold over 1,000,000 feet of the product.

What are the properties of the butyrate that recommend it for this purpose? For one thing, it is non-corrosive, whereas metal pipes may rust and cause an admixture of foreign particles in the conducted fluid. Pure distilled water can be chemically affected by metal but not by plastics tubing, nor have fruit juices, lactic acid and syrups experienced any deleterious effects. It is non-electrolytic with metals, a factor in cost cutting, as metal pipes may require special coating for insulation. Again, the plastics tubing is transparent so that its fluid contents may be observed. The various tints that can be chosen to harmonize with wall and furnishings offer a pleasant contrast to the ugly coils of pipe characterizing metal plumbing. . . .

Seamless plastics tubing, unlike metal, is extruded in continuous lengths. The thermoplastic material is forced by heat and high pressure through a forming die and, theoretically, there is no limit to the length that can be manufactured. Coils up to 10,000 feet are commercially available, the diameters ranging from .04" (inside diameter) to ½" (outside diameter). One concern stocks it in long length coils for sizes up to ½" in diameter with a wall thickness of .035"; for greater diameters, 12-foot lengths are available. Special sizes and shapes in round, square, oval and rectangular form can be obtained on special order.

An important factor is that the tubing is practically unbreakable and can be curved or bent to satisfy almost any requirements. Another advantage over metal pipes is the elimination of weld marks and joints. And the same tools used for copper tubing are employed in adjusting its ends to standard flared fitting; for tubes with a greater diameter, standard thread cutting tools can be used. . . .

---

[4] Philip Pollack. "Indestructible Piping," *Plastics* (August, 1945), p. 42.

The disadvantages of plastics tubing as compared with metal pipes are in rigidity, bursting point, and resistance to extreme temperatures. Although plastics piping has replaced block tin in many cases for cooling coils in draft beer dispensing apparatus and is adaptable for commercial ice-cooling systems and direct draw systems with automatic refrigeration, it is no real substitute for copper refrigeration tubing. Again, it softens up when the temperature climbs beyond 150°F. and cannot withstand the heat of steam cleaning.

Metal is superior, also, in the matter of bursting pressure. At the same time, extruders and fabricators point out, the butyrate functions with complete satisfaction under the conditions of pressure and temperature normally prevailing in the beverage dispensing industry. One laboratory report showed that the bursting pressure is reduced 60% when the temperature rises to 150°F.

There is no significant difference between the butyrate plastics and metal tubing in the matter of cost, as the relative lightness of the plastics makes up for its higher cost per pound. Thus, steel may cost 50 cents a pound as against $3 a pound for cellulose acetate butyrate. But one foot of steel, ½″ square in cross section, weighs 0.668 lb., as against only 0.1 lb., for the butyrate. The steel bar would thus cost $.334 as against $.30 for the plastics. These figures are approximate only, but they serve to illustrate the economic advantage of lightness in plastics. One manufacturer pointed out that one pound of his company's plastics tubing is equivalent to approximately eight pounds of copper, block tin, or stainless steel or 2½ lbs. of aluminum and rubber. . . .

What of the post-war future of plastics tubing? In general, extruders, manufacturers and distributors express confidence in the existence of a large, potential market for the product. . . .

The limitations that have been pointed out for cellulose acetate butyrate and vinyl tubing can probably in large measure, if not entirely, be overcome by the use of reinforcement, especially inorganic reinforcement; and no discussion of the future of plastics tubing should overlook what reinforcement of cloth, other fiber forms, etc., can do for it in increasing its resistance to heat and in making it tougher and stronger. Persons who have laboriously chopped ice off their sidewalks in winter well know how much tougher and more resistant ice that has a few twigs imbedded in it is than unreinforced ice.

The ice example gives only a rough idea of what a fibrous reinforcement can contribute to plastics—innumerable products other than tubing—and the real proof must arise from the developmental work now known to be under way in a number of laboratories, including those particularly concerned with the development of resins as well as those concerned with the development of various types of reinforcement.

In spite of developments, however, most manufacturers and distributors agree that the outlook is for a slowly rising market rather than a sensational advance in sales. As a manufacturer expressed it: "In spite of its limitations the decisive factor for the beverage and food industry in the choice of piping is the fact that plastics tubing is neutral to beverages and is not fouled up with use. This important point is bound to persuade an increasing number of dealers to change from metal to plastics tubing."

APPENDIX D
NOTES ON MARKETING STEEL PRODUCTS

It was generally recognized and agreed in the steel industry that there were no significant differences in the quality of steel products as between the various producers. Steel prices quoted by the major producers tended to establish prices for the entire industry. The industry was very sensitive to prices, and a price change by one of the large companies was almost immediately followed by the entire industry. With the usual competitive factors of quality and price standardized, sales were based to a considerable extent on service, personal acquaintanceship between salesmen and customers, and reciprocity agreements. It was the belief of many salesmen that a majority of steel products were sold because a salesman was intimately acquainted with the buyer. These relationships between buyers and sellers were so strong in many instances that salesmen retained their customers regardless of the producer they represented.

In addition to personal relationships, dealers considered it important for steel salesmen to be capable of handling customer problems regarding the use of steel. This ability included a knowledge of the various types of steel and steel products and their uses and limitations, and competence in dealing with engineering, metallurgical, and other technical problems relating to the products. Some dealers believed that increasing emphasis was being placed on salesmen with some degree of technical ability and knowledge. This ability was considered especially important in the sales of specialty steel products such as pipe, tubing, welding rods, and wire. An experienced and successful steel salesman usually earned over $5,000 a year.

One dealer said that a good salesman for tubular products was a man who could go into a shop or manufacturing plant and see applications for tubing which would be advantageous to the customer. He gave as an example an instance where a salesman, observing a process in which lengths of tubing were being used in the manufacture of a finished product, noticed that nearly one tube in five was split in the process and had to be discarded. The salesman inquired about this tubing and, after briefly studying the problem, he was able to tell the manufacturer the exact specification tubing to use virtually to eliminate this waste. The dealer said that this customer was very appreciative of the unsolicited advice and thereafter the manufacturer regularly purchased his total steel requirements from this dealer. Such incidents, according to the dealer, were not unusual and the wide variety of uses for tubular products made it possible for new uses or improved applications for tubing to be found frequently.

The major steel companies maintained their own sales offices in important cities throughout the country. Company salesmen working from these offices actively solicited sales within their regions. Typically, the salesmen were specialized in particular products such as sheets, nails, tubes, or structural shapes, which they sold direct to large ultimate users. These salesmen concentrated on large tonnage orders which were placed on the company's mills for direct delivery to the customer. Some regional warehouses were owned and operated by the important producers to facilitate deliveries of standard items in quantities not warranting special scheduling for mill production.

In addition to district sales offices of the principal producers, there were many independent steel dealers serving each locality or region. These dealers or supply houses carried inventories for making rapid local deliveries, and solicited orders which they placed with the producer they represented for direct delivery to the customer. In such cases it was customary for the producer to bill the dealer, while the dealer in turn billed the customer. Some, but not all, dealers operated under exclusive sales arrangements with a producer whereunder no other dealer was allowed to carry that company's product in the locality, and in turn the dealer carried no competing products. Irrespective of these exclusive arrangements, however, producers often solicited direct orders in the same area by their own sales organization. Dealers typically dealt directly with producers. In the case of a few specialty steel items, especially those not involving large tonnages, however, manufacturers sometimes sold through manufacturers' agents who carried no stock and merely represented producers, but only a relatively small volume of the steel industry's business was handled in this manner. As has been pointed out, Castengo used manufacturers' agents almost entirely and had no sales force of its own. One dealer remarked that manufacturers' agents who sold steel products generally were the type of individuals who could "sell anything" and that their success in the steel line was due more to their wide personal acquaintanceships among potential users rather than to technical knowledge of the products they were selling.

Dealers received commissions on sales made direct, and discounts from the list price for items carried in stock. These discounts and commissions varied from 40% on special items regularly carried in inventory to 5% for sales of standard products shipped directly from the producer's mill. Discount and commission schedules, however, were so arranged that prices to the customers were the same whether purchased from a dealer, direct from the producer, or through an agent. Even during times of depressed business activity these standardized prices to customers were maintained within close limits.

Instruments Incorporated

DURING ITS FIRST YEAR and a half of operations, ending September 30, 1949, Instruments Incorporated of Bridgeport, Connecticut, showed steady growth (see Exhibit 1) and on October 1, the company's back-

Exhibit 1

INSTRUMENTS INCORPORATED

Sales, Employees, and Backlog of Orders by Quarters

Year	Quarter	Approximate Sales	Employees	Approximate Backlog of Orders: at End of Period
1948				
3/15–6/30..............	1st 3 months	(No Operations)		
7/1–9/30..............	2nd 3 months	$ 40,000	26	$ 50,000
10/1–12/31..............	3rd 3 months	45,000	32	75,000
1949				
1/1–3/31..............	4th 3 months	57,000	45	90,000
4/1–6/30..............	5th 3 months	87,000	50	185,000
7/1–9/30..............	6th 3 months	115,000	65	310,000

Source: Company letter to prospective investors.

log of orders aggregated over $300,000 (see Exhibit 2). Mr. Arthur Johnson, the company's president, stated that the most pressing and critical problem at that time was a shortage of funds which was inhibiting the company's growth, and that his efforts to solve it were consuming a large portion of his time.

At the time of incorporation the cofounders of the company, Mr. Johnson and Mr. Henry Brown, the vice-president, expressed the intention to specialize primarily in ". . . engineering development, design, and fabrication of electromechanical precision instruments such as . . . gyroscopes, automatic pilots, special indicators and mechanical instruments, and hydraulic and electric control systems." Mr. Johnson and Mr. Brown believed they could apply these instruments and controls to industrial processes. They were especially interested in hydraulic and electric control systems and thought these could include, in addition to

Exhibit 2

INSTRUMENTS INCORPORATED

Backlog of Orders as of September 30, 1949

CUSTOMER	TYPE CONTRACT	PRODUCT	OPERATIONS	CONTRACT PRICE	Material	Labor	Administration	Total	Number of Units
						Manufacturing Expense			
								EXTENT IN PROCESS	
Armed Forces........	Prime	Electronic equipment	Machining and assembly	$ 33,000	5,711	6,907	7,918	20,536	100 + spares
Armed Forces........	Prime	Mechanical controls	Machining and assembly	24,000	0	1,502	1,371	2,873	766
Armed Forces........	Prime	Development	Study contract	22,600	5,446	2,352	3,023	10,821	2
Armed Forces........	Prime	Mechanical measuring equipment	Machining and assembly	4,750	2,068	2,306	2,875	7,249	109
Development, Inc.....	Subcontract	Aircraft instrument	Development	16,300					model
Development, Inc.....	Subcontract	Electronic control system	Development	22,000	3	99	134	236	model
Bendix..............	Purchase order	Mechanical assemblies	Machining and assembly	25,185	4,018	2,903	3,742	10,663	60
Westinghouse........	Purchase order	Electromechanical equipment	Machining and assembly	135,000	821	934	1,333	3,088	94
Electronics, Inc......	Purchase order	Precision parts	Machining fabrication	5,750	169	607	778	1,554	102
Rensselaer Polytechnic Institute.........	Purchase order	Miscellaneous laboratory equipment	Machining and assembly	6,000	1,084	1,587	2,112	4,784	50
Electronics, Inc......	Purchase order	Signal generator	Machining and assembly	10,000					1
Miscellaneous........	Purchase order	....	....	6,000	0	93	88	181	
Total.........				$310,585	19,321	19,291	23,375	61,987	

Source: Compiled from company records.

adaptations of the special indicators and instruments noted above, ". . . new elements which will apply to the control of machine tools and to the chemical process industry." Both men had resigned from promising positions with a large manufacturer of mechanical and electronic equipment and had formed their own company in order to be unfettered in putting into effect their own ideas.

As of the end of September, 1949, practically all the company's income had been from government contracts or contracts with other companies engaged in government work. The rapid growth of this business, however, had produced a continuous strain on working capital. This shortage, besides actually restricting the company's rate of expansion, had limited funds for the research and development of the company's own products (referred to by the executives as "commercial development") to somewhat less than the amount of company earnings.

In July, 1949, Mr. Johnson said he had "learned enough politics" while he was negotiating unsuccessfully for a loan with the Reconstruction Finance Corporation the previous year to justify a second attempt, and planned again to negotiate for a loan of $150,000 which he contemplated using as follows: working capital, $25,000; research and development of company's own new products, $25,000; refinancing of outstanding indebtedness, $40,800; purchase of equipment previously leased from War Assets Administration, $45,500; and new equipment, $13,700.

The following analysis was prepared by Mr. Johnson for submission to the RFC:

Instruments Incorporated is in a rapidly expanding field with multitudinous opportunities. The company, without additional financial aid, is in an awkward position. It has expanded its personnel and organization to the point that short-term orders and contracts may not be sufficient to provide a stable continuity of employment and scale of operations (fortunately, not a major problem to date). Yet, on the other hand, large, extended-term contracts cannot be bid, or subsequently financed, without an improved working capital position. Although the company can and will expand, and increasingly profit without such new funds over a longer period of time, temporary slack periods and the resulting difficulties therefrom can probably be expected in the period of general adjustment ahead.

This company has expended a great deal of time and effort in attempts to obtain financial assistance from other sources. The risk-capital tree in general, and in New England decidedly, is markedly barren of fruit these days—a discouraging handicap to new enterprises. The banking situation in New England is similarly described. Numerous contacts have been made with New York banks as well, without satisfactory solution.

Cost-of-sales figures show that approximately 50%–60% of Instruments Incorporated's gross sales dollar is spent on payroll. Our present working capital position ($30,000) is producing (based on just-ended, last-quarter results) a yearly gross sales volume of about ten times that amount ($360,000). Of this amount, payroll amounts to over half ($200,000 on a 12-month extension of current payroll figures).

The physical facilities, including building and tools presently at hand, are capable of supporting a severalfold increase in productive output, without major increases in the amount of tooling or in present fixed charges, such as depreciation, real estate tax, etc. For this and other reasons, it is estimated that doubling the present working capital position will much more than double gross sales. With the earmarking of $25,000 of the additional funds for working

Exhibit 3

INSTRUMENTS INCORPORATED

Comparative Statement of Profit and Loss and Earned Surplus for Selected Periods

	9 Months Ending March 31, 1949	April 1949	May 1949	June 1949	12 Months Ending June 30, 1949	15 Months Ending Sept. 30, 1949
Net sales	$141,368	$18,189	$38,766	$30,586	$228,909	$345,521
Less: Cost of goods sold:						
Raw materials	$ 18,621	$ 4,289	$ 7,688	$ 4,063	$ 34,661	$ 61,060
Direct labor	62,852	10,086	9,336	9,758	92,032	126,391
Manufacturing expenses	52,318	7,214	7,326	7,530	74,387	104,463
Total	$133,791	$21,589	$24,350	$21,351	$201,080	$291,914
Add: Inventories at beginning:						
Work in process	.....	$17,396	$24,014	$17,652	.....	
Commercial products in process	.....	2,822	6,022	7,381	.....	
Commercial products development	.....	6,708	6,708	6,708	.....	
Total	.....	$26,926	$36,744	$31,741	.....	
Less: Inventories at end:						
Work in process	$ 17,396	$24,014	$17,652	$22,748	$ 22,748	$ 61,987
Commercial products in process	2,822	6,022	7,381	9,097	9,097	11,543
Commercial products development	6,708	6,708	6,708	6,708	6,708*	6,708*
Total	$ 26,926	$36,744	$31,741	$38,553	$ 38,553	$ 80,238
Cost of goods sold	$106,865	$11,771	$29,353	$14,539	$162,527	$211,676
Gross profit on sales	$ 34,503	$ 6,418	$ 9,413	$16,047	$ 66,382	$133,845
General and administrative expenses	25,424	2,886	3,006	4,540	35,856	48,740
Net income from operations	$ 9,079	$ 3,532	$ 6,407	$11,507	$ 30,526	$ 85,105
Less: Discounts on sales	.....	107	139	302	548	1,692
Net income before federal and state taxes	$ 9,079	$ 3,425	$ 6,268	$11,205	$ 29,978	$ 83,413
Less: Federal and state taxes	900	....	....	8,300	9,200	30,206
Net profit to earned surplus	$ 8,179	$ 3,425	$ 6,268	$ 2,905	$ 20,778	$ 53,207
Less: Organization expenses	650	....			650	3,457
Earned surplus before adjustments	$ 7,529	$ 3,425			$ 20,128	$ 49,750
Add: Income tax adjustment					450	
Earned surplus after adjustments					$ 20,578	

* From the company's records it could not be readily determined exactly how this item was carried on the company's balance sheets.

Source: Company records.

capital, the new working capital position would allow bidding-in and financing, with available progress payment assistance, of new longer term government contracts up to $750,000 face value. This would be expected to at least double present employment and payroll.

The results to be expected from the use of $25,000 earmarked for new commercial products are not as readily predictable, but it is deemed to be in the best interest of the general economy actively to develop and enlarge nongovernment sponsored business activity. Because of the barely scratched applications to industrial processes of new control and instrumentation techniques, the potentialities of our planned developments are considered excellent. This has been confirmed by considerable and continuing contact with and inquiries from the potential market. An important aspect is the fact that application of the devices and equipment planned for development and sale will result in higher manufacturing productivity at a lower cost. Such equipment is salable in our country even during depressions; and contrary to disproved theories, new technological developments always result in an increased general economy and employment. (See Exhibits 3 and 4 for comparative income statements and balance sheets.)

Exhibit 3a

INSTRUMENTS INCORPORATED

Profit and Loss Analysis—Percentage

	9 Months Ending March 31, 1949	April 1949	May 1949	June 1949	12 Months Ending June 30, 1949	15 Months Ending Sept. 30, 1949
Net sales	100.0%	100.0%	100.0%	100.0%	100.0%	100.0%
Less: Cost of goods sold:						
Raw materials	13.2	23.6	19.8	13.3	15.2	17.6
Direct labor	44.4	55.4	24.1	31.9	40.1	36.6
Manufacturing expenses	37.0	39.7	18.9	24.6	32.5	30.2
Total	94.6%	118.7%	62.8%	69.8%	87.8%	84.4%
Add: Inventories at beginning:						
Work in process	...	95.6%	62.0%	57.8%	...	...
Commercial products in process	...	15.5	15.5	24.2	...	...
Commercial products development	...	36.9	17.3	21.9	...	...
Total	...	148.0%	94.8%	103.8%	...	...
Less: Inventories at end:						
Work in process	12.3%	132.0%	45.5%	74.4%	9.9%	17.9%
Commercial products in process	2.0	33.1	19.1	29.8	4.0	3.3
Commercial products development	4.7	36.9	17.3	21.9	2.9	1.9
Total	19.0%	202.0%	81.9%	126.0%	16.8%	23.1%
Cost of goods sold	75.6%	64.7%	75.7%	47.6%	71.0%	61.3%
Gross profit on sales	24.4%	35.3%	24.3%	52.4%	29.0%	38.7%
General and administrative expenses	18.0	15.9	7.8	14.9	15.7	14.1
Net income from operations	6.4%	19.4%	16.5%	37.5%	13.3%	24.6%
Less: Discounts on sales	...	0.6	0.3	0.8	0.3	0.5
Net profit before federal and state taxes	6.4%	18.8%	16.2%	36.7%	13.0%	24.1%
Less: Federal and state taxes	0.6	...	...	27.2	4.0	8.7
Net profit to earned surplus	5.8%	18.8%	16.2%	9.5%	9.0%	15.4%

Source: Compiled by case writer.

Exhibit 4

INSTRUMENTS INCORPORATED

Comparative Balance Sheet for Selected Dates, May 15, 1948, to September 30, 1949

Assets	May 15, 1948	December 31, 1948	June 30, 1949	September 30, 1949
Current Assets:				
Cash on Hand and in Banks	$14,734	$ 2,465	$ 5,211	$ 21,906
Accounts Receivable	3,500	20,611	22,309	11,898
Work in Process	....	7,519	22,748	61,987
Commercial Products in Process	....	....	9,097	11,543
Finished Goods	....	1,463	....	....
Prepaid Expenses	4,330	7,465	7,790	9,144
Total Current Assets	$22,564	$ 39,523	$ 67,155	$116,478
Fixed Assets:				
Land	$ 1,000	$ 1,013	$ 1,013	$ 1,013
Building and Structures	$54,300	$ 62,980	$ 64,448	$ 64,448
Less Reserve for Depreciation	....	1,262	2,263	....
	$54,300	$ 61,718	$ 62,185	
Machines and Tools	$15,258*	$ 24,204*	$ 32,704*	$ 35,660*
Less Reserve for Depreciation	....	2,499	4,890	....
	$15,258	$ 21,705	$ 27,814	
Laboratory Equipment	$ 2,075	$ 2,345	$ 3,175	$ 5,613
Less Reserve for Depreciation	....	507	959	....
	$ 2,075	$ 1,838	$ 2,216	
Furniture and Equipment	....	$ 2,736	$ 3,145	$ 4,197
Less Reserve for Depreciation	....	99	252	....
	....	$ 2,637	$ 2,893	....
Total Land, Plant, and Equipment at Cost	....	....	....	$110,931
Less Reserve for Depreciation	....	....	....	10,855
Total Fixed Assets	$72,633	$ 88,911	$ 96,121	$100,076
Other Assets:				
Commercial Products Development	....	....	$ 9,474	$ 13,903
Organization Expenses	$ 539	$ 650	....	....
Total Other Assets	$ 539	$ 650	$ 9,474	$ 13,903
Total Assets	$95,736	$129,084	$172,750	$230,457
Liabilities and Net Worth				
Current Liabilities:				
Accounts Payable	$ 5,971	$ 7,716	$ 9,767	$ 17,524
Accounts Payable, Long Term	2,705	6,130	5,995	4,733
Other Accrued Payables	560	6,125	21,455	41,944†
Total Current Liabilities	$ 9,236	$ 19,971	$ 37,217	$ 64,201
Mortgage Payable on Real Estate	27,000	35,200	34,400	34,000
Net Worth:				
Class A Common Stock	$31,100	$ 45,000	$ 48,000	$ 50,100
Class B Common Stock	25,400	27,400	29,200	29,200
Stock Subscribed	3,000	3,954	3,355	2,805
	$59,500	$ 76,354	$ 80,555	$ 82,105
Surplus (Deficit)	....	(2,441)	20,578	50,151‡
Total Net Worth	$59,500	$ 73,913	$101,133	$132,256
Total Liabilities and Net Worth	$95,736	$129,084	$172,750	$230,457

* Does not include approximately $50,000 of machine tools leased from WAA for purchase of which the company was negotiating.

† Provision for state and federal taxes, $30,206.

‡ Includes $400 paid-in surplus.

Source: Company records.

ORGANIZATION

In October, 1949, the company employed over 60 people and was organized as indicated in Exhibit 5.

Each of the company's executives or supervisors was an engineer by training or experience except Mr. Robbins, who had graduated from the Harvard Law School in 1943. Mr. Johnson, after receiving his Master's degree in physics from the University of Chicago in 1936, had worked with the Philco Radio and Television Corporation on vacuum tube application and radio receiver design and from there had gone to Westinghouse to do commercial engineering on receivers and then to General

Exhibit 5

INSTRUMENTS INCORPORATED

Organization Chart

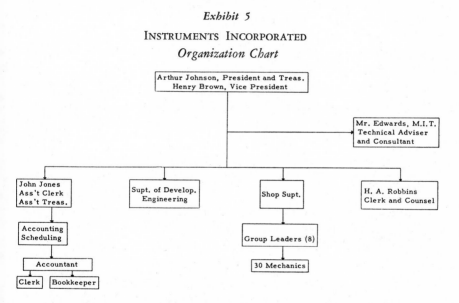

Electric as manager of a research, development, and production group of 160 people working on special radar equipment. Mr. Johnson and his associates believed this latter experience to be the equivalent of engineering and management responsibilities of a business firm of about the same size.

Mr. Brown had received an A.B. degree in chemistry from Purdue in 1936 and had subsequently worked in the research laboratory of the Allied Chemical Company as chief instrument designer and machine-shop superintendent. During the war he was in charge of test work on ammunition and various mechanical and electronic equipment, including radar and antiaircraft gun control. Mr. Brown had gone to General

Electric after the war as senior engineer, designing servo mechanisms.

Mr. Jones, after receiving his degree in engineering from Harvard, served in the Navy as an engineering officer and later in a liaison group responsible for engineering compliance with contract requirements.

The shop superintendent had held positions as plant superintendent of a small machinery company, and, consecutively, as assistant shop superintendent, head tool designer, and shop superintendent with three small manufacturing companies in the Bridgeport area.

The company's consultant, Mr. Edwards, associate professor at Massachusetts Institute of Technology in the instrumentation section of the Aeronautical Engineering Department, had had experience in his field in industry and in the service and was a specialist in gyroscopics and vector kinematics.

Several other men whom Mr. Johnson and Mr. Brown contemplated adding to this management group as the company grew possessed similar backgrounds, or at least comparable experience.

Mr. Johnson and Mr. Brown, through stock ownership, held voting control as well as the management of the company between them. Their purpose in organizing Instruments Incorporated had been to create a company run by engineers for engineers. Their previous experience had convinced them that good engineering supervision would enable them to compete with other organizations, large or small. Mr. Brown considered the market which the company intended to invade so large and new that "a half-dozen companies like it could exist side by side and all prosper."

Within three months of incorporation, the company had a $150,000 plant in operation, consisting of a modern, well-lighted building with 14,000 square feet of floor space, more than adequate for the company's 1949 volume of production, and machine tools and test equipment necessary for precision production. Mr. Brown stated that this relatively large investment in fixed assets was designed to "keep the company's feet on the ground." Both he and Mr. Johnson agreed they did not want to have their company's existence dependent upon someone "having a new idea a minute." They intended to develop manufacturing skills and a reputation for quality and precision which would bring production orders to the company, and foresaw their commercial development as contributing new machines and control devices to be manufactured by means of these skills. They stated that they were not interested in products for a mass market. Mr. Johnson believed his employees possessed a high degree of skill and intelligence so that, as a result, operations were efficient and there would be no "administrative communication" problem. He believed "administrative headaches" would develop if the company became involved in production line operations employing unskilled labor.

Mr. Johnson expressed no interest in becoming a "financial tycoon." He stated that he and Mr. Brown wanted to enjoy running the business and could do this only if it were small enough to be supervised personally. It was his opinion that large companies operated on the wrong side of the "efficiency curve" and that Instruments Incorporated's peak efficiency would be reached at about 400 to 450 employees. He said he had no desire to operate above this point, where he believed output per machine and per man would tend to go down.

During June, July, and August, while sales continued to increase and backlog to grow, commercial development on the company's own products was stopped as all available funds were channeled into working capital. Negotiations with the War Assets Administration for transfer of the $45,900 worth of surplus machinery to Instruments Incorporated were completed, although title was not transferred, and one foreman and twelve workers were added as a night shift.

A large part of Mr. Johnson's time during this period was devoted to raising additional funds or helping Mr. Brown, whose time was spent scheduling orders and directing production so as to take advantage of progress payments[1] on partial shipments in order to meet current obligations. Mr. Brown maintained a close watch over production to insure against last minute errors that would jeopardize the shipping schedule. Both men felt these exigencies were dictating their activities to an undue extent. Mr. Johnson believed additional funds were justified if for no other reason than on the grounds that they would free both men from worry and unnecessary unproductive activities, and allow them time to study and take care of the company's operating problems and commercial research. Both men were anxious to get into the laboratory themselves to work on their own ideas for new products. From the beginning they had each worked seven days a week and evenings. They received the same salaries paid them in their previous positions, but to help financially had taken, to the limit of their means, stock in lieu of a portion of these salaries.

---

[1] The government would provide advances called "progress payments" of up to 90% of actual direct labor and material, payable upon receipt of portions of a contract completed and shipped. In case of fixed-price contracts these costs as well as all others were subject to renegotiation.

PRODUCTION

Next in importance to the critical shortage of working capital, according to Mr. Brown, was a shortage of the "best engineering supervision." The company had a nucleus of three men, considered to have good engineering and production abilities, who acted as project engineers. Each was assigned a specific project, such as a government contract or a commercial product, and given responsibility for its development or production engineering from raw materials through processing and manufacture to shipment. A fourth man, the shop superintendent, also acted as project engineer on some jobs. His main duty was to supervise the actual work of the groups which were of various sizes depending on the magnitude of individual projects. Mr. Brown considered the night-shift foreman capable of supervising the workmen, but not capable enough to develop schedules and appraise an entire project. Mr. Brown was proud of both supervisors and workers. The average age of the entire group was 31 years. Most of them had come from the community in which the company was located or from nearby towns and had been upgraded considerably since coming to the firm. Mr. Brown stated that many of the men were approaching a highly skilled level and possessed enough intelligence to co-operate in scheduling work on various machines used jointly. An exception to this general efficiency occurred on the night shift where, according to Mr. Brown, the right type of worker had not been secured. Although a 10% premium over day wages was paid, the best workers could work days elsewhere for approximately the same wage. This shift did not measure up to day-shift standards of productivity or quality. The plant was not unionized and Messrs. Johnson and Brown believed it would not be. They both contended that this nonunionized working force constituted one of Instruments Incorporated's most important competitive advantages.

ACCOUNTING

Mr. Brown estimated that raw material cost was perhaps 8% of total selling price, whereas total payroll expense approached 55%. (The work-in-process figures show higher material costs than this, because of carrying vendor subcontract work, such as heat-treating, plating, and gear cutting, as a material charge.) He therefore believed the latter deserved the closest watching and control. Mr. Jones was in charge of the company's accounting, records, and office personnel and until August, 1949, had also been acting as purchasing agent. In August a man was brought in to perform this latter function under Mr. Jones's direction. Purchasing generally was on a project-requirement basis, since the variety of materials used was too great to permit stocking raw materials. Invoices were paid net 30 days in order to conserve working capital. According to Mr. Brown, the large diversity of materials purchased in small quantities constituted a continuing problem which often determined the production rate on rush jobs.

Direct material, labor, and manufacturing overhead costs were collected in considerable detail by Mr. Jones, who had devised an actual job-order cost system to provide the information necessary for government contract work. Because of the production organization, it was relatively easy to provide such costs by product or by contract. Labor costs and hours worked were collected by months and cumulatively, and by type (such as shop mechanics, junior draftsmen, senior engineers, etc.) From these was developed a current cost per hour for each type of labor, to be used for contract negotiation (see Exhibit 6). Manufacturing expense, comprising indirect expenses, factory overhead, and all depreciation, also included any employee's time not assignable to projects. These expenses were collected monthly and cumulatively and were related percentagewise to both total direct-labor dollars and hours. General administrative expense (executive salaries, office salaries and financial expenses) were treated similarly. Manufacturing expense and general and administrative expense were then divided by total direct labor hours charged to projects to give a per hour figure which, when added to the actual cost for any type of labor, could be compared to the government allowance for that type and thus furnish a rough check on company efficiency. This system also provided Messrs. Johnson and Brown and stockholders with monthly income statements and balance sheets and the former two men with material, labor, and overhead figures by month and by completed contract. In addition Mr. Jones also furnished Mr. Johnson with daily data on cash on hand, accounts payable, and accounts receivable.

Mr. Brown believed that the diversified nature of the products precluded the use of any standard costing system but that good estimates were essential for bidding. Mr. Johnson estimated hours for various types of labor on each new contract and, using the current total cost per hour, computed an over-all estimate for the contract. This estimate for the contract as a whole was broken down into shippable units, and the actual cost on completion of each such unit was checked against the

Exhibit 6

INSTRUMENTS INCORPORATED

Selected Data from Cost Accounting Record for Government Contract Negotiations

	I	II	III	IV	V	VI	VII
	PRODUCTIVE LABOR COSTS			MANUFACTURING EXPENSE PER DIRECT LABOR HOUR[d]	GENERAL AND ADMINISTRATIVE EXPENSE PER DIRECT LABOR HOUR[e]	(III + IV + V) TOTAL EXPENSE PER HOUR	GOVERNMENT APPROVED ALLOWANCE PER HOUR[g]
	Dollars	Actual Hours	Average Dollars per Hour				
Shop Mechanics:							
1949—first six months	$41,661	26,292	$1.585	$1.317	$0.598	$3.50	$3.62
Total since inclusive through 6/49	71,037	44,810	1.59	1.362	0.657	3.61	
Junior Engineers:							
1949—first six months	5,357	3,488	1.54	1.317	0.598	3.46	3.75
Total since inclusive through 6/49	8,169	5,372	1.52	1.362	0.657	3.54	
Senior Engineers:							
1949—first six months	5,716	1,548	3.69	1.317	0.598	5.61	6.92
Total since inclusive through 6/49	10,416	2,590	4.02	1.362	0.657	6.04	
Laboratory Technicians:							
1949—first six months	2,228	1,604	1.39	1.317	0.598	3.31	3.61
Total since inclusive through 6/49	2,793	2,045	1.365	1.362	0.657	3.38	
Total Productive Labor[a]:							
1949—first six months	$55,688	33,240	$1.675				
Total since inclusive through 6/49	93,142	55,247	1.685				

Manufacturing Expense

	Total Dollars	Per Cent of Productive Labor Dollars[c]	Dollars per Direct Labor Hour[f]
1949—first six months	$43,802	78.7%	$1.317
Total since inclusive through 6/49	75,286[b]	80.8%	1.362

General and Administrative Expense

	Total Dollars	Per Cent of Productive Labor Dollars[f]	Dollars per Direct Labor Hour[f]
1949—first six months	$19,886	35.7%	$0.598
Total since inclusive through 6/49	36,292[b]	38.9%	0.657

a Total of dollars and hours shown above but reflecting also cost of one senior and one junior draftsman after May.
b This item shows a relatively small variation from the amount as given in the operating statement (Exhibit 3).
c Manufacturing expense as percentage of total productive labor costs,
d Manufacturing expense divided by the total productive labor hours for corresponding period.
e General and administrative expense divided by the total productive labor hours for corresponding period.
f General and administrative expense as a percentage of total productive labor costs.
g This rate was set from experience to cover all costs plus profit allowance and was open to renegotiation after and re-examination prior to each contract.

Source: Company records.

estimate. In September the company began including these estimates on the job cost sheet, thus making the estimate part of a permanent record to be used subsequently in estimating similar contracts. On no large contract had the company failed to make a profit, although on several smaller fixed-price contracts the bid price had been slightly lower than the company's actual costs.

Until March, 1949, company officers estimated that from 70% to 80% of prime and subcontract work had been on a cost-plus-fixed-fee basis, but after that date the percentage of fixed-price contracts had increased until in September fixed-price contracts accounted for an estimated 90% of sales. The company was still very much interested in "cost-plus" contracts, especially development contracts which called for a large amount of the time of senior engineers and draftsmen. Cost-plus was also preferred because such contracts, according to company officers, involved lower estimating risks. Company bids had usually been in the lower 5% to 10% of those submitted, but Mr. Johnson stated that by August the range of bidding was beginning to narrow. Bids were being decided on the basis of a few dollars, and he believed some companies were bidding on the basis of direct costs alone.

The executives indicated that they were not interested in taking a job on which they could not make a profit. Mr. Johnson stated that up to September there had been no trouble, principally because ". . . We've got an engineering management that can do some cute tricks in the plant and get the stuff out."

PRODUCTS

The company's backlog of unfilled orders at the end of September was representative of orders to that time. Most of these were the result of personal visits and the reputations of Mr. Johnson and Mr. Brown. Both of the men had friends in the armed services and in various companies with whom they had worked during the war. In addition, a part-time representative who worked in behalf of the company in securing contracts was stationed at Wright Field. Another representative sold Instruments Incorporated abilities and products along with other noncompeting products to some industrial concerns in the Middle Atlantic area. A third representative was located in Washington, D.C. Sales by these men had not been large; indeed, up to September, sales expense had not been deemed large enough to justify its segregation from the general expense category.

In addition to production and development contract work for others,

Instruments Incorporated had in the early months begun development of its own commercial products, limiting itself to those requiring a small amount of funds to develop. A strain-gauge pressure transducer for measuring rapidly changing pressures had been invented and pat-ented by a faculty member of the Rensselaer Polytechnic Institute. Instruments Incorporated had developed the invention to the point where it could be placed on the market, and by March, 1949, began to promote its sale. Work on a complete line of pressure transducers,[2] a fluid flowmeter, and several small items, such as instrument relays and hydraulic valves, had been halted by the shortage of funds while they were still in the developmental stage. Mr. Johnson and Mr. Brown had personally observed the need for, or application of, these products over the period of their employment prior to coming to Instruments In-corporated, and Mr. Johnson believed each had a market in labora-tories, industries, and the military services.

The company's pressure transducer was reported by management to have technical qualities for precision measurement which surpassed competitive products. It consisted of: (1) a sensitive metal gauge, precision-machined, capable of translating engine pressures into an electrical signal; and (2) a compact and sensitive electronic amplifier capable of enlarging the signal for presentation on a Du Mont oscillo-scope. The company's price of $500 per unit did not include the oscillo-scope. Without the amplifier the unit price was $325.

The pressure transducer had been purchased in pilot quantities of one or two by such firms as Ethyl Corporation and General Motors (see Exhibit 7), both for laboratory work in analyzing the properties of fuels and engines and as an aid in engine production and tuning. A small advertising program was launched in July, 1949. In September, the instrument still presented production difficulties, and three or four had been returned. If the hardness of the steel in some of the parts varied, the established tolerances were not sufficient for proper opera-tion. One gauge had for unknown reasons cracked in operation. A problem of corrosion of some parts had been overcome by the com-pany, and work was being done to correct the other difficulties. Of-ficers stated that they believed it would be some time before sales of the instrument resulted in an over-all profit to the company and that, although it was sold on customer demand, sales should not be pushed until technical difficulties had been overcome. The instrument was first

---

[2] A device to give accurate pressure reading at a location other than where the pressure itself existed.

Exhibit 7

APPROXIMATE CHRONOLOGICAL SALES
RECORD OF PRESSURE TRANSDUCER
April 25 to September 30, 1949

Quantity	Customer	Accessories
1	General Electric Co.	(With amplifier)
1	General Electric Co.	
4	Pratt-Whitney Aircraft	(With amplifier)
1	Univ. of Michigan	(With amplifier)
1	Univ. of Michigan	
1	Nash Kelvinator	(With amplifier)
2	Ethyl Corporation*	(With amplifier)
2	E. I. Du Pont de Nemours	
1	U.S. Dept. of Interior† (Bureau of Mines)	
1	General Motors Corp.	(With amplifier)
1	General Motors Corp. (Electro Motors Division)	
1	U.S. Navy	
1	Mack Manufacturing Co.	(With amplifier)
3	Demonstrators	

* One of these was a replacement.
† Later replaced.

Source: Company records.

used in Rensselaer laboratories where it was observed by some of its subsequent purchasers. From the latter others learned of its characteristics. In August, 1949, Mr. Brown estimated total market for the pressure transducer at between 500 and 1,000, and believed several hundred could be sold annually. He believed the market was known and easily reached. He anticipated using direct-mail promotional material but believed the best and primary source of sales would be through "word of mouth." Mr. Brown stated that, lacking expensive market-research facilities, only very general estimates of market potential for company products could be determined. These estimates, however, he believed sufficiently accurate, and he explained further that a capable man who knew the product could generally tell whether it had an extensive, medium-size, or small market, and that from the company's standpoint, in view of its scale of operations, this was probably all that was necessary.

Mr. Johnson stated that, although none of the foregoing developments was likely to "mushroom into a mass market," collectively they could provide a sizable commercial business and a steady and profitable sales volume.

These items, however, were considered by the executives to be "specialty" products and of minor importance as compared with the possibilities of the company's plans in the field of automatic machine-tool controls. In the latter part of August, 1949, Mr. Johnson wrote: ". . . The economies of mass production under current high labor costs are such that automatic equipment which will produce a better product at a lower cost is extremely salable, leasable, or profitable to operate in a competitive market. The whole machine tool industry is aware of the potentialities in this direction. We have discussed some of our ideas and the control devices which we have in hand, with major tool manufacturers. These discussions have definitely outlined specific areas in which need for such developments is real and current. At the expense of losing our potential patent position, we could undoubtedly close a deal with some of these firms to finance our development costs. To date, we have not thought this desirable for obvious reasons. . . ."

In the latter part of 1948, Instruments Incorporated had bid on and received an order for the machining of a quantity of precision-instrument gears. This order offered an opportunity to study production techniques for this part and resulted in several new ideas for a basically different automatic precision gear cutter and new ideas for employing servo controls and precision positioning devices. Since Mr. Brown's and Mr. Johnson's ideas were more specific with regard to this machine, the company's entrance into the machine-tool field was planned by way of the development of such a gear cutter. Mr. Johnson stated that millions of dollars worth of such gears were produced yearly at high unit labor cost and that Instruments Incorporated contemplated building and operating the gear cutter since he believed the company had the subsidiary equipment and know-how to "make a dent in the gear market."

He anticipated that by the end of 1950 the company's own commercial specialty products, such as the pressure transducers, microrelays and flowmeters, would comprise 30% of total sales, the remainder coming from government contracts. He hoped that by the end of 1951 this percentage would have increased to 50% of total sales and that Instruments Incorporated would be well on its way into the production of new machine tools also.

FINANCE

Mr. Johnson stated that this projected rate of growth was dependent upon the funds available. For instance, if $30,000 were secured, only a modest development program could be undertaken, while if $500,000 became available, the company could immediately begin work in the machine-tool field.

Originally the company's financing had been solely through equity capital. To retain voting control in the hands of the two founders and to secure the funds necessary for operations, two classes of stock were authorized: (1) 10,000 shares of Class A nonvoting common at $20 par value and having preference on liquidation with regard to assets; (2) 5,000 shares of Class B voting common no par, issued at $20 per share. The first issue for 5,000 shares of Class A and 2,470 shares of Class B was not subscribed in full. Mr. Johnson and Mr. Brown each received 500 shares of Class B for services rendered in incorporating and were to receive 60 shares a year for a period of five years. In addition Mr. Johnson purchased 500 shares of Class B at $20 per share and Mr. Brown bought 100 shares of Class B at $20 per share with an option to purchase at the same price another 400 shares within a five-year period. Mr. Jones purchased 250 shares of Class B and was to receive 30 shares per year for a period of five years for services rendered in incorporating. By July, 1948, 2,430 shares of Class B stock had been issued to seven individuals, all either active in company management or intending to take an active part sometime in the future. By this time, 2,080 shares of Class A stock had been sold to 23 individuals, including all the holders of Common B with the exception of Mr. Johnson and Mr. Brown. Although no single individual held more than 250 shares of Class A, the family of one member of the board held the largest block. By April, 1949, this family held 650 shares.

Despite the efforts of the company executives between July, 1948, and April, 1949, only 320 more shares of Class A and no additional Class B stock had been sold. In addition to specific factors, such as changes in stock market quotations affecting potential investors, Mr. Johnson attributed this lag in equity financing to the fact that he was not a salesman. "I told investors the truth—that it was a long-term pull and they could not expect dividends for three or four years, but that we were in a field with unlimited opportunities." Mr. Johnson was further restricted in that both he and Mr. Brown wanted to know their stockholders. Several individuals expressed interest in investing sums large enough to dwarf contributions by other individual stockholders, but Mr. Johnson stated, "I do not want anyone who might try to finagle control when times get better."

When it became evident that sufficient funds would not be forthcoming through sale of stock, Mr. Johnson investigated the possibilities of debt financing. Actually, as sales and profits grew, he had become less inclined to sell stock at all. Banks and commercial credit institutions were willing to lend up to 80% of accounts receivable, but both requested, along with other requirements such as purchase by the company of accounts overdue by 30 days, the personal signatures of Mr. Johnson, Mr. Brown, and Mr. Jones. On this basis, however, the company refused to borrow and Mr. Johnson stated, "Of what benefit is the limited liability of a corporation under such circumstances?"

Preparations for a second attempt at negotiation with the RFC were abandoned in August, 1949, when a group of New York businessmen who had organized to invest in small businesses on a speculative basis sent a representative to the plant in response to an approach made by the company early in the year. The visit resulted in considerable interest on the part of this group in Instruments Incorporated, and in September Mr. Johnson was preparing a letter to them outlining the company's plans and a basis for financing. He was inclined to favor the typical method of financing employed by the group, which generally invested a relatively small amount, perhaps 5% to 20% of total funds furnished, in common stock and the rest in preferred stock, debentures, or notes. On this basis Mr. Johnson believed $100,000 should be considered, one-third to be used for working capital, one-third for fixed assets, and one-third for commercial development. Mr. Johnson was favorably impressed with this group of businessmen. He stated that advice and contacts provided by them might be well worth the price of the loan and that he would welcome one or two of the men as additions to his board of directors. This group had successfully backed several small companies, helping them to grow into sizable and profitable concerns.

STOCKHOLDERS AND DIRECTORS

Mr. Johnson believed that any sizable investment, whether through equity or debt, should be represented by a membership on the company's board of directors. The board was composed of Messrs. Johnson, Brown, and Robbins from the company and the following outside directors: Mr. Steven L. Leslie, president of a small textile-finishing company, trustee of the Committee for Economic Development, and president of the American Business Congress (formerly the Smaller Business Association for New York, New Jersey, and Connecticut, an association of several hundred small businesses in the area); Mr. Ralph Newman, associate counsel and auditor for the firm of Arthur Andersen & Co.; and Mr. Joseph McLennen, vice-president of the Fairfield County Trust Company of Stratford, Conn. This board had several times expressed confidence in the management by helping to furnish information and contacts necessary in carrying out policies decided upon by the company officers. In fact the board had left the direction of the company almost exclusively in the hands of its management, giving help only in the direction which the officers indicated they desired to take.

COMPETITION

Depending upon the product considered, Instruments Incorporated competed with a wide range of companies in several industries possessing diverse characteristics.

Electronic control devices for industry had their inception in the early thirties and prior to the war accounted for about $15,000,000 at factory prices, or about 5% of the total output of the electronics industry. During the postwar period the annual total industry average was about $1,000,000,000; 15% or $150,000,000 of this was accounted for by industrial control systems and allied devices. By 1944,[3] approximately 17,000 devices were reported in use by 796 industrial manufacturers, and about 8,500 of these were in use in the metalworking industry. Most important other users were metal-producing, chemical-processing, and electric-utility industries. Control devices and measuring and analysis instruments were by far the most important applications, accounting for about 6,000 instruments each. Companies competing for this business ranged from such firms as General Electric, Radio Corporation of America, Westinghouse and Raytheon, to smaller specialists such as Woodward Governor, or to smaller one- or two-man companies fostered by the war. Altogether there were about 500 companies capable of producing major electronic equipment and about 2,000 to 2,500 manufacturers of component parts. Not all of these were engaged in industrial work; in fact, most such companies manufactured communications equipment, but very few produced only one type of equipment. The war, however, had fostered a rapid trend toward vertical integration within the industry.

The metalworking industry was also marked by a large number of competing companies varying widely with regard to size. Major machine-tool companies such as Ex-Cell-O Corporation of Detroit, Heald of Worcester, Massachusetts, or Jones and Lamson of Springfield, Vermont, known for the design and manufacture of high-quality machine tools, in both standard and special-purpose types, obtained a large per-

---

[3] "Present and Potential Applications of Electronic Devices in Industry," Research Department, McGraw-Hill Publishing Company, Inc., 1944. Gordon K. Bell, Jr., "Electronics from War to Peace," *Industrial Record* (National Industrial Conference Board), Vol. V, No. 3 (April 30, 1946).

centage of their income from the machining and heat-treating of precision parts. These large companies (and others such as the Cincinnati
Milling Machine Company, Gisholt Machine Company, Brown &
Sharpe Manufacturing Company) maintained mechanical, metallurgical, and electronic engineering staffs sometimes numbering in the hundreds. In addition, in the Bridgeport area alone there were over 200
machine shops of varying capabilities. About 20% of the latter claimed
to qualify as experimental shops. Products such as gears for which extensive markets existed were manufactured not only by many of the
foregoing companies and many machinery and instrument manufacturers but by a sizable number of nationally advertised companies specializing in this product. Thus, there were approximately 10 manufacturers specializing in gear-cutting machinery about equally divided
geographically between the Midwest, Middle Atlantic, and New England areas and over 25 specialists in gear production. Approximately
50% of these companies were located in the Detroit-Chicago area, 30%
in the New York and Pennsylvania area, and 20% in New England.[4]

---

[4] *Thomas' Register of American Manufacturers* and *American Machinist*.

PART III

Organizing Administrative Personnel and Putting Plans into Action

Portland Company

In 1957 The Portland Company of Portland, Maine, was a leading producer of architectural porcelain enamel on metal products and industrial ceramic coatings. The product line was sold to a variety of industries and included ceramic-on-steel bathroom tiles, gas station signs, ceramic coatings for jet engine parts, and monumental building wall panels. Pictures of the products are shown in Exhibit 1.

The company was founded in 1919 and until 1947 remained a small job shop subcontractor of porcelainized sheet metal and cast iron products, producing principally stove parts for a single customer. The company did not solicit war contracts nor expand during World War II; it lost money in 1941, 1942, 1944, and 1945 before hitting its first sales peak in 1946 with $326,000 sales and $19,000 profit after taxes.

In 1947 Mr. Robert A. Black took over the control and presidency of Portland, brought in a new management team, and embarked on a 10-year expansion program. From 1947 to 1952 all effort was devoted to developing people and products; from 1952 to 1955 the emphasis shifted to plant development; and from 1955 to 1956 concentration was on production and profit.

During the second phase of its 10-year program, Portland expanded in three stages into what the president termed "the Portland Family of Companies" (see organization chart, Exhibit 2):

1. Portland acquired three subsidiary corporations. In 1947 Portland had received 51% of the stock from the Lisbon Porcelain Company, Lisbon Falls, Maine, in exchange for technical services. In 1952 the company bought 100% of the capital stock of the Detroit Porcelain Company, Detroit, Michigan, for $68,000 in Portland common stock and $184,450 in cash. In addition, Detroit stockholders were given warrants representing rights to buy 8,500 shares of Portland common stock at $5 a share between August 1, 1953, and July 31, 1955. In 1953 Portland made a 25-year royalty and technical-fee agreement with the Dana Company, Toronto, Canada. Dana received technical advice for which it agreed to pay royalties ranging from 2% to 10% on all products sold, plus a $1,000 monthly fee. After the Toronto plant

Exhibit 1

PORTLAND COMPANY

Pictures, Sales, and Expected Profit of Portland Products, 1953–56

Markets and Principal Products	Pictures of Principal Products	Portland Sales (thousands)				Expected Profit
		1953	1954	1955	1956	
I. Architectural:		*All Sales to Monumental Building Field*				
1. Curtain wall panels for the the monumental building field	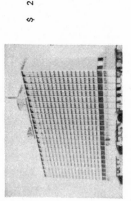	$ 232 11.7%	$ 528 26.3%	$ 706 34.8%	$ 926 32.0%	20%
2. Ceramic-coated magnetic steel chalkboard for the school field		*Chalkboard Sales Only*				
		$ 172 8.7%	$ 120 6.0%	$ 278 13.7%	$ 363 12.5%	25%

Source: Company records.

$ 420   14.5%   20%

Tile made only at Lisbon, which became wholly owned in 1956; 1955 tile sales were $286,000

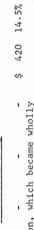

3. Ceramic-on-steel wall tile for the the home field

Roofing Sales Only

$ 90   4.5% $ 49   2.4% $ 64   3.2% $ 75   2.6%   33%

4. Porcelainized corrugated steel roofing and siding materials for the industrial field

Exhibit 1—Continued

PORTLAND COMPANY

Sales of All Miscellaneous Architectural Products

5. Fireproof, cement-coated honeycomb paper cores for curtain wall panels - principal miscellaneous product

$ 17	0.9%	$ 14	0.7%	$ 15	0.7%	$ 22	0.8%	25%

Total Architectural Sales

| $ 511 | 25.8% | $ 711 | 35.4% | $ 1,063 | 52.4% | $ 1,806 | 62.4% | |

All Industrial Ceramic Coating Sales

II. Industrial ceramic coatings. These coatings had a variety of applications, including jet engine parts (shown)

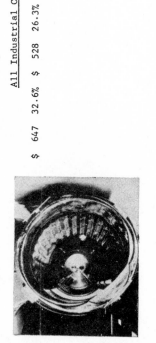

| $ 647 | 32.6% | $ 528 | 26.3% | $ 154 | 7.6% | $ 84 | 2.9% | 30% |

Sales of Signs Only

III. Miscellaneous Products. Principal items were signs (shown) and bathtubs for trailers

| $ 154 | 7.7% | 67 | 3.3% | $ 53 | 2.6% | $ 139 | 4.8% | 25% |

Other Sales

| $ 673 | 33.9% | $ 692 | 34.5% | $ 693 | 34.1% | $ 741 | 25.6% | 25% |

Royalties

| - | - | $ 10 | 0.5% | $ 67 | 3.3% | $ 125 | 4.3% | 25% |

Total Sales

| $ 1,985 | 100% | $ 2,008 | 100% | | 100% | $ 2,030 | 100% | |

burned down in 1954, Portland helped arrange a public stock offering and received 18% of the common stock through a stock exchange; Portland gave 50 shares with a market value of $250 for 50,000 shares of Dana common with a market value of $125,000. In addition, Dana stockholders assigned voting rights to Portland for 56% of their stock for 10 years.

Exhibit 2

PORTLAND COMPANY

The Portland Family of Companies—Organization Chart, 1957

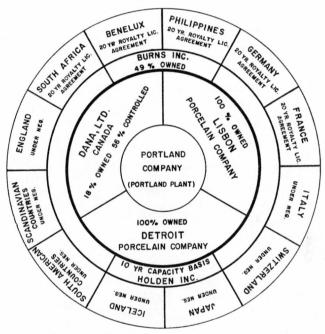

Source: Company records.

2. Portland became associated with two small corporations. In 1954 it gave technical advice and $100 to Burns, Inc., Putney, Vermont, makers of insulating cores for building wall panels, and received a 49% ownership interest in return. It also obtained exclusive rights for 10 years to the production capacity of Holden, Inc., Dover, Massachusetts, which was to make porcelain enamel on aluminum products.

3. Portland licensed foreign manufacturers to make and sell its products. Beginning in 1955, Portland granted 20-year exclusive license agreements; the terms were similar to those in the agreement with

Dana and included an initial fee, a monthly technical fee, and royalties on sales. Agreements had been made with five companies by 1957. Mr. Black pointed out that the arrangements with Holden and foreign companies permitted Portland to enter new fields without capital investment.

During the expansion program sales increased 7.5 times from 1947 to $2.9 million; net profits grew nine times to $87,000; total assets increased 11 times to $2.5 million; and net worth multiplied 49-fold to $1.2 million. Net profit generation over this period was only $96,-108; most of the expansion was financed with outside public stock issues and loans. Balance sheets and income statements for years 1947 to 1956 are shown in Exhibits 3 and 4.

In February, 1957, the president, Mr. Black, planned future expansion. He was preparing to take three important steps: privately place $350,000 in debentures and $140,000 in common stock; rent a new plant in a projected industrial park or buy an abandoned wool mill; and consolidate company stationery with one letterhead, listing the Detroit, Lisbon, and Dana plants as divisions for the first time and containing the words "Portland International Family of Companies— World Leaders in Ceramic-on-Metal Products." The change in the stationery was in recognition of the consolidation of the subsidiaries with the parent company and to facilitate customer identification of the members of the Portland family of companies.

PRODUCT LINE

Porcelain enamel, which is essentially a glass surface fused to a metal base, is resistant to acid, abrasion, corrosion, heat and shock, and is flexible as to color and texture. Mr. Black pointed out that such properties made hosts of household, architectural, and industrial applications attractive possibilities, but until World War I porcelain enamel had been used primarily for kitchenware, hospital equipment, and signs. Architectural sheets had been produced in the middle 1920's, and the first all-porcelain White Tower restaurant was built in 1928. According to Mr. Black, the industry did not exploit the possibilities of the process until after World War II.

The production of porcelain enamel products was in four main steps: product fabrication, pickling, spraying, and baking. (1) Most of the items produced by the Portland plant were made in its sheet metal shop, but about 2% of the dollar volume was delivered prefabricated and ready for pickling. (2) Pickling solutions removed foreign material from the products and etched a surface to insure adherence of the coating material. (3) The parts were sprayed with or dipped in porcelain enamel which was a mixture of "frit," a gravel-like glass, and clay, fluxes, colored metallic oxides, and water. Frit manufacturers, including Mr. Black's father, supplied mix formulas. (4) The parts were baked at about 1,500 degrees in two box-type oil-fired furnaces. At this temperature the enamel became cherry red and was fused to the metal; the result was a smooth, glass-like surface. Steps three and four were sometimes repeated two or three times to obtain certain textures and colors.

Portland manufactured three basic types of porcelain enamel products: architectural, industrial ceramic coatings, and miscellaneous items.

Architectural products were used in five major ways:

1. Monumental building field: Office buildings, hotels, theaters, hospitals, and municipal buildings were included in this category. Portland's major product was curtain wall panels which stretched from floor to window sill and from the top of the window to the ceiling. The panel consisted of two sheets of porcelainized enamel steel with an insulating core of cement-coated paper sandwiched between them. It became both the exterior and interior wall of a building. Mr. Black said Portland pioneered the panel field with the Administration Building of the General Motors Technical Center, Warren, Michigan, and was the recognized leader. He added that Portland had yet to solve problems of strict building codes which required fireproof laminating material. Other products for monumental buildings included window sills, louvered panels, and sculptured murals. Portland sometimes took charge of all or part of the installation of products or hired local contractors.

2. School field: Schools used the same products as monumental buildings. In addition, Portland manufactured a magnetic, ceramic-coated steel chalkboard with a plywood backing. It was manufactured in various standard sizes and was guaranteed for the life of the building in which it was installed. United States Plywood Corporation laminated the board to plywood and was the sole marketing agent under a license which expired in 1957.

3. Home field: The Lisbon plant manufactured two types of steel wall tiles. One was a porcelain-on-steel tile, installed by fitting it into a slotted foundation board. Another, introduced in February, 1956, was a lighter, cheaper, ceramic-on-steel tile, installed on any flat surface with a special adhesive. Mr. Black said both tiles would not craze,

Exhibit 3

PORTLAND COMPANY

Comparative Balance Sheets for Fiscal Years Ending December 31, 1947–56

Assets	1947	1948	1949	1950	1951	1952	1953	1954	1955	1956
Current Assets:										
Cash	$ 2,608	$ 3,303	$ 3,092	$ 3,501	$ 15,160	$ 43,702	$ 85,349	$ 36,218	$ 92,911	$ 155,890
Notes and Accounts Receivable	41,003	93,877	80,274	137,508	133,292	170,970	154,242	316,055	303,500	532,772
Inventories	40,096	52,439	47,293	108,343	124,507	202,192	222,963	276,464	337,340	555,003
Prepaid Expenses		2,799	16,104	5,603	11,615	18,829	12,973	12,337	18,393	54,598
Income Tax Claims	2,308	9,929	4,556						58,907	
Total Current Assets	$ 86,015	$162,347	$152,320	$254,955	$284,574	$435,693	$475,527	$641,074	$811,060	$1,298,263
Investments:										
Investments in Subsidiaries		$ 2,856	$ 16,711	$ 33,543	$ 34,858	$ 31,300	$ 38,800	$ 41,000	$ 41,350	$ 2,850
Notes and Accounts Receivable from Subsidiaries						15,565	103,650	134,061	167,371	20,154
Total Investments		$ 2,856	$ 16,711	$ 33,543	$ 34,858	$ 46,865	$142,450	$175,411	$208,721	$ 23,004
Fixed Assets:*										
Land and Building	$100,001	$ 94,601	$111,965	$111,965	$132,846	$296,952	$303,836	$298,515	$301,506	$567,117
Machinery and Equipment	45,795	44,140	58,977	133,489	132,471	284,711	301,836	316,373	318,829	749,696
Furniture and Fixtures	1,753	2,819	3,710	6,408	6,970	15,332	16,393	19,781	15,393	23,630
Automobiles	1,621	3,653	1,621	4,015	4,443	4,442				5,384
Total Fixed Assets (Gross)	$149,170	$145,213	$176,273	$255,877	$276,730	$601,437	$622,065	$634,669	$635,728	$1,345,827
Less Accumulated Depreciation	18,898		41,183	55,637	68,503	179,831	207,595	237,327	268,927	384,387
Total Fixed Assets (Net)	$130,272	$145,213	$135,090	$200,240	$208,227	$421,606	$414,470	$397,342	$366,801	$961,440
Other Assets:										
Goodwill from Consolidation	$	$	$	$	$	$	$	$	$	$ 127,211
Deferred Sales Expense	1,722			23,340	17,233	14,279	7,925	13,119	15,209	14,825
Life Insurance			1,078	375	2,215	4,458	7,723	10,413	13,186	15,979
Recapitalization Expense			2,713	2,739	2,199	1,659	1,119	579	39	348
Deferred R & D Expense								35,940	29,002	86,017
Total Other Assets	$ 1,722	$	$ 3,791	$ 26,454	$ 21,647	$ 20,846	$ 16,767	$ 60,051	$ 57,436	$ 117,169
Total Assets	$218,009	$310,416	$307,912	$515,192	$549,306	$925,010	$1,049,214	$1,273,878	$1,444,018	$2,527,087

Liabilities and Net Worth

Current Liabilities:									
Mortgage Due and Notes Payable	$ 17,032	$ 45,788	$113,119	$ 35,490	$ 46,063	$ 39,263	$ 56,157	$104,500	$ 341,219
Accounts Payable	37,370	55,302	116,788	51,341	79,842	81,895	279,452	263,013	497,314
Accrued Expenses	12,068	12,328	20,427	23,552	41,464	56,759	75,472	86,756	136,246
Employees' Retirement Fund	6,744			5,357	8,159	18,868	14,639	1,216	18,965
Reserve for Income Taxes	4,354	7,161	1,706	19,994	35,775	47,649	48,926		12,480
Due to Officers	2,930	1,874							
Unearned Technical Service Fees								29,500	
Total Current Liabilities	$ 73,754	$122,453	$252,040	$135,734	$211,303	$244,434	$474,646	$484,985	$1,006,224
Long-Term Notes and Mortgages	$119,373	$134,135	$105,876	$ 90,175	$ 93,767	$159,504	$124,500	$234,250	$ 272,972
Minority Interest (5% Preferred)					28,000	28,000	28,000	28,000	28,000
Net Worth:									
7% Cumulative Preferred	32,400	40,400	40,400						
Common Stock	17,838	17,838	44,883	100,000	175,000	175,000	175,610	212,307	220,302
Capital Surplus	(23,331)	8,873	33,054	134,100	327,863	327,863	330,303	477,091	509,071
Appraisal Surplus			63,232	54,832	46,432	38,032	29,632	21,232	422,756
Earned Surplus	(2,025)	(6,641)	16,107	34,465	42,645	76,381	111,187	(13,847)	67,762
Treasury Stock	10,292	(31,403)							
	(31,403)	(31,403)							
	$ 29,067								
Total Net Worth	$ 24,882	$ 46,000	$157,276	$323,397	$591,940	$617,276	$646,732	$696,783	$1,219,891
Total Liabilities and Net Worth	$218,009	$310,416	$515,192	$549,306	$925,010	$1,049,214	$1,273,878	$1,444,018	$2,527,087

* Fixed assets were carried at cost except on the bases of independent appraisals: $67,507 in machinery and equipment entered on the books on April 30, 1950; $117,397 in all fixed assets except land and automobiles entered on the books on December 31, 1952; and $409,920 in all fixed assets except land and automobiles entered on the books on December 31, 1956.

NOTE: The 1952 and subsequent consolidated balance sheets included the Detroit subsidiary while the 1956 statement included both the Detroit and Lisbon subsidiaries.

Exhibit 3a

PORTLAND COMPANY

Balance Sheet Analysis—Percentages

Assets	1947	1948	1949	1950	1951	1952	1953	1954	1955	1956
Current Assets:										
Cash	1.2	1.1	1.3	0.7	2.7	4.7	8.1	2.8	6.4	6.2
Notes and Accounts Receivable	18.8	30.2	26.1	26.7	24.3	18.5	14.7	24.8	21.0	21.1
Inventories	18.4	16.9	15.4	21.0	22.7	21.9	21.3	21.7	23.4	22.0
Prepaid Expenses		0.9	5.2	1.1	2.1	2.0	1.2	1.0	1.3	2.1
Income Tax Claims	1.1	3.2	1.5						4.1	
Total Current Assets	39.5	52.3	49.5	49.5	51.8	47.1	45.3	50.3	56.2	51.4
Investments:										
Investments in Subsidiaries		0.9	5.4	6.5	6.4	3.4	3.7	3.2	2.8	0.1
Notes and Accounts Receivable from Subsidiaries						1.7	9.9	10.6	11.6	0.8
Total Investments		0.9	5.4	6.5	6.4	5.1	13.6	13.8	14.4	0.9
Fixed Assets:										
Land and Buildings	45.9	30.5	36.4	21.7	24.2	32.1	29.0	23.4	20.9	22.5
Machinery and Equipment	21.0	14.2	19.2	25.9	24.1	30.8	28.8	24.8	22.1	29.7
Furniture and Fixtures	0.8	0.9	1.2	1.3	1.3	1.6	1.5	1.6	1.0	0.9
Automobiles	0.7	1.2	0.5	0.8	0.8	0.5				0.2
Total Fixed Assets (Gross)	68.4	46.8	57.3	49.7	50.4	65.0	59.3	49.8	44.0	53.3
Less Accumulated Depreciation	8.7		13.4	10.8	12.5	19.4	19.8	18.6	18.6	15.2
Total Fixed Assets (Net)	59.7	46.8	43.9	38.9	37.9	45.6	39.5	31.2	25.4	38.1
Other Assets:										
Goodwill from Consolidation	0.8									5.0
Deferred Sales Expense			0.3	4.5	3.1	1.6	0.8	1.0	1.1	0.6
Life Insurance			0.9	0.1	0.4	0.5	0.7	0.8	0.9	0.6
Recapitalization Expense				0.5	0.4	0.1	0.1	0.1	0.0	
Deferred R & D Expense								2.8	2.0	3.4
Total Other Assets	0.8		1.2	5.1	3.9	2.2	1.6	4.7	4.0	9.6
Total Assets	100.0	100.0	100.0	100.0	100.0	100.0	100.0	100.0	100.0	100.0

Liabilities and Net Worth

Current Liabilities:										
Mortgage Due and Notes Payable	7.8	9.6	14.9	21.9	6.5	5.0	3.8	4.4	7.2	13.5
Accounts Payable	17.1	24.8	18.0	22.7	9.3	8.6	7.8	21.9	18.2	19.6
Accrued Expenses	5.5	3.8	4.0	4.0	4.3	4.5	5.4	5.9	6.0	5.4
Employees' Retirement Fund		2.2			1.0	0.9	1.8	1.2	0.1	0.8
Reserve for Income Taxes	2.0	1.4	2.3	0.3	3.6	3.9	4.5	3.9		0.5
Due to Officers	1.4	0.2	0.6							
Unearned Technical Service Fees									2.1	
Total Current Liabilities	33.8	42.0	39.8	48.9	24.7	22.9	23.3	37.3	33.6	39.8
Long-Term Notes and Mortgages	54.8	43.2	50.8	20.6	16.4	10.1	15.2	9.8	16.2	10.8
Minority Interest (5% Preferred)						3.0	2.7	2.2	1.9	1.1
Net Worth:										
7% Cumulative Preferred	14.8	13.0	13.1	8.7	18.2	18.9	16.7	13.8	14.7	8.7
Common Stock	8.2	5.7	5.8	6.4	24.4	35.5	31.2	25.9	33.0	20.2
Capital Surplus	(10.7)	2.9	2.9	12.3	10.0	5.0	3.6	2.3	1.5	16.7
Appraisal Surplus			(2.2)							
Earned Surplus	(0.9)	3.3	(10.2)	3.1	6.3	4.6	7.3	8.7	(0.9)	2.7
Treasury Stock		(10.1)								
Total Net Worth	11.4	14.8	9.4	30.5	58.9	64.0	58.8	50.7	48.3	48.3
Total Liabilities and Net Worth	100.0	100.0	100.0	100.0	100.0	100.0	100.0	100.0	100.0	100.0

Source: Prepared from Exhibit 3 by Harvard Business School staff.

Exhibit 4

PORTLAND COMPANY

Comparative Statements of Profit or Loss for Fiscal Years Ending December 31, 1947–56

	1947	1948	1949	1950	1951	1952	1953	1954	1955	1956
Net sales	$387,873	$574,595	$605,712	$742,271	$1,055,955	$1,215,373	$1,985,179	$2,007,522	$2,029,752	$2,894,657
Cost of goods sold	304,644	458,379	503,261	620,314	844,406	966,857	1,616,067	1,642,684	1,910,336	2,428,124
Depreciation	5,490	9,211	9,899	14,454	11,197	20,491	25,603	26,382	27,814	115,480
Gross profit	$ 83,229	$116,216	$102,451	$122,456	$ 211,549	$ 248,516	$ 369,112	$ 364,838	$ 119,416	$ 466,533
Selling and administrative expense	$ 61,430	$ 89,691	$110,120	$108,052	$ 152,895	$ 182,891	$ 266,436	$ 281,908	$ 314,514	$ 382,951
Operating profit	21,798	26,524	(7,670)	14,404	58,654	65,625	102,676	82,930	(195,098)	83,582
Deductions	10,301	9,266	13,820	12,885	19,298	9,205	13,267	5,251	(7,330)	(15,500)
Net profit before taxes	11,497	17,258	(21,490)	1,519	39,356	56,420	89,409	77,679	(187,768)	99,082
Federal income taxes	1,700	4,345	......	1,300	20,000	36,216	47,500	34,700	(70,907)	12,000
Net profit	$ 9,797	$ 12,913	$(21,490)	$ 219	$ 19,356	$ 20,204	$ 41,909	$ 42,979	$(116,861)	$ 87,082

Percentage Analysis

	1947	1948	1949	1950	1951	1952	1953	1954	1955	1956
Net sales	100.0	100.0	100.0	100.0	100.0	100.0	100.0	100.0	100.0	100.0
Cost of goods sold	78.5	79.8	83.1	83.5	80.0	79.6	81.4	81.8	94.1	83.9
Depreciation	1.4	1.6	1.6	1.9	1.1	1.7	1.3	1.3	1.4	4.0
Gross profit	21.5	20.2	16.9	16.5	20.0	20.4	18.6	18.2	5.9	16.1
Selling and administrative expense	15.9	15.6	18.2	14.6	14.5	15.0	13.4	14.1	15.5	13.2
Operating profit	5.6	4.6	(1.3)	1.9	5.5	5.4	5.2	4.1	(9.6)	2.9
Deductions	2.7	1.6	2.3	1.7	1.8	0.8	0.7	0.3	(0.4)	(0.5)
Net profit before taxes	2.9	3.0	(3.6)	0.2	3.7	4.6	4.5	3.8	(9.2)	3.4
Federal income taxes	0.4	0.8	...	0.2	1.9	3.0	2.4	1.7	0	0.4
Net profit	2.5	2.2	(3.6)	0	1.8	1.6	2.1	2.1	(5.8)	3.0

NOTE: The operating results of the Detroit subsidiary, subsequent to its acquisition in June, 1952, were included in the consolidated profit and loss statements. The operating results of the Lisbon subsidiary for 1956 were included in the consolidated 1956 statement.

Source: Company records.

Exhibit 4a

PORTLAND COMPANY

Selected Balance Sheet and Operating Ratios

		1947	1948	1949	1950	1951	1952	1953	1954	1955	1956
(R)	Current ratio	1.2	1.2	1.2	1.0	2.1	2.1	1.9	1.3	1.7	1.3
($)	Net working capital	12,261.0	32,066.0	29,900.0	2,900.0	148,800.0	224,400.0	231,100.0	166,400.0	326,100.0	292,039.0
(R)	Acid test ratio	0.6	0.8	0.9	0.6	1.2	1.1	1.0	0.8	1.0	0.7
(%)	Current assets to total assets	39.5	52.3	49.0	49.0	52.0	47.0	45.0	50.0	56.0	51.4
(%)	Total fixed assets to total assets	59.8	46.8	44.0	39.0	38.0	46.0	40.0	31.0	25.0	38.0
(R)	Net worth to debt	12.9	17.4	0.1	0.4	1.4	1.8	1.4	1.0	0.9	93.3
(%)	Net worth to total assets	11.4	14.8	9.0	31.0	59.0	64.0	59.0	51.0	48.0	48.0
(days)	Receivables turnover*	38	59	48	67	45	51	28	57	54	66
(days)	Inventory turnover†		36	36	45	50	61	47	55	58	66
(%)	Total assets to net sales	56.2	54.0	51.0	69.0	52.0	76.0	53.0	63.0	71.0	87.3
(%)	Fixed assets to net sales	33.6	25.2	22.0	27.0	20.0	35.0	21.0	20.0	18.0	33.2
(%)	Operating profit to net worth	87.6	57.66	(26.4)	9.2	18.1	11.1	16.6	12.8	(28.0)	6.9
(%)	Net profit to net worth	39.4	28.07	(73.9)	0.1	6.0	3.4	6.8	6.6	(16.8)	7.1

* Accounts receivable $\times$ 360/net sales.
† Average inventory $\times$ 360/cost of goods sold.
Source: Prepared from Exhibits 3 and 4 by Harvard Business School staff.

crack, or change color; were resistant to heat, moisture, chemicals, and other corrosive elements; and were lighter in weight and cheaper to install than ordinary clay tiles. Comparative prices per square foot were: clay tiles, 63 cents; ceramic-on-steel tiles, 48 cents; and plastic tiles, 38 cents.

4. Industrial field: Portland's principal product was ceramic-coated corrugated steel roofing and siding material, made at Detroit. It had resistance to extreme atmospheric conditions, gases, fumes, moisture, smoke, and other corrosive elements.

5. Miscellaneous: These products included outdoor movie screen panels, window sills, escalator step risers, covering for church steeples, and the fireproof cement-coated honeycomb core used for insulating and stiffening curtain wall panels.

Industrial ceramic coatings, Portland's second basic type of product, had a variety of applications. High-temperature coatings extended the heat range of metals, provided resistance to corrosion or erosion by gases, and allowed low-grade metals to be substituted for high-grade ones. In 1957 these coatings were principally used for aircraft jet engine parts, but Portland was concentrating on increasing the use of ceramic coatings on automotive and marine mufflers, exhaust systems, and industrial furnaces. Mr. Black said Portland could coat a $500 turbo-supercharger part for $50 and extend its life two to three times. He hoped to expand into the field of atomic energy by coating reactor linings; in 1956 the company hired an atomic scientist as a part-time department manager. Portland also produced miscellaneous industrial products such as chemical tanks and oil refining equipment where protection from acid and heat corrosion was needed.

Miscellaneous products were similar to other Portland products but did not fall into the company's long-range product program. The principal items were signs, distributed nationally by a sign company. Other products included gas station fronts, fireplaces, commercial baking oven panels, home trailer bathtubs, and conventional porcelain enamel items.

Mr. Black had a basic product philosophy. Portland should (1) enter only expanding fields with large market potential even if the company's percentage share were small, (2) diversify into several markets in hopes of avoiding the cyclical fluctuations of any one of them, and (3) try to have products in every major segment of the markets entered. "We didn't have a product for the home, so we worked hard and finally found the steel wall tiles," he said in 1956. In explaining his product philosophy, he said:

> We've either got to have a product that's different or be the leaders and so carve a niche for ourselves. We definitely stay away from products which the big companies can produce better. Any product we take on must be one that will fit our equipment or experience; however, we don't turn away business if we need business. We produce bathtubs for trailers but we're emphasizing the bathtub business, and we'll gradually ease out as we did the original stove parts business. Movie screens are another example. They seem a foolish sort of thing for us to do, but they are made and erected the same way as our curtain wall panels. The only trouble is that it costs money to finance a broad product line.

COMPETITION

Portland had started in the competitive porcelain enameling business, but on broadening into the field of ceramic coatings on metal the company had produced some products for which there was little or no direct competition. Mr. Black said that for such products as the steel wall tile, the honeycomb cores, and the ceramic-coated corrugated roofing and siding material there was little competition from other companies making the same product line. Other items, such as chalkboard or high-temperature coatings, had limited direct competition. Portland was the established leader in architectural ceramic-coated products; however, some of the company's miscellaneous products, such as signs, encountered heavy competition from companies having equal advantages.

In 1956 there were approximately 238 porcelain enameling companies in the United States competing in an industry which had nearly doubled over the previous 10 years (see Exhibit 5). Mr. Black noted that this growth had occurred despite competition from a variety of materials, including aluminum, stainless steel, and plastics. He said that sales of major appliances and housing and industrial construction were indicators for forecasting that he watched carefully. These are graphed in Exhibits 6 and 6a for 1946 through 1956.

The size of porcelain enameling companies varied from organizations such as General Motors and General Electric, that maintained plants for enameling their household appliances, to one-man shops making porcelain enamel jewelry. There were 62 appliance manufacturers with porcelain enameling facilities, 87 specialty manufacturers, 14 companies producing oddities, and 75 porcelain enamel job shops.[1] Of

---

[1] *Thomas' Register of American Manufacturers.*

Exhibit 5

PORTLAND COMPANY

Sales of Porcelain Enamel Parts, 1953–56

(Millions of Dollars)

Porcelain Enamel	1953	1954	1955	1956
Household appliances (ranges, refrigerators, washers, dryers, etc.)	$191	$182	$210	$218
Architectural products	25	28	48	60
Other building products (plumbing fixtures, hot water tanks, signs, etc.)	79	82	88	90
Industrial equipment	32	29	32	36
Cooking utensils and hospitalware	28	28	29	30
Jobbing and miscellaneous	29	27	33	34
Total	$384	$376	$440	$468

Early in 1957 The Porcelain Enamel Institute, a trade association, estimated the industry's 1957 total dollar volume would approach $500 million, with architectural products reaching $66 or $67 million. These estimates were a revision of an early 1956 forecast that predicted 1960 total volume at $488 million and architectural products at $50 million.

Source: Published reports and news releases of the Porcelain Enamel Institute. Reprinted by permission.

the 87 specialty manufacturers 29 produced signs only, 28 made sanitary ware, 12 made reflectors, 11 produced glass tanks, and 7 manufactured hospital equipment and kitchenware. Some job shops, such as Portland, offered varied products but many tended to concentrate in one or more areas as shown in the following table:

Product	*Number of Shops*
Signs	47
Architectural	40
Stoves	18
Ceramic coatings	13
Sanitary ware	10
Refrigerator panels	9
Glass-lined tanks	9
Kitchenware	7
Wall tile	6
Laundry equipment panels	6

The industry was geographically concentrated with 46% of the manufacturers located in three states: Illinois, Ohio, and Pennsylvania. In New England there were approximately 17 porcelain enameling plants of which four were job shops, and of these three were included in the Portland family. Mr. Black said, "The small number of plants in New England is a competitive advantage for Portland, since shipping costs usually prevent competition outside a seven- or eight-hundred-mile radius of the plant location." He added that this was not

Exhibit 6

PORTLAND COMPANY

Factory Sales of Major Appliances, 1946–56

(Thousands of Units)

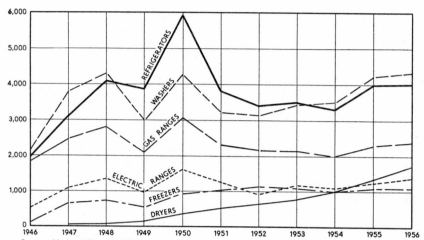

Sources: National Electrical Manufacturers Association; Gas Appliance Manufacturers Association; American Washer & Ironer Manufacturers Association.

Exhibit 6a

PORTLAND COMPANY

Building Construction, 1946–56

(Millions of Dollars)

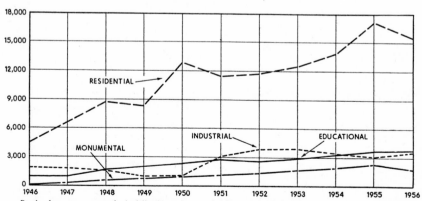

Portland management made the following estimates of market potentials based on past experience and published data: The dollar value of curtain wall panels averaged 3% of total monumental building construction and 6% of school construction. Each school classroom required about $125 of chalkboards; there were an estimated 500,000 new classrooms needed within five years, and an equal number would require replacement boards. The dollar value of tiles averaged 0.66% of residential construction, while the dollar value of corrugated roofing and siding material was about 16.6% of industrial building construction.

Source: U.S. Department of Commerce; Statistical Abstract of the United States; company records.

always the case, since Portland supplied panels for a bank building in St. Louis, but here design and service were considered before price.

Despite the industry's growth, many companies were unprofitable. Mr. Black said that a Porcelain Enamel Institute study of its architectural division members revealed that in 1955, 40% of the companies lost money, 30% broke even, and 30% made a profit. He explained that the losses were due largely to the inexperience of a new manufacturer in construction bidding and running a business and not to lack of volume. Mr. Black said others thought their industry suffered from overcapacity and believed losses resulted from competing with (1) companies specializing in one or two products, (2) large firms wanting jobs in slack periods to help cover overhead, and (3) companies trying to gain prestige by submitting low bids for jobs outside their geographic area. Pricing methods were discussed at an industry seminar held at Ohio State University in June, 1956, but Mr. Black noted no significant improvements in the situation.

ORGANIZATION

In 1957 Mr. Black described the home office, located at the Portland plant, as a co-ordination and development center and himself and his fellow officers as a consulting group for the rest of the Portland family of companies. He stressed that instead of having a tiered form of organization with one level reporting to the next the Portland companies were grouped in a circle with the Portland plant as the hub (see Exhibit 2). They were all interrelated. Mr. Black explained:

> The narrow band represents a catalyst of ideas that flow in both directions between the affiliates and licensees and the companies we run. None of the companies have to go through us; rather, they can contact any of the others directly. The Portland plant has become a pilot plant for testing and improving processes, and we provide a constant flow of information to the other companies. We will always have this form of organization because we feel that Portland will always be a developmental company in addition to being a large and—we hope—profitable producer.

Similarly, Mr. Black tried to create an atmosphere of teamwork and flexibility within the Portland plant with his "crossways" organization. He said:

> A chart-type organization gets in the way just when you need your employee talent the most, especially for a fast-growing company like ours. Whenever abilities are needed on a problem we work crossways, not up and down, to get the maximum value out of the talents we have in the company. Nobody's nose gets

out of joint, and a lot of people grow up in the process. It's a natural way to help them. As a result—and this may sound trite, but it's true—we have a team company.

An example of how management worked is given in Exhibit 7.

Exhibit 7

PORTLAND COMPANY

Promotion of Coffee Tables with Porcelain Enamel Tops

On the afternoon of March 25, 1957, Mr. and Mrs. Herbert N. Carter, Portland's full-time artists, dropped in to show Mr. Black a coffee table; the top was a mural of enamel. During the ensuing conversation about the importance of artists to business, it developed that Mr. Carter was going to give a speech at the Artists Equity Convention, Washington, D.C., on March 28.

BLACK: I'll call Koerper & Koerper, our public relations firm, and tell them to pick this up and make something of it. Maybe Herb could meet Bill Koerper on the way to the convention. Of course, we've got to get a release out ahead of the speech.

FOWLER (*who just entered*): Bill must have known about the convention, and maybe he's planning something.

BLACK: They'll need to have something for a news item.

CARTER: I could stop at a gas station outside New York and dictate my speech to Bill.

FOWLER: When are you leaving?

CARTER: Thursday morning.

FOWLER: Couldn't you get something about the speech in the mail to K & K before then?

CARTER: Perhaps, but I've got to work on my murals.

BLACK: How do you like the table, Nat?

FOWLER: Very nice. I am just preparing a price for 300 of them.

BLACK: Has a hotel chain asked for one of them?

FOWLER: No, but we've been asked to quote on lots up to 300.

BLACK: I think we've really developed something. The Sheraton people seem really interested. (*Portland had redecorated a Sheraton hotel room using porcelain-enameled furniture and thrown a party for Sheraton executives.*) We ought to get Fred Hannon in here, but before we do my feeling would be to have the tables made at Lisbon; they need the business and are going to concentrate on such jobbing.

FOWLER: Good point. (*Mr. Hannon entered.*)

BLACK: Don't mean to bother you, Fred, but Nat's been working on these tables with Sheraton Hotels, Tish Hotels, Schine Hotels, and Hotel Corporation of America. Nat is preparing a bid on 300 tables, and the Carters want to talk about producing them.

Exhibit 7—Continued

HANNON: I'll talk to Bob Wood (*a Portland plant foreman*).

BLACK: But wouldn't it be better to make them at Lisbon?

HANNON: If it's a matter of 300, we could do them at both plants.

FOWLER: You wouldn't get all 300 at once.

HANNON: If we did it at Lisbon, we would still have to do some here.

FOWLER: Only when we're experimenting.

HANNON: Lisbon needs the work badly.

BLACK: They'll be damn interested in lots of 300.

The telephone rang, and, while Mr. Black talked with Mr. Bill Koerper, Mr. Hannon discussed production plans with the Carters and then left to make arrangements with the Lisbon plant.

BLACK (*on the telephone*): . . . We were discussing this convention, and it looked as if there might be something of a "news hook" along a prediction line —you know, something to the effect that within 10 years every manufacturer will have to have an artist. This is not conjecture. Everything's being painted these days, even oil storage tanks have designs on them; color dynamics is the technical term. Besides, the Carters have talked with businessmen and our foreign licensees, and they get kind of a general reaction that art is increasingly important to business. They are really authorities. I think you've got to start working on this now to get the news value out of the speech. You know, we can send reprints to industry, architects, even financial men. I wish you'd really get on to it today. . . .

BLACK: Bill Koerper thinks this idea has promise. You know, maybe we have taken the wrong approach by directing our mural advertising to architects and artists and not to industry. Nat, you'd better follow up this call tomorrow—you can tell Bill Koerper what time the Carters are leaving as an excuse. If Art Farley weren't tied up, we could ask about the Carters' request for increasing their draw another $500. But we must talk about it as soon as he's through—it's very important.

CARTER: We've drawn $3,000, but when the murals are finished we'll have $3,600 coming to us. We could use $500 until other jobs come through.

BLACK: In preparing your speech, be as dramatic as you can.

CARTER: Don't forget this is an artists' convention, with artists, dealers, students. . . .

BLACK: You might be fairly blunt on the other side of the picture: tell the businessmen about the importance of artists to industry but also tell the artists about the importance of businessmen in developing work for artists.

CARTER: That information would be of importance to teachers, for example.

BLACK: Maybe we can plan a couple of articles signed by you and us to run side by side or in different magazines. One article would be addressed to businessmen, the other to artists, and both would stress the importance of each to the other. Let's work on it.

FOWLER: Herb, will you come in my office so I can get an idea of your speech and plan your meeting with Bill Koerper?

Five minutes later Mr. Black called Mr. Fowler into his office.

Exhibit 7—Continued

BLACK: Give the Carters $50 towards the trip. Say it's not for travel expense but because of the public relations angle.

One hour later Mr. Fowler entered Mr. Black's office to discuss some problems.

FOWLER: I was in a hotel last week and saw little mosaic tables about two thirds the size of the Carters' which cost $75. I think we can get $100 for our tables.

BLACK: I think we should get the price down to at least $75.

FOWLER: We can, I think. The Carters estimated costs are $33, and they want 5% of the selling price in exchange for making the stencils, supplying personnel, and giving technical advice.

BLACK: They've got to make more than that; it's too conservative.

FOWLER: All right, 10% or 15%.

BLACK: That $33 cost doesn't include the sign spraying cost.

FOWLER: Fifteen dollars, at the most.

BLACK: Yes, but that adds up to $75.

FOWLER: No. Look, $63, and that's padding it.

BLACK: But that doesn't include any overhead or selling and administrative expense. We'll have to give the Carters $10 a table.

FOWLER: On 300 tables that's still $3,000.

BLACK: Right. We've got to do better than 5% for the Carters; still, the price ought to be below $100.

One hour later Mr. Farley looked into Mr. Black's office on his way home. Mr. Black told Mr. Farley about the planned promotion for the tables, which Mr. Farley admired. The treasurer said he had arranged to advance the Carters $500.

Mr. Black made the following comment about the above conversations:

I think that's typical of the way we work together. I can never predict when we'll have such meetings or what will be discussed; they just happen. I think it's important to do things immediately when they arise. For example, I'd just returned from a 10-day trip and hadn't finished opening the mail when the Carters dropped in. Seeing them wasn't important to me, but it was to Nat and terribly important to the Carters; I guess I spent two hours discussing the tables.

Under the president were three top executives: Mr. Arthur Farley, age 39, vice-president and treasurer; Mr. Frederick Hannon, age 51, vice-president and general manager; and Mr. Nathaniel Fowler, age 38, general sales manager. These men were responsible for the functions of finance, production, and sales respectively at the Portland plant and, according to Mr. Black, acted as advisors to the subsidiary corporations. For example, Mr. Farley contacted the president of Detroit Porcelain Company at least weekly on financial matters, while Mr. Fowler would discuss sales with the sales manager. Descriptions of these executives and their duties given by them or their colleagues follow.

Mr. Robert Black, President. Mr. Black joined the Portland Company in December, 1945, as a 25-year-old vice-president and sales manager. While serving in the Canadian Army in Europe the previous year, Mr. Black had bought 50% of the outstanding Portland common stock for approximately $14,000 on the advice of his father, president of a corporation producing enameling materials and equipment. The president and owner of the other 50% of the common gave Mr. Black a free hand in making all operating decisions. Although Mr. Black said he was not satisfied with the work of some of the supervisory personnel, he deferred any major staff changes until 1947.

During 1946 Mr. Black took several steps to strengthen the company. After the 1945 loss, he got the OPA to allow Portland a 28% price increase, a move which lost Portland two small customers. He instructed salesmen to refuse orders for certain items that seemed unprofitable. As he secured contracts for signs, gasoline station fronts, elevator cab panels, and commercial baking ovens, he decreased the amount of stove enameling. He and the president each loaned the company $13,500 with money raised from savings and friends and received in return 6% notes. Mr. Black persuaded a local bank to loan the company $36,000 on a six-year note at 4%, secured by the owners' signatures. The bank required a 2:1 current ratio. Part of the loan was used for machinery and part for building a new metal shop, when the old one burned down in March. Mr. Black visited workers' homes and induced some of them to leave higher-paying jobs to fill vacancies in Portland's skilled labor forces. In April he established a profit-sharing plan for all nonsupervisory personnel; 10% of the net profit before taxes was to be distributed on the basis of individual gross earnings.[2] Worn out by his work, in the spring of 1947 Mr. Black went to Florida for a month's rest.

An appointment by Mr. Black in 1947 brought a hidden conflict to a head. The president had disagreed with Mr. Black's ambitious diver-

---

[2] This plan was not a success and was discontinued; however, Mr. Black said a second plan, introduced in 1951, had proved successful. In the 1951 plan, the company paid 15% of the before tax net profit into a fund, while the employee contributed 3% of his gross pay (up to $120). The employee's share was prorated annually on the basis of one point for each dollar contributed and one point for each year of service.

sification and expansion plans for Portland but had not interfered with the latter's decisions; however, he openly opposed Mr. Black's hiring Mr. Hannon as general manager in January, 1947. After six months of bickering Mr. Black proposed the 50–50 stock ownership arrangement be dissolved by either he or the president buying out the other. Mr. Black and Mr. Hannon, with the help of Mr. Farley who came in to handle the firm's financial affairs, bought the president's stock, and Mr. Black assumed the presidency.

Portland soon needed more money than the management could raise or borrow; Mr. Black turned to public financing as the only available source of funds. In 1956 he expressed the belief that he could make Portland, or any small company, grow by using public financing "generally considered to be reserved for big business." Mr. Black said:

> Generally speaking, I've found that small businessmen have avoided public financing for these reasons: First, they don't have a clear picture of the specific advantages. Second, they don't know how to go about getting such financing. Third, they're afraid they will lose control of their businesses. Fourth, they don't know where their appeal to the investor lies. Fifth, they misunderstand the role of the underwriter and are shocked by his seemingly high fees. And finally, they are overawed by SEC regulations.

Mr. Black thought a small company should consider offering stock to the public if it met one of the following requirements: (1) good earnings record, (2) a product with a unique potential or high demand, (3) good management, and (4) strong possibilities of growth.

According to Mr. Black, Portland's growth potential made it an attractive issue for investors who wanted capital gains. Such persons, he believed, appreciated the importance of reinvesting profits in product development rather than paying dividends. He pointed out that a public offering entailed no fixed interest charges and by increasing Portland's net worth enlarged its line of credit. With an established market price, the stock might contribute to the process of acquiring other companies. Mr. Black thought that practical control was more likely to be diluted when a big minority interest in a company was sold to a small group than when a public offering was made to a larger group. The only major disadvantage he saw to a small company using public financing was its relatively high cost. He said, "The investment banker's cost of investigating a company is hardly a function of its size; however, we get values that make the cost worth it."

Between 1947 and 1956 Portland raised almost $700,000 through sale of common stock to the public. The first offering was in 1949 and raised over $200,000 through sale of 82,162 shares of $1 par common stock at $2.50 a share. A small Portland investment firm handled the issue under a "best efforts" agreement.[3] The second offering, in 1952, was for 58,000 shares of common stock and 58,000 warrants representing rights to buy 29,000 shares of common at $5 a share between August 1, 1953, and July 31, 1955. One share of common and one warrant sold for $4; a large investment banking firm underwrote the issue. Approximately 99% of the warrants were exercised before their expiration.

Mr. Black thought that his job as president was to concentrate on long-range planning and be available to work on the most important problems that might arise in any area of the business. He said he was more interested in getting ideas than in filling in the details; his other executives were to decide if the ideas were feasible from a financial, sales, or production viewpoint. He said that in a sense the 1947–56, 10-year plan "came off the tops of our heads." He explained, "It was more of a plan in retrospect than a plan in prospect; by that I mean we set up a goal of where we wanted to be in ten years and later on divided the ten years into periods." Without exception, Portland management had the highest praise for Mr. Black's enthusiastic planning; however, two management men felt that Mr. Black paid too little attention to so-called "details," especially cost. One executive countered this comment when he said, "If Bob stopped to think of all the realities, he wouldn't be as creative as he is."

When he worked on the implementation of a plan with his executives, Mr. Black said he felt he was working for them, rather than they for him. "I take a lot of directions from my people, although they are charitable in listening to my ideas." Mr. Black thought he spent equal time in all functional areas, but his associates said he spent most of his time in those areas in which he was interested and excelled; that is, sales and promotion. They noted that he used to handle the large clients himself; however, for the past three years the sales manager had taken care of all the accounts. According to his management, Mr. Black sold much of the stock Portland offered in 1947 and 1952.

Mr. Black worked closely with the company's public relations firm (see Exhibit 7). He did not believe that magazine advertising was nearly as effective for Portland as having favorable mention or articles in business and trade publications. The public relations firm wrote ar-

---

[3] A "best efforts" agreement meant the firm would not underwrite the issue and that Portland would take back any unsold stock.

ticles for his or Mr. Hannon's signature. Reprints were sent to clients; for example, the sales department sent architects a folder containing 14 separate reprints. Portland executives had a stack of reprints of articles beside their desks and frequently quoted from them when describing the company or its policies.

Mr. Arthur Farley, Vice-President and Treasurer. Mr. Farley, who came to Portland after being a division controller for Mr. Black, Sr.'s, company, said he had a variety of jobs. He explained:

> In a small company you have to be a jack of all trades. As treasurer and controller I okay all financial matters and policies and do most of the work with the banks, although Bob Black gets involved on loan discussions. I think we're a pretty good combination: I'm more equipped to handle the figures, while he's more of a salesman and has the sales information the banks are interested in. I handle a lot of the details for Bob. He's interested in setting the general picture, such as planning out 1957 financing, but he's not interested in working out the details of the plan; he leaves that to me.
>
> I get involved in setting prices, sales administration, labor negotiations, insurance, some purchasing, and the administration of the foreign licensees.

Because of Portland's financial situation, the treasurer was consulted on many decisions. Fellow executives agreed that Mr. Farley with his M.B.A. degree and love of figures was well suited to the treasurer's job. They thought his down-to-earth approach to ideas was a necessary stabilizing influence for the company.

All Portland incoming mail went first to Mr. Farley who passed it on to the appropriate person. "It's sort of a control," he explained. "I've thought of having someone else do it, but it doesn't take long and it keeps me informed on the different aspects of the business and gives me a chance to keep Bob's mail to a minimum. Now, if I don't read all the mail in the morning, I take it home to read at night."

Mr. Farley said he did not believe the three banks Portland used really understood his company's problems; he was trying to get a loan from a different prominent Portland bank that would enable him to sever his present connections. Two banks that had the term debt and the mortgage once were eager for business but now wanted to shorten the repayment period, while Portland wanted to extend the loans. Likewise, Mr. Farley did not think the bank that discounted the Lisbon accounts receivable had a co-operative or understanding attitude. He said:

> A fellow from that bank just happened to be here when I wanted to stretch the accounts receivable; he got the business! We overdrew our account, were late

paying, and so forth. It was just a matter of squeezing out the money we needed. But that bank has an impractical approach. Just when we needed the money last January (1956), they tried to change the period from 90 to 60 days and the amount from 80% to 75%. We'd talked them out of that idea three times and we did it again. We pointed out it was not logical and so on, but they've got that holier-than-thou attitude most bankers have. They want to run our business or protect us—we'd rather go busted than be told how to run our business, and we don't aim to go busted either. We've been a small, growing business with financial problems, and I guess we'll continue to be one.

The Portland plant cost system was run by the office manager under Mr. Farley's over-all supervision. The system had three purposes: to provide historical data for estimating, to produce reports which would highlight production problems and areas for improvement, and to insure correct valuation of work in process and finished goods. Management was particularly anxious not to make clerks out of the production force.

Almost all costs were collected on job order cards. Material costs were calculated from the quantities shown on the perpetual inventory cards which were kept on a FIFO basis. The cost of enamel used was found by relating spray labor time to enamel material and preparation costs.[4] Direct labor and engineering costs were figured with the help of an electronic call system whereby each worker called in every time he started or stopped a job. The overhead rate was expressed as a percentage of direct labor hours. Management attempted to use efficient labor standards in estimating the total hours. The rate for 1955 and 1956 was 125% and for 1957, 135%. A 17% selling and administrative charge was calculated from an historical percentage of sales.

Mr. Farley said he was more interested in the gross than the net profit because the selling and administrative expense was not allocated by jobs. For example, he said the chalkboard had a 10% gross, but, because United States Plywood was the sole customer and handled all the marketing, the item made a profit, not a 7% book loss. The gross profits were compared with the "normal" which, according to Mr. Hannon, were competitive guidelines "with a little bit of wishful thinking to spur the men on" (see Exhibit 1). Gas station jobs were broken

---

[4] The previous month's total dollar value of enamel used plus preparation labor was divided by the spray labor time to find the dollar rate of enamel used per dollar of spray labor. The price of the particular enamel used on a job was expressed as a percentage of the average enamel costs. For example, if the ratio of the specific enamel used to average enamel was 3:2, or 150%, the ratio of average enamel to spray labor was 2:1, and spray labor was $1.50 an hour, then one hour of spraying a certain enamel that was 150% of the average would be: 150% of $2 (average enamel) × $1.50 (spray labor) equals $4.50.

down by production process because the competition was so stiff; Portland's gross for gas stations ranged from a 50% profit to a 25% loss on different jobs.

The office manager pointed out that the cost system was simple but useful. The job cards showed the chronological cost of each job; when a job was completed, the cards were circulated among top management. In addition, the system provided raw data for several reports which were a monthly raw steel summary, a monthly work-in-process summary by categories such as architectural, a finished goods summary by categories showing normal and actual gross profit, a daily and monthly report of labor dollars expended, an end-of-the-month incomplete job data report, and a sales forecast.

Mr. Farley said he was uncertain how much of the R & D expenses should be capitalized, how much expensed to the Portland plant, and how much charged to the Lisbon and Detroit plants. In 1956 a management consulting firm estimated that Portland's R & D program had cost a total of $2.5 to $3 million since 1947; they observed that most of these costs had been charged to expense and in effect had reduced potential profits.

Mr. Frederick Hannon, Vice-President and General Manager. Mr. Hannon, who had gone into the porcelain enamel business and risen to be vice-president of a stove company after his graduation from Massachusetts Institute of Technology, supervised production, gave technical advice, and acted as a co-ordinator between sales, engineering, and production for all plants. Reporting to him were the plant superintendent with 8 foremen and 100 men, the chief engineer with 7 engineers, and the R & D lab manager. Mr. Hannon pointed out that great care had to be exercised in the production process because slight bends or faulty welds produced scaly surfaces and poor fusing while slight variations in the furnace temperature warped parts and changed colors. Portland would match any color if one of its 48 standard colors was unsuitable. Since Mr. Black was adverse to refusing orders, Mr. Hannon said he had to keep close watch on the promises made and the prices quoted. The production department was flexible, he said, and cited how during the Korean War they had built a new plant and started production of high-temperature coatings within six weeks; however, there had been times when promises could not be fulfilled.

Prices posed a problem because Portland usually based its quotations on competition, not on costs. In January, 1947, the following conversation took place:

FARLEY: We quoted $88,000 to do eight ovens for a large baking company with whom we used to do business. We wanted the job, so when we were high to the tune of $20,000 we bid $65,000 and got the contract. We won't make any 25% gross, but perhaps we'll have a $5,000 contribution to selling and administrative expenses.[5] We think it's all right to take the job at that price if we're not jammed to the teeth. To bid properly, we have to predict our volume three or four months ahead.

HANNON: Bob Black got in on this bidding—we usually toss the ideas around at lunch. He wanted the job, and you know Bob, when he gets your ear bent it stays bent!

FARLEY: If we can deliver the ovens without crating, we'll save some $3,000. Fred, I guess you'll have to see where we can improve construction and sharpen the pencils to keep the costs down.

HANNON: We'll have to spend some $7,000 for dies.

FARLEY: Wait until you check with Detroit before getting dies because they may have them. It's worth a phone call. When you already have the dies, it's a cost advantage.

HANNON: Our first order for this company was $80,000 and then on the $125,000 second order we made a 53% gross, remember?

FARLEY: Maybe they thought we gouged them. . . .

HANNON: I don't think they figured the costs that closely; it was during the steel shortage.

Portland had had several strikes since 1947, but Mr. Hannon thought labor relations were good in 1957. The company was anxious to retain its employees because training porcelain enamel workers was a lengthy process. Portland was unionized in 1950 over the question of shorter working hours. Mr. Hannon said the company wanted to keep the men's take-home pay high by long hours and later raise the hourly rate when it was financially more feasible. He added that Portland's real weakness had been its paternalism: "We closed down on hot days, bought ice cream for the men, and gave many benefits including eight paid holidays, but we soon learned such an approach doesn't improve employee morale." After a three-day strike, the company reduced the work week from 47½ hours to 45 hours with the same pay, "something we

---

[5] Mr. Fowler thought the ovens would yield a 5 to 10% profit "because everybody is conscious that the price is low and will really do some production planning." Mr. Hannon and Portland engineers visited the baking company and effected several cost savings by getting the customer to approve some specification changes. The additional dies cost under $1,000, the finished panels were shipped uncrated, and Mr. Black said Portland made a profit on the job.

were about to do anyway." In 1952 there was a 21-day strike over wages. Protracted negotiations culminated in a three-day strike in 1954 over union demands for a 40- instead of a 45-hour week at the same pay; a compromise was finally agreed upon. In 1955 there was a seven-week strike over wages. Mr. Hannon blamed the intransigence of the union's regional officer for the company's inability to reach an agreement with the union. The next year a labor relations consultant reached and agreement in two meetings with the union officer for a 7-cent raise and an extra half-day holiday.

According to Mr. Hannon, the union had been both harmful and beneficial to the company. Management blamed the 1955 loss on the seven-week strike and said union rules had forced it to give up having its own erection crew. On the other hand, Mr. Hannon said union pressure had forced "job bidding" on the company. This meant that any employee could bid for any vacant job. The plant superintendent, the former shipper, said, "Job bidding caused a lot of headaches, but having the men bounce around makes the company more flexible, and you find out how many jobs a man can do."

Mr. Nathaniel Fowler, General Sales Manager. Mr. Fowler, who started as Portland's sole salesman and engineer in 1938, was responsible for sales. Under him directly were five men: an assistant, two sales engineers, and two New York salesmen. Mr. Fowler handled the larger accounts and spent most of his time away from the office calling on customers and attending technical conferences. He followed reports and graphs on sales by product to date, forecasts by customer and product, and comparisons of Portland sales with the industry. The general sales manager summarized his job as follows:

> I'm Johnny-on-the-spot, and I have the ability to stimulate salesmen. I have to be able to talk slang with the contractor from whom I learn how to improve our products, give technical papers at conferences where I learn about new products, and converse with a president who prefers to talk with a Portland executive than with a salesman.

A variety of dealers and distributors handled the Portland products. (1) Approximately 12 building material distributors, including glass and window specialists, served the monumental building market. Portland engineers worked closely with architects and contractors. (2) The chalkboard was marketed solely by United States Plywood under a license which expired in 1957. Mr. Fowler visited United States Plywood about every two weeks. "It's a fairly new product for them, and they require a lot of handholding," he explained. (3) About 23 distributors and dealers of building materials carried the tile lines. In order to promote sales of this product, Portland salesmen asked officers of hotels and other monumental buildings if they might demonstrate the wearability and colorfastness of ceramic-on-steel tiles. Portland quoted special prices for this purpose. (4) Corrugated roofing was distributed by some 15 roofing and siding distributors. The Detroit sales manager asked chemical companies and others with corrosion problems if his company might install a section of its roofing to demonstrate its qualities. (5) Almost all of the other products were sold direct.

Mr. Fowler envisioned Portland entering many markets and becoming known as the "corrosion people" (see Exhibit 7). He said he was constantly looking for new products using the process; for example, he was experimenting with coatings for fire alarm boxes.

Messrs. Farley, Hannon, and Fowler were responsible for the functional areas of finance, production, and sales, but each did not hesitate to perform jobs outside his area in accordance with Mr. Black's conception of a crossways organization. In explaining how well this system worked, Mr. Hannon said:

> The duties of the executives and supervisors overlap at all levels of the organization. We have no staff departments, so in a sense we're performing staff functions for each other. Each one of us does the things we can do best, and we certainly fit together well. For example, Nat Fowler is a terrific salesman but not so good at writing letters and handling administrative details. Art Farley, on the other hand, is not such a good salesman but has a real head for figures and writes fine letters. Therefore, Nat does the selling, while Art checks the prices and writes some of Nat's letters, and Nat's assistant handles the day-to-day administrative matters.
>
> In addition, it's perfectly all right to cut across lines of authority. For example, Bob Black might give orders to the lab man who's under me. It would then be the lab man's responsibility to keep me informed and he always does. In the same way, I might call one of the salesmen directly and give him instructions. I hope we never grow so big or so highly organized that we can't continue this overlapping.

All executives expressed enthusiasm for these operating policies, but some pointed out that in a different kind of organization where the executives did not work so well together Mr. Black's dislike of organization charts could cause misunderstandings. For example, the estimator's salary was charged to the accounting department, but Mr. Farley said the estimator worked for production, Mr. Hannon said he worked for sales, while Mr. Fowler said he reported to Mr. Hannon.

RELATIONSHIP BETWEEN THE HOME OFFICE AND OTHER PORTLAND COMPANIES

Mr. Black believed that the home office worked for the rest of the Portland family as consultants. He said:

> With the attitude that we're working for them rather than they for us, Lisbon, Detroit, and Toronto naturally come to us for advice. We delegate to them enormous amounts of responsibility. When we get to the point where as far as I'm concerned they've got to do something—if it's that important—we set the stage and sell them the idea.

Mr. Farley said of this relationship:

> We don't tell them how to run their businesses, but we do make suggestions, and they usually agree with them. They are still profit-responsible, separate corporations, but we treat them as divisions. At Lisbon, where we are also officers, the suggestions are more likely to be interpreted as instructions.

Control over the subsidiary companies was exercised in three ways: personal visits, reports, and review of correspondence. (1) The executives of the subsidiaries in charge of finance, production, and sales were responsible respectively to Messrs. Farley, Hannon, and Fowler, each of whom visited the subsidiaries monthly. The presidents or senior executives in each company had the right to make general administrative decisions that did not concern the over-all operation of the Portland family. Mr. Black visited any executive he felt needed his help. (2) Each subsidiary sent the home office various reports that included weekly production schedules, forecasts of monthly shipments, actual results for the month, monthly profit and loss statements, and monthly balance sheets. (3) The Portland office received a daily file of all the correspondence mailed by each of the subsidiaries. These files, together with a similar home office one, were circulated to Messrs. Black, Farley, Hannon, and Fowler. Mr. Farley pointed out that such files kept him informed of the other companies' problems. One day he called Detroit to suggest that they make their sales letters less blunt, and another time he phoned Toronto "to give the engineering department a great big push to get the orders out."

The three subsidiary companies differed from each other in product line and organization. Descriptions of these companies are given below, and selected financial data for the years 1952 to 1956 are shown in Exhibit 8.

Lisbon was the smallest of the three subsidiaries, nearest to Portland,

Exhibit 8

PORTLAND COMPANY

Selected Financial Data for Portland's Subsidiaries, 1952–56

	1952 $	1952 %	1953 $	1953 %	1954 $	1954 %	1955 $	1955 %	1956 $	1956 %
Lisbon:										
Total assets	$479,913	...	$ 555,868	...	$ 620,049	...	$ 524,397	...	$ 655,508	...
Net worth	13,284	...	(59,275)	...	(90,551)	...	(199,212)	...	(176,471)	...
Net sales	$160,037	100.0	$ 594,245	100.0	$ 534,623	100.0	$ 546,604	100.0	$ 600,958	100.0
Cost of goods sold	156,430	97.7	573,561	96.5	491,608	92.0	540,122	98.8	506,532	84.3
Gross profit	$ 3,607	2.3	$ 20,684	3.5	$ 43,015	8.0	$ 6,482	1.2	$ 94,426	15.7
Selling and administrative expense	$ 29,947	18.7	$ 80,122	13.5	$ 95,799	17.9	$ 89,578	16.4	$ 101,970	17.0
Net operating income	(26,340)	(16.4)	(59,438)	(10.0)	(52,784)	(9.9)	(83,096)	(15.2)	(7,544)	(1.3)
Additions, deductions, and taxes	11,464	7.2	20,621	3.5	(21,508)	(4.0)	25,565	4.7	(30,285)†	(5.0)
Net income	$(37,804)	(23.6)	$ (80,059)	(13.5)	$ (31,276)	(5.9)	$ (108,661)	(19.9)	$ 22,741	3.7
Detroit:										
Total assets	$327,022	...	$ 339,395	...	$ 423,745	...	$ 393,606	...	$ 816,734	...
Net worth	257,376	...	236,996	...	236,266	...	238,530	...	605,455‡	...
Net sales	$401,309	100.0	$ 672,146	100.0	$ 692,259	100.0	$ 877,559	100.0	$ 896,877	100.0
Cost of goods sold	358,939	89.4	620,232	92.3	597,297	86.3	766,059	87.3	782,533	87.3
Gross profit	$ 42,380	10.6	$ 51,914	7.7	$ 94,962	13.7	$ 111,500	12.7	$ 114,344	12.7
Selling and administrative expense	$ 61,409	15.3	$ 62,900	9.3	$ 92,185	13.3	$ 101,318	11.5	$ 92,918	10.3
Net operating income	(19,029)	(4.7)	(10,986)	(1.6)	2,777	0.4	10,182	1.2	21,426	2.4
Additions, deductions, and taxes	(5,590)	(1.4)	1,221	0.2	2,107	0.3	6,518	0.8	11,161	1.3
Net income	$(13,439)	(3.3)	$ (12,207)	(1.8)	$ 670	0.1	$ 3,664	0.4	$ 10,265	1.1

Dana:

Total assets	$394,696	··	NA	··	NA	··	$1,008,145*	··	$1,251,161	··
Net worth	55,874	··	NA	··	NA	··	460,757	··	463,970	··
Net sales	$706,945	100.0	$1,239,941	100.0	$1,127,657	100.0	$1,833,723	100.0	$1,951,098	100.0
Cost of goods sold	652,861	92.3	1,110,563	89.6	1,017,560	90.2	1,572,398	85.8	1,701,243	87.2
Gross profit	$ 54,084	7.7	$ 129,378	10.4	$ 110,097	9.8	$ 261,325	14.2	$ 249,855	12.8
Selling, administrative and financial expense	$105,701	15.0	$ 94,419	7.6	$ 111,886	9.9	‡ 220,865	12.0	$ 244,545	12.5
Net operating income	(51,617)	(7.3)	34,959	2.8	(1,789)	(0.1)	40,460	2.2	5,300	0.3
Additions, deductions, and taxes	····	··	739	0.1	······	··	17,069	0.9	2,088	0.1
Net income	$(51,617)	(7.3)	$ 34,220	2.7	$ (1,789)	(0.1)	$ 23,391	1.3	$ 3,212	0.2

* In 1955, Dana ended its fiscal year on September 30, instead of March 31 as heretofore. For the six months ending September 30, 1954, sales were $541,162 and the net loss $5,431.
† Included cancellation of $50,500 indebtedness applicable to prior years.
‡ Appraisal increase in the value of buildings and equipment of $358,060 was entered on the books on December 31, 1956
Source: Company records.

and under the tightest home office control. Mr. George Underwood was general manager and responsible for production; a sales manager handled sales, and Mr. Underwood's assistant and an accountant collected figures for home office use. Housed in an old streetcar barn, the 27,000-square foot, 60-man plant had a continuous conveyor system for production of bathroom tile. Mr. Underwood pointed out that daily measurements of ceramic-coating usage, line output, and spoilage made relatively accurate cost estimating possible. He said the new tile line lost money because it was still in the development stage and volume was low; selling prices were based on market demand, not on initial production costs; spoilage ran between 3 and 35% and far exceeded the monthly average of 5% allowed for. The $400-a-day overhead was largely fixed. About 25% of the plant's dollar volume was in jobbed items consisting of street signs or overflow from the Portland plant.

Mr. Underwood had started Lisbon in 1947 with technical advice from Portland; in return the latter received 51% of the outstanding Lisbon common stock. After a 1952 refinancing Portland invested $38,500 to make up a 55% ownership. In December, 1956, Portland acquired the remaining minority stock interest and debentures in exchange for 7,995 shares of common and warrants, expiring September 1, 1962, to buy 14,307 common shares at $5.50 a share. Mr. Underwood favored this transaction and pointed out he had never controlled the company. He was willing to commute the 100 miles to work since he was looking forward to the consolidation of the Portland and Lisbon production in a new plant nearer home. Meanwhile, he made sure any capital items were movable.

The Detroit plant was the largest of the three and the sole producer of the ceramic-coated roofing and siding material. It was 54,000 square feet and had both box furnaces and a continuous furnace. Both the president and the general manager had resigned shortly after Portland acquired the company; Mr. Black said that they had not agreed with Portland philosophy. In 1957 Detroit had (1) a president, (2) a vice-president and general manager in charge of 85 production employees, (3) a sales manager with three salesmen under him, and (4) a secretary responsible for the cost and accounting departments.

The Toronto plant was the newest of the three, farthest from Portland, and under loosest home office control. The 60,000-foot plant was completed in 1955. One of the three former owners, who was interested in research, remained president, while the other two became vice-presidents. Executive authority was exercised by Mr. Nason whom Portland brought in as executive vice-president.

The Portland management said they had difficulty persuading their subsidiaries, especially Detroit, to adopt Portland ideas of management. Mr. Farley said Detroit executives seemed to understand crossways organizations when attending company meetings, but on returning to Detroit they continued to operate within well-defined functional areas. In addition, he thought Detroit did not recognize the necessity of bidding on a contribution-to-overhead basis during forecast slack seasons or for deliveries to be made in such periods. Mr. Black cited an incident that occurred in March, 1957; the correspondence files showed that Detroit had refused certain orders for so-called "lack of production." The home office disagreed with this decision and believed that with slight rearrangements in schedule and facilities the production manager could have accommodated this order. Portland executives believed this decision was a result of too formal an organization. Mr. Black said he recognized that "we can't make them do things our way merely by picking up the telephone," and he planned to have home office top executives spend a week at Detroit. Mr. Farley commented, "I'll go out there and live with their problems; they'll either see the light or go busted."

FUTURE PLANS

Portland executives hoped to solve their biggest problems, lack of production capacity and high costs, by building a new plant in 1957 or 1958. Mr. Farley noted that diversified products insured the company against cyclical fluctuations but entailed small lots and noncompetitive costs; often competition capitalized on Portland's R & D because the latter was unable to produce large quantities quickly. The treasurer expected continuous furnaces and automatic spraying would be the major cost advantages of a new plant. Mr. Black, Sr.'s company had designed a plant for Portland which for about $360,000 of equipment would increase furnace capacity $6\frac{1}{4}$ times and reduce enameling and materials handling labor from 70 men to 60 men. Mr. Farley said, "With such a plant and an increased sales force, we could have a policy of never being undersold in New England, make a profit, and produce items heretofore impossible to make on our machines even though we accepted the orders."

Plans for the plant were still unsettled in March, 1957. Its size had been considerably reduced after discussions with Portland bankers.

The plan of including the Lisbon tile line was dropped, but Portland was thinking of moving the Burns operation from Putney, Vermont. Mr. Burns, who owned the patent rights, wanted to stay in Putney; Mr. Black said Portland would operate the Burns' equipment and he would ask Mr. Burns to be a consultant. The three alternatives being discussed for the new plant were: (1) lease a $400,000, 75,000-square-foot plant in a proposed industrial park from a realtor, (2) buy an abandoned wool mill for $248,000 or less, or (3) lease a prefabri-

Exhibit 9

PORTLAND COMPANY

Sales and Net Profit Forecast, 1957–59

	1957		1958		1959	
	$	%	$	%	$	%
Total revenues	4,055,000	100.0	6,200,000	100.0	8,700,000	100.0
Cost of sales	3,198,178	78.9	4,800,000	77.4	6,500,000	74.7
Gross profit	856,822	21.1	1,400,000	22.6	2,200,000	25.3
Sales and administrative expense	498,835	12.3	720,000	11.6	760,000	8.7
Net operating profit	357,987	8.8	680,000	11.0	1,440,000	16.6
Additions and deductions	69,180	1.7	115,000	1.9	180,000	2.1
Net profit before tax	288,807	7.1	565,000	9.1	1,260,000	14.5
Federal income tax	118,000	2.9	225,000	3.6	630,000	7.25
Net profit	170,807	4.2	340,000	5.5	630,000	7.25

Current order backlog at February 15, 1957: $1,550,000.
Source: Prepared by Mr. Farley.

cated metal building. Mr. Hannon had estimated that a new plant would break even at the 1956 level of operations, sale of the Portland building would net $100,000, and moving costs would be about $50,000.

To pay for the new equipment, Portland in February, 1957, privately placed $350,000 of 5¾% convertible subordinated debentures due in 1971 and 35,000 shares of $1 par common stock at $4 a share.[6] The debenture purchasers included investment bankers, industrial retirement programs, and a college. Each $1,000 bond could be converted into 210 shares of common stock. The $490,000 raised was used actually for working capital; Mr. Farley thought Portland might try to raise another $360,000 for the equipment when needed.

[6] In March, 1957, the bid price for Portland stock sold over the counter was $4⅞.

Mr. Black expressed faith in Portland's ability to expand capacity and meet forecast sales (see Exhibit 9). Since the Portland plant was operating at a capacity of dollar volume and the Lisbon and Detroit plants at about 75% capacity, it would be necessary to build the projected new plant or acquire new subsidiaries to meet the 1958 sales goal. Early in April, 1957, Mr. Black told the press that 1957 sales would be "substantially better than 1956." He had to estimate 1956 figures because the company statements were not ready until toward the end of the month; the delay was due partly to difficulties involved in including the Lisbon plant in the consolidated statement for the first time. Mr. Black said:

We now look forward to large and expanding markets for which we will produce products used by a wide variety of industries. Some day there will be a big company in our field. I don't know if Portland will be that company or not, but we're sure going to try.

Flawless Foundry
and Equipment Company

IN MARCH, 1950, an incident occurred which caused Henry D. Williams, chief executive of Flawless Foundry and Equipment Company of Cleveland, Ohio, to wonder about the effectiveness of his management organization. The sales manager, personnel manager, and plant superintendent had become sufficiently concerned over the increasing frequency of late delivery to customers of Flawless' products to insist that the general manager, Joseph D. Stocker, hold an executive meeting at which they would endeavor to get at the roots of the trouble.

Henry Williams had known about the increase in late deliveries during the past year, and that two large customers had been lost consequently. He had not worried previously about the company's operation, however, because Flawless had been operating at a profit. Too, he realized that Joseph D. Stocker, a former castings salesman and general manager since 1948, needed time in which to learn how to handle his new job.

The demands on Stocker made by the subordinate executive group in March did disturb Williams, however, and caused him to wonder about the effectiveness of his management organization.

For a year prior to the March meeting, the foremen of Flawless' six production departments reported directly to general manager Stocker. Mr. Stocker still devoted a great deal of his time to casting sales work. He expected each foreman and department head to run his own department and to work directly with other departments with only occasional checks on his part. Stocker's assistant in production management, plant superintendent William D. Miller, was responsible for interdepartmental scheduling and for product deliveries, but held no authority over the production foremen (see Exhibit 1).

The numerous late shipments of orders in the past year had been due primarily to material shortages and to late deliveries of work-in-process between departments. The material shortages had resulted not so much

Exhibit 1

FLAWLESS FOUNDRY AND EQUIPMENT COMPANY

Organization Chart, July, 1949

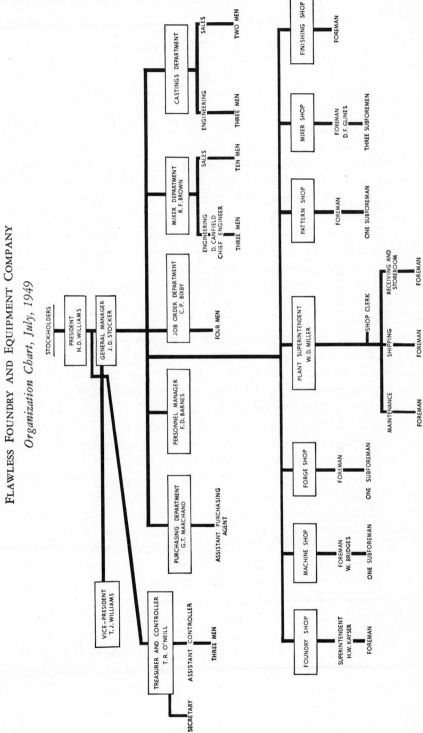

from lack of these items in the open market, according to Miller, but rather from the inadequacy of material inventory controls and from the difficulty of procuring the special parts which many orders required. Operated on a functional basis, the departments were interdependent; a holdup at one place could cause delays in several departments. Such occurrences had increased substantially in 1949 and early 1950.

At the request of the subordinate executive group, John Stocker had held an executive meeting in March to discuss the increase in late deliveries of orders. At this meeting he announced that Miller was responsible for the delays. The latter stated that this surprised the whole group; he then requested authority over the foremen and was granted it by Stocker (see Exhibit 2).

Henry Williams, chief executive of Flawless since 1946, had prior experience only in the accounting department and did not feel that he knew enough about the operation of the company to judge the effectiveness of his management organization. Therefore, in April, 1950, he hired a management consultant to study the problems of the company for him.

In July, 1950, Flawless Foundry and Equipment Company was engaged in the custom manufacture of (1) gray iron castings, (2) industrial mixing machines, and (3) industrial machinery parts of many varieties. Since 1939, the company had tripled its sales volume with sales of $2,984,000 and profits of $99,000 in 1949 (see Exhibits 3 and 4). During the same period the organization had expanded from 173 to 276 employees with the addition of employees, equipment, and buildings in random fashion as the needs increased.

During 1950, four of the company's six production departments were running below full capacity because of the dwindling of the gray iron castings business. Industrial mixer orders were at a higher level than in 1949, compensating somewhat for the low volume of gray castings orders and keeping the machine shop busy. Stocker estimated that, regardless of high volume in the mixer line, about 25% of the company's equipment was not being utilized.

Stocker felt that gray iron castings would never again be the most important factor in the company's business. He stated that his thinking and planning were shifting away from this part of the business on which the company had been built to mixer and industrial parts production, and that he had given considerable thought to the acquisition of a new product which would be suitable for production with the idle facilities.

Exhibit 2

FLAWLESS FOUNDRY AND EQUIPMENT COMPANY

Organization Chart, July, 1950

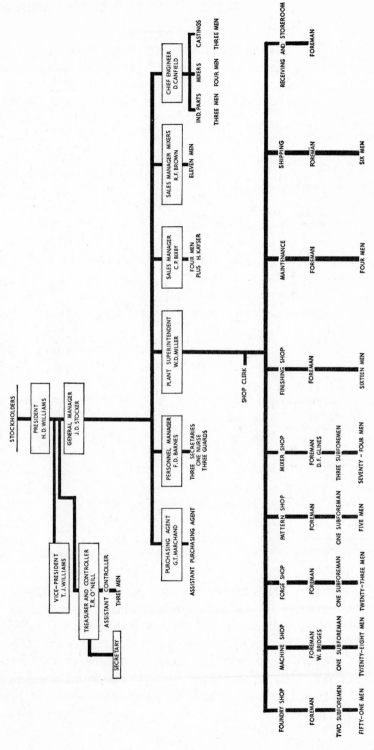

Exhibit 3

FLAWLESS FOUNDRY AND EQUIPMENT COMPANY

Comparative Balance Sheets for Selected Years Ending December 31

(In Thousands)

Assets	1949	1948	1947	1946	1944	1941	1937	1933	1927	1924
Cash	$ 116	$ 33	$ 8	$ 46	$ 153	$ 5	$ 31	$ 15	$ 51	$ 11
Accounts Receivable (Less Reserve)	320	244	189	188	114	215	125	55	179	123
Notes Receivable	...	...	...	...	82	3	6	19	...	8
Accounts—Officers and Employees	19	14	...	24	14	...	...	23	...	...
Stock Investments	23	22	22	114	188	49	61	61	29	37
Inventories	711	1,076	937	627	574	505	137	120	157	114
Total Current Assets	$1,189	$1,389	$1,156	$ 999	$1,125	$777	$360	$293	$416	$293
Other Assets	15	31	39	21	14	17	33	57	6	...
Fixed Assets	827	823	768	684	632	613	564	486	439	394
Less: Reserve for Depreciation	603	584	574	539	423	465	359	277	129	47
Net Fixed Assets	$ 224	$ 239	$ 194	$ 145	$ 209	$148	$205	$209	$310	$347
Total Assets	$1,428	$1,659	$1,389	$1,165	$1,348	$942	$598	$559	$732	$640
Liabilities										
Accounts Payable	$ 25	$ 67	$ 105	$ 53	$ 59	$ 78	$ 9	$ 3	$ 28	$ 3
Notes Payable	...	123	258	240	70	57	1	26	...	31
Accrued Liabilities	138	120	154	139	7	62	49	20	16	5
Accounts—Officers and Employees	112	214	71	6	199	163	24	15	55	36
Taxes Payable	79	159	62	35	184	25	12	...	...	...
Total Current Liabilities	$ 354	$ 683	$ 650	$ 473	$ 519	$385	$ 95	$ 64	$ 99	$ 75
Capital	123	123	123	123	123	123	123	122	122	123
Surplus	951	853	616	569	706	434	380	373	512	443
Total Liabilities	$1,428	$1,659	$1,389	$1,165	$1,348	$919	$598	$559	$732	$640
C.A./C.L.	3.36	2.03	1.78	2.11	2.17	2.02	3.77	4.58	4.20	3.91
N.C.A./C.L.	1.35	0.46	0.34	0.79	1.06	0.71	2.35	2.70	2.62	2.39

HISTORY

E. A. Williams founded Flawless in 1900 and soon began the custom manufacture of cast iron vessels and parts for plumbing, stove, and furnace manufacturers. In 1910 he was joined by his brother, D. R. Williams, forming a brother team which ran the company until 1942. E. A. Williams controlled finances and always held final authority. D. R. Williams, as general manager, made all decisions concerning operations. The latter was described by Henry Williams, his nephew, as a man of "dynamic personality" who inspired personal loyalty from the

Exhibit 4

FLAWLESS FOUNDRY AND EQUIPMENT COMPANY

Comparative Operating Statements for Selected Years Ending December 31

(In Thousands)

	1949	1948	1947	1946	1944	1941	1937	1933	1927	1924
Sales	$ 2,984	$ 3,933	$ 2,716	$ 2,441	$ 3,427	$ 1,554	$ 1,041	$ 398	$ 767	$ 459
Cost of sales	2,340	3,035	2,422	2,450	2,999	1,379	905	312	677	415
Gross profit	$ 644	$ 898	$ 294	($ 9)	$ 428	$ 175	$ 136	$ 86	$ 90	$ 44
Selling and administrative expense	412	414	161	151	168	85	81	80	86	43
Net profit from operations	$ 232	$ 484	$ 133	($ 160)	$ 260	$ 90	$ 55	6	4	$ 1
Other income	9	14	25	14	16	15	3	3	11	14
Gross income	$ 241	$ 498	$ 158	($ 146)	$ 276	$ 105	$ 58	9	15	15
Other deductions	76	158	91	24	115	59	35	6	9	3
Net income before taxes	$ 165	$ 340	$ 67	($ 170)	$ 161	$ 46	$ 23	3	$ 6	$ 12
Income taxes	66	139	20		109	16	5			
Net profit	$ 99	$ 201	$ 47	($ 170)	$ 52	$ 30	$ 18	3	$ 6	$ 12

	1949 %	1948 %	1947 %	1946 %	1944 %	1941 %	1937 %	1933 %	1927 %	1924 %
Sales	100.00	100.00	100.00	100.00	100.00	100.00	100.00	100.00	100.00	100.00
Cost of sales	78.42	77.16	89.18	100.37	87.51	88.74	86.94	78.39	88.27	90.41
Gross profit	21.58	22.84	10.82	(0.37)	12.49	11.26	13.06	21.61	11.73	9.59
Selling and administrative expense	13.80	10.53	5.93	6.18	4.90	5.47	7.78	20.10	11.21	9.37
Net profit from operations	7.78	12.31	4.89	(6.55)	7.59	5.79	5.28	1.51	0.52	0.22
Other income	0.30	0.35	.92	0.57	0.46	0.97	0.29	0.75	1.43	3.05
Gross income	8.08	12.66	5.81	(5.98)	8.05	6.76	5.57	2.26	1.95	3.27
Other deductions	2.55	4.02	3.35	0.98	3.35	3.80	3.36	1.51	1.17	0.65
Net income before taxes	5.53	8.64	2.46	(6.96)	4.70	2.96	2.21	0.75	0.78	2.62
Income taxes	2.21	3.53	0.73		3.18	1.03	0.48			
Net profit	3.32	5.11	1.73	(6.96)	1.52	1.93	1.73	0.75	0.78	2.62

Exhibit 5

FLAWLESS FOUNDRY AND EQUIPMENT COMPANY

Sales by Products

(In Thousands)

	6 Mos. 1950	1949	1948	1947	1946	1945	1944	1943	1942	1941	1940	1939	1938	1937	1936	1935	1934
Castings	$ 294	$ 979	$1,255	$ 828	$ 708	$ 762	$ 458	$ 536	$ 638	$ 767	$ 642	$ 469	$ 370	$ 699	$ 683	$ 588	$ 597
Mixers	649	1,172	1,583	1,180	1,374	1,419	1,355	776	441	460	209	218	89	88	99	19	8
Industrial machinery parts	155	776	1,043	637	307	330	286	100	109	207	283	204	217	254	138	91	11
Miscellaneous	25	57	52	71	52	31	24	38	18	9	6	……	……	……	……	……	……
War products	……	……	……	……	……	73	1,304	3,696	2,680	110	……	……	……	……	……	……	……
Total sales	$1,123	$2,984	$3,933	$2,716	$2,441	$2,615	$3,427	$5,146	$3,886	$1,553	$1,140	$ 891	$ 676	$1,041	$ 920	$ 698	$ 616
	%	%	%	%	%	%	%	%	%	%	%	%	%	%	%	%	%
Castings	26.2	32.8	31.9	30.5	29.0	29.1	13.4	10.4	16.4	49.4	56.3	52.6	54.7	67.1	74.2	84.2	96.9
Mixers	57.8	39.3	40.2	43.4	56.3	54.3	39.5	15.1	11.3	29.6	18.4	24.5	13.2	8.5	10.8	2.7	1.3
Industrial machinery parts	13.8	26.0	26.6	23.5	12.6	12.6	8.3	1.9	2.8	13.3	24.8	22.9	32.1	24.4	15.0	13.1	1.8
Miscellaneous	2.2	1.9	1.3	2.6	2.1	1.2	0.7	0.8	0.5	0.6	0.5	……	……	……	……	……	……
War products	……	……	……	……	……	2.8	38.1	71.8	69.0	7.1	……	……	……	……	……	……	……
Total sales	100.0	100.0	100.0	100.0	100.0	100.0	100.0	100.0	100.0	100.0	100.0	100.0	100.0	100.0	100.0	100.0	100.0

Backlog of orders August 1, 1950:

Castings	$ 164
Mixers	520
Industrial parts	239
Total	$ 923

Estimated* total sales for 1950, $2,243

*By plant superintendent Miller.

men, and whose philosophy was to encourage competition between individuals and between departments. As one of the older foremen recalled, "In the old days under D. R., Flawless was a hard-driving outfit from top to bottom."

The depression of the early thirties hit the gray iron business hard. Flawless sales dropped from a peak in 1927 of $767,000 to $398,-000 in 1933. New products were sought to maintain employment and to hold the company together. In 1933, Flawless began custom production of industrial mixing machines. In 1936, Flawless began production of machinery parts on a job order basis for nearby industrial customers. By 1939, Flawless had doubled its 1933 size, employing 173 men.

In 1941, Flawless received its first war contracts. A wartime sales peak of $5,146,000 was reached in 1943. During the wartime period the company received several citations for its service in the building of ordnance parts.

In 1943, a national independent labor union, after two unsuccessful attempts, organized the workers of the company though this was done against the opposition of D. R. Williams and his production manager, Paul S. Hofstetter, who felt that such action was an encroachment on their management prerogatives. The following year production was halted for 35 days by a strike in protest of department transfer of a worker by Hofstetter. During the strike, workmen demonstrated their protest by overturning Hofstetter's car.

In 1942, the bachelor president, E. A. Williams, died, leaving half of his stock to Henry D. Williams, son of a deceased third brother, and dividing his remaining stock equally between D. R. Williams and a sister. Henry D. Williams thus became the largest stockholder in the company.

D. R. became president upon his brother's death. Later in the same year, however, his health failed, and on doctors' orders he relinquished active management of the company to his production manager, Paul Hofstetter. Henry Williams later described Hofstetter as a good production man, hard driving and very decisive. "Paul's doing the job was the most important thing to him."

"During these years under Hofstetter," said Henry Williams, "discord increased between management and employees; the former had little respect for the union and the union grew in favor with the men so that although production continued high, trust between management and the workers had largely disappeared by 1946."

Henry D. Williams returned from three years' Navy service in 1946 to become vice-president and executive head of Flawless with his uncle, D. R., acting in an advisory capacity. Educated in liberal arts and interested in business chiefly as a "human community," Henry Williams stated that he disliked the conflict which he saw in the company and was determined to bring it to an end.

In 1946, he allowed Hofstetter to resign because of a "basic disagreement" in their management philosophies. Henry Williams then promoted the head of the castings department, Joseph O'Brien, to the post of general manager. Intending to exert no pressure on the organization, Mr. Williams gave O'Brien full charge of the company's operations while he concerned himself with the problems of management-union relations. Mr. Williams later described O'Brien, who remained in office until 1948, as having been a good salesman but inadequate as a general manager, getting bogged down in details.

In the spring of 1948, D. R. Williams died; Henry Williams became president and O'Brien resigned to take the post of sales manager for a large foundry company. A few months later Henry Williams chose Joseph D. Stocker, a castings salesman for the company, as the man best qualified to become general manager. Stocker was given the same broad powers of full, free control which had been granted to his predecessor.

"Since Henry took over in 1946," said general manager Stocker, "things have been a lot different. When Paul Hofstetter was here, it was his word or else. Henry went to the other extreme to correct this situation, allowing others to have a hand in running the company with as much leeway as possible. In the last two years the workers have taken advantage of Henry's leniency and the company has suffered. Now we must tighten up."

PRODUCTS—GRAY IRON CASTINGS

Flawless' original products, cast iron vessels and plumbing, stove, and furnace parts, as well as other gray iron machinery parts, were manufactured in many different shapes and sizes. These gray iron products were used by other manufacturers as parts for a large variety of applications.

Flawless made gray castings largely on a custom basis, although certain shapes were of standard design. Gray cast iron parts, as opposed to malleable shapes (not made by Flawless), were relatively brittle and less apt to stand up under strong impact. Malleable shapes and alloys adapted to individual needs and conditions had made inroads into fields formerly served by gray iron products.

INDUSTRIAL MIXERS

Flawless built on a custom basis a line of industrial mixing machines, mainly for the mixing and blending of liquids in the chemical, plastics, and related industries. Certain basic designs of the mixers were standard, and although a variety of sizes and types was offered, the same general production routines were followed for most of the mixers produced. Flawless would build almost any mixer that a customer desired—lined with stainless steel, alloy metals, plastic, rubber, or something else.

The most common type of mixer built consisted of a large cylindrical tank with agitator mechanisms built on the sides or on the top. Other types included conical or horizontal cylinder machines. Most mixers had a capacity of 500 gallons and over. The assembly of the machines involved plate and sheet metal work, a certain amount of precision machining of moving parts, and construction of suitable bracketing. At times special orders called for unusual designs or materials with specified characteristics to fulfill unique and difficult needs of the customer.

INDUSTRIAL MACHINERY PARTS

Located in a heavily industrialized region, Flawless did a large volume of job order casting, machine work, and welding fabrication to produce machinery parts for industrial customers of all kinds. "Anything we think we can build, we quote on," said chief engineer Donald Canfield.

OWNERSHIP

Flawless was owned jointly by the D. R. Williams estate, a Williams sister, and Henry D. Williams. Henry Williams stated that the sister placed full reliance upon him and that he held unquestioned authority of ownership in the company.

Thomas J. Williams, son of D. R., was vice-president representing his father's estate, a trust for Mrs. D. R. Williams and three children. "No major disagreement with Tom is possible," said Henry Williams. "We always agree, working well together, and discussing freely all matters."

All major stockholders were represented on the payroll of the company. Consequently, it had been the policy of the company not to pay dividends as none had been paid since 1938.

ORGANIZATION

Henry D. Williams, president of Flawless, was a tall, slender man of 38, immaculate in dress and mild in manner. His conversation indicated a wide command of the English language and a close acquaintanceship with the literature and arts of Western culture.

Aware of his lack of technical training and his stated lack of aptitude or desire for it, he approached his job as one of general administrative supervision, leaving the operational management to his subordinates. Mr. Williams considered his primary function as a human one, to serve as a catalyst that would blend the human elements into a smooth organization to work toward his own and the company's end. He did not keep in touch with the daily operations of the company except for matters where subordinates judged that company policy was involved, thereby requiring his attention. He had no scheduled report from anyone, although in July, 1950, at the suggestion of the management consultant, he was considering the installation of some control reports to keep himself more closely informed on the company's operation. He talked with the chief officers along very general lines every day and kept closely informed on personnel and labor matters, frequently talking with the personnel manager and listening to the men's personal problems.

"It is hard to say how good a job we are doing now," said Henry D. Williams. "I don't know whether Joseph Stocker is doing a good job, or whether anyone is. Perhaps none of us is doing as good a job as if driven—though I doubt it. If each man is allowed to find his own level, to express himself as he sees fit, I think that in the long run we can accomplish more and have a better time doing it than if we were working under pressure.

"I personally abhor conflict and competition. Sometimes I wish that I had some of it in my nature. Nevertheless, I do not believe in it as an end in itself—as such it is evil.

"This love of 'drive' pervades our whole life—a nation of gladiators; if we win, O.K.; if not, thumbs down. It's vicious. It presupposes an ability by all of us to fit into that system, and all of us don't. Those who do not fit are made to feel inadequate, whereas actually they may be entirely adequate. I don't like this game spirit, this get-in-there-and-fight, but I may abhor it for a wrong reason.

"I think the life that one builds for himself must be judged on its own merits and not in juxtaposition to that of Henry Ford!

"The drive itself is not evil, but the system that deifies that drive I'm inclined to be skeptical of. The only excuse for material development is to make it possible for men to think about something else. Shaw expressed it well—first acquire an independent income, then practice virtue . . . he may have them backwards, however, overlooking the material rewards of ethical living. It is necessary that men have enough, but what they do with the residue appalls me."

Thomas J. Williams, vice-president and son of the late D. R. Williams, took little active part in the management of Flawless. He was in close touch with his cousin, Henry, on matters of policy, acted occasionally as a representative for Henry, and did favors for the men such as making personal loans in times of individual distress. He concerned himself primarily with the matters of his father's estate and with the general supervision of a real estate business of his own.

Joseph D. Stocker, general manager since 1948, was a quiet, calm man in his late 40's who had been a casting salesman for the company since 1942. A graduate mechanical engineer, he had worked for a similar company since 1927 as salesman and later as sales manager.

"My job here," said Mr. Stocker, "is chiefly a checking job. Unless there's friction, the departments work directly together, and when they get into trouble I step in to smooth things out. I'm not tied down to anything. Of course, there are some things that I must handle myself. I make some big selling trips. I will still have to fool with castings sales from now on; Charles Bixby [sales manager and former manager of job order department] doesn't know how to handle them, and it's no trouble to me."

Mr. Stocker received a monthly report of sales by products; he did not receive any other regular written reports. Each day he checked all castings orders and did the necessary sales managerial work on these orders. Typically, Mr. Stocker did not visit the department heads but would discuss their problems when they brought them to him.

In 1949 he had created a "policy committee" composed of the five major department heads. With the exception of the meeting called in March when they discussed the late delivery problem, no meetings of this committee had been held in 1950.

"I tried to run the company without bothering Henry with details—that's what he wants, I believe, isn't it? This is a one-man job; if he's going to take a more active part, then I don't see what there is for me to do here."

During the past year general manager Stocker had made several changes in the organizational setup of Flawless. Formerly, (see Exhibit 1) Stocker had had 16 direct subordinates, including all production foremen and the castings department personnel—an arrangement inherited from his predecessor. The changes reducing his direct subordinates to six in number, consolidated all sales, except mixers, under one man, Charles P. Bixby; placed all engineering under the chief design engineer, Donald Canfield; and transferred authority over the production foremen to plant superintendent Miller (see Exhibit 2).

BOARD OF DIRECTORS

The owners of Flawless (H. D., T. J. and his two brothers, T. J.'s mother and aunt) plus the treasurer, Thomas R. O'Neill, comprised the board of directors. Regularly scheduled meetings of the entire board were very infrequent.

COMPETITION

Foundry Industry. In 1950, there were 5,300 foundries in the United States engaged in the manufacture of castings ranging from gray iron castings (which tonnagewise accounted for the highest share of the output), malleable iron and alloys, to casting in nonferrous metals like nickel and aluminum. In recent years there had been a noticeable trend towards alloys and nonferrous castings inasmuch as the number of companies specializing in these fields had increased at the expense of the gray iron foundries. Flawless to some extent had followed suit when part of its foundry was devoted to the making of alloy and nonferrous castings for its job order division.

About half of the foundries in 1950 were strictly jobbing shops of the type Flawless had represented in its past, while one-sixth were "captive shops" being departments of larger corporations making castings used for their own products. The remaining one-third were establishments producing for both their own needs and for sale on the outside. The size of the 5,300 foundries ranged from the tiny owner-run "neighborhood operation" with a limited product line to the large, multimillion dollar establishments, offering any conceivable cast shape made efficiently on mechanized equipment.

Mr. Stocker stated that in recent years it had become increasingly difficult for the smaller foundries to get the business of large customers because of the powers of reciprocal buying possessed by the larger integrated companies. Flawless had to compete by giving personalized service and quality but could not match the reciprocity arrangements.

Furthermore, the larger companies had been continually successful in developing new and more efficient casting techniques.

Industrial Mixing Machines. Machines for the mixing and blending of liquids, powders, and viscous substances were used in large numbers by the growing chemical, drug, plastic and food industries, as well as by the various building trades. In 1950, there were over 200 companies engaged in the manufacture of a variety of devices to serve mixing and blending needs.

The smallest of these machines were so-called laboratory "stirrers," a "beater" on a long rod, turned by air or electricity, which could be immersed in barrels or pails of liquid and held by hand. The largest of the mixing machines were huge tanks, with capacities of hundreds or thousands of gallons, fitted with agitator mechanisms or consisted of power-driven vibrating or rolling containers. Other examples were the familiar stationary or truck-mounted concrete mixers used in the building trade.

Some of the larger companies in the field, like Eastern Industries or Patterson Foundry & Equipment Company, manufactured mixers for the whole range of conceivable applications. Other smaller companies, including Flawless, specialized in a more limited field, making machines for solids or liquids only, or specializing in concrete mixers, hand mixers, or dough kneading machines, and the like. Sales of industrial mixers had expanded along with the industries served, and new developments like plastic-lined vessels or new heating methods had been pioneered.

Most of the companies, including many firms which offered a standardized line of mixers, made "tailored-to-order" machines upon request by the customer. Meeting the special needs of many customers required engineering skill and quality production, and Flawless was able to compete along these lines. This offset the fact that it did not offer a standard line of products. Flawless thus was typical of the smaller producer in the industry and sold directly to users on a custom basis.

PRODUCTION

Flawless had six production departments: foundry shop, machine shop, forge shop, pattern shop, mixer shop, and finishing shop (see Exhibit 2).

William D. Miller, plant superintendent, explained in July, 1950, that two production departments were in excellent shape with regard to orders: there were 254 mixers on order, enough to last the mixer department until the first of the year; and the machine shop had industrial parts ordered sufficient to carry it through November. Among the other departments the situation was not so good; the forge shop and the finishing shop which finished plumbing, stove, furnace, and some other cast iron parts each had only five weeks' work. The foundry and pattern shops had two weeks' work in standard parts but were better situated for the nonferrous work and job order iron casting, with a two-month backlog of orders.

FOUNDRY

Oldest of Flawless departments, the foundry for most of its history had made cast iron vessels and plumbing, stove, and furnace parts. Flawless, however, was not equipped to produce the steel parts which had gained in favor with many customers in recent years. With the decline of these products, foundry operations had been diversified to include production of soft-iron machine and parts casting and nonferrous castings. Most recently, permanent mold casting of nonferrous metals on a job order basis appeared to be a promising field, according to Miller and Stocker.

About half of the foundry floor was devoted to rows of standard parts molds; the rest was used for smaller soft-iron and nonferrous castings. Two 40-foot-high cupolas were used to melt iron, and two small electrical furnaces melted the nonferrous metals. Pouring of large castings was done by snap molders[1] who used ladles suspended from overhead monorails. Other workers poured smaller castings with 100-pound-capacity hand ladles. Molds were prepared in the morning and pouring was done in the afternoon. In July, with a shortage of orders, snap molders were working only two days a week.

The foundry was supervised by one foreman and two subforemen. About half of the men in the foundry were laborers who were shifted from one phase of the operations to another as the labor needs changed during the day. The management consultant felt that although there were three supervisors, the foundry was only about 60% efficient. President Williams believed the foundry was only moderately profitable at best, though there were no separate department records to substantiate this feeling.

Part-time technical adviser to the foundry was Herbert W. Kayser who had been with Flawless for 27 years and who had been foundry superintendent for several years prior to 1950. In January, 1950, Stocker relieved Kayser of authority over the foundry and placed him

---

[1] Snap molding is a process which employs molding flasks consisting of two halves which are closed with a snap fastener.

in the sales department "to cut down on the number of foundry supervisors and to gain a solicitor for foundry orders."

Kayser had a knowledge of metallurgy which no one else in the company possessed; thus, when difficult foundry problems arose, it was necessary that he be called back to the foundry as a technical adviser. Kayser maintained a primary interest in the foundry, dropping his sales work when foundry troubles materialized. Neither sales manager Bixby nor plant superintendent Miller considered himself to have authority over Kayser while the latter held this dual capacity. Both men wanted general manager Stocker to clarify Kayser's position.

The most recent job in the foundry involving "permanent" molds had been the production of 500 intricate, thin-walled aluminum castings. Two engineers had tried to design the mold without success, and Kayser was called in to aid. After conducting experiments for five weeks, he remedied the flaws in the mold design so that volume production could be begun in late July.

FINISHING SHOP

Vessels, standard plumbing, and stove and furnace parts made in the foundry were taken to the finishing shop where, under the supervision of one foreman, these parts, as well as some of the gray iron machine parts, were machined, cleaned, and made ready for delivery to outside customers.

MACHINE SHOP

The nonferrous castings from the foundry generally were taken to the machine shop for finishing operations. Equipped with all conventional machine tools, the machine shop handled most industrial machinery parts orders.

With the aid of one subforeman, this department was run by foreman Walter Bridges, a thin, energetic New Englander who was continually worried about the lack of ambition of the men: "They just don't seem to want to improve themselves." Bridges planned all of his department's operations, did most of the cost and time estimating for bids on machine work, and designed the department's tools and jigs. The latter work, he said, was taking too much of his time. He had formerly kept job times by machining operations which aided greatly in estimating. Upon a complaint by the labor union that this was unfair, general manager Stocker, without consulting Bridges, had ordered the discontinuance of this recording of incremental operation times. "They won't tell me why they do things and they don't give a damn whether you like it or not," said Bridges in reference to this incident. "They won't allow me enough control, but they sure raise hell when something goes wrong."

FORGE SHOP

The forge shop was the starting place for most of the parts used in mixing machine manufacture. It was equipped with plate and bar shears, metal punches and saws, heavy drill presses, bending machines, hot working forges, and a blacksmith shop. Most of the equipment was old, and the area was crowded, with the result that the aisles were usually blocked with wagonloads of work-in-process materials. A shop foreman with the aid of one subforeman controlled the flow of materials visually. Materials were moved from machine to machine on small steel wagons which were pushed by hand and which sometimes required six men or more to move. Aisles were considered too narrow for lift trucks, and the ceiling too low to install a bridge crane. With inadequate space and a great variety of heavy materials to be moved, the material-handling problem contributed to frequent temporary bottlenecks which in turn caused delays in production in the mixer shop.

MIXER DEPARTMENT

Located on the other side of, and adjacent to the forge shop, was the mixer department, biggest of Flawless' production departments. This department was under the supervision of Daniel F. Glines, Jr., and three subforemen. Glines was a son of the forge shop foreman. The department consisted of a single production line with six stations, several subassembly areas, a mixer repair area, and a paint shop. Mixers of every type were built on the one production line. Subassemblies such as frames, bracketing, and agitator assemblies were built in side areas and fed into the main production line.

The work of the mixer department was an assembling operation done chiefly by welding and riveting. The work at the first two stations was nearly standard, with the custom variation in the mixing machines being handled at the later stations. More than half of the mixers produced were tank type mixing machines. Even with these semistandard jobs, however, the necessary variations in production time hampered uniform flow of work from station to station. Also, there might be six different types of mixing machines on the line at one time, with the slowest job setting the pace for the whole group. Mixer production averaged slightly more than two per day.

In addition to handling the mixing machine work, Glines with one of his subforemen supervised welding operations on industrial orders. In June, at the suggestion of the management consultant, part of this work had been shifted into a separate area.

The plant superintendent in charge of all production departments was William D. "Bill" Miller, 35-year-old mechanical engineer. After several years with the company as an engineer before the war, he became production control manager in 1946; in 1947, he was named plant superintendent, but with no substantial change in his duties of production control and with no authority over the foremen, this authority being vested in the general manager.

Shortly after becoming plant superintendent in 1947, Miller installed a "Productrol" system for control of production scheduling. The Productrol boards with the accompanying records and one clerk served as a message center through which all orders and information came into the shop. Records were kept of all orders moving between departments. Miller asserted that the system, coupled with frequent checks with the foremen, had afforded good control on long orders but had been less effective on short-run orders.

In April, 1949, Miller requested another clerk to help in operating the Productrol system. Stocker felt that the system was inadequate and too expansive; rather than grant Miller's request, he discontinued the Productrol system completely. As a substitute each foreman was to control his own department completely and was to be responsible to general manager Stocker. All orders were handled directly between foremen and the engineering department without any central control point such as had existed under the Productrol system.

Miller continued to be responsible for interdepartmental scheduling of work and for the prompt delivery of orders to customers. He conferred with each foreman daily to keep informed on the progress of work and to try to smooth the flow of work-in-process between departments.

After the discontinuance of the Productrol system, the number of late deliveries to customers of products increased. "By March, 1950, the situation had become intolerable and very confusing to all. There was no co-ordination between departments," said Miller. "I was bypassed by the foremen and by those in the engineering office so that I had no real control of production scheduling, and Joseph Stocker was still acting like a castings salesman.

"We had an executive meeting last March when the late orders' problem became acute," continued Miller. "Much to everyone's surprise, Joseph Stocker told us that I had the full responsibility for the plant. Then I demanded, and got, authority over the foremen. We still have a lot of educating to do, but the foremen are getting to know now that I am their boss. No one gives them orders except me, and no one is going around me anymore—either up or down. The consultant has helped me a lot in organizing my work. Now that I know what my job is, and just what my bounds of authority are, this change of command is going to work or else."

In May, 1950, Miller had installed biweekly foremen's meetings at which mutual problems were discussed and at which the foremen were informed of developments and company policies which affected them. "A good foreman will stand on his own hind legs; we haven't got but three who do so now. The rest usually try to shift responsibilities wherever possible; for example, if a worker tells a foreman to 'go to hell,' he just takes it to Floyd (personnel manager). That's no way for a foreman to act. There has been a lot of apathy among foremen and workers. Since the 'renaissance,' however, I believe that they will come around."

After the March meeting Miller decided to confer with the sales and purchasing departments twice weekly. The status of all orders was reviewed, and the information of all three was pooled regarding material needs, sales prospects, production facilities available, and the expected delivery time on orders. Miller carried a clip board with him on which the status of work in every department was noted. He conferred daily with each production foreman, checking on the progress of new and late orders and helping them with their problems.

Delivery time estimates were asked by most industrial parts and mixing machine customers, with less frequent requests for such promises from castings customers. These estimates were given to the sales manager by Miller. With the aid of the production foreman he would make such estimates after consideration of production requirements of an order and the current availability of production facilities.

Because of the custom nature of the shop and the consequent great variety of jobs, no production standards had been employed. Labor times by whole jobs[2] were collected through a job-card time-clock system and recorded by a shop clerk. No record of elemental work times had been kept except in the instance of Mr. Bridges' efforts in the machine shop. Delivery time estimates, as well as cost estimates, were made on the

---

[2] Whole jobs might include several products.

basis of previous work for whole jobs, with the limited aid of the job-card information. Such estimating was considered satisfactory for jobs closely similar to previous work, according to treasurer O'Neill who was responsible for the collection of time and cost information. The lack of elemental work standards, however, greatly limited the accuracy of estimates on new types of work. "Our products are so varied that we can't establish standard costs," said Mr. O'Neill. "I wish someone could devise a system for us which wouldn't require a whole flock of men to operate it."

ENGINEERING

Donald Canfield, chief engineer, age 38, came to Flawless in 1935 as a draftsman-engineer with a degree in mechanical engineering. He was named chief design engineer in 1941. Subsequently he had been concerned primarily with mixer design and engineering until all engineering was consolidated in the fall of 1949 and placed under his direction.

This department, containing ten engineer-draftsmen, was responsible for most of the price estimating work for product design, for plant engineering, and for inspection of finished mixers. In addition, Canfield made infrequent selling trips.

When customer inquiries were received, the engineering department made price estimates for the sales manager with the aid of the accounting and purchasing departments. The accounting department supplied labor cost information on past work completed, which was used as an aid in estimating the labor cost of new work. Material cost estimates were obtained from the purchasing department. On items concerning which the purchasing agent had to make outside inquiries, Canfield complained that action had usually been slow. Overhead rates were fixed by the accounting department, expressed as a fixed percentage of direct labor for most departments. Canfield stated that overhead rates had been changed only three times in the past 15 years and that he doubted the accuracy of these rates.

All customer orders came to Canfield. There, shop orders were written up, materials were requisitioned from the purchasing department, the necessary engineering work was done, and the order was sent to the shop for production. The engineering department had no control over the production department except indirectly in an advisory capacity and in an inspecting capacity.

The required engineering work usually consisted of adapting a standard design to meet the specific requirements of the customer. Engineering work usually was necessary on every mixing machine order. Most of the industrial machinery parts required no engineering work as designs were supplied by the customer. In cases where original design work had to be done, this work was performed sometimes at the time of customer inquiry but more usually after the receipt of a firm order. In the past year they had developed two new agitator assemblies for mixing machines, a new stainless steel mixer, and had improved the present mixing machine designs. "We seem to be just one jump ahead of the sheriff all the time around here," said Canfield. "There is no time to plan for the future."

ACCOUNTING

Thomas R. O'Neill, controller and treasurer, was a slight man of about 60 years who said that he had been trained by the first president, E. A. Williams, to "keep the figures close to himself." An executive with the company since 1925, O'Neill was the financial adviser to Henry Williams, supervisor of all accounting and financial work, and personal handler of the private ledger (profits, officers' salaries, etc.).

An assistant controller and four other men completed the department. Conventional company accounting was practiced. The department kept all Flawless records and handled most financial transactions.

There was no interdepartmental accounting, and no records were made of departmental profitability. Total costs by product were not kept. "We just throw it all together and see how it comes out at the end of the year," said the assistant controller.

PURCHASING

George T. Marchand, purchasing agent, stated that he was responsible for all purchases. With an assistant to handle local purchases and routine work, Marchand concerned himself with major items of supply, inventory control, and the making of purchase inquiries.

On receiving a material requisition from engineering, he would determine whether the material could be taken from stock or must be ordered. In the latter case he would make outside inquiries, getting price and delivery date from material suppliers. "Getting special stuff is a headache, and we seem to need a lot of it—odd-sized bolts for some mixers, special material for an industrial part, and so on. The engineering department always wants it in a hurry, and I have to keep pushing the suppliers to get the stuff here on time."

Inventory control was decentralized and nearly all visual. Marchand kept records of plate, shape, and bar stock (steel), checking frequently with the foremen to insure adequate supply of the right sizes, and taking quarterly actual inventories. Foremen kept inventories on less critical items such as sand or limestone for the foundry. The plant superintendent kept castings inventories, and the sales manager for mixers, R. F. Brown, kept inventories of mixing machines and accessories. "Inventory control is sort of a joint responsibility among the foremen, Stocker, Brown, and myself," said Marchand. "If it had been my full responsibility, we wouldn't have run out of stainless steel sheet here last month like we did; they just didn't tell me that the supplies were low. Then the market tightened up, and we couldn't get nearly enough."

SALES

When responsibility for all the sales (except mixers) had been consolidated in late 1949, the job of sales manager was given to 33-year-old Charles Bixby, who had previously been head of the job order sales department. Henry Williams considered him to have been an excellent man in handling these industrial orders and in handling government war contract negotiations during World War II.

There were four engineer salesmen under Bixby. Formerly, three of these had been castings salesmen exclusively and one had been a parts salesman. After consolidation all four were authorized to sell both lines of products, but actually there had been little change in their work, the three still being "99% castings salesmen." Bixby also sold industrial parts about 25% of his time.

The salesmen were paid on a commission basis with a small drawing account. Bixby in his new capacity did not believe that he should continue to draw sales commissions since it put him in an embarrassing position with his salesmen at the time. He wanted his salary tied to the sales of the whole department and had made such a proposal to Stocker in late 1949, but as yet no action had been taken.

Prior to the new sales setup general manager Stocker had been castings sales manager in addition to his job as general manager. When the sales switch had been made, Bixby had understood that Stocker was to transfer the castings business gradually to him. In July, 1950, Stocker was still handling all castings sales work. The two castings salesmen had been told of the new setup but were confused because Stocker still handled their accounts. "I haven't pushed this castings control," said Bixby. "It will work out eventually. As long as the castings orders are being handled, it's O.K. by me."

At the time of the consolidation of sales, the handling of all mixer sales was transferred to Robert S. Brown, a former mixer salesman. Henry Williams described Brown as a "wonderful salesman—the alpha and omega of the mixer division." The mixing machines made by Flawless had been successful in gaining a good reputation in the market, according to Brown, and were well received by old and new customers alike.

Brown operated with three office men and eight salesmen who called on customers directly. "During the past few years we could have sold all of our mixing machines over the telephone but we need the contacts so we have maintained the sales force. We sell mixing machines for a few hundred dollars more than our big competitors at times, but we give quality custom service and the customers know it. We haven't had a serious failure of our machines in 14 years," said Mr. Brown.

Mr. Brown added that their chief customers had been the large chemical and food manufacturers who bought both on price and quality. "We can't keep mixers in stock because of the custom nature of our work and because of the expense, but we can deliver within about five weeks after an order is placed."

Bixby stated that the production co-ordination meetings with Miller and Marchand were working reasonably well. "We get expediting and delivery promises pretty accurately from Miller now. This has been a sore subject in the past, but we are rocking along all right now. We still fall down on a few promises, but it isn't as bad as it was last year.

"These production meetings are the only ones of any sort that we have in this company," continued Bixby. "We need more meetings. They would prevent lots of our problems. No one ever asked my advice on company problems. I don't like to keep running and complaining, but I would like my thoughts heard nevertheless. Also, we shouldn't have to ask what's going on; we ought to be informed automatically. I don't see how a company runs without the executives getting together once in a while."

The Flawless sales program was almost entirely direct selling by engineer salesmen. Occasional advertisements were run in trade journals, and some direct-mail advertising was used, including calendars and product brochures.

LABOR RELATIONS

Floyd D. Barnes, age 32, had been personnel manager since the spring of 1949. An engineer, previously he had been assistant to Charles Bixby in the industrial job order department. He was familiar with every phase of the company's operations, acting as plant superintendent for two weeks in July when Miller was on vacation. Common interests in the human problems of the business and in philosophical matters had drawn him close to Henry Williams. The latter felt that Floyd was one of the few men in the company with whom he had much in common and was one of the few whom he knew well.

In July, 1950, Barnes had just completed a wage negotiation with the union granting a 5-cent-per-hour general wage increase plus six paid holidays.

Year-end profit bonuses had been paid to the men for the past two years, 11 cents per hour and 5¼ cents per hour, respectively. The men stated that they did not want such bonuses but would rather have the money in their regular pay envelopes. With the negotiated raise the company did not intend to grant any further such bonuses.

Bonuses were to continue, however, for office and supervisory personnel. These bonuses had been on an arbitrary basis "according to a man's value to the company," as decided by president Williams.

"There was a complete lack of trust in the early days of the union," said Barnes. "Things are much better now, but some of that distrust still exists among the workers. In trying to overcome this, we have been actually too lenient. No one has been fired for inefficiency or insubordination in over a year. Petty grievances have multiplied. I now believe that we must handle the men with a firm but fair hand.

"The men don't have any enthusiasm for the work as they did before the war," Barnes added. "The snap molders are only putting out 60 molds a day each, where we know they can do 100 easily. In the mixer shop the men did put on a little drive in June to increase production while the consultants were here, but now they have slipped into their old complacent ways; furthermore, the supervisors have done little to get more work out of the men. I don't know—perhaps the basic trouble is that no one knows exactly what he is supposed to do."

OPERATIONS AND PLANS

In the spring of 1950, Flawless designed a special casting for a prospective customer who intended to buy 1,200 units. The design was approved by the customer's engineering department; this design was given to a large competitor for bidding. Flawless quoted a lower price than the other firm, and the Flawless bid was accepted tentatively. When sent to main company headquarters for final action, however, the order was changed, going to the large competitor presumably for reasons of reciprocity, according to Stocker.

With the memory of this incident freshly in mind and the knowledge of developments in the foundry industry, general manager Stocker was searching for new ways and ideas to make use of the idle casting facilities and men.

By July, 1950, the management consultant firm, which had been hired by Mr. Williams to analyze the operations of the company, had studied the mixer shop and the foundry and expected to complete the study of the management organization and of the whole company by early fall.

In the mixer department the consultants believed that production could be doubled on the single assembly line without any basic changes. Because of the great variations in work they stated that close supervision was needed for efficiency and that foreman Glines previously had not been spending enough time in direct work supervision. During June, the consultants put three extra supervisors on the mixer line for methods study; the workmen made a sustained effort to increase production, turning out 67 units, an increase of 18% over the months of 1950. Foreman Glines did not receive the help of the consultants willingly. Miller asked that he congratulate the men on the June performance, but Glines refrained from doing so. In early July the consultants had made several minor suggestions about improvements in production methods, but none had been acted on. In July, mixer production dropped to 38.

In June, 25 of the mixers produced had to be taken off the line incomplete for lack of certain rubber parts; in July, the production line was held up three days for lack of rivets of a special size. An improvement on the visual control of mixer parts inventory was being devised by the consultants with written records and one man to act as a full-time stock chaser. It was hoped that this new system of inventory control would eliminate holdups from material shortages and would allow Glines more time in the future for direct work supervision.

The consulting firm was also devising a standard cost system and production control system for the mixer department. The methods would be to set standards for the basic fundamental operations performed in the shop and then to synthesize a set of job standards from these elements for each variety of mixer that was produced. Use of the system would require the services of one timekeeper; it was hoped to extend this system later to all departments.

After studying the foundry, the consultants made recommendations in July to rearrange the layout, reducing the floor area assigned to standard molds and increasing the nonferrous area. It was recommended that two bridge cranes be installed to replace the present single-rail system and that a separate building be constructed for the permanent mold work. It was further recommended that the pattern shop be combined with the foundry and that the combined supervision be reduced from five to two foremen. Mr. Stocker said that at least the physical changes would be made in the near future.

With an old plant, overcrowding had become a serious problem, particularly in the forge and mixer shops. Several plant layout revisions had been made by the consulting firm. On the one hand, a new mixer building was considered. "Stainless steel mixers are going extremely well," said Stocker, "and to get volume production on them it would be best to have a new building." On the other hand, Stocker was considering moving the forge shop out under the adjacent craneway and expanding the mixer shop with two parallel production lines into the present forge shop area. This revision would give these departments much needed additional space and would allow the establishment of a second mixer line, mitigating the problems of building so many different types of mixers on one production line. Mr. Stocker stated that he wanted to get a full plant revision worked out before taking any action on an individual department layout.

Old equipment was another problem, much of it being over 20 years old. It was realized that this contributed to high cost production, though no figures had been accumulated to substantiate this feeling. "When the money is available out of earnings, we will buy new equipment as we can," said Mr. Stocker; "we don't want to borrow to buy equipment." In recent months new mixer shop tools and an automatic turret lathe had been purchased. Most critical needs were considered to be a new plate punch, a plate shear, and a milling machine. The new plate punch would effect labor savings which would pay off its cost in three years. At present, however, there was not an adequate space in the forge shop in which to put it.

Returning from a week's selling trip on July 26, 1950, general manager Stocker beamingly presented Henry Williams with the first big order for standard castings which the company had received in over a year; "I sewed it up just before the big boys arrived!"

The Rose Company

MR. JAMES PIERCE had recently received word of his appointment as plant manager of Plant X, one of the older established units of the Rose Company. As such, Mr. Pierce was to be responsible for the management and administration at Plant X of all functions and personnel except sales.

Both top management and Mr. Pierce realized that there were several unique features about his new assignment. Mr. Pierce decided to assess his new situation and relationships before undertaking his assignment. He was personally acquainted with the home office executives, but had met few of the plant personnel. This case contains some of his reflections regarding the new assignment.

The Rose Company conducted marketing activities throughout the United States and in certain foreign countries. These activities were directed from the home office by a vice-president in charge of sales.

Exhibit 1

THE ROSE COMPANY

Old Organization

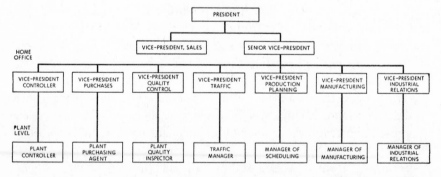

Manufacturing operations and certain other departments were under the supervision and control of a senior vice-president. These are shown in Exhibit 1. For many years the company had operated a highly centralized functional type of manufacturing organization. There was no general manager at any plant; each of the departments in a plant re-

276

ported on a line basis to its functional counterpart at the home office. For instance, the industrial-relations manager of a particular plant reported to the vice-president in charge of industrial relations at the home office, the plant controller to the vice-president and controller, and so on.

Mr. Pierce stated that in the opinion of the top management the record of Plant X had not been satisfactory for several years. The board had recently approved the erection of a new plant in a different part of the city and the use of new methods of production. Lower costs of processing and a reduced manpower requirement at the new plant were expected. Reduction of costs and improved quality of products were needed to maintain competitive leadership and gain some slight product advantage. The proposed combination of methods of manufacturing and mixing materials had not been tried elsewhere in the company. Some features would be entirely new to employees.

According to Mr. Pierce the top management of the Rose Company was beginning to question the advisability of the central control of manufacturing operations. The officers decided to test the value of a decentralized operation in connection with Plant X. They apparently believed that a general management representative in Plant X was needed if the new experiment in manufacturing methods and the required rebuilding of the organization were to succeed.

Prior to the new assignment Mr. Pierce had been an accounting executive in the controller's department of the company. From independent sources the case writer learned that Mr. Pierce had demonstrated analytical ability and general administrative capacity. He was generally liked by people. From top management's point of view he had an essential toughness described as an ability to see anything important through. By some he was regarded as the company's efficiency expert. Others thought he was a perfectionist and aggressive in reaching the goals that had been set. Mr. Pierce was aware of these opinions about his personal behavior.

Mr. Pierce summarized his problem in part as follows: "I am going into a situation involving a large number of changes. I will have a new plant—new methods and processes—but most of all I will be dealing with a set of changed relationships. Heretofore all the heads of departments in the plant reported to their functional counterparts in the home office. Now they will report to me. I am a complete stranger and in addition this is my first assignment in a major 'line' job. The men will know this.

"When I was called into the senior vice-president's office to be informed of my new assignment he asked me to talk with each of the functional members of his staff. The vice-presidents in charge of production planning, manufacturing, and industrial relations said they were going to issue all headquarters instructions to me as plant manager and they were going to cut off their connections with their counterparts in my plant. The other home office executives admitted their functional counterparts would report to me in line capacity. They should obey my orders and I would be responsible for their pay and promotion. But these executives proposed to follow the common practice of many companies of maintaining a dotted line or functional relationship with these men. I realize that these two different patterns of home office–plant relationships will create real administrative problems for me."

Exhibit 2 shows the organization relationships as defined in these conferences.

Exhibit 2

THE ROSE COMPANY
New Organization

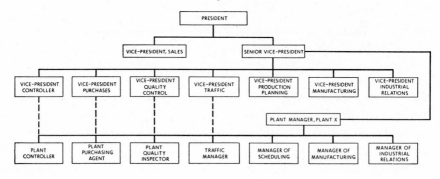

The Larger Company (A)

THE PHONE RANG, and highly indignant words blared: "Masters, what do you mean by submitting a report to all the executives without first talking it over with the division manager!"

Masters replied, "My men made every effort to see him. They never got past his secretary. He instructed her to have them talk to the works manager."

"I don't believe a word of it. Vining is up in arms. He says the report is vindictive. What are you trying to do—embarrass the division manager? I don't believe your men ever tried to see Vining and I question the veracity of their statements!" The phone on the other end was hung up with a bang.

Masters said to himself, "Gunn must be hot under the collar or he wouldn't have called me when I was away from my own office, visiting another plant."

The next day Masters' office received Gunn's letter confirming this telephone conversation and demanding an explanation. A week later Masters received a letter from Gunn's superior, a Mr. Jordan, stating, "I have read the aforementioned report and discussed it with Mr. Gunn. He has advised me that the report is essentially untrue, inaccurate, and overstated. I am not satisfied to have such wide differences of opinion and have scheduled a meeting to be held in my office on ———. I would appreciate it if you would be present."

In light of the phone call and the two letters, Mr. Masters decided to reassess all events leading to this climax.

. . . .

The cast of characters is as shown in Exhibit 1. The Larger Company had an elaborate organizational structure as a result of its scale of operation. At the headquarters office of the corporation the president had a group of staff vice-presidents in charge of functions. Mr. Masters was a staff department head reporting to the vice-president, manufacturing. The headquarters staff departments assisted in policy formulation and made staff studies for the operating organization when requested. Members of such departments were encouraged to offer ideas for the good

Exhibit 1

THE LARGER COMPANY (A)
Organization Chart

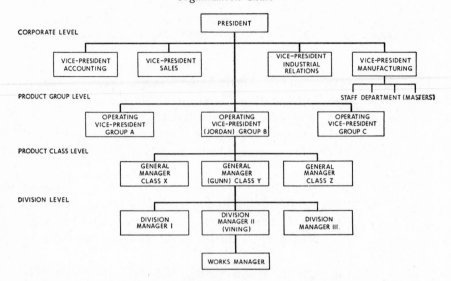

of the company. Their proposals were considered by a management committee consisting of the vice-presidents at the headquarters level and the operating vice-presidents in charge of product groups. Mr. Jordan of this case was the operating vice-president, Product Group "B."

Under the product groups there were general managers of product classes. They supervised the division managers, who were in charge of the sales and manufacturing operations of one or more plants. Mr. Gunn was general manager of Product Class "Y." One of the four division managers under him was Mr. Vining of Division II.

. . . .

Two years before this incident occurred, Mr. Masters' staff department proposed to the management committee, with the approval of the vice-president, manufacturing, that representatives of Mr. Masters' office join with representatives of the vice-president, accounting to make studies in each plant of the procedures for and actual practices regarding expense control. The suggestion was approved, and enthusiastically endorsed by the general managers. They sent a letter through channels to each division manager advising that periodically a team of two men would visit each plant to make a comprehensive analysis of expense-control practices and systems.

After a visit these field representatives of headquarters were to prepare a report giving findings and recommendations. They were to discuss it with the appropriate division manager and his staff. Thus they would be able to incorporate any specific plans of action set in motion by division managers. Next, a report was to be submitted to Mr. Masters. Both his department and the accounting office were to make comments. The final document was then to be submitted to the vice-president, accounting; the vice-president, manufacturing; the operating vice-president, product group; the general manager, product class; and the division manager concerned.

This general procedure had worked smoothly within the company until general manager Gunn of Product Class "Y" exploded. In the first plant studied, the two team members spent approximately four weeks examining documents, interviewing line management, interrogating industrial engineers, observing operations, etc. The employees of this plant were very co-operative. Some of the facts revealed by them could have been embarrassing to the division manager. The team was enabled to make specific recommendations for improvement to the division manager. His reception of the report was good. According to him, the study had given an opportunity to review his situation and get his house in order. He intended to implement the recommendations unless they were changed in the review process at the higher level. Sixteen other plants were visited with reasonably good acceptance of the work of the team.

. . . .

In his review of the Division II situation, Mr. Masters found that the team had observed all the required organization routines. Mr. Sawyer, representing Mr. Masters, had a master's degree in industrial engineering and had twelve years with the company. Mr. Peters, from the accounting office, had served that department for thirty years. Both men had shown ability to gain confidences and to use them discreetly. They were considered straightforward, conscientious, and unobtrusive in their work. In Division II the team obtained from plant personnel considerable information which pointed up a number of practices and procedures requiring improvement. In the opinion of the team members, the operating organization at the lower levels sincerely wanted to make these changes. The team thought that there was some resistance at some level within the division to these suggestions and, in fact, to any from headquarters.

While the study was in process, Mr. Sawyer advised Mr. Masters about the possible impact of the information which was being collected.

Mr. Masters emphasized the necessity to report to the division manager, and Mr. Sawyer promised that he and Mr. Peters would do so.

The team made several efforts to see the division manager, but his secretary informed them that he was busy. They questioned the secretary closely to learn if the manager had knowledge of the procedural requirement that he and his staff go over the report with the team. She replied that he knew the requirements, but was too busy to discuss a headquarters program. He would ask his assistant, the works manager, and several staff members to go over it, and what they approved would be all right with him. Eventually this meeting was held.

The members of the local management staff took a very reasonable attitude; they admitted the bad situation portrayed in the analysis and offered their assurances that immediate steps would be taken towards improvement. The team members thought that the local management staff was glad to have their problem brought out in the open, and were delighted to have the suggestions of the headquarters representatives.

. . . .

When Mr. Masters reviewed the report, both team members expressed their complete dissatisfaction with the brush-off they got from the division manager. Masters took this as a cue to question them extensively concerning their findings and recommendations. In view of the sensitive character of the situation and the possible controversy that it might create, he was reluctant to distribute the report. It was the consensus of the remainder of the staff and the representatives of the accounting office that the usual transmittal letter should be prepared, and distribution made. Mr. Masters signed this letter and took no other action until the telephone call came from Mr. Gunn.

The Larger Company (B)

MR. JORDAN, operating vice-president, Product Group "B" of the Larger Company, called a meeting to review the report submitted by Mr. Masters' staff department and the accounting office. Mr. Jordan, Mr. Gunn, Mr. Masters, the vice-president, accounting and the vice-president, manufacturing attended. In a very constructive, two-hour meeting, the report was evaluated and many conclusions were confirmed.

Division manager Vining was not present. Mr. Jordan had not invited him because he wanted to keep "heat" out of the meeting. Mr. Jordan regarded Mr. Vining as an "individual operator" who on more than one occasion had shown definite disrespect for headquarters' functions and programs.

There was some heat in the meeting, nevertheless. Mr. Gunn stated that Mr. Masters should have discussed the report with him. Thus he might have had an opportunity to take executive action at his level. When a division manager failed to consider a report the superior should have a chance even though the formal procedure did not provide for it. Mr. Gunn said that Mr. Masters should have known that. Mr. Gunn also read a letter that had been prepared by Mr. Vining. It generally and categorically denied most of the statements in the report that were unsatisfactory to him. The vice-president, accounting and Mr. Masters, however, had certain information and supplementary reports which seemed to discount the effectiveness of the letter of rebuttal.

Before too much time elapsed, Mr. Jordan turned the discussion into ways of bringing about improvement in the future. "Where there was so much smoke," he observed, "there might be some fire." He suggested that men of higher rank review the work of the two team members; this would serve either to confirm or modify their findings. This step seemed advisable in order to assuage the feelings of the local division manager.

The meeting ended on a very harmonious note. Mr. Jordan asked Mr. Gunn to see Mr. Vining. "He needs to understand and appreciate

283

that he has a responsibility to find time to review and comment on the type of reports being made by team members."

Mr. Masters was pleased by the results of the meeting and the follow-up actions. Mr. Gunn must have talked with Mr. Vining. Whatever was said may have contributed to better working relationships. Plant co-operation immediately improved. The division manager cleared any obstacles interfering with the success of the program. His influence was particularly noticeable in its effect on the behavior of the line supervisory organization. According to Mr. Masters, co-operation rather than resistance was now encouraged. The home office team became the advisory team it was intended to be.

In reviewing this experience Mr. Masters said, "There was bound to be some form of blow-up because Vining had the reputation of thinking he did not have to conform to company-wide programs unless it was to his advantage. Further, he was more rugged in nature than Gunn. On many occasions Gunn was inclined to support Vining. There has been a very definite change in this respect during the latter part of this year."

Potter Drug and Chemical Company

THE POTTER DRUG AND CHEMICAL COMPANY, founded in Boston in 1883, was in 1946 the largest and one of the oldest manufacturers of proprietary[1] medicinal soaps and ointments in the United States. Its products were distributed in the United States and abroad under the trademark Cuticura, a name formulated by combining the Latin words "cutis," meaning skin, and "cura," meaning care (see Exhibit 1).

In 1932, following the death of his predecessor, Mr. S. M. Best became president of the company. At that time there was considerable doubt among the company's board of directors regarding the possibility of re-establishing former sales volume. Though the concern had never failed to earn a yearly profit, sales had dropped from a peak of $4,000,-000 in 1919 to a low of $1,476,000 in 1932. After 1932, sales of Cuticura preparations did increase, however, and reached a 26-year peak of $3,195,000 in 1945; in 1946 an even larger total volume was in prospect.

COMPANY PRODUCTS

Cuticura ointment and Cuticura soap were the company's original preparations. Although the variety of products manufactured by the company had increased, over 86% of the sales volume in 1945 still resulted from sales of soap and ointment. An analysis of current Cuticura products is shown in Exhibit 2.

Cuticura ointment was composed of the following active ingredients: petrolatum, unbleached paraffin and mineral oil, beeswax, and oxyquinoline—an antiseptic coal-tar derivative. The ointment was recommended by the company for temporary relief of itching caused by eczema; also for the relief of chapping, windburn, and diaper rash. Cuticura medicated soap was made of a high-quality soap stock in combination with the active ingredients of the ointment. Its suggested uses

---

[1] Any such drug, chemical, or similar preparation used in the treatment of diseases, if such article is protected against free competition as to name, product, composition, or process of manufacture by secrecy, patent or copyright, or by any other means. (Council on Pharmacy and Chemistry, American Medical Association.)

Exhibit 1

POTTER DRUG AND CHEMICAL COMPANY

Cuticura Products

Cuticura Preparations

KNOWN AND USED THE WORLD OVER FOR MORE THAN THREE GENERATIONS···

CUTICURA SOAP ··· LUXURIOUS IN QUALITY YET ONE OF THE MOST ECONOMICAL FINE SOAPS YOU CAN BUY. Because Cuticura is one of the most mild and gentle of soaps as well as one of the most pure and reliable, it may be used with confidence on a new born baby and right on through life. Cuticura has the essential ingredients of an exceptionally fine soap, is mildly medicated—and has, in addition, a delicate fragrance that is pleasing to the most discriminating men and women, and suitable to infants and children. Another quality that distinguishes Cuticura Soap is that it is hard-milled and therefore surprisingly long-lasting and economical. Cuticura should be used not only for the daily care of your face and hands, but as your regular bath and shampoo soap as well.

CUTICURA OINTMENT ··· AN EMOLLIENT HELPFUL IN MANY WAYS THE YEAR AROUND. Cuticura Ointment is a pure, fragrant, mildly medicated emollient that justly deserves its wide use and recognition, for it goes beyond the ordinary toilet requirements of skin and scalp care. Its soothing, comforting and palliative qualities furnish prompt aid in relieving such irritations as diaper rash, chafing, heat rash, rough red skin due to weather or work, small cuts, minor burns and temporary relief of the itching of eczema. So varied are its purposes that Cuticura Ointment should be in regular use in every household. Always use Cuticura Soap also where cleansing is indicated.

IMPORTANT NOTE REGARDING CUTICURA SOAP AND OINTMENT INGREDIENTS: The "Unbleached Paraffin" and "Unbleached Mineral Oil" designated in the formulae of Cuticura Soap and Ointment contain traces of sulfur and coloring materials, thus differing from U.S.P. Paraffin and U.S.P. Mineral Oil.

For over 60 years "Unbleached Paraffin" and "Unbleached Mineral Oil" have been a part of the Cuticura Soap and Ointment formulae.

CUTICURA TALCUM ··· A SUPERIOR YET INEXPENSIVE DUSTING POWDER. Made of the highest grade "air float" talcum, borated and delicately perfumed, Cuticura Talcum is mildly medicated to help make it soothing and comforting to the skin as well as a safeguard against chafing and similar minor irritations. Cuticura Talcum should be used as a dusting powder after the bath. It overcomes the unpleasant effects of perspiration, removes after-shaving shine, is comforting to babies and children — particularly during the summer — and is cooling and soothing to sunburn.

Victory Package

Exhibit 2

POTTER DRUG AND CHEMICAL COMPANY

Active Products—1946

Cuticura Products	Year Introduced	Size (in Ounces)	Price	Production Status	Sales Market
Ointment........	1878	¼, ¾, 1¾, 4¾	10¢, 25¢, 50¢, $1.00	Regularly in production	Domestic and foreign
Soap...........	1878	1½, 3½	10¢, 25¢	Regularly in production	Domestic and foreign
Talcum powder...	1920	1¾, 4	10¢, 25¢	Regularly in production	Primarily foreign
Shaving stick....	1923	2	25¢	Production on demand	Primarily foreign
Shaving cream...	1929	2½	25¢	Production on demand	Domestic
Shampoo........	1936	½	10¢	Production on demand	Foreign
Cold cream......	1936	4	$1.00	Production on demand	Domestic
Hand cream.....	1936	4	$1.00	Production on demand	Domestic
Liquid antiseptic	1946	3	60¢	Regularly in production	Domestic and foreign

were for general skin care and for relieving externally caused pimples and blackheads. Cuticura shaving cream and shaving stick also included the same base used in Cuticura soap and ointment. Cuticura talcum was an all-purpose powder which the company recommended for a variety of purposes including after-shave use; also as a dusting powder for babies.

In 1936 three new items were added to the Cuticura line: shampoo, hand cream, and cold cream. None of these products achieved sales success in the United States, and in 1946 they were being manufactured only upon the receipt of orders from wholesalers.

In 1946, after a two-year trial sales program in Canada, Cuticura liquid antiseptic was being distributed on a trial basis in the New York City and Detroit areas.

Three proprietary preparations, formerly manufactured by the company, were no longer produced. Cuticura blood pills and Cuticura chest plasters had been withdrawn in the twenties. Resolvent, a liquid blood medicine sold as a tonic, was a popular product which rivaled Cuticura soap in sales volume during the thirties, but its distribution and sale had been halted in 1938. The passage of the Pure Food, Drug and Cosmetic Act (1938) had made necessary the relabeling and repackaging of Resolvent, and the company consequently stopped its manufacture.

COMPANY HISTORY

At the outset the Potter company manufactured all its Cuticura products except soap. Soap was produced for Potter on a contract basis by Robinson Brothers and Company in Malden, Massachusetts. In 1892 Potter Drug purchased the Robinson firm in order to have its own soap manufacturing facilities and at that time moved from Boston to Malden. In 1919 the manufacturing plant at Malden was doubled in size in anticipation of rising domestic and foreign sales of Cuticura products.

Cuticura preparations were first advertised in 1883 in Boston daily papers; in 1886 a limited amount of international advertising was instituted. Foreign outlets were established in Great Britain (1916), Australia (1916), Canada (1921), Ireland (1936), and South Africa (1937).

COMPETITIVE SITUATION

Prompted by the success of Cuticura preparations, numerous companies began early to manufacture and sell medicinal soaps and ointments. Many of these companies failed, and after 1938, only a small number of new concerns attempted to enter the industry. In 1946 there were five competitors for Potter Drug among concerns manufacturing both medicated soaps and ointments. Most of these competitors were small companies with limited financial resources. Potter was the largest manufacturer of medicated soaps and ointments in the field.

Cuticura soap was sold both as a medicated soap for skin care and as a toilet soap. Competition for Cuticura soap sold as a medicinal product was threefold: (1) from standard medicated soaps such as Resinol, Mazon, and Poslam; (2) from special medicinal soap preparations containing materials such as sulfa and iodine, which appeared and disappeared rapidly from the market; and (3) from health soaps which were sold on the basis of contributing to the health of the skin rather than of having medicinal qualities (such as vitamin soaps and superfatty soaps). Prices of competitive medicinal and health soaps ranged from 25 cents to 50 cents a bar.

Competition for Cuticura, as a toilet soap, came from approximately 70 companies.[2] Some of these were small plants serving local markets; others were national concerns such as Procter & Gamble, Lever Brothers, and Colgate-Palmolive-Peet Company. The latter companies engaged in active competition evidenced by large advertising expenditures, constant introduction of new products, intensive missionary sales work, and in depression periods, price cutting. Prices of their toilet soaps ranged from 8 cents (occasionally less) to 15 cents a bar.

Cuticura ointment faced competition (1) from the five companies in the medicated soap and ointment field, and (2) from numerous companies which produced ointments as well as other proprietary items

---

[2] Thomas' *Register of Manufacturers,* December, 1945.

(Zemo, Peterson's Ointment, and Noxzema). Prices for medicated ointments, depending on the size of the container, varied from 25 cents to $1.75.

Cuticura shampoo and shaving preparations were sold in competition with thousands of other branded products. Though new items were constantly being introduced into this market, most sales were made by older, well-advertised and established brands.

In the matter of retail prices, the Potter company had had a great deal of difficulty with cut-rate drugstores selling Cuticura products as loss leaders. One large cut-rate drug chain sold Cuticura soap for 17 cents a bar; however, most retailers sold Cuticura soap at prices ranging from 22 cents to 25 cents a bar.

SALES

Mr. W. C. Hamilton, sales manager of the Potter company, remarked that his company had picked the "skin trouble" market as its area of concentration. He stated, "The general usage and beauty markets were well covered by Ivory, Swan, Lux, and Camay; we concentrate on selling people who have externally caused skin disturbances."

The Potter Drug and Chemical Company did not employ any salesmen; nor did any of its officials call regularly on the trade. The company's sales and advertising departments consisted of Mr. Hamilton and five clerks who read and checked newspaper advertisements. The company relied primarily on its consumer advertising to obtain and hold its patronage. Mr. Hamilton said the company's sales plan worked as follows: (1) our advertisements sell the consumer on Cuticura products; (2) the consumer goes to the drugstore and asks for Cuticura; and (3) this creates a demand which comes back to the company through the wholesalers.

Cuticura soap, ointment, and talcum powder were carried, in small quantities, by almost every wholesale and retail druggist in the United States. An average druggist's supply of medicated soap and ointment consisted of one or two bars of the minor brands of medicated soaps and perhaps a dozen bars of Cuticura soap; supplies of ointment were stocked in approximately the same ratio. Spot checks made from time to time indicated that retailers seldom displayed Cuticura products; they sold them only on request.

Mr. Hamilton attributed this lack of active dealer promotion to the margins allowed by Cuticura. "We ignore traditional trade margins in the drug field. Ordinarily a wholesaler gets discounts of 16⅔%, and the drug retailer gets discounts of 33⅓%. Cuticura products are sold on a combined wholesaler-retailer margin of between 25% and 30%." No definite breakdown of this combined gross margin as between the wholesaler and the retailer was specified by the company. Wholesalers handling Cuticura products, however, typically took gross margins of 13%; retailers received the 20% gross margin if they secured the full 25-cent retail price for the item (see Exhibit 3). "Wholesalers and retailers do some kicking about these margins, but we intend to continue the policy."

Exhibit 3

POTTER DRUG AND CHEMICAL COMPANY

Price Schedules—Regular-Size Preparations

	Unit Selling Price	Unit Cost	Gross Margin*
Retailer:			
Direct purchase from manufacturer (2-gross minimum).....................	$0.25	$0.1736	30.5%
Purchase through wholesaler (typical)...	$0.25	$0.2000	20.0%
Wholesaler:			
Sales to retailer.......................	$0.20†	$0.1736	13.2%

* Gross margins were the same on all sizes and types of Cuticura products with the exception of Cuticura liquid antiseptic. On that item a combined wholesaler-retailer gross margin of 42.13% was allowed by the company.
† Minus any trade discounts given for special list sales or cash discounts for payment within 20 days of invoice date.

The Potter company would sell to wholesalers or retailers who ordered at least $50 worth of merchandise per order. Freight charges were paid on all shipments; terms for payment were net cash 20 days from date of invoice. The company did not give discounts either for quantity purchases or to secure promotional advantages with large accounts. Mr. Best, president, said that in 1945 the company had had less than $50 in bad debts on all domestic sales. "We don't sell to any firm which we believe to be a doubtful credit risk."

Mr. Putnam, assistant to Mr. Best, believed that a major problem of the company was its fixed retail selling price. Cuticura soap retailed at 25 cents for the standard 3½-ounce bar; this had been the price for the same quality and size bar since the company had started in business. "While the sales price has remained constant, cost of production has gone up," Mr. Putnam continued. "Tallow, the primary ingredient of soap, formerly cost as low as 6 cents a pound; in 1946 it cost us 22 cents a pound. I believe the only solution to the problem is an increase in productive efficiency."

In addition to standard sizes of Cuticura products, supplementary sizes had been added to meet consumer demands. In 1934 the company marketed miniature (10-cent) sizes of Cuticura soap, ointment, and talcum powder for sale through variety and chain stores. Mr. Putnam noted that chain stores had wanted the small size product for many years. "We resisted them however, until the depression cut out sales. Production costs for the 10-cent items," he continued, "are almost the same as they are for the larger, more profitable sizes."

The company's program to secure promotion of Cuticura products was (1) distribution twice a year of retailer counter displays, and (2) mailing of a letter outlining ways by which a retailer could increase his sales of Cuticura products. Both these programs were administered by the company's advertising agency. The counter displays were sent out by the agency to business managers of newspapers which carried Cuticura advertisements. These newspapers in turn distributed the cards to druggists in their immediate localities and, in addition, reported back to the Potter company as to whether the stores visited carried Cuticura products. The newspapers did not try to sell co-operative advertisements for Cuticura products, nor did they attempt to persuade any retailer to carry Cuticura products. During the summer months a form letter suggesting ways of promoting Cuticura products was mailed to local radio stations handling Cuticura spot advertisements. These stations readdressed and mailed copies of this letter to druggists. No measurement of the success of these promotional programs was attempted.

The minor products manufactured by the Potter company, from the standpoint of sales volume, were talcum powder, shaving cream, shaving sticks, and shampoo. With the exception of shaving cream, these products had been marketed successfully in foreign markets. Mr. Hamilton commented that Cuticura talcum powder never had caught on well in the domestic market. "We just don't know why. In the foreign market our talcum powder sells because people like its odor. As far as the shaving stick is concerned, the price of the product is out of line; it is a high-priced item, and demand is low. We don't push sales of our shaving cream because the trend is away from this type of cream and toward the brushless variety. Powdered shampoo is a popular English item which we had hoped to popularize for the domestic dime-store trade; the idea just never took hold in America."

ADVERTISING

An agency in New York City handled the complete administration of the company's advertising contract. The primary responsibility of the Potter company was to approve the advertising copy submitted by this agency. In addition, for the purpose of analyzing the company's advertising expenditures, Mr. Hamilton had divided the country into nine districts. He correlated advertising expenditures with sales volume by these advertising districts. If the sales volume was low in an area, advertising expenditures would be reduced to insure profitable operation for the company in that district.

Since Mr. Best became president in 1932, there had been three significant developments in the company's advertising program. First, the amount of money expended for advertising purposes had been increased. Each year since that date an estimate of the coming year's sales had been formulated, based on existing sales volume plus an anticipated gain. A sum equaling one-third of this total was allocated for advertising purposes. Second, the type of advertising copy employed in the United States had been shifted from testimonial letters written by satisfied consumers of Cuticura items to advertisements stressing the value of Cuticura products for externally caused skin trouble. Third, the company increased its use of radio spot announcements.

The original Pure Food and Drugs Act (1906) had provided limited federal regulatory control over the proprietary drug industry. In 1938 two additional regulatory laws governing the proprietary drug field were enacted by the Congress of the United States: the Pure Food, Drug and Cosmetic Act of 1938[3] and the Wheeler-Lea Amendment (1938) to the Federal Trade Commission Act.[4] These laws sharply increased federal

---

[3] The new Federal Food, Drug and Cosmetic Act prohibits the marketing of a drug that is adulterated or dangerous to health, and it also provides that a preparation used in self-medication is misbranded and subject to regulatory action if its label does not contain information required by law concerning its description and use. In addition to the net weight, fluid measure, or numerical count of the contents of the packages and the name and address of the manufacturer and distributor, the label of a drug product must bear a declaration of all the active ingredients (drugs upon which the product depends for therapeutic efficacy) in the preparation. (F. J. Cullen, *Behind the Contents of the Home Medicine Chest,* published by the Proprietary Association of America, 1946, p. 26.)

[4] The new Federal Trade Commissions Act (Wheeler-Lea Amendment) grants the commission authority to stop the advertising of products which are dangerous to health. The Act provides criminal punishment for those convicted of disseminating advertisements that are intentionally false. A false advertisement as defined by the Act is "an advertisement, other than labeling, which is misleading in a material respect; and in determining whether any advertisement is misleading, there shall be taken into account (among other things) not only representations made or suggested by statement, word, design, device, sound, or any combination thereof, but also the extent to which the advertisement fails to reveal facts material in the light of such representations or material with respect to consequences which may result from the use of the commodity to which the advertisement relates under the conditions prescribed in said advertisement, or under such conditions as are customary or usual."

supervision and control over proprietary medicines, both as to the quality and medicinal content of the proprietary medicine and the manner in which it advertised.

To assure strict compliance with provisions of these laws, the Potter company in 1938 employed the services of a New York laboratory to test the clinical effects of Cuticura preparations. Since the company now had, for the first time, clinical reports on the effectiveness of Cuticura, it revised its advertising program to conform with the results of this investigation. Instead of testimonial letters (which were subject to increasingly strict regulatory control) the company began to stress the ability of Cuticura ointment to relieve temporarily the itching caused by eczema and the beneficial effects of Cuticura soap on externally caused pimples. "The pimple field," Mr. Hamilton noted, "was a large, ever-recurring market. Externally caused pimples could be mentioned in all newspaper advertisements, but the radio industry would not allow this practice." All Cuticura advertisements were checked for compliance with Federal Trade Commission requirements: (1) by the company's advertising agency, (2) by the Boston legal counsel of the firm, (3) by the corporation's legal counsel in Washington, and (4) for radio announcements, by the radio station accepting the spot announcement.

Over the past decade advertising claims made by proprietary drug companies had become less sensational. Since 1938, this trend had been accelerated by the increasingly strict regulatory action of the Federal Trade Commission. The Commission had drastically reduced the scope of statements which proprietary drug manufacturers could make and required them to submit impartial research records to substantiate advertising copy. In foreign countries advertising regulations were not as severe, and medicated soap and ointment advertisements were more extravagant. Mr. Best stated that the federal regulatory agencies were constantly limiting the effectiveness of his company's advertising program.

In 1934 Potter Drug first began to use radio advertisements. By 1937, 25% of the company's advertising budget was expended for radio spot announcements; in 1946 over 60% of the advertising budget was allocated to this medium.

Cuticura newspaper layouts consisted of one column, one-inch or two-inch advertisements (see Exhibit 4). "The most important factor is not the size," Mr. Hamilton concluded. "It is to get the words 'pimple' and 'skin trouble' before the public, and the reader will find the advertisement."

PRODUCTION

The Potter company's plant, located at Malden, Massachusetts, included three adjoining multistoried brick buildings with a combined floor space of approximately 100,000 square feet. The main and largest building was occupied by the manufacturing department and company offices; the two smaller ones were used for warehousing raw materials and finished goods.

With the exception of soap manufacture, production of Cuticura products was confined to simple mixing and packaging operations. For low-volume products, production operations were carried on by hand. In the production of ointment, a high-volume item, manufacturing operations were highly mechanized.

Manufacture of Cuticura soap was accomplished by the following method: (1) Fat and a weak solution of caustic were pumped into a two-story soap kettle; each charge of fat and caustic was sufficient for 40,000 pounds of soap. This liquid mass was boiled, by the admission of steam, for approximately one week to clean the soap and remove impurities. (2) The finished kettle soap was pumped to mixing machines called "crutchers." Here the semiliquid soap was mixed with an emulsion of Cuticura ointment. (3) The liquid soap then flowed through pipes to a cooling machine, was converted to soap ribbons, and then conveyed to drying machines which removed excess moisture. (4) The ribbons of semifinished soap were compressed into loosely compacted pellets of soap milled to incorporate the perfume and to make the soap uniform in consistency. (5) The milled soap was extruded in the form of a long bar of soap which was cut into desired sections. (6) The blank bars of soap were shaped, lettered, and packaged.

The equipment used for kettle soap making was extremely bulky and required a great deal of plant space. Furthermore, the time necessary for the conversion of raw materials into finished product ranged from ten days to two weeks. To speed up these processes, some other members of the soap industry had developed a continuous saponification process whereby soap could be manufactured with compact equipment in a matter of hours. Most commercial soap, however, was still manufactured by the proven kettle process. In 1946 the company's soap machinery consisted of seven soap kettles, two soap-processing lines (mixing, cooling, drying, milling and extruding), and the necessary packaging equipment. This machinery occupied the basement and first two floors of the main building of the Potter factory.

Mr. Putnam estimated that the Malden plant was currently operating

Exhibit 4

POTTER DRUG AND CHEMICAL COMPANY

Representative Cuticura Advertisements

BODY FRESHNESS
Banish odor this pleasant easy way
Why endure strong-smelling soaps when a daily bath with fragrant, mildly medicated Cuticura Soap banishes grime and odor instantly, leaves you feeling wonderfully clean and confident! Finish with fragrant, borated Cuticura Talcum to absorb perspiration, guard against offending. Buy Cuticura today!

RED, ROUGH HANDS
Enjoy soothing comfort, prompt relief with world-known, mildly medicated, emollient
CUTICURA OINTMENT

HERE'S REALLY PROMPT RELIEF!
TEEN AGE PIMPLES
when externally caused. Use Cuticura—preferred by many doctors, nurses and certain hospitals—to quickly relieve embarrassing externally caused pimples, rash, blemishes. Softens blackhead tips for easy removal! Buy today!
CUTICURA SOAP AND OINTMENT

RASHES
For soothing relief by external means, apply pure, emollient
CUTICURA SOAP and OINTMENT
Cuticura is mildly medicated, dependable, world-known. Start using Cuticura today! Buy BOTH at your druggist's!

FEET "KILLING" YOU?
HERE'S REAL RELIEF!
Bathe in Cuticura Soap suds. Apply Cuticura Ointment, then Cuticura Talcum. Great!
CUTICURA SOAP, TALCUM OINTMENT

PIMPLES-BLACKHEADS
TRY THIS PROMPT RELIEF FOR EXTERNALLY CAUSED BLEMISHES
Cuticura contains valuable, scientific medical ingredients to promptly relieve, help nature heal. Satisfaction guaranteed. Buy today!
CUTICURA SOAP & OINTMENT

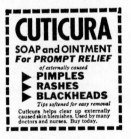

CUTICURA
SOAP and OINTMENT
For PROMPT RELIEF
of externally caused
▶ PIMPLES
▶ RASHES
▶ BLACKHEADS
Tips softened for easy removal
Cuticura helps clear up externally caused skin blemishes. Used by many doctors and nurses. Buy today.

PROMPT, ALMOST AMAZING RELIEF
PIMPLES-BLACKHEADS
when externally caused, try Cuticura—preferred by many doctors, nurses and certain hospitals! Relieves pimples, rash, blemishes; softens blackheads for easy removal. Buy today!
CUTICURA SOAP AND OINTMENT

BABY CHAFING
For prompt relief use world-known Cuticura. Fragrant, mildly medicated. 65 years success. All druggists. Buy!
CUTICURA SOAP, TALCUM OINTMENT

at about 60% of capacity. "This plant was originally constructed to manufacture Cuticura products for all domestic and foreign markets. Since a high percentage of the world market is now supplied by branch factories overseas, our home plant has been left with a great deal of excess capacity."

In an attempt to utilize this plant capacity, the Potter company began in 1933 to solicit outside manufacturing contracts. This program had met with limited success; approximately 20% of the company's domestic production volume during depression years was contract work, and in 1946 about the same dollar volume was being realized. Although the company in 1946 was not pushing contract manufacturing, it was handling work for seven different companies, making white soap, baby oil, liquid shampoo, and flea soap, which those companies then sold under their own brand names. "We don't try to bid competitively where a one-eighth cent difference in the bid will give you the contract," Mr. Putnam noted. "We prefer contracts where the brand name of the product allows the selling company a comfortable resale margin."

In 1946 the Potter company planned to expend $100,000 to replace one of its two soap processing lines. Mr. Putnam estimated that with the new equipment the factory could produce an additional 80% of soap by volume, if the necessary manpower could be secured. New machinery had also been secured for the talcum powder department; also new packaging equipment.

LABOR

The Potter company had a labor force of 115 employees. Since manufacturing operations were performed mechanically, the majority of the company's 67 production employees were unskilled persons used in wrapping and packaging operations. Over 50% of the company's employees had been with the Potter company for over 25 years; company officials referred to anyone who had been with the company less than five years as a "youngster."

During the war, wages had been under the prevailing rates in the state. However, by 1946 the average pay for a male employee, including overtime, had risen to $43 a week; for a woman employee, to $25 a week including overtime. Mr. Putnam believed these rates to be above the state average.

Potter employees were not unionized, and Mr. Putnam believed employee morale to be high. Employees were given work clothing, and the company maintained a kitchen and dining room where food was sold at cost. As a further gesture of goodwill, the company had recently established a chicken ranch which sold employees eggs and poultry at cost.

RESEARCH AND PRODUCT DEVELOPMENT

The research laboratory of the Potter company had three primary functions: (1) testing the quality of current production runs, (2) developing new products, and (3) handling plant first-aid work. Mr. Baade, a registered pharmacist, had recently been hired by the company to handle this laboratory work.

Mr. Putnam believed that the function of the laboratory as a product research center was threefold: (1) keeping the management up to date on new proprietary products and ideas, (2) improving present products, and (3) carrying out development work on new products. He noted, however, that the primary purpose of the laboratory was to maintain control of product quality. "Any developmental work which Mr. Baade does is pure profit."

INTRODUCTION OF NEW PRODUCTS

In 1936, after considerable experimentation, the Potter laboratory developed Cuticura cold cream and Cuticura hand cream. Both products were high-quality items and were attractively packaged in smartly designed containers. The creams retailed for $1 a jar; usual trade discounts were given to wholesalers and retailers. Initial distribution was made directly by the company to representative department stores from coast to coast. Advertising was carried on by inserting circulars describing Cuticura cold cream and hand cream in other Cuticura product packages. In 1938, following the passage of the Pure Food, Drug, and Cosmetic Act, both products were withdrawn from the national market, since their labels did not contain certain information required by law. Limited intrastate sales of both the cold cream and hand cream were being made in 1946. Neither before nor after 1938, however, did either of these items achieve very substantial volume.

Cuticura liquid antiseptic was first introduced on a trial basis in Canada. As a result of this test sales program, the company changed the package design of the product and increased the quantity in each bottle. This antiseptic was introduced in the United States in 1946. The Potter company employed a special sales organization with branches in New York City and Detroit to secure initial distribution in these two cities. This sales organization visited drug wholesalers and retailers and, through the use of free merchandise, attempted to secure dealer support for the new product. Usual trade discounts of 16⅔% and 33⅓% were given to wholesalers and retailers during the introductory campaign. Local publicity campaigns consisting of radio, newspaper, and subway advertisements were also employed.

On the basis of its introductory campaign, the Potter company was planning to extend the sale of liquid antiseptic as rapidly as possible. Mr. Hamilton commented that sales to date had been satisfactory. "We have been running into some criticism and complaint on the part of retailers who want the same discounts on other Cuticura products as we allow them on the new product. We do not believe, however, that this criticism is serious." A combined wholesaler-retailer gross margin of 42.13% was to be allowed on the antiseptic after the introductory period was over. While the company planned to continue advertising in support of the liquid antiseptic, it did not contemplate further use of the sales organization to secure product distribution.

"We are very interested in the introduction of new products; however, our schedule calls for the promotion of one product at a time— we don't want to branch out in numerous directions at once," said Mr. Putnam. He pointed out that the introduction of a new product requires capital outlay. In 1946 the company was using a hand-labeling machine which cost $1,300. If sales of the liquid antiseptic were high, the company would, he said, be forced to buy a $6,500 automatic machine.

Potter was currently marketing baby oil and baby talcum powder in Canada with considerable success. The company was deliberating, however, whether to introduce it in the American market since Mennen's and Johnson & Johnson would provide strenuous competition. The company was also contemplating the sale of a boxed set of two unwrapped large (¾-ounce) bars of Cuticura soap which would retail for $1. The soap would be stamped Cuticura bath soap and sold for general toilet use; Cuticura bath soap would be manufactured from the identical components as Cuticura medicated soap.

COMPANY MANAGEMENT

Exhibit 5 shows the company's executive organization plan.

The executive staff of the Potter company had always been characterized by (1) its small size, (2) the long service of each executive with the company, and (3) the close relationships among the executives by reason of family or marriage.

Mr. Best, who was in his mid-sixties, had been associated with the Potter company for 40 years, having joined it upon graduation from the Massachusetts College of Pharmacy in 1906. In 1932, upon assuming the presidency, he had initiated a three-point program to improve company sales procedures: (1) increased emphasis on securing foreign sales, (2) sharply increased advertising expenditures, and (3) increased emphasis on radio spot advertisements. Mr. Best said that this program had been successful and remarked, "The company is doing exceptionally well."

Mr. William C. Hamilton, son of a former company president, had been with the company for 26 years. He had first directed its office staff; in 1934 he was appointed vice-president in charge of the sales department.

Mr. William D. Gooch had joined the Potter company in 1907. Thirteen years later he became company treasurer, succeeding Mr. F. T. Bradbury, a brother-in-law of former president G. R. White. Mr. Gooch's assistant, Mr. Place, had joined the Potter organization in 1936.

Exhibit 5

POTTER DRUG AND CHEMICAL COMPANY

Executive Organization, 1946

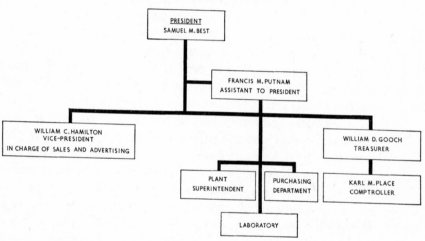

Mr. Francis M. Putnam had been until 1946 in charge of the company's manufacturing activities. Under his supervision the company had modernized its manufacturing operations. Mr. Putnam had had experience in drug retailing before becoming associated with Potter Drug and Chemical Company in 1930. In 1946 he was made assistant to Mr. Best. In this new position he was still in charge of manufacturing and was also responsible for liaison work with all foreign outlets of the company.

COMPANY OWNERSHIP

The two major beneficiaries of profits earned by the Potter company were the Massachusetts General Hospital and the Boston Museum of Fine Arts. Mrs. F. T. Bradbury (a sister of Mr. G. R. White, former president of the company) had been the majority stockholder of the concern from 1922 until her death in 1930. According to the provisions of her will, a trust was created to hold her stock for the benefit of the Massachusetts General Hospital and the Boston Museum of Fine Arts. Administration of the trust stock was assigned by the will to a designated board of trustees: Mr. S. M. Best, Mr. W. D. Gooch, and Mr. W. C. Hamilton.

The board of trustees was a self-perpetuating group. If one member died, the other two would appoint a successor, subject to the approval of the court administering the will. Under the will, the board of trustees in 1946 had the sole power to recommend either sale or continued ownership of the Potter stock. The two beneficiary institutions had only the right to make suggestions to the trustees. Since the minority stockholders (one-third of the outstanding stock) were not active in company affairs, the trustees, as representatives of the majority stock interests (two-thirds of the outstanding stock), elected the company's board of directors. The Potter board of directors in 1946 was composed of Mr. S. M. Best, Mr. W. D. Gooch, and Mr. E. H. Talbot, legal counsel for the Potter concern. Mr. Best said that the trustees to date had preferred to have working members of the Potter company on the board.

When, under Mrs. Bradbury's will, the trust was first set up, the officers of Massachusetts General Hospital wanted the trustees to sell the Potter stock and give the Hospital and the Museum the money derived from such a sale. This, however, was not possible at the time because of a provision in the will preventing any sale of the stock before 1935. As time went on, the officers of the hospital recognized the fact that they were receiving a substantial income from this investment. They did occasionally, once as late as 1937, refer to the trustees prospective purchasers of the Potter company. None of these offers was accepted, however, and they no longer attempted actively to urge the trustees to sell the stock. In 1932, Mr. Best concluded an arrangement with the hospital whereunder it agreed to use only Cuticura soap for toilet purposes. Mr. Best, in turn, agreed not to make this the basis of flamboyant advertising; it did, however, give him a basis for his advertising statement that Cuticura products were used by some hospitals and doctors. Mr. Best at that time outlined his plans to the officials of Massachusetts General Hospital for increasing company sales, pointing out that if he were given co-operative assistance, he could assure extremely profitable operation for the Potter company, which meant regular income for the hospital.

In 1946, Mr. Best believed that the two institutions were well satisfied with the substantial profits which they were getting from the Potter company.

INTERNAL CONTROLS

The company developed its first cost accounting system in 1936, when Mr. Place, comptroller of the concern, joined the Potter organization. Mr. Place noted that cost control had not been stressed by the Potter company since "costs were not of great importance to the company."

The company followed a meticulous procedure in inventory control; inventory totals were proved each day, both by units and by dollar value. If actual inventory did not balance with the perpetual inventory cards, the inventories were retaken the same day and all balances were proved before affected employees were allowed to leave the building.

"Our company does not use cash budgets," Mr. Place concluded, "since we always have plenty of cash." The comptroller's staff included 11 clerks.

To secure discussion of company problems, Mr. Best held a meeting once a week with all of his executive staff. "We work together as a team," he concluded. Mr. Best received (1) a daily report on domestic sales and a monthly report of both foreign and domestic sales, (2) a monthly report of advertising expenditures, (3) a written report from Mr. Putnam on general company activity, and (4) a monthly and quarterly report on company finances.

PURCHASING

To secure centralized procurement the company organized a purchasing department in 1946. Theretofore, company officials and section chiefs had purchased materials needed for their individual departments. The agent in charge purchased 750 items and was currently engaged in a program of standardizing the cartons and packages used by Potter Drug.

FOREIGN ORGANIZATION

Cuticura products had been sold abroad since 1883, and foreign sales (export sales from the United States plus sales of foreign outlets) for many years had constituted an important part of total company volume. This had been increasingly so during the period 1936–45. In fact, in 1945 foreign sales constituted approximately 50% of the company's total volume.

Originally the Potter company handled all foreign sales directly from the United States. Restrictions arising from World War I had prompted the company to establish a London branch office in 1916. As tariff barriers, questions of nationalistic pride in home manufacture, and export-import regulations began to make international trade more difficult, the company extended its chain of foreign outlets.

To secure the most advantageous financial position for the Potter company under various foreign countries' taxation and monetary exchange laws, three different types of foreign outlets were employed: (1) branch office (England), (2) wholly owned subsidiary companies (Australia and South Africa), and (3) sales representatives (Ireland and Canada). Whereas the type of organization employed abroad varied, the basic policies under which Potter operated its foreign units were the same. These policies were (1) limited use of Potter employees at its overseas outlets, (2) production of Cuticura products in the foreign country by contract manufacturers, and (3) the use of established foreign sales organizations for the promotion and marketing of Cuticura products.

Since all sales and manufacturing operations in foreign countries were handled under contract by established firms in the various countries, the Potter company needed few foreign operating employees of its own. In fact, with the exception of the branch office in London, where a group of clerks (employees of the United States organization) handled routine correspondence and reports, the Potter company did not have any overseas operating personnel in the United States corporation's direct employ. In other countries the company at times borrowed employees from its contract sales organizations to handle occasional nonsales matters.

In order to secure quality control over production by contract manufacturers in foreign countries, all perfumes, coloring compounds, and the Cuticura medicinal base were manufactured at the Malden, Massachusetts, plant and shipped to the contract manufacturer overseas. Moreover, quarterly samples of Cuticura products made by foreign contract manufacturers were shipped to the Malden plant for testing.

A foreign sales agent's organization, typically, handled the promotion and distribution to wholesalers and retailers of Cuticura products and of eight or ten other proprietary preparations. Sales agents were given the exclusive sales rights for Cuticura products in their domestic markets as well as in specified areas of other foreign markets. They carried on missionary sales work which included distribution of counter cards, setting up Cuticura displays in stores, and arranging for promotional campaigns.

On the basis of sales forecasts supplied by these sales agents, Potter let contracts for the manufacture of Cuticura products. Goods were shipped directly from the contract manufacturers to the warehouses of the sales agents. The latter organizations assumed all warehousing costs and credit risks on shipments made to wholesalers and retailers.

Exhibit 6

POTTER DRUG AND CHEMICAL COMPANY
Income Information—Selected Years, 1932–46
(In Thousands)

Year	Net Sales*	Net Profit Before Taxes†
1932	$1,476	$111
1936	1,776	166
1937	1,709	158
1938	1,674	175
1939	1,961	287
1940	1,912	316
1941	2,172	440
1942	2,189	446
1943	2,495	522
1944	2,822	589
1945	3,195	726

* Excluding wholly owned subsidiaries.
† From all operations of company including wholly owned subsidiaries.

Prices of Cuticura products in foreign countries were about the same as prices of competitive products in those countries. This meant that in 1946 they averaged 20% to 30% more than prices for the same items in the United States. Trade discounts allowed on Cuticura products were specified by the Malden office for both the wholesale and retail trade. These discounts were lower than the usual trade discounts in the countries of sale, with the exception of Canada, where Cuticura discounts conformed with usual allowances. The company's officials believed that their company had good coverage of drug retailers in the foreign countries in which it was represented.

Most of the dollar volume of export sales resulted from sales of Cuticura soap and ointment. Cuticura talcum powder was the next best selling product. Potter Drug had marketed the first medicated soap and ointment of its type in the English markets. Following its introduction there, many new medicated soaps and ointments appeared as time went on. In 1946 there were some 48 ointments and 12 competitive soaps; three of these soaps were outselling Cuticura. In other foreign countries, as well, Cuticura products, shortly after their appearance, faced increasingly severe competition.

The foreign sales representatives submitted directly to the Potter company trimonthly, monthly, and quarterly sales reports as well as

Exhibit 7

POTTER DRUG AND CHEMICAL COMPANY

Balance Sheet Information as of December 31—Selected Years, 1933–45

(In Thousands)

Assets	1933	1936	1937	1938	1939	1940	1941	1942	1943	1944	1945
Current Assets:											
Cash	$ 213	$ 261	$ 295	$ 271	$ 148	$ 149	$ 153	$ 345	$ 428	$ 462	$ 460
Accounts Receivable	393	290	243	267	267	461	441	302	285	364	325
Merchandise Inventory	342	308	280	264	380	344	517	513	599	492	454
Securities	302	311	311	311	311	311	311	311	341	350	602
Prepaid Expenses	11	38	30	39	30	21	37	18	20	19	15
Investment in Other Companies at Par	5	25	25	25	25	25	25	25	57	57	57*
Accounts Receivable—Other Companies					39	33	39	38	8	4	3
Loans Receivable				20†	20	20	20	21	21	21	20
Fixed Assets (Depreciated):											
Land	31	31	31	31	31	31	31	31	31	31	31
Building	32	19	50	34	36	40	41	35	22	8	9
Total Assets	$1,329	$1,283	$1,265	$1,262	$1,287	$1,435	$1,615	$1,639	$1,812	$1,808	$1,976
Liabilities											
Accounts Payable	$ 199	$ 209	$ 185	$ 220	$ 295	$ 442	$ 530	$ 566	$ 725	$ 727	$ 842
Reserve for War Loss							86	25			
Capital Stock	200	200	200	200	200	200	200	200	200	200	200
Surplus	930	874	880	842	792	793	799	848	887	881	934
Total Liabilities	$1,329	$1,283	$1,265	$1,262	$1,287	$1,435	$1,615	$1,639	$1,812	$1,808	$1,976

* Includes investment in Robinson Brothers and Company ($5,000), South African subsidiary ($10), and Australian subsidiary ($51,990).

** Working capital loan to South African subsidiary, 1938-45.

NOTE: Includes parent company and outlets in England, Ireland, and Canada. Investments in wholly owned subsidiaries are found under the account Investments in Other Company at Par. Undistributed profits from operations of wholly owned subsidiaries are shown in the account Accounts Receivable—Other Companies.

quarterly reports of inventory on hand. The company's chartered accountant in each foreign country submitted directly to the Potter company monthly analyses of the sales agents' expenditures for marketing Cuticura products. They also sent quarterly financial reports. Mr. Putnam handled any inquiries which foreign contract manufacturers and sales agents made of the Malden office.

Mr. Best did not believe that management of foreign sales units entailed any special problems. "It is just the same as running a factory across the street. We get reports and a copy of every bit of their Cuticura correspondence, no matter how trivial the subject of the letter might be." Before World War II Mr. Best had made yearly inspection trips abroad. Following the war the company planned to bring its sales representatives to the Malden office once every year for general discussions.

EXPORT TRADE FROM THE UNITED STATES

During the five-year period 1941–45 never less than 20% of Potter's domestic production had been exported to the Far East, to Central and South America, and to the west coast of Africa.

Inasmuch as Cuticura products were exported to foreign markets both from the company's foreign branches and from the home plant in the United States, initially some overlapping of exports occurred. For instance, in British Honduras, Cuticura products were at one time being sold by importers who secured the lines from British, Canadian, and American exporters. As a result, three different types of Cuticura packages could be purchased under a variety of sales terms. The company later assigned this territory exclusively to the Canadian branch.

FUTURE PLANS

"The life of most proprietary drug companies," said Mr. Best, "is very short. The item or items which these companies manufacture lose public favor, and the company is forced out of business. I have great faith in the future sales of our soap and ointment; I know we have the best products in these lines which any firm can manufacture. There is always the possibility, however, of these products becoming obsolete. The introduction of new products therefore is an insurance policy for the continuing success of Potter Drug. We already have our minor products (shaving preparations and shampoo) which, when the time is right, we will advertise and promote."

The Potter company was considering the establishment of foreign sales outlets in South American countries, and discussions were already being conducted by the company with an Argentine firm.

Consolidated Vultee Aircraft Corporation

CONSOLIDATED VULTEE AIRCRAFT CORPORATION was in 1944 the largest single producer of aircraft in the world. Before the end of World War II, the company was manufacturing 14 different types of airplanes, ranging in size from the small Sentinel Flying Jeep to the giant XB-36 and the Dominator (B-32), companion to the Super-Fortress (B-29). Among the better-known planes designed and manufactured by Consolidated Vultee were the Liberator (B-24), Catalina (PBY), Coronado (PB2Y-3), Privateer (PB4Y-2), and Valiant (BT-13). The com-

Exhibit 1

CONSOLIDATED VULTEE AIRCRAFT CORPORATION

Location and Activities of Divisions as of January, 1945

Division	Location	Principal Activities
San Diego Division	San Diego, Calif.	Manufactured PBY, PB2Y, RY-3, B-32, B-24, PB4Y-2
Fort Worth Division	Fort Worth, Texas	Manufactured B-24, C-87, XB-36, B-32
Vultee Field Division	Vultee Field, Calif.	Manufactured BT-13, 15; parts for B-32, B-24, PB4Y-2, P-38
Allentown Division	Allentown, Penn.	Manufactured TBY-2
Elizabeth Division	Elizabeth, N.J.	Modification center for Navy planes
Louisville Division	Louisville, Ky.	Modification center for B-24
Intercontinent Aircraft Corporation	Miami, Fla.	Manufactured parts for A-31, A-35, B-24, F4U, P-38
Nashville Division	Nashville, Tenn.	Manufactured A-31, A-35, P-38, parts for B-24
New Orleans Division	New Orleans, La.	Manufactured PBY, modification center for PB2Y-3
Stinson Division	Wayne, Mich.	Manufactured AT-19 and L-5, "Flying Jeep"
Tucson Division	Tucson, Ariz.	Modification center for B-24
Stout Research Division	Dearborn, Mich.	Experimental and development
Consairways	Fairfield, Calif.	Operation of Consairways, ATC contract airline

pany had 13 divisions located in various parts of the United States, employing over 100,000 workers. Exhibits 1 and 2 indicate the location and activities of the company's divisions and the aircraft sales volume during the period of 1940–44.

306

Exhibit 2

CONSOLIDATED VULTEE AIRCRAFT CORPORATION

Net Sales for the Period 1940–44

(In Millions)

Year	Consolidated	Vultee	Consolidated Vultee
1940....................	$ 9.3	$ 5.6	....
1941....................	94.8	34.0	....
1942....................	304.0	109.7	....
1943....................	....	....	$797.2*
1944....................	....	....	960.0

* The Consolidated and Vultee organizations merged in March, 1943.

Consolidated Vultee, formed in 1943 as a merger of Consolidated Aircraft Corporation and Vultee Aircraft, Inc., was an associated company of the Aviation Corporation,[1] a manufacturing and holding company owning 30% of Consolidated Vultee common stock. Through its stock ownership the Aviation Corporation had the controlling interest in the management of Consolidated Vultee. The Aviation Corporation acquired Vultee in 1934 when it was a small designer and manufacturer of light planes. By 1940 Vultee was known as one of the major producers of training planes for the armed forces.

Consolidated Aircraft Corporation, founded in 1923 by R. H. Fleet, first specialized in the design and manufacturing of Army and Navy training planes, and then expanded into the field of large, multiengine aircraft. In December, 1941, Vultee purchased Mr. Fleet's stock interest, and Consolidated became an associated company of the Aviation Corporation. Consolidated and Vultee operated independently until March, 1943, when they were merged, forming Consolidated Vultee Aircraft Corporation.

After 1940, aircraft production expanded rapidly and both Consolidated and Vultee encountered numerous management problems. The Aviation Corporation enlisted management personnel from outside the aircraft industry to assist in its expanding production program. Mr. T. M. Girdler, well-known industrialist and chairman of the board of directors of the Republic Steel Corporation, became a director of Aviation Corporation; subsequently he became chairman of the board of

[1] The Aviation Corporation had five manufacturing divisions and three associated companies. The manufacturing divisions produced aircraft products and some automotive parts. The associated companies were Consolidated Vultee; the New York Shipbuilding Corporation, one of the country's largest producers of naval combatant ships during the war; and the American Central Manufacturing Corporation, manufacturers of household kitchen equipment. The Aviation Corporation also held substantial investments in American Airlines, Inc., and Pan American Airways System.

directors of Vultee and Consolidated, and later of Consolidated Vultee. An associate of Mr. Girdler, Mr. Harry Woodhead, whom Mr. Girdler succeeded as chairman of Vultee's board of directors, became president of Vultee and Consolidated, and later of Consolidated Vultee. Under Mr. Woodhead's management, Vultee pioneered the use of powered assembly lines in the aircraft industry.

While Vultee's expansion during 1940 and 1941 was rapid, Consolidated's expansion as a major producer of heavy bombers was even greater. During this period, Mr. R. H. Fleet, Consolidated's chairman and president, maintained personal control over the company's operations. In January, 1942, however, Mr. Girdler became chairman of the board of directors of both Consolidated and Vultee. The following quotation from *Fortune* magazine indicates some of the circumstances incident to this change in management:

There were no brass bands or welcoming committees waiting for Tom Girdler one Saturday last January when the Board Chairman of Republic Steel arrived at San Diego to take charge of the Consolidated Aircraft Corporation, producer of long-range flying boats and four-engine bombers. He came over the Rockies in Republic's private airplane and next day walked through the plant with several men directly responsible for Consolidated production. Monday morning he called all the department heads together, two dozen or more, to lay down his plans. Among them were men who had been in aviation since their youth, and some who were with Consolidated when it had nothing but a few thousand dollars, mostly borrowed, "Rube" Fleet's colossal nerve, and "Mac" Laddon's designs.

Mr. Girdler sat at a big desk, feet up, hat slanted rakishly over owlish horn-rimmed glasses, as he set forth what he proposed to do. . . . In the hush that followed, a Vice President, one of the powers of the old Fleet regime, stepped forward. He called the steelman "an interloper," a money man who, with gross impertinence, had bought his way into an art of craftsmen and pioneers, and in accents sharp with rage he told Girdler that the best thing he could do was to go back where he came from.

If T. M. Girdler had ever before tolerated a tongue-lashing, there is no record of it. But this time he made no answer. The man whose boast is "I put together Republic" understood. After his castigator had finished, he turned to one of the Fleet men and said quietly, "You straighten this out. . . ."

. . . .

The events that persuaded this toughest of industrial operators to change careers at sixty-five, to sacrifice a sure berth in steel for the "hot seat" of a war production job, have curiously passed almost unnoticed. They begin with the difficulties in which Major Reuben H. Fleet, founder and boss of Consolidated, found himself a year ago after the President had called for a concentration of production behind the heavy-bomber program. This meant a terrific expansion for Consolidated, whose B-24 (Liberator) was one of only two four-engine

American land bombers, and whose two-engine PBY's (Catalina) and four-engine PB2Y's were the only long-range flying boats then in production. From 1939 to the summer of 1941, Consolidated went from 1,500 to over 30,000 workers, and floor space increased many times.

Rube held almost a third of the stock and absolute control. He had married a young wife, his second, and it was no secret that he wanted to sell out—partly to convert his equity into cash while tax schedules were comparatively easy, partly to spread responsibility in a war corporation where he had such a heavy stake in every dollar. Also, the Army and Navy, with hundreds of millions of dollars worth of airplanes in Consolidated's backlog, wanted to see him replaced with a first-class industrialist. While the services were grateful to Rube for having run a shoe-string hawker of trainers into a potential source of enormous striking power, he had taxed their patience with his continuous wrangling with labor and his bullheaded arguments over tactical changes. Worst of all, his inability or disinclination to shake Consolidated down into something more substantial than a one-man show was injecting grave doubts into the stability of the heavy-bomber program.

From the point of view of Mr. Robert A. Lovett, Assistant Secretary of War for Air, and Rear Admiral John H. Towers, chief of the Bureau of Aeronautics, who took a hand in the task of showing up Consolidated, the problem was not to find a purchaser with money, but rather one with the production experience and intestinal fortitude to man perhaps the most crucial single strong point on the whole production battle line. Several companies were tempted, but eventually shied away; their managements already had their hands full. Then . . . Mr. Victor Emanuel [The Aviation Corporation] secretly entered the negotiations. . . .

.   .   .   .

The deal . . . was closed last December [1941]. Vultee, now 76 percent owned by Aviation Corporation, was the purchaser. . . .

As Mr. Emanuel tells the story:

"When we finally took Consolidated over, I was deeply worried, since we knew nothing about big airplanes and the situation was almost a danger to the country. . . . I became more and more concerned, and finally told him [Tom Girdler] that he'd have to take over—and fast.

"After the facts were laid before him, Tom finally said he would. He never bothers much about details—he knew there was a stipulated production rate and that was all that mattered."

As Chairman of the Board and chief executive officer of both Consolidated and Vultee, while still retaining the chairmanship and policy direction of Republic, Mr. Girdler has moved into one of the top production assignments of the war. His interests extend from coast to coast. Already an estimated 130,000 workers are on the payrolls of the three companies that he managed directly; the companies' assets at the end of 1941 stood at nearly $600 million, and their backlog runs into the billions. . . .

.   .   .   .

Girdler, by his own definition, is an executive rather than a production man —"and there's a hell of a difference." An executive is one who lays down general policy and then delegates to other men responsibility of execution. "The trick," he once advised Victor Emanuel, "is in putting a man in a job, giving him complete responsibility, not bothering him, and not letting anyone else bother him." In theory, this leaves the executive free to ponder long-range problems, and Girdler believes that he has so nearly approached the ideal that, when testifying before the La Follette Committee about who in Republic reported to him, he said, "The President, . . . two secretaries, and one airplane pilot.". . .

.   .   .   .

A quick look [at Aviation Corporation] convinced him that aviation could be a big market for his [Republic's] light steels. And with the double purpose of forearming Republic while also helping his friends, he lent them Mr. Harry Woodhead, Vice President and General Manager of a subsidiary, Truscon Steel, to apply the "Republic touch."

Under the combined drive of the first rearmament orders and of Mr. Woodhead, a tireless, amiable, towering Yorkshireman, what is now Aviation Corporation began to right itself productionwise. . . . Except for keeping "a friendly eye" on Mr. Woodhead's progress . . . Girdler remained pretty much out of sight. He did not emerge as a power behind Aviation Corporation until . . . Victor Emanuel swung his great coup: the purchase of Consolidated.

.   .   .   .

As Mr. Girdler points out: "A lot of people think we busted in here to salvage a broken-down plant. That's bunk. We bought Consolidated because it already had the kind of strength we could use." The 3,000-foot assembly line that Rube started, though radically modified, remains the beginning and end of everything, and many of his executives, whose light had lain under a bushel, have moved up. One is thirty-four-year-old George J. Newman, a factory manager, whom Girdler put in charge of the Texas plant; another is the Major's thirty-two-year-old son, David Fleet, now Executive Vice President of Vultee. And the third and most important is I. M. (Mac) Laddon, designer of the B-24, the PBY, and the PB2Y, now Executive Vice President and General Manager. Mac Laddon learned his profession in the last war at McCook Field where he worked on some of the earliest armored and turbosupercharged warplanes, and where he eventually designed the first all-metal airplane produced in this country. "You're my kind of guy," the steelman said impulsively, after their first fishy-eyed exchange. It is a good thing, for the services rightly cherish Mac Laddon, a gentle, self-effacing soul.

On the other hand, Mr. Girdler has crowded his own brand of management around the top. To be Vice Chairman and No. 2 man of Vultee, he imported Mr. G. M. (Monte) Williams, President of Russell Manufacturing Co. (textiles), before the head of the now defunct Marmon Motor Car Co. . . . Mr. Woodhead was brought down from Vultee to be President of Consolidated. Young Mr. C. W. Perelle, Vultee's production strategist, whom Girdler calls "a tough cookie," was drafted to "help knock the man-hours out of the B-24." And Mr. Francis A. Callery, an Emanuel man, was made Vice President in charge of finance. Major Fleet, who is still around under a five-year, $60,000-a-year contract as "adviser," remarked one day, "Well, it's taken five men, including Tom Girdler, to fill my shoes."

.   .   .   .

. . . Girdler, after breaking several Army schedules, has pushed his potential well beyond the government's ability to supply him with parts and materials. This has been the result of introducing a straightline production system; of pushing more and more of the final assembly back into the subassemblies; of patient worker education; of introducing incentive bonuses; and of delegating authority. . . . By fall [1942], Consolidated will have the final assembly lines moving continuously, if slowly, under power. "The only thing that can stop production," Mr. Girdler has said, "will not be management or brain power, but the gadgets over which we have no control."[2]

.   .   .   .

After January, 1942, there were several changes in the top management personnel in Consolidated and Vultee as indicated in the foregoing statement. Mr. Woodhead and Mr. Laddon became officers of both Consolidated and Vultee, and Mr. Perelle was made vice-president in charge of production for Consolidated. Mr. Girdler made the following statements concerning Mr. Laddon and Mr. Perelle:

Rich though [Consolidated] is in talent, and especially in engineering talent, I. M. Laddon is the genius. Laddon's is the fundamental creative force which the Consolidated organization is expressing. Laddon now is our executive vice president. Each kind of business has to have its emphasis on some special talent; in a mail order house the emphasis probably is on merchandising; it would be on showmanship in a circus; but in aircraft manufacturing the emphasis is definitely and unmistakably on engineering and design. Mac Laddon is an engineer who became a great designer.[3]

Woodhead brought [to Vultee] C. W. Perelle, a young engineer with a superb understanding of production. Perelle did a swell job. He never rested until he had Vultee making more pounds of airplane per man-hour than any other plant in the world. Before he worked for us, Perelle had worked in the Boeing plant in Seattle. He is forty-one and looks twenty-five. As if by instinct he knows that he can't get the best done unless every man under him knows only one boss—Perelle. . . . That is the way I [Girdler] have always felt.[4]

In addition to Woodhead and Perelle, several other Vultee executives were brought to Consolidated to strengthen the latter's organization. Consolidated's organization by March, 1942, is shown in Exhibit 3.

Both Consolidated and Vultee continued to expand rapidly during 1942. Consolidated's employment reached 44,300 during that year. Two new plants commenced operations producing B-24's—one in Fort Worth, Texas, and the other in San Diego. The latter plant supple-

---

[2] "Tom Girdler's Truce," *Fortune*, Sept., 1942, pp. 89 ff.

[3] Tom M. Girdler, *Boot Straps* (New York: Charles Scribner's Sons, 1943), pp. 425–26.

[4] *Ibid.*, p. 424.

Exhibit 3

CONSOLIDATED AIRCRAFT CORPORATION

Organization Chart, March 26, 1942

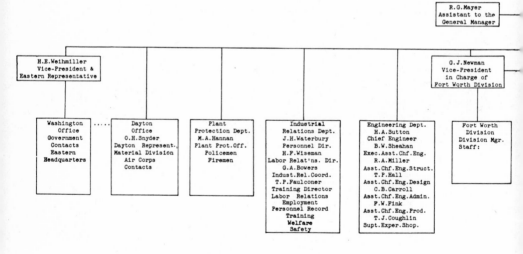

Exhibit 3—Continued

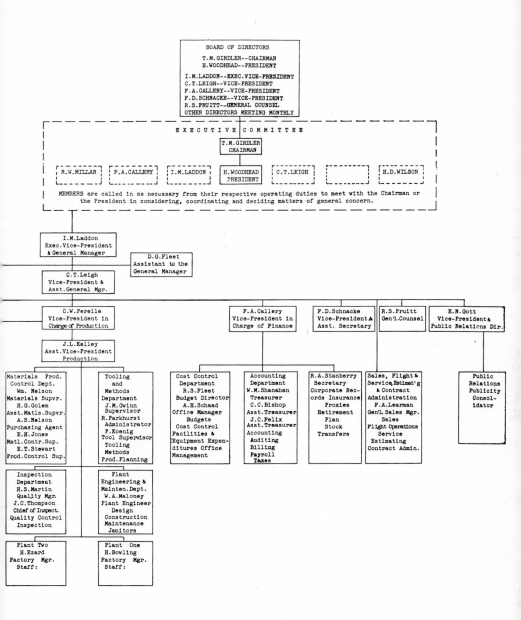

BOARD OF DIRECTORS

T.M.GIRDLER--CHAIRMAN
H.WOODHEAD--PRESIDENT

I.M.LADDON--EXEC.VICE-PRESIDENT
C.T.LEIGH--VICE-PRESIDENT
F.A.CALLERY--VICE-PRESIDENT
F.D.SCHNACKE--VICE-PRESIDENT
R.S.PRUITT--GENERAL COUNSEL
OTHER DIRECTORS MEETING MONTHLY

EXECUTIVE COMMITTEE

T.M.GIRDLER
CHAIRMAN

R.W.MILLAR   F.A.CALLERY   I.M.LADDON   H.WOODHEAD   C.T.LEIGH   H.D.WILSON
                                        PRESIDENT

MEMBERS are called in as necussary from their respective operating duties to meet with the Chairman or
the President in considering, coordinating and deciding matters of general concern.

I.M.Laddon
Exec.Vice-President
& General Manager

D.G.Fleet
Assistant to the
General Manager

C.T.Leigh
Vice-President &
Asst.General Mgr.

C.W.Perelle
Vice-President in
Charge of Production

F.A.Callery
Vice-President in
Charge of Finance

F.D.Schnacke
Vice-President &
Asst. Secretary

R.S.Pruitt
Gen'l.Counsel

E.N.Gott
Vice-President &
Public Relations Dir.

J.L.Kelley
Asst.Vice-President
Production

Materials Prod. Control Dept. Wm. Nelson Materials Supvr. H.G.Golem Asst.Matls.Supvr. A.S.Nelson Purchasing Agent E.H.Jones Matl.Contr.Sup. E.T.Stewart Prod.Control Sup.	Tooling and Methods Department J.M.Gwinn Supervisor R.Parkhurst Administrator P.Koenig Tool Supervisor Tooling Methods Prod.Planning	Cost Control Department R.S.Fleet Budget Director A.H.Schaad Office Manager Budgets Cost Control Facilities & Equipment Expen- ditures Office Management	Accounting Department W.M.Shanahan Treasurer C.C.Bishop Asst.Treasurer J.C.Felix Asst.Treasurer Accounting Auditing Billing Payroll Taxes	R.A.Stanberry Secretary Corporate Rec- ords Insurance Proxies Retirement Plan Stock Transfers	Sales, Flight & Service,Estimat'g & Contract Administration F.A.Learman Gen'l.Sales Mgr. Sales Flight Operations Service Estimating Contract Admin.	Public Relations Publicity Consol- idator

Inspection
Department
H.S.Martin
Quality Mgr.
J.C.Thompson
Chief of Inspect.
Quality Control
Inspection

Plant
Engineering &
Mainten.Dept.
W.A.Maloney
Plant Engineer
Design
Construction
Maintenance
Janitors

Plant Two
H.Ezard
Factory Mgr.
Staff:

Plant One
H.Bowling
Factory Mgr.
Staff:

Exhibit 4

CONSOLIDATED VULTEE AIRCRAFT CORPORATION

Organization Chart, March 30, 1943

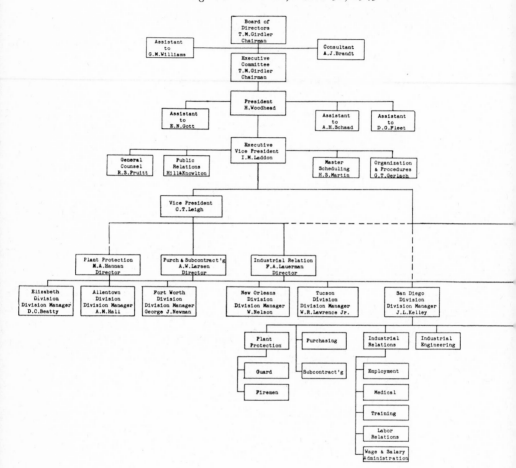

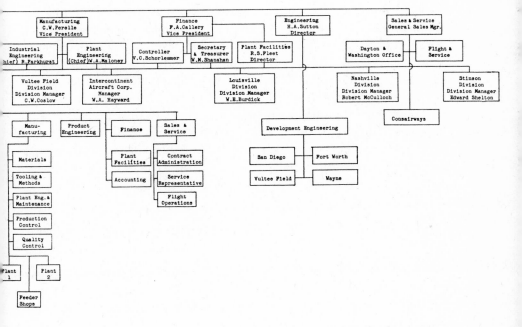

mented the company's existing plant facilities in San Diego. Modification centers were established at Tucson, Arizona, and Elizabeth, New Jersey, to handle war-theater modifications of B-24's and PBY's. Vultee added a modification center at Louisville, started the Allentown Division (manufacturing), acquired Intercontinent Aircraft at Miami, and increased production at its home plant (Vultee Field), at the Nashville Division in Tennessee and at the Stinson Division (Wayne, Michigan). During this period, preliminary to the eventual merger, efforts were made to standardize company procedures and organizations.

Consolidated Vultee Aircraft Corporation was formed in March, 1943. The company's organization chart at the time of the merger is shown in Exhibit 4. There were 11 divisions of the company operating throughout the country, in addition to Consairways, an airline operated by the company, and the research activities located at Dearborn, Michigan. In order to standardize the organizations within each division, a standard division organization was established. Each division was to conform with this organization, and any deviations were subject to the approval of the executive vice-president, Mr. Laddon.

To supervise all company operations, a central staff was formed consisting of the directors of the various company functions. Frequent meetings of the central staff officers and division managers were held to discuss mutual problems, among which were matters relative to the company's form of organization. The first meeting, held in San Diego on March 29, 1943, served primarily to introduce this new form of organization. The following statements are excerpts and notes taken from the minutes of this and subsequent meetings of Consolidated Vultee's division managers:

DIVISION MANAGERS' MEETING—SAN DIEGO—MARCH 29, 1943

In opening this meeting Mr. Girdler stated that a lot of time had been spent on the setting up of the new organization chart in an effort to work things out so that they would function smoothly. The chart represented the combined thinking of Mr. Woodhead [President], Mr. Laddon [Executive Vice President], Mr. Leigh [Vice President], and some others. He emphasized that now that the merger had taken place, there was neither a Vultee outfit nor a Consolidated outfit, but rather it represented the Consolidated Vultee Aircraft Corporation.

Mr. Girdler stressed the fact that the management wanted everyone to feel that he could talk to everyone else but that he wanted him to do it logically. In [explaining] the division manager's setup, Mr. Girdler spoke as follows:

"As far as Consolidated Vultee is concerned I have one President and one secretary and no one else reports to me. Mr. Woodhead has two secretaries and two or three assistants. I have a couple of assistants but they do not report to me; they spend most of their time reporting to Mr. Woodhead and Mr. Laddon. Everybody else in the company, other than the few I mentioned, report to Mr. Laddon as Executive Vice President. Now I want to give you this organizational setup as I see it—this is what I call a straight line organization. If a Division Manager talks to Mr. Woodhead about something, that is perfectly all right, but if he forgets to talk to the people he is supposed to report to on the subjects they have in hand, and forgets to tell his boss in that line about it, that is something for his boss to handle in his own good way. In other words, if Mr. Coslow [Division Manager, Vultee Field] or Mr. Newman [Division Manager, Fort Worth] or Mr. Burdick [Division Manager, Louisville] takes something up with Mr. Woodhead or Mr. Laddon and forgets to take it up with Mr. Perelle, if it is in Perelle's line, then Mr. Perelle has a perfect right to raise Cain about it. Mr. Perelle has no right to object to them talking to Mr. Woodhead and Mr. Laddon about it but he does have a perfect right to insist that he be kept informed. On some matter of purchases or some matter of credit or some matter of finance, he should, of course, take it up with Mr. Schorlemmer [Controller] or Shanahan [Secretary-Treasurer] or Callery [Vice President—Finance] or whoever he should take it up with. He is subject to censor if he does not do it. In other words, there is a straight line way of doing it and a straight line should be followed. I hope that when you gentlemen leave here and go back to your respective locations that you will have everything perfectly clear in your mind as to how this organization is to function. I think they say in law that ignorance of the law is no excuse. I think everybody will have time before he goes back to go to people and ask for interpretations on certain subjects so that there will be no ignorance of the law. I am very glad to have men talk to me. Don't consider that you have talked to anybody but me because I don feel any responsibility to passing it on to anyone else. You should talk to Mr. Perelle, Mr. Laddon or Mr. Callery or even to Mr. Woodhead through the proper channels, and then if I don't hear what I am supposed to hear, I will raise the dickens with them and not with you. To get down to brass tacks, there is only one man to tell me everything I ought to know, and that is Mr. Woodhead."

Mr. Woodhead next stressed the fact that one of the main reasons for the merger was to give authority to the Division Manager. The central staff affords men who can furnish guidance in the handling of specific problems. Again loyalty to the Corporation was emphasized.

Mr. Laddon was then asked to explain the basic idea of the new organization. He pointed out that the various divisions of the company were bolstered by the addition of a central staff. The people on this central staff were the people regarded as the best brains in the organization for the specific function to which they were assigned. In answer to the question "For whom do I work" it was stated that the Division Managers would work for everybody on the staff. In other words if there were a division that had nothing but manufacturing in it, it would be working 100 percent for Perelle. If there were a division having only engineering work, it would be working for Sutton [Engineering Director]. The plan did not mean that the staff man was going to come down to the division to specify every move that was to be made—it meant that the Division Manager was to act to the best of his ability and, when he needed help, a staff man would be available to look over the situation and to make suggestions as to what should be done to improve the function. It was emphasized that these suggestions were to be complied with. The Division Managers were to have responsibility and reasonable authority. This method of organization was felt to be the basis for operating a big corporation, and it was stated that other large companies had operated very successfully along this line. The central staff plan makes it possible to make better brains available to the entire corporation than would otherwise be the case.

It was announced that the purpose of the meeting was to go over the general form of organization taking it point by point and answering any questions that the Division Managers might have. It was felt that specific details growing out of this meeting would aid in the preparation of a more detailed functional write-up. The meeting was then thrown open to questions.

[The] question was raised concerning the organization chart which showed a line running from Laddon to Kelley [Division Manager, San Diego], bypassing all the staff. The question was whether the Division Managers reported through central staff representatives only. The answer was that on most things the Division Manager should report to the staff representative concerned, but that on a small percentage of general policy matters they should report directly to Mr. Laddon.

The following . . . statement was made [Mr. Girdler] in amplification of the above discussion:

"If you [Laddon] issued an executive order to each Division Manager and it affected production, you would send it also to Perelle [Vice President—Manufacturing] or, in the matter of finance, to Callery [Vice President—Finance], but over your signature as Executive Vice President."

The Division Managers were requested to make up an organization chart of their divisions, not paying particular attention to titles at this stage of the game, as it was intended to standardize titles throughout the Corporation.

By way of illustration of the way plant departments would work in relation to division managers and central staff heads, the title of "Chief of Plant Protection" was discussed. Each plant has its own Chief of Plant Protection; he was required to report everything with reference to plant protection to the Division Manager and it was also stated to be the duty of that Chief of Plant Protection Officer to report to the Director of Plant Protection at San Diego in order to keep the central office thoroughly in touch with everything that was going on.

Mr. Woodhead stressed the fact that the Plant Protection Officer had to be sure that he reported everything to the Division Manager, but nevertheless paralleled this to report to the Plant Protection Chief of the whole Corporation.

With regard to Engineering, the Division Engineer was responsible to the Division Manager for producing the drawings in time to meet the schedule as set. The Division Manager was not in any sense responsible for design. The design of the airplane was something that was controlled by the Director of Engineering. The fact that the Division Engineer does parallel his report to the Division Manager and the central office does not take away any of the responsibility or authority of the Division Manager. He was responsible for the discipline and for the fact that the engineering department functioned as a part of his organization.

One Division Manager raised the following question: "Suppose I have a man in my organization who gets an answer from a staff representative of which I have also received a copy. He doesn't put that into effect until he checks with me,—is that right?" The answer given this Division Manager was that he was still the Division Manager and the man in his organization was still working for the Division Manager but receiving guidance and suggestions from the central office. It was again emphasized that the central staff group was responsible for the successful conduct of their line of activity at the divisions. The question was answered negatively in that it was stated that the directions from the central staff officer constituted a direct order on both the department head and the Division Manager and that the department head didn't have to wait to talk to the Division Manager about it but rather could put the instruction into effect. The question was then posed as to whether such action relieved the Division Manager of responsibility for the specific matter. . . . It was said that if the Division Manager disagreed with instructions issued by the central office he could bring it to the Executive Vice President's attention or go directly himself to the central staff officer involved and try to work out a better course of action.

Mr. Laddon said that he believed there were many things that the Division Managers would have to contact him on directly—matters of general policy which affected the whole division. He felt that that was all right but that they should not contact him on anything that had to do with a specific function for which there was a staff man. On those things the Division Manager should work through the staff representative. He further pointed out that only one report per week was wanted from each Division Manager, that report to be a discussion of weekly progress with decisions arrived at, etc. If definite and special reports were requested by a central staff man those reports should be sent to the person in charge of that particular function by the division department head concerned but simultaneously a copy of the report should go to the Division Manager.

The question was raised as to whether the Division Engineer was responsible for scheduling engineering to meet production and whether the engineering schedule would have to be approved by the Director of Engineering. The answer was that the Division Engineer should submit the schedule of what he promises he can do. After all he was the man on the job who knew local conditions and it was then up to him to live up to it. It was not felt that the Director of Engineering could be responsible for that schedule because he couldn't keep in close enough touch with it. If things did not work out satisfactorily then probably the Division Engineer was not the man for the job. There was no reason under this arrangement why a Division Engineer should accept a larger work assignment from the Director of Engineering than he felt he could handle.

Another example of relationship was that the Division Flight man supervised the Flight Operations but that there was one man on the central staff particularly concerned with flight operations. It was stated that he did not have the right to order the Division men around without going through the Division Manager. The Division Flight Operations Department reported "directly, concurrently, simultaneously, instantaneously" to the Division Manager. It was then said that the central staff man had a right to ask the Division Flight Operations people questions about a particular problem and that the Division Manager would get a copy of the response. . . . It was said that 99 times out of 100 the central staff man would not give the Division Flight Operations Department a direct order. . . .

Delivery schedules were to be set up by Master Scheduling with Perelle, Martin [Scheduling Director] and the Division Manager taking part in their formulation. The Division Manager should look over what the Army or Navy calls for and advise the central office as to what they think they can do.

Mr. Woodhead injected the thought that the Division Managers didn't want to get the idea that the central office was going to run the Division Manager's plant. He said that the Division Manager should bother the central office the smallest amount possible but use them when necessary. Otherwise the company might as well separate into subsidiary companies and there wouldn't be a reason for the Consolidated Vultee Aircraft Corporation. He suggested that they not worry too much about authority. He said he had gone into Division Managers' offices where the desk was littered with papers and everything was beautifully bottlenecked because the Division Manager didn't want anybody to do anything until he had told them to do it. This simply illustrated the need for greater delegation.

The staff people were, to the best of their ability, to work through the Division Managers and there was to be no intent to work without them. However, in order to speed up action and to prevent bottlenecking, it was felt that it might help for the central staff men to go direct to their corresponding department heads with coordination through the Division Manager; for if all negotiations went through the Division Manager only, it might easily be held up for several days.

Another point that was raised was in regard to schedules. Take, for instance, a modification center where the Air Force representative asks if a division can turn out some additional airplanes. The situation was to be handled by the Division Manager saying that he would investigate it. He was then to report to San Diego what he felt he could do and San Diego would, in 99 cases out of 100, okay the proposed action and the Division Manager could then report the proposed schedule to the A.A.F. The Division Managers were not to say "we can't tell you what the schedule is until we get in touch with San Diego." The idea of the San Diego check was so that the central office could coordinate the whole program. It wasn't a matter of asking permission of San Diego but merely reporting what it was felt could be done.

With regard to procedures or standard practices, any one of the staff heads could issue a procedure. If it affected plant protection or purchasing or subcontracting, it would come out over Mr. Leigh's signature and, in the case of manufacturing, would come out over Mr. Perelle's signature.

On the matter of the Division having no responsibility for engineering schedules discussed earlier, Mr. Laddon said that he thought Sutton should have a staff assistant assigned particularly to that problem. He felt that engineering schedules were difficult to establish and that there should be a certain amount of staff supervision and responsibility over them. Mr. Girdler did not see how Sutton could take full responsibility or how the Division Manager and the Division Engineer could take full responsibility for such schedules. He felt that it had to be a cooperative thing and if Sutton could have an assistant who spent his whole time checking on such schedules it would be a substantial help.

Labor matters were considered definitely a matter of Corporation policy and in that connection it was stated that Mr. Lauerman [Industrial Relations Director] would sit in on all negotiations of contracts with labor. He was to cover all divisions in person.

DIVISION MANAGERS' MEETING—SAN DIEGO—MAY 3, 1943

. . . .

It was proposed that all company general policies should be issued in the form of Corporation Standard Practice Instructions. . . . By way of explanation it was stated that a Corporation Standard Practice Instruction was to be issued only when it affected more than one function. If Mr. Perelle wished to issue a directive with regard to the Production Department it was to be issued as a directive covering the functioning of the Production Department. If, however, it affected production and also contract administration, in other words, more than one department, it should be issued as a C.S.P.I. over Mr. Laddon's signature or Mr. Leigh's. On the subject of organization charts it was stated that they were not to be taken too seriously. The functioning of the organization as a whole was said to be dependent upon the people in the organization wanting to do the job.

Mr. Woodhead said that no matter how perfect you make an organization chart, if the disposition to make the organization work isn't there, it won't work. The original chart was a tentative outline of how the organization was supposed to function for the following few months, and there would probably be a considerable number of changes as things were found not to be exactly as they should be.

Mr. Laddon again emphasized that he did not want the Division Managers coming to him on things that should be handled through the staff. If the matter had to do with production it should go through Perelle; if it had to do with engineering the Division Manager should go through Sutton. If it concerned Industrial Relations they should go through Lauerman. There were, however, certain things as relations with the customer and matters of general policy that should continue to come to Mr. Laddon.

Mr. Woodhead stated that they were going to discourage any deliberate effort to go around and not through the channels they were supposed to go through.

. . . .

Many questions were directed by the Division Managers concerning accounting, cost matters and contractual matters. It was stated that no satisfactory clarification of the accounting structure could be accomplished until the functional organization had been set up on a uniform basis throughout all divisions.

It was stated that a typical organization chart for any division was being developed and that it should be ready for the next Division Managers' meeting.

DIVISION MANAGERS' MEETING—DOWNEY, CALIFORNIA
—JUNE 30, 1943

Mr. Laddon announced that the decision had been made that the Division Managers should not appoint key personnel such as assistant managers, general superintendents, etc., without first clearing with the general office at San Diego. One reason why this was requested was that smaller divisions would not require as many top personnel as larger divisions. It was emphasized that this was not so much a matter of receiving permission to appoint new personnel but was rather a matter of organization. Everyone should remember that he was part of a large organization; that a man might be placed in a particular position and for reasons known to the general office it might be advisable to move him. This would have to be done, of course, from the standpoint of over-all good for the organization. It would not be a case of taking away the Division Manager's authority but rather of having Division Managers recognize the fact that they are part of a large organization. There seemed at this time to be a tendency on the part of some of the smaller divisions to adopt the organization which existed at San Diego and Fort Worth. There was no justification for this as many functions could be combined and thus simplify the smaller divisions' operations. This meant that the Division Managers should follow the general outline of the chart but would not necessarily have identical positions. The necessity for approval of changes on the part of San Diego would go down only to the point where the functions corresponded to the major functions on the central staff. Below those positions it was not necessary for the Division Managers to refer to San Diego.

Mr. Girdler pointed out in this connection that it wasn't a question of the Division Managers getting permission but rather giving the central staff heads a chance to make suggestions. In most cases the Division Manager would probably get the man he wanted anyhow.

.   .   .   .

DIVISION MANAGERS' MEETING—SAN DIEGO—
JANUARY 18–19, 1944

Relation Between Corporation Staff and Corresponding Personnel in Divisions

MR. COSLOW [Division Manager]: In directing department heads in a Division just how far down the line should the staff man go in selecting the personnel of the department? It was your statement at one Division Managers' Meeting that control should go as far as the top man. Since that time there has been some change in thinking on that—at least I have indications that the staff man is interested further down in the organization.

MR. LADDON: When the merger took place we eliminated the job of General Manager. The staff as it exists fulfills the function of a General Manager. They are my representatives with regard to their particular functions and function as a General Manager functions in their particular field. For instance, the staff man on industrial relations has the responsibility in that field that the General Manager would have. Say you want to appoint the head of a department. It is a good idea for you to consider the staff man's opinion in picking a candidate for that office. If the staff man is not satisfied that the job is properly handled in your Division and comes to you and suggests a change in personnel, you should listen to him. He is the one to whom I have assigned the responsibility. If he desires he can go down a man or two below the department head. He can step in to the degree he deems necessary to make the function work at your Division. If you want to appoint a new man to any function call the staff man concerned and get his suggestion. Take his advice. If you get the basic idea that the staff man is part of the General Manager you will be all right. This Corporation is too big to have any one man as General Manager. I found that out on numerous occasions. We have got to have people consider the accomplishment of the individual job more and forget their personal situations and prerogatives. Stop worrying about whether someone is stepping on your toes. Your personal advancement will be based on accomplishment and not on anything else. The corporate organization is well charted. I can answer any question about it. What we need is better team work. Worry about getting a thing done in the best and fastest way. There has been considerable improvement in the past six months but there is room for a lot more.

MR. WOODHEAD: Personal prestige in this Corporation means less than nothing. The thing that counts is the Corporation's success. A team success. There will be very little sympathy for the Division Manager who creates a situation and it is found the only thing that suffers is his own prestige and feelings. There is enough glory and reward for everyone to get his share. Personal prestige means nothing.

MR. McMAHON [Division Manager]: Agreed that you can and must have harmony. Just suppose the staff man says something can go and the Division Manager says it can not?

MR. WOODHEAD: You may have a difference of opinion with the staff man. You have a perfect right to straighten it out. You don't have to take everything the staff man says. Be sure it is an honest difference of opinion and for the good of the Corporation and not a difference because you feel your own prestige is affected.

MR. LADDON: Every employee has the right of appeal. Go up through channels and state the case. I don't anticipate we should get many of these. There have been only two or three in the last four months. They usually get resolved by common sense meeting of minds. No one can take an unreasonable stand and get away with it, whether Division Manager or staff man.

Utilizing Staff and Division Experience

MR. MARTIN: The matter that brought this to my attention was a recent trip to Fort Worth in connection with inspection. They were having the same troubles San Diego had a year or so ago. It seemed to me that instead of trying to find their own solution they might have wondered if other Divisions had run into those troubles and how they had solved them. For example, Fort Worth was trying to write an inspection manual. San Diego had written several thousand pages of inspection procedure and it seems to me it would have been a big start on an inspection manual if Fort Worth had asked what had been done here along that line.

MR. LADDON: There is a very natural tendency on the part of everybody to endeavor to work out their own problems in their own way. We should bear in mind that there is a great deal of experience available in the Corporation and before we start experimenting on a particular problem it would speed things up immeasurably if we talked it over with those Divisions where experimentation on that item has already taken place. This is one of the major advantages of a large Corporation and it is the specific responsibility of staff function concerned to see that all Divisions utilize to the fullest degree the entire corporate knowledge and experience.

DIVISION MANAGERS' MEETING—STINSON DIVISION (WAYNE, MICHIGAN)—AUGUST 14–16, 1944

Issuance of Directives by Staff Members to Department Heads at Divisions

MR. LADDON: At our very first staff meeting we defined what we considered to be the staff responsibility and we said at that time that it would not be necessary for every staff man to do all of his work through the Division Manager. We said at the time that he would work directly with his counterpart at the Division but that he should be very careful that the Division Manager was kept informed. We have had a number of instances where directives are issued or phone calls made to the department head or the staff counterpart involved without informing the Division Manager and that practice must be discontinued. The staff has a definite responsibility but nevertheless in fulfilling that responsibility they must do it in such a fashion that they do not belittle the authority of the Division Manager. He still is to function as the boss. We have in our Corporation a couple of people who have had considerable experience with a staff setup, F. A. Lauerman and M. A. Hannan. We have had little or no trouble with them. They decide on the proper course of action and tell their counterpart to talk it over with the Division Manager and, if he has no objections, put it into effect, or, if he has any, to call them. On the other hand, we have people who call up and give orders and the Division Manager does not know about it. In the final analysis the Division Manager is responsible for the functioning of the entire Division. The staff man involved may want a particular person hired to take care of a particular function in the best possible way, but getting that man may upset the over-all wage scale in the Division. Before any final action is taken it should be taken up with the Division Manager. That is particularly true in matters of organization. We have had situations where directives have been issued or changes of organization made by the staff man involved and the information sent directly to his counterpart in the Division. In the case mentioned it was issued in its final form and a copy was sent to the Division Manager. This is not the way to do it. In a number of cases conflicting directives have been issued. When a directive is issued by a staff man it should be okayed by the head of that function. Industrial relations or purchasing or materials or plant protection matters should all go through one place and follow the same procedure. . . . I am sure these are not issued with the idea that they will conflict with any other directive, but, in many cases, they do not know what directives have been issued.

MR. WOODHEAD: I would like to raise a point. When a staff man goes to a Division, the first thing he should do, for no other reason than common courtesy, is to check in with the Division Manager. After he talks with the man who is handling his particular phase of activity it would seem to me the right thing for the staff man to check out with the Division Manager so that he is familiar at all times with what is going on. One of the reasons for having a big Corporation rather than having a lot of small companies is to have the benefit of the added strength and talent by combination staff activities,—that is the primary purpose of having a Corporation. There are certain rules and regulations laid down because of the Corporation's setup. There is nothing to stop the Division Manager from working through the particular staff man. When there is something which you think is wrong or you object to, the party you must object to is the party that is responsible for it. If the matter is something to do with the Contract Department, go to Frank Watson and not through other sources. The thing which we do not like is that there is too much criticism and too much conversation in the wrong direction. There is absolutely no reason why the Division Manager should continue with something which he thinks is wrong and just keep his mouth shut, nor do we like people who open them too wide. That is the policy which we have set up and that is what we are going to follow.

MR. LADDON: The staff man is always thinking of his particular function; the Division Manager has to think of the whole Division. If the staff man insists that his directive be followed and the Division Manager does not agree, call Mr. Woodhead or me and get a decision on it. I get few such calls. I have had about two in a year and a half. The right of free speech still exists. Go to the top. Mr. Girdler's door is always open. So are Mr. Woodhead's and mine. We definitely do not want the staff to become consultants, to give advice but have no responsibility. That is not the way we want them to operate. If you cannot get together with the staff man and settle your difference of opinion, come to us. There has been a lot of behind-the-scenes complaining, and I want to see an end to it. Bring your complaints out in the open. All of the fault is not with the staff. We have had several instances where the Division Managers made changes in personnel without consultation with a staff man. That has to be stopped.

MR. WOODHEAD: With reference to this business of working together with the staff, I served as Division Manager for approximately seven years for Republic Steel under the same setup that we are working under here. In all that time I never once found a situation embarrassing to me or belittling to my position or which took away my authority. If two reasonable people, the staff man and the Division Manager, want to make the situation work, they can make it work perfectly without subordinating themselves or abdicating any of their authority. The Industrial Relations Manager for Republic Steel would come first to my office at Truscon Steel and say whom he came to work with. He would spend two or three days working with the man and then come back to my office and say how the man was working and then leave. We had the same thing with the Purchasing Department and with the Accounting Department. We had a good Chief Accountant who worked for me, who took my orders. When the Central Office

Auditor would come out, he would come into my office and say he was going to work with Jack Stanton. He would work with him three days and, if they had changes to make, he would present them to me when he was leaving but wouldn't go into detail. I never felt for one moment that I didn't have any control over that department. If I found out that anything had happened, how long do you think it would have been before I would have been on the phone finding out what was going on? I had the combined power of the whole Republic Steel Corporation to back me up. That was how I felt about it. I had all this strength behind me to use. The success of Consolidated Vultee isn't Louisville, or Nashville, but it is Consolidated Vultee. The success of a Division Manager is going to be the success of Consolidated Vultee. The thing we have to put over is the Corporate setup. Any time any little thing comes up like a conflict in orders or if a staff man comes into your Division and says something he shouldn't have said, we don't want to hear it from five different people. It is to be settled right on the spot between the Division Manager and the staff man. There has been altogether too much of this business of telling somebody else of the difficulties which you have had with a staff man. There is too much trying to play the individual game. This conversation is not meant for any particular individual. We do not want to know these things through a number of individuals. We want to hear them direct. We don't want to hear about it from anyone whose job has nothing to do with it. When we had trouble in the Police Department at Republic, we called up James Williams. We didn't call up the Police Department who would call up the Accounting Department. We called up James Williams and got it settled right then. Ninety-nine percent of our difficulties, irritations, complaints and criticisms will clear up if you fellows will work direct. I am going to go one step further and say this. If you do not do this, we are going to begin to question your motives and think you are trying to cross things up. If you persist in doing it, we are definitely going to question you as to whether you are really honestly trying to do the job and play the game as it should be played. We are going to be less charitable. When we get to the reconversion period and we have to begin to shrink operations, we are going to shrink it back corporation-wise. The organization that will be with this Corporation postwar is the organization which has earned its right to be with the Corporation. No one has an inside track. We are going to determine the permanent organization based on the record, ability and the personality of the individual.

MR. LADDON: Is there any discussion on that subject? I believe Mr. Coslow has some definite ideas on it.

MR. COSLOW: My thoughts on the matter were expressed in the memo which I wrote in answer to Mr. Martin's request. I used the word "consultant" which was wrong. My only thought was that when a staff man comes in to see you once in three or four months, he can't be too familiar with every little detail and can't watch things too closely. I work with every staff man that comes in, in nearly every case. The staff man is willing to work with and through the Division Manager. The only trouble is that they give their counterpart information which I don't learn about.

MR. LADDON: We said at our very first meeting that we didn't want to have everything flow through the Division Manager. We didn't want to get in the position where one man was a bottleneck. When important changes are to be made, they should be decided tentatively between the staff man and his counterpart and then confirmed with the Division Manager. When the staff man calls the counterpart he should not give him instructions on important changes which have not first been talked over with the Division Manager.

MR. GIRDLER: I have been functioning under this system for a good many years. It is pretty hard to lay down any rule which does not have a few exceptions and you can't wear people out by trying to set it up so every minute detail has to go through a straight channel. If Mr. Hannan [Plant Protection Director] calls up the Plant Protection Department at Nashville and says he just got some information on one of the men and wants him fired right away, in my opinion it isn't necessary to find Joe Hennen [Division Manager] to fire that particular guard. Say Hennen has a foreman in the plant who fires a man, he does not tell Hennen,—that is a relatively commonplace case. But on the other hand if Hannan has a Plant Protection man in Nashville and wants to transfer him from Nashville to Allentown, he cannot talk to the man about it until he has talked to Hennen about it. The spirit of cooperation is the most important part of this setup.

MR. WOODHEAD: Mr. Coslow mentioned the fact that a staff man may only go into a Division once every three or four months and therefore he is not too familiar with what is going on. How often do the Division Managers call up the staff men—not wait for the staff man to call them? Ask the staff man for assistance and help. The staff man is responsible for his particular function in the Corporation. How often do you ask for that assistance? Again, if a Division Manager is having trouble with his Engineering setup, does that Division Manager try to work with his Division Engineer or does that Manager call up Mr. Sutton? Do they go right to the staff man who would help them at that time?

MR. LADDON: It is all part of the idea that we do not want the staff to work just as consultants. When the Division Manager is in trouble, we want him to call the staff for help and when he isn't getting help, we want to know about it. We want the staff people to have responsibility, not be just advisors and consultants. They may know someone who can be spared at some other Division to help out. The staff man can demand that help be given. I want to get away from this idea of a consultant.

.   .   .   .

In discussing the corporation's organization, Mr. Laddon stated that one of top management's difficulties concerned the selection of division managers. It was desirable for a division manager to possess both outstanding administrative ability and wide manufacturing and engineering experience. Such men were difficult to find, and frequent compromises were made as between desired abilities and available men with somewhat lesser qualifications. An example concerned a manager of a major manufacturing division assigned to that position because of his ability as a strong administrator. Although associated with the aviation industry for several years, this man had had no previous experience with large-scale manufacturing operations. He effectively brought together an organization which functioned well for a time. After a change in production to a new and more complicated type of plane, however, some serious production shortcomings developed, notably in the control of quality. Mr. Perelle, central staff officer in charge of manufacturing, first tried to solve the division's manufacturing problems by advising and making suggestions to the manager and his organization. Progress was slow, however, and Mr. Perelle became dissatisfied with his lack of direct authority over manufacturing operations which he believed required immediate attention. He later received temporary authority from Mr. Laddon and Mr. Woodhead to assume direct control of production at this division in order to deal effectively with this immediate problem. Significant improvements in manufacturing efficiency followed, although major changes in operating personnel and manufacturing methods were required. During the period of Mr. Perelle's direct management of manufacturing operations the division manager resigned.

Mr. Perelle resigned on September 1, 1944, to become vice-president and general manager of the Hughes Tool Company at Houston, Texas, and manager of the Hughes Aircraft Company at Los Angeles. In these positions, Mr. Perelle was to have sole responsibility for manufacturing at the two companies.

In April, 1945, Mr. Girdler resigned as chairman of the board of Consolidated Vultee. The following statement was published in the *American Aviation Daily* at the time:

Consolidated Vultee Aircraft Corporation announces the resignation of Tom M. Girdler as chairman of the board and a director after almost three and a half years of service. Consolidated directors accepted Girdler's resignation "with profound regret."

In his letter of resignation, Girdler said that when he accepted the position with Consolidated he did so with the understanding that he would relinquish it "when I felt my portion of the job was finished. I believe that the time has now come. The defeat of Germany is assured."

Girdler said that "the urgent need for large production of aircraft will remain until Japan falls, but the industry is now geared to meet every production requirement. All that is necessary is for production lines to keep moving."

Girdler continues as chairman of the board of Republic Steel Corporation. He became chairman of the Consolidated and Vultee aircraft corporations in December, 1941, to help accelerate military aircraft production.[5]

---

[5] *American Aviation Daily,* April 24, 1945, p. 270.

In comparing the organizations of Consolidated Vultee and Republic Steel, Mr. Girdler said:

> The splendid performance of Republic Steel Corporation during the war is to be explained by one simple fact. For thirteen years Republic has been "boiling out." We got rid of all those who could not or did not fit. Up and down the line the men in Republic have learned where their authority ends, where that of another begins. Lines of demarcation are respected. Since there is no friction, the whole enterprise runs as a well-oiled machine. Every man in it seems to delight in doing his best.
>
> Of course, there has not been time for such a "boiling out" in the big aircraft companies. For one thing, they have expanded so greatly, as much as fortyfold and more within a couple of years. Yet at Consolidated I found an organization far better than I had expected, one that was extraordinarily rich in talented men.[6]

Mr. Girdler was succeeded at Consolidated Vultee by Mr. Irving B. Babcock. Mr. Babcock, formerly a vice-president of General Motors and president of Yellow Truck and Coach Manufacturing Company, had joined the Aviation Corporation as president in February, 1945. The Aviation Corporation's annual report for 1944 included the following statement concerning Mr. Babcock:

> The addition of Mr. Babcock to the organization greatly strengthens it because of his wide general manufacturing and commercial experience. He not only has first-hand knowledge of production, but is familiar with the problems of finance, sales, engineering and development. It is evidence of Mr. Babcock's belief in the future of The Aviation Corporation that he should sever his long association with the automotive industry to apply his executive abilities in a new field. His background of experience will be of value not only during the war, but also in the postwar program on which The Aviation Corporation will embark when the end of the war permits the resumption of normal activities.[7]

Consolidated Vultee's organization by July, 1945, is shown in Exhibit 5.

Exhibit 6 is an analysis of changes in division manager personnel during the period March, 1943—July, 1945.

---

[6] Girdler, *op. cit.,* p. 425.

[7] The Aviation Corporation and Associated Companies, *Annual Report for the Fiscal Year Ended November 30, 1944,* p. 10.

Exhibit 5

CONSOLIDATED VULTEE AIRCRAFT CORPORATION

Organization Chart, July 25, 1945

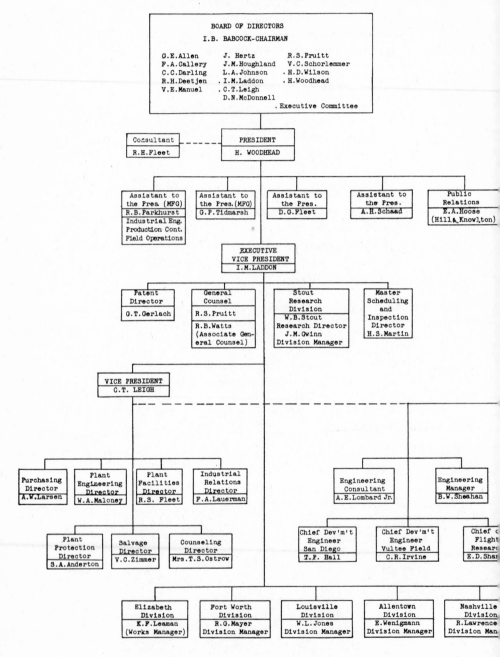

BOARD OF DIRECTORS

I.B. BABCOCK-CHAIRMAN

G.E.Allen	J. Hertz	R.S.Pruitt
F.A.Callery	J.M.Houghland	V.C.Schorlemmer
C.C.Darling	L.A.Johnson	. H.D.Wilson
R.H.Deetjen	. I.M.Laddon	. H.Woodhead
V.E.Manuel	. C.T.Leigh	
	D.N.McDonnell	

. Executive Committee

Consultant
R.H.Fleet

PRESIDENT
H. WOODHEAD

Assistant to the Pres. (MFG)
R.B.Parkhurst
Industrial Eng.
Production Cont.
Field Operations

Assistant to the Pres.(MFG)
G.P.Tidmarsh

Assistant to the Pres.
D.G.Fleet

Assistant to the Pres.
A.H.Schaad

Public Relations
E.A.Hoose
(Hill & Knowlton)

EXECUTIVE VICE PRESIDENT
I.M.LADDON

Patent Director
G.T.Gerlach

General Counsel
R.S.Pruitt
R.B.Watts
(Associate General Counsel)

Stout Research Division
W.B.Stout
Research Director
J.M.Gwinn
Division Manager

Master Scheduling and Inspection Director
H.S.Martin

VICE PRESIDENT
C.T. LEIGH

Purchasing Director
A.W.Larsen

Plant Engineering Director
W.A.Maloney

Plant Facilities Director
R.S. Fleet

Industrial Relations Director
F.A.Lauerman

Engineering Consultant
A.E.Lombard Jr.

Engineering Manager
B.W.Sheahan

Plant Protection Director
S.A.Anderton

Salvage Director
V.C.Zimmer

Counseling Director
Mrs.T.S.Ostrow

Chief Dev'm't Engineer San Diego
T.P. Hall

Chief Dev'm't Engineer Vultee Field
C.R.Irvine

Chief of Flight Research
E.D.Shar

Elizabeth Division
K.F.Leaman
(Works Manager)

Fort Worth Division
R.G.Mayer
Division Manager

Louisville Division
W.L.Jones
Division Manager

Allentown Division
E.Wenigmann
Division Manager

Nashville Division
R.Lawrence
Division Man

Exhibit 5—Continued

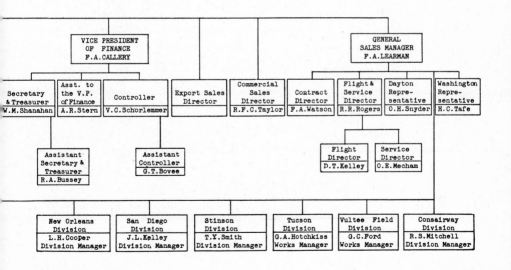

Exhibit 6

CONSOLIDATED VULTEE AIRCRAFT CORPORATION

*Analysis of Changes in
Maunfacturing Division Manager Personnel
March, 1943—July, 1945*

Divisions	March, 1943	July, 1943	December, 1943	May, 1944	July, 1945
San Diego	J. L. Kelley				
Fort Worth	G. J. Newman			R. G. Mayer	
Vultee Field	C. W. Coslow				G. C. Ford
Allentown	A. M. Hall	R. J. McMahon			E. Wenigmann
Elizabeth	D. C. Beatty		L. H. Cooper		K. F. Leaman
Louisville	W. E. Burdick	W. L. Jones			
Intercontinent Aircraft Corporation	W. A. Hayward		N. C. Sather		
Nashville	R. McCulloch	J. W. Hennen			R. Lawrence
New Orleans	W. Nelson				L. H. Cooper
Stinson	E. Shelton				T. Y. Smith
Tucson	W. R. Lawrence				G. A. Hotchkiss

PART IV

Control

A Note on the Manufacture and Distribution of Portland Cement in the United Kingdom[*]

CEMENT MANUFACTURE

PORTLAND CEMENT was developed from an invention of a laborer in Leeds, England, in 1824. It was called "portland" cement because the concrete made from it resembled the well-known portland building stone in color and texture. Its manufacture is today a major world industry. World consumption has risen from 81 million tons in 1938 to 315 million in 1960 and is still rising.

Cement itself is manufactured from a closely controlled mixture of calcium carbonate, alumina, and silica. Calcium carbonate is found in various forms of limestone fairly liberally throughout the world. To be suitable for the manufacture of cement, the calcium carbonate content of the limestone must be relatively free from impurity. Soft chalk, which is very high in calcium carbonate, is found uniquely on either side of the English Channel toward the southern part of the North, Sea. Chalk is easier to process than hard limestone, and its availability accounts, in part, for the fact that nearly half of British production is located in southeastern England.

Alumina is found in some forms of clay or shale. A relatively small amount of sand supplies the silica requirements.

From 3,000 to 3,600 pounds of raw materials are required to make a ton of cement. These are quarried with large diesel or electric power shovels and conveyed to the works, which is normally placed nearby. There they are crushed and ground to a fine powder, and—in what is known as the "wet process"—mixed in strictly controlled proportions with water to form cement slurry. (Slurry normally contains about 40% water by weight.) The liquid state of the mixture is necessary to

---

[*] Much of the material included in this description was taken, with permission, from a paper "The Manufacture and Distribution of Cement" prepared by the Chairman of The Rugby Portland Cement Company Ltd., Rugby, England.

facilitate a perfectly homogeneous mixture of the raw materials and to permit rapid adjustment of the proportions by merely adding materials which quickly become uniformly dispersed throughout the liquid.

The slurry, when chemically correct, is fed to the kiln, which in a modern works is a large steel cylinder from 3 to 500 feet in length and 9 to 14 feet in diameter. It rotates at the rate of approximately once every 45 seconds, on a slightly inclined axis. The slurry is fed in at the higher end.

Near the lower end of the kiln is the burning zone, where fuel is injected into the kiln and fired to produce a temperature of about 2,500°F. Pulverized coal is the usual fuel in Britain, but oil and natural gas are used in other countries where these fuels are readily available. The water in the slurry is driven off as steam, together with the carbon dioxide content of the calcium carbonate and minor quantities of other gases. The remaining materials are fluxed in the intense heat and leave the kiln in the form of pea-sized nodules called cement clinker. The chemical part of the process, completed at this point, is closely controlled throughout by chemists who test the raw materials, the coal, and the slurry every hour, day and night.

Thereafter, the process is largely mechanical. The cement clinker is ground in large water-cooled mills to a predetermined fineness, and a small amount of calcium sulphate, or gypsum, is added in order to control the "setting time" of the resultant powder, now finished cement.

As it leaves the mills, the cement is weighed automatically and then pumped through pipes by compressed air to the large concrete silos in which it is stored. It remains in storage until it is withdrawn by mechanical means to the packing plant, where it is packed into paper sacks, which are automatically fitted, sealed, weighed and delivered by means of conveyors to the truck, the rail car, or the ship. It may be withdrawn from the silos into special bulk trucks which deliver it unpacked.

THE USES OF CEMENT

Cement is used as the binding agent in concrete and in mortar. Concrete, one of the world's primary construction materials, is composed of cement, sand, aggregate (clean gravel and stones), and water. Cement reacts chemically with the water and hardens within a few hours after mixing, binding the sand and gravel particles in a solid mass. Concrete can be used without reinforcing (as in highway pavements which contain only wire matting for temperature stresses), or it can be used with steel reinforcement, as in buildings and bridges.

STRUCTURE OF THE INDUSTRY IN THE UNITED KINGDOM—1960

The cement industry in the United Kingdom consists of nine financially independent groups, all of which have been members of the Cement Makers' Federation since its establishment in 1934.

The three largest interests held, in 1960, about 83% of the home market and have provided much of the leadership within the federation. Associated Portland Cement Manufacturers Limited is considerably the largest company, with about 62% of the United Kingdom market. The Tunnel Group has about 12.4%, and The Rugby Portland Cement Company Limited 7% of the United Kingdom market. Practically all the United Kingdom export trade is conducted by these three makers, which are also the only companies having manufacturing subsidiaries abroad.

The federation regulates the internal affairs of the industry and arranges an interchange of technical information and industry-wide statistics. By far its most important function, however, is establishing the basis of selling prices and conditions of sale, in order, it is asserted, that the costs of distribution—which average nearly 20% of delivered cost of cement—can be controlled. Membership is voluntary and voting power is proportionate, although not directly, to the previous year's home deliveries. Approval of any proposal, however, requires the concurrence of at least four of the nine members. The federation has no control over the production of any manufacturer, nor is it concerned with the export trade.

The British cement industry also maintains a large research and promotional organization, the Cement and Concrete Association, part of whose function is to increase the use and uses of concrete. Cement itself has no substitute; however, it is used only to form concrete, which is in competition with steel, brick, stone, tile, timber and many other materials.

The industry also organizes its conduct of labor relations. For more than 35 years it has operated a National Joint Industrial Council at which industry-wide wage rates and working conditions are set. The industry has never had a national strike or lock-out. Holidays with pay and profit-sharing plans were features of the industry for many years before World War II.

POSTWAR GROWTH OF THE INDUSTRY

The postwar progress made by the industry is shown in the following exhibit:

Exhibit 1

THE MANUFACTURE AND DISTRIBUTION OF PORTLAND CEMENT IN THE UNITED KINGDOM

United Kingdom Cement Deliveries
(000 tons)

	Home	Export	Total
1961 (est.)	13,800	800	14,600
1960	12,463	1,000	13,463
1959	11,683	1,088	12,771
1958	10,675	1,145	11,820
1957	10,709	1,382	12,091
1956	11,275	1,600	12,875
1955	10,759	1,766	12,526
1954	10,079	1,769	11,848
1953	9,335	1,917	11,253
1952	9,147	2,055	11,202
1951	8,144	1,974	10,119
1946	5,479	1,095	6,574
1939	7,587	665	8,252

THE ECONOMICS OF THE INDUSTRY

Siting of the Plant. It is considered a matter of prime importance that cement plants be located as close as possible to raw material deposits. Adequate water supplies, fuel, and electricity, and access to road, rail, and water transport must also be available. Thorough technical investigation is required since both the physical and chemical properties of the raw materials will influence the design of many of the factory components.

Costs of Production. The manufacture of cement is a highly mechanized process and employs comparatively little labor. The capital investment is among the highest for any industry; it equals almost £20,-000 per man employed, which is over six times what it was before World War II. Depreciation is therefore a heavy charge, and will become progressively heavier as prewar plants are replaced.

Coal is the largest individual item in the cost of production. It takes approximately 800 pounds of coal, including the coal used to generate electricity, to make a ton of cement.

In general, industry production costs are distributed as follows:

```
Coal and power.............................45–50%
Direct labor...............................10–15%
Consumable equipment....................... 9–12%
Depreciation (installed cost).............. 9–12%

Indirect factory labor and other overheads (super-
    vision, testing, maintenance, cost accounting,
    etc.)..................................15–20%
Manufacture cost........................... 100%
Average haulage............................20–30% of Manufacture Cost
Sales expense.............................. 5– 8% "        "        "
General administrative overhead............10–15% "        "        "
```

Profit margins are not disclosed. It has been asserted that current prices allow profits only because the manufacturers are still using, in part, equipment installed in the late 1930's. As greater proportions of new, more expensive plant installations are brought into use, prices may rise to cover increased depreciation charges.

Leaders of the British cement industry have repeatedly stated that manufacture of cement in the United Kingdom has for years been conducted with the highest efficiency and one of the lowest unit costs of any producing country in the world.

Distribution. The distribution of cement to the site where it will be used is a more technical and complicated problem than at first sight appears, for it is not the cost of production at the place where the cement is made but the cost at the site where it will be used that is important. The geographical distribution of demand, which in itself varies quite considerably from year to year (and can be materially distorted at different times by large airport programs, road works, reservoirs and similar forms of construction using large quantities of cement) is not coincident with the geographical distribution of the works.

Most companies in the industry maintain a fleet of trucks for road delivery. Little goes by rail, owing to the costs of double-handling. Delivery in bulk (in special vehicles) has rapidly increased in recent years and now accounts for nearly 50% of the home trade.

PRICING AND THE ROLE OF THE CEMENT MAKERS' FEDERATION

The manufacturers feel that a joint policy of distribution and price can avoid the severe price competition which, in the early 1930's created difficulties for both producers and users. For example, a works near to a large consuming area might be able to supply only one-third of the demand in that area, leaving the remaining two-thirds to come from a much greater distance. If there were not a co-ordinated price policy, it has been said, a builder taking his supplies from the nearer works would pay one price, while his competitor would have to pay a higher price for cement coming from a more distant works. This would assertedly lead to endless complications in bidding for construction projects.

The federation's pricing arrangements, therefore, have the following objectives:

1. To sell and distribute cement throughout the country in the most efficient and economical manner commensurate with the interests of the country as a whole, of the users of cement, and of the manufacturers—in particular by:
   a) Encouraging the delivery in any particular area from the nearest works with the object of avoiding unnecessary and wasteful haulage.
   b) Eliminating depots (except where these perform useful functions) and delivering straight from works to construction sites.
   c) Providing a stable system of prices which takes into account the high proportion of the cost of transport in the price of cement and avoids disproportionate price differentials which would otherwise arise between various parts of the U.K.
2. To provide a price system giving sufficient stability to enable manufacturers individually and collectively to plan production in advance efficiently and economically, and individually to undertake the heavy expenditure required to meet increasing demand for cement.
3. To ensure during any temporary shortage of cement that prices remain at a reasonable level.
4. To eliminate unnecessary and expensive advertising.
5. To provide for standard forms of packages, bulk delivery and the like.
6. To arrange for the convenience of both manufacturers and buyers, standard conditions of supply and forms of quotation and contract.
7. To facilitate joint research and exchange of information to improve the standard and the potential utility of cement.[1]

To achieve these aims, the federation's present system provides for the same delivered price at the same point of delivery for all brands of cement, irrespective of the works from which the cement may come.

There are 48 cement works in the United Kingdom. (Cement works very near one another usually have the same base price.) There are 37 base prices, one for each location where cement is manufactured, and one for each cement importing center on the coast. These base prices are nearly the same at every factory, although there are slight variations made for the type of raw materials used, and the delivered

---

[1] Summarized from a policy statement of the federation.

price of fuel to the works. For the former, for instance, plants using chalk as their source of calcium carbonate have base prices about 5% lower than those using limestone, since all limestone crushing and grinding expenses are eliminated. In 1961, the base factory price (delivered within five miles of plant) of ordinary portland cement ranged from 111/6d. to 127/6d. per ton.

Radiating from each works is a series of concentric circles at four- or five-mile intervals, the circles from any particular works continuing until they meet the circles radiating from another works. The delivered price within each of these circles increases by 1/6d. for each circle. (See Exhibit 2.)

These price increments do not, in fact, cover actual transportation costs; therefore, manufacturers allow 10–15% of the base price plus the zone price increments for covering haulage costs. As a result, between 20 and 30 miles from a producing unit is considered the "breakeven" haulage distance, below which haulage costs are less than the allowance in the base price plus the incremental price increases, and above which the converse is true. The more efficiently a producer can operate his truck fleet, the greater will be his breakeven haulage distance.

The pricing scheme means that every buyer at a particular point will pay exactly the same price for his cement. It also means that there is every inducement for a manufacturer to save transport costs by selling as much of his production as possible within the circles controlled by his own works. The further he delivers cement from his own works, the more likely he is to run into the circles controlled by another works, where the price he will receive will begin to decrease. The federation asserts that the effect of this arrangement is to save as much as possible of the heavy transport costs and so maintain throughout the country, on the average, a lower level of prices than would otherwise be the case.

There exist standard merchant discounts. Retail building material suppliers are entitled to a merchant's discount, but they in turn must sell cement at the same prices, in the particular zones, which apply to the manufacturers. Thus, a buyer pays the same price whether he buys from a manufacturer or a merchant. Merchants play a major role in supplying small orders, since the minimum order normally accepted by a manufacturer is 6 tons. A relatively small percentage of industry sales is made directly to merchants for their own accounts, but much more cement is delivered to the customer "on site" at a merchant's order.

Exhibit 2

THE MANUFACTURE AND DISTRIBUTION OF PORTLAND CEMENT IN THE
UNITED KINGDOM

Illustration of the Federation's Pricing Agreement

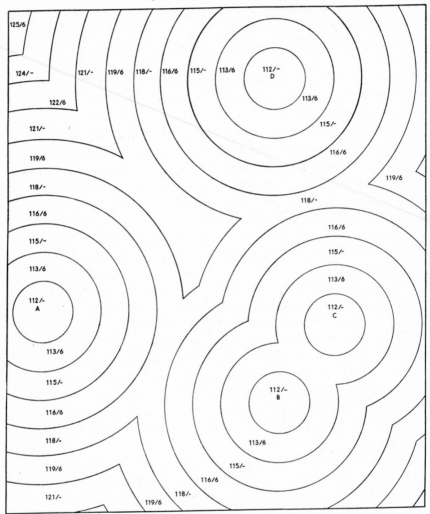

Sales price in shillings and pence per ton shown for each four- or five-mile zone.

THE RESTRICTIVE TRADE PRACTICES ACT

In 1956, England passed the Restrictive Trade Practices Act, which required that all trade agreements be registered with the Registrar of the Restrictive Practices Court. These agreements subsequently had to be justified before the Court, which would decide whether they were contrary to the public interest. On March 16, 1961, the Restrictive

Practices Court handed down its decision: it upheld the federation's price agreements with only minor modifications.

In essence, the federation argued that, because of its price-fixing agreement, U.K. cement manufacturers could operate with more certainty of profit than under free competition. Because of this greater security, they were willing to accept a lower return on investment and thus could sell cement appreciably lower than if prices had not been fixed.

Experts on both sides agreed that, in order to attract new capital into the industry, a net return on investment of at least 15% would have to be available. The federation proved that, in order to yield such a return, a new cement plant would have to price its cement at least 25 shillings per ton higher than the current average price. It also established that federation members were earning, on the average, less than 10% return on investment. The Court therefore concluded that, had the price-fixing arrangement not existed, the price of cement would have been "significantly" higher, and the public would have suffered accordingly. Thus the Court upheld the main price-fixing clause. It found that the industry was efficient and had acted with a sense of responsibility.

The presiding judge was concerned only that the price-fixing agreement should be as honorably administered in the future as had been true in the past. Thus he requested, and the federation agreed, that if at any future date the Registrar should wish to determine whether prices were still being kept at a fair level, the federation would cooperate fully by making cost and price data available for inspection.

The federation's practice of giving quantity discounts based on total annual purchases from *all* federation members was disallowed by the judge, on the grounds that it did not reflect true economies from volume sales.

The court also scrutinized, and upheld with one exception, minor agreements regarding terms of sale. In summing up his decision, Mr. Justice Diplock remarked:

> In the result, therefore, the Respondents have satisfied us that the main price-fixing conditions, other than those providing for general rebates to large users and large merchants, are not contrary to the public interest, and that the ancillary restrictions, other than that relating to the prohibition upon the quotations and contracts for the supply of cement for periods exceeding twelve months, are also not contrary to the public interest. . . .[2]

---

[2] *Judgement in the Restrictive Practices Court on an Agreement between Members of the Cement Makers' Federation*, printed by the Cement and Concrete Association, 1961.

In commenting on the Court's decision, Sir Halford Reddish observed:

I am not being wise after the event if I say that the judgement accorded closely with our expectations, for we were confident throughout that a detailed examination of our arrangements would show conclusively that they were in the public interest. And the cement makers were not alone in their satisfaction with the outcome of the case. Over four thousand buyers of cement sent us replies to a questionnaire before the hearing: something like 97 per cent of them were strongly in favour of a continuation of the present system.[3]

---

[3] *Investors Chronicle,* March 24, 1961.

The Rugby Portland Cement Company Limited (A)

HISTORY, GROWTH, AND ORGANIZATION

THE RUGBY COMPANY began producing lime in the early nineteenth century at a works near Rugby, England. Cement manufacture, under the company's "Crown" Cement trade-mark began at the works in the 1820's, and thereafter became its principal product. In 1925, the company, which hitherto had been a partnership, became a private limited company with share capital of £100,000 owned by descendants of the previous partners. In 1929, Mr. (now Sir[1]) Halford Reddish, a young chartered accountant with a consulting practice, joined the board which previously had comprised only representatives of the two descendant branches of the original owners. Four years later, upon the death of the general manager, Mr. Reddish became managing director, and shortly afterward, chairman.

At that time, the cement industry was in the middle of a deep depression. Prices were at a very unprofitable level. In spite of this crisis, the chairman decided to expand and modernize the company's production facilities. Contrary to previous industry tradition, he also decided to operate the plant 52 weeks per year, thus ensuring steady employment for the workers. Despite the depression and difficulties of selling the increased output, a profit was realized at the end of the first year of the new management. A second manufacturing site was obtained when a nearby company went into receivership. Erection of a new factory at the second site plus the modernization and expansion of the Rugby works required substantial fresh capital. In 1935, the company became a public company with its shares quoted on The London Stock Exchange, and additional capital of £140,000 was introduced. Since that time, additional equity capital had been raised by occasional "rights" issues.

---

[1] In early 1958, Her Majesty Queen Elizabeth II knighted Mr. Halford Reddish for his public services.

In 1936, Rugby acquired a third site and erected its Rochester works. In 1939, another company was purchased and its facilities were combined with those at Rochester. In 1945, Rugby acquired another company, and although its production facilities were closed, Rugby used its brand name and distribution organization.

Rugby made major additions to its three plants in Great Britain after 1946.

During the immediate postwar years, export trade was very profitable, with unit margins several times those of the home market sales. The proportion of Rugby's deliveries accounted for by exports reached a maximum in 1951 and 1952 at about 43%. In 1961, however, Sir Halford Reddish said that in recent years export sales had become almost marginal because of the increased competition (much of it subsidized) from non-British manufacturers and the growth of cement industries in areas formerly importing cement. Rugby had itself established overseas subsidiaries and built manufacturing plants in Trinidad and western Australia. The former started production in 1954, and the latter in 1955. Both units were able to supply cement at substantially lower prices than existing imported cement and made useful contributions to Rugby's consolidated profits.

With a rapidly developing local market plus export trade in the eastern Caribbean, the Trinidad factory required the doubling of its capacity within less than five years of starting its operation. Management decided in 1961 to extend the Australian plant in the near future.

In highlighting Rugby's growth, Sir Halford said in 1961:

In 1933 we had the one not very modern works at Rugby and total net assets with a book value of £109,250. Today all our works at home and abroad are modern and up-to-date and the total net assets of the company at book values amount to £13,404,369. (The real value is probably in excess of £18,500,000.) Additional capital introduced from 1st January 1933 to 31st December 1960 amounted to £13,295,119. Here's how the money has been found.

Shareholders have subscribed for shares (including
    premiums and loan stock)..................£ 5,890,863
    by leaving profits in the company..............   5,666,076
And others (by minority interests in, or loans to,
    subsidiary companies) have found...........   1,738,180
                                 £13,295,119

Net profit before taxes rose from less than £4,000 to almost £1.8 million in the same period. Postwar growth produced 11 years of successively record deliveries from 1945 to 1956 and 16 years of successively record group profits, 1946–61 (see Exhibits 1–3).

Exhibit 1

THE RUGBY PORTLAND CEMENT COMPANY LIMITED (A)

Consolidated Balance Sheet Statements 1946 and 1951–61

(1,000's of £)

Assets	1946	1951	1952	1953	1954	1955	1956	1957	1958	1959	1960	1961
Current Assets	576	1,847	1,982	2,616	3,836	4,211	4,521	4,195	4,692	6,744	7,597	*
Fixed Assets (1937 Valuation or Cost If Subsequently Acquired)	1,673	3,271	3,591	3,876	6,171	7,861	8,613	9,309	9,487	9,809	10,627	
Less Accumulated Depreciation	436	987	1,125	1,261	1,562	1,635	1,969	2,306	2,601	3,008	3,456	
Net Fixed Assets	1,237	2,285	2,466	2,616	4,609	6,226	6,644	7,003	6,886	6,801	7,171	
Investment in Subsidiary Companies (Not Consolidated)	209	33	393	793	760							
Total Assets	2,022	4,165	4,841	6,025	9,205	10,437	11,165	11,198	11,578	13,545	14,768	
Liabilities and Net Worth												
Current Liabilities	367	1,355	814	776	1,327	1,498	1,759	1,292	1,190	1,191	1,364	
Debt Capital:												
4% Debenture	420											
Mortgage Loans						400	480	560	640	720	800	
4½% Unsecured Loan 1957–62			1,000	1,500	1,500	1,500	1,500	1,500	1,500	1,500	1,500	
Total Debt	420		1,000	1,500	1,500	1,900	1,980	2,060	2,140	2,220	2,300	
Share Capital:												
4% and 6% Preference Shares	325	825	825	825	825	825	825	825	825	825	825	
Ordinary Shares 5/par	325	500	500	750	1,250	1,500	1,500	1,500	1,500	1,750	2,000	
"A" Shares 1/par					50	50	50	50	50	50	50	
Capital Reserve	325	610	563	810	1,265	1,300	1,358	1,415	1,275	2,133	1,950	
Revenue Reserves:												
General Reserve	100	500	500	750	1,125	1,500	1,750	2,000		1,000	1,217	
Reserve for Future Taxation		249	408	504	352	390	320	303	350			
Reserve for Ordinary and "A" Share Dividend Payment (Net)	161	52	55	55	115	201	230	230	276	329	383	
Undistributed Profit		73	175	56	120	106	275	451	2,947	3,067	3,741	
Total Capital and Reserves	1,236	2,809	3,026	3,750	5,102	5,873	6,308	6,774	7,223	9,154	10,166	
Interest of Outside Shareholders in a Subsidiary Company					1,277	1,165	1,117	1,072	1,025	980	938	
Total Liabilities and Net Worth	2,022	4,165	4,841	6,025	9,205	10,437	11,165	11,198	11,578	13,545	14,768	
Net Working Capital	210	491	1,168	1,841	2,510	2,712	2,762	2,903	3,502	5,553	6,233	
Equity/Debt Ratio	2.9/1	no debt	3.0/1	2.5/1	3.4/1	3.1/1	3.2/1	3.3/1	3.4/1	4.1/1	4.4/1	

* Balance sheet information for 1961 not available.

Exhibit 2

THE RUGBY PORTLAND CEMENT COMPANY LIMITED (A)

Consolidated Profit and Loss Account 1946 and 1951–61

(1,000's of £)

	1946 £	1946 %	1951 £	1951 %	1952 £	1952 %	1953 £	1953 %	1954 £	1954 %	1955 £	1955 %	1956 £	1956 %	1957 £	1957 %	1958 £	1958 %	1959 £	1959 %	1960 £	1960 %	1961 £	1961 %
Consolidated trading profits	213		522		656		744		904		1,256		1,369		1,397		1,500		1,877		2,183		2,569	
Other income			19		20		24		27		39		65		51		52		57		99			
Less depreciation	79		124		142		136		210		270		340		342		381		443		506		550	
Net profit before taxes	134	100	417	100	534	100	633	100	721	100	1,025	100	1,093	100	1,106	100	1,171	100	1,491	100	1,777	100	2,019	100
Taxation—profits tax‡			100		102		125		62		115		109		135		60		45		88			
Income tax‡	39		150		255		300		313		325		255		235		260		475		550		776	
Total taxes	39	29	250	60	357	67	425	67	375	52	440	43	364	33	370	34	320	27	520	35	638	36	776	
Net profit after taxes	95		167		177		208		346		585		729		736		851		971		1,139		1,244	
Preference dividends	12	9	21	5	21	4	22	3	22	3	23	2	23	2	23	2	23	2	24	2	24	1	24	
Ordinary dividends (net)	22	16	52	12	55	10	55	9	115	16	172	17	194	18	194	18	230	20	268	18	306	17	306	
"A" share dividends (net)											29	3	36	3	36	3	46	4	61	4	77	4	77	
Retained in business	61	46	94	23	101	19	131	21	209	29	361	35	477	44	484	44	553	47	618	41	732	41	837	
Ordinary dividend per share (gross)	7½d		1/-d		1/-d		1/-d		1/-d		1/-d		1/1½d		1/1½d		1/3d		1/3d		1/3d		1/3d	
Capital distribution per share (gross)																								
"A" share dividend per share (gross)	3d		3d		3d		3d		..		1/-d		1/3d		1/3d		1/6d		2/-d		2/6d		2/6d	
Net profit before taxes as return on total capital and reserves	10.85%		14.87%		17.65%		19.50%*		17.65%†		17.42%		17.30%		16.30%		16.20%		16.29%		17.48%			
Gross ordinary dividend as return on capital employed, i.e., ordinary plus disclosed reserves (less reserves credited to "A" shares)	4.36%		5.04%		4.54%		4.12%*		6.20%†		6.09%		6.36%		5.84%		6.06%		5.43%		5.56%			

* Excluding the £500,000 of additional capital introduced at end of 1953.
† Excluding the £1,000,000 of additional capital introduced at end of 1954.
‡ *Profits Tax* was the estimated liability for the year ending with the statement. *Income Tax* was the estimated liability for the subsequent two-year period. This procedure gives rise to the Reserve for Future Income Tax in the balance sheet. The estimated income tax for the future period is put into this reserve; and at the end of each year, the actual tax liability for the year is withdrawn from the reserve and put into current liabilities, from which the actual remittance is made.

Exhibit 3

THE RUGBY PORTLAND CEMENT COMPANY
LIMITED (A)

Indices of Deliveries, Profit, and Net Worth 1946–61
(Base: 1946 = 100)

Year	Deliveries*	Capital†	Profits
1946	100	100	100
1947	105	184‡	140
1948	138	203	195
1949	139	208	214
1950	155	219	262
1951	168	227	311
1952	208	245	398
1953	214	303§	473
1954	238	413‖	538
1955	302	475	765
1956	307	510	816
1957	294	548	825
1958	296	584	874
1959	319	741¶	1,113
1960	357	822	1,326
1961	388		

* These are total group deliveries, in tons, used as an index basing point.
† "Capital" here equals total equity capital, including reserves.
‡ In 1947, £1,000,000 of new capital was raised: £500,000 from new preference shares sold, and £500,000 from new common shares. Without this sale of shares, the index would have remained at 100.
§ In 1953, £500,000 of new common shares were sold. Without this sale, the index would have been 265.
¶ In 1954, £1,050,000 of new capital was raised, £50,000 by the sale of "A" shares, £1,000,000 by the sale of new common shares. Without this new capital, the index would have been 330 at the end of 1954.
‖ In 1959, £1,075,000 of new capital was raised through sale of common shares. Without this sale, the index would have been 655 at the end of 1959.

Late in 1961, a new kiln, with an annual capacity of 180,000 tons, was installed at the Southam works. After this addition, the five company works and their annual capacities in tons were:

Southam (England)	500,000
Rochester "	400,000
Rugby "	320,000
Trinidad	165,000
Australia	120,000

The company also maintained a chalk quarry at Totternhoe, some 48 miles from Rugby.

At the end of 1961, The Rugby Cement Company had about 1,600 employees in its three United Kingdom factories, other U.K. subsidiaries, overseas operations, and headquarters in Rugby, England. The headquarters was organized into seven functional departments: accounting, production, engineering, transportation, domestic sales, export sales, and legal. There was also a secretarial department. Above these departments was a small control and co-ordination group called the administration department. This group, consisting mostly of assistants to top management, directed and co-ordinated the activities of the functional departments and served as the intermediate link between subsidiary companies, which addressed all inquiries and reports to Sir Halford Reddish, who was the chairman of each, and to the headquarters staff departments.

The board of directors comprised seven members, three of whom were top executives in the company. These three were: Sir Halford Reddish, chairman and managing director; Mr. R. L. Evans, deputy managing director; and Mr. M. K. Smith, head of the legal department. Sir Halford and Mr. Evans worked closely with one another attempting to attain an interchangeability of talents. Sir Halford played a leading role in all major policy decisions, but was particularly concerned with financial management and public relations. Mr. Evans' background was also in accounting; he was considered the expert on accounting and technical phases of the operations. As second in command, he in effect headed the administration department. Mr. Smith generally confined himself to the company's legal matters and did not become involved in routine company operations.

Sir Halford, who served on the boards of three other corporations and on a number of semipublic councils, spent the greater part of each week in London. His days in Rugby included the weekend, and he normally met with Mr. Evans on Sunday morning to discuss current operations and problems, and also to do financial planning up to "two or three balance sheets ahead."

REASONS FOR GROWTH

Sir Halford felt that the company's growth and profitability were attributable to several interrelated activities.

1. *Emphasis on operating efficiency* was considered one of the most important of these activities. Sir Halford said that the key to lower unit costs when producing with expensive, continuous process equipment was keeping the plant operating as close to full capacity as possible and minimizing every element of operating and overhead costs. Therefore, avoiding down time, improving efficiency of men and machines, and fuel and power economies were all important. To accomplish these ends, Rugby employed an elaborate monthly cost reporting system which facilitated pin-pointing the items of excessive costs. The factory

managers were held responsible for costs under their control, and the chief engineer and production manager were continually watching fuel and power costs and working on means of increasing machine efficiency. Excess overtime, costly repairs, stores usage and factory staff costs were other items which attracted the attention of the central cost control department. One manager said: "We continually work on the weakest point reflected by the cost analyses."

The company's research on improvement of its manufacturing process produced several cost savings. The major outcome of such research was the recent development of a "wetting" agent for the slurry. Without affecting the chemical properties of the finished product, this agent produced the same "liquidity" and thus the same mixing and handling properties in a slurry containing only 35% water contrasted with 41% previously required. The smaller amount of water to vaporize meant appreciable fuel savings.

Worker efficiency was also a matter of continuous attention. Because of the expensive equipment and need to operate without stoppages, misconduct on the job, unexcused absences, and excessive tardiness were considered grounds for release. Such strictness was necessary because, for example, a kiln burner[1] could, through 10 minutes' neglect, permit many thousands of pounds' worth of damage to the equipment. Sir Halford said that his insistence that all employees "play the game according to the rules of the organization" was not only necessary for efficiency but was also a matter of loyalty. "But," he added, "I hold firmly to the view that loyalty should be two-way traffic. If the head of a business expects a man to be loyal to him, then I say that man has every right to expect the same loyalty from the head of the business."

Finally, emphasis was placed on clerical and procedural efficiency. Sir Halford said that greater use of mechanized accounting and invoicing, and continuous analysis and improvement of office procedures had slightly reduced the head office staff in the past few years. Periodic evaluation of the forms and paper work systems was conducted to eliminate unnecessary ones. "We have even had our competitor friends," he said, "come to look over our reporting and accounting systems. They are amazed by the fact that we get our data faster than they do with a proportionately smaller clerical staff."

2. *An effective sales organization* was the second contributing factor to growth and profits. Manufacturing savings effected by maintaining

---

[1] The kiln burner was the worker in charge of operating one or more kilns.

peak production were attainable only as long as the output could be sold. Mr. Yeatman, the general sales manager, remarked, "Since the industry sells on a common price arrangement, you don't sell cement by selling cheaper than the next man. You sell on delivery service, goodwill, product quality, and on contact with the customer. We like to think that we rate very high on all these counts. Selling cement is very much of a team effort, and we have a fine organization here, which naturally makes my job much easier." Under Mr. Yeatman were two area sales managers, one for midland sales and one for southern and export sales. Each manager had eight salesmen, most of whom worked from their homes. Three of the southern salesmen were located in the London office. The salesmen were paid entirely by salary, because, Mr. Yeatman said, "It's very difficult to say who's responsible for an individual sale. Most of our orders are sent in to one of our four offices: London, Birmingham, Rochester, or Rugby, rather than through the salesman. Our salesmen sell the company in general rather than the product; they are chiefly purveyors of goodwill."

Mr. Yeatman added that many customers bought from two or more manufacturers as a matter of policy. "I might mention," he added, "that all the U.K. cement manufacturers make cement which is so much higher in quality than standard British specifications that our customers have come to expect such quality from us. Accordingly, all manufacturers are constantly checking one another's product quality. Finally, since most large users have their own expert technical information on cement, we find ourselves giving technical advice only to an occasional small user. It's not an important tool in our sales kit."

3. *Overseas manufacture and other subsidiary activities* accounted for much of the company's growth and its increased profits in the past five years. Rugby was continually conducting site investigations and negotiations in search of new overseas opportunities for expansion.

4. *Transportation* of the U.K. cement sales was another reason for RPC's growth and profitability. Rugby's fleet had grown from 52 trucks in 1946 to 196 in 1961 (77 flat-bed trucks, 17 bulk tippers, and 102 pressurized bulk wagons)[2] plus extra trucks hired in the peak construction season. Rugby was proud of the efficiency of its fleet, the operating costs of which remained below the transportation allowance in the delivered price. During 1960, the fleet averaged less than 7% delays for

---

[2] Flat-bed trucks carried cement in bags; pressurized bulk wagons carried loose cement in large tanks which were slightly pressurized to remove the cement at the delivery site; bulk tippers were fully enclosed dump trucks which carried loose cement.

repair, less than 10% nonoperating idleness, and 6% on-the-job delays. Company officials believed that their truck fleet was one of the most efficient in the industry. The major reason for this efficiency, the directors believed, was the highly centralized scheduling of truck dispatches. Each day the central transportation department, working with the sales department, prepared schedules of the following day's dispatches of all trucks from each of the three works. Scheduling attempted to maximize the number of deliveries by each truck and to make as uniform as possible the work-load at the packing and loading plants.

5. *A philosophy of teamwork:* Sir Halford and the other directors of Rugby believed that the most important reason for the company's success was the achievement of company-wide teamwork through the chairman's human relations philosophy and application of profit-sharing and employee-shareholding plans. Rugby had no "personnel" department; development of teamwork was the job of managers at all levels within the firm. The impersonal term "personnel" and the word "welfare," with its connotation of charity, were banned from the Rugby vocabulary.

During the course of his career, Sir Halford had developed a philosophy of business as a team effort. A concrete expression of this philosophy was his introduction at Rugby of employee shareholding and profit-sharing plans. Commenting on the relationship between his philosophy and these plans, he said:

> I am convinced that no scheme of profit-sharing or employee shareholding can succeed unless it is built on a firm foundation of confidence within the business and of real esprit de corps, of a strong feeling on the part of all employees of pride in the company and its achievements. The goodwill of those working together in an industrial enterprise cannot be purchased for cash—of that I am sure. A scheme which is put in with the primary object of buying goodwill is almost certainly doomed to failure from the start. It may indeed not only do no good but may even do positive harm by creating suspicion, however ill-founded.[3]

Teamwork, commendable in any organization, was held to be doubly important in the cement industry where production in large units of continuous-process plant made it impossible to associate individual effort with specific product output. Mutual confidence was felt to be the basic ingredient of teamwork: the board's confidence that all employees would put forth a fair day's work, operate and maintain the plant in-

---

[3] Quotation from "This is Industrial Partnership," a pamphlet written by Sir Halford in 1955 explaining his philosophy and the profit-sharing and employee share-holding schemes of Rugby.

telligently, and follow the leadership of the company; the employees' confidence in the capability and integrity of the directors and that discipline "which is as fair as it is firm" will be maintained.

ESPRIT DE CORPS AND COMPANY POLICIES

The following paragraphs summarize the most important company policies which Sir Halford felt had established *esprit de corps* within Rugby.

1. Personal contact between top executives and operating people all over the world was relatively frequent. Sir Halford visited the Trinidad and Australian plants at least once a year, and someone from the central headquarters staff visited them, on an average, every two or three months. At home, Sir Halford not only delivered his annual "Message to My Fellow-Workers," but he always personally made presentations which were given to men with 25 years' service and again after 50 years' service. Such presentations were made in the presence of the recipients' colleagues, and Sir Halford usually gave a brief review of the recent progress of the company.

2. In his annual messages to the employees, he described recent developments within the company, emphasizing the co-operative roles played by employees and shareholders. He frequently discussed the importance of profits. The following is part of his message following the 1951 operations:

> I want now to say something about profits, because a lot of nonsense has been talked about profits in the last few years, often by politicians of all parties who have never been in industry and have no practical knowledge of industry.
>
> You and I know that profits are the reward and the measure of economy and efficiency, and are essential to the maintenance and expansion of a business. They are, in fact, the real and only bulwark behind our wages and salaries, for if this company ceases to make profits it can be only a comparatively short time before you and I are out.
>
> Let us recognize that it is up to every one of us in this team to go all out all the time, to give of our best, to maintain and increase our production with economy and efficiency, and, in turn, the profits of the company: first—and note that I put this first—because it is the job we are paid to do, and it is only common honesty to our shareholders to do it; and secondly in our own interests to safeguard our jobs for the future.

3. Another aspect of the teamwork was the "works committee" at each plant. Composed of the works manager, the works engineer, the safety officer, and five representatives elected from the factory work force, the committee met without exception each month with a senior

member of the headquarters staff in attendance. The committee discussed matters of particular interest to the works concerned, and suggestions for operational improvements. The head office staff took this opportunity to clarify and discuss newly announced changes in policy and other company developments such as the annual financial statements.

Late in 1961, an IMEDE[4] researcher had the opportunity to attend a works committee meeting at the Rochester works. Mr. R. L. Evans was the representative of top management in attendance. The committee chiefly discussed matters of plant safety and of amenities for the workers, such as a sink and hand towels for workers at a remote plant location. Mr. Halfden Lav, the Rochester works manager, said that this meeting was typical, especially insofar as it was primarily concerned with safety and working conditions. The researcher was impressed at the free and easy manner in which the workers entered into the discussions. Mr. Evans explained in great detail some minor points of company policy on tardiness and vacation time. Mr. Lav commented that the worker representatives occasionally brought up very minor points in the committee; "I think," he added, "that some men do this just to show that they are on their toes and doing a good job for their fellow-workers. We let them talk as long as they want to, and the result is that the committee functions very well, and in a very good spirit."

4. Another policy was that no one but Sir Halford had the authority to release people during slack periods. He had in fact never authorized a layoff. For instance, the rail strike in 1955 almost closed the Rochester factory as coal reserves ran low. As the shutdown date approached, Sir Halford announced that no one would be laid off, but that:

a) Some men would have to take their vacations during the shutdown.

b) Everyone would have to agree to do any job given him (at his usual pay rate) during the shutdown.

(Last minute settlement of the rail strike saved Rugby Cement from its contemplated shutdown.)

5. Since 1954, the company had offered its weekly paid employees the option of having their contract of employment determinable not by the usual one week's notice but by one month's notice by either side for employees having 10 years' service, two months for those having

---

[4] IMEDE is the abbreviation of l'Institut pour l'Etude des Méthodes de Direction de l'Entreprise at Lausanne, Switzerland.

15 years, and three months for those having 20 years. Of those to whom the offer applied, over 85% had accepted one of these options.

In commenting on the fact that 15% of the workers had not chosen to take one of these options, company officials said that some workmen preferred the independence of being able to leave on short notice. "Our employee turnover is, however, quite low," one executive pointed out. "If we set aside employees with less than two years of service, our average worker has been here about 13 years. We do find that some new employees, especially young men, are not prepared for the demanding work in a cement plant, and such men leave, usually within 12 months. Thus new employees should not be fairly included in our average turnover figure. Incidentally, taking total annual wages and bonuses as an indicator, the cement industry ranks in the top half-dozen British industries in terms of earnings."

6. The final key policy of the company was summarized by Sir Halford:

If there is to be a lively interest and pride in the company and its doings, then it is necessary that all employees be kept informed as far as possible about what is going on. . . .

We try as far as we can to ensure that everyone has an opportunity of reading on the company's notice boards a few hours *before* it appears in the newspapers any release issued to the Press. We do not think it right that a man should learn from the newspapers something which he could quite properly have heard at first hand within the company.[5]

Besides all of the aspects of teamwork within an organization, two other features of any profit-sharing or employee-shareholding plan were felt necessary by Sir Halford. The first was that any such scheme must be tailored to suit the circumstances of the company and the outlook, philosophy, and intention of its leader. The second feature was simplicity.

THE PROFIT-SHARING SCHEME

Sir Halford said that the Rugby profit-sharing scheme, inaugurated in 1935, was designed to emphasize two things:

a) That the efforts of the employees are the efforts of a team—that we are all working to one end.

b) The essential partnership which exists between the ordinary shareholders and the employees.[6]

---

[5] "This Is Industrial Partnership."
[6] *Ibid.*

In speeches both to shareholders and workers, Sir Halford referred to the partnership between capital and employees. He said that capital was nothing more than the "labour of yesterday—the production of yesterday which was surplus to the consumption of yesterday."

Fundamental to the partnership was the following bargain:

. . . the labour of today is guaranteed payment for its services and the profit is calculated only after the remuneration of that labour has been paid. Capital, therefore, takes the risk and in return takes such profit (or loss) as arises *after* the labour of today has been paid in full.

But to my mind this difference in the basis of their respective remuneration in no way destroys the conception of industrial enterprise as essentially a part-nership between the labour of yesterday (capital) and the labour of today. Nor is it destroyed if the "bargain" is varied slightly by guaranteeing the greater part of labour's remuneration irrespective of profit or loss and by making an addi-tional but smaller part of it dependent on the results of the enterprise as a whole.[7]

The employees' profit-sharing scheme provided for an annual bonus in excess of industry-negotiated wages (wage-earners) or contracted salary (staff) for all Rugby workers. Basic points of the scheme are summarized below:

1. To qualify for the profit-sharing bonus, an hourly or salaried employee must have completed, on December 31, twelve months' unbroken service to the satisfaction of the Directors.

2. For the purpose of calculating the bonus, each qualified employee is treated as if he held a certain number of ordinary shares in the company. A staff employee received two "notional shares" for each £1 of annual salary. An hourly worker received shares in proportion to his length of service. For exam-ple, a worker with one year's service had 250 "notional shares"; a worker with five years' service, 375; a worker with 20 years, 750; and a worker with 40 or more years had 1,250.

3. The bonus is calculated at the full rate per share of the gross dividend de-clared and paid to the ordinary shareholders for the financial year in question and is paid immediately after the Annual General Meeting. For example, in 1960 the ordinary dividend declared was 1s.3d. per share. Thus a worker with five years' service, holding 375 notional shares, would receive a bonus of (375 × 1/3d.) or £23/8/9.

4. Certified sickness or compulsory National Service are ignored in calcu-lating the number of years of unbroken service.

5. Any employee who leaves or is under notice to leave prior to the date of payment forfeits his bonus.

6. The scheme confers no rights in respect of any capital distribution, or distributions other than those declared as dividends on the ordinary shares of the company out of profits.

[7] *Ibid.*

7. The scheme is subject to modification or withdrawal at any time at the discretion of the Directors.[8]

Sir Halford emphasized that the bonus was not automatic. In a very small number of cases each year, bonuses were withheld completely or in part because service was not "to the satisfaction of the directors." If a man's record for the year was questionable, including several unexplained tardinesses, for instance, it was submitted, without name, to the works committee of the factory. In all cases, the directors had abided by the committee's recommendation. Sir Halford said that withholding the bonus was not so much a penalty to the slack worker, but was necessary in fairness to those who gave 100% service during the year.

Summarizing, Sir Halford said:

I believe that this is important: the bonus must be something that is earned —not something which becomes a right. I also feel that the link with the ordinary shareholders' dividend is fundamental: if the dividend per share goes up, so does the bonus; if the dividend is reduced, the bonus falls too—which is as it should be.

THE "A" SHARE SCHEME

After the war, Sir Halford saw two factors that made the profit-sharing scheme inadequate in emphasizing the partnership between capital and labor. He felt that the twin virtues of hard work and thrift no longer assured a man of personal savings for his old age—*taxation* restricted savings and inflation *devalued* them. Unlike the ordinary shareholder's income which flowed from an asset whose market value reflected both the company's prosperity and inflationary pressures, the employee's profit-sharing bonus was not reflected in a realizable capital asset. Thus he did not have a "hedge" against inflation.

To supply this need, Sir Halford presented his "A" share plan, in late 1954, for approval by the ordinary shareholders. He said that the scheme was designed to do three things:

To give practical form to the unity of interest which I have always held to exist between the ordinary shareholders and the employees; to give a return to the ordinary shareholders on profits "ploughed back" in the past; and to give to every full-time employee the opportunity to have in his hands a capital asset readily realizable on death or retirement. It was received enthusiastically by shareholders and employees alike.[9]

---

[8] This explanation of the profit-sharing scheme contains only the major aspects. Full details are available in Sir Halford Reddish's booklet, "This Is Industrial Partnership."

[9] Explanation of "A" share plan summarized from "This Is Industrial Partnership."

One million "A" shares of 1*s.* each were created with the following conditions attached to them:

1. For any financial year after 31st December 1954 for which (*a*) the net profits before tax are not less than £900,000, and (*b*) the gross amount distributed as dividend to the ordinary shareholders is not less than £300,000, the holders of the "A" shares shall be entitled to an amount of £70,000 plus 20% of any excess of the said net profits over £900,000 (see Exhibit 4). However, (*i*) the amount attributable to the "A" shares shall not exceed 12½% of the net profits; and (*ii*) in the event of the issue of additional ordinary share capital by the company after 31st December 1954, otherwise than by way of a capitalization of reserves or undistributed profits, the said figure of £900,000 shall be increased by a sum equal to 6% of the proceeds or other consideration received by the company.[10]

2. Any amount attributable to the "A" shares as ascertained under (1) above may be distributed as dividend or carried forward in the books of the company to the credit of the "A" shares for subsequent distribution, as the Directors may decide.

3. The holders of "A" shares have no voting rights.

4. In a winding-up, the "A" shares may participate only insofar as the amount of their paid-in capital value and the "A" share credit carried forward on the company books, but no further participation in assets.

5. No further "A" shares shall be created without the sanction of an Extraordinary Resolution passed by the holders of the "A" shares.[11]

Half of the "A" shares were offered to the ordinary shareholers at par and half to the employees.

"*All* full-time employees of the company were included: this was not a get-rich-quick exercise for the favoured few," said Sir Halford.

Allocation to the employees was done by dividing all employees into groups according to remuneration, responsibility, and status within the company (length of service was not a factor). Those in the first group were offered 250 shares, followed by groups of 500, 750, 1,000, 1,500, 2,000, and so on. (Most factory production workers were in the first group, for example.) Over 90% of Rugby's employees had exercised their option and purchased the "A" shares.

Sir Halford was particularly concerned about two aspects of the scheme. About the first, he said:

I was anxious that there should be no element of a "gift" from one partner (the holders of the ordinary shares) to the other (the employees); and that the equity owned by the ordinary shares should be unimpaired. I was convinced that the holders of the ordinary shares could have no legitimate cause for complaint

---

[10] Because additional equity had been introduced since 1954, the "A" shares now began participating at net profits of £964,500.

[11] Explanation of "A" share plan summarized from "This Is Industrial Partnership."

if the profits were so substantially increased in the future and some comparatively small part of the increase went to the employees as a reward for their efforts.

The "A" shares should be worth no more than was paid for them when issued, so that the employees could feel that whatever increased value accrued thereafter was due to their teamwork, with, I do not forget, nor do I allow them to forget, the capital provided by their partners in the enterprise.[12]

This reason, and tax considerations (discussed later) dictated that the minimum profit level at which the "A" shares would start participating (£900,000) should be well above the profit levels when the "A" shares were issued.

The second aspect was that the main object of the scheme was to insure employees of a capital sum on death or retirement. Sir Halford foresaw that the "A" shares might have some speculative attraction to the general public and he did not want the employees to be tempted into selling and thus depriving themselves of retirement or death benefits from the plan. He also felt that anyone leaving the firm be required to sell his shares back at par and thus enable newcomers to participate. To accomplish these ends, Sir Halford designated that the shares allocated to the employees were held in their behalf by Staff Nominees Limited which was accountable to the employees for dividends declared and authorized to act in their behalf in all matters relating to the "A" shares. The following conditions applied:

1. Initially and whenever an employee moves upward to a new group, he is given the opportunity to buy his allocation of shares at par. Failing to do so, he is not given a subsequent opportunity.
2. "A" shares may be sold by the employee at any time *at par* to Staff Nominees Limited and *must* be sold any time he leaves the company.
3. An employee's share may be sold at market value (market price was established by quotation on The London Stock Exchange of the "A" shares allotted originally at par to the ordinary shareholders) *only* in the event of the employee's death while in the service of the company, or upon his reaching the age of 65 (55 for women).
4. Any dividend declared on the "A" shares is paid immediately to the employee.

Fifty thousand shares remained unallocated to the employees after the initial sale. The Directors felt that this block of shares and those shares which Staff Nominees Limited bought back, at par, from employees who left, would be sufficient to offer shares to new and promoted employees for the foreseeable future.

---

[12] *Ibid.*

In his message to his fellow-workers in the company following the 1958 operations, Sir Halford said the following about the "A" share plan:

. . . Quite often a man will say to me: "This 'A' share scheme of yours—tell me, has it increased production?" And I reply: "I haven't the slightest idea, but I shouldn't think so." So he says: "But surely that was the object. It's an incentive scheme, isn't it?" "On the contrary," I tell him, "I have always insisted that it should *not* be called an incentive scheme, because that to my mind would imply that we in Rugby Cement were not already doing our best, were not doing our duty in return for our wages and salaries. And that I will not have."

What our "A" share scheme does is to give to the employees the opportunity to build up capital available on retirement or on earlier death, and to promote the feeling that we are all one team working to the same end in partnership with our shareholders. The value of the "A" shares depends in the long run on the success of our efforts in making profits. And don't overlook the fact that half the "A" shares were issued, also at par, to the holders of our ordinary shares. They very rightly benefit too, as they have seen these 1s.0d. shares change hands on the Stock Exchange at prices up to 42s.0d.[13]

Apart from the capital aspect, the holding of "A" shares by the employees of the company, and also, of course, our "profit-sharing" schemes, give some reward for successful endeavour—which is surely right.

The Taxation Aspect. For the company, the profit-sharing bonus was considered a wage bonus and therefore a before-tax expense. The "A" share dividends, however, were similar to ordinary dividends, being paid out of after-tax profits.

For the employees, the profit-sharing bonus was taxed as ordinary wage or salary income. Taxation of the employees in connection with "A" share distribution was a most difficult problem and one for which Sir Halford spent many hours in consultation with the Board of Inland Revenue.

The law held that if at the time of issue the value of the shares was greater than the amount the employees paid for them, the difference was taxable as a "benefit" arising from employment. The Rugby "A" share sale to its employees, however, had two characteristics which affected any ruling under this law:

1. "A" shares were not quoted on the market until two months after issue; thus it was a matter of discussion whether at time of issue they were worth more than the par value paid for them.
2. Employees were not free to sell their shares at market price except on retirement or death.

---

[13] In 1961, "A" shares were quoted on the stock exchange at up to 100 shillings per share.

Final agreement with the Inland Revenue was reached which assessed the value of the "A" shares at time of issue slightly above par.

Tax assessment for shares issued subsequently to newcomers or to promoted employees required a different arrangement with the Inland

Exhibit 4

THE RUGBY PORTLAND CEMENT COMPANY LIMITED (A)

Profit Participation of the "A" Shares
Graph of Participation "Formula"
and
Schedule of Gross Profits *before* Taxes

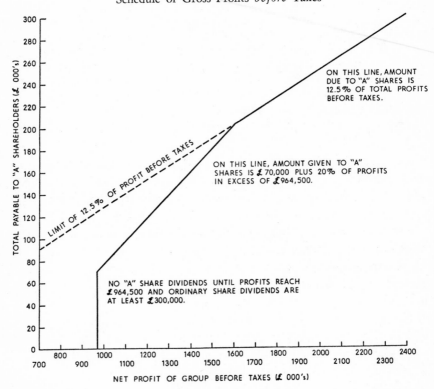

ON THIS LINE, AMOUNT DUE TO "A" SHARES IS 12.5% OF TOTAL PROFITS BEFORE TAXES.

ON THIS LINE, AMOUNT GIVEN TO "A" SHARES IS £70,000 PLUS 20% OF PROFITS IN EXCESS OF £964,500.

LIMIT OF 12.5% OF PROFIT BEFORE TAXES

NO "A" SHARE DIVIDENDS UNTIL PROFITS REACH £964,500 AND ORDINARY SHARE DIVIDENDS ARE AT LEAST £300,000.

TOTAL PAYABLE TO "A" SHAREHOLDERS (£ 000's)

NET PROFIT OF GROUP BEFORE TAXES (£ 000's)

Revenue, since by that time a market value was established. Final agreement resulted in considering a variable fraction of the difference between current market value and par value as taxable income. The fraction varied inversely with the length of time between the recipient's age and 65 when he could realize the market price of the "A" shares. For instance, a 25-year-old newcomer receiving 500 "A" shares would have to consider as income, for income tax purposes, only 10% of the

Exhibit 4—Continued

THE RUGBY PORTLAND CEMENT COMPANY LIMITED (A)

Summary of Earnings and Gross Dividend Payments 1954–61

(1,000's of £)

Year	1954	1955	1956	1957	1958	1959	1960	1961
Profit before tax	721	1025	1093	1106	1171	1491	1777	2020
Gross ordinary dividend	200	300	338	338	375	437	500	500
Gross payable to "A" shares	..	95	109	111	124	179	222	252
Actual "A" share dividend	..	50	63	63	75	100	125	125
Difference carried forward as "A" share credit	..	45	46	48	49	79	97	127
Cumulative "A" share credit*	..	45	91	140	189	268	365	493

* The "A" share credit was contained in the Undistributed Profit account in the balance sheet. The directors considered this credit as a "dividend equalization reserve" to supply "A" dividends if they were not earned according to the formula (i.e., if pretax profits were below £964,500).

difference between market value and the price paid (one shilling per share), because he could not realize the market value for 40 years. On the other hand, a 50-year-old man receiving 500 "A" shares would have to consider 60% of the difference as taxable income, because he was much closer to realizing the gain. (The United Kingdom had no "capital gains" tax, but all dividends received by employees on their "A" shares up to retirement age were treated, for tax purposes, as "earned" income and therefore taxed at income-tax rates.)

Overseas. An employee profit-sharing plan, similar to that existing for Rugby workers in the United Kingdom, had been established for workers in the Trinidad and Australian plants. "A" shares were offered only to workers in the United Kingdom, including staff assigned temporarily to the overseas operations.

The Rugby Portland Cement
Company Limited (B)

LATE IN 1961, an IMEDE[1] research team decided to attempt to expand the Rugby Portland Cement case by adding information on the ways in which various employees of the company viewed their jobs. To this purpose, an IMEDE researcher toured each of the company's three cement works in England; he also conducted interviews with a number of hourly paid workers and with a substantial number of middle- and top-management executives. This case includes excerpts from some of these interviews, as well as some of the researcher's impressions of what he saw.

VIEWS OF SOME RUGBY WORKMEN

Rugby's management was very co-operative in helping the researcher to interview some of the workmen. Although in theory it would have been useful to interview a rather large number of workers selected at random, this was not practicable for certain reasons:

1. There were limitations on the research time available for these interviews.
2. There was a chance that some men, if chosen at random, might:
   a) Not be able to articulate their views.
   b) Be less than wholly frank.
   c) Be unable to leave their work posts at the desired time.

Accordingly, Mr. R. L. Evans (deputy managing director) and Mr. Baker (works manager of the Rugby works) selected from the Rugby work force four workers who, they thought, would be articulate, honest, and as representative as possible of the general sentiments of the entire Rugby worker group. The researcher interviewed the four men separately, in an office at the Rugby plant; nobody else was present during the interviews. The names of the four men interviewed have been disguised.

---

[1] Once again, IMEDE is an abbreviation for l'Institut pour l'Etude des Méthodes de Direction de l'Entreprise at Lausanne, Switzerland.

INTERVIEW WITH MR. RYAN

Mr. Evans and Mr. Baker, in arranging the interviews, mentioned that Mr. Ryan should provide a highly entertaining and useful interview, that he was outspoken and highly articulate. Mr. Ryan, who had been working for the company since 1956, was an Irishman; he appeared to be about 40 years old. He worked in the transport department of the company as a truck driver and had been a member of the Rugby works committee for some time. The researcher asked each of the four men only one question to begin: what did the man think about working for the company, what were the bad points and the good points? Mr. Ryan began:

Well, I might tell you I'm an old union man, been a sort of union agitator all my working life. Before I came here I never held a job longer than eighteen months. I've been here almost six years now and I can tell you this, I'm going to stay here the rest of my life. And, mind you, I got a lot less to gain by staying here than most of the men. I have no A-shares, because you know you only get one chance to buy them A-shares, and when I had to buy them, I didn't have the money because my wife just had to have an operation. So now for the rest of my life I got to work here knowing that I'll never have no A-shares, and I think this is unfair, and I keep fighting to get me shares, and maybe I will and maybe I won't, but I'll stay on here no matter what.

And another thing is I'm a very bad timekeeper—sometimes it's my fault, and sometimes it was because I had to take my wife to the doctor and so I'd come in late, and so for three straight years I lost my profit-sharing bonus on account of being late so much. [Mr. Ryan had actually lost his bonus in two nonconsecutive years, management reported.] So you can see what I mean when I tell you that I got much less to gain by working here than the other men.

But even though there's lots of little things could be done, this is a wonderful place to work, and that's the Lord's own truth. I'm not saying anything to you I wouldn't say right to the Chairman's face if he asked me—I'm not a man to say what he doesn't mean.

You got to remember this: it's no good coming down to a cement works if you don't want to work hard. But they pay you good and, the main thing is, you always get treated fair. If you got a complaint, you can take it as high as you want, right up to the Chairman himself, but it's no good complaining unless you give 'em the facts. That's what they want to see: facts.

Another thing you ought to write down is this: in this company, I'm just as good as anybody, as good as the Chairman or Mr. Evans—that's what you won't get anywhere else. We all know this here, and we know you've got to work as a team. And I'll tell you this, I know the Chairman would let me buy my A-shares if he could, but you see he's got to be fair to the other workers too. But I do think that you get punished awful hard for being late. [Mr. Ryan's profit-sharing bonus would have amounted, in those years when he lost it, to about £30. His weekly wages were about £15.]

Over in Coventry, you know [about 15 miles away], in the car and airplane factories a man can make £30 a week while here he'll only make about £15, but we get the £15 for 52 weeks of the year, plus the profit-sharing, the A-shares, and lots of other benefits. The company buys up lots of clothes for us so we can get them cheaper. I once compared what I earned in a year with a friend of mine who works in Coventry for £29 a week, and you know what? I came out £48 ahead of him for the year, because those fellows are always getting laid off.

And let me tell you this: you'd never get a better firm to work for, no matter where you went; there isn't another company like this, at least none I've ever heard about.

You know, when I tell you we work hard here, you've got to remember that the Chairman doesn't ask us to to do anything he doesn't do himself. You know, he works eighteen hours a day, and when he come down sick recently and had to have that operation, his doctors told him to take it easy, and so he did—he only worked ten hours a day.

[Mr. Ryan then gave the researcher a very detailed description of what was involved in his truck-driving. He stressed that the equipment was the best obtainable, that the company paid much more attention to driver safety than to delivering a maximum daily tonnage of cement, that scrupulous care was taken at great expense, to be certain that the customer received all the cement he had been billed for.]

You see my truck out there? That truck, it's brand new, and it cost £10,000, and they expect me to take care of it like if it was my own, and I do. [The truck in fact cost slightly over £3,500.] And I know I've got 42 hours a week guaranteed, and more hours on weekends if I want to make extra money, and that's a hell of a nice thing for a truck driver. And as soon as I've driven 11 hours in a single day, even if I didn't get home with the truck by the time my 11 hours was up, the company would send out another lorry with two drivers to drive me and my truck home, that's how careful they are about the 11-hour rule. And you see them fine overalls we drivers got, and them jackets? Mr. Reddish, I believe, bought them for us out of his own pocket. That's just the kind of man he is. [In fact he didn't: they are provided by the company.]

I told you I used to be a union man, but I tell you this, if a union came in here now, it would hurt the workers—they'd get less pay, they couldn't touch anything they weren't supposed to. That's the kind of a union man I am today.

In summing up, and this is God's own truth, I think Sir Halford Reddish ought to be England's Prime Minister, and Mr. Evans ought to be the Secertary for Foreign Affairs.

INTERVIEW WITH MR. MASON

Mr. Mason was a foreman in the "raw plant," where the slurry was made. He had been working for the company about 14 years and appeared to be about 50. He began:

Well, wherever I went, I don't think I could better myself, that's what I'd say. The Chairman puts us in the picture about what's going on, he has more of a fatherly concern for us, I think. I've known the Chairman 30 years and if he says a thing he means it. He's put in some wonderful plans for the men, he has. For example, when my father died, we got about £1000 for his A-shares, and this was a big help, because I've got a sister who isn't very well, and this money pays for her. From the workman's point of view, if you want it, I find that they're very, very satisfied. I've got 30-odd men working for me, and I get all the points of view, so to speak, and I think I can say that they're all happy to be working here. Now, of course, there's some men as will always find something to complain about, you're going to have that anywhere, but in the main I think that the men like working here very much.

You're an American, so I'll put it in American: damn it all, we're on to a good thing here and we know it.

I've got a brother, a son, and two brothers-in-law working here, and my father before he died. They all came to work here after I did. Now do you think they'd have come if this wasn't a good place to work?

I do believe honestly, and I'm not handing you any bull, that we couldn't better ourselves. And you've got to remember this: Sir Halford will give any of his men a proper hearing anytime. And what's astonishing is that as the firm gets larger, the company seems to give us more attention, when you'd think it'd be the other way around.

Now you take your average Englishman, he's the biggest grumbler in the world, about anything at all. But you won't find much grumbling here. You'd have to kick them out to get the men here to leave.

INTERVIEW WITH MR. TOOT

Mr. Toot, who appeared to be about 50, had been with Rugby about seven years. The researcher received the distinct impression that Mr. Toot was temperamentally a sort of cynic who only grudgingly would admit that a workingman's life could be decent, although this impression was formed on the basis of very little evidence. Mr. Toot began:

Taken all around, I should say that this is a very good place to work. A workman here knows that he can go as high as he likes, if he has the ability. You get fair treatment here. I suppose that work here is 80% satisfactory. For the other 20%, it's hard to say what the objections might be. But one thing is, when a man first came to work here, he didn't get enough participation in the bonus system (the profit-sharing scheme), but they've changed that now.

If a man's willing to do an honest day's work, he'll generally be satisfied here. I suppose I could say this: the longer a man's been here, the more he wants to stay.

Now, you get some fellows, especially young ones, come in and they can't stick the work; it's too heavy or too hard for them. They usually leave, if they're this type, in 12–18 months. If a man sticks it a year or a year and a half, he'll probably stay here until he's through working.

This is a long-term policy job, so to say. It's good if you're thinking about your old age, because the company really takes care of you after you retire. I don't suppose you know this, but all the company's pensioners [retired workers] get a ton of coal from the company at Christmas. There's a Christmas party for the pensioners. And men like Mr. Evans and Mr. Baker visit the pensioners very regularly. The company doesn't just forget you when you've stopped working for them—they take care of you.

I suppose when I think of it, it's hard to say what kind of objections, you might say, a man could have to working here, if he's not just a casual laborer who doesn't care about doing an honest day's work, if he doesn't care about doing a good job. This is a good place to work.

INTERVIEW WITH MR. FORSTER

Mr. Forster had been working for Rugby for 48 years, and he worked in the quarry. He talked rather little, much less than the previous three men.

Well, I've been working here all my life, and that's a fact. It's hard work, and no doubt about it, but it's a wonderful company to work for. I was here, you know, when Sir Halford took over, and it was wonderful when he did. He promised us steady work, and we've had it ever since. Some of your casual lads, now, who come here looking for an easy day's work and high pay, they don't stay, but a real man, a man who doesn't mind work, he'll be happier here than anywhere else I've ever heard of.

RANDOM IMPRESSIONS OF THE RESEARCHER

In the course of his tour of the three different works, the researcher spent a great deal of time with Mr. R. L. Evans, who toured each plant with him, and with the works managers. The researcher was especially struck by two facts. First, Mr. Evans and the works managers appeared to know a great deal about the background of every company employee. The researcher was, while walking through the plant, introduced to one worker who had been a chef in Wyoming some years ago. Another worker was pointed out as having been (he was now 72) a good Rugby player in his youth. These and similar details were forthcoming quite frequently from Mr. Evans or the works managers. Second, the workers all said "hello" to Mr. Evans as he passed through the plant, and Mr. Evans would chat with them about their families and how things were going.

Another impression, although a difficult one to justify with explicit evidence, was that the various managers were more than superficially concerned with their workers and their lives. Words and phrases which often recurred in the four days of conversation included: "fair treatment," "decent work for a man," "take care of our men," "except them to work as part of a team." Workers and managers alike constantly referred to themselves as being part of a single team; they did so either implicitly or explicitly.

Sawyer & Ward, Inc.

SAWYER & WARD was a professional firm of consulting radio and electronic engineers. It was organized as a two-man partnership in 1930, was incorporated in 1953, and merged with another firm in 1955. Originally, the company specialized in problems involving the selection and allocation of broadcast station sites and frequencies, but in later years it branched out into other communications fields, especially applied research, design and development of equipment (R & D). According to the former partners, Mr. J. C. Sawyer, now chairman of the board, and Mr. Paul M. Ward, president, the firm was consistently profitable until the 1956 loss. Gross operating income, which is the equivalent to gross sales in a manufacturing company, is shown for the partnership from 1930 to 1950 in Exhibit 1. Balance sheets and income statements for the partnership from 1951 to 1953 and the corporation from 1954 to 1956 are given in Exhibits 2 and 3 (with Exhibit 3A giving selected balance sheet and operating ratios), while the 1955 and 1956 statements of surplus are shown in Exhibit 4. A company organization chart is reproduced in Exhibit 5.

Mr. Sawyer was one of the first to explore the possibilities of radio-telephone broadcasting.[1] In 1913, as an undergraduate at a Midwestern university, Mr. Sawyer helped establish America's first broadcasting station. After receiving an S.M. in Physics, he taught radio engineering from 1920 to 1929. Meanwhile, he was asked to participate in four government radiotelephone conferences to discuss the need for legislation on station number, location, and broadcast frequency used; the work of these meetings formed the basis for the Radio Act of 1927, which set up the Federal Radio Commission, forerunner of the Federal Communications Commission.

From 1928 to 1930 Mr. Sawyer, as a consultant, gave technical advice to applicants for a fast diminishing number of frequencies available to radiotelephone broadcasting and also testified as an impartial witness before the Federal Radio Commission.

---

[1] Radiotelephony, as contrasted with radiotelegraphy, involves the electrical transmission of *sounds,* usually voice (not signals), between points by radio waves.

Exhibit 1

SAWYER & WARD, INC.

*Gross Income, Expenses, Bonuses, Net Income,
Partners' Withdrawals, and Partners' Account, 1930–50*

	1930	1931	1932	1933	1934	1935	1936
Gross income........	$ 7,140	$ 21,256	$ 20,702	$ 23,631	$ 36,987	$ 43,792	$ 36,737
Expenses..............	1,364	8,098	11,632	12,969	19,015	20,571	22,200
Employee bonuses......	....	.....	.....	.....	795	1,083	1,655
Net income...........	5,776	13,158	9,070	10,662	17,177	22,138	12,882
Partners' withdrawals..	2,100	10,650	10,980	10,889	10,800	13,850	13,675
Net over or under.......	3,676	2,508	(1,910)	(227)	6,377	8,288	(793)
Partners' account*......	6,676	9,184	7,274	7,047	13,424	21,712	20,222†

	1937	1938	1939	1940	1941	1942	1943
Gross income..........	$ 45,145	$ 46,471	$ 70,203	$116,841	$104,370	$ 82,570	$ 96,527
Expenses..............	24,818	23,694	28,861	41,723	50,251	45,569	59,603
Employee bonuses......	2,011	2,146	3,353	7,092	5,380	2,957	.....
Net income...........	18,316	20,631	37,989	68,026	48,739	34,044	36,924
Partners' withdrawals..	16,962	17,580	34,415	24,577	62,929	19,175	23,969
Net over or under.......	1,354	3,051	3,574	43,449	(14,190)	14,869	12,955
Partners' account*......	21,576	24,627	28,201	71,650	57,460	72,329	85,284

	1944	1945	1946	1947	1948	1949	1950
Gross income..........	$130,025	$262,890‡	$224,085	$192,599	$197,549	$159,921	$190,821
Expenses..............	83,166	99,486	131,696	150,513§	149,514	143,016	151,981
Employee bonuses......	.....	13,241	24,220	19,871	23,400	.....	.....
Net income...........	46,859	150,163	68,169	22,215	24,635	16,905	38,840
Partners' withdrawals..	31,900	45,149	100,079	46,800	27,000	25,600	28,800
Net over or under.......	14,959	105,014	(31,910)	(24,585)	(2,365)	(8,695)	10,040
Partners' account*......	100,243	205,257	173,347	148,762	146,397	137,702	147,742

* From 1930–35 includes $3,000 in Mr. Sawyer's investment account.
† Tax adjustment of $2,303 added in here.
‡ Includes sale of radio station.
§ Includes $86.68 loss on sale on fixed assets.
Source: Company records.

Associates said, in 1956, that Mr. Sawyer had remained prominent both in and outside his field and his company. "You have to talk to J. C. (Sawyer) before you can begin to understand Sawyer & Ward," one commented. Mr. Sawyer's former partner, Mr. Ward, said: "J. C. is a very stimulating, imaginative engineer, who has come up with many ideas and made many friends. While it is difficult to say that this or that job came in because Sawyer was president of this or that technical society, still we have certainly built up a reputation." A director, whom the former partners said was a good friend and guide, had a colorful personality, and made apt but dramatic statements, added: "J. C. has connections with all sorts of generals and admirals, and yet he often sits there in his office figuring bar charts. Just last year I told him, 'Don't do any more bar charts or graphs—I just want to see the cash coming in.' "

Mr. Ward, starting as a student of Mr. Sawyer's in 1923, developed much of the original equipment used in testing radiotelephone systems. In describing his functions at Sawyer & Ward, he said, "J. C. (Sawyer) started in the broadcast field, was better known in it than I and so brought the business in, while I saw to it that what came in went out. Each of us also built up our own accounts." Mr. Ward emphasized the importance of "accurate field measurements" as opposed to what he dubbed "table-top engineering" and in evaluating the performance of radio antennas he developed what he said was the first practical mobile equipment for measuring radio field strength when using standard broadcast frequencies. Using this equipment, he and Mr. Sawyer compiled the *Standard Coverage Market Data Service,* which they said were the first standards to recognize the difference between day and night station coverage and to make a distinction between field strength requirements for city and rural service.

Company engineers, in 1956, commented on Mr. Ward's established reputation in the communications field, his capacity for hard work, and his administrative ability; however, they pointed out that final decisions had been explicitly made by Mr. Sawyer, who in so doing had appeared to second-guess Mr. Ward. During World War II the latter had a chance to run the company, and about June, 1955, Mr. Sawyer turned all his administrative functions over to Mr. Ward and began attending an almost constant succession of overseas technical conferences. Mr. Sawyer said:

Paul had been prevented from taking real responsibility, although I didn't realize it at the time. For a long time I'd tried to get rid of executive responsibility, but it kept coming right back to me. This really came to a head when, on the advice of our lawyer, I decided to attend an important international conference. I just said, "Paul, I'm going," and left. He rose beautifully to the situation and handled things well.

The lawyer said to Mr. Ward at this time, "You are responsible for everything in this corporation; you are the boss. Don't call meetings, don't worry, just decide, and if you don't I'll call a meeting and I'll 'can' you."

Mr. Sawyer and Mr. Ward, together with other members of the company, thought of themselves as professional people. Mr. Sawyer explained:

Exhibit 2

SAWYER & WARD, INC.

Partnership Comparative Balance Sheets for Years Ending December 31, 1951–53

Corporate Comparative Balance Sheets for June 1, 1953, and Years Ending May 31, 1954–56, and Four Months Ending September 30, 1956

Assets	Partnership Dec. 31, 1951	Partnership Dec. 31, 1952	Partnership Dec. 31,* 1953	June 1, 1953	May 31, 1954	Corporation May 31, 1955	May 31, 1956	Sept. 30, 1956
Current Assets:								
Cash	$ 59,646	$ 89,983	$ 71,004		$ 21,927	$ 19,713	$ 25,019	$ 22,813
Accounts and Notes Receivable:								
Clients			$ 2,683		$120,704	$117,998	$103,111	$140,382
Officers and Employees			514		14,687	8,066	200	
Miscellaneous			712		556	553		1,749
Total	16,629	20,376	$ 3,909		$135,947	$126,617	$103,311	$142,131
Unbilled Income—R & D					$ 31,727	$ 52,644		
Inventory:								
Parts and Material					$ 9,550	$ 8,684	$ 8,505	$ 9,601
Work-in-process					60	119	14,456	6,038
Total Inventory	4,322	8,120		$ 6,509	$ 9,610	$ 8,803	$ 22,961	$ 15,639
Notes Due from Stockholders						$ 2,640		
Total Current Assets	$ 80,597	$118,479	$ 74,913	$ 6,509	$199,211	$210,417	$151,291	$180,583
Cash Value of Life Insurance	$ 10,004	$ 10,004			$ 31,873†	$ 36,778†	$ 41,719†	$ 41,719
Fixed Assets:								
Land			$ 26,481					
Buildings and Improvements			87,719					
Furniture, Fixtures, Equipment	138,788	146,092		$ 80,239	$ 63,293	$ 45,964	$ 19,269	$ 21,565
Total Fixed Assets			$114,200	$ 80,239	$ 63,293	$ 45,964	$ 19,269	$ 21,565

	(1)	(2)	(3)	(4)	(5)	(6)	(7)	(8)
Other Assets:								
Prepaid Charges	1,473			$ 410	$ 20,403	$ 18,858	$ 23,249	$ 9,994
Organizational Expense	1,224				476	520		
Notes Due from Stockholders		407				23,760‡		
Goodwill				242,842	242,842	242,842		
Total Assets	$230,862	$275,799	$189,520	$330,000	$558,098	$579,139	$235,528	$253,861

Liabilities and Net Worth

	(1)	(2)	(3)	(4)	(5)	(6)	(7)	(8)
Current Liabilities:								
Notes Payable—Secured					$115,195	$40,000	$40,000	$42,126
Notes Payable						69,080	53,890	21,445
Accounts Payable:								
Trade	$16,912				$ 8,293	$ 6,618	$ 41,823	$ 14,500
Pension Plan Premium					23,172	11,620		
Federal and State Taxes					7,268	9,261§		
Mansfield Electronics Corp.							50,000	100,000
Total		$ 11,018			$38,733	$27,499	$ 91,823	$114,500
Withheld Taxes and Insurance					4,680	5,105	2,745	5,460
Accrued Expenses			$ 910		31,685	29,223	10,483	19,436||
Long-Term Debt Installment	5,000	5,000	5,000					
Total Current Liabilities	$ 21,912	$ 16,018	$ 5,910	....	$190,293	$170,907	$198,941	$202,967
Long-Term Debt	$ 22,500	$ 43,750	$ 38,750					
Partners' Capital	$186,450	$216,031	$144,860					
Capital Stock				$330,000	$370,000	$409,000	$119,702	$119,702
Deficit					(2,195)	(768)	(83,115)	(68,808)
Total Net Worth	$186,450	$216,031	$144,860	$330,000	$367,805	$408,232	$ 36,587	$ 50,894
Total Liabilities and Net Worth	$230,862	$275,799	$189,520	$330,000	$558,098	$579,139	$235,528	$253,861

* On December 31, 1953, the partnership was liquidated; fixed assets were transferred to the Mayflower Building Corporation, and the partners divided the remaining assets.

† The values stated represented the cash value as of December 18, 1953, 1954, and 1955, the anniversary dates of the policies. The cash value as of September 30, 1956, as confirmed by the National Life Insurance Company was $46,744. These policies were assigned to the Niagara Trust Company as collateral for the secured loan of $40,000.

‡ The notes due from stockholders represented the balance due on subscriptions to 208 shares of capital stock of the corporation. The corporation held the stock certificates as security for the notes. Of the total amount due, $2,640 was due within one year. After merging with Mansfield, Mr. Ward and Mr. Sawyer assumed these notes because it was not legal for a manufacturing corporation to accept notes in part payment for stock in Mansfield's state.

§ An application for carry-back adjustment of federal income taxes of $14,105.67 paid for the fiscal years ending May 31, 1955, under the provisions of the Internal Revenue Code, was filed with the Director of Internal Revenue. The claim was awarded in 1956.

|| Includes $17,718 in accrued payroll.

Source: Company records.

Exhibit 3

SAWYER & WARD, INC.

*Partnership Comparative Profit or Loss Statements for Years Ending
December 31, 1951–53*

*Corporate Comparative Profit or Loss Statements for Years Ending May 31,
1954–56, and Four Months Ending September 30, 1956*

| | Partnership | | | Corporation | | | |
	Dec. 31, 1951	Dec. 31, 1952	Dec. 31, 1953	May 31, 1954	May 31, 1955	May 31, 1956	Sept. 30 1956
Operating income:							
Research and development contracts:							
Government..................	$137,277	$237,477	$139,327	$283,817	$378,077	$298,845	$164,288
Commercial.................	.....	.....	.....	84,925	33,365	17,752	4,891
Consulting sources:							
Broadcast..................	96,774	127,316	68,075	162,297	163,253	96,134	49,674
Nonbroadcast*..............	65,898	86,765	76,077	41,092	38,355	37,772	19,026
Gross operating income......	$299,949	$451,558	$283,479	$572,131	$613,050	$450,503	$237,879
Operating expense:							
Compensation†..............	$163,816	$263,453	$138,992				
Officers...................				$ 70,999	$ 74,995	$ 89,904	$ 29,610
Others....................				311,347	321,591	292,327	119,771
Provision for vacation........	.....	.....	.....	7,294	2,754	(7,773)	(2,276)
Reimbursable direct expense‡....	.....	.....	.....	61,468	82,518	56,693	40,096
Leasehold expense...........	.....	.....	.....	29,385	38,931	38,315	13,016
Building and office operating expense	15,881	17,398	14,459				
Heat, light, and power§........	.....	.....	.....	3,451	3,690	3,499	840
Pension plan...............	4,212	7,128	3,480	16,026	28,295	27,801	9,300
Supplies and expense.........	3,723	5,017	1,976	12,592	11,542	13,232	6,359
Depreciation...............	3,022	3,905	2,649	9,266	10,926	12,193	2,702
Taxes.....................	5,104	6,820	8,299	8,350	8,926	7,110	2,293
Advertising and promotion expense.	3,760	4,683	2,934	8,221	4,082	4,736	2,845
Professional meetings.........	1,992	3,191	3,552	5,370	3,493	4,621	935
Telephone and telegraph.......	3,351	4,162	2,147	4,303	5,065	5,614	2,042
Legal and tax accounting.......	190	2,119	13,225	2,658	3,717	3,193	1,836
Maintenance and repairs—equipment	611	763	355	1,980	2,581	.....	.....
Insurance..................	662	1,268	681	1,604	2,334	2,331	780
Subscriptions and publications....	1,593	1,544	977	1,239	1,710	1,788	398
Travel....................	2,573	1,075	411	733	1,286	1,852	780
Miscellaneous‖..............	3,271	5,303	6,356	2,766	3,336	3,461	3,562
Total operating expense......	$213,761	$327,829	$200,493	$559,052	$611,766	$560,897	$234,889
Net operating income (loss)........	$ 86,188	$123,729	$ 82,986	$ 13,079	$ 1,284	($110,394)	$ 2,990
Other income¶................	.....	.....	891	10,914	9,380	6,256	211
Other deductions—interest........	940	455	.....	3,702	5,005	4,241	1,065
Life insurance premiums.........	7,359	9,852	4,941	2,366	6,892	5,965	1,935
Miscellaneous...............				857	63	.....	.....
Net (loss) income before taxes.....	$ 77,889	$113,422	$ 78,936	$ 17,068	($ 1,296)	($114,344)	$ 201
Prior period adjustment**........					$ 19,972		
Federal income tax..............				6,201	7,906		
Net profit (or loss) after taxes......				$ 10,867	$ 10,770	($114,344)	

* For period 1951–53, some commercial R & D included.
† Included bonuses of $37,809 paid in 1952 and $19,184 paid in 1953; no bonuses were paid 1954–56.
‡ For period 1951–53, these charges distributed to other accounts.
§ For period 1951–53, included in building and office operating expense.
‖ In September, 1956, included $1,635 for engineering services performed for Mansfield.
¶ In 1954, included $10,740 charged to the partnership for accounting and administration services. In 1955, included royalties of $8,978 on photo printer.
** From government contract determined 18 months previously.

Source: Company records.

My original concept of Sawyer & Ward was that it would be similar to a professional law firm, governed by professional ethics. You see, we represented the *users,* not the manufacturers, of radio and electronic equipment. We made it clear to the manufacturers that if we bought any equipment for our clients and received a discount we would pass that discount on to the client. We didn't want people to think we could be influenced in making equipment recommendations. As servants of the radiotelephone broadcasting field, we felt we should not own any stock in broadcast stations or in equipment manufacturers. When we testified before the FCC, we acted as impartial witnesses, but before

Exhibit 3A

SAWYER & WARD, INC.

Selected Balance Sheet and Operating Ratios, 1951–56

		1951	1952	1953	1954	1955	1956
(R)	Current ratio....................	3.68	7.40	12.68	1.05	1.23	0.76
($)	Net working capital..............	$58,685	$102,461	$69,003	$8,918	$39,510	($47,650)
(R)	Acid test ratio...................	3.48	6.89	12.68	1.00	1.18	0.65
(%)	Current assets to total assets.......	34.91	42.96	39.53	35.69	36.33	64.23
(%)	Total fixed assets to total assets....	60.12	52.97	60.26	11.34	7.94	8.18
(R)	Net worth to debt................	4.20	3.61	3.24	2.93	2.39	0.18
(%)	Net worth to total assets..........	80.76	78.33	76.44	65.90	70.49	15.53
(Days)	Receivables turnover*.............	199.58	162.45	496.42	85.54	74.35	82.56
(%)	Total assets to gross income.......	76.97	61.08	66.86	97.55	94.47	52.28
(%)	Fixed assets to gross income.......	46.27	32.35	40.29	11.06	7.50	4.28
(%)	Operation profit to net worth......	46.23	57.27	57.29	3.56	0.31	(301.73)
(%)	Net profit to net worth...........	41.77	52.50	54.49	2.95	2.64	(312.53)

* Accounts receivable × 360/net sales.
Source: Prepared from Exhibits 2 and 3 by Harvard Business School staff.

Exhibit 4

SAWYER & WARD, INC.

Statement of Surplus (Deficit) for the Years
Ending May 31, 1955, and 1956, and
Four Months Ending September 30, 1956

	May 31, 1955	May 31, 1956	Sept. 30 1956
Balance (deficit):..	$ (2,195)	$ (768)	$(83,115)
Add: Net loss for the year..............................		114,344	
Unamortized portion of appreciation of fixed assets sold..	40	8	
Amortization of appreciation of fixed assets..........	12,647	9,472	
Write-off of organization expense...................		520	
	$(14,882)	$(125,112)	$(83,115)
Less: Net income for the year..........................	10,770		201
Adjustment for error in the amount of officers' life insurance expense written off in prior period..........	394		
Increase in cash value of officers' life insurance........	2,950	4,941	
Elimination of goodwill, excess of appreciated value of fixed assets over book value, and adjustment of capital stock.....................................		37,056	
Refund of federal income taxes received for the fiscal years ended May 31, 1954, and 1955................	......	......	14,106
	$ 14,114	$ 41,997	$ 14,307
Balance (deficit):..	(768)	(83,115)	(68,808)

In 1954, $13,062 for amortization of the appreciated value of fixed assets over net book value of June 1, 1953, was charged to earned surplus and not expensed for tax purposes. This transaction was included in the profit and loss statement; no separate statement of surplus was prepared.

Source: Company records.

the testimony we tried to get our client in such a position that the *facts* of the case spoke in his favor. We wanted our client to win, but we also had to maintain our professional position. We adopted a standard of ethics, but if we

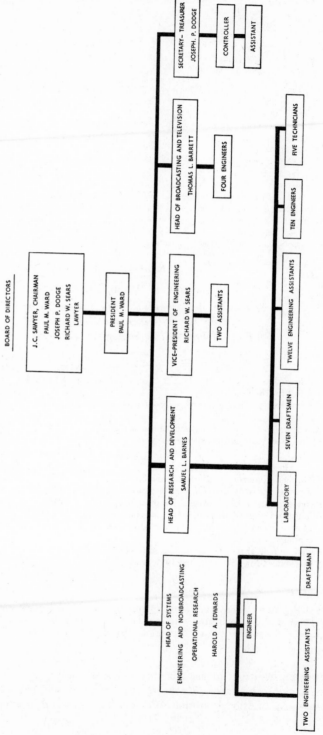

Exhibit 5

SAWYER & WARD, INC.

Proposed Company Organization Chart, June, 1956

Source: Company records.

had charged the real value of our services by taking payment in stock, for example, we'd be millionaires today. Some of our competitors are.

COMPANY HISTORY, 1930—JUNE, 1953

To expand his radiotelephone consulting, Mr. Sawyer formed a partnership with Mr. Ward in 1930, and over the span of ten years gave him a 50% share of the partnership equity. One executive later summed up the beginning of Sawyer & Ward as follows: "Radio stations used to roam from one location to another and one frequency to another like a carnival side show; the reason we're here is because the FCC is here—it needed standards for administrative purposes."

The partners broadened the scope of their broadcast services as opportunities developed. They entered the new field of Frequency Modulation (FM) soon after a personal friend of Mr. Sawyer's and Mr. Ward's discovered it. In 1938 they built the third FM station in the United States and operated it until 1945. During World War II Mr. Sawyer became a special consultant to the Secretary of War and worked on the use of radar and radio communication in air defense. Meanwhile, the firm, with Mr. Ward in charge, concentrated on war work, studying mobile point-to-point communications, antenna characteristics, and the jamming of radio signals. After the war, Sawyer & Ward started giving technical advice to TV station applicants and had helped file 100 applications by September, 1948, when the FCC froze the number of stations and frequencies, pending completion of tests on color TV and Ultra High Frequency (UHF) and an investigation into the opportunities for new TV stations. The "TV Freeze" lasted until July, 1952. Company engineers, in 1956, saw an increasing demand for help in TV station and frequency allocation once set, manufacturers started adding the 70 possible UHF channels to the basic 12 TV channels; they pointed out that with 1,879 available assignments there were 472 TV stations, of which 100 could broadcast UHF.

Broadcast and TV services fell into 12 general activities: (1) determination for clients of unallocated suitable channels; (2) selection of transmitter locations; (3) preparation of the engineering portions of applications for FCC construction permits; (4) proof of performance measurements, especially of directional antenna systems to ensure no spurious radiation; (5) determination of coverage area; (6) station valuation; (7) networks systems planning; (8) experimental activities, such as the use of booster stations; (9) testimony before the FCC; (10) co-operation with industry and government groups; (11) broadcast station equipment design; and (12) broadcast station planning.

The partners had also branched out during the 1930's into four related fields. "We never resisted entering other fields if it tied in with our know-how," Mr. Ward said. The first of these areas was "systems engineering," which was defined as the planning and integration of a communications system as a whole, distinguished from the design, manufacture, or installation of single or multiple pieces of equipment. A company brochure explained:

> In the absence of systems engineering on behalf of the user, the characteristics of a system are often determined by what happens to be the characteristics of the apparatus selected for the job. This puts the cart before the horse. The object of efficient systems engineering is first to establish their requirements with due regard to the *capabilities* of the art and then to select the equipment best adapted to meeting those requirements.

One of Sawyer & Ward's major systems engineering projects was the design and activation in the 1930's of a co-ordinated and integrated mobile multipurpose radiotelephone system for an inland waterways association. In 1956 Sawyer & Ward continued to do work for the association. Contracts for systems engineering had ranged between $3,000 and $120,000.

Sawyer & Ward began R & D, the second new field, for three reasons: (1) they wanted to develop their own measuring equipment; (2) they received many requests from other firms to do R & D work on predetermined problems of communications equipment design; and (3) they wanted to continue working on particular systems engineering projects by doing the R & D work through the prototype stage. "We began by developing our own measuring equipment and certainly had no intention of producing anything for sale," Mr. Ward said, in explaining how they got into R & D. Sawyer & Ward was hired to work on specific problems; the results, including any patent rights, belonged to its clients. The company's first major job was perfecting an electronic radio typewriter for a large company; however, since World War II most of the R & D work had been for the government.

The third new field was "operational research," which management defined as an objective field study of the efficiency of the equipment and the effectiveness of the operation of an already established system with a view to improving the methods of operation and organization. An example of operational research was a study of the engineering and technical facilities of a broadcasting network. The report recommended improvements in the techniques and changes in the organization of the engineering department. Fees for such work were similar to those for systems engineering.

Selling marketable products was the fourth new field and accounted for about 1.5% of Sawyer & Ward's gross income. Such products included a $900 midget radio transmitter the size of two cigarette packages; a $250 FM adapter for use with communications equipment; and a $99.50 mechanical lettering machine for marking chassis and resistor cards.

The company grew physically while expanding its activities. The number of employees increased from 3 in 1930 to 61 in 1953, and to 71 in 1956. In 1946 the company bought a building downtown, and the next year moved all personnel except Mr. Sawyer and his secretary into it. A director explained the reasons for this separation: "J. C. has to have a well-appointed office uptown for speech writing and meeting clients. He should not be in the lousy downtown atmosphere where everyone ran in and out and he could keep on distracting himself by asking them questions." In April, 1954, Mr. Sawyer together with the broadcasting, systems engineering, business, and accounting departments moved to another uptown building. Mr. Ward felt this second move had raised some problems:

> At times I was disturbed, because he felt that since he was situated uptown he was going to run the broadcast and systems engineering departments, and because I was situated downtown I was going to run the R & D end of the business. After a while he encouraged this, but the people working for us felt there were two bosses in fact—two bosses who felt it necessary to give orders in the other's domain. It was not clear who was responsible for the over-all operations of the company. Neither of us had the desire to take over; what happened was the outfit just never did get run.

The partners came to believe that because of the company's growth and size it was necessary to hire a trained man to handle the administrative details of Sawyer & Ward and so relieve the scientific personnel of many nonengineering problems. Mr. Richard W. Sears, head of R & D, recommended Mr. Joseph P. Dodge, who was hired as business manager and assistant treasurer in June, 1952. "I read a book about the Mayo clinic hiring a doctor with a flair for business to be the administrative head, and it seemed logical that we, too, should get someone in the business field," Mr. Sawyer said.

Mr. Dodge was not given definite duties and responsibilities. Mr. Ward said:

> Joe's position is business manager, but we're not sure what we mean by that. We probably never did spell out for Joe what his duties or responsibilities were. He must take on the responsibilities of the chief officer but still remem-

ber that he is not the chief officer. J. C. has worried a lot about the details of financing and so forth, and really he shouldn't worry; it's not good for his health. I want to arrange it so he doesn't have to worry—and I don't want to have to do it either. Joe shows a certain reluctance to go ahead and make decisions for fear they might be reversed, but I'd be tickled to have him do it; in fact, that's what I'd hoped he'd do when I hired him.

Mr. Sawyer agreed with Mr. Ward:

We didn't define Joe's job 100%; that was really up to him to do. But I thought it would include accounting, housekeeping matters, working out plans for delegation of authority, setting procedures, and the contract and cost work connected with selling. I was in no position to give him directives; I respect business but I am conscious business is not my field. Hiring Joe was like getting a doctor. If I don't agree with the doctor, I get another one, but I don't tell him how to do his job.

In June, 1956, Mr. Kaye, assistant treasurer of the company with whom Sawyer & Ward merged in 1955, wrote a job description for Mr. Dodge (see Exhibit 6).

Mr. Dodge had received an S.B. degree in 1932 and an M.B.A. degree two years later. From 1935 to 1947 he worked for the government, to which he had returned in 1951 after doing economic and statistical work

Exhibit 6

SAWYER & WARD, INC.

Mr. Kaye's Definition of Mr. Dodge's Job

This is to attempt to define in general the job of business manager and to specifically define the duties and responsibilities that go with the job. In general, the job is one of service. It is not management, in the normal sense of the word, but rather to provide the ways and means so that everything that is not engineering may be expeditiously taken care of.

Cash:

The primary responsibility for the cash of the corporation rests on the Treasurer. This means constant attendance to the ageing of the accounts receivable and the accounts payable. This also means helping the president in his relations with the bank. This arrangement, although not normal to the job of treasurer, is necessary in view of the personal aspects attached to the present Sawyer & Ward, Inc., banking relations. The treasurer should supply the president with all of the background information as often as necessary on the collection and disbursement of money and on the necessity for borrowing same.

In a small company, particularly in S & W's present circumstances, almost everything that is done affects the cash account. It should be the responsibility of the treasurer to watch with close scrutiny those things which affect this. On this particular point there is the matter of billings and collections which must be kept current.

Exhibit 6—Continued

Assets:

Purchases should be under the control of the treasurer. Dividing these purchases down further, it would probably be well to delegate responsibility for job and stock material purchases under $50 to someone in the organization under the treasurer. Purchase material for jobs over that amount should be only with authorization from the treasurer. Machinery should be set up to see that material purchases are obtained as advantageously as possible. The dividing line between assets and expense should be at the same $50, and assets should be subject to the approval of the president. A particular note of importance is the always necessary reminder to the people of the organization that financial commitments should not be made without permission of the president or treasurer!

Sales:

The business function here is to aid the engineering sales effort whenever possible. The treasurer is "on call" to aid in bidding and pricing. It is suggested that perhaps some type of standard bid form with advance notification to those people involved in pricing would be advantageous. It would also be desirable to develop a series of average rates for bidding purposes. The treasurer should be aware of the commitments necessary in bidding, such as furnishing financial data and cost breakdowns that may be necessary.

During negotiations for a contract, prices should be maintained by engineering involved and should only be changed after consultation with those who made the prices to begin with. The engineering and financial aspects of contract negotiations should not be mixed.

It should be the responsibility of the engineering department to advise the treasurer when changes or alterations in contracts have been made that influence the amount of money to be spent. No engineering should be undertaken at the expense of S. & W., Inc., without the permission of the president and treasurer.

Inventory and Purchases:

Control over the inventory and purchases should be the responsibility of the treasurer. The present method of inventory can be simplified, and it is planned to investigate ways and means of doing this. The present procedures for purchasing as discussed above need slight modification to insure that there is adequate control over items purchased and that there is adequate follow-up afterwards.

Expenses:

The treasurer must be a "no" man on expenses, where necessary. It is essential that the treasurer with the advice and counsel of the president have the complete say on expenses. This will include such items as travel, operating materials, etc. The hiring of people should be done only with the permission of the president. All pay increases should be cleared with the treasurer who will take them up with the president. All plant and physical property other than technical equipment should be under the treasurer for his care and maintenance. All outside service or rental contracts should come under the cognizance of the treasurer.

Exhibit 6—Continued

Personnel:

In line with the aforementioned program of providing service to the engineering function of the company, the treasurer or business manager becomes also the personnel manager. In a company the present size of S. & W., Inc., this calls for the maintaining of relations such that there are smooth and harmonious working conditions.

The personnel function does not override the importance of the individual department head. It is the responsibility of a department head to hire people and to fire them if necessary. The function of personnel is to do the preliminary screening for security checks, supplying an applicant with brief job descriptions so that misunderstandings do not occur. The responsibility for ultimately selecting the right man rests in the department head.

Accounting:

It is the responsibility of the treasurer to oversee the accounting department. Further, the accounting department answers only to the president and treasurer. The accounting department should provide service to the president and treasurer in the same manner as the treasurer provides service to engineering.

In view of the changes that have been made in the basic accounting system, there should be more time available for attention to billings and the obtaining of current statements. Constant decisions must be made to differentiate between the important and the unimportant. Items affecting sales and cash certainly take precedence over nonoperating items such as reserves.

Office Management:

The general job of office management should be done by the treasurer. This includes supervision of systems and records not mentioned above.

Security:

As security officer all aspects of both plant and personnel security are the treasurer's responsibility.

for nonprofit organizations. Mr. Dodge described himself as aggressive but said he had failed to get the business and engineering functions completely delineated and separated, because the engineering executives did not seem to understand the importance of the business functions in Sawyer & Ward. Mr. Dodge explained:

I think that Paul and J. C. are not primarily interested in making a profit but in just doing engineering. Here, any engineering problem, no matter how small, is more important than any business problem, no matter how large. When I joined the company, the partners couldn't understand that I was interested in making a profit, and only recently has Paul decided that we should grow. I tried to explain the importance of business concepts, but they were often unwilling even to discuss my recommendations. For example, I was responsible for sales, and I wanted to discuss the idea of hiring a sales engineer to initiate a sales program. I had initiated a series of weekly meetings, each of which lasted about three hours. Maybe we shouldn't have talked so long. At first I put my sales recommendation third on the agenda so as not to appear boastful. But we never got to my recommendation, so I started putting it first. Then Ward would say,

"This is going to take a lot of discussion; let's go on to the next topic." We never did discuss it at all. Nothing got done about a lot of my recommendations; I guess the easy procrastinating way of avoiding decisions naturally wore off on me, too. Of course, if I had the authority to make the decisions, that would have been different.

I suppose a really aggressive guy would have knocked their heads together and made them do things, but I don't like to work that way. You can't teach people by force; you have to be patient and keep prodding. I like to lay the groundwork first by discussing functions and responsibilities, so that each knows who is responsible for what. I'm not like Dick Sears, who when he found no one making decisions stepped in, made them all over the lot, and told J. C. and Paul afterwards. Responsibility gets very fuzzy with that sort of behavior.

Looking back, I can claim credit for Sawyer & Ward incorporating and merging, and I think I've done an outstanding job of running the corporation on so little capital—although few here realize how difficult that is to do.

Some company engineers agreed that their tendency to procrastinate on decision making "might discourage an aggressive man full of ideas and pep" but said that Mr. Dodge had done a disappointing job in such areas as security, contract administration, and the collection of project costs. "I kind of kid him about a lot of things he was going to do but never got done just so he'd know we remembered. But he just laughs, so apparently it doesn't affect him," one said. One day a department head to whom the downtown building janitor reported asked Mr. Dodge to take some action on the janitor's complaints of needing a helper. Mr. Dodge said he'd have his new assistant investigate when he joined the company the next month.

"Engineers don't understand my job," Mr. Dodge said. He continued:

To have an accurate project cost available at any time, I would have to have a schedule of what each man was to do and that's an engineering function. They should think ahead and plan their work; I don't see why I should do it for them. These engineers think I'm responsible, for profits, don't they? Well, Ward is really responsible, for he makes the final decisions. If I were responsible for profits, I'd do a lot of things. I'd delineate functions and responsibilities, cut costs, trim overhead and lost time, and see if we couldn't adhere to a budget.

Mr. Dodge said he spent considerable time interviewing prospective employees and had hired an assistant who would handle internal personnel problems. In addition, this man was to be security officer and supervise plant operations, maintenance, and affiliated functions.

FROM PARTNERSHIP TO CORPORATION, JUNE, 1953–OCTOBER, 1955

After two years of management discussions, Sawyer & Ward was organized as a corporation on March 20, 1953, and started operations as successor to the partnership on June 1, 1953. The company was incorporated at $330,000, and 330 shares of common stock were issued to each partner. This value was reached as follows: The partners and lawyers had evaluated radio stations and newspapers, where they said assets did not measure earning power, and thought that Sawyer & Ward stock valued at $500 a share would represent a fair going-concern valuation. All unfinished contracts, except those to be completed in 60 days, were transferred to the corporation, which bought all the partnership's assets except cash, accounts receivable, and real estate. Lawyers advised the former partners that if they loaned any cash to the newly formed corporation, any repayment of principal on the loan might be taxable as a dividend. Thereafter Sawyer & Ward, Inc., rented the engineering building from the Mayflower Building Corporation, owned by Mr. Sawyer and Mr. Ward.[2] The fixed assets purchased were appreciated $46,456, or 51% greater than the depreciated cost to the partnership. Assets were written up in varying amounts ranging from 0.5% for the top equipment to 81% for the technical apparatus; these values were determined without independent appraisal. Since this was considered a tax-free sale under the Internal Revenue Code, the corporation did not claim depreciation on this appreciation as a deduction for income tax purposes. Goodwill was determined at $242,842.[3]

Incorporation held several advantages for Sawyer & Ward, but the idea was distasteful to the partners because other professional people, such as lawyers or doctors, who have close personal relationships with their clients may not legally incorporate. "We kicked this around for a long time, longer than I like to think," Mr. Ward said. "To our surprise, all we got from our notices of incorporation were congratulations," Mr. Sawyer added. He pointed out the advantages of incorporation: (a) It was a good way to insure the company's continued existence. Government contracts were the majority of Sawyer & Ward's business, and the government preferred to give contracts to corporations; a contract given to a partnership might not be finished, since the partnership is legally dissolved on a partner's death. Similarly, bank loans are more

---

[2] This corporation netted $12,000 after corporate taxes in 1956.

[3] In certifying the statement for the year ending May 31, 1954, the auditors wrote: "In view of the fact that we are unable to appraise management's judgment in its valuation of capital assets and goodwill as of June 1, 1953, we are unable to express an opinion on the statement as a whole. In all other respects, except that the corporation derived benefit from certain expenses prepaid by the predecessor partnership ($2,800 in pension plan and insurance premiums), the accounts are fairly stated in accordance with generally accepted accounting principles."

readily available to corporations than to partnerships. (*b*) Incorporation enabled the partners to include themselves in the company's retirement program with before-tax money. (*c*) The partners had promised the senior men a share in the company. "You want to do something for the men who have been with you for a long time but who cannot afford to buy an equal interest in the partnership," Mr. Ward explained. Under the partnership senior men had received annual bonuses of as much as 50% of their salary.

Shortly after Sawyer & Ward became a corporation, Mr. Sawyer and Mr. Ward decided to enlarge the stockholder group and the board of directors. At the constant urging of Mr. Sears, the former partners agreed in March, 1954, that five senior men should become stockholders. In April, 1955, the five men bought 260 shares of stock at a "fair" price of $150 per share with terms of 15% down and ten-year, 4% notes for the balance (see Exhibit 6). The following September the former partners personally sold these five key men a total of 40 more shares. In December, 1954, Mr. Sears and the company attorney had joined Mr. Sawyer, Mr. Ward, and Mr. Dodge on the board of directors. (See Exhibit 7.)

The corporation in March, 1954, took over the major portion of the life insurance policies on the two principal officers. The face value of the policy on each man was $130,000. Of this amount, the corporation assumed $100,000 and the individuals retained $30,000. The corporation exchanged 80 shares of stock, valued at $500 a share, for the two policies with a total cash value of $33,828 and $6,172 in cash. The partners, in turn, sold 40 of these shares to the five key men at $150 a share. Under the partnership the policies had been payable to the heirs of the other partner with an agreement that this money was to be used to buy the deceased partner's share of the company, while under the corporation these policies were payable to the corporation.

In appraising the company's future in 1955, as owners, the new stockholders agreed with the former partners that at least three problems remained unsolved: lack of manufacturing facilities and capital and small size. They felt there was more money to be made in manufacturing equipment, called "hardware" in the trade, than in R & D work, but they thought manufacturing was a different type of business and were uncertain if Sawyer & Ward could be successful at it. Mr. Sawyer said:

The problem with straight R & D work is there's no money in it; the 7% above costs given in government contracts soon gets swallowed up in expenses the government later disallows and won't let you charge for. Most of our competitors doing R & D have access to manufacturing facilities and do the R & D in hopes that it will result in equipment orders running into millions of dollars.

In addition, the stockholders thought there was a real future for a company three to five times the size of Sawyer & Ward. Mr. Ward

Exhibit 7

SAWYER & WARD, INC.

Ownership of Common Stock, 1953–56
(Shares)

	Sawyer & Ward, Inc., Common				Mansfield Common		
	June 1, 1953	March 1, 1954	April 26, 1955	Sept. 1, 1955	Oct. 1, 1955	June 8, 1956	July, 1956
J. C. Sawyer........	330	370	370	350	1,505	15,050	16,555
P. M. Ward.........	330	370	370	350	1,505	15,050	16,555
J. P. Dodge.........			52	66	284	2,840	3,124
R. W. Sears.........			52	66	284	2,840	3,124
S. L. Barnes.........			52	56	241	2,410	2,651
H. A. Edwards......			52	56	241	2,410	2,651
T. L. Barrett........			52	56	241	2,410	2,651
Total..........	660	740	1,000	1,000	4,301	43,010	47,311

The first column shows the division of stock at the start of the corporation, June 1, 1953. On March 1, 1954, the former partners received 80 shares, valued at $500 a share, in exchange for the life insurance policies and cash. Five key employees bought 260 shares from the corporation at $150 a share on April 26, 1955. In September these five employees bought 40 shares from the former partners at $150 a share.

When Sawyer & Ward merged with Mansfield Electronics on October 1, 1955, 4.3 Mansfield shares were exchanged for one Sawyer & Ward share. On June 8, 1956, Mansfield split its stock ten for one in a recapitalization plan designed to increase employee ownership and create a market for the stock, while at the same time retaining ownership control in the same hands. The next month Mansfield declared a 10% stock dividend. In the fall of 1956 Mansfield stock sold over-the-counter for $1.60 a share, and there were 338,736 shares outstanding.

Source: Company records.

pointed out that work was "going begging," but his firm was too small to get it either as a government contractor or subcontractor for another manufacturer. Both former partners agreed that the firm would continue to do high-quality work and not increase in size merely by adding people to the payroll. Mr. Sawyer explained that the term "engineer" embraced a variety of people from the technician, who took a night course in electronics, to the Ph. D., and therefore he believed that a small, select group of highly qualified engineers was more valuable than a large group of engineers with more dubious qualifications. According to Mr. Sawyer, many clients and some competitors seemed to believe in the "American philosophy" that "appointing a man to a job qualifies him to do it." Other competitors, he said, impressed clients with the "shotgun" approach of assigning a large number of men to a job on the theory that some of them are bound to come up with an answer. Mr. Ward added, "It's hard to tell a client that you can put 100 engineers on the job tomorrow and, after signing the contract, go out and hire those 100 engineers, but some competitors do it." Mr. Sawyer believed his firm must find a "middle ground" between locating "just the right man" and hiring "warm bodies."

As a first step towards dealing with these shortcomings of lack of manufacturing facilities and size, Sawyer & Ward thought of merging with another company.

STOCK EXCHANGE WITH MANSFIELD ELECTRONICS, INC., OCTOBER 1, 1955–JUNE, 1956

Sawyer & Ward was "ripe for a merger" when it was approached by a representative of Mansfield Electronics, Inc., in 1954. After a year and a half of "courtship," the firms agreed to merge on October 1, 1955. The final agreement included these points: (1) For the first year, at least, Sawyer & Ward was to be free to do consulting work and continue as a separate corporate entity, operating autonomously as a wholly owned subsidiary. (2) Mansfield was to assume all Sawyer & Ward's obligations, including bank loans personally endorsed by Mr. Sawyer or Mr. Ward, and to furnish additional working capital during the first five or six months, if necessary. (3) Sawyer & Ward was to retain its retirement plan. In addition, it was to institute a management incentive plan for the fiscal year ending May 31, 1956, providing distribution of 20% of the net profit before taxes to key employees selected annually by the directors. (4) Each company was to be represented on the other's board of directors.[4] (5) All of Sawyer & Ward's stock was to be exchanged for Mansfield common on the basis of adjusted book value at the end of the Sawyer & Ward and Mansfield fiscal years, which were May 31 and September 30, respectively. The finally agreed upon ratio was 4.3 to 1; Mansfield exchanged 4,301 shares for Sawyer & Ward's 1,000 shares (see Exhibit 6).

The terms of this final agreement were made explicit during the summer of 1955; Mansfield made some concessions, including the length of

[4] As of January, 1957, Sawyer & Ward had not enlarged its board of directors.

time that working capital would be supplied. In August, five-year employment agreements were drawn up between Mr. Sawyer, Mr. Ward, and their company, Sawyer & Ward, Inc. Annual salary for each was fixed at $30,004 to be paid in 26 installments; a year's salary was to be paid to heirs in case of death. In September agreement was reached on the book value of the stocks:

1. Mr. Dodge estimated that if goodwill and the remaining $18,879 of the original $46,456 asset appreciation were written off Sawyer & Ward had a stated book value of at least $146.51 plus $160 in other values not in the balance sheet, for a total of $306.[5] He thought Mansfield was thinking of appraising book value at $175 a share, which increased by the $160 a share for other values would be $335 a share. Taking Mansfield's book value of $45 a share without independent verification, Mr. Dodge suggested to Mansfield in September, 1955, that the exchange ratio should be $7\frac{1}{2}$ to $6\frac{4}{5}$ Mansfield shares to one Sawyer & Ward share.

2. Mr. Kaye, assistant treasurer of Mansfield, made some calculations. He reexamined Mansfield's book value, disregarding some "worthless" assets, and arrived at a book value of $42.50 a share; he reappraised the Sawyer & Ward stock, eliminated some $225,442 of goodwill, and came up with a value of $182.79. This value was the basis for the final ratio of 4.3 to 1.

Both companies had expected certain definite advantages from the exchange of stock. Before agreeing to the transfer, the Sawyer & Ward directors sent Mansfield a list of questions about the company's general aims and the advantages it expected from the merger. These questions included: "Does Mansfield expect J. C. Sawyer and P. M. Ward to be salesmen?"; "Does Mansfield contemplate joining their R & D and ours?"; "How many Mansfield employees are classified as engineers?"; and "What are Mansfield's plans for growth—buying companies, etc.?"

From discussing the answers to such questions, Sawyer & Ward concluded that the reasons for the merger were: (1) The companies and products were different but complementary. Mansfield was a firm of 200 people, located 500 miles from Sawyer & Ward, and both manufactured electronic products and did specialized R & D research on their own and on contract. Such manufacturing facilities could be used for Sawyer & Ward developments, while Mansfield could call on its new subsidiary for needed engineering help. In communications equipment research the two companies also complemented each other; Sawyer &

---

[5] Mr. Dodge said he obtained the other values, which totaled $160,000 or $160 a share, by valuing the key man insurance at $25,000; the pension plan at $50,000 (he said for Mansfield to start funding a similar plan would cost over $100,000); a year's potential sales of two electronic devices, $35,000; and the Sawyer & Ward name, $50,000.

Ward worked in the low end of the frequency spectrum around 1,000 megacycles or less, while Mansfield was in the 10,000 megacycles range. Neither company felt qualified to enter the other's field unassisted. (2) Sawyer & Ward wanted assistance in selling their services: "We don't have continual contact with the right people in other R & D centers. We know the top men, but these are not the people who do the buying," Mr. Ward explained. (3) Sawyer & Ward needed capital for physical expansion. (4) Although Sawyer & Ward thought they had space for a 300% physical expansion, they felt they lacked the necessary management skills for such a move; they liked the Mansfield management.

Several Sawyer & Ward executives expressed the view in 1956 that it was too early to judge or even to expect results from the merger. One department head explained, "We needed cash and help. They've given us working capital, left us on a divisional basis, tried to help us, and leaned over backwards not to butt in. We appreciate all this but we still say, 'Don't tell us how to do engineering, brother, because we can do that, but if we didn't need your help we wouldn't have merged.' " Mr. Sawyer said the companies had pooled engineers for common problems, but as yet neither firm had passed on business to the other. Sawyer & Ward had evaluated some of Mansfield's own projects as "outsiders."

Sawyer & Ward followed some of Mansfield's suggestions and adopted a modified accounting system compatible with Mansfield's. The partnership had operated on a cash basis, while the corporation had used an accrual system. After the merger, Sawyer & Ward changed to a modified accrual system and at the same time reduced somewhat its accounting manpower requirements. Under the new system income consisted solely of billings, but some expenses were accrued. Mr. Ward pointed out that with this system the profit and loss statements could be misleading if there was much unbilled, but expensed, work in process.

Mr. Dodge also agreed with Mr. Kaye, of Mansfield, to (1) have the 1955 accounts audited; (2) eliminate the asset appreciation and goodwill from the books as of May, 1956; and (3) change the Sawyer & Ward 1957 fiscal year to coincide with Mansfield's (October 1 to September 30).

Mansfield was anxious to have Sawyer & Ward save $17,195 in rent by consolidating operations in the downtown building. In June, 1956, Mr. Dodge and the accounting department moved to the downtown building, but Mr. Ward was unwilling to move the systems engineering department prior to Mr. Sawyer's return from a world trip. Company engineers pointed out that the downtown building was crowded, that it was logical to separate consulting and R & D because they were different types of businesses, and that this separation simplified security measures. In any event, they thought Mr. Sawyer would remain uptown.

Mr. Kaye, assistant treasurer of Mansfield, agreed it was too early to really evaluate the success of the merger; however, he pointed out that Mansfield was still providing Sawyer & Ward working capital at the end of 1956 through a $100,000 bank loan. He said, "Cash is scarce here, too. The acquisition of Sawyer & Ward enabled us to get into fields we were never in, but we had not counted on losing money. We agreed to leave them autonomous, but keeping that agreement will depend on the profit situation; we're looking for just one quarter in the black. After all, they made a profit for 25 years; why did they have to stop now?"[6]

THE SITUATION, JUNE–SEPTEMBER, 1956

During 1956 Sawyer & Ward management discussed among themselves three areas they thought needed attention: company organization, sales department, and overhead rates. Several senior men felt certain aspects of the partnership relationship explained some of the problems existing in 1956. One director said:

> Most of the present troubles grew out of a long pleasant agreement between J. C. (Sawyer) and Paul (Ward); if they'd fought, all would be all right now. Nobody knew who was in charge; nobody knew whom to blame for what— so everybody blamed everybody.

Another officer pointed out that the partners' actions affected the rest of the organization:

> J. C. and Paul acted as foils for each other. They developed the idea that if either had a problem he put it on the table, and if it didn't go away it would solve itself sooner or later. This approach carried over to the key personnel with the result that to preserve this "one big happy family" men did not go slugging and take definite action on problems.

Mr. Ward agreed: "We never had a really tight organization. J. C. and I had equal say in all decisions; we never had a major difference of opinion on policy." Mr. Kaye, of Mansfield, once told Mr. Sawyer and Mr. Ward: "You have lived together too long; you aren't frank. You will treat engineering problems impersonally and objectively but won't discuss business problems the same way."

---

[6] Mr. Sawyer commented on reading the case: "I've asked the same question many times."

In June, 1956, Mr. Ward prepared an organization chart. He and Mr. Dodge had made such a chart the previous September, but although some engineers, particularly Mr. Sears, urged that he post it, he had deferred to his former partner and not done so. Mr. Sawyer did not want all engineering decisions channeled through Mr. Sears, although he agreed with the latter that organization charts were useful to delineate functions and avoid personnel conflicts. Mr. Ward commented, "I have trouble with organization charts. You can draw the best darn functional charts, and then you put in the names and the charts are no good because of the personalities involved. So then you adjust the personalities to the functions."

In the new chart, Mr. Ward designated five department heads: Mr. Samuel L. Barnes, head of R & D; Mr. Harold A. Edwards, head of systems engineering and operational research (SE & OR); Mr. Thomas L. Barrett, head of broadcasting and TV (BTV); Mr. Sears, vice-president of engineering and head of sales; and Mr. Dodge, business manager and secretary-treasurer. Mr. Barnes, who joined Sawyer & Ward in 1939 and received his S.B. a year later, was to handle all laboratory work for R & D and for Mr. Edwards' department. Mr. Barnes had succeeded Mr. Sears but would now report directly to Mr. Ward. "It will take quite a bit of co-ordination to know what Dick Sears' problems are," Mr. Barnes said and added that he believed in letting project supervisors run their groups without direct supervision from him while he played the role of adviser and acted as liaison to the accounting department.

Mr. Edwards (SE & OR) planned to generate his own business, although other executives thought this might be difficult, because he said many equipment manufacturers offered free services *"called* systems engineering or operational research." Mr. Edwards said although such services were not strictly comparable with this, they might be a selling block. He had received his S.B. in 1941, and after five years in the Army had joined Sawyer & Ward in 1947. He had reported to Mr. Sawyer but now was to report to Mr. Ward. Mr. Edwards said he was pleased to be given responsibility and freedom of movement: "It's a lot better to have it all clear. If I need something, I figure I'm going to tell people. If I need equipment, I'll talk to Sam Barnes." In the fall of 1956 the department had several thousand dollars worth of service contracts, and Mr. Edwards was looking for an assistant.

Mr. Barrett (BTV) said he had three objectives for his department: (1) to maintain the "doctor-patient" relationship in dealing with clients;

(2) to grow in a professional way by giving clients superior advice and by staying in the forefront scientifically; and (3) to participate actively in the industry associations "where the innovations are developed." He thought it was especially important from a long-range viewpoint for company engineers to work on the frontiers of scientific knowledge through publishing papers, heading specialized groups, and contacting other professionals. He wanted to allow himself time for such work and therefore was training an assistant to handle the departmental detail work. Mr. Barrett had joined Sawyer & Ward after receiving a B.E.E. in 1939 and had worked in the broadcast field ever since. "I came as a man who could jump on a roof and install FM antennas for the new station we were building," he said.

Mr. Sears was picked in June, 1956, to set up a R & D sales department and plan Sawyer & Ward's first sales program; executives agreed he was the company's most imaginative engineer. He had joined the company in 1936, a year before receiving his S.B.; two years later he got his S.M. Mr. Dodge said of him, "When Dick saw what needed to be done, he'd grab the ball and do it; why, even the janitor was responsible directly to him." From the outset, Mr. Sears' department was to consist of himself, an engineer who had applied for Mr. Sears' job, and a woman, who because she had had "considerable experience in sales in previous employments" was to establish the office routine and organize the contact files.

Sawyer & Ward personnel believed that a professional firm such as theirs was restricted as to selling methods, especially when selling consulting. They agreed with Mr. Sawyer's comment:

> Like a lawyer, we have to sell without selling—it's all indirect, a matter of keeping in contact with clients. You can't go out and pound on doors to sell our services because you've got to beat the client over the head at times, and you can't do that if you've sold him. I've always said that the best client is the one in trouble that has to come to you.

The senior men disagreed as to the necessity of such "selling." Several, including Mr. Ward, disliked the idea of selling. Mr. Dodge said, "When I came here in 1952, there was a definite feeling that we shouldn't sell, and, in fact, we've never had to go out and sell until the past two or three years; I guess we still shudder at the word 'sell.'" In both 1948 and 1956 the R & D department lacked work when large contracts were finished. Mr. Sears thought that, unlike consulting, there was considerable room for selling R & D if social contact with top executives provided good leads for technical salesmen to follow up. Mr.

Sawyer, in 1956, said, "I always have stood for selling our services, but my view was not fully understood by the rest of the organization." He continued:

I believe in selling all right; I've had to do most of it, although I don't like it. Ward hates to sell, and some of the other men do too. Anyone who has had to meet a payroll, and I carried a large part of that burden for Sawyer & Ward, knows you have to be commercial to stay alive. An engineer lacks sales sense— too many assume that their ability is self-selling; it is not. Just recently I read in the papers that one of our clients, one whom we had on a retainer basis, had bought two TV stations. When I got to the office, I asked Barrett when he'd last spoken to that client. He replied, "Oh, about six months ago." I picked up the phone, called the client, and, after congratulating him on the purchase, asked, "When do we start work? We're ready tomorrow." The client said he'd call us after he'd visited the stations. I told Barrett, "If he doesn't call you next week, you call him."

According to Mr. Sears, the "new sales department would be responsible first for the securing of new R & D projects and, second, for the development of additional engineering talents, services, or products." The department would select, plan, and co-ordinate the face-to-face, telephone, and written contacts which sales personnel would usually make, although "all employees should automatically respond to a possible lead that might arise from their daily work." In addition, the sales department would channel bid requests to the engineering department for writing the proposal and to the business department for pricing and other contract information. All price quotations together with the technical proposal were to be submitted to a pricing committee for final review. In cases where the pricing committee could not agree Mr. Ward would have final approval; in his absence Mr. Sears was authorized to act in his stead. The engineering department ordinarily was to make the final decision whether to bid on a particular project. If Mr. Sears did not agree with this decision and wanted further consideration, the proposal might go to Mr. Ward for a review. Mr. Sears eventually hoped to expand the force to include field representatives.

Although Mr. Sears admitted it would be a "conscious effort" for him not to do any engineering, he was eager to try the job:

I insisted sales be an executive job so I wouldn't have to go to Paul for permission every time I wanted to move. . . . Everyone likes to feel he has something of the salesman in him. I'd like to find out how far we can go in trying to sell something. We are trying to sell services, and you don't sell them the same way as something you hold in your hand.

We seem to have made a mistake by relying so heavily on our background. We have an entry into places on the strength of our name and past reputation, but on the strength of work done now we cannot convince people.[7] It's most important that we keep up our research and develop new ideas or we'll have nothing to sell. Right now we don't have any sure-fire ideas or quick capital, so we must keep on doing contract work. We must increase volume and keep on working and hope something will come along. If our sales program is not successful, what is there to go back to? I am under no illusions.[8]

Mr. Barnes of R & D had mixed feelings about Mr. Sears' proposal to have Barnes' engineers write the proposals besides carry them out:

This is good in that the engineers are in on the proposals, and this gives them an insight into the type of work we make bids on. Also, the engineer who *writes* the proposal might later be the project head. On the other hand, when we are on proposals, we are on nonproductive work, and this is tough to swallow. We are fighting to get overhead down; every unpaid hour takes several productive hours to make up. Even if you rule out all proposals, you still have some unpaid time in meetings, preparing work, reading technical magazines, and so forth. With the lab fully loaded we should be able to work between 90 and 95% of efficiency, but a good many weeks we're not up to 50%. You see, the extent to which one can charge more productive time to direct labor depends upon the project.

One director, in reply, said: "If 50% of your time is unproductive, you have twice as many engineers as you need. You approach a problem with an engineering mind."

The matter of engineering efficiency and overhead, of which Mr. Barnes spoke, was the subject of a series of reports by Mr. Dodge in 1956. First he reviewed Sawyer & Ward's fees. For office work and FCC hearings the charge was $20 an hour, while the field rate was $12.50 an hour for the first man, $7.50 an hour for the assistant. The rate for office time of Mr. Sawyer and Mr. Ward was $30 an hour and for Mr. Sears $25. "Statistical engineers" and draftsmen were billed at $7 an hour. Mr. Dodge thought the fees were comparable to those charged by lawyers.

Mr. Dodge tried to show the relationship between efficiency and overhead charges. Using Sawyer and Ward's fees, he had the controller prepare a schedule of potential gross income and cash requirements, based on each engineer working at maximum assumed efficiencies. Using the most recent wage rates and overhead figures, he found the overhead rate would be 145% of direct labor at maximum efficiency. In 1956

---

[7] Mr. Sears said he did not mean to imply that the *quality* of work had declined over the years, but rather that the *type* of work done had not changed with the times.

[8] In February, 1957, Mr. Sears commented, "I'm beginning to enjoy selling, although I don't tell anybody lest they think this is an easy job. Making contacts takes money and time; the best chance I have to do any engineering is on trains."

the actual overhead rate was 160.49%, and the average efficiency, 67.8%. Efficiency, Mr. Dodge said, would have to be increased to 72.1% for the overhead to be 145%. Mr. Dodge commented:

To accomplish these results would require a continuing effort to relieve the executives and senior engineers of a substantial portion of their present non-productive responsibilities, except in the realm of broad policy and supervision, and also a careful budgeting of time devoted by all productive personnel to professional, educational, and miscellaneous activities.

Mr. Dodge also calculated that additions to the staff would reduce the overhead rate, but only if sales were such that these additions could be used at maximum efficiency within a short time after employment.

FUTURE PLANS, SEPTEMBER, 1956

In looking at the past with an eye to the future, Mr. Sawyer said he had often asked himself, "Why hasn't an organization as old as ours with the very high reputation we have, coupled with the highest ethical standards, grown as fast as many of the younger electronic companies?" He said there were four reasons for his firm's slow rate of growth, which were:

(1) Engineers are lousy businessmen—it was a long time before we realized that as you get bigger you must delegate authority and functions. (2) We lacked sales sense. (3) We had no access to manufacturing facilities. And (4) we adopted standards of ethics and conduct which were higher than industry wanted or was willing to pay for.

For the future, Mr. Sawyer expressed uncertainty about the ability of his firm to get government research contracts or bid on part of a contract under the cost plus fixed fee method. He said the contracting officer usually let the contract to a low *initial* bidder and not to experienced firms like Sawyer & Ward who bid higher, knowing that a low bid would only have to be negotiated later. "I suggested we be 'realistic' and cut our bids by, say, 40%, but then again that's not right. We'd know they would have to be renegotiated. As a result, we've got a reputation for being high priced, and it's led us to be more interested in subcontracts from larger firms who value our experience and professional attitude," Mr. Sawyer said. Mr. Ward added that he thought the government requirement that each bidder submit with each bid a separate technical proposal describing his method of attacking the problem was "an appalling drain on engineering man power." He cited an example of 30 companies bidding for one contract and using a total of 45 to 65 man-years to prepare the 30 proposals. He quoted Mr. J. M. Bridges, director of electronics in the Office of the Assistant Secretary of Defense (application engineering), as saying in a public address: "We need to establish a method of selecting developmental contractors that will not require this waste . . . a sound choice can be made on the basis of experience, record of accomplishment, available facilities and engineering man power, and management attitudes." Mr. Ward commented, "Agreed, provided that the people who make the choice are, first, qualified and, second, willing to accept the responsibility for such a decision."

"We've done a lot of swimming upstream, and we still have a real educational job to do, especially in the broadcast-TV area," Mr. Sawyer said.

The advertising agencies and the consumer surveys and recorders of commodity movements in distributions channels have killed much of our work. We think it's more important to measure who *can* listen before you try to estimate whether people are listening to a particular program. It's important to know your coverage; many times I've seen clients who reached one area with their programs and distributed to another. In the technical area there is much to be done, too. Long ago we discovered that the station range depends most on the frequency, less on the antenna, and least on the electrical power. Yet, today, one station advertises it is the only 50 kw. station in the city. This statement is meaningless unless you know the broadcast frequency, because the higher the frequency the more power is needed.

Mr. Ward thought Sawyer & Ward could expand in its present line of activities. He said R & D would grow through Mr. Sears' efforts and the use of Mansfield's facilities and thought the small marketable products had possibilities. Because it did not compete with any manufacturers, Sawyer & Ward had received an Air Force contract to test all antennas submitted by manufacturers; Mr. Ward and Mr. Sears thought the company should do more impartial evaluation work. Mr. Ward pointed out that FM, UHF, and the various proposed TV arrangements, such as educational, closed circuit, community, and pay-as-you-go, were promising fields for the broadcast-TV department.

Some outsiders commented that the requirements for a R & D firm were different from those doing the type of work Sawyer & Ward were doing in communications. One scientist said:

You can judge a R & D company or department pretty well if you know how many of the men are under 30. You need young men to keep on top of scientific developments. It's not that the older men are lacking in ability or imagination to grasp new ideas; rather, the older ones have an approach which prevents them asking the most useful questions. The older scientist accepts transistors as a substitute for radio tubes, but the young scientist wonders why one needs tubes or transistors at all and has the time, opportunity, and physical stamina to work day and night and follow through his ideas.

Mr. Ward and R & D senior engineers agreed that the requirements for R & D work differed from those for communications consulting and that further expansion into R & D would be built by young men under their supervision. They pointed out that while their consulting needed relaxed men with mature judgment to solve specific problems before them R & D required men who would generate problems and find unique solutions. The senior men said that even if they didn't understand the field they could by asking questions be sure the young engineers were on the right track. One said:

I'm at my best when I'm tossing ideas back and forth with young engineers. An idea will come up, and I'll tell him to work on it and report next week. I can't do it any more—I just don't have the time to concentrate. Anyway, I much prefer to think up ideas and let someone else work them out.

This man added that, with one exception, only since 1954 had Sawyer & Ward realized the value of hiring superior R & D engineers who could create and make decisions on their own.

Mr. Ward said in summary, "There is the right-sized company for every sized job. The questions facing us now are: What size should we be? and What jobs should we do?"

Linton Company, Inc.

"I THINK lack of capital is our biggest problem," Mr. Frank Corbett, president of the Linton Company, a wholesale grocery firm, told a case writer from the Harvard Business School in April, 1954. "We need additional sales volume, but our present capital is not large enough to finance additional receivables and inventory. We could make a substantial incréase in profits by increasing sales, because most of our expenses are fixed or would rise very little with higher volume. I have prepared some figures that show you how this looks (see Exhibit 1). At present gross margin and other income just cover our operating expenses. For five years now, we've been trying to get volume over this 'break-even' point to where we will be making sizable profits. At first I thought our break-even point was about $2,500,000. Then it increased to $3,000,000, and now it seems as though we need about $4,000,000 sales before we'll show real profits!

"Each time our bank loan comes up for renewal, the loaning officer, Mr. Eaton, asks us when we are going to make some money. I've been giving him this same explanation since 1947. Last time Mr. Eaton saw Bob, who is my brother and partner; he said, 'Your brother Frank sounds like an old broken record being played over and over. When is he going to have something new to tell me?'

"One reason we haven't made larger profits is that we took the calculated risk of lowering margin and prices to increase volume. If I had an additional $100,000 capital I could risk cutting margins even further. This, I am positive, would enable us to secure additional large customers and increase sales to a point where we would really be making money. What I couldn't do with this business if I only had some capital to use!" (See Exhibits 2, 3, 4, 5 and 6 for financial data.)

The Linton office and main warehouse were in Elgin, Illinois, a city of 44,000 population, approximately 30 miles northwest of Chicago. The company rented a smaller frozen-food warehouse in another suburb about 15 miles nearer Chicago. The grocery line, which included over 2,000 grocery products, was sold to 405 retail accounts within a

Exhibit 1

LINTON COMPANY, INC.

Estimates of Projected Weekly Income and Expense Figures

	WEEKLY							
	1	2	3	4	5	6	7	8
YEAR	Mr. Frank Corbett's Assumptions of Sales Volume		Grocery Income*	Frozen-Food* Income	Total Income	Expense†	Profit or (Loss)	Annual Profit or (Loss)
	Groceries	Frozen Foods						
	$32,000	$16,000	$2,410	$1,690	$4,100	$4,400	$(300)	$(15,600)
	32,000	18,000	2,410	1,740	4,150	4,400	(250)	(13,000)
	32,000	20,000	2,410	1,950	4,360	4,400	(40)	(2,080)
	32,000	22,000	2,410	2,180	4,590	4,400	190	9,880
	35,000	16,000	2,635	1,690	4,325	4,400	(75)	(3,900)
	37,000	16,000	2,795	1,690	4,485	4,400	85	4,420
	40,000	16,000	3,010	1,690	4,700	4,400	300	15,600
	40,000	18,000	3,010	1,740	4,750	4,400	350	18,200
	VERY LIKELY VOLUME IN 1954							
	37,000	18,000	2,795	1,740	4,535	4,400	135	7,020
	POSSIBILITY IN 1954							
	37,000	20,000	2,795	1,950	4,745	4,400	345	17,940
	GOAL							
	40,000	22,000	3,010	2,180	5,190	4,400	790	41,080
	ACTUAL RESULTS 1950–53							
1950....	25,500	3,500	2,702	357	3,059	2,950	109	5,668
1951....	22,800	8,600	2,572	809	3,381	3,268	113	5,876
1952....	22,900	13,100	2,054	1,465	3,519	3,428	91	4,732
1953....	29,000	16,600	2,186	1,927	4,113	3,921	192	9,984

* Total income includes gross margin, advertising allowances, and purchase discounts as estimated by Mr. Frank Corbett.
† This was Mr. Frank Corbett's estimate of "highest conceivable operating cost" at these volumes.

Source: Mr. Frank Corbett.

50-mile radius of Elgin, in Illinois and Indiana. Linton was also the distributor for Apex Frozen Foods in the same territory.

HISTORY UNDER PREVIOUS MANAGEMENT, 1903–45

Linton was founded in 1903 by Messrs. S. F. Linton and J. C. McIvor, wholesale flour, grain, and feed dealers. After their original warehouse burned down in 1914, the company built a new warehouse and added

Exhibit 2

LINTON COMPANY, INC.

Balance Sheets, 1945–53

Assets	Dec. 31 1953	Dec. 31 1952	Dec. 31 1951	Dec. 31 1950	Dec. 31 1949	Dec. 31 1948	Dec. 31 1947	Dec. 31 1946	June, 1945
Cash on Hand and on Deposit	$ 54,659	$ 27,923	$ 18,240	$ 26,906	$ 11,818	$ 6,030	$ 5,873	$ 12,841	$ 14,380
Accounts Receivable—Trade	86,875	73,436	53,550	62,813	37,506	50,028	40,485	35,989	28,077
Accounts and Claims Receivable—Nontrade	174	4,095	395	388	1,402	1,105	2,441	1,121	....
Inventories: Groceries	201,954*	176,180*	179,599*	200,251*	116,021*	128,777	159,364)	201,142	58,805
Frozen Foods	20,027	13,777	6,679	10,751	14,485	29,381	0)		
Total	221,981	189,957	186,278	211,002	130,506	158,158	159,364	201,142	58,805
Total Current Assets	$363,689	$295,411	$258,463	$301,109	$181,232	$215,321	$208,163	$251,093	$101,262
Cash Surrender Value—Life Insurance	2,180	1,563	1,020	276	20				
Land	1,500	1,500	1,500	1,500	1,500	1,500	1,500	1,500	1,500
Buildings	15,437	16,150	16,863	17,575	18,288	19,000	19,713	20,425	21,494
Improvements	5,105	4,525	3,201	3,783	4,365	4,948			
Total Real Estate	22,042	22,175	21,564	22,858	24,153	25,448	21,213	21,925	22,994
Furniture and Equipment	2,643	3,291	2,901	2,763	3,217	7,833	9,232	3,560	98
Delivery Truck	100	320	699	1,937	2,970	3,734)	7,820)	3,632)	3,739
Automobiles	2,886	3,174	4,242	1,521	1,117	1,866)			
Total Fixed Assets	$ 27,671	$ 28,960	$ 29,406	$ 29,079	$ 31,457	$ 38,881	$ 38,265	$ 29,117	$ 26,831
Miscellaneous Receivables			310	612					
Deposit Premiums and Unexpired Insurance	2,734	1,743	2,080	2,393	1,261	1,648	1,913	542	610
Other Deferred Charges	199	199	341	106	104	240	186		636
Officers and Employees' Accounts	2,064	1,696			978				77,339
Total Other Assets	$ 4,997	$ 3,638	$ 2,731	$ 3,111	$ 2,343	$ 1,888	$ 2,099	$ 542	$ 78,585
Total Assets	$398,537	$329,572	$291,620	$333,575	$215,052	$256,090	$248,527	$280,752	$206,678

Exhibit 2 (Continued)

LINTON COMPANY, INC.

Balance Sheets, 1945–53

Liabilities	Dec. 31, 1953	Dec. 31, 1952	Dec. 31, 1951	Dec. 31, 1950	Dec. 31, 1949	Dec. 31, 1948	Dec. 31, 1947	Dec. 31, 1946	June, 1945
Notes Payable—Unsecured	....	....	$ 1,215	....	$ 4,000	$ 13,000	$ 20,000	....	....
Notes Payable—Autos	....	....	715	$ 461	....	....	....	....	....
Due Officers							682		$ 26,784
Accounts Payable—Trade	$150,871	$113,880	77,684	113,810	37,970	55,897	39,992	$ 82,814	33,000
Notes Payable—Bank (Secured by Inventory)	120,000*	90,000*	90,000*	100,000*	73,500*	106,479	102,844	124,606	....
Notes Payable—Secured by Equipment	310	400	....	....	256				....
Provision for Taxes	6,342	6,621	4,261	7,150	6,739	7,830	11,279	8,645	6,484
Accrued Expenses and Other Liabilities	4,032	1,953	3,340	3,353	980	1,590	2,261	2,187	1,254
Amortization of Mortgage Payable	1,500	1,500	1,500	1,350	1,500	1,500	1,500	1,500	....
Total Current Liabilities	$283,055	$214,354	$178,715	$226,124	$124,945	$186,296	$178,558	$219,752	$ 67,522
Mortgage Payable—Real Estate	24,000	25,500	27,000	28,650	23,625	25,125	28,500	28,500	20,000
Capital Stock	75,300	74,200	70,000	63,800	53,000	32,500	32,500	....	24,000
Earned Surplus	16,182	15,518	15,905	15,001	13,482	12,169	8,969		95,156
Total Capital	$ 91,482	$ 89,718	$ 85,905	$ 78,801	$ 66,482	$ 44,669	$ 41,469	$ 32,500†	$119,156
Total Liabilities and Capital	$398,537	$329,572	$291,620	$333,575	$215,052	$256,090	$248,527	$280,752	$206,678

* Inventory of $116,021 pledged to secure note of $ 73,500 on 12/31/49.
    " $194,834   "   "   " $100,000   "   12/31/50.
    " $173,388   "   "   " $ 90,000   "   12/31/51.
    " $169,829   "   "   " $ 90,000   "   12/31/52.
    " $195,971   "   "   " $120,000   "   12/31/53.

† Partner's capital.

Source: Company records.

Exhibit 3

LINTON COMPANY, INC.

Breakdown of Capital Stock

Capital Stock:

First Preferred, 7% Cumulative, Par...........$	100		
Authorized: 800 shares			
Issued: 426 shares.....................		42,600	
Subscribed: 2 shares.....................		200	$42,800
Second Preferred, 4½% Cumulative, Par........$	100		
Authorized: 300 shares			
Issued: 300 shares.....................			30,000
Common, No Par Value			
Authorized: 1,000 shares			
Issued: 100.........................			2,500
Total Capital Stock.......................			$75,300

Source: Auditors' report.

groceries to the line. Regarding the previous management, Mr. Corbett stated:

"The company as managed by Linton and McIvor was a slow-moving, low-volume, high-markup operation. Neither management nor the salesmen were merchandising-conscious: they thought a sale was complete when the goods were delivered and did little to help move products off the retailer's shelf. They bought at the best prices available and added a high enough margin to ensure a net profit of 4% or 5%. This high-price policy, coupled with a sales emphasis on the company's own private brands, resulted in a profitable record until the early 1940's when the company began to have difficulties. Mr. Linton nevertheless continued to run the business on these policies until the day he retired."

In the early 1930's two trends emerged in the grocery business, stated Mr. Corbett. First, margins dropped as increasing chain-store competition caused many independent retailers to turn to higher-volume, lower-markup co-operative and voluntary chain wholesalers. Secondly, advertising by large manufacturers promoted consumer acceptance of national brand names, often at the expense of local wholesalers' private brands.

Continuing, Mr. Frank Corbett said, "Linton's policies, which resulted in high prices, private-label emphasis, and inadequate service to retailers, made the fast-growing, merchandising-conscious, independent supermarket operator stay away from them."

After losses in 1943 and 1944, Mr. Linton sold out to Mr. Frank Corbett in June, 1945. Net sales and net profits had declined slowly

Exhibit 4

LINTON COMPANY, INC.

Graphs of Cost of Goods Sold, Gross Profit, Total Operating Expenses, and Net Profit

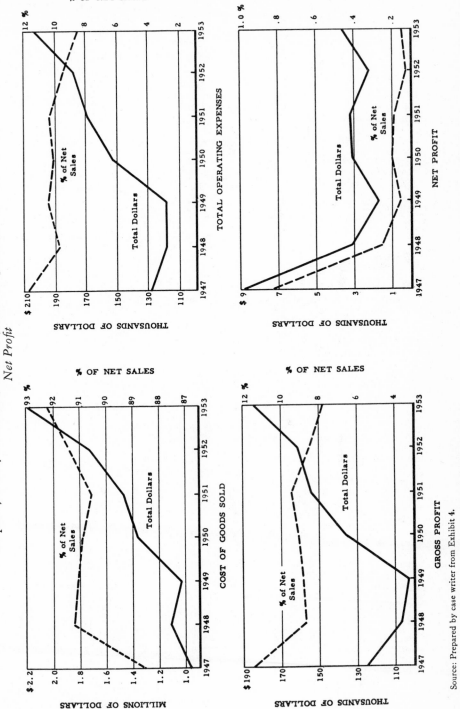

Source: Prepared by case writer from Exhibit 4.

Exhibit 5

LINTON COMPANY, INC.

Operating Statements—Years Ending December 31, 1950–53

	1953 Combined Dollars	Per Cent	1953 Groceries Dollars	Per Cent	Frozen Foods Dollars	Per Cent	1952 Combined Dollars	Per Cent	1952 Groceries Dollars	Per Cent
Sales.........................	2,403,389	101.44	1,526,533	101.43	876,856	101.45	1,899,760	101.34	1,209,359	101.4
Returns and allowances..........	34,126	1.44	21,577	1.43	12,549	1.45	25,182	1.34	17,809	1.4
Net sales.......................	2,369,263	100.00	1,504,956	100.00	864,307	100.00	1,874,578	100.00	1,191,550	100.0
Cost of goods sold										
Beginning inventory..........	189,957		176,180		13,777		186,279		179,599	
Net purchases.................	2,210,991		1,440,655		770,336		1,712,742		1,098,814	
Freight and other expense.......	5,535		5,535				4,723		4,723	
	2,406,483		1,622,370		784,113		1,903,744		1,283,136	
Closing inventory.............	221,981		201,955		20,026		189,957		176,180	
	2,184,502	92.20	1,420,415	94.38	764,087	88.40	1,713,787	91.42	1,106,956	92.9
Gross profit....................	184,761	7.80	84,541	5.62	100,220	11.60	160,791	8.58	84,594	7.1
Operating expenses:										
Selling expense:										
Advertising................	1,813	0.07	1,813	0.12			*		*	
Payroll—sales	41,482	1.75	17,270	1.15	24,212	2.80				
Sales promotion.............	5,412	0.23	1,603	0.11	3,809	0.44				
Payroll burden..............	1,591	0.07	661	0.04	930	0.11				
Incentive commissions.......	.....	....								
Total selling expenses..........	50,298	2.12	21,347	1.42	28,951	3.35	45,114	2.41	23,489	1.9
Warehouse and handling expense:										
Building expenses:										
Taxes—real estate........	898	0.04	898	0.06			*		*	
Mortgage interest.........	1,188	0.05	1,188	0.08						
Repairs..................	1,612	0.07	1,612	0.11						
Depreciation.............	1,545	0.06	1,545	0.10						
Insurance................	283	0.01	283	0.02						
Total building expenses.......	5,526	0.23	5,526	0.37						
Rent......................	2,889	0.12			2,889	0.34				
Light and heat..............	1,993	0.08	1,993	0.13						
Burglar alarm...............	449	0.02	449	0.03						
Fire and extended coverage on										
inventory..............	585	0.03	456	0.03	129	0.01				
Payroll—warehouse........	17,631	0.75	9,074	0.60	8,557	0.99				
Payroll—burden............	959	0.04	494	0.03	465	0.05				
Cornwall Warehouse Company										
payroll................	3,491	0.15	3,491	0.23						
Maintenance and miscellaneous	229	0.01	229	0.02						
Total warehouse and handling...	33,752	1.43	21,712	1.44	12,040	1.39	26,774	1.43	16,418	1.3
Delivery expenses:										
Gas, oil, repairs, dry ice.......	3,141	0.13	2,159	0.14	982	0.11	*		*	
Truck rentals...............	13,316	0.56	5,238	0.35	8,078	0.93				
Insurance—autos, trucks.....	1,179	0.05	1,138	0.08	41	0.01				
Depreciation—autos, trucks...	1,308	0.06	1,308	0.09						
Total rolling stock expense......	18,944	0.80	9,843	0.66	9,101	1.05				
Payroll—delivery...........	20,951	0.88	12,169	0.81	8,782	1.02				
Payroll—burden............	1,124	0.05	654	0.04	470	0.06				
Cornwall Warehouse Company										
payroll.................										
Total delivery expenses.........	41,019	1.73	22,666	1.51	18,353	2.13	41,573	2.22	24,012	2.0

* Subtotals not available for 1952.

Frozen Foods		Combined		1951 Groceries		Frozen Foods		Combined		1950 Groceries		Frozen Foods	
Dollars	Per Cent	Dollars	Per Cent	Dollars	Per Cent	Dollars	Per Cent	Dollars	Per Cent	Dollars	Per Cent	Dollars	Per Cent
90,401	101.08	1,655,196	101.31	1,206,445	101.51	448,751	100.77	1,531,189	101.35	1,348,946	101.46	182,243	100.55
7,373	1.08	21,348	1.31	17,898	1.51	3,450	0.77	20,392	1.35	19,400	1.46	992	0.55
83,028	100.00	1,633,848	100.00	1,188,547	100.00	445,301	100.00	1,510,797	100.00	1,329,546	100.00	181,251	100.00
6,680		211,002		200,251		10,751		130,506		130,506			
13,928		1,449,650		1,050,903		398,747		1,446,945		1,273,787		173,158	
		4,539		4,137		402		7,548		7,265		283	
20,608		1,665,191		1,255,291		409,900		1,584,999		1,411,558		173,441	
13,777		186,279		179,599		6,680		211,002		200,251		10,751	
06,831	88.85	1,478,912	90.52	1,075,692	90.51	403,220	90.55	1,373,997	90.95	1,211,307	91.11	162,690	89.76
76,197	11.15	154,936	9.48	112,855	9.49	42,081	9.45	136,800	9.05	118,239	8.89	18,561	10.24
*	*	5,195	0.32	5,149	0.43	46	0.01	5,408	0.36	5,253	0.39	155	0.08
		26,405	1.61	23,736	2.00	2,669	0.60	36,165	2.39	30,545	2.30	5,620	3.10
		1,060	0.06	698	0.06	362	0.08	1,160	0.08	1,017	0.07	143	0.08
		1,247	0.08	1,122	0.09	125	0.03	1,170	0.08	920	0.07	250	0.14
		305	0.02	305	0.03			88	0.00	88	0.01		
21,625	3.16	34,212	2.09	31,010	2.61	3,202	0.72	43,991	2.91	37,823	2.84	6,168	3.40
*	*	1,019	0.06	1,019	0.09			1,047	0.07	1,047	0.08		
		1,324	0.08	1,324	0.11			1,145	0.08	1,145	0.08		
		1,330	0.08	1,330	0.11			945	0.06	945	0.07		
		1,294	0.08	1,294	0.11			1,295	0.08	1,295	0.10		
		134	0.01	134	0.01			140	0.01	140	0.01		
		5,101	0.31	5,101	0.43			4,572	0.30	4,572	0.34		
		225	0.01			225	0.05	2,019	0.13	2,018	0.15	1	0.00
		1,254	0.08	1,254	0.10			1,638	0.11	1,638	0.12		
		449	0.03	449	0.04			412	0.03	412	0.03		
		297	0.02	211	0.02	86	0.02	414	0.03	378	0.03	36	0.02
		15,294	0.94	6,512	0.55	8,782	1.97	17,750	1.17	14,848	1.12	2,902	1.60
		959	0.06	428	0.04	531	0.12	1,022	0.07	856	0.06	166	0.09
		2,270	0.14	2,270	0.19			1,656	0.11	1,656	0.13		
		197	0.01	158	0.01	39	0.01	158	0.01	141	0.01	17	0.01
10,356	1.52	26,046	1.60	16,383	1.38	9,663	2.17	29,641	1.96	26,519	1.99	3,122	1.72
*	*	3,789	0.23	3,075	0.26	714	0.16	6,630	0.44	3,767	0.28	2,863	1.58
		10,139	0.62	4,284	0.36	5,855	1.32						
		1,127	0.07	1,119	0.10	8	0.00	1,073	0.07	1,073	0.08		
		1,927	0.12	1,927	0.16			1,670	0.11	1,670	0.13		
		16,982	1.04	10,405	0.88	6,577	1.48	9,373	0.62	6,510	0.49	2,863	1.58
		17,008	1.04	10,757	0.90	6,251	1.40	12,025	0.80	9,326	0.70	2,699	1.49
		985	0.06	623	0.05	362	0.08	658	0.04	510	0.04	148	0.08
								318	0.02	318	0.02		
17,561	2.57	34,975	2.14	21,785	1.83	13,190	2.96	22,374	1.48	16,664	1.25	5,710	3.15

Exhibit 5—Continued

LINTON COMPANY, INC.

Operating Statements—Years Ending December 31, 1950–53

	1953 Combined		1953 Groceries		1953 Frozen Foods		1952 Combined		1952 Groceries	
	Dollars	Per Cent	Dollars	Per Cent	Dollars	Per Cent	Dollars	Per Cent	Dollars	Per Ce
Administrative expenses:										
Office and clerical expenses:										
Payroll—clerical and IBM..	15,293	0.64					*	*	*	*
Payroll—burden..........	444	0.02								
IBM rentals.............	5,852	0.25								
IBM supplies.............	1,632	0.07								
Other office and clerical supplies..................	5,377	0.23								
Total office and clerical expenses................	28,598	1.21								
Payroll—executive..........	22,790	0.96								
Payroll—burden............	693	0.03								
Miscellaneous insurance......	716	0.03								
Legal and audit.............	2,226	0.10								
Telephone.................	3,994	0.17								
Travel....................	2,045	0.09								
Dues and subscriptions.......	543	0.02								
Depreciation—furniture and fixtures..................	617	0.03								
Miscellaneous administrative expenses...............	433	0.02								
Cornwall Warehouse Company payroll.................	3,491	0.15								
Miscellaneous taxes and licenses................	491	0.02								
Intracompany charges (red)...										
Total administrative expenses...	66,637	2.81	42,328	2.81	24,309	2.81	55,975	2.98	35,694	3.00
Financial expenses:										
Bank service charges.........	729	0.03					*	*	*	*
Cornwall Warehouse Company expenses...............	2,200	0.09								
Interest expense (except mortgage interest)..........	6,706	0.29								
Estimated loss on accounts receivable................	2,369	0.10								
Donations and contributions..	190	0.01								
Total financial expenses........	12,194	0.52	12,194	0.81			8,820	0.47	8,820	0.7
Total operating expenses........	203,900	8.61	120,247	7.99	83,653	9.68	178,256	9.51	108,433	9.1
Gross operating profit or (loss).....	(19,139)	(0.81)	(35,706)	(2.37)	16,567	1.92	(17,465)	(0.93)	(23,839)	(2.0
Other operating income:										
Promotional advertising........	5,876	0.25	5,876	0.39			4,284	0.23	4,284	0.3
Purchase discounts...........	22,892	0.97	22,892	1.52			17,911	0.95	17,911	1.5
Miscellaneous................	342	0.01	342	0.02			17	0.00	17	0.0
Total other operating income......	29,110	1.23	29,110	1.93			22,212	1.18	22,212	1.8
Net income or (loss) before taxes and other expenses.......	9,971	0.42	(6,596)	(0.44)	16,567	1.92	4,747	0.25	(1,627)	(0.1
Federal and state taxes.........	3,945	0.17					2,331	0.12		
Net cost of life insurance........	2,406	0.10					177	0.01		
	6,351	0.27					2,508	0.13		
Net profit for year..............	3,620	0.15					2,239	0.12		

* Subtotals not available for 1952.

Frozen Foods		Combined		1951 Groceries		Frozen Foods		Combined		1950 Groceries		Frozen Foods	
Dollars	Per Cent	Dollars	Per Cent	Dollars	Per Cent	Dollars	Per Cent	Dollars	Per Cent	Dollars	Per Cent	Dollars	Per Cent
✧	*	12,444	0.76	12,444	1.05			12,510	0.83	11,326	0.85	1,184	0.65
		370	0.02	370	0.03			530	0.03	480	0.04	50	0.03
		4,685	0.29	4,685	0.39			4,254	0.28	4,254	0.32		
		3,048	0.18	3,048	0.26			1,215	0.08	1,215	0.09		
		2,084	0.13	1,935	0.16	149	0.03	2,659	0.18	2,516	0.19	143	0.08
		22,631	1.38	22,482	1.89	149	0.04	21,168	1.40	19,791	1.49	1,377	0.76
		28,860	1.77	28,860	2.43			20,280	1.34	20,280	1.53		
		436	0.03	436	0.04			270	0.02	270	0.02		
		415	0.02	371	0.03	44	0.01	376	0.03	347	0.03	29	0.02
		2,007	0.12	2,007	0.17			1,046	0.07	1,046	0.08		
		2,974	0.18	2,790	0.23	184	0.04	2,751	0.18	2,672	0.20	79	0.04
		1,467	0.09	1,467	0.12			272	0.02	272	0.02		
		484	0.03	484	0.04			499	0.03	495	0.03	4	0.00
		490	0.03	490	0.04			453	0.03	453	0.03		
		606	0.04	506	0.04	100	0.02	483	0.03	461	0.03	22	0.01
		3,405	0.21	3,405	0.29			1,529	0.10	1,529	0.12		
		(15,000)	(1.26)	15,000	3.37			(1,040)	(0.08)	1,040	0.58
20,281	2.97	63,775	3.90	48,298	4.06	15,477	3.48	49,127	3.25	46,576	3.50	2,551	1.41
•	*	499	0.03	499	0.04			444	0.03	444	0.03		
		2,051	0.13	2,051	0.17			1,416	0.09	1,416	0.11		
		6,356	0.39	6,356	0.54			4,937	0.33	4,937	0.37		
		1,655	0.10	1,206	0.10	449	0.10	1,353	0.09	1,171	0.09	182	0.10
		350	0.02	350	0.03			129	0.01	129	0.01		
		10,911	0.67	10,462	0.88	449	0.10	8,279	0.55	8,097	0.61	182	0.10
69,823	10.22	169,919	10.40	127,938	10.76	41,981	9.43	153,412	10.15	135,679	10.20	17,733	9.78
6,374	0.93	(14,983)	(0.92)	(15,083)	(1.27)	100	0.02	(16,612)	(1.10)	(17,440)	(1.31)	828	0.46
		4,187	0.26	4,187	0.35			3,268	0.22	3,268	0.24		
		16,331	1.00	16,331	1.38			18,758	1.24	18,758	1.41		
		384	0.02	384	0.03			227	0.01	227	0.02		
		20,902	1.28	20,902	1.76			22,253	1.47	22,253	1.67		
6,374	0.93	5,919	0.36	5,819	0.49	100	0.02	5,641	0.37	4,813	0.36	828	0.46
		2,788	0.17					2,132	0.14				
		(23)	(0.00)					464	0.03				
		2,765	0.17					2,596	0.17				
		3,154	0.19					3,045	0.20				

Exhibit 6

LINTON COMPANY, INC.

Condensed Statements*—Years Ending December 31, 1947–53

	1953		1952		1951	
Net Sales	$2,369,263	100.00%	$1,874,578	100.00%	$1,633,848	100.00%
Cost of Goods Sold	2,184,502	92.20	1,713,787	91.42	1,478,912	90.52
Gross Profit (Before Purchase Discounts)	184,761	7.80	160,791	8.58	154,936	9.48
Total Operating Expenses	$ 203,900	8.61%	$ 178,256	9.51%	$ 169,919	10.40%
Gross Operating Profit or (loss)	(19,139)	(0.81)	(17,465)	(0.93)	(14,983)	(0.92)
Other Operating Income Including Purchase Discount	29,110	1.23	22,212	1.18	20,902	1.28
Net Income before Taxes and Other Expenses	9,971	0.42	4,747	0.25	5,919	0.36
Net Profit for Year	$ 3,620	0.15%	$ 2,239	0.12%	$ 3,154	0.19%

* See Exhibit 7 for industry averages.
Source: Company records.

from their peak in 1928 until 1944, when sales of $475,000 brought a loss of $4,870. Sales in the first six months of 1945 were $220,000.

Speaking of the business when he took it over, Mr. Corbett said, "Because Linton was a tightfisted old man who saved everything he made, he spent little on the upkeep of the buildings. The warehouse was dark and dingy. Warehousemen who had been employed by the company as long as 10 years were being paid $30 per week, and there were office girls making $25 per week. I sometimes think Linton was forced to sell out because his employees were disgruntled and the organization was going stale."

PURCHASE OF THE BUSINESS

The purchase of the business by Mr. Frank Corbett in June, 1945, was negotiated through Mr. Thomas Kahn, a broker and personal friend of both the Corbett brothers. At that time, Mr. Frank Corbett was general manager of the National Wholesale Company, a large Chicago co-operative grocery wholesaler.

After preliminary negotiation a price of $108,200 was set for the building (subject to a mortgage of $20,000), inventories, and other assets. Since Mr. Corbett had only $800, he obtained a 30-day option for which he paid $500, and then set out to borrow the rest of the purchase price. His first step was to approach the bank he dealt with on behalf of the National company. This bank agreed to lend him $50,000 secured on the Linton inventory. Mr. Corbett described his further money-raising efforts as follows:

	1950		1949		1948		1947	
	$1,510,797	100.00%	$1,140,752	100.00%	$1,216,110	100.00%	$1,089,120	100.00%
	1,373,997	90.95	1,038,473	91.03	1,109,612	91.24	964,536	88.56
	136,800	9.05	102,279	8.97	106,498	8.76	124,584	11.44
$	153,412	10.15%	$ 119,481	10.47%	$ 119,663	9.84%	$ 128,099	11.76%
	(16,612)	(1.10)	(17,202)	(1.50)	(13,165)	(1.08)	(3,515)	(0.32)
	22,253	1.47	18,282	1.60	19,366	1.59	15,163	1.39
	5,641	0.37	1,080	0.10	6,201	0.51	11,648	1.07
$	3,045	0.20%	$ 1,801	0.16%	$ 3,199	0.26%	$ 8,969	0.82%

"My brother Bob was overseas in the navy, but I knew he would come in with me as a partner. We both were reared in our father's wholesale grocery business, and after we got out of college, Bob took a job as sales manager for a large Detroit grocery wholesaler, and I went to work for National. We often talked about how much we would like to be in business together. After I was sure of the bank loan on Linton, I cabled him in Italy and soon had his answer that he would put $6,000, nearly all his savings, in the venture. I then approached friends and relatives, and several of them lent me amounts varying from $500 to $10,000. A final loan of $14,800 from Tom Kahn enabled me to complete the purchase of the business."

OPERATION UNDER NEW MANAGEMENT

"When I took control," Mr. Corbett stated, "I retrained employees in new sales, merchandising, order handling, and billing routines. I attempted to increase efficiency and lower costs in every department. We also exerted every possible effort to increase sales volume. In the 24-month period beginning June, 1945, when certain types of merchandise were still in short supply, stock turnover was more rapid, and markups were higher than in 1953. We earned a net profit of $40,000 on sales of $1,600,000."

Mr. Corbett believed these results were mainly owing to his good friends who stood by him with generous credit lines and extra supplies of hard-to-get merchandise. Because of his contacts and record of increasing sales volume at National, he received preferential treatment from many manufacturers and salesmen.

Exhibit 7

LINTON COMPANY, INC.

Financial Data for Linton Company and Wholesale Grocery Trade

(In Per Cent)

Grocery Wholesalers with Asset Size $250,000 to $1,000,000

	Linton Co.	Industry		
Year	Dec., 1953	1952	1951	1950
Number of statements analyzed	.....	93	80	79
Assets:				
Cash	13.72	5.25	5.45	4.22
Marketable securities	....	0.42	0.56	1.48
Receivables (net)	21.84	21.13	20.05	21.16
Merchandise (net)	55.70	51.92	53.32	52.02
All other	....	1.33	1.18	0.90
Total current	91.26	80.05	80.56	79.78
Plant and equipment	6.94	14.23	13.05	13.45
All other	1.80	5.72	6.39	6.77
Total noncurrent	8.74	19.95	19.44	20.22
Total	100.00	100.00	100.00	100.00
Liabilities:				
Due to banks	30.11	12.45	12.34	13.68
Due to trade	37.86	17.10	13.96	15.44
Federal income taxes	1.59	1.80	2.33	1.80
All other	1.46	7.05	7.93	5.42
Total current	71.02	38.40	36.56	36.34
Due to banks (long term)	6.02	1.39	1.81	1.10
Other long-term debt	....	3.71	3.98	4.54
Total debt	77.04	43.50	42.35	41.98
Reserves	....	0.48	0.52	0.78
Net worth	22.96	56.02	57.13	57.24
Total	100.00	100.00	100.00	100.00
Income data:				
Net sales	100.00	100.00	100.00	100.00
Cost of sales	92.20	92.24	91.51	91.42
Gross profit	7.80	7.76	8.49	8.58
All other expense (net)	7.48	7.02	7.24	7.42
Profit before taxes	0.32	0.74	1.25	1.16
Federal income taxes	0.17	0.34	0.54	0.39
Net profit or loss	0.15	0.40	0.71	0.77
Ratios:				
Current	1.28	2.09	2.20	2.20
Net worth/total noncurrent assets	2.80	2.81	2.94	2.83
Net worth/total debt	0.30	1.29	1.35	1.36
Sales/receivables	27.22	26.13	24.93	21.88
Receivables turnover (days)	13.00	14.00	14.00	16.00
Sales/merchandise	10.67	10.64	9.38	8.90
Merchandise turnover (days)	34.00	34.00	38.00	40.00
Sales/total noncurrent assets	72.53	27.69	25.72	22.89
Sales/net worth	25.90	9.86	8.75	8.09
Profits/net worth	3.96	4.00	6.24	6.21
Sales/total assets	5.94	5.52	5.00	4.63
Profits/total assets	0.91	2.24	3.57	3.55

Source: Adjusted data from Robert Morris Associates Statement Studies (1948 to 1952, inclusive).

In January, 1946, Mr. Robert Corbett received his discharge from the Navy and joined the company. He immediately assumed responsibility for sales and merchandising efforts.

During 1947 the merchandise heretofore hard to get became more plentiful. Pricing became more competitive, and the company cut margins to maintain volume. Selling effort and service were also increased with resultant extra costs. Profits as a percentage of sales declined over the next six years until in 1953 they were 0.15%.

During 1950 Mr. Frank Corbett succeeded, after considerable effort, in obtaining an exclusive distributorship for Apex Frozen Foods, a popular nationally advertised brand. Apex was a subsidiary of the Oshawa Foods Corporation, a large integrated manufacturer with a varied product line. Apex sold all its products through exclusive wholesale distributors until 1952, when it started selling direct to all grocery chains. Former exclusive distributors, however, continued to sell Apex products to all food retailers except chains, and they voluntarily continued to maintain territorial boundaries previously in effect.

"One of our biggest problems is whether we can hold out long enough financially to get the increased volume we need to cover costs and show a better profit," said Mr. Frank Corbett in August, 1953. "We have placed our emphasis on securing large new customers who run modern supermarket-type stores and this policy has kept us in an ever-widening vicious circle of getting more and more volume and at the same time, of needing to cut costs in order to sell these customers on a low-margin basis."

For 1953, Linton Company showed a net profit of $3,620 on sales of $2,369,262 (see Exhibit 5). "The low net profit of 0.15% for 1953 re-emphasizes the fact that our most pressing task is to get the business showing a better net profit," said Mr. Frank Corbett. (See Exhibits 7 and 8 for related industry statistics and information.)

CAPITAL SOURCES

Earnings from June, 1945, to June, 1947, enabled Mr. Frank Corbett to repay all the individuals from whom he had borrowed except those who agreed to transfer their loans to a preferred stock equity. In June, 1947, the capital structure of the business was changed to provide for three different classes of stock (see Exhibit 3). Common stock was owned 90% by Frank Corbett and 10% by Robert Corbett. Voting power was vested in the common unless the first and second preferred dividends were unpaid for two and three years respectively. The Cor-

Exhibit 8

LINTON COMPANY, INC.

Excerpts from Robert Morris Associates
1952 Issue of "Highlights of the Wholesale Grocery Trade"

SUMMARY

The year 1951 marked the sharpest decline in profitability for wholesale grocers in postwar years. Gross profit on sales decreased. Net profit on sales fell from .70% to .45%. Net profit on worth was reduced from 6.1% to 4.3%.

Inventory and receivables turnover rates increased with the increase in sales volume. Turnover of working capital improved without much detrimental change in the working capital position. This again emphasizes the importance of the increased sales volume. Again firms with extremely high turnovers in inventory and receivables earned a higher return on worth. Purchase discounts surpassed the profits before taxes. Percentage of purchase discounts to total purchases declined with an increase in size.

The industry is still characterized by long-established firms with seasoned management. Lower current ratios and a higher proportion of debt characterized the larger firms. Smaller firms showed higher equity. Percentage of wholesale grocers with outstanding bank loans at some time during the year fell from 95% to 93%. Peak borrowing was in the winter and early spring months. Effects of competitive conditions, higher cost of sales, and continued taxation were evidenced in the extremely low profits of the wholesale grocery trade during 1952.

INTRODUCTION

The wholesale grocery business unit is apt to be a one-man operation. The low margin on each product magnifies the importance of small savings in cost and slight improvements in turnover rates. This emphasis on detail may have a tendency to dim perspective on major policy decisions. Good organization and controlled delegation of authority are at a premium.

This study includes 229 companies most of whom are located in the North Central region of the United States. Of these, four are affiliated with a holding company engaged in food distribution; 54, 24%, are in a voluntary group; five are operated as a retailer-owned cooperative; 72, 31% of the sample, sell at cost plus a fixed markup or service charge fee. The information was so incomplete concerning the type of operation that it did not support special tabulation of financial patterns by these types.

Wholesale grocers are generally the most active group of bank borrowers.

The gross profit ratio is highly significant in this business. Oddly enough, a decrease in the ratio can be a signal of greater efficiency. An increase could result from speculation. Sometimes a company with sales that are declining (or at least increasing less rapidly than others) may show an increase in gross due to taking on lines that, while having a better gross, are harder to sell, develop slower turnover of inventory and carry credit problems. Outstanding companies in this business have had an almost steady decrease in gross profit, but the in-

Exhibit 8—Continued

crease in turnover of inventory and receivables has given as much or greater return on invested capital.

The ability of the wholesaler to survive depends upon his capacity to adjust to changing conditions in the performance of his basic economic function of distribution. The credit man should be on the alert for changes in individual companies and judge them in relation to competition. Credit guideposts of the wholesale grocery trade include: the age of the company and the tenure of the present management, the trend of the gross profit ratio, turnover of inventory, purchase discounts earned, receivable turnover, size of average receivable and area sold, aging of accounts and bad debt experience, turnover of working capital seasonal borrowing pattern, and comparative financial progress. In addition, it has been suggested that the credit man should be aware of transportation and selling costs, investments in or loans to retail outlets, changes in proportion of private brand sales and sales to public institutions.

MANAGEMENT

One clue to the quality of management is the age of the business. Another clue may be provided by the length of tenure of present management.

While not statistically provable, there is the belief in informed quarters that the going concern value of a wholesale grocery business is deteriorating. This follows from the rather unique characteristic of more modest but rather constant profits on capital. Under today's tax laws rarely will there be found a case of glamour from a capital gains standpoint. Hence, the capital value suffers from this limited market for transfer of ownership. As a creditor, however, the banker can be reassured on the liquidation value of inventory if it is well balanced and does not contain an important amount of own brand or other stock less advertised and marketable.

betts owned all the stock except $6,000 of the first preferred and $10,000 of the second preferred. Stock owned by outsiders was distributed among eight of their friends and relatives in amounts ranging from $300 to $6,000. For some of these people this investment was a substantial portion of their savings.

Increasing sales had substantially multiplied the need for working capital to enlarge inventories, carry receivables, and provide cash to enable the firm to take discounts. The main sources of funds were increased bank loans and trade credit.

BANKING RELATIONSHIP

In 1946, the original line of credit was increased from $50,000 to $75,000. In 1947, the bank that granted this line merged with another bank, which subsequently withdrew from the Linton arrangement and referred Mr. Corbett to a third bank. Upon reviewing the situation this bank's officers stated that they did not wish to take over the Linton line. They referred Mr. Corbett to Mr. Eaton, vice-president and loaning officer of the North West Bank. After investigating Mr. Corbett's case, Mr. Eaton agreed to have the $75,000 line of credit transferred to the North West Bank. The line of credit, which had gone as high as $160,-000, stood at $120,000 as of April, 1954.

FIELD WAREHOUSING ARRANGEMENT

The bank loan was secured by a field warehousing arrangement involving the entire grocery inventory. Ordinarily warehouse receipts were accepted as collateral by the North West Bank only when they were issued by a bonded warehouse in which the merchandise was clearly marked, segregated, and inventoried. Merchandise was withdrawable from the warehouse only on repayment of the warehouse receipts[1] which had been assigned to the bank as security. Because of the increased labor and paper work entailed in handling merchandise under an ordinary field warehousing arrangement, Mr. Frank Corbett and Mr. Eaton worked out what Mr. Corbett said was a unique system they called "bulk field warehousing." Under this arrangement, which had been in effect since 1947, the Cornwall Warehousing Corporation, a warehouse service organization, was engaged by the bank to be responsible for the segregation, storage, and inspection of the pledged goods,[2] which were all kept in the Linton warehouse. Two Linton employees were placed in the employ of the Cornwall company. One was a warehouse worker, who padlocked all the doors every night; the other worked in the office and checked the IBM inventory system report on the total merchandise. The Linton Company reimbursed the Cornwall company for the salaries of these two men.

Under the warehousing agreement Linton was allowed a shipping leeway of 10,000 case units amounting to a $45,000 weekly volume. The office manager examined the IBM records of the units shipped each

---

[1] For example, if 10,000 cases of salmon valued at $5 per case were put in a field warehouse and the bank specified a margin of 25% on the loan, the company would be able to borrow $37,000 on the $50,000 worth of salmon kept as security by the bank. The warehouse manager would then, in effect, sell the salmon back to the wholesaler or grocer for $3.75 per case. In this manner the bank lent the grocer funds to pay for inventory and the grocer repaid the bank in proportion as he drew on the inventory.

[2] Large signs in the warehouse stated, "The merchandise in this warehouse is the property of the Cornwall Warehousing Corporation." Stickers on the merchandise also identified it as belonging to the Cornwall Warehousing Corporation. The company padlocked all the doors of the warehouse every night as required by law. In accordance with the bank's insurance requirements, a sprinkler system had been installed throughout the office and warehouse.

day to make sure that the company was not shipping more than the quota allowed. Every Friday a special report of the total units shipped and received daily for the past week was sent to the bank and the ware-housing company.

"Mr. Eaton understands our problem and is a real help in managing our financial situation," stated Mr. Corbett. "However, he is anxious about the loan and has to justify the amount to the bank's board, which seems to be putting pressure on him to get out of the loan so that the money can be lent to a more profitable business under a simpler and more secure collateral arrangement. I don't know what I would do if the loan were called."

"Our long-term objective," said Mr. Corbett, "is to pay the bank loan off and own the business free of debt."

SUPPLIER CREDIT RELATIONS

In Mr. Corbett's opinion Linton received more generous credit ac-commodations than the average grocery wholesaler. The Oshawa Food Company, for example, extended $45,000 and $25,000 lines of credit on Apex frozen foods and grocery items respectively.

Supplier's credit departments ordinarily checked closely on whole-salers' financial conditions and required certified copies of all financial reports. Grocery manufacturers generally maintained strict terms of 2% discount 10 days from invoice date, net 30 days, except in unusual situations. The nondiscounting of an invoice by a wholesaler was a serious indication of financial weakness. When an invoice was not paid within 30 days, grocery manufacturers had been known to cancel all credit and place the wholesaler on a cash-payment basis. Terms on frozen foods were typically net 10 days. Mr. Corbett stated that the average wholesaler was considered to have made par on discounts if he averaged 1.5% of grocery purchases.

Since cash discounts were one of the most important sources of "in-come" or cost savings to a grocery wholesaler, it was vital that the com-pany take discounts. "We've been in a few jams in the past when our cash was so low we weren't able to take discounts," said Mr. Corbett.

POSSIBLE SOURCES OF CAPITAL

To obtain more permanent capital Mr. Frank Corbett was investi-gating the possibility of a sale and lease-back arrangement on the ware-house and office building. Although this building was mortgaged for $26,000, he thought it could be sold for $70,000 to $80,000, which would give the company additional capital amounting to approximately $50,000. It had been appraised at $165,000 by an engineering consultant in February, 1953, and was insured for $130,000.

The Corbetts thought they might be able to sell more stock to some of their friends and relatives but had not yet approached anyone in this matter. "We both have too much pride to ask any of our friends or relatives for money. Possibly some of them could help us, but this is about the fastest way I know to lose their friendship," said Mr. Frank Corbett.

SALES

Mr. Corbett stated that grocery wholesaling was extremely competitive. Brand merchandise was the same no matter which wholesaler sold it, and a price difference of only a few cents on a $100 purchase would cause a retailer to change suppliers unless he received some important service for the additional cost. "There are about 25 dry grocery wholesalers, 3 frozen-foods wholesalers, and 3 wholesalers carrying both lines that compete with us in some area of our territory," said Mr. Corbett.

"In order to keep our product line up to date with the retailer's needs," said Mr. Corbett, "we usually take on about 20 new items each month and drop 10 to 15 old ones. Most of these changes are in package sizes, but we do add some new products every month. In 1954, new products seem to have been mostly baking mixes and drug items. All new products are taken on an experimental basis and continued permanently only if results warrant."

"Private labels," stated Mr. Corbett, "are 'a thing of the past' because advertising has made the consumer want national brand names. Fifteen years ago Linton made a good profit on private brands because the firm was able to sell at a price differential of $2 or $3 a case. Now, because of increased costs for small manufacturers and cost savings by large-volume producers, we are able to undercut name brands by only 25 to 30 cents per case of 24 cans. When figured on a per can basis, the private-brand price differential has fallen so much it can't overcome name-brand appeal."

Because of limited working capital Linton concentrated its sales efforts on customers who were able to pay on short terms, rather than on the type of retailer who required extended credit. The latter usually purchased in small quantities and could be charged higher prices, stated Mr. Corbett.

In addition to Mr. Robert Corbett, who covered 25 of the best accounts, the company had 2 other grocery salesmen. Number and size of accounts covered by each are shown in Exhibit 9. There were also 4 frozen-food salesmen who were order takers only and were paid on a salary-plus-bonus basis.

A policy of reduction on the number of retail accounts and salesmen began in 1952 as the result of a survey which showed that 80% of sales volume came from less than 20% of the customers. Since this survey also showed that most customers split their purchases between two or three different wholesalers, the Corbetts concluded that they could increase volume and cut cost by dropping their smaller accounts and trying to obtain a larger percentage of their large customers' business. The total number of customers had been reduced from about 700 to 405 between September, 1952, and July, 1953. The company had also reduced the number of grocery salesmen from 6 to 2 in the same period. The objective was to cut back further to 60 customers who without a salesman's call would make purchases amounting to at least $500 weekly by mail or phone.

The 1952 customer survey was made as a preliminary study before Linton initiated a "cost plus 3, plus 9" plan under contract with the Nation-Wide voluntary chain of wholesale and retail grocery outlets. Under the Nation-Wide plan prices to selected retail customers were cost plus freight in before discounts, plus a 3% markup and a flat $9 weekly service charge, f.o.b. Linton's warehouse. There was in addition a transportation fee of 4 cents a case. For example, if a retailer bought $1,000 worth of merchandise weekly, he would pay $30 for markup plus the $9 service fee, or a total of $39 plus transportation and the basic cost of merchandise. For accounts of $300 and $1,000 weekly volume, this plan gave a markup of approximately 6% and 3.9%, respectively. The objectives of the plan were to effect an increase in the size of accounts and attract larger ones on which the company could operate profitably with a much smaller margin. Sales and delivery expenses on "cost plus 3, plus 9" business were reduced because the customer ordered weekly on an order sheet without a salesman calling. Also, the number of deliveries was set at one per week plus a limited number of emergency deliveries. A policy of a $100 minimum order for each delivery was strictly enforced under the plan. "Cost plus 3, plus 9" customers paid for merchandise by sending signed "blank" checks with each order.

The Nation-Wide organization was one of the oldest voluntary

Exhibit 9

LINTON COMPANY, INC.
Grocery* Customer Analysis—September, 1953

VOLUME OF PURCHASE

Class	Purchases per Week
A+	$300 or over
A	$100 to $300
B	$ 50 to $100
C	$ 25 to $ 50
D	$ 15 to $ 25
E	Under $15

SALESMAN	NUMBER OF CUSTOMERS ON BOOKS	TOTAL SALES	CLASS A+			CLASS A			CLASS B			CLASS C			CLASS D			CLASS E		
			Number	Per Cent	Approximate Weekly Volume	Number	Per Cent	Approximate Weekly Volume	Number	Per Cent	Approximate Weekly Volume	Number	Per Cent	Approximate Weekly Volume	Number	Per Cent	Approximate Weekly Volume	Number	Per Cent	Approximate Weekly Volume
Office	178	$ 5,009	2	1%	$ 700	6	3%	$1,200	11	6%	$ 825	13	7%	$ 494	33	18%	$660	113	65%	$1,130
Cost +3 +9†	25	8,000	20	80	7,000	5	20	1,000	..	..	..	..	..	..	..	..	..	..	..	..
W. F. Keeler	92	7,736	3	3	1,050	16	17	3,200	28	30	2,100	32	35	1,216	4	5	80	9	10	90
D. C. Manio	110	9,768	4	4	1,400	22	20	4,400	32	29	2,400	36	32	1,368	4	4	80	12	11	120
	405	$30,513	29	7%	$10,150	49	12	$9,800	71	18%	$5,325	81	20%	$3,078	41	10%	$820	134	33%	$1,340

* Frozen-food customer analysis not available.
† Sold on the basis of a weekly order sheet mailed or phoned to the office.
Source: Company records.

wholesaler-retailer co-operative groups. Under the Nation-Wide plan selected wholesalers were granted a franchise for an exclusive territory. Each wholesaler paid the Nation-Wide organization a fee based on annual sales volume. The wholesaler granted local grocery stores a retail franchise in the Nation-Wide Food Store Service Fee Plan.

Under the Nation-Wide contract with the retailer Linton agreed: to allow the retailer the use of Nation-Wide store signs and insignia; to service the retailer's merchandise needs satisfactorily; to supervise retailer merchandising efforts; to supply advertising material; to assist in planning store layout; to educate and train retail store personnel by means of letters, bulletins, and meetings; and to furnish store signs on a rental basis. In return the retailer agreed: to pay for merchandise on Linton's terms; to pay for other services and material on a nominal fee basis; to order merchandise on a weekly basis; and to co-operate in advertising and merchandising plans, including local newspaper advertising.

Since joining the organization Linton had succeeded in getting 25 large independent supermarket accounts on this plan. "Naturally," said Mr. Corbett, "we signed up our best and most co-operative customers first, and from now on it undoubtedly will be much harder to get additional customers on the "cost plus 3, plus 9" plan. Mr. Robert Corbett stated that he was planning to retrain the two remaining grocery salesmen as sales supervisors under the Nation-Wide sales plan. Their main job then would be to check displays, floor planning, and other merchandising aspects of the stores on the "cost plus 3, plus 9" plan.

Exhibit 9 shows an analysis of retail customers by volume of purchases according to the company's IBM records as of September 20, 1953.

Exhibit 10 shows a customer breakdown by frequency of purchase as of September 20, 1953. From this exhibit it can be seen that customers who, according to Mr. Corbett, were practically valueless made up 50% of the customer list. Mr. Corbett stated that extra profits could be made if invoicing, delivery, selling, and other services, which were of a "roughly fixed-cost nature" for each customer, could be eliminated for this 50% of Linton outlets. Nevertheless, there were important practical difficulties in dropping the smaller customers, stated Mr. Corbett. A "D" or "E" customer was often in the same vicinity as an "A" or "A plus" customer, and under these circumstances a salesman could call and delivery could be made to handle the business at practically no additional cost.

Exhibit 10

LINTON COMPANY, INC.

Grocery Customer Analysis by Frequency of Purchase—1953

Mr. Frank Corbett's Classifications	Number of Customers	Percentage of Customers
Customers who all buy once a week ("Cost + 3 + 9").....................	25	6%
Regular customers who buy every week......	89	22
Buy regularly at least twice a month........	76	19
Buy regularly once a month................	27	7
Buy irregularly less than once a month— practically no value.....................	72	18
Buy irregularly and very seldom—hardly worthy of the name "customer".........	116	28
Totals.............................	405	100%

Source: Company IBM records.

Mr. Frank Corbett went over an IBM sales analysis summary sheet with each of the salesmen every Friday afternoon. This sheet listed customers by name, address, amount of sales for the week, and amounts owed to the company. Except for "cost plus 3, plus 9" customers, the company sold to retail outlets on a net 7-day basis. Institutions were allowed net 30-day terms. The average collection period of accounts receivable had been kept down to approximately 15 days through enforcement of a strict credit policy, stated Mr. Corbett.

Because of the small net profit, Mr. Frank Corbett had been searching for some plan to increase sales volume over what he called the "break-even point" which he believed was $3,500,000 in October, 1953. He thought that exceeding this volume would make the difference between a substantial net profit and the marginal profits the company was earning.

Mr. Robert Corbett had made the suggestion of trying to increase profits by raising markup on all products 1%. This action was not feasible, Mr. Frank Corbett said, because such an increase would price many products out of competition. He stated, however, that they were always trying to raise total markup by increasing the margin on some items as much as 3% and edging it up possibly ½ of 1% even on competitive staple items. Mr. Frank Corbett stated that he and his brother studied all markup and turnover ratios regularly to eliminate slow moving or low-profit products.

The 1953 net profit proved, said Mr. Frank Corbett, the need for a sales increase in the more profitable large-volume customers. He estimated that, if the company could sell an extra $2,000 weekly in frozen foods at only 5% gross margin, instead of the regular 10%, gross income would increase $100 per week. If $5,000 extra grocery volume could be sold at 2% instead of the regular 6%, there would be an additional $100 gross margin, or a total of $200 per week. Mr. Corbett said that the cost of the total additional volume could not possibly exceed $100 per week. This meant that the $7,000 extra weekly volume would give an additional net profit before taxes of $5,200.

The foregoing line of reasoning caused Mr. Corbett to consider whether the company should enter into a *sub rosa* agreement with one or two large independent supermarkets. Under such an agreement the supermarket would buy in large volume at a lower price than regular customers. Because this type of supermarket did a heavy volume, Mr. Frank Corbett thought his company might possibly sell as much as $15,000 a week to any one of them. He thought that within 10 miles of the warehouse there were seven or eight stores of this type that might be agreeable to such an arrangement. Many wholesalers, he said, were turning to this expedient of offering a price advantage to a few large independent supermarkets to induce them to buy in large volume that could be handled at a low cost, while at the same time they tried to maintain, and break even on, sales to their regular customers to whom they sold on their usual terms. Thus these wholesalers were able to increase sales over the break-even point and realize an added profit.

Because a wholesaler was ultimately dependent on retailers, Mr. Frank Corbett was thinking of eventually entering the retail business by owning or leasing a chain of supermarkets. In order to do this, the company would have to enlarge its facilities to handle perishables, dairy products, health and beauty aids, and other items formerly carried mainly by drugstores. A meat department would also be necessary. Mr. Corbett stated that he and his brother did not know the meat business, and that in five to ten years they might be in a position to hire a man who knew this business.

WAREHOUSE AND OFFICE FACILITIES

Grocery warehouse and office space in Elgin totaled 21,000 square feet on three floors (see Exhibit 11). Because the Elgin warehouse had no cold storage, Linton rented a frozen-food warehouse, 7,000 square feet in area. In March, 1954, every available inch of warehouse and office space was being used for storage. Even in the garage cases of merchandise were stacked to the ceiling. "To attain sales of $4,000,000,

Exhibit 11

LINTON COMPANY, INC.

Plan of Elgin Warehouse and Offices

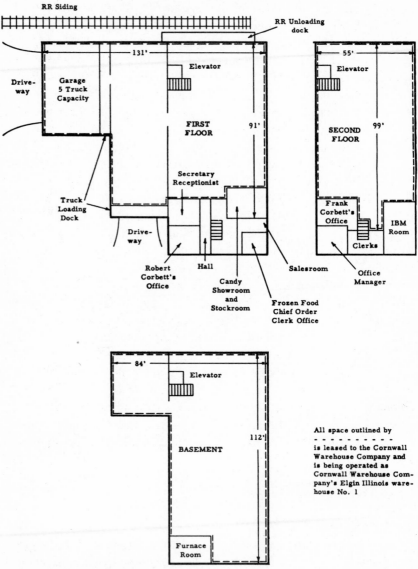

Source: Company records.

which is our immediate goal, we definitely need extra space," Mr. Corbett said. "In addition, we are severely hampered by the multiple-story building, which prevents the use of a modern conveyor system, lift trucks, or other new techniques of merchandise-handling. At present we are handling merchandise five or six times before it reaches a customer, whereas competitors handle their merchandise only two or three times on the average." Mr. Corbett estimated that warehouse salaries could be cut by $7,500 annually if space were available to use more modern methods. "This extra salary cost is a direct drain on profits," he said.

Mr. Corbett had recently asked a carpenter to estimate the cost of building an additional 3,000 square feet of warehouse space adjoining the present building. In his opinion, however, what the company actually needed was a one-floor warehouse of at least 35,000 square feet in area. Mr. Corbett had seen estimates of $5 per square foot to build an ordinary cement-block building without offices. "Eventually," he said, "we wish to sell the building and move."

"The present location," Mr. Corbett stated, "is not the best possible in 1954 because the center of the company's market area has shifted toward the South. On goods sold south or west of Chicago there is a double haul because we have to transfer nearly all merchandise from Chicago, which is the lake port and shipping terminal, to Elgin and then back again." Mr. Frank Corbett thought the best location would be in Chicago or possibly Springdale, where the frozen-food warehouse was located.

Because of the company's restricted financial position and the risk of losing volume if the business were moved, Mr. Frank Corbett thought the bank would not allow a move until the walls were actually "bulging." He considered the move at least five years away and was not looking for another building at present. He was reluctant to talk to Mr. Eaton on this subject.

Lack of space and capital made it impossible for the company to add to its line the meats, perishables, or beauty items[3] which were becoming increasingly a necessity to a wholesaler serving the large supermarket-type store. Candy products and various sundries, however, had been added to fill out the line during the previous year.

OFFICE OPERATION

The office staff handled all the paper work necessary in processing accounts payable, invoicing, collections, and general accounting.

In 1947 the company began to change its accounting operation to IBM machines. Inventory accounting was the first to be put on IBM

---

[3] Items such as deodorants, lipsticks, cold creams, lotions, etc.

and it required one and one-half years to get the new system functioning smoothly. Sales and invoicing were put on IBM in 1950, and in the
spring of 1953 the accounts receivable tabulation for frozen foods was
added. The frozen-food receivables tabulation had worked out so well
that in July, 1953, the company changed grocery receivables accounting to IBM. When the transition from the old manual system of bookkeeping to IBM had been completed, five people would be able to do
the work that six were previously doing. Moreover, because all accounting personnel would be trained on all IBM operations, jobs would be
interchangeable and the company would not have to keep an extra
worker to allow for absences. When the switch to IBM was complete,
over one-third more work could be handled in the office without addition to the present staff, stated Mr. Frank Corbett, since the company
was "practically on a minimum-charge basis" with respect to expenses
for IBM operation. Commenting further on the company operations in
general, Mr. Corbett stated, in August, 1953, "We have just reached
the break-even point. Right now our volume just gets rid of cost. With
a higher volume and the same expense we'll be making a better profit."

Weekly office payroll included Mr. Davis, office manager, at $75, a
billing clerk working for the Cornwall warehouse company at $52, two
IBM girls at $47 each, and two clerks at $40 each.

CONTROL

In an effort to find where he could save on cost to increase profits,
Mr. Corbett had studied the cost breakdowns on the operating statements carefully. He thought that costs could not be lowered appreciably
and that an increase in volume was necessary. "I am no longer interested in percentages," he said, "because the trend in the grocery business
is to take a lower profit percentage on a higher volume. If we strive for
lower margins and higher volume, competitors in the territory would
be squeezed out," he stated. As volume increased, Mr. Corbett said,
overhead expenses became less in proportion, and the company could
cut costs still more and therefore get a higher volume, which ultimately
meant more profit.

ORGANIZATION

As shown in Exhibit 12, Mr. Frank Corbett, the president and Mr.
Robert Corbett, vice-president and sales manager, shared the management function of the business. Each could handle the other's job without difficulty; but, Mr. Frank Corbett stated, his brother took more of

Exhibit 12

LINTON COMPANY, INC.

Organization Chart

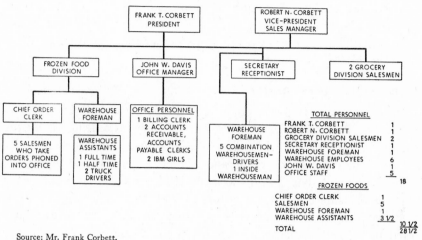

Source: Mr. Frank Corbett.

the responsibility for the grocery division. Mr. Robert Corbett did most of the grocery purchasing and spent a good deal of his time on grocery sales, warehousing, and delivery operations. Mr. Frank Corbett spent a large amount of his time supervising the office staff that handled payments and billing. Mr. Frank Corbett also took the major responsibility for the frozen-foods division. Under him were the chief frozen-food order clerk, the frozen-food warehouse foreman, two warehouse assistants and two truck drivers who also worked in this division. Although each brother spent most of his time on these respective duties, each usually knew what the other was doing and they talked over problems many times a day.

The office manager, Mr. John W. Davis, age forty-two, was with the company when Mr. Frank Corbett bought it. Under Mr. Corbett's almost constant supervision he was responsible for seeing that the routine payment and invoicing work was done by the office staff.

"If he or his brother were taken from the business suddenly," Mr. Frank Corbett stated, "one of the older warehouse hands could come in and perform most of the jobs except buying." This he thought could be done only by himself or Robert. He said that there were "three or four warehouse men who knew the business well." They had been trained under Mr. Linton. "The organization would be capable of carrying on adequately if either Bob or I had to leave for some time," said Mr. Corbett.

In 1953 the board of directors was composed of Frank and Robert Corbett and Mr. Davis. It functioned, said Mr. Corbett, in name only. He wanted to ask both Mr. Eaton and Mr. Kahn to serve on the board but hesitated because he thought it might take too much of their time. "There is also the question of whether they would consider it an honor to be asked to serve on our board and whether they could do anything for us at present," he stated.

DUTIES OF MR. FRANK CORBETT

"The first thing I do every morning, usually between 8:00 A.M. and 8:15 A.M., is to talk with Mr. Davis to see what his schedule is for the day," said Mr. Frank Corbett. "I check back several times each day to see what the office staff is doing and whether payments and billing are being kept up to date. I also check the IBM operators once or twice a day to make sure they are not falling behind. Every morning I go over credit accounts with Mr. Davis to see that payments are up to date. I often phone overdue accounts myself to put pressure on them to pay bills. Another major aspect of my work is scheduling the payment of all bills. Mr. Davis might be able to do this, but I don't let him because it requires my judgment to decide which bills should be paid quickly and which can go for two or three days longer. I keep a running summary of all receipts and disbursements so that I know what the bank balance is at any time during the day. This helps avoid overdrawing our account." In handling this task Mr. Corbett examined with Mr. Davis all incoming invoices, checks from customers, and adding-machine tapes of cash receipts two or three times each day. Mr. Corbett was also in charge of payroll, an activity which took four or five hours of his time each week. He stated that about 30% of his time was spent on careful control of the credit and financial aspects of the business. This control was necessary, he said, because of the company's lack of working capital. In conference with his brother he made daily checks on turnover, markup, and pricing statistics, and they discussed markup and turnover ratios and any complaints received on pricing, delivery, or quality of the merchandise.

He also checked with the frozen-foods chief order clerk to keep posted on total sales and sales by each salesman. In the frozen-foods division, Mr. Frank Corbett set prices and handled all the purchasing except for basic staple items, on which the chief order clerk could purchase up to seven days' supply in advance. He received two calls a day from each of the salesmen regarding complaints, questions, and prices. He often talked to salesmen in the office regarding complaints or other matters. He also supervised the frozen-food warehouse man and with him checked the drivers' routes and mileage, since the frozen-food drivers were paid by mileage. He received visits from customers and suppliers, averaging about five a day.

Mr. Frank Corbett very seldom had time to work on even a 10-minute job straight through until it was finished and was nearly always working on two or three problems at the same time. His secretary counted 72 telephone calls that he handled in one day from 8:30 A.M. to 5:00 P.M.

Mr. Frank Corbett handled the company's bank relationship and worked with the auditors. He left the office at about 6:00 P.M. daily except for one or two nights a week when he worked until 11:30 P.M. or 12:00 midnight. Since the regular help left at 5:00 P.M., he used the time from 5:00 to 6:00 to finish odd jobs and talk over the events of the day with his brother. He and Robert both came in every Saturday morning to discuss general policy questions and finish up work they had not been able to do during the week.

DUTIES OF MR. ROBERT N. CORBETT

Mr. Robert Corbett came to work every morning at 6:00 A.M. His first job was to pick up merchandise invoices that had come in the previous day and plan the early morning Chicago pickup trips by the company's trucks.[4] About 7:00 A.M. the shipper came to work and together they planned the truck routes for the day and attended to the paper work of filling orders. After the truck routing was started, Mr. Robert Corbett looked over the mail and checked the previous day's cash-and-carry sales. As grocery sales manager he dealt with problems of the grocery salesmen and customer complaints, except those that were referred to his brother. He also was responsible for the Nation-Wide "cost plus 3, plus 9" program. He passed on customers brought into the program and handled all details and problems arising from it. On Mondays and Tuesdays, which were the heaviest days of the week for telephone orders, he helped take telephone orders. Two days a week he spent on the road handling directly 25 of the company's biggest-volume customers. He set all grocery-division prices and markups and kept customers and salesmen posted on changes. He worked closely with the grocery-warehouse foremen to make sure that orders were being shipped promptly and that stock was being moved out quickly.

---

[4] By doing its own trucking from Chicago to Elgin, the company saved approximately $40 per week on the haulage of goods from Chicago warehouses to Elgin.

On Wednesdays from 9:00 to 11:00 A.M. and from 1:00 to 3:00 P.M., he interviewed suppliers' salesmen and did the buying. Most afternoons were spent working on promotion plans and making up advertisements for retailers. He also planned the company's bulletin, a small newspaper that under the Nation-Wide heading was sent to the Nation-Wide Plan retailers.

"I like working the long hours and often stay at the office until 11:00 P.M.," said Mr. Robert Corbett. "I have done it all my life and find it thoroughly enjoyable. This is the usual thing in the wholesale grocery business and many of our competitors do the same. It is nothing to stay late and finish up the work that hasn't been done when there aren't enough hours in the day." Mr. Frank Corbett stated that "Bob was into everything" in some way, that he was generally the first one in the office every morning and the last out every night. He handled a minimum of 50 incoming phone calls each day and made about 25 himself to handle the business he was responsible for.

.   .   .   .

Following are two incidents which the case writer recorded in his notes on the Linton Company:

A

After receiving his mail one morning in March, 1954, Mr. Frank Corbett hurriedly called his brother Robert into his office. The following conversation then took place:

FRANK CORBETT: Bob, here's a check for $7,000 from Tom Kahn. It just came through the mail. He wants this much of our first preferred stock.

ROBERT CORBETT: Well, that's good news! But what are we going to do with it? (*Points to the check.*)

FRANK CORBETT: Well. . . .

ROBERT CORBETT: How about buying some of that frozen broccoli? We could make an extra two cents a package on it because the price is going up again next week. We could take 90 cases,[5] and that would be . . . let's see (*figures on a piece of paper*) . . . an inventory profit of $43.20. On second thought, Frank, don't you think we should just slap this in the bank?

FRANK CORBETT: Well . . . yes, I guess we should, but I was talking to the

---

[5] A case of frozen broccoli contained 24 packages and cost Linton $2.91. The company's policy was to pass cost increases on to customers one week after the manufacturer changed his price regardless of what the company paid for the merchandise it already had in inventory when the price increase was announced. Since inventories purchased at the old price were seldom sold out during the week the company made an "inventory profit" on the remaining stock purchased at the lower price.

Federal Foods salesman on the phone this morning, and three of their canned baby foods are going up 10 cents a case tomorrow. If we ordered today, we could take 50 cases of each.

ROBERT CORBETT: Wait just a minute till I check the IBM clerk to see what we have on hand. (*Phones clerk regarding stock on hand.*) We've already got plenty of broccoli and baby foods in stock so this would all be extra.

FRANK CORBETT: Well, we don't have much space to put it in, but I hate to pass this up. It's the easiest way there is to make money in this business!

ROBERT CORBETT: Say, that's my phone, and I've got to get right over to Silver's. Why don't we talk this over at lunch?

FRANK CORBETT: Okay, see you then!

The sale of $7,000 of the Linton Company's first preferred stock to Mr. Kahn had been accomplished as a result of a long talk about the business that Mr. Frank Corbett had with Mr. Kahn during a game of golf in Florida earlier in the winter.

"I explained the difficulties we were having because of our lack of capital, and Tom offered to help us out to this extent. He has been a good friend to Bob and me for many years now, and this probably was an important factor in his risking $7,000 in our business," said Mr. Corbett. Mr. Kahn had interests in several businesses and owned a large office building in Chicago. He was considered by both the Corbetts to be a very astute businessman.

.   .   .   .

B

In April, 1954, Mr. Robert Corbett received the following letter at his home:

PATTERSON FOODS, INC.[6]

Office of the President

April 5, 1954

PERSONAL - CONFIDENTIAL

Mr. Robert N. Corbett
732 Irving Drive
Elgin, Illinois

DEAR MR. CORBETT:

In our program of investigating possible candidates for the newly created executive position of merchandising manager in the Ready-Mix division of

---

[6] The Patterson Foods Company was one of the nation's largest grocery product manufacturers with sales over $100,000,000 annually.

our company your name has been recommended to me from several sources in the grocery trade. In this regard I am wondering if you would be interested in meeting with me and several other members of our management sometime before Friday, April 23, to discuss the possibility of your joining our company in this capacity.

The position of merchandising manager of the Ready-Mix division has been created as a result of a definite need for someone to assume responsibility for the combination of sales promotion and advertising efforts at the wholesaler and retailer levels of our business.

From inquiries made in our own organization and other trade sources we feel that your background and experience in the grocery business are ideally suited to the requirements of this position.

We expect that this position would lead, in a short time, to a top-management position in the marketing department of our business.

We are prepared to offer you a salary in the five-figure bracket with a substantial increase over your present earnings.

May we hear from you on this?

> Sincerely,
> /s/ JEFFREY C. ROBBINS
> *President*

When he came to work the next morning, Mr. Robert Corbett showed the letter to his brother Frank. After Frank had read and studied the letter for several minutes, the following conversation took place:

FRANK CORBETT: That's some letter, Bob! What do you think of it?

ROBERT CORBETT: Well, my first reaction was "no"! We've put so much time, effort, and money into this business that now it seems like part of us . . . (*pause*).

FRANK CORBETT: Sure.

ROBERT CORBETT: I would never pull out if I didn't think that would be the best move in the long run for you and me and the business. But you know, Frank, I got to thinking about the possibilities here for you if I took this job. You could take over sales, let Davis take over responsibilities for the office and bank balances, break in Bill or Tony on purchasing, and run the business by yourself. Without my salary and expenses, profit would take a real jump.

FRANK CORBETT: You're saying this is really a one-boss business? And that I could make more. . . .

ROBERT CORBETT: I don't know. I'm really just thinking out loud—but what do you say? I should reply to this letter sometime in the next day or two at the most. I could get enthusiastic about this job (*points to letter*), but if we could make out better in the long run together here I'd sooner stay put. What do you think?

Research, Inc.

IN EARLY 1958 Research, Inc., commonly referred to as Searchco, with home offices in Waltham, Massachusetts, and three branch offices in the Northeast, was primarily engaged in research and development, largely under government contract. Commercial business—mainly a limited line of gamma radiography equipment[1] together with some research and development for commercial concerns—accounted for about 8.2% of the approximately $2.2 million gross income for 1957. Another 7.1% of gross income came from partly owned subsidiaries working on company-developed electrical power supply and photographic products. (See Exhibits 1 and 2 for selected financial data.)

In 1958 the company, founded in 1951, employed about 190 people, 70 of whom were administrative, the rest technical. The latter, about one-fourth of whom held Ph.D.'s, were trained and experienced in such fields as operations research, physics, chemistry, nucleonics, electronics, and applied mechanics. In its six-year history, however, the company had specialized in operations research. A layman's definition of this term was provided by one company scientist as follows:

> Operations research is an analytical process in which several people representing several different scientific disciplines get together to solve a problem They may spend some time defining the problem in a way they can handle it, determining the kinds of data they will need, and selecting the best way or ways of analyzing these data. The big advantage of operations research lies in the interdisciplinary talents it brings to the problem. A physicist, for example, can see the limitations of the way an electronics engineer would usually approach the problem, and vice versa. Between them, they should be able to devise a better way of solving a particular problem than they could severally. This approach is particularly good for very complex technical problems requiring high-powered computing equipment.

---

[1] Gamma radiography is a nondestructive method of testing solids by using the rays of radioactive isotopes to produce radiographs which reveal internal flaws in the material being tested. It resembles radiography by X rays, except that the equipment is typically smaller, requires no reliance on electrical power, and is hence more flexible. In 1958 Research, Inc., was one of very few producers of a standard line of gamma radiography equipment. The cost of a typical installation was about $2,500.

Exhibit 1

RESEARCH, INC.

Selected Financial Data

(Dollars in Nearest Thousands)

OPERATING RESULTS	PERIOD ENDING SEPTEMBER 30	
	1952	1957
Gross income:		
R & D contracts (government)..........	$160	$1,902
Commercial........................		185
Subsidiaries*		
Watts, Inc.........................		149
Developers Company................		10
Total.............................	$160	$2,246
Operating profit on R & D contracts.......	$ 4	$ 122
Operating profit on commercial sales.......		$ 32
Total net operating profit before federal income tax†..............	$ 1	$ 131

* These amounts were paid to the company for technical services performed, at cost.
† Total operating profit less "other expenses."

Net Income after Taxes for the Five Years, October 1, 1952 to September 30, 1957

	PERIOD ENDING SEPTEMBER 30				
	1953	1954	1955	1956	1957
Net income....................	$9	$10	$17	$40	$66
As % of gross income..........	3.0%	2.1%	2.8%	3.2%	2.9%
Shares of common stock outstanding................	114,541	106,266	107,282	230,595	230,595
Net income per share of common (in actual dollars)....	$0.08	$0.09	$0.16	$0.17	$0.28

Source: Company records.

According to company officers, Searchco was highly regarded, especially among the various government contracting officers, for its competence in this field.

FACILITIES

Company-owned facilities in Waltham, Massachusetts, included approximately 70,000 square feet of laboratory, shop, and office space in a building of modern design constructed in 1956. The laboratories were equipped with the latest standard devices for experiments in electronics,

Exhibit 2

RESEARCH, INC.

Balance Sheets, as of September 30, 1952, and 1955–57
(Dollars in Nearest Thousands)

Assets	1952	1955	1956	1957
Current Assets:				
Cash..	$ 46	$ 31	$ 106	$ 41
U.S. Government Securities, at Cost..............	...	10	72	...
Accounts Receivable:				
U.S. Government............................	24	37	117	437
Other......................................	24	9	19	75
Unbilled Expenditures on Research and Development Contracts and Estimated Profits Thereon..	50	100	156	101
Inventories, at Lower of Cost or Market.........	10	42	41	45
Prepaid Expenses.............................	6	7	22	12
Total Current Assets......................	$160	$236	$ 533	$ 711
U.S. Government Securities, at Cost..............	...	...	$ 400	...
Investments in and Advances to Affiliates..........	...	...	5	$ 151
	...	...	$ 405	$ 151
Property, Plant and Equipment, at Cost...........	$ 21	$ 75	$ 206	$ 681
Less: Reserves for Depreciation and Amortization..	2	30	49	84
	$ 19	$ 45	$ 157	$ 597
Total Assets.............................	$179	$281	$1,095	$1,459
Liabilities				
Notes Payable.................................	...	...	...	$ 275
Other Current Liabilities........................	$ 9	$ 80	$ 199	208
	$ 9	$ 80	$ 199	$ 483
Reserve for Deferred Federal Income Taxes..........	...	...	...	$ 14
Stockholders Equity:				
Common Stock Outstanding, Par Value $0.10 per Share...................................	$ 12	$ 12	$ 23	$ 23
Capital Surplus...............................	163	166	799	799
Earnings Retained in the Business..............	(5)*	34	74	140
	$170	$212	$ 896	$ 962
Less: Treasury Stock, at Cost..................	...	11	...	...
	$170	$201	$ 896	$ 962
Total Liabilities........................	$179	$281	$1,095	$1,459

* The figure for earnings retained in the business in 1952 was subsequently adjusted to approximately $1,000.

Source: Company records.

physics, nucleonics, and chemistry, as well as with special apparatus designed by the company staff.

The company's machine shop, designed for research and versatility rather than volume production, included only very flexible general-purpose equipment. It was capable of handling work ranging from heavy radiation shields to precision electronic-optical instrumentation. Part of the shop facilities was devoted to producing the gamma radiography equipment.

The building also housed a large number of individual offices, equipped with desks and blackboards, and a library containing standard reference works and texts as well as a representative collection of specialized volumes on nucleonics, photography, atomic medicine, and current issues of a number of research periodicals. Included in the company's equipment were an analog and a digital computer.

OWNERSHIP

Until 1956 Research, Inc., was largely owned by its three founders, Drs. Henry R. Garrard, William S. Scott, and Willis M. Wharfedale. Due to the company's rapid growth, however, the founders began in 1956 to feel restricted by limited capital, and started to search for additional funds. Their efforts resulted in a major recapitalization in 1956. Two large institutional investors together contributed, for slightly less than one-half of the stock, funds amounting to about 320% of the approximately $201,000 owner's equity as of September 30, 1955.

BOARD AND OFFICERS

After the recapitalization, the company's board, which had previously comprised only the three founders and two lawyers and two industrialists without significant ownership interest, was expanded to include three representatives of each of the two institutional investors. In 1958 board meetings were being held monthly, and according to Dr. Scott, the new directors demonstrated a very active interest in company affairs.

In mid-1957 a vice-president for administration, Mr. Robert Marcello, was added to the ranks of company officers, which previously included only the three founders. According to the latter, Mr. Marcello was hired to assume some of the administrative burdens that had resulted from the company's rapid expansion, and that were becoming too heavy for the founders' time, experience, and interest.

Immediately prior to forming Searchco, all three founders had held responsible technical positions (for example, project director, physics and electronics division) in a large New England research and development organization, Trajectories, Incorporated. Each had become at least moderately dissatisfied with what one termed "the bureaucracy of a large organization," and had decided that he could find greater fulfillment in a company where he would have more control over his own and the organization's activities.

Before joining Trajectories, each of the founders had spent several years on the staffs of highly regarded research and academic institutions.

Each had earned his Ph.D. before 1940. All three became special technical consultants to the U.S. Air Force in 1951. Dr. Scott differed from the others in that he had also had two years of experience as assistant to the president of a small development company, a job which encompassed a wider range of responsibilities than those typically involved in technical (project) administration. The ages of the founders ranged from 35 to 41.

Mr. Marcello, age 41, came to Searchco with a broad background in government contract administration. After receiving his license as a certified public accountant, he spent several years in public accounting. For about five years he worked for the government, first negotiating contracts for the purchase of Army transport vehicles, later handling the procurement and supply of truck and automotive spare parts as a deputy branch chief in the Ordnance department. In 1948 he joined the research office of a large university as chief accountant, and six years later became business manager. The research office was principally engaged in research and development for the Navy. Mr. Marcello left it to join Searchco.

ORGANIZATION

A visualization of the company's organization is presented in Exhibit 3. The management did not maintain a formal organization chart or manual.

Dr. Garrard, president, and Dr. Scott, executive vice-president and treasurer, regarded themselves as sharing "top executive responsibilities." In addition, Dr. Scott was responsible for the administrative departments headed by Mr. Marcello; for the group of scientists specializing in electronics, and for the radiography equipment department. Both of the latter were headed by managers. Dr. Garrard was technical director for operations research projects performed in the home offices in Waltham ("on site"), and was responsible for the mechanical engineering and chemical groups. Both these groups were headed by program chairmen, who co-ordinated, controlled, and supervised the individual projects. Dr. Wharfedale, vice-president, worked as technical adviser or project leader on projects, usually in the field of physics, of interest to himself.

Prior to 1957, the technical personnel located in Waltham—approximately 80% of the total of 120—worked as individual scientists with no departmental or group affiliation. As the company grew, however, the difficulty of fixing responsibility in this type of setup was beginning to present some real problems, according to Dr. Scott. Consequently in 1957 almost all technical personnel were organized into research "groups," each of which was to specialize on problems in one of the scientific disciplines. With the aim of fixing financial responsibility on the group managers and program chairmen, the company's accounting system was modified to yield dollars and cents performance data by group.

Dr. Garrard stated that, prior to the establishment of the research "groups," company personnel had taken an interdisciplinary approach

Exhibit 3

RESEARCH, INC.

Organization Chart, Early 1958

Source: Prepared by case writer from interviews with company executives.

to a large portion of the research problems. This practice continued, according to Dr. Garrard, in that individuals frequently shifted from group to group, "usually without troublesome formality."

Besides the headquarters in Waltham, in 1958 the company included three "off-site" offices, located in leased facilities at or near government units with which the company had long-term contracts. Established for work on specific contracts, these offices would not be maintained when the contracts were terminated. The managers of these off-site locations reported directly to a director of operations research, a post established in early 1958. All three offices worked exclusively in the field of operations research.

Also included in the organization were four technically trained part-time salesmen who reported directly to Drs. Garrard and Scott. These salesmen, who worked about one-half of the time as scientists, called on government and commercial offices in an effort to secure requests for bids on planned projects or in an effort to stimulate the formulation of new projects on which the company might later bid. They did not sell the company's radiography equipment, which was distributed through a separate organization.

SALES

According to Dr. Garrard, about "one-half to two-thirds" of the company's business resulted from contract renewals. The rest resulted from successful bids on new projects. Contracts ranged in amount from $10,000 to $650,000.

Requests for bids on projects came from commercial and government offices either through a "sale" by the salesmen or founders, or simply as a result of the company's reputation for competence in a certain field. Contracts were generally awarded to the lowest bidders. Under government cost-plus-fixed-fee arrangements, the bid and accepted price supposedly amounted to a maximum reimbursable cost-plus-fee figure. This price might, however, be adjusted upward with the approval of the government contracting officer, once work under the contract had begun. Because of the prevalent practice of underestimating overhead costs in order to turn in a low bid, many government offices had bids audited before deciding which one to accept.

At the end of February, 1958, the company had a backlog of government work amounting to slightly less than $1 million. Dr. Garrard regarded this backlog as unsatisfactorily low, and thought that the company's estimated overhead rate was too high to meet the competition on bids. This condition was largely the result, according to Dr. Garrard, of having recently expanded the company's facilities and personnel at a rate faster than business had expanded. In early 1958 two new part-time salesmen were added to the previously existing two-man sales force, and Drs. Scott and Garrard resolved to focus more of their attention on obtaining new business.

COSTING

On the basis of a project description accompanying a request for a bid, an estimate was made of direct labor costs—that is, salaries of technical personnel who would work on the project—to which overhead costs were added. Overhead accounted for about 60% of the total cost of work performed by Searchco in 1957. Two classes of expense were included: indirect costs such as heat, light, depreciation, and fringe benefits; and general and administrative costs such as financial expenses, officer salaries, and nonproductive labor time.

Overhead cost estimates were made for the period in which work under the contract would be performed. Mr. Marcello stated that in making these estimates he projected the company's past cost performance into the future, making adjustments for all foreseeable changes in salaries, average amount of nonproductive labor hours, facilities, and so forth.

RESEARCH "PRODUCTS"

According to company officers, research, particularly operations research, was Searchco's major "product." Several members of the organization suggested that, although they could define operations research in scientific terms, not much effort had been made in the company to define it in terms of what it could do for various potential users. As one of the company's salesmen put it, "The government has come to us to ask us to do some operations research work for it, and our approach has been to conclude that the government is our market for operations research."

In early 1958 an operations research group, specially formed for this project, was working on a study of the best tactics for the civilian populace to employ in minimizing the effects of radioactive fall-out. This study was being performed for the Federal Civil and Defense Agency. Dr. Garrard stated that he was very interested in the problems of minimizing the devastation from an atomic attack, and was hoping that the company's performance on the Federal Civil and Defense Agency project would result in additional work in this area.

Projects in the field of operations research at Searchco ranged from the formulation of analytic models of motor vehicle convoys, to the evaluation of insect eradication problems, to the development of safety programs for nuclear power plants. Some of the techniques used by company personnel in operations research projects were: operational simulation (tactical gaming); cost-effectiveness analysis; queueing theory; and the design and analysis of experiments for studying behavior in terms of Monte Carlo models.

In the fields of physics, chemistry, nucleonics, and applied mechanics, company personnel had been involved in a variety of projects. For example, one project of the chemical group involved determining the sources of photographic "fog" and the mechanisms of superadditive photographic development. According to members of the group, the data being collected were expected to aid in the formulation of new and more active chemical developers, leading to increased photographic sensitivity. Projects of the electronics group, which had turned out more "physical" products than any other, involved the development of radiation detection devices, electro-optical instruments, and weapon simulators. Projects of the mechanical engineering group involved working on the theoretical analysis of the use of high energy fuels to power armored vehicles, and on the determination of the causes of wear and galling in submarine gear couplings. In the past, projects handled by the physics group had ranged from the theoretical calculation of the "transport" of radiation through finite scattering media, to the analysis of the physics underlying the operation of technical instruments. The theoretical study of radiation "transport" resulted in a new theory which, according to members of the physics group, proved to be more accurate than the widely adopted radiation-diffusion theory, especially when studying highly absorbent media and regions close to radiation sources.

COMPETITION

The company faced competition from a number of research and development organizations, most of which had come into existence in the early 1950's, from government research offices, from educational institutions, and from the research departments of industrial concerns. Mr. Marcello, in citing a National Science Foundation study, stated that in 1953 approximately 20,000 companies contributed $3.7 billion to the country's research and development effort. About 3,700 of these supported projects performed by outside organizations; the remainder conducted research and development in their own facilities. Total expenditures for research and development amounted to more than $5 billion in 1953, $1.4 billion of which was spent by the federal government.[2] Mr. Marcello estimated that expenditures of private companies for research and development had increased from about $3 billion in 1951 to over $9 billion in 1957.

Mr. Marcello stated that these figures were not very useful to him in getting a clear idea of the market for the company's products, or of the company's performance in relation to its competitors. "About all we know, and we are not too sure of that," said Mr. Marcello, "is that

---

[2] *Science and Engineering in American Industry, Final Report on a 1953–1954 Survey,* National Science Foundation, NSF 56–16, October 10, 1956, p. 3.

Searchco is the largest publicly owned research and development organization in the field of operations research."

COMMERCIAL PRODUCTS AND PRODUCT DEVELOPMENT

"In addition to the fact that product development work is almost frowned on around here," stated one member of the administrative staff, "a product that the technical people want to develop is usually not the kind of product that might turn out well from a marketing standpoint." Since its founding the company had produced three products which the founders believed had enough commercial potential to warrant exploitation.

The first of these products was the gamma radiography equipment, which derived from an idea conceived during a research project for the government very early in the company's history. It was developed by the founders on company time, and the first piece of such equipment was sold in 1953. Sales of the line accounted for most of the company's commercial business in 1957.

The next product derived from some new concepts developed by the company in transistorized electrical power circuitry. These concepts found their practical application in a small volume of special-purpose equipment designed for several industrial firms.

To produce and sell its transistorized power supplies, Searchco in 1956 joined with Electronic Tubes, Inc., a nearby company which had become a leader in the field of microwave tubes, to form a subsidiary, Watts, Inc., in which each parent had a half interest. Searchco allocated technical personnel to the new company, and Electronic Tubes allocated production personnel and facilities. As of September 30, 1957, Searchco had made investments in and advances to Watts, Inc., amounting to $107,000, and Searchco's share of the accumulated losses to date was approximately $51,800. Company officers, however, believed that Watts would show a moderate profit in fiscal 1958. Sales, which had expanded rapidly, were expected to reach a level of $600,000.

Since transistorized electrical power supplies were not yet competitive on a cost basis with the conventional vacuum tube, rotary, and vibrator power supplies, their use had been mostly in applications where extreme operating conditions had forced the user to reject conventional circuitry for the more reliable transistorized type. The concept of transistorized circuitry, according to Dr. Garrard, was "revolutionary," and the possibilities of its application to commercial products were "unlimited."

The last of the products developed and exploited by Searchco was a new machine for processing Kodachrome film. Previously, all Kodachrome had been processed by Eastman Kodak Company by a complex method which required accurate and continual control of temperature and flow rates, and continuous chemical analysis of developing solutions. The machine developed by Searchco meant lower labor and equipment costs, and greater quality reliability. The idea for this machine was developed by company personnel who had previously worked on a number of government projects in the field of photographic chemistry.

To exploit this new film processing technique, the company in 1957 joined with an investment group to found Developers Company, 60% owned by Searchco. Personnel experienced in the field of film processing were hired by the investment group to operate the plant in Cranston, Rhode Island, while technical assistance was provided by Searchco personnel. Losses, attributed by Searchco's management to "start-up" costs, were sustained in the first year. Searchco's share of these losses was $15,900. The company's investment in and advances to Developers amounted to $44,000 as of September 30, 1957. Developers' sales were expected to reach $200,000 in fiscal 1958.

Prior to creating Developers, according to Dr. Scott, the founders of Searchco spent considerable time discussing organizational means of exploiting the new film processing machine. The alternatives discussed were licensing the new machine to an existing firm; processing film with it in Searcho's existing facilities and organization; and creating a subsidiary such as Developers. The founders chose the last alternative after long debate, principally between Dr. Scott and Dr. Garrard. The first alternative of licensing was quickly dismissed, according to Dr. Scott, because of the limited royalty payments which could be expected. Since both Drs. Garrard and Scott believed that keeping the new development in the existing organization would provide additional management opportunities for company personnel and greater control over operations, the issue turned, according to Dr. Scott, on whether it "could be done." Dr. Scott summarized his point of view as follows:

We are scientists. We have had no training or experience in production methods and techniques. We don't have the basic production skills. It would have been foolish for us to try to produce anything other than the limited amount of radiography equipment we turn out.

Dr. Garrard thought, however, that "there is nothing so difficult about production, especially film processing, if you make up your mind to do it." He indicated that he did not continue to press the issue because Dr. Scott felt so strongly opposed to processing the film in the present organization, and because, financially, he did not think it would make much difference either way.

In commenting on the founders' decision to form Developers, one of the company's technical personnel said:

It seems very wise to me to keep production out of the operation here as much as possible. We just don't have a production atmosphere around here. Most of us would go nuts in a controlled, orderly, efficient, and sterile production atmosphere.

In fiscal 1957 the company spent approximately $16,000 on its own research and development projects. Dr. Garrard thought that some of these projects would result in additional contracts for the company's direct research and development activity. In addition, Dr. Garrard thought there was some "slight" possibility that an idea with commercial potential would arise from work on these projects. Expenditures by the company for its own research and development projects were allowable costs under most government contracts.

OBJECTIVES

When asked about their objectives for the company, the three founders and Mr. Marcello replied as follows:

DR. GARRARD: Our objective is to reach a volume of $10 million within the next three years. In achieving this objective, we want to stay out of commercial business. You know, you can't get into too much trouble with C.P.F.F. [cost-plus-fixed-fee] work, while you could really get into a mess in doing work for commercial concerns. If the government procurement agents have the money, they will want to spend it and they have no vested interests which would prevent us from doing what we think is best on each project. Commercial concerns, on the other hand, do have vested interests and would always be running in here to tell us what to do, and to prevent us from spending too much money.

Before the Sputnik, I didn't think we had a chance of reaching $10 million just doing government work. But now I am certain that government funds will free up and we will be able to get more work than we can handle for a long time to come.

DR. SCOTT: In my opinion, the company doesn't have a well-defined set of objectives. Oh! We talk about objectives such as a volume of $10 million. But to me, the way we talk about them is very general and very subjective. The three founders of the company have three different personalities, three different sets of motivations in life. Fortunately, though, the divergencies in our motivations are not so great that we can't come to some kind of decision on the questions we have to consider.

I believe that we would all rather do the technical work than run the business. But at the level of $10 million, for example, I don't believe we will be able to get into the technical end at all. If we get that big, we will just have to be satisfied with being surrounded by the stimulation of scientific atmosphere.

Dr. WHARFEDALE: We talk about a volume of $10 million, but I'm not too sure I would want the company to get that much bigger. Already the volume of business is getting almost too big for us to handle. The job I have carved out for myself is to get some of the projects that come in here outlined for others to work on. And this job is not one that you can delegate any more than a judge can delegate his job.

MR. MARCELLO: My objectives for Searchco are for it to grow into a bigger and more profitable company and to keep growing. As far as I'm concerned, the profit motive is the greatest factor influencing my decisions. Of course, I also want the company to turn out very high quality work, but primarily because it is necessary to turn out good work to get more and more business.

I don't think the founders get together very often to decide how the company is going to grow in the future. They have come up with an objective of $10 million, but it doesn't seem to me that they have really worked out how they are going to get it. As I see it, there are several ways this volume could be achieved. It certainly won't happen by continuing to engage exclusively in government research, which is dangerous as well. One of these ways would be to take on commercial jobs as well as government jobs in the same place. This would be hard to do because those companies big enough to have the money to put into R & D usually already have their own research units. Another—and I think the more probable—way of being able to do it would be to take on new products, either producing them ourselves or setting up subsidiaries to produce them. This would mean that we would probably have to concentrate more on research which would be likely to result in developable products.

Drs. Garrard, Scott, and Wharfedale, and Mr. Marcello were characterized by several members of the organization as follows:

> Dr. Garrard: He is the most competent, nonanalytical, and confident administrative scientist I have ever seen.

Dr. Scott: He actually is the only one of the founders of the company who *worries* about the business aspects of the operation.

Dr. Wharfedale: He refuses to be concerned about the business side of the company. He is a top notch scientist and obviously wants to remain just that.

Mr. Marcello: He has experience in working with us eggheads, so some of the things we do don't really upset him. He can be trusted to see our viewpoint.

PART V

Follow-up and Reappraisal

Bay State Abrasive Products Company

INTRODUCTION

THE BAY STATE ABRASIVE PRODUCTS COMPANY of Westboro, Massachusetts, was founded "on a shoe string" in 1922 and grew steadily thereafter. For the first 14 years it was managed by its three founders, Messrs. Key, Finch, and Lindsay. In 1936, upon the death of Mr. Lindsay, Mr. McKelvey bought approximately a one-third interest in the company. These three men made all major decisions as an executive committee; no one of them had final authority, although Mr. Key was chosen president by lot for legal purposes.

Messrs. Key, Finch, and McKelvey were in charge of production, finance, and sales respectively (see organization chart—Exhibit 1). In 1945 they created a personnel policies committee as a training ground for their subordinates. Later each of the three owners gradually transferred operating responsibility for his respective department to a subordinate who was a member of the committee. In 1955 these three subordinates were placed on the executive committee and given complete responsibility for sales, production, and finance. The three owners then took on the roles of very active directors. Under this committee system of management, company sales quadrupled between 1939 and 1947, quadrupled again between 1947 and 1956, and Bay State became the third largest company in the industry (see Exhibits 2 and 3). Figures in the case have been slightly modified.

In November, 1956, Mr. Key said that the company faced two major problems: (1) an educational problem of acquainting all potential customers with Bay State's excellent abrasive products, and (2) a perennial shortage of funds to finance improvements and expansion. There were never enough funds after taxes and dividends to do all the things they wanted to do. The latter problem was a natural result of company policy to remain a closed family corporation and had a number of consequences. Many opportunities for diversification into coated abrasives could not be followed up; production facilities had not expanded as

447

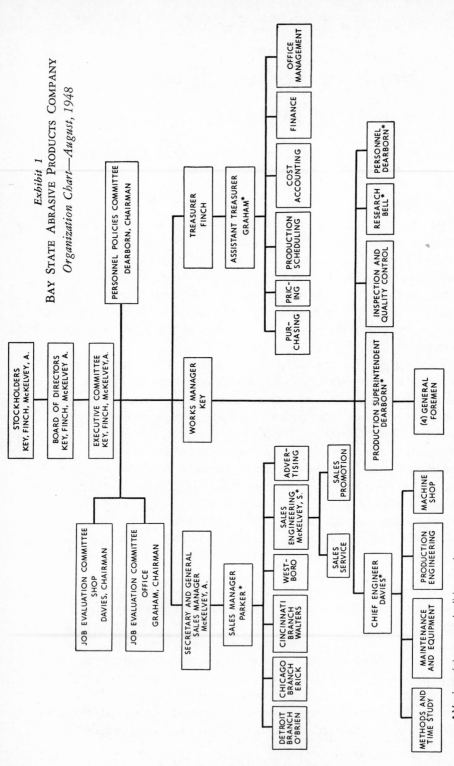

Exhibit 1

BAY STATE ABRASIVE PRODUCTS COMPANY

Organization Chart—August, 1948

* Members of the personnel policies committee.
NOTE: The office of president was not shown on the company's organization chart.
Source: Company records.

Exhibit 1a

BAY STATE ABRASIVE PRODUCTS COMPANY

Organization Chart—February, 1957

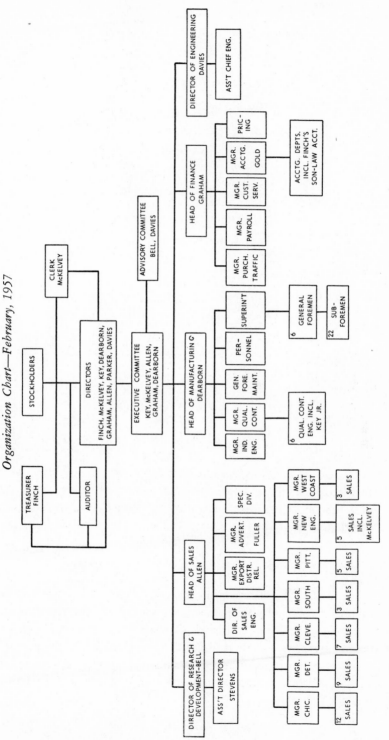

Source: Company records.

Exhibit 1b

BAY STATE ABRASIVE PRODUCTS COMPANY

Contemplated 1960 Organization Chart

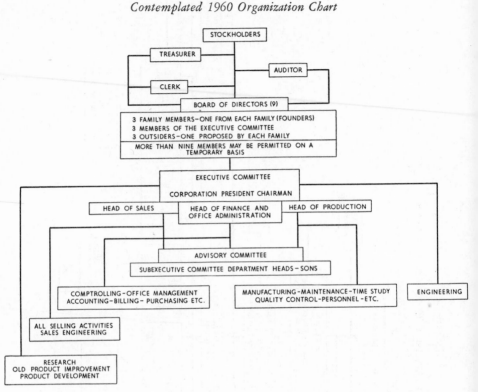

Source: Company records.

rapidly as sales, and as a result several sections of the plant were over-crowded. In addition, there were not enough funds to meet the need for a new manufacturing plant on the West Coast. Mr. Key said that, nonetheless, he "was not dissatisfied with the growth of the last eight years."

INDUSTRY

Products. The abrasive industry was comprised of three major sub-industries: bonded abrasives, coated abrasives, and abrasive grain, or grit. Coated abrasives consisted of paper or cloth coated with grit, and bonded abrasives consisted of wheels, discs, and sticks of various shapes which were composed of a homogeneous mixture of grit and a bonding agent. The bonded abrasive industry was further divided partly by the

Exhibit 2

BAY STATE ABRASIVE PRODUCTS COMPANY

Comparative Profit or Loss Statements for Selected Fiscal Years Ending December 31, 1931 to 1956*

(In Thousands)

	1931	1940	1944	1946	1948	1950	1952	1953	1954	1955	1956
Gross sales	NA	NA	$4,265	$3,078	$5,418	$7,875	$11,203	$13,591	$10,738	$14,651	$16,178
Less: Returns, allowances, discounts	NA	NA	258	162	213	314	433	675	497	543	611
Transportation out					121	163	227	309	227	296	289
Royalties paid					31	35	47	51	33	34	56
	NA	NA	$ 258	$ 162	$ 365	$ 512	$ 707	$ 1,035	$ 757	$ 873	$ 956
Net sales	$176	$1,003	$4,007	$2,916	$5,053	$7,363	$10,496	$12,556	$ 9,981	$13,778	$15,222
Cost of goods sold	117	569	2,675	2,082	3,290	4,726	7,288	9,287	7,362	9,674	10,388
Gross profit	$ 59	$ 434	$1,332	$ 834	$1,763	$2,637	$ 3,208	$ 3,269	$ 2,619	$ 4,104	$ 4,834
Selling expense	40	181	488	541	660	905	1,313	1,572	1,462	1,783	2,034
Selling profit	$ 19	$ 253	$ 844	$ 293	$1,103	$1,732	$ 1,895	$ 1,697	$ 1,157	$ 2,321	$ 2,800
General administrative expense	14	70	174	193	250	317	415	486	452	584	767
Net profit from operations	$ 5	$ 183	$ 670	$ 100	$ 853	$1,415	$ 1,480	$ 1,211	$ 705	$ 1,737	$ 2,033
Other income	2	2	26	35	29	79	88	76	114	189	411
Gross income	$ 7	$ 185	$ 696	$ 135	$ 882	$1,494	$ 1,568	$ 1,287	$ 819	$ 1,926	$ 2,444
Other deductions	3	4	59	22	14	14	49	57	63	30	43
Net income before taxes	$ 4	$ 181	$ 637	$ 113	$ 868	$1,480	$ 1,519	$ 1,230	$ 756	$ 1,896	$ 2,401
Federal income taxes		67	462†	52	342	771	1,008	777	388	981	1,245
Net profit	$ 4	$ 114	$ 175	$ 61	$ 526	$ 709	$ 511	$ 453	$ 368	$ 915	$ 1,156
Dividends	$ ...	$ ...	$ ...	$ ...	$ 31	$ 92	$ 120	$ 121	$ 120	$ 118	$ 154

* Figures in the case have been slightly modified.
† Excess profits tax of $448,000 included.
Source: Company records.

Exhibit 2a

BAY STATE ABRASIVE PRODUCTS COMPANY

Profit or Loss Statement Analysis—Percentages

	1931	1940	1944	1946	1948	1950	1952	1953	1954	1955	1956
Gross sales	100.0%		106.4%	105.6%	107.2%	107.0%	106.7%	108.2%	107.6%	106.3%	106.3%
Less: Returns, allowances, and discounts			6.4	5.6	4.2	4.3	4.1	5.3	5.0	4.0	4.0
Transportation out					2.4	2.2	2.2	2.5	2.3	2.1	1.9
Royalties					0.6	0.5	0.4	0.4	0.3	0.2	0.4
			6.4	5.6	7.2	7.0	6.7	8.2	7.6	6.3	6.3
Net sales	100.0%	100.0%	100.0	100.0	100.0	100.0	100.0	100.0	100.0	100.0	100.0
Cost of goods sold	66.7	56.7	66.8	71.4	65.1	64.2	69.4	74.0	73.8	70.2	68.2
Gross profit	33.3	43.3	33.2	28.6	34.9	35.8	30.6	26.0	26.2	29.8	31.8
Selling expense	22.7	18.1	12.2	18.6	13.1	12.3	12.5	12.5	14.6	13.0	13.4
Selling profit	10.6	25.2	21.0	10.0	21.8	23.5	18.1	13.5	11.6	16.8	18.4
General administrative expenses	7.8	7.0	4.3	6.6	4.9	4.3	4.0	3.9	4.5	4.2	5.0
Net profit from operations	2.8	18.2	16.7	3.4	16.9	19.2	14.1	9.6	7.1	12.6	13.4
Other income	1.4	0.3	0.7	1.2	0.6	1.1	0.8	0.6	1.1	1.4	2.7
Gross income	4.2	18.5	17.4	4.6	17.5	20.3	14.9	10.2	8.2	14.0	16.1
Other deductions	2.1	0.4	1.5	0.8	0.3	0.2	0.5	0.4	0.6	0.2	0.3
Net income before taxes	2.1	18.1	15.9	3.8	17.2	20.1	14.4	9.8	7.6	13.8	15.8
Federal income taxes		6.7	11.5	1.7	6.8	10.5	9.6	6.2	3.9	7.1	8.2
Net profit	2.1	11.4	4.4	2.1	10.4	9.6	4.8	3.6	3.7	6.7	7.6
Dividends					0.6	1.2	1.1	1.0	1.2	0.9	1.0

Source: Prepared from Exhibit 2 by Harvard Business School staff.

type of bonding agent used: vitrified, resinoid, and rubber. Reinforced products had resinoid bonding agents.

Bay State produced a full line of bonded abrasives, which accounted for about 95% of its production in recent years. The remainder was in coated abrasives. Very few companies in the bonded abrasive industry had full lines. The Grinding Wheel Institute, with 35 members producing about 95% of all bonded abrasives, reported in 1955 that 34 companies were producing resinoid bonds; 26, vitrified; 10, rubber; and 4, other products such as diamond and reinforced abrasives.

In 1956 bonded abrasive industry sales continued at the record level of 1955 and amounted to $124 million in the first nine months. Exhibit 4 shows company and industry sales as a percentage of total sales by product classes. Exhibit 4a shows other industry data. (See p. 458.)

Since World War II the bonded abrasive industry had witnessed a large demand for the new reinforced abrasives. Mr. Stevens, assistant director of research at Bay State, said that they had been a leader in the development of these reinforced wheels since 1946, when they purchased a sublicense from the developer of a reinforced cut-off wheel.

Bay State entered the coated abrasive industry in 1952 when Mr. Key decided that the company should develop a novel coated abrasive, which he had heard discussed technically. He assigned the problem to the research department, and they came up with a unique manufacturing process for what Bay State called Gritcloth. Gritcloth looked much like a window screen, and the "threads" were coated with abrasive particles. Its open-mesh structure permitted particles ground or rubbed off to pass through it, rather than clog the surface, as they did in such solid coated abrasives as sandpaper. This factor was supposed to extend useful life 10-fold.

The introduction of this product received large editorial write-ups in almost every metalworking trade paper and stimulated immediate competition throughout the industry. Executives at Bay State thought that Gritcloth was superior to similar products brought out by competitors and attributed this to their secret coating process. Mr. Graham, head of finance, said that they had a patent for producing the cloth which they coated. A few textile companies that had helped them develop the cloth manufactured it for Bay State.

Almost all of Bay State's production of Gritcloth was sold to the automotive industry to prepare vehicle bodies for paint. The rest of the company's production was sold through normal distributor channels. Mr. Key commented that there was an opportunity for great diversifica-

Exhibit 3

BAY STATE ABRASIVE PRODUCTS COMPANY

Comparative Balance Sheets for Selected Years Ending December 31, 1931 to 1956*

(In Thousands)

	1931	1940	1944	1946	1948	1950	1952	1953	1954	1955	1956
Assets											
Current:											
Cash	$ 7	$ 85	$ 136	$ 168	$ 427	$ 674	$1,111	$ 814	$ 613	$ 770	$1,423
Accounts Receivable (Less Reserve)	28	156	420	400	713	1,049	1,463	1,117	1,267	1,643	1,681
Marketable Securities	13	28	367	92	12	79	148	146	144	143	214
Inventories: Finished Goods	$ 56	$100	$ 73	$ 139	$ 184	$ 249	$ 376	$ 572	$ 507	$ 656	$ 652
Goods in Process	6	33	141	106	152	195	192	200	178	246	318
Raw Materials and Supplies	14	84	174	247	368	684	839	967	880	1,236	1,306
Total Inventories	$ 76	$217	$ 388	$ 492	$ 704	$1,128	$1,407	$1,739	$1,565	$2,138	$2,276
Prepaid Expenses	2	2	7	4	9	39	40	39	34	30	29
Total Current Assets	$126	$488	$1,318	$1,156	$1,865	$2,969	$4,169	$3,855	$3,623	$4,724	$5,623
Fixed Assets: Cost	$128	$334	$ 831	$1,263	$1,557	$2,105	$3,290	$3,900	$4,162	$4,728	$5,611
Less Reserves for Depreciation	29	95	401	439	572	703	1,217	1,556	1,915	2,328	2,769
Net Fixed Assets	$ 99	$239	$ 430	$ 824	$ 985	$1,402	$2,073	$2,344	$2,247	$2,400	$2,842
Goodwill	50	……	……	……	……	……	……	……	……	……	……
Total Assets	$275	$727	$1,748	$1,980	$2,850	$4,371	$6,242	$6,199	$5,870	$7,124	$8,465
Liabilities and Capital											
Current:											
Federal Income Tax Payable	$ ..	$ 67	$ 248	$ 52	$ 342	$ 816	$1,008	$ 778	$ 388	$ 780	$ 670
Accounts Payable	23	54	95	101	124	203	234	277	235	370	412
Notes Payable—Banks	……	25	25	240	167	58	103	130	184	327	……
Notes Payable—Officers	8	66	22	35	……	……	……	……	……	……	……
Accrued Liabilities	1	29	128	83	164	255	387	375	308	490	591
Total Current Liabilities	$ 32	$241	$ 518	$ 511	$ 797	$1,332	$1,732	$1,560	$1,115	$1,967	$1,673

Fixed Liabilities:

Mortgage Payable	$ 45	$ 20	$ 5	$	$	$	$	$	$	$ ....
Notes Payable—Banks	....	....	....	....	220	812	646	575	419	832†
Notes Payable—Officers	31	50	33	....	....	....	....	....	....	....
Total Fixed Liabilities	$ 76	$ 70	$ 38	$	$ 220	$ 812	$ 646	$ 575	$ 419	$ 832
Capital:										
Common Stock (Authorized 250,000 Shares)	$160	$ 160	$ 160	$ 157	$ 154	$ 150	$ 152	$ 150	$ 148	$2,942‡
Preferred Stock (100,000 Shares, $100 Par, Unissued)										
Paid-in Surplus	....	....	249	146	81	....	73	72	71	70
Earned Surplus	7	1,000	1,022	1,750	2,584	3,548	3,768	3,958	4,519	2,948
Total Net Worth	$167	$1,160	$1,431	$2,053	$2,819	$3,698	$3,993	$4,180	$4,738	$5,960
Total Liabilities and Net Worth	$275	$1,748	$1,980	$2,850	$4,371	$6,242	$6,199	$5,870	$7,124	$8,465

* Figures in the case have been slightly modified.

† $668,000 loan balance to be drawn February 1, 1957; total loan to be $1,500,000 payable 10% per year 1957-67.

‡ Par value of common changed to $20 per share in 1956.

Source: Company records.

Exhibit 3a. BAY STATE ABRASIVE PRODUCTS COMPANY

Balance Sheet Analysis—Percentages

	1931	1940	1944	1946	1948	1950	1952	1953	1954	1955	1956
Assets											
Current:											
Cash	2.5%	11.7%	7.8%	8.5%	15.0%	15.4%	17.8%	13.1%	10.4%	10.8%	16.8%
Accounts Receivable (Less Reserve)	10.2	21.5	24.0	20.2	25.0	24.0	23.5	18.0	21.6	23.1	19.9
Marketable Securities	4.7		21.0	4.6	0.4	1.8	2.4	2.4	2.5	2.0	2.5
Inventories: Finished	20.4	13.7	4.2	7.0	6.5	5.7	6.0	9.2	8.6	9.2	7.7
In Process	2.2	4.5	8.1	5.4	5.3	4.5	3.1	3.2	3.0	3.5	3.8
Raw Materials and Supplies	5.1	11.6	9.9	12.5	12.9	15.6	13.4	15.7	15.0	17.3	15.4
Total Inventories	27.7	29.8	22.2	24.9	24.7	25.8	22.5	28.1	26.6	30.0	26.9
Prepaid Expenses	0.7	0.3	0.4	0.2	0.3	0.9	0.6	0.6	0.6	0.4	0.3
Total Current Assets	45.8	67.1	75.4	58.4	65.4	67.9	66.8	62.2	61.7	66.3	66.4
Fixed Assets—Cost	46.5	46.0	47.5	63.8	54.6	48.2	52.7	62.9	70.9	66.4	66.3
Less Reserves for Depreciation	10.5	13.1	22.9	22.2	20.1	16.1	19.5	25.1	32.6	32.7	32.7
Net Fixed Assets	36.0	32.9	24.6	41.6	34.5	32.1	33.2	37.8	38.3	33.7	33.6
Goodwill	18.2										
Total Assets	100.0%	100.0%	100.0%	100.0%	100.0%	100.0%	100.0%	100.0%	100.0%	100.0%	100.0%
Liabilities and Capital											
Current:											
Federal Income Tax Payable	8.4%	9.2%	14.2%	2.6%	12.0%	18.7%	16.2%	12.6%	6.6%	10.9%	7.9%
Accounts Payable		7.4	5.4	5.1	4.3	4.6	3.7	4.5	4.0	5.2	4.9
Notes Payable—Banks		3.4	1.4	12.1	5.9	1.4	1.7	2.1	3.1	4.6	
Notes Payable—Officers	2.9	9.1	1.3	1.8							
Accrued Liabilities	0.4	4.0	7.3	4.2	5.8	5.8	6.2	6.0	5.3	6.9	7.0
Total Current Liabilities	11.7	33.1	29.6	25.8	28.0	30.5	27.8	25.2	19.0	27.6	19.8
Fixed Liabilities:											
Mortgage Payable	16.3		1.1	0.2							
Notes Payable—Banks											
Notes Payable—Officers	11.3		2.9	1.7							
Total Fixed Liabilities	27.6		4.0	1.9		5.0	13.0	10.4	9.8	5.9	9.8
Capital:											
Common Stock	58.2	27.0	9.2	8.1	5.5	3.5	2.4	2.5	2.6	2.1	34.8
Paid-in Surplus				12.6	5.1	1.9		1.2	1.2	1.0	0.8
Earned Surplus	2.5	39.9	57.2	51.6	61.4	59.1	56.8	60.7	67.4	63.4	34.8
Total Net Worth	60.7	66.9	66.4	72.3	72.0	64.5	59.2	64.4	71.2	66.5	70.4
Total Liabilities and Capital	100.0%	100.0%	100.0%	100.0%	100.0%	100.0%	100.0%	100.0%	100.0%	100.0%	100.0%

Source: Prepared from Exhibit 3 by Harvard Business School staff.

Exhibit 3b

BAY STATE ABRASIVE PRODUCTS COMPANY

Selected Balance Sheet and Operating Ratios

		1931	1940	1944	1946	1948	1950	1952	1953	1954	1955	1956
Current ratio	(R)	3.9	2.0	2.5	2.3	2.3	2.2	2.4	2.5	3.2	2.4	3.4
Net working capital	(000's)	94	247	800	645	1,068	1,637	2,437	2,295	2,508	2,757	3,950
Acid test	(R)	1.5	1.1	1.8	1.3	1.5	1.4	1.6	1.4	1.8	1.3	2.0
Current assets to total assets	(%)	45.8	67.1	75.4	58.4	65.4	67.9	66.8	62.2	61.7	66.3	66.4
Fixed assets to total assets	(%)	36.0	32.9	24.6	41.6	34.6	32.1	33.2	37.8	38.3	33.7	33.6
Net worth to debt	(R)	1.5	2.0	2.0	2.6	2.6	1.8	1.5	1.8	2.5	2.0	2.4
Net worth to total assets	(%)	60.7	66.9	66.4	72.3	72.0	64.5	59.2	64.4	71.2	66.5	70.4
Long-term debt to total assets	(%)	27.6		4.0	1.9		5.0	13.0	10.4	9.8	5.9	9.8
Receivables turnover*	(days)	NA	51	37	46	51	51	48	32	46	43	40
Inventory turnover†	(days)	NA	NA	NA	74	69	77	74	61	81	69	77
Total assets to net sales	(%)	156.3	72.5	43.6	67.9	56.4	59.4	59.5	49.4	58.8	51.7	55.6
Net fixed assets to net sales	(%)	56.3	23.8	10.7	28.3	19.5	19.0	19.7	18.7	22.5	17.4	18.7
Operation profit to net worth	(%)	3.0	37.7	57.8	7.0	41.5	50.2	40.0	30.3	16.9	36.7	34.1
Net profit to net worth	(%)	2.4	23.5	15.1	4.3	25.6	25.2	13.8	11.3	8.8	19.3	19.4
Dividends to net worth	(%)					1.5	3.3	3.2	3.2	2.9	2.5	2.6
Dividends to net profit	(%)					5.9	13.0	23.5	26.8	32.6	12.9	13.3

* All accounts and notes receivable (net) × 360/net sales.
† Average inventory × 360/cost of goods sold.
Source: Prepared from Exhibits 2 and 3 by Harvard Business School staff.

Exhibit 4

BAY STATE ABRASIVE PRODUCTS COMPANY

Industry and Company Bonded Abrasive Sales by Product Line
Selected Years, 1947–56

(% of Net Sales)

Products	1947	1954	1955	1956	Industry Sales*
Vitrified	57	41	42	39	45
Resinoid	31†	45	46	47	38
Diamond abrasives	5	8	8	8	†
Rubber bonded wheels	2	2	2	2	5
Gritcloth	0	3	4	3	‡
Other	5	1	1	1	12
	100%	100%	100%	100%	100%

* Net sales of 35 companies reporting to Grinding Wheel Institute by product line in 1955–56.
† Industry figures on diamond abrasives included in "Other."
‡ A coated abrasive not included in industry figures.
Source: Bay State sales from company records; industry sales from Grinding Wheel Institute.

Exhibit 4a

BAY STATE ABRASIVE PRODUCTS COMPANY

Production and Value of Two Abrasive Grains*

(In Thousands of Dollars and Thousands of Short Tons)

YEAR	SHORT TONS		PRODUCTION AS A % OF CAPACITY	% USED IN ABRASIVES	TOTAL VALUE	VALUE PER SHORT TON
	Average Annual Capacity	Production				
Silicon Carbide						
1944–48 (avg.)	72	60	..	..	$ 5,185	$ 86.41
1949	81	68	83	76	6,056	89.73
1950	84	65	77	76	7,304	112.38
1951	107	100	94	54	11,735	116.76
1952	111	92	82	54	12,041	131.39
1953	111	62	56	59	8,190	131.46
Aluminum Oxide						
1944–48 (avg.)	233	156	..	..	$ 9,921	$ 63.59
1949	237	126	53	97	8,500	67.46
1950	239	140	59	ɩ 98	11,958	85.41
1951	249	216	87	96	21,444	99.22
1952	255	180	72	97	17,814	98.95
1953	273	244	89	97	23,808	97.54

* U.S. and Canadian combined.
Source: Bureau of Mines, *Mineral Year Book*, 1950–53, "Abrasive Grains."

tion in other coated abrasives, which Bay State had not been able to follow up for lack of funds.

Competition. The majority of companies in the bonded abrasive industry were small and did not produce a full line; they devoted themselves to a few products and often competed only on a regional basis. Bay State officials estimated that the nine largest members of the Grinding Wheel Institute produced about 90% of all bonded abrasives. The two largest manufacturers, Norton Company and The Carborundum Company, produced about 62%, of which Norton got about 38% and Carborundum 24%. Bay State and two or three other companies each accounted for about 5% to 10% of total sales. About five other companies sold between 1% and 3% each.

Norton and Carborundum, while dominating the bonded abrasive industry, were also large producers of allied products. Norton produced a wide line of coated abrasives through its subsidiary, the Behr-Manning Company, and was a large producer of grinding machinery. Norton's total asset figure was about 15 times Bay State's. Carborundum was also a large producer of coated abrasives and produced abrasive grain, as did Norton and the Simonds Abrasive Company. Bay State purchased all its grain from a few specialized manufacturers located near Niagara Falls.

Norton's domestic sales organization, in 1956, included over 315 distributors, 127 salesmen, 8 district sales offices, and 5 warehouses. In addition, its subsidiary, Behr-Manning, had 16 district sales offices. Norton employed over 200 research personnel and spent over $1 million in research and development.[1] Carborundum had over 300 distributors and 11 district sales offices and warehouses. It initiated an expansion of its research and development department in 1956; the department had 106 men and budgeted an expenditure of $2.4 million. It planned to employ 270 men and to spend $4 million on research and development by 1958.

Both Carborundum and Norton were expanding facilities. In 1954–55 Carborundum spent $9.3 million on new and improved office and plant facilities. In 1954 they built, sold, and leased back two warehouses to supplement sales offices in Los Angeles and San Francisco. In 1953 Norton built a plant in California for the production of bonded abrasives, and in 1956 it was finishing a new $6 million plant in Worcester, Massachusetts.

---

[1] Data on Norton and Carborundum were from publicly available company brochures and articles in the *Christian Science Monitor,* December 14, 1956.

Markets. Bay State asked *Iron Age,* a major metalworking trade journal, to make a survey of the markets for grinding wheels and coated abrasives in 1955. The general market for abrasives was the metalworking industry, but the survey indicated that three groups of that industry bought about 85% of bonded abrasives:

1955 Purchases of Grinding Wheels and Coated Abrasive Belts and Discs by the Metalworking Industry as Expanded from the Field Sample

SIC*	Industry Groups	Grinding Wheels Purchased	Coated Abrasive Belts and Discs Purchased
19	Ordnance	$ 1,013,380	$ 496,172
25	Metal furniture	303,622	1,305,681
33	Primary metals	43,060,930	7,195,377
34	Fabricated metal products	14,572,545	10,890,934
35	Machinery	54,977,377	8,687,348
36	Electrical equipment	4,475,193	3,177,588
37	Transportation equipment	40,285,090	34,519,185
38	Instruments	1,209,621	569,165
39	Miscellaneous metal products	905,689	1,755,631
	Total metalworking	$160,793,607	$68,591,341

* Standard Industrial Classification.

Each of these nine two-digit subclassifications of the metalworking industry were broken down into about 50 four-digit classifications for Bay State, giving the purchases of bonded abrasives for each. The major buyers under "Machinery" were manufacturers of motors, tractors, machine and cutting tools, and roller and ball bearings; under "Primary Metals," steel works, rolling mills, and iron and steel foundries; under "Transportation Equipment," motor vehicles and aircraft engines and parts. These major buyers purchased about 70% of bonded abrasives sales in 1955. This survey also indicated that more than $70 million worth of coated abrasives were sold in 1955, about 40% going to the automobile and aircraft industries.

Customers of the abrasive industry varied greatly in size, from large steel mills and automobile manufacturers to thousands of small foundries, tool and die shops, and automobile repair and welding shops. The smaller customers tended to buy standard wheels from one supplier, while the larger purchasers often wanted specialized wheels. Skilled salesmen with the ability to solve difficult engineering problems were a big factor in making sales.

The existence of about 250,000 bonded abrasive items precluded the maintenance of a complete stock of finished products. Consequently, the majority of production in the industry was on a job-order basis, and rapid delivery was possible only on those standard lines which sold in such large quantities that they could be produced for stock. Norton kept 25,000 such items in stock, but few other companies kept as large an inventory.[2]

ORGANIZATION

In 1945 the three principal owners established a personnel policies committee as a management-training device and to lighten their own administrative work. They appointed to this committee the following: Mr. Graham, assistant treasurer; Mr. Parker, sales manager; Mr. Dearborn, production superintendent; Mr. Davies, chief engineer; and Mr. Bell, director of research. The committe was directly responsible to the executive committee, which was composed of the three principal owners (see Exhibit 1), and made major recommendations on such matters as: a pension plan for a few employees not included in the regular pension plan; a stock bonus plan for junior executives; and a general wage increase at a time when a union was soliciting membership. They also studied the question of whether a warehouse in Cleveland should be purchased or rented.

In 1948 Mr. Finch had a heart attack, and his assistant, Mr. Graham, had to assume more responsibility in the treasurer's department. In 1953 Mr. Allen, district sales manager at Detroit, was named sales manager under Mr. McKelvey and became at that time a member of the personnel policies committee (Mr. Parker had been named head of quality control). By 1955 Messrs. Graham, Dearborn, and Allen had taken on more and more of the management of their three sections as the owners took more time off from direct supervision of operations. On November 1, 1955, official recognition was given to this change in authority: Mr. Graham was named head of finance; Mr. Dearborn became head of production; and Mr. Allen was appointed head of sales. Mr. Key and Mr. McKelvey were titled president and executive vice-president respectively, but they both acted like "full-time directors." They kept an eye on everything and served on the executive committee along with Messrs. Graham, Dearborn, and Allen. Committee management was maintained, and each of the five men had one vote. Mr. Finch was not on the executive committee but was named chairman of the board.

The personnel policies committee was abolished, and the three members of that committee who were not on the new executive committee

---

[2] *Ibid.*

(Parker, Bell, and Davies) were named to an advisory committee (see Exhibit 1a).

The owners were concerned with the distant future and wished to make some arrangements for the management of Bay State in the years to come. All members of the executive committee were specifically concerned with the future roles the owners' sons would assume in the company.

Control of Bay State had always been divided approximately evenly by the three owners, and it was generally agreed that only one member from each family should have a top position in the company at any one time. In 1956 Mr. McKelvey's son was working in Pennsylvania as a salesman for Bay State after spending two years in the sales engineering department; Mr. Finch's son-in-law was in the accounting department; and Mr. Key's son was in quality control. It was planned that within three to five years the two active owners, who were in their mid-sixties, would retire completely. Messrs. Graham, Dearborn, and Allen (so-called "interim management"—see Exhibits 1b and 5) would then constitute a three-man executive committee, and an advisory committee with added membership would prepare to succeed the "interim management group." This revised advisory committee would be

Exhibit 5

BAY STATE ABRASIVE PRODUCTS COMPANY

Extracts from Interoffice Memos

1. To: MR. FINCH   8/2/55

From: MR. GRAHAM

In line with your request, we (Messrs. Allen, Dearborn, and Graham) have compared notes and given considerable thought to the question of what our organization should be in the future. . . . Not only is there a problem that has to be faced when you retire, but also the additional problems that will develop when an additional member of the present Executive Committee retires and when all three are no longer active. Then on top of these problems is the additional question of how to smoothly pave the way for the second-generation members of your families to take over control when that day comes. All of these questions are so interrelated that no satisfactory solution to any one problem can be reached without completely facing up to all of them. . . .

The passing forward of the responsibilities of management to the second generation will be a disturbing and trying period and will create many problems of its own. We must therefore at this time adequately provide for these problems both monetary and otherwise by the formulation of a complete employment program.

Exhibit 5—Continued

2. To: MR. FINCH   11/4/55
   MR. KEY
   MR. MCKELVEY

From: MR. GRAHAM

I think that we agreed that we have a mutual problem [succession] that
should be resolved between the founders and the interim management people
[Allen, Dearborn, and Graham] before the retirement of any one of you. I
believe that we also reasonably agreed:

1. One objective was to insure the continuity of the management of the
   company until the second generation is ready to take over.
2. Secondly—that the interim management should protect and enhance
   the results of your work for the past thirty-five years and your sizeable
   personal investment in Bay State.
3. Thirdly—that it should be insured in the minds of the interim management group in concrete form that the indications of the founders intent
   be fulfilled.
4. Fourth—that any plan to fulfill these objectives should be separate and
   not confused with normal compensation.
5. Fifth—that any solution must be in the interest of the founders, the
   interim management group, the second generation, and the corporation.

To meet these objectives it is our thinking that you should expect:

1. That we not only perform the duties normally expected from us, but
   also through enthusiastic and conscientious effort train the second
   generation individuals to take over the management of the company.
2. That we agree not to leave or go into the abrasive business against the
   will of the Board of Directors during the twenty year period.
3. That we undertake to fulfill objective number two as though the investment were our own.
4. That we indicate that we will carry out to the very best of our ability,
   the indicated intent of the founders.

3. To: MANAGEMENT AND STOCKHOLDERS   11/7/55

From: FINCH
      KEY
      MCKELVEY

. . . Since the basic reason for forming and operating the company has
been the earning of profits, there will arise the question of what are normal
profits and what portion of them should be retained by the company for its
expansion needs and what portion should be paid to the stockholders. Up to
the present, our goal has been to earn from 7% to 8% of net sales after federal taxes. During the first 25 years all net earnings were retained and no
dividends were paid. During the last 10 years about 80% of the profits was
plowed back into the business. It seems desirable to continue this general
policy for some time into the future, though perhaps less drastically. . . .

Exhibit 5—Continued

As the original founders near retirement age, the active daily management of the company is to be turned over to an Executive Committee composed of younger men. . . .

Active in the business are people whose abilities have been partially proven and many whose abilities have still to be proven. It is the desire of the founders that each successive management in years to come will have the foresight necessary to recognize the needs of younger able employees. They should be anxious to delegate the responsibilities and authority necessary for expression of these needs. . . .

If the growth of the company continues at a reasonable rate, it is foreseen that the problem of ascension to positions of responsibility will not be a problem. Rather the problem for the Board will be one of finding enough capable men to fill the responsible jobs. This is said with the belief that in ten years the company will be making coated products and its own abrasives, and in another ten years will have started to expand into other fields as well. Thus, many opportunities will exist for all.

These thoughts are recorded as a guide to the thinking of the Board of Directors and the younger group will gradually take over the management of the company.

Exhibit 6

BAY STATE ABRASIVE PRODUCTS COMPANY

Bonded Abrasive Industry Sales, 1948–56

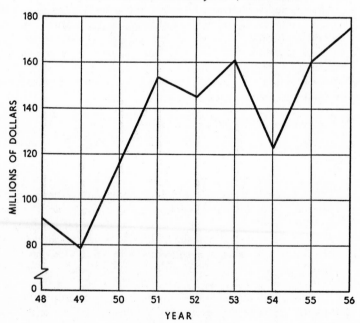

composed of major department heads and the three sons of the current owners (see Exhibit 1b).

In order to insure adequate interim management and to make future changes smoothly, the owners were considering the granting of stock options and other guarantees to provide a degree of security of tenure for the interim management group.

Exhibit 6a

BAY STATE ABRASIVE PRODUCTS COMPANY

Sales as a % of Industry Sales, 1948–56

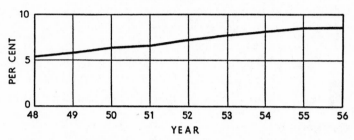

Source: Exhibit 6, Bonded Abrasive Trade Association; Exhibit 6a, calculated by Harvard Business School staff from Exhibits 2 and 6.

PRODUCTION

In November, 1956, the company employed about 975 people, including about 680 plant workers; 130 executives, engineers, and other staff on monthly salaries; 110 clerical workers; and 50 salesmen. In 1944 the company had employed about 600 men in production, although sales were about one quarter 1955 sales. Mr. Davies, chief engineer, said in 1956 that their larger competitors might be slightly more efficient in their operations than Bay State. He pointed out that Norton and Carborundum spent many times the dollar amount on research, engineering, and new equipment that Bay State did and that the larger companies could gain from longer production runs.

Mr. Dearborn felt the whole industry was primarily on a job-order schedule and that skilled engineers were the determining factor in maintaining and improving efficiency. The engineering staffs designed to keep Bay State production at optimum efficiency are discussed below.

In manufacturing abrasive wheels, a mix of ingredients was pressed into a wheel shape and baked. The mix consisted of a bonding agent and grit, with some water and filler. There were four major specifications for each wheel mix: (1) type of grit, (2) size and hardness of the grit, (3) the type of bonding agent, and (4) the structure of the mix after pressing. Since each of these specifications had many possible variations, the number of possible combinations was almost infinite.

The making of bonded abrasive wheels was the major part of all Bay State production. A sheet of specifications accompanied each order through its manufacturing process. There were approximately 10,000 orders, referred to as checks, at any one time passing through the plant in a four- to six-week manufacturing cycle. The average check was for about 10–20 wheels. First, in the mixing area the proper weights of the designated types of grit and bond were mixed in small tubs. These tubs were then sent to the pressing area where the mix was put in the specified molds and pressed under the designated amounts of pressure. The pressed, or green, wheels were then taken out of their molds and were baked for a predetermined time, depending upon the type of wheel. After the wheels had been baked, they were carefully checked, finished, tested, and shipped. The finishing operations often required tolerances of a few thousandths of an inch. (See Exhibits 6 and 6a.)

COST CONTROL

The great variety of items thus produced were not subjected to accurate cost control. The accounting department accumulated and analyzed costs on a quarterly basis for 80 product groups. These were subdivisions of the major product lines: resinoid, vitrified, and so on. For example, there were nine vitrified product groups classified by sizes of sticks, wheels, or mounted points. Little effort was made to analyze the costs of the many items within a product group. Mr. Gold, head of the accounting department, expressed the opinion that undoubtedly some such items were unprofitable. Payroll for direct and indirect labor was distributed to each of the product groups. The spec sheets, which accompanied each check through the plant, gave the exact materials used in each product group. Overhead charges were made to each group by direct charges for some supplies and by allocation of other expenses. Mr. Gold said that he generally expected the summary of costs for each group to equal 65% of the net sales of that group, except in diamond abrasives where the costs typically ran higher. He indicated that cost control of every product within the 80 groups might be possible with the use of electronic machines and that experiments along this line were under way.

EMPLOYER-EMPLOYEE RELATIONS

Mr. Dearborn stated that the small size of the company and management's consideration for everyone's opinion created a friendly atmosphere throughout the organization. The maintenance of confidence and co-operation among everyone was one of his special interests. Constant communication among executives was maintained by the committee-type system of management. There was close communication between factory workers and management. For example, whenever any change in the physical plant was contemplated, all the workers who would be affected were notified and asked for specific suggestions regarding the change. Mr. Dearborn thought that worker satisfaction and interest were promoted in this manner and many helpful ideas were obtained.

Bay State had an employee suggestion plan that paid $680 to 11 persons in December, 1956. One of the workers who received $150 that month had been awarded $145 the month before. The company also introduced a "floating" seventh paid holiday in 1956 which occurred on December 24, a Monday, to give a long Christmas week end. In the future, the date of this floating holiday was to be chosen by the workers. In 1956 Bay State voted a week's pay bonus to all workers employed for six months or more, and the remainder received half a week's pay.

By 1956 a policy had developed to place as many employees as possible on incentive pay. At that time 85% of the hours of direct labor were on piece rates, and 85% of the people on indirect labor were on piece rates. Everyone on monthly salary was on an incentive plan; it paid a bonus based on the level of selected operating expenses in relation to sales, over which the persons involved had some form of direct or indirect control. It was believed that under normal conditions this plan would pay bonuses of 20 to 50%. Top executives were on a bonus system based upon company profits and growth of sales as a percentage of industry sales. There were many fringe benefits for all employees. The company was not unionized.

SALES DEPARTMENT

Distributor Organization. Bay State had about 100 full-line distributors, principally mill supply houses, in 1948. Since then it has added about 90 and divided these distributors into two classes: "A" and "B." The A distributors were distinguished from the B distributors by their employment of a full-time abrasive specialist who concentrated his selling efforts on Bay State products. In addition, there were approximately 300 limited-line distributors and jobbers which had contact with segments of the abrasive market.

In the fall of 1956 the company had about 40 A distributors selling about $6 million worth of its products and about 150 B distributors selling about $2 million. The 300 smaller distributors sold about $700,000 of Bay State products. The six largest A distributors sold nearly one-half of total A distributor sales, or nearly 20% of company sales.

Bay State gave no exclusives to distributors and selected as many in each area as the sales management thought were needed to cover the territory. Mr. Allen, head of sales since 1953, believed the gross margins received by the company's distributors were competitive. Bay State quoted list prices less quantity discounts to its distributors and direct customers (see Exhibit 7). The A distributors received an additional discount to compensate for the employment of a full-time abrasive specialist. Distributors in turn granted quantity discounts to their customers. On the average, the company estimated that distributors realized gross margins between 15% and 20% on sales of Bay State abrasives. The range of gross margin that a distributor might earn on a particular order varied widely; if they bought at the largest discount from Bay State and resold at the smallest discount to customers, they would realize a gross margin of over 50%; if they bought at the largest discount from Bay State and resold at the largest discount to customers, they would realize a 9% gross margin, although the dollar amount involved would be larger.

Exhibit 7

BAY STATE ABRASIVE PRODUCTS COMPANY

List Prices and Discounts

The company published a book ¼ inch thick containing the list prices of its thousands of items. These lists were established for convenience of quotation and were changed infrequently. An extract from part of one page of the list dated January, 1956, is shown in Figure 1.

The description of the class of items was in the heading. An item consisted of a particular wheel of a given diameter, size hole, if any, and thickness as shown. The figures, A40, B80, and so on, at the top of a block referred to the required size of quantity orders; the letter identified column headings on product and quantity multiplier sheets.

The company issued product and quantity multiplier sheets that were applicable to list prices. These enabled customers and billing clerks to figure net prices per wheel applicable to an order of a particular size. These sheets were issued whenever necessary to effect a change in prices offered. The date of the multiplier list applicable to the item illustrated below was October 1, 1956; for instance, on a straight wheel, type 1-A face, 3 inches in diameter, and ⅛ inch

Vitrified Bond—1/2" to 20" Diameters—1/8" to 4" Thicknesses

LIST PRICES—Straight Wheels—Type 1—"A" Face—Subject to Discount

DIAM / HOLE	THICKNESS																			
	1/8	1/4	3/8	1/2	5/8	3/4	7/8	1	1 1/4	1 1/2	1 3/4	2	2 1/4	2 1/2	2 3/4	3	3 1/4	3 1/2	3 3/4	4
	A40	B80	C200	D400	E1000	A30	B60	C150	D300	E750	A20	B40	C100	D200	E500	A10	B20	C50	D100	E250
1/2	.50	.50	.55	.55	.60	.60	.70	.70												
1	.70	.70	.80	.80	.85	.85	.95	.95	1.30	1.65	2.00	2.35	2.70	3.05	3.40	3.75	4.10	4.45	4.80	5.20
1 1/2	.90	.90	1.00	1.00	1.05	1.05	1.15	1.25	1.70	2.10	2.55	2.95	3.40	3.80	4.25	4.70	5.10	5.55	5.95	6.40
2	1.05	1.05	1.15	1.25	1.35	1.35	1.40	1.50	1.95	2.40	2.85	3.30	3.80	4.30	4.80	5.30	5.80	6.30	6.80	7.40
2 1/2	1.55	1.55	1.65	1.75	1.85	1.95	2.05	2.15	2.65	3.20	3.80	4.40	5.00	5.60	6.20	6.80	7.40	8.05	8.70	9.40
3	1.85	1.85	1.95	2.15	2.25	2.45	2.55	2.65	3.30	3.90	4.60	5.30	6.00	6.70	7.40	8.10	8.80	9.50	10.20	11.00

Figure 1

Exhibit 7—Continued

thick, the list price was $1.85. The consumer multiplier for a quantity of 40 was 0.315, thus yielding a net price of $0.58; the jobber multiplier for the same quantity was 0.2835, yielding a price of $0.52; the ordinary distributor multiplier for the same quantity was 0.2268, yielding a price of $0.41; and the A distributor paid the same price for this quantity.

Thus on an untreated aluminum oxide vitrified bond 120 or coarser for the foregoing item the net prices paid by each class of customer in the quantities made available to them were as follows:

Quantity	Consumer	Net Price per Wheel in Quantities		
		Jobber	B Distributor	A Distributor
Less than 40...........	$0.77	$0.69	$0.62	$0.62
A—40................	0.58	0.52	0.41	0.41
B—80................	0.54	0.48	0.41	0.41
C—200...............	0.50	0.45	0.40	0.40
D—400...............	0.46	0.42	0.40	0.38
E—1,000.............	0.42	...	0.38	0.37

Ordinarily, industrial users were expected by the company to pay the consumer net price whether they purchased from the company directly, the jobber, or either class of distributor. The company made very few sales to so-called "jobbers," though it quoted a price to them. Typically, they did not carry stock but performed the function of breaking up a quantity order into small delivery units. The A and B distributors have already been defined in the body of the text.

Mr. Allen said that while this discount policy fostered large orders it was aimed primarily at getting the distributors to carry large stocks of the company's products. The existence of large stocks, and the consequent facility of rapid delivery, was an important selling point to users. Mr. Allen said that about half of Bay State's distributors carried adequate stocks but the other half was very reluctant to do so. He felt that the burden of taxation, lack of capital, and a fear of obsolescence kept these distributors from maintaining larger stocks, even though the discount policy made large orders very profitable.

Bay State distributors were at a disadvantage in many areas because the older, larger supply houses handled the lines of Norton and Carborundum. Norton was founded in 1858, and Carborundum in 1891; by the time Bay State was founded in 1922 the two older companies had already established a sizable distributor organization. This long historical base gave a great deal of strength to both Norton and Carborundum and their distributors. In some cases Bay State distributors gave better service than those of Norton and Carborundum, but Mr. Allen said the majority of customers in such cases would still go to the older supply houses.

Mr. Allen thought that Bay State distributors, because they were smaller and younger than those of Norton and Carborundum, were more aggressive, more efficient, and had to give better service than their larger competitors. This was slowly resulting in new users for Bay State products. Mr. Allen said that Bay State was, compared to Norton and Carborundum, much like its own distributors; that is, small, aggressive, and able to give good service. He said this resulted in better distributor relations for Bay State, because distributors felt more important and got more personal attention in the Bay State management than they did in larger organizations.

Mr. Key, in commenting on market conditions, said that many of the key personnel of their major competitors' distributors had set up supply houses of their own and asked for Bay State's line. A new generation of customers, less wed to the traditional supremacy of Norton and Carborundum, was emerging, and Bay State had a better chance of selling these people than the older firms in the business.

Salesmen. In November, 1956, Bay State had about 50 salesmen, or about double their 1948 number. Most of these men worked in the company's four major sales districts: Cleveland, Chicago, Detroit, and Pittsburgh. Each of these districts had a branch office, a warehouse, and five to 10 salesmen. In addition, there were three salesmen on the West Coast, five in New England and eastern New York, and three in the South. There was also a district manager in each of the seven districts mentioned.

Salesmen spent their time both selling direct to ultimate users and working with distributor salesmen. Sales compensation consisted of base salary, commission, and expenses; it was administered under four or five related plans that had varying amounts of base pay and commissions. For example, under one plan salesmen received $200 a month base pay, 3% of sales up to $10,000, 2% from $10,000 to $20,000, and 1½% over $20,000, while under another plan men received $500 per month plus 2% of all sales over $20,000. Under all systems, commissions were paid on total monthly sales of items that were shipped into the salesman's territory, regardless of whether the salesman, or a distributor in his territory, made the sales. This was done to prevent competition between salesmen and distributors and to encourage company salesmen to turn over their accounts to distributors and go after new customers. The salesmen were also given expense accounts and spent from a few hundred dollars to eight or nine thousand per year. Management was still experimenting with its sales compensation plans and was not satisfied it had the final answer.

Advertising and Promotion. Advertising and promotion were under the direction of Mr. Fuller. He believed his advertising should "pave the way for the selling force" and make it easier for them to gain access to customers. He thought the best way to do this was to advertise unique and new products, to point out technical progress, and in 1957 he planned to publicize case histories of how Bay State engineers had solved specific problems for its customers.

The major parts of Mr. Fuller's program were space advertising in metalworking trade journals and direct mail to present and prospective customers. He had the assistance of an advertising agency in planning and setting up advertisements and checked the effectiveness of these by means of reader services—Starch, Mills Shepard, and Readex. Copies of the advertisements and numerous brochures were sent to a large mailing list (30,000) every two months, as well as to the homes of all salesmen and distributors' salesmen.

Mr. Fuller was also working on a market analysis of sales districts. Before 1956 sales had been estimated by the sales manager according to district managers' expectations, past sales records, and the general outlook. With the assistance of *Iron Age,* a major metalworking trade journal, Mr. Fuller was making a statistical analysis of the abrasive sales potential in each district (see Exhibit 8). A survey conducted by *Iron Age* indicated abrasive sales to each of about 150 groups in the metalworking industry. Mr. Fuller expected to pinpoint abrasive sales to counties by relating these figures to the regional census data of the metalworking industry.

Norton published a house organ, *Grits and Grinds,* which was, according to Mr. Fuller, the bible of the industry's publications. Bay State had been considering publishing one, but most officials felt it could not put out one that would compete with *Grits and Grinds.* A great backlog of newsworthy information was considered essential for the success of a house organ, and Bay State was gathering such data, but no house organ was contemplated in the near future. The difference in Bay State's resources compared to its two big competitors really prevented total competition, Mr. Fuller said. He referred to the house organ and space advertising to illustrate this. Carborundum, in 1956, was placing multicolored ads on glossy paper as inserts in many trade papers. If Bay State used such expensive methods, it would severely affect the frequency of its advertisements. Carborundum maintained an insertion frequency several times that of Bay State.

Exhibit 8

BAY STATE ABRASIVE PRODUCTS COMPANY

Analysis of Bay State Sales and Industry Potentials by Districts

(% of Total or Estimated Sales)

1	2	3	4	5	6	7
District	Direct Sales Bay State	Estimated Industry Potential*	Bay State Sales			Column 6 Column 3
			1954	1955	1956	
Chicago.............			18	18	17	
Detroit..............			16	18	15	
Cleveland............	26	13.0	11	11	12	92
Pittsburgh...........			13	15	15	
New England†			NA	18	21	
West Coast...........	20	7.1	NA	4	4	56
South...............			NA	5	5	
Other‡..............			NA	11	10	
	average	100.0	58	100	100	

* Gives districts' potential as a % of total bonded abrasive industry sales as computed by Bay State for 1955.
† Included New England, Philadelphia, and New York.
‡ Included Gritcloth, specialties, and exports not sold through districts.
Source: Company records.

STAFF DEPARTMENTS

Bay State employed about 60 engineers and trained technicians in its five major staffs. A brief outline of the duties of these staffs follows.

Research and Development. This department, headed by Mr. Bell, was directly responsible to the executive committee, although Mr. Key directed them to some extent due to his background and interest in research. Under Mr. Bell and his assistant, Mr. Stevens, there were eight engineers with technical college backgrounds and 14 technicians trained by Bay State after high school graduation. About one-half of the department's effort was directed toward improving manufacturing processes and maximizing efficiency in existing, renovated, and new sections of the plant. Of the other half of their efforts, 20% was in pure research and 80% in product development, which consisted of improving existing abrasive products. In 1948 this department employed six people, and 90% of their efforts were aimed at product development.

Sales Engineering. Mr. McKelvey, a brother of one of the owners, was head of sales engineering from 1936, when this staff was created, until his death in 1950. At that time one of the sales engineers was temporarily put in charge. In 1954 Mr. Parker was placed in charge of this staff after about a year as head of the quality control department. In August, 1956, Mr. Parker took a leave of absence from the company, and his assistant, Mr. Simson, took over. At that time Mr. Allen, to whom this department was directly responsible, outlined the scope and function of sales engineering: "To serve as liaison between Sales and Manufacturing Departments and Research and Development. To direct our efforts toward satisfying the customer by assisting our salesmen and distributors and expanding our sales volume."

Mr. Simson said that special customers' problems were referred to his men by company and distributor salesmen. His engineers spent about one-half of their time in the field and one-half in their Westboro offices working on such problems. As in the research department, the sales engineers specialized along product lines and worked with their counterparts in other staffs to solve their problems.

Industrial Engineering. This department, in 1956, had nine persons on work classification, or methods study, and 10 time-study engineers. In both cases, the men were specialists in certain products. Mr. Dearborn said that this group, which was responsible to him, had made many improvements in method and had gradually placed more and more workers on piece rates.

Engineering. The engineering department had been managed by Mr. Davies since 1943. Prior to that, he had been superintendent of production. Mr. Davies said that the main job of his department was to provide buildings and equipment and to design the production layout. This department also operated the machine shop, which made the molds for the pressing sections of the plant and some machinery and parts.

Mr. Davies said that the work of his department on plant layout overlapped the work of the industrial engineers to some extent. The industrial engineers worked with his project engineers in planning layout and then took over the supervision of manual operation of the facilities. The research department, in working on processes, often had to work with both the methods engineers and Mr. Davies' men. The quality control engineers were sometimes involved in this planning, as they had to determine the effect of process changes on quality.

COMPANY FINANCIAL POLICY AND GROWTH

Financial Policy. The owners maintained a definite policy of keeping the company a closed family outfit. They followed a policy of retaining all earnings for reinvestment until 1948. Mr. Key commented that because they had decided to remain a closed company there had always been a shortage of funds to meet opportunities for expansion and diversification. Mr. Graham pointed out that the company was forced to review all investment possibilities, pick out the best ones, and postpone those with the least potential.

After 1948 dividends were paid every year (see Exhibit 2). In order to supplement retained earnings, the company borrowed from banks and in 1956 arranged for its largest total debt of $1.5 million. Mr. Graham thought that Bay State should not borrow any more than this amount for the foreseeable future. He believed that there would be sizable amounts of retained earnings for further expansion in a few years. Future dividend policy was to be determined by the changes in the classes of stock, which were taking place in 1957. In essence, these changes were going to turn one-third of the outstanding stock into $4\frac{1}{2}\%$ preferred. It was expected that annual dividends equal to 3% of the book value of the remaining common stock would be paid.

The company expected to make a tax-free reclassification of stock during the year 1957. There would be three classes: class A voting common, class B nonvoting common, and the $4\frac{1}{2}\%$ preferred stock. Class A stock would be used to maintain voting control and would be made available to present stockholding interests. Class B common stock would be available for sale to employees or outsiders if need be and for stock options to employees. The $4\frac{1}{2}\%$ preferred was to be issued to present stockholders and was to provide semiguaranteed fixed incomes for its holders. Early in 1957 the company was awaiting approval of federal and state authorities regarding the tax-free status of the proposed reclassification.

The management had not determined the total number of shares of class A and class B stock which it would seek to have authorized by its stockholders under the terms of the state laws affecting the company. The executives believed that more shares of nonvoting stock should be authorized than would be issued under the reclassification conversion program that they were planning for existing stockholders. They wanted adequate authorized, unissued stock so as to have corporate flexibility. Such unissued stock might be used, for instance, to raise cash by sale, provide stock for options to officers and employees, or for use in connection with mergers.

PHYSICAL EXPANSION SINCE WORLD WAR II

Since 1946 the introduction of new products and the change in proportion of sales, combined with a general increase in demand for all lines, had continually put pressure on manufacturing space. In those sections of the plant producing coated abrasives, reinforced products, and snagging wheels, greatly expanded production had caused congestion, and in many cases, sections of the plant had been spread into contiguous sections. Mr. Fuller commented that the great demand for Gritcloth, which followed its announcement, required expansion "in a vest pocket," and advertising on Gritcloth had to be stopped in 1953 because production was so far behind demand.

In 1951–52 the truing and bushing (finishing) section of the plant was greatly expanded. Mr. Graham said that they had deliberately overexpanded T & B so that they would not have to expand it in four to five years. He said that due to the great expense involved in moving equipment this overexpansion would save them money in the long run. He pointed out that as a result of modest beginnings in 1922 the plant was built on piles over swampland; this had increased foundation costs. In order to provide for expansion of T & B in the distant future, the stock room was located at the end of the new T & B area, so that T & B could be enlarged without moving any old equipment.

In 1953 a warehouse program was initiated. Formerly, the company had rented warehouses in its four major sales districts, but, as Mr. Allen said, it was more convenient, and in the long run more economical, to own your own. A warehouse was built in Chicago in 1953, one in Detroit in 1955, one in Pittsburgh in 1956, and one was nearing completion in Cleveland in early 1957. These warehouses each cost between $200,000 and $300,000.

In 1952 Bay State bought 83 acres adjoining its plant. This land was referred to as the "island" because it was half swamp, with an island of high ground adjacent to the Boston & Albany Railroad. In 1953 the company erected a $100,000 building there intended for Gritcloth production but actually used as a warehouse and added to the factory for Gritcloth. In 1956 they were building a wash plant and a resinoid burnout on the island.

In 1956 a $2 million expansion program was initiated. It was expected to be completed by early 1958. It consisted mainly of enlarging the existing plant and rearranging some of the sections. Its purpose was to increase the room for resinoid, rubber, snagging, inspection and packaging, storage of grain, mixing of vitrified bonds, research, vitrified pressing and maintenance, and the machine shop.

PLANNED GROWTH

Mr. Graham, while discussing company policy on the allocation of reinvested earnings, stated that the company must spend enough each year in plant improvements to guarantee continued peak efficiency. After such expenditures, remaining funds could be applied to new facilities. A budget was prepared annually to determine the amount of money needed to improve existing facilities. The foreman in each department estimated needs for his section, and these estimates, after review by Mr. Dearborn and Mr. Davies, were worked into a budget by the executive committee. The amount usually spent on such improvements was approximately equal to depreciation charges, leaving retained earnings for new facilities.

The capital expenditure budget of 1957 consisted of ordinary and "expansion" capital costs, totaling $1,445,000. There was $313,000 to improve existing facilities; $427,000 for a Cleveland warehouse, Westboro office, a wash plant, and a resinoid burnout; $705,000 to complete the $2 million expansion program. Sources of funds were earnings, estimated depreciation charges of $50,000, and the remainder of a bank credit amounting to $575,000.

A $1,500,000 debt to an insurance company and a Boston commercial bank was to be paid back at $150,000 a year for 10 years starting in February, 1958. At the end of 1956 only $925,000 of this had been used, but the remainder was to be taken by the company in February, 1957.

By 1956 Bay State had grown about 10% per year measured on a square-foot-of-plant basis (see Exhibit 9). Mr. Graham felt that a review of the company's history and future expectations indicated that this rate of growth would probably continue. He pointed out that since the company had plans to produce its own raw materials, diversify into new lines, and also to seek an ever-increasing share of the market in its current line it was possible that they could grow faster than they had.

Mr. McKelvey said that "while we have more ideas than money" it is all for the best that we grow no faster than 10% per year because of the great difficulty involved in adapting an organization to a rapidly growing enterprise.

POSITION ON THE WEST COAST

Mr. Fuller, in November, 1956, sent a report to his superiors in which he indicated that the company's competitive position on the West Coast was being seriously threatened. The market for abrasives on the West Coast had increased more substantially than in any other area of the country since World War II. In order to give this market rapid service and provide intensive coverage, a larger competitor was building an abrasive factory in Santa Clara, California. Mr. Fuller indicated that this might be a threat to West Coast sales.

Mr. Fuller's report read:

The big problem at the moment is what we can and should do to combat the situation . . . the best solution would be to have our own manufacturing facilities on the Coast. The second best step . . . is to increase our direct man power and to add additional distributors. The question of wheel stocks is also important.

Exhibit 9

BAY STATE ABRASIVE PRODUCTS COMPANY

Growth of Factory Space
1940–56

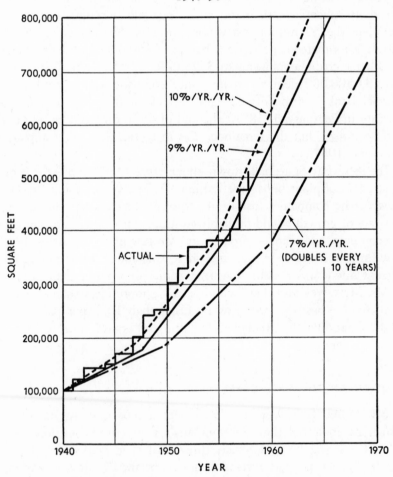

Source: Records of Mr. Graham.

To combat faster deliveries, which are possible through manufacture on the Coast, it will be necessary to increase our stocks of standard shelf items and to keep a good supply of special customer hold stock either at our distributors or at a warehouse. This, of course, involves some risk, as always, but it appears to be necessary.

Mr. Fuller said that it would also be necessary to aim some ads at the West Coast market and increase direct mail there.

Mr. Allen, commenting on this situation, said that Bay State was in the process of buying land on the West Coast and that they might have a warehouse and a sales office there by early 1958 and perhaps by 1960 could be producing wheels. He added that at first they could only produce a limited line of wheels but would plan to add facilities gradually.

Patterson & Swift, Inc.

PATTERSON & SWIFT, INC., of Philadelphia, produced two lines of electrical relays[1] that it sold to manufacturers of communications equipment and industrial, aircraft, and missile controls. One line, with 15 basic types and many hundreds of variations, was considered "specialized" and was engineered to work under conditions of shock, vibration, and extreme temperatures. These relays reacted to electric impulses of fractions of a watt, or to small amounts of light in photoelectric applications. According to a government survey, the company produced almost 30% of United States output of these relay types.

The other line consisted of about 20 standardized relay types designed to work under less extreme conditions. In addition, the company manufactured some industrial control systems on a custom order basis and produced an electronic household timer in limited numbers.

Specialized relays generally required modification to fit particular customer requirements. Company executives believed that design, quality, reliability, and service were of greater importance than price in competing with six larger manufacturers having diversified lines, and with about 100 smaller companies specializing in certain relay types. Executives further believed the company had a technical lead of a year or more in several specialized relay types.

The standard relays competed through price as well as through rigid adherence to standards, service, and innovations in design. There were numerous large competitors in this field. Household timers were made by a limited number of manufacturers. The company's product was a high-priced quality item sold through better mail-order and department stores.

In the fall of 1956, company sales reached an $8 million level, of which 62% went to military uses. Relays accounted for about 86% of total sales. (For financial statements and an analysis of sales, see Exhibits 1, 2, and 3.)

---

[1] Circuit breakers or switches activated by electric current.

Exhibit 1

PATTERSON & SWIFT, INC.

Sales Analysis

(Thousands of Dollars)

	9 Months Ended 9/30/56	1955	1954	1953	1952	1951	1950	1949	1948	1947	1946	1945
Relay sales	$5,318	$5,544	$5,547	$8,342	$5,820	$2,348	$1,001	$ 870	$533	$390	$228	$613
Other products	866	879	731	571	433	442	463	301	176	86	70	27
Total sales	$6,184	$6,423	$6,278	$8,913	$6,253	$2,790	$1,464	$1,171	$659	$476	$298	$640
Relay sales	86%	86%	88%	94%	93%	84%	68%	74%	81%	82%	77%	96%
Other products	14	14	12	6	7	16	32	26	19	18	23	4
Total sales	100%	100%	100%	100%	100%	100%	100%	100%	100%	100%	100%	100%
Sales to military	$3,836	$4,065	$3,961	$6,914	$4,979	$1,852	$ 877	....	....	....	....	$416
Civilian sales	2,348	2,358	2,317	1,999	1,274	938	587	$1,171	$659	$476	$298	224
Total sales	$6,184	$6,423	$6,278	$8,913	$6,253	$2,790	$1,464	$1,171	$659	$476	$298	$640
Sales to military	62%	63%	63%	78%	80%	66%	60%	NA	NA	NA	NA	65%
Civilian sales	38	37	37	22	20	34	40	100%	100%	100%	100%	35
Total sales	100%	100%	100%	100%	100%	100%	100%	100%	100%	100%	100%	100%
Backlog—relays	$1,613	$1,915	$1,824	$3,574	$8,105	NA	NA	NA	NA	NA	NA	NA
Backlog—other products	137	75	43	61	19							
Total backlog	$1,750	$1,990	$1,857	$3,635	$8,124							
Inventory—relays	$1,118	$ 867	$ 508	$1,009	$ 715	$ 517	$ 167	$ 93	$ 36	$ 28	$ 22	$ 21
Inventory—other products	275	269	233	144	65	84	52	38	16	8	5	4
Total inventory	$1,393	$1,136	$ 741	$1,153	$ 780	$ 601	$ 219	$ 131	$ 52	$ 36	$ 27	$ 25

(Military Sales Dropped)

NA Not available.

Source: Company records.

Exhibit 2

PATTERSON & SWIFT, INC.

Balance Sheets as of December 31, 1945–55, and September 30, 1956
(Thousands of Dollars)

	Sept. 30, 1956	Dec. 31, 1955	Dec. 31, 1954	Dec. 31, 1953	Dec. 31, 1952	Dec. 31, 1951	Dec. 31, 1950	Dec. 31, 1949	Dec. 31, 1948	Dec. 31, 1947	Dec. 31, 1946	Dec. 31, 1945
Assets												
Cash	$ 385	$ 423	$ 268	$ 220	$ 178	$ 100	$ 73	$ 66	$ 21	$ 31	$ 13	$ 17
Accounts Receivable—Trade	1,004	834	682	854	310	250	193	112	77	28	57	86
Accounts Receivable—Assigned	…	…	…	190	681	352	…	…	…	…	…	…
Loans to Employees	50	24	11	21	4	5	…	…	…	…	…	…
Notes Receivable	6	11	3	3	…	…	…	…	…	…	…	…
Notes Receivable—Employees	60	62	62	69	…	…	…	…	…	…	…	…
Inventory	1,393	1,136	741	1,153	780	601	219	131	52	36	27	25
Total Current Assets	$2,898	$2,490	$1,767	$2,510	$1,953	$1,308	$485	$309	$150	$ 95	$ 97	$128
Land and Buildings—Net	160	215	265	303	357	447	36	38	21	23	20	21
Machinery and Equipment—Net	127	120	158	171	164	152	48	36	24	20	11	13
Goodwill	…	…	…	…	…	…	…	…	7	7	7	7
Other Assets	12	20	16	13	16	5	12	9	5	4	2	4
Total Assets	$3,197	$2,845	$2,206	$2,997	$2,490	$1,912	$581	$392	$207	$149	$137	$173
Liabilities												
Accounts Payable—Trade	$ 291	$ 343	$ 253	$ 475	$ 161	$ 206	$ 97	$ 87	$ 58	$ 14	$ 24	$ 24
Notes Payable—Bank	…	…	…	176	157	608	…	…	…	11	12	…
Accrued Payroll and Taxes	178	336	243	194	164	138	34	28	13	9	8	7
Accrued Profit Sharing	84	23	115	231	78	30	18	1	…	…	…	…
Reserve for Year End Adjustment	133	…	…	…	…	…	…	…	…	…	…	…
Reserve for Federal and State Taxes	542	475	214	726	856	166	89	57	6	11	4	43
Total Current Liabilities	$1,228	$1,177	$ 825	$1,802	$1,416	$1,148	$238	$173	$ 77	$ 45	$ 48	$ 74
Reserve for Past Emergency Costs	50	90	90	90	90	…	…	…	…	…	…	…
Mortgage Payable—Real Estate	…	27	84	84	259	316	…	…	…	…	…	…
Notes Payable—Employees	183	122	89	61	78	54	62	45	24	…	…	…

Capital Stock—Common	7	7	7	7	7	7	19	19	19	19	19	19
Capital Stock—Class A	16	16	1	1								
Paid in Surplus	33	9	16	16	12	12						
Earned Surplus	1,830	1,397	1,094	936	628	376	262	155	87	85	70	80
Total	$1,886	$1,429	$1,118	$960	$647	$395	$281	$174	$106	$104	$89	$99
Less: Treasury Stock	150					1						
Total Capital Stock and Surplus	$1,736	$1,429	$1,118	$960	$647	$394	$281	$174	$106	$104	$89	$99
Total Liabilities	$3,197	$2,845	$2,206	$2,997	$2,490	$1,912	$581	$392	$207	$149	$137	$173
Working Capital	$1,670	$1,313	$942	$708	$537	$160	$247	$136	$73	$50	$49	$54
Current Ratio	2.4:1	2.1:1	2.1:1	1.4:1	1.4:1	1.1:1	2.0:1	1.8:1	1.9:1	2.1:1	2.0:1	1.7:1
Acid Test	1.2:1	1.2:1	1.2:1	0.8:1	0.8:1	0.6:1	1.1:1	1.0:1	1.3:1	1.3:1	1.4:1	1.4:1
% Earned on Net Worth after Taxes	25.0%	22.2%	14.1%	32.1%	52.9%	29.2%	37.4%	43.6%	1.9%	14.4%		26.3%

Source: Company records.

Exhibit 3

PATTERSON & SWIFT, INC.

Statements of Income and Expense

(Thousands of Dollars)

	9 Months Ended 9/30/56	1955	1954	1953*	1952	1951	1950	1949	1948	1947	1946	1945
Net sales	$6,184	$6,423	$6,278	$8,913	$6,253	$2,790	$1,464	$1,171	$659	$476	$298	$640
Cost of goods sold:												
Direct labor	$ 692	$ 823	$ 712	$ 900	$ 710	$ 363	$ 186	$ 152	$101	$ 65	$ 59	$ 85
Materials	1,891	2,058	1,622	4,006	2,091	1,072	438	397	226	122	87	196
Factory burden	1,554	1,782	1,821	2,092	1,581	854	419	308	184	145	95	156
Total	$4,137	$4,663	$4,155	$7,078	$4,382	$2,289	$1,043	$ 857	$511	$332	$241	$437
Inventory adjustment	257	394	(413)	373	180	382	88	79	16	8	3	2
Cost of goods sold	$3,880	$4,269	$4,568	$6,705	$4,202	$1,907	$ 955	$ 778	$495	$324	$238	$435
Gross profit	$2,304	$2,154	$1,710	$2,208	$2,051	$ 883	$ 509	$ 393	$164	$152	$ 60	$205
Operating expenses:												
Selling and administration	$ 708	$ 844	$ 732	$ 706	$ 551	$ 364	$ 198	$ 185	$110	$101	$ 90	$101
Commissions	441	463	452	548	390	239	134	86	51	31	21	35
Total	$1,149	$1,307	$1,184	$1,254	$ 941	$ 603	$ 332	$ 271	$161	$132	$111	$136
Net operating profit	$1,155	$ 847	$ 526	$ 954	$1,110	$ 280	$ 177	$ 122	$ 3	$ 20	($ 51)	$ 69
Profit sharing	280	228	217									
Net income before federal taxes	$ 875	$ 619	$ 309	$ 954	$1,110	$ 280	$ 177	$ 122	$ 3	$ 20	($ 51)	$ 69
Provision for federal income taxes	442	301	151	646	768	165	72	46	1	5		43
Net income after taxes	$ 433	$ 318	$ 158	$ 308	$ 342	$ 115	$ 105	$ 76	$ 2	$ 15	($ 51)	$ 26

Net sales	100.0%	100.0%	100.0%	100.0%	100.0%	100.0%	100.0%	100.0%	100.0%	100.0%	100.0%	100.0%
Cost of goods sold:												
Direct labor	11.2	12.8	11.3	10.1	11.4	13.0	12.7	13.0	15.3	13.7	19.8	13.3
Materials	30.6	32.0	25.9	45.8	33.4	38.4	29.9	33.9	34.3	25.6	29.2	30.6
Factory burden	25.2	27.8	29.0	23.5	25.3	30.7	28.6	26.3	27.9	30.5	31.9	24.4
Total	67.0%	72.6%	66.2%	79.4%	70.1%	82.1%	71.2%	73.2%	77.5%	69.8%	80.9%	68.3%
Inventory adjustment	4.2	6.1	(6.6)	4.2	2.9	13.7	6.0	6.8	2.4	1.7	1.0	0.3
Cost of goods sold	62.8%	66.5%	72.8%	75.2%	67.2%	68.4%	65.2%	66.4%	75.1%	68.1%	79.9%	68.0%
Gross profit	37.2%	33.5%	27.2%	24.8%	32.8%	31.6%	34.8%	33.6%	24.9%	31.9%	20.1%	32.0%
Operating expenses:												
Selling and administration	11.4%	13.1%	11.6%	7.9%	8.8%	13.0%	13.5%	15.8%	16.7%	21.2%	30.2%	15.8%
Commissions	7.2	7.2	7.2	6.2	6.2	8.6	9.2	7.3	7.7	6.5	7.0	5.4
Total	18.6%	20.3%	18.8%	14.1%	15.0%	21.6%	22.7%	23.1%	24.4%	27.7%	37.2%	21.2%
Net operating profit	18.6%	13.2%	8.4%	10.7%	17.8%	10.0%	12.1%	10.5%	0.5%	4.2%	(17.1)%	10.8%
Profit sharing	4.5	3.6	3.5	.....	.....	.....	.....	.....	.....	.....	.....	.....
Net income before taxes	14.1%	9.6%	4.9%	10.7%	17.8%	10.0%	12.1%	10.5%	0.5%	4.2%	(17.1)%	10.8%
Provision for federal income taxes	7.1	4.7	2.4	7.2	12.3	5.9	4.9	4.0	0.2	1.0	.....	6.7
Net income after taxes	7.0%	4.9%	2.5%	3.5%	5.5%	4.1%	7.2%	6.5%	0.3%	3.2%	(17.1)%	4.1%

* Subcontracts of about $1.0 million let to other companies are included.

Note: Figures in parentheses indicate loss.

Source: Company records.

HISTORY

The company was founded by its president, Chester F. Patterson, and the engineering manager, Henry T. Swift. Friends since the early thirties, the cofounders started business before the war, first producing a jointly developed navigational instrument, and thereafter experimenting with job-order manufacturing. During the war they acquired control of a small company making specialized relays which was put on a paying basis after considerable experiment. It reached a peak in 1945, with 150 employees and sales of well over $500,000.

After the war, loss of Navy contracts and the two-year lead time generally required to develop products for a low-margin commercial market proved to be difficult, but by 1949 the company had been successfully converted. The Korean conflict brought back military contracts, and by 1953 the company employed 700 people and reached a sales volume of almost $9 million. This expansion was accomplished with the help of a $725,000 V-Loan that was paid off in 18 months. However, financial stress during these years was so great that "reasonable salaries were not paid to management until after 1953," according to Mr. Patterson. "But today the banks are looking for business with us," he said.

During expansion additional difficulties arose from moving to the present building and from the use of subcontractors, some of whom could not master the technical intricacies of the product. "In short, we were the third bottleneck in the United States electronics industry, and the government was furious," said Mr. Patterson.

ORGANIZATION AND OWNERSHIP

"We don't like titles around here," said Mr. Patterson. He stated that Mr. Fritz ("Red") Gruber was in charge of sales, Henry Swift of all engineering, James Clark of accounting, and Joseph Adams of "everything else." (See Exhibit 4.)

Mr. Patterson was the major stockholder, owning just over 50% of the company's stock, while his brother Thomas and Henry Swift together owned just under 50%. A recent proxy arrangement gave voting supremacy to any two of the three major stockholders. These three men composed the board of directors, together with James Cooper, company clerk, who was a partner in a local law firm.

Mr. Patterson characterized the board, which met infrequently as a "very minor vehicle for gripe sessions and a means to tease the president." He said it rarely made decisions of any consequence. In his opinion,

Exhibit 4

PATTERSON & SWIFT, INC.

Organization Chart

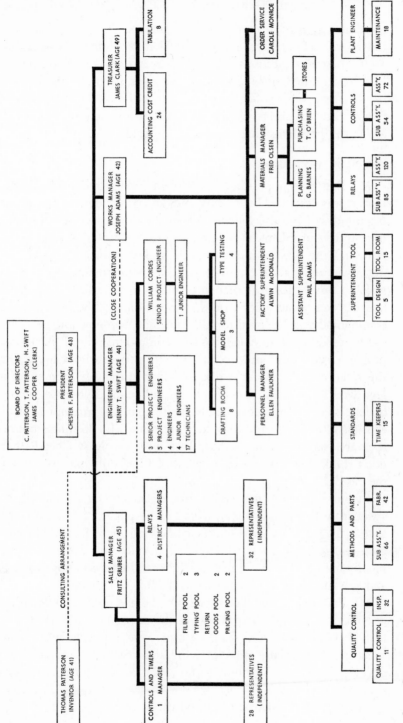

Source: Company executives.

there was no need for any outside members. For example, he said had the board deliberated on the expansion of civilian business back in 1946, the main questions would have been technical, so outsiders could have contributed little. Similarly, the issue of profit sharing was not handled as a "vast policy decision," but was talked about informally in two or three meetings. "We consider ourselves able to reason carefully about the problems that come up," he said.

PRESIDENT PATTERSON

Mr. Patterson, a philosophy major in college and a self-educated engineer, was described by his associates as a gifted designer with a searching mind that could get at the core of the most difficult technical or administrative problems by isolating key issues through sharp questioning. Although he was admired for this ability, some executives believed there was reluctance, especially in the middle-management group, to seek his advice for fear of being shown up. He had a reputation for keeping somewhat aloof from his subordinates. Mr. Patterson himself commented that he loved to talk, and that "some people get scared because I tend to talk too loud, too fast, and too insistent. I like to discuss a problem 'coequally,' and I get along with people who manage to rise to this relationship. I prefer to discuss things in the way roommates in college would do it, and I don't like to pull rank. But some people here believe that my influence counts more than my attempt to avoid authoritative behavior and that there are some who do things not because they are convinced, but because they wish to please Chet Patterson. I don't think this is true; I try to act as if I had only one vote along with the rest."

In building his organization, the president was attempting to "get away from having all the answers," as he put it. "Some time ago," he said, "I began to feel the effect of knowing more than other people. I then realized that this condition could develop yes-men around me, and luckily managed to avoid that. In the past, I used to know every person and job in the place, but this was a long time ago."

Mr. Patterson stated that at one time he had found an effective means of control in taking direct charge of the disposition and handling of returned goods. By investigating customer complaints, he was able to spot weaknesses, especially in engineering and production. As new technical developments grew in number, however, he was forced to assign this responsibility to the engineers.

Mr. Patterson currently received three monthly reports at which he looked if he was "concerned about something." Two one-page summaries showed orders on hand, shipments, backlogs, and materials on order. The third statement, which he called "blueprint," contained detailed balance sheets and operating statements that compared actual with budgeted performance by months and gave cumulative totals to date.

Most of Mr. Patterson's activities, he said, reflected his particular interests. "I look over the shoulders of the engineers who are working on new products or new processes, and I pinch-hit there once in a while."

Another interest was advertising for the sensitive relay line; he personally supervised this activity, suggesting ideas or writing copy, often of a conversational, witty character for the advertisements that appeared from time to time in magazines like *Scientific American* and *Electronics* (see Exhibit 5). Over a period of two years he had delegated most of the detail work here to his secretary, and he had recently appointed her advertising manager, but the job still took about 10% of his time. Occasionally, to test customer response, he advertised new products still in the development or prototype stage. This at times resulted in a frantic effort by engineering and production to overcome "bugs" in the new item in time to fill the orders pouring in.

A private hobby, which Mr. Patterson believed was shaping up as a commercial possibility, took almost one-half of his productive time. He had developed a new method of using plastic foam for making large, high-strength, light-weight panels and molded shapes, and he believed this method might eventually find application in production of aircraft and automotive parts. About $30,000 had been spent on this development, largely for experiments.

Occasionally Mr. Patterson concerned himself with tax or financial matters. For example, he participated in a particularly involved contract renegotiation; he also originated the idea of the profit-sharing plan which the company was currently using.

A large part of his time was, he said, "wasted" on walking around talking to people, or on business reading. "In this, like everything else, I follow my tastes and interests, and I tend to spend a disproportionate amount of time with persons working on something that fascinates me. My contacts are thus not balanced, and I know that this is not what the textbooks on management recommend a president should do, but one has to live with shortcomings."

Mr. Patterson believed the best way to direct a company was to select competent people to head the various subdivisions. He said he had succeeded in doing this in general, although the executives varied in com-

Exhibit 5

BENJAMIN DELANO ELECTRON
1791-1942
FOUNDER*

We take our share of pompous pride, shyly calling attention
to our own contribution, in fatuously welcoming the Billenium. General Motors
has built 50,000,000 self-propelled hydrocarbon energy converters, General-
Whats-his-name has gotten his family of scientists to develop the prestige-pump.
The BEV is dashing the modesty of the nucleus, and the lowly potato,
long the friend of the TV-less, deepfreezeless proletariat, now coyly
minces garbed in snobba-peel.

Our own bosom-swelling pride stems from our tradition of back-slapping familiarly with the greats of electricity and magnetism, whose august names are memorialized by the lower-case initial — joe volt, sam ampere, ed gauss, john henry, fred faraday — to us, each of these is a saint of science, their spirits blazoned on our banners boldly.

And now, in our humble way, we place on the altar of science at the epicenter of the Billenium our intellectual contribution for posterity. We are memorializing one of our staunchest researchers, who has reduced to hitherto unknown limits of accuracy, the measurement and observation of energy loss (or FRICTION), both magnetic and mechanical.

The New Unit is equal, for obvious reasons of national pride, to the friction overcome when the Battleship Missouri was pulled off the mud. As with the farad, in ordinary use, it is prefixed micro, or micro-micro, and for export to Europe, pica. It is the mccarthy (micromccarthy, micromicromccarthy, picamccarthy). M. K. S. and C. G. S. adherents may obtain metric conversions from Navy Bu-Ships data on the big Mo. Absolute units are of course the abmccarthy and the statmccarthy.

Sensitive relays with good repeatability of operating characteristics never have more than 130 centimeter-micromicromccarthys (50 inch-micromicromccarthys) of pivot friction at all extremes of temperature. Our relays don't even have that much.

*THIS ISN'T OUR FOUNDER, BUT WE THINK HE SETS THE RIGHT TONE, AND IS MORE PICTURESQUE THAN OURS, WHO ISN'T EVEN DEAD YET!

Source: Company records.

petence. "Things get done here like in a company with committee management, where the committee never meets," he said. "People with sufficient influence, and not necessarily by sheer authority, get things accomplished in their respective area. For instance, if I left here for six months, the company would encounter no operational difficulties. Hank Swift, who is highly respected, understands how to handle engineers and is skilled in analyzing problems and finding solutions. He and Joseph Adams, who is a very able man, would have no trouble directing the company in my absence.

"I run this company by the 'exception principle,' which means that I get into the act when something is out of line," he continued. "For instance, when expected sales increases did not materialize last summer, and the 'blueprints' showed a deviation from expected performance, I instigated a budget revision. But I made sure by talking to people that I had concurrence of opinion. Usually I find, however, that the people responsible for a job have taken corrective action by the time I get around to them."

When Mr. Patterson disagreed with current policies or arrangements, he often made this known by dropping subtle hints in casual conversations. He believed this method usually worked, since he thought the "grapevine" was a very effective method of communication, one on which he relied himself as a good indication of people's feelings. "I have never known the grapevine to get excited without reason," he said.

Occasionally, however, Mr. Patterson's hints were not understood. For example, in 1953, he had discussed his plan for a reorganization of engineering with the chief engineer and believed that the grapevine had carried the news to the rest of the department. However, many engineers were shocked when the new setup was announced. In speaking of this episode, Mr. Patterson commented, "There I was the closest to a solo decision that I ever came to."

Some of Mr. Patterson's subordinates believed he acted by "creating crises," either when he felt his hints had not been understood or when he wanted to jar members of the organization out of what he thought were unproductive or complacent ways of thinking. The engineering reorganization was dubbed such a crisis. Similarly, some engineers believed Mr. Patterson's premature advertising created small crises, and they were careful to hide developments from him until workability was assured. "It's Chet's way of putting on the heat," they said; Mr. Patterson, however, denied the intention of upsetting anyone.

DEVELOPMENT AND ENGINEERING

The general comment was that a majority of the company's successful products had been created by Mr. Thomas Patterson, brother of the president, and one-time head of the former development engineering section. He was unanimously described as a mechanical genius with a flair for conceiving of brilliant and simple solutions to "any technical problem." Somewhat eccentric, Thomas Patterson shunned "red tapey" engineering organizations and preferred to have his way in group efforts. Currently he had arranged to be retained by the company on a part-time consulting basis where he set his own pace, working in spontaneous spurts and alternating between the invention of relays and his major interest, the construction of harpsichords.

"My brother and I share a funny disease," commented Chester Patterson; "we don't mind explaining things, but we quickly get annoyed at superficiality. Neither of us can stand a 'stuffed shirt' or people who don't know what they are talking about. Tom is much worse in this respect than I am." He went on to tell how Thomas had caused friction by showing his annoyance at several electrical engineers who displayed only a superficial knowledge of mechanical aspects of the product. "Tom is a mechanic of whose quality there are not five in this whole country, but he must be left alone," he added. He explained that in past years he had quarreled with his brother about the latter's "government work," or private hobbies carried on during working hours, but he had found that his brother's mind worked best when allowed to pursue ideas of his own. "It took me longer than most people around him to realize that," he said.

The engineering department was currently headed by Henry Swift, self-educated engineer and cofounder of the company. He assumed this position in the spring of 1956 when the former chief engineer, William Cordes, relinquished most of his administrative functions after prolonged illness and overstrain. Mr. Cordes remained in charge of the drafting room, model shop, and testing facilities only.

During 1953, the organization of the engineering department had been substantially changed by the president. Prior to that time, the engineers had worked as groups or teams: A development group did research on relay applications and new product ideas; a product group took over at this point, transforming prototypes into models with specifications acceptable to production as well as customers; an applications group worked closely with the sales department in analyzing customers' problems and adapting standard products to their use. Each engineering group had electrical, mechanical, and other specialists who worked co-operatively together.

While this system was in effect, a number of difficulties arose. Increasingly, special problems or ideas forwarded by the sales organization were shelved and lost. At times products were designed which could not be manufactured profitably; poor service, delays, errors, and embarrassing situations resulted. Furthermore, no sales manual had been drawn up, although the increasing numbers of basic relays and common variations called for a comprehensive survey and presentation.

In the summer of 1953, the president unexpectedly announced a number of changes. He dissolved the application engineering group and abolished the existing group system. From that point on, he said, each of the five senior engineers was to be responsible for one or more relay types. Theoretically, one engineer now decided on all aspects of design, specifications, and materials used; he assisted customers and field representatives, as well as foremen in the plant. Under this "King Theory," responsibility for success of the product was his alone.

By this move, Mr. Patterson intended to force the engineers to take a broader view, in fact to make them "businessmen" interested in serving the customers.

However, upset and confusion attended the change, since, as one engineer pointed out, it forced former specialists to cope with problems outside their experience.

One of the senior engineers later said he had been against the idea, since he believed that groups could accomplish more than individuals. Thomas Patterson opposed the change because it caused unrest. Another engineer thought making one person responsible for a product was a risk because he might become ill or quit. Mr. Cordes stated that the "King Theory" prevented a co-ordinated program. A member of the sales department thought it facilitated pursuit of fruitless projects.

On the other hand, it was conceded that some good emerged quickly from the shake-up. "Before the change, we never knew the whole product in all its aspects, but afterward we had to see it," commented one senior engineer. Also, customer service was improved, and the sales manual, which Mr. Patterson had ordered completed in six months, was made ready within the year.

After 1953, further development took place. Gradually the engineers began to consult informally among themselves, with specialists helping each other on problems. After Mr. Swift took over the department, he started a series of monthly meetings and newsletters in order to improve co-ordination and to familiarize the project engineers with each other's activities. In speaking of the "King Theory," Mr. Swift stated that he thought it worked well, but required modification by introducing group effort. Consequently he tried to put at least two people of different skills on any one project.

In 1956 there were 11 project engineers, including Mr. Swift and Thomas Patterson, assisted by 28 other engineers and technicians.

Mr. Swift described his duties as two-thirds supervision and one-third working on engineering projects of his own. Advising on technical questions and handling "political" problems took about equal amounts of time, he said. The latter included problems arising from the reorganization, questions of procedure, and the relationships between the engineers and the factory. "The political problems are the hardest," said Mr. Swift; "for instance, I find that some engineers want to do projects all by themselves, while spreading the task among at least two people makes things easier and better. The problem is how to do it without hurting individual pride."

Members of the engineering staff indicated that they welcomed Mr. Swift's efforts to achieve co-ordination through newsletters and meetings. They also felt that working in a small department allowed them to achieve unusually close contact with all aspects of the product, and that this gave the company a competitive advantage over larger manufacturers.

Mr. Patterson stressed that engineers were encouraged to travel in order to keep up customer contact. He said that new product ideas came from "exposure" to present and potential customers, and that he "raised hell" if the engineers did not travel enough. Expense accounts were not questioned. "I myself and many others just pick up enough money and bring back the change, and no questions asked," he said. Similarly, Mr. Patterson strongly urged the use of long-distance calls instead of letters, since he believed the engineers could learn more and faster by talking to a customer directly.

Mr. Cordes said the company had to take exceptional care in selecting engineers, as they became its symbol. "Every company has its strong group around which it is built, and with us it is engineering." He regretted that steps had not been taken earlier to hire more young engineers, since men with the qualifications desired had become scarce. Mr. Cordes believed recruiting activity had been slowed up by Mr. Patterson's requirement that he personally interview every incoming engineer. On this the president commented that it was a general and necessary policy to screen applicants through a committee consisting of Messrs. Patterson, Gruber, Swift, and others.

Mr. Cordes also thought the company's competitive advantage of making specialized products was slowly decreasing, as the growing market attracted more competitors, and that the company thus had to rely on self-generating engineers with business sense to help it move ahead.

Mr. Patterson said that new product development utilized a "shotgun approach," but he believed the money frequently spent on projects that turned out to be useless or obsolete was a necessary cost, especially since the experience gained could be usefully applied in different projects.

PRODUCTION

All products of the company were manufactured in a two-story building of 100,000 square feet in northern Philadelphia, adjacent to a railroad and a highway. The first floor contained office space and laboratories as well as the relay manufacturing area, while the second floor contained part of the accounting department, a cafeteria, additional assembly space, and rooms for the experiments with plastics. Materials and finished goods were stored in side rooms on the ground floor. An 18,000-square-foot addition for office space was currently under construction.

Joseph Adams, works manager since 1945, had joined the company in 1942 as an expediter in the purchasing department. He had previously managed restaurants and food stores for the Food Products Co., during which period he acquired a degree in industrial management by attending night school.

Mr. Adams described his job as including all contacts and procedures involved in manufacturing; in addition, he supervised budgeting and capital expenditures. Reports going to him on a monthly basis included operating statements, inventory status by parts, subassemblies and finished products, and variance analyses. Weekly reports showed backlog on hand, orders past due, orders held, and materials on order. Daily shipments were also reported. In addition, the personnel manager presented a monthly report on absenteeism and labor turnover, and she reported frequently on exit interviews. Every three weeks or oftener the planning section furnished a forecast of allocation of plant capacity to the various relay types, based on statistical analysis plus "seat of the pants estimates."

As the company expanded, Mr. Adams had delegated certain duties; for example, a former employee interviewer, Mrs. Ellen Faulkner, was made personnel manager, while a former project engineer, Alwin McDonald, was made factory superintendent. As the latter described it, Mr. Adams told him "to find out for himself what it entails to run the factory," and to come back to him should he encounter problems. Mr. McDonald commented that he later used the same approach successfully in building his own factory "staff group." Mr. Adams said that he believed in a firm chain of command, but was careful to give his subordinates full responsibility for the execution of their jobs once he had defined them.

Mr. Adams said he generally spent about two hours daily with the factory superintendent, one hour each with the materials manager and the treasurer, and one-half hour each with the order service manager and the personnel manager. Other executives sought him out for consultation, and he worked especially closely with Henry Swift, the engineering manager. "Hank and I consult on major steps I take, or we talk over operating statements. We discuss also what we can do to improve the company in general," he said.

Mr. Adams considered it one of his main problems at present to help the new engineering manager take over the leadership in his department after the past reorganization. Of this event he said, "No matter what one hears about the whole thing, no real change took place except that the responsibility of the engineers was focused. It also fostered better understanding between the formerly separate engineering sections. But now Hank is trying to put back the teamwork which had gotten lost when the engineers began to pursue individual projects." Mr. Adams went on to tell of instances where duplication of engineering effort had formerly resulted in spending several thousand dollars on excess tooling. "McDonald put in an 'Iron Curtain' to avoid similar occurrences, and there has been a lot of improvement in the last six months," he said.

Mr. Adams, together with Henry Swift, served as a mediator of conflicts between project engineers and the factory superintendent: If an engineer should be dissatisfied with the method of production used for a particular relay, the foreman in charge brought the matter first to Mr. McDonald; if he could not settle it, then Mr. Adams and Mr. Swift settled it jointly. Mr. Adams explained, "Although the engineers were decreed to have full authority over their relays, the important factors are whether you can build it and whether you can sell it. Under the theory as developed by Chet, the engineer could stop production if he was not satisfied. However, as far as I know, that has not happened. To the contrary, there were instances in which I personally ordered production halted to force the project engineer to redesign or modify his relay because 90 out of 100 relays made did not work. Similarly, customer acceptance starts or stops production of a relay."

Looking to the future, Mr. Adams spoke of the main problem confronting the company as that of getting more "idea men" to develop new products, inasmuch as most of the successful products of the past had been invented by the two owner-brothers. Visualizing a potential sales volume of $12 million within the next five years, Mr. Adams felt that "the thing to do is to keep our sales volume of the present products and to get the engineers to develop more products the world can use."

Mr. Adams stated that another job of vital importance was the planning, scheduling, and control of production; upon it hinged the size of inventories, materials purchases, labor requirements, and delivery schedules. At any one time, about 700 orders were in process, or 18,000–24,000 relays per week. In the course of a month, 1,000 orders were handled, averaging 28 basic types and thousands of variations.

Orders were expedited on the manufacturing floor by special order clerks, but there was confusion in many cases. According to the planning manager, Glen Barnes, the company's rapid growth was responsible for many control practices not best suited to the purpose. For example, he felt that production schedules were at times unduly influenced by the order service department's efforts to placate or help particular customers. This department had been set up especially to handle customer inquiries and complaints. It had been determined that each customer on an average checked two and a half times on his order, and frequently confusion resulted before the status of a particular order, or the reason for delays, could be traced through the various departments. As a special project for the future, Mr. Adams was planning an examination of the paper flow used in keeping customers informed of the progress of their orders.

Both Mr. Barnes and Mr. Adams believed that excessive duplication and red tape were present in production control. Mr. Barnes ascribed this to a "reaction" from having almost no formal procedures in the period five years earlier. A project to improve paper work, or "red tape flow," as it was called, had recently been set on foot by Mr. Adams, who delegated this responsibility to his brother, Paul Adams, and to Mr. Barnes. As Mr. Adams put it, "For all I know, we may have too little in the way of papers, but we are going to find out and eliminate wasted effort, which arose when, during the last four years, the nature of our business changed from a few high-volume items to a great variety of products." Mr. Adams stated that timekeepers on the production floor were maintaining essentially the same records which the cost department kept independently. "I believe," he injected, "that once the staff people are doing a good enough job, the factory people will cease to make their own efforts."

Mr. Barnes was planning the introduction of a formal production control system. In conjunction with this he hoped to consolidate the forms used by each department. "It is just like one department not trusting the other, and therefore each makes up its own forms," he said. To illustrate this problem, he pointed to the difficulty of making sure that alterations in blueprints reached the production floor, since engineering and production records were essentially separate.

Until recently, most relays had been manufactured on an order basis. In order to alleviate scheduling problems and because the company could now finance it, an increasing percentage of the more common relays and subassemblies was kept in stock. By the fall of 1956, about 60% of orders, accounting for 15% of dollar volume, were shipped from inventory.

Inventory control, under Mr. Olsen, had to cope with 6,000 to 7,000 parts and subassemblies, about double the number of five years before. It had formerly been the policy to write off as obsolete any parts or subassemblies not sold after three months, but recently policy here had grown more flexible. Mr. Adams said the growing number of products forced a steady increase in inventories, but he had found that competing companies were carrying even higher inventories relative to sales volume. He estimated that finished goods accounted for about 17% of inventory, work in process for 35%, the rest being raw materials and parts either procured outside or made by the company.

Delivery schedules generally called for a seven- to eight-week manufacturing period, which was about average for the industry. This time allowance, greater than actual manufacturing time, enabled the foremen to schedule the work force to best advantage. Many customers desired delivery spaced over a period of time which conformed with their own manufacturing operations. The company found that a backlog of orders of about three months was necessary to keep scheduling efficient.

In managing the production department, Mr. Adams frequently initiated special projects, carried on under his direct supervision, such as those planned to "improve red tape flow" and the paper work for checking on customer orders.

Partially completed was a project for establishing standard operation times for many different products and processes—though Mr. Adams saw the possibility of conflict between an emphasis on time standards and the company's traditional emphasis on quality.

Another special project, already accomplished, was a survey of job requirements for all operating and clerical personnel, through which job definitions and wage ranges were established. A similar survey of supervisory and executive positions was planned.

For use in determining employment policies, a survey of opinions on personnel practices had recently been carried out among all ranks. Mr. Adams' interest in employee and wage problems had resulted in the practice of clearing everyone's wages through his office.

LABOR RELATIONS

The company employed about 600 persons, 60% of whom were women whose skill and dexterity were required in assembling the many intricate metal, glass, and plastic parts. Each relay required a number of adjustments and tests during and after assembly. "Our products work only because the girls on the benches *want* them to work," said an engineer.

Labor relations in the company were characterized by all as friendly and peaceful. The plant was not unionized, a fact which Mr. Adams considered a great advantage because he or any other executive or supervisor was under no restriction about visiting the manufacturing area, talking to the workers, and examining products at various stages of completion. He believed these circumstances made it much easier to keep close liaison between production and other departments interested in quality and progressive innovation.

According to Mr. Adams, the company's employment policy helped to promote the friendly spirit among the workers. Stable employment was emphasized, and to avoid layoffs, production schedules were frequently stretched, and workers were shifted between jobs. The company relied on "natural turnover" among its employees to cut back in slow periods, and new workers were hired only if an increase in orders indicated a long-term rise in sales. Many employees brought relatives or friends to work for the company. Mrs. Faulkner interviewed each new employee and administered a vocational interest test to assure correct placement.

Wages averaged at or slightly above the going rate in the community, and, in addition, the company had instituted a profit-sharing plan several years ago, under which one-third of profits before taxes were distributed among all employees of two years' uninterrupted service. About five-sixths of the employees were eligible under the plan. Bonuses generally amounted to 20% or more of annual wages. The company had established a trust, administered by Messrs. Adams, Swift, and a senior engineer, into which all bonuses up to 15% of wages were paid for investment in general market securities. The balance of the bonus was paid in cash.

BUDGETING AND CAPITAL EXPENDITURES

In addition to his production duties, Mr. Adams was in charge of financial planning. Drawing up the budget involved co-ordination of forecasts made by the sales department with departmental spending estimates obtained from foremen and supervisors, and past performance as shown on Mr. Clark's cost records. Mr. Adams commented that he set the budget as he saw fit and was not forced to seek Mr. Patterson's approval. "Chet often displays the attitude, 'Don't bother me unless I ask you,'" he said.

Mr. Patterson received a copy of the budget at the same time the other executives did. He said he thought the problems of budgeting in the past few years had consisted mainly of determining the capacity of the plant and filling in the orders from the large backlog on a first-come, first-served basis. Then it was a matter of estimating the expenses. Mr. Adams concurred, adding that the company was still riding the boom in the electronics business. "We have had no worries yet—but the real test for this place will come should we experience a recession in our industry."

Mr. Adams also handled most requests for capital expenditures. No formal system of project appraisal was used for the yearly capital outlays of $60,000–$75,000, and Mr. Adams served as a clearing center. For instance, when Mr. Gruber, Mr. McDonald, and the purchasing agent complained about the lack of office space, Mr. Adams arranged the preparation of a master plan for a $180,000 addition to the building. After discussing this plan thoroughly with Mr. Swift and Thomas Patterson, he submitted it to the board. It was on this level that Chester Patterson first reviewed and voted on the plan.

SALES

The sales department had been developed by Mr. Fritz Gruber, who had joined the company in 1946 as the only sales engineer, after spending over eight years with the Factory Insurance Corporation. Reporting directly to him were five district sales managers who supervised a total of about 35 sales representatives working as independent agents on a commission basis.

Selling the company's products required considerable understanding of the customer's technical problems and requirements. Since the salesmen worked for independent agents, the district managers spent much time visiting the representatives and accompanying salesmen on their calls. District managers enjoyed a high degree of independence in the pursuit of their duties, having authority to "hire and fire" representatives. "It looks like I have successfully worked myself out of a job," was Mr. Gruber's comment on the amount of delegation practiced in his department.

Mr. Gruber, an "applications engineer at heart," disliked purely administrative duties. He said about one-third of his time was spent on personnel matters, since he considered it highly important to get people who fitted into the company's spirit of independent thinking. Another third of his time went to administrative duties that consisted mainly of approving new sales representatives, "pinch-hitting" for his district managers, and preparing sales forecasts. The remainder of Mr. Gruber's time was spent on the problem of new product development, which he considered, along with selling, one of the two chief responsibilities of his department.

In making sales, salesmen looked first to see if customer specifications could be met by one of the semistandard relays listed in the company's sales manual. This volume listed all basic relays and over a thousand variations that had a relatively wide or steady market. If, however, the sale required a special application, the salesman referred the problem to the company's district manager, who in turn sought advice from whichever company engineer he considered expert in the field involved.

After the product had been selected or designed, the sales department wrote up the orders and the specifications obtained from the engineer. The order was then handed to the planning and scheduling group, which arranged for materials and production.

In pricing the company's products, Mr. Gruber relied on cost data supplied by Mr. Adams and Mr. Clark to set a "floor" below which business was considered unattractive. Actual selling prices varied with the size of the order, and depended on market conditions.

The company did not always try, however, to meet competitors' prices. For example, in a conversation with Mr. Patterson, Mr. Gruber referred to a sizable order lost because of price cutting by a smaller competitor. After rapid questioning, Mr. Patterson agreed with Mr. Gruber's decision not to meet the lower price, but he urged the sales manager to protect the company from getting the reputation of a high-price concern impervious to market pressure. Mr. Gruber replied he felt strongly that it was time to re-examine the pricing policy for relay types on which the company no longer held a technical advantage. Mr. Patterson agreed, and he asked to be informed if steps were taken to adjust pricing policy to the basic changes in the growing relay field, which attracted more and more competitors.

So far, no prices were listed in the company's sales manual, but Mr. Gruber hoped in the long run to change this situation.

NEW PRODUCTS COMMITTEE

Mr. Gruber believed that seeking out new product ideas was as important a part of his job as selling. As chairman of a "new products committee," which consisted of himself and the five district managers, Mr. Gruber every two or three weeks reviewed a number of the 200–300 new ideas in his files.

This committee, composed exclusively of sales personnel, had developed about a year ago out of a larger committee which had consisted of Messrs. Patterson, Gruber, Adams, Cordes, and Thomas Patterson. Mr. Gruber said the old committee fell into disuse because its members were too far removed from detailed knowledge about customer problems, and because the five men were difficult to assemble at one time. He characterized the new group as an "idea screening committee" whose members, all engineers by training, were intimately familiar with the capacity of the plant and its people as well as with the demands of the market. He believed that more efficient selection of product ideas could result in reduced effort and man-hours wasted.

In speaking of new products selection, Mr. Patterson commented that "every once in a while someone in the company wants a new products committee." He said that he was not aware of the need for such a group at present, since facilities of the engineering department were now adequate to permit the engineers to pursue all new ideas that sufficiently fascinated them. "Should we not be able to do this any more, then I can see a need for a screening committee, although I always think of the saying: 'Had Moses been a committee, the Israelites would still be in Egypt today.'"

The former chief engineer, Mr. Cordes, stated that in his experience, committees of this nature were doomed to failure because the interest of all participants could not be sufficiently aroused, because there was lack of authority, and because no really new information could be given.

Mr. Adams said the sales department was the right place for a new products committee should there be a need for one. He could not recall seeing any information on the activities of the present group. He commented that the first committee described by Mr. Gruber had functioned for about a year in the early 1950's when Mr. Thomas Patterson had "dreamed up" so many new product ideas that a committee was needed to classify them in order of importance. But the need dwindled when no new products were forthcoming for a longer period. "I think it is necessary to distinguish between real innovations or just improvements, and a committee should really deal only with the former," he said.

ACCOUNTING AND FINANCES

James Clark, treasurer and controller, joined the company in 1945 as assistant treasurer, and became treasurer shortly thereafter. His department consisted of 32 people who prepared the company's general accounting records and maintained a job-cost system which analyzed actual production costs, departmental overhead, and inventories.

Mr. Clark was greatly interested in the application of mechanical tabulation and had introduced it to the company when he joined it. Progressively he rented IBM equipment until he completed the system with a high-speed tabulator. Rental charges amounted to about $2,000 per month. The IBM equipment required the services of six full-time employees, but Mr. Clark said mechanization had brought more than proportionate reductions in the office force.

In the fall of 1956, conversion to card tabulation was not yet complete. Major projects still to be tackled included inventory controls and accounts receivable records. Mr. Clark indicated that the equipment made possible speedy completion of monthly operating statements and detailed analyses of sales, orders, commission statements, territorial backlogs, etc.

Mr. Clark was concerned with the problem of selling the use of mechanized equipment down through the ranks. He expected to hold an "open house" for everyone in the company once he had completed the accounting system. "I think when people see what can be done, there will be questions," he said.

The peak load on the machines occurred around the first of each month, when monthly reports and statements were run. This was a stumbling block to using the equipment in areas like production scheduling or analyses of orders in process. Mr. Barnes commented that successful use of IBM methods for production purposes would require some control over the equipment, since tabulations would have to be made as needed, at any time during the month. However, he had begun studies on the application of the equipment for production purposes.

Furnishing data for renegotiation purposes was another duty of the treasurer, especially important for the company because of the high percentage of military contracts. Mr. Clark had spent considerable time in past years on preparing cost analyses to support the company's profits on military orders. The allocation of overhead costs had proved difficult because the regular accounting records did not contain such allocations, but the company had finally been cleared every year.

Mr. Clark had received full authority to run his department as he saw best fit, and this authority continued to be maintained. "I can run my machines with pink cardboard if I want to, and no one would bother me," he said. In running his operation, he had little contact with most other phases of the company. "I am rather isolated here," he commented, "and I see no outsiders at all; sometimes I wish I were in purchasing to see more people."

THE FUTURE

In discussing the future, Mr. Patterson commented on planning:

We—or maybe I better say "I"—generally prefer to work and plan ahead in small steps. We think of the immediate situation, spending as much time and money as we can afford at the moment on the problem, and then take a look again. We may not like a particular situation, such as a decline in orders for a particular product, but there is nothing drastic to do—we kick ideas around until we find the best thing in our reach. For instance, when Clark wanted some IBM equipment, we did not decide on the over-all installation right then and there, but each part was justified at the time by him. It is just like building a wall—the basic decision to put the wall up was made when I decided to go into business; now it is a matter of putting the stones in squarely, one at a time. Or take the plastic foam: Every one of us sees each dollar that is being put in the experiments, and we all see the results as they come. Now and then we take a look to see what opportunities are coming up.

We try to justify our decisions as they arise. At times we must establish basic policy, like going into the manufacture of industrial controls. But we avoid going into a new area or a competitive field with full steam. We would rather drive a small car of our own than ride the tail gate of a fast moving truck driven by some of the big firms in the business. This is how we would feel by committing ourselves heavily into the future.

Mr. Patterson considered the most important problem of the company to be the high percentage of government work. He felt that he should actively seek more civilian business. "We exist all right on government contracts," he said, "but I hate to trust it. It is not so much a question of the additional red tape; rather, there is no sense of achievement in producing for outside inspectors. For instance, I am sure I could turn my ideas on plastic foam processing into military applications, but frankly, I don't want to do it. It is just not a pleasant way of doing business."

Another problem cited by the president was that of finding the right people for his company as it grew. "We are generally aware of the need for bringing people along," he said, "and there are prospects for young people with us." He referred to his policy of putting no pay ceilings on jobs, but he was conscious of the fact that promotions in rank could not be given as fast as desirable, since the company was still small. "We have consistently promoted from within whenever possible, and have had a number of conspicuous successes. But we have some people in positions who are not able to go further, which may become even more of a problem, since their jobs grow bigger as we grow."

A DAY WITH MR. PATTERSON

On this particular day Mr. Patterson spent considerable time with four individuals. First, he conferred with a senior project engineer for about an hour on a new product. In Mr. Patterson's own words, he "pretty strongly urged him to use a different approach to the technical problem involved."

The rest of the morning Mr. Patterson spent with the engineer in charge of the plastic process, actively participating in experiments. Both men solicited reactions to new ideas from each other; in several instances the case writer thought Mr. Patterson helped to clarify the engineer's suggestions by thorough questioning.

Shortly before lunch, Mr. Patterson was asked by the sales manager, Mr. Gruber, about a trip he had made some time ago. The conversation developed into a discussion of the loss of a contract due to price cutting by a competitor, moving from there to pricing policy in general.

About half the afternoon was spent on a series of product tests which Mr. Patterson conducted, together with the project engineer in charge, for the benefit of Mr. Gruber, who had inquired about the characteristics of this product some time ago. Thereafter, Mr. Patterson returned to the plastics experiments. The last half hour of the day was spent on reading mail and reworking a sales pamphlet.

"This day was more typical than yesterday would have been, if there is such a thing as a typical day," commented Mr. Patterson. He had spent more than half of the previous day with two visitors who presented him with "some hare-brained product idea" for diversification. Mr. Patterson had finally declined to invest in the new product. "While you might consider that a typical problem with which I concern myself every day, it certainly is not," he said.

A DAY WITH MR. SWIFT

The case writer observed that the major part of Mr. Swift's time was spent walking about the department talking to his engineers. Several times he chatted with a particular engineer engaged in modifying a prototype relay, asking technical questions and making suggestions. Another time he was called by a laboratory technician to attend a test of three samples of a new product. Mr. Swift participated in testing, suggested changes, and inquired into the possibility of compiling statistics on the variations encountered. After the senior project engineer in charge had mentioned ways of implementing such research, Mr. Swift walked away.

Later he met another project engineer who was weighing the merits of several suppliers of plastic parts for his product. Mr. Swift sat down with him to analyze the pros and cons. Finally the engineer decided to call personally on one supplier to insure correct production of the intricate part. At no time did Mr. Swift overrule an opinion by authority, or ask for a follow-up report.

In the afternoon one of the senior engineers asked Mr. Swift about a request by Mr. Patterson to list specifications in the manual on a new series of relays. After discussing the technical merits of the product, they jointly decided that such a listing was not yet feasible. This same engineer then raised the issue of getting an assistant, and Mr. Swift said he would see the personnel manager about it.

While in his office, Mr. Swift was visited by one of the district sales managers who presented a customer's request for a guarantee of rather tight specifications on a relay. Mr. Swift went to see the plant superintendent and the chief inspector, who agreed to his suggestion that the product be inspected for the purpose. Later in the day Mr. Swift attended tests of the relay and told the district manager that he could give the guarantee.

A district sales manager came in to ask about procedures for notarizing a bid for the City of Chicago. Mr. Swift, a notary public, proceeded to supply the information through a series of phone calls.

Intermittently, Mr. Swift read pamphlets on the shortage of engineers and dictated letters in connection with the last directors' meeting. Then he discussed one of his own projects with the chief tool designer who asked for a change in specifications. Mr. Swift decided to request a sample product with the new specifications to test personally the effects of the change.

Later, Mr. Swift discussed with the senior engineer sharing his office two memos received from the plant superintendent. The memos inquired about the status of a parts cleaning procedure suggested by production "a long time ago," and further asked for a listing of each engineer using a certain expensive raw material. Mr. Swift was tempted to let the memos "die," but after some consideration he decided to pass along the first one to the project engineer in charge of the product, "to see what he thought of it." Technical discussions accounted for the remainder of his time.

A DAY WITH MR. ADAMS

The case writer observed in the works manager's office that Mr. Adams mainly made himself available for counsel and advice. "Your presence scares off quite a number of people who would ordinarily come here to talk to me about their jobs, as well as their own personal problems," Mr. Adams said. Nevertheless, he had several visitors: Mr. Gruber came in to talk about the change in pricing policy which he had been discussing with Mr. Patterson the previous day. A lengthy conversation developed during which both men commented that the company was undergoing a basic change as its products met increasing competition. Mr. Adams listened to the arguments of the sales manager, who supported his views by drawing price-cost curves, and stated that he would turn the matter over in his mind for a few days.

Thereafter Mr. Adams spent two hours with a company accountant to review the profit-sharing arrangement in the light of a new tax ruling. Mrs. Faulkner, the personnel manager, dropped in to ask Mr. Adams' views on a want-ad for a testing engineer. After hearing his criticisms, she suggested a more unusual approach. Mr. Adams gave suggestions as to where help for the ad could be obtained.

The engineering manager came to Mr. Adams' office to ask whether the time-payment policy for the office force was also applicable to engineering personnel. Mr. Adams said it was, but that so far it had not been possible to reduce a general policy to writing.

A spontaneous meeting of the planning and order service heads in

the superintendent's office next door drew Mr. Adams' attention. It involved the fact that "short orders" (rush orders) were increasing in
number and that a change in scheduling these special requests might be
warranted. Mr. Adams suggested that no changes be initiated until
completion of the current study of the paper flow.

Later the treasurer stopped by to announce that the next monthly
statement would be available shortly. Finally, Mr. Adams authorized a
request for a $6,000 machine tool after the factory superintendent ex-
plained briefly the need for the machine and his search for the best possible supplier.

Blakeston & Wilson

BLAKESTON & WILSON, of Chicago, Illinois, was a manufacturer of medium-price, high-quality chocolate candy. Its chocolates, sold under the brand name "Perfection," were distributed through company-controlled stores and by candy wholesalers (usually called "jobbers" in the candy trade).

The company was organized in 1938 when it purchased the assets of the bankrupt Sidwell Wilson Company. Mr. Wilson, who had been president of the defunct company, was instrumental in securing necessary capital and in organizing the new firm, of which he also became president. Whereas the original company had had an unsuccessful profit record, Blakeston & Wilson achieved immediate financial success. Profits were earned each year from 1938 through 1946. Mr. Wilson believed that the failure of his first company resulted from excessive sales costs; in turn, he believed that the success of the new company resulted from the fact that lower sales costs had been achieved. Profits for the first quarter of 1947 were the highest in the firm's history.

During 1947, Blakeston & Wilson planned to double the number of Perfection Chocolate Shops which marketed its candy. This expansion in retail store operations was the outgrowth of a policy adopted in 1943. Prior to that time, the company had sold its chocolates solely to wholesalers and large chain buyers. Mr. Wilson stated that his company had entered the retail sales field in 1943 to assure a stable, profitable postwar market for a part of his factory's manufacturing capacity. The opening of these Perfection Chocolate Shops was a real innovation in the company's distribution procedures; Blakeston & Wilson executive personnel had not had previous experience in retail store operation. Operating results from 1943 through April of 1947, however, had convinced Mr. Wilson of the success of the policy, as well as of the wisdom of further retail sales expansion.

PREDECESSOR COMPANY

The Sidwell Wilson Company, incorporated in 1923, had sold packaged and bulk chocolates under several brand names. Sales volume had averaged $700,000 annually, with selling expenses of approximately $100,000 (see Exhibit 1). The company had employed eight salesmen, who, under the direction of Mr. Wilson, served wholesalers and buying syndicates in the Middle West and the East.

Stock ownership had been originally divided between Mr. Wilson (25%) and the majority stockholders (75%). By borrowing money from a company supplier, Mr. Wilson had purchased complete ownership of the company in 1926. Serious losses during the early thirties made repayment of the loan impossible, and in 1937 company assets were sold to satisfy creditor claims.

Exhibit 1

PREDECESSOR COMPANY—SIDWELL WILSON COMPANY

Profit and Loss Statement for the Year Ending December 31, 1935

	Amount	Percentage of Net Sales
Net sales	$623,069.97	....
Less: Cost of sales	520,616.71	83.56%
Gross profit	$102,453.26	16.44
Less: Selling, general, and administrative expenses:		
Freight and cartage outward	$ 22,618.72	3.63
Shipping wages and supplies	10,505.42	1.69
Advertising	4,373.97	0.70
Selling expenses	40,536.91	6.50
Administrative expenses	19,740.40	3.17
Miscellaneous expenses	9,015.74	1.45
Total expenses	$106,791.16	17.14
Net loss for period	$ 4,337.90	0.70

Source: Company records.

"The company failed," Mr. Wilson stated, "primarily because our selling expenses were too high. Moreover, we were selling to wholesalers who played one manufacturer against another to force prices down. We worked and sweated to make a few dollars manufacturing candy while the wholesalers and retailers took large margins for distributing and selling our products. Consequently, the consumer paid a high price for candy on which we did not make profits." The company had also been troubled by shortages in working capital. "We had just $3,000 plus equipment when we started in 1923, and, when we did occasionally make money, the stockholders took it all out in dividends."

FORMATION OF BLAKESTON & WILSON

After analyzing the difficulties which he had encountered in his first business, Mr. Wilson concluded that by reducing sales expense he could successfully compete in the candy business. To secure capital for his new enterprise, Mr. Wilson approached Mr. Blakeston, a director and operating executive of a large Midwestern variety chain. Mr. Blakeston and three of his associates furnished the minimum amount required, $30,000. They received 500 shares of preferred stock; in addition, when all preferred stock had been retired from earnings, they were to be issued 48% of the company's authorized common stock. For services rendered, Mr. Wilson was then to receive 52% of the common stock.

By March of 1938, necessary machinery had been installed and production was initiated. Company offices, located in the factory building, were furnished simply; all administrative and overhead expense was kept to a minimum. The executive organization of the new company consisted of two men: Mr. Wilson, president and general manager, who was in charge of sales and promotion work, financial administration, and supervision of administrative personnel; and Mr. Herman Smith, production manager, who directed manufacturing, purchasing, and cost accounting work, in addition to performing some other miscellaneous duties.

PRODUCT

Blakeston & Wilson, in 1947, manufactured quality boxed and bulk chocolates. The company's boxed chocolates were packed in attractive, but inexpensively designed, paper boxes. All Blakeston & Wilson candy was hand-dipped, a process normally used only for expensive packaged chocolates; medium-price and some expensive chocolates were usually dipped by machine. Hand-dipping was reputed to create thicker, creamier chocolate coatings over the candy centers—qualities which the company believed were recognized and appreciated by consumers. Mr. Wilson stated that his chocolates (75 cents per pound) were equal in quality to those sold in the high-price range ($1.00–$2.50) and superior in quality to other medium-price chocolates ($0.75–$1.00). "The difference in price between medium- and high-price chocolates lies primarily in expensive boxes and decorations and in large promotional expenditures, not in the quality of the candy," he stated.

Prior to World War II, the company had manufactured some standard hand-dipped chocolates for variety chains and grocery chains. Shortages of raw materials had forced the company to reduce sharply production for these outlets during the war years.

ORIGINAL SALES PLAN OF BLAKESTON & WILSON

Blakeston & Wilson, until 1943, sold chocolate candy under a variety of brand names only to wholesalers and to two large chains. The company sold to 121 wholesalers in an area bounded by Madison, Wisconsin, Rock Island, Illinois, Louisville, Kentucky, and New York City. Wholesalers were given usual trade discounts (wholesale, 20%; retail, 33⅓%) and exclusive sales rights for a specified area. A typical wholesaler's sales varied in volume from $4,000 to $25,000, with an average of $8,000. He, in turn, sold to outlets such as drug and department stores, clubs, and grocery stores. Wholesalers did not carry other brands of chocolates in a competitive price range. They did, however, carry both lower-price and higher-price chocolates.

"My theory was that there were more people who would buy our product because of its quality value than there were people who would have to be coaxed into buying it by expensive sales efforts," said Mr. Wilson. In carrying out his policy to cut sales expenses, Mr. Wilson personally handled all sales work; he had no salesmen or sales representatives. Mr. Wilson periodically visited wholesalers and syndicate buyers, determined credit policies, supervised sales accounting work, selected candy items, and designed candy packages. "My selling costs for the wholesale and syndicate trade vary between 1.5% to 2% of gross sales," Mr. Wilson stated, "whereas usually costs in the industry for selling to that trade amount to 6%." He attributed the industry's high selling costs to its use of numerous salesmen, expensive missionary sales work, and high promotional expense. "We do very little promotional work for our wholesalers, and the wholesalers do not do any promotional work on our candy. They have recognized our effort to shave expenses and therefore place the best box of candy in the consumer's hands at the lowest price." Company sales promotional material initially consisted of circulars describing candy manufacturing processes and counter display cards. "The quality of our candy will sell these chocolates without sales promotion," Mr. Wilson emphasized.

Mr. Wilson had personally selected his wholesalers when the new company was first organized. Thereafter, he visited each distributor approximately three times a year. These visits were informal and frequently amounted to a game of golf with the executives of the concern. Mr. Wilson knew each executive personally, and all business relations were on a first-name basis. During World War II, his visits to company wholesalers became more infrequent, since selling at that time consisted of allocating scarce supplies of candy among these firms.

In 1947, commenting on the excellence of his original wholesaler selection, Mr. Wilson noted: "We haven't gained or lost a new account in over nine years." Shortages of candy, as well as a heavy personal work load, had prevented Mr. Wilson from returning to his prewar schedule of visits to wholesalers.

ENTRANCE INTO RETAIL SALES OPERATIONS

During the depression years of the early thirties, the candy industry had been described as "sick"; its chief symptom was overcapacity with its attendant pains of price cutting, secret rebates, and overextension of credit. Since the incorporation of Blakeston & Wilson in 1938, however, candy production, as well as the price per pound received by the manufacturer, had increased substantially (see Exhibit 2). Company sales, following the general industry pattern, increased from $286,000 in 1938 to $909,000 in 1942. Although wartime sugar rationing had hampered production, this difficulty had been partially eliminated through the increased use of nonrationed substitute materials. Moreover, manufacturers of medium- and high-price packaged chocolates had benefited greatly from the sharply increased national income. Consumers were willing to buy these more expensive candies, on which the manufacturer realized excellent margins, instead of cheaper bulk candy formerly purchased in variety stores.

Mr. Wilson, despite his firm's prosperity, was apprehensive over future prospects for sales to the wholesaler trade. On the basis of the experience with his former company, he believed that competition would first appear and be most severe on sales made to wholesaler organizations. Manufacturers selling through wholesalers, Mr. Wilson stated, could never be certain how much they could sell, and they had little control over prices received for their products. Mr. Wilson believed that a market for at least a part of his productive output could be secured at a controlled price by opening company-operated candy stores. He was not sure of making profits in these stores. "If we could just break even on store operations, our profits would come from manufacturing the candy."

Mr. Wilson, although he had worked in the candy industry since 1909, had not had any experience in retail sales work or in retail store management. He therefore discussed his idea for retail candy stores with his board, company bankers, and associates in the industry; they were unanimous in their disapproval of his plan. Despite these objections, Mr. Wilson announced that he planned to open a retail store, if necessary by supplying funds from his personal resources. The board of directors, after this statement, reluctantly approved the new policy.

Perfection Candy Stores, Inc., was organized to finance operations of the new retail store; the necessary capital was subscribed by

Exhibit 2

AVERAGE WHOLESALE VALUE PER POUND OF CONFECTIONERY SOLD BY
MANUFACTURER-WHOLESALERS AND MANUFACTURER-RETAILERS, 1925–45

YEAR	MANUFACTURER-WHOLESALERS*		MANUFACTURER-RETAILERS	
	Number of Firms	Average Value per Pound	Number of Firms	Average Value per Pound
1925	386	$0.229	96	$0.392
1926	386	0.226	96	0.396
1927	369	0.222	113	0.348
1928	381	0.224	118	0.319
1929	394	0.210	123	0.335
1930	405	0.196	113	0.386
1931	404	0.174	114	0.366
1932	337	0.136	81	0.340
1933	301	0.131	44	0.376
1934	354	0.137	44	0.387
1935	308	0.142	48	0.385
1936	308	0.143	40	0.420
1937	265	0.153	33	0.451
1938	265	0.144	33	0.453
1939	244	0.143	29	0.449
1940	244	0.144	29	0.436
1941	224	0.153	24	0.468
1942	235	0.188	29	0.489
1943	258	0.218	26	0.414
1944	258	0.232	40	0.490
1945	353	0.244	51	**

* Includes cocoa-bean processors specializing in solid chocolate items.
** Applicable information not available.
Source: U.S. Department of Commerce, *19th Annual Report on Confectionery Sales and Distribution* (1946), p. 23.

Mr. Blakeston and his associates. They received the preferred stock of the new corporation plus 48% of its common stock. Mr. Wilson received the remaining 52% of the common stock for "services rendered." The 6% cumulative preferred stock did not have voting power unless three consecutive annual dividend payments were passed. The new corporation had the same management and board of directors as did

Blakeston & Wilson; it was a separate corporate entity only for tax purposes and as a method of limiting the financial liability of Blakeston & Wilson.

The first Perfection Chocolate Shop was opened in Chicago in the fall of 1943. At that time all former brand names of the company, with the exception of those used for the syndicate trade, were abandoned, and the name "Perfection" was adopted for chocolates sold to the company store and to the wholesale trade.

OPERATION OF RETAIL STORES

Success in the operation of the first Perfection shop led to further expansion during 1946. Between January and August of that year, five

Exhibit 3

BLAKESTON & WILSON

Intercorporation Relationships

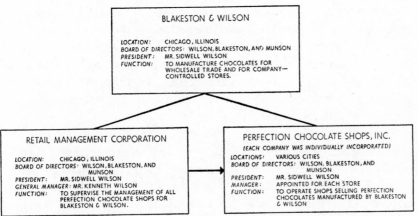

NOTE: Stock ownership of all companies was held by Mr. Wilson, Mr. Blakeston, and Mr. Blakeston's associates. Over-all management of all companies was handled by Mr. Sidwell Wilson.

additional Perfection shops were opened in the business section of Chicago. Each new shop was organized, financed, and individually incorporated, as was done in the case of the original store. (See Exhibit 3.)

Perfection Chocolate Shops were located in sections of Chicago where pedestrian traffic passing each store was heavy, as well as where the possibilities that passers-by would purchase candy were high, i.e., near hotels, department store shopping areas, and financial districts. Shops featured Perfection packaged chocolates in ½ pound, 1 pound, and 2 pound boxes, in addition to Perfection bulk chocolates; they sold only Blakeston & Wilson products and did not handle accessory lines, such as nuts and novelties. Most chocolates were 75 cents a pound or $1.45 for a 2 pound box. A few specially packed boxes of chocolates retailed at higher prices—$1.25–$1.50 a pound.

Each shop had a manager and, usually, four clerks. These were all girls and they were selected with regard to their appearance, character, and education. Starting weekly wages were $30, which were advanced to $35 after three months' service; competing firms started their sales girls at $22 a week. Managers were paid between $40 and $50 a week. In addition, both clerks and managers were paid a bonus if each girl sold over $480 of candy per week; clerks averaged between $2 and $14 per week in bonuses. Managers were eligible for an additional supervisors' bonus.

Mr. Wilson believed that any Perfection Chocolate Shop was in a strong competitive position because (1) it sold high-quality, reasonably priced candy; (2) all stores were efficiently operated; and (3) each store had a large sales volume.

Perfection chocolates were superior in quality to other medium-price chocolates. They were five cents less per pound, however, than chocolates sold by the leading competitor of Perfection Candy Shops—a seminational chain of retail candy stores. Savings resulting from reduced retail selling costs and efficient manufacturing operations were passed on to the customer through the use of highest-quality candy ingredients, Mr. Wilson stated.

Perfection Candy Shops were operated more efficiently than competitive shops, Mr. Wilson said, because of several unique operating features which he had developed. He had designed all Perfection shops with a small display window, in which several boxes of candy were highlighted. Traditionally, retail candy stores had large display windows which, he believed, took several hundred dollars of display stock, as well as many hours of time for decoration. Furthermore, Perfection bulk chocolates were packed in specially designed 5 pound boxes at the factory; these boxes fit into display cases in the retail stores without rehandling. Competitive stores, said Mr. Wilson, packed their candies in stock boxes at the factory, and the candy had to be repacked for store display. Moreover, he continued, through the operation of the bonus-payment plan for store clerks, there was an incentive upon their part to keep store personnel at a minimum—the fewer clerks in a store, the higher the individual bonus payments to each girl.

He believed that Perfection sales volume per store (1947) was substantially higher than the sales volume of competitive candy outlets.

Originally Mr. Wilson (1943 through August of 1946) personally directed all retail store operations. He visited each store daily to check on operations and to assure himself that everything was being handled satisfactorily. He hired all store personnel, supervised advertising and promotion campaigns, and determined details of operating procedures. Daily reports of cash and sales, as well as a weekly report of inventory, constituted his formal check on store operations. "It worked out beautifully," said Mr. Wilson. The primary management difficulty during this period was to find sufficient supplies of candy to meet the accelerated wartime demand for quality products.

To secure critically short materials, such as butter, sugar, and chocolate, which were necessary for the manufacture of Perfection chocolates for his retail trade, Mr. Wilson reduced production of all low-margin chocolates sold to chain buyers; this sharply diminished sales to those two customers. Sales to wholesalers were maintained at varying percentages of their 1941 purchases. These material sources were not sufficient, however, to fill the retail store demand for Perfection chocolates, and a wartime customer ration of one pound per day was instituted. In April, 1947, the improved materials situation permitted the removal of this wartime customer ration in all shops.

RETAIL MANAGEMENT CORPORATION

To relieve a heavy personal work load, as well as to prepare for intensive postwar competition, Mr. Wilson organized the Retail Management Corporation; that company was to supervise the operations of all Perfection Chocolate Shops. "My usual business day was fifteen hours long," he stated. "With conditions in the industry returning to normal I knew that more intensive management efforts were going to be required. I did not have the time to supervise retail store operations, in addition to my regular work." Retail Management Corporation was incorporated on August 1, 1946; it was organized and financed in the same manner employed in the incorporation of Perfection shops. Mr. Wilson, as president of Retail Management Corporation, made all major decisions for the new concern.

Mr. Wilson appointed his son, Kenneth, as manager of the new company. Kenneth, upon graduation from college in 1937, had been employed by the Sidwell Wilson Company as a salesman. He was assigned to develop wholesale business in the Michigan area. After a six months' trial period, this attempt had been abandoned as unprofitable. Kenneth later worked in the leather industry until his induction into the army. He returned to work for his father in November of 1945. At that time Mr. Wilson planned to have his son handle sales to wholesalers in the Middle Atlantic states. "Sugar rationing continued during 1946, however, and selling to wholesalers was still primarily a matter of ordertaking," said Mr. Wilson, "so we placed Kenneth in charge of the Retail Management Corporation." Kenneth's experience with retail sales and with the candy industry was limited to his earlier work with his father. "I wanted to give my son a chance at the business. He doesn't know much about it, but the way I look at it, I would have to teach either a stranger or my son. I might as well gamble on my son."

The staff of Retail Management Corporation consisted of four persons, in addition to Kenneth Wilson. A supervisor of stores inspected (weekly) the appearance of store property, displays, and personnel and filled out an inspection report which noted the results of his investigation; this report was given to the store manager with a duplicate copy forwarded to Kenneth Wilson. To correct any inadequacies noted on the inspection report, each manager checked her *Perfection Operating Manual*. This manual, written by Sidwell Wilson, outlined in detail approved operating procedures to be used in his retail stores. He believed that, through the use of this manual, store operations and activities were so systematized that necessary supervision was limited to an occasional check by the supervisor of stores, Kenneth Wilson, or himself. Sidwell Wilson's daughter, Thelma, was director of merchandising and purchasing. She determined inventory requirements for the shops and purchased supplies of chocolates from Blakeston & Wilson. A commercial artist developed display and counter card promotional material; radio and newspaper advertisements were prepared by a Chicago advertising agency. A bookkeeper kept necessary accounting records. Neither of the Wilson children had had previous experience in retail sales work.

Retail Management Corporation, in supervising the management of all Perfection Chocolate Shops, hired personnel, inspected the appearance of stores and store personnel, kept necessary accounting records, purchased candy and supplies, and furnished necessary financial service and advice. It received 10% of the gross sales of all Perfection shops as a management fee. Retail Management agreed to spend at least one-half of this sum for advertising purposes, the exact amount to be determined by Blakeston & Wilson.

The number of Perfection Chocolate Shops supervised by Retail Management increased from six to seventeen between August, 1946, and April, 1947. Store sales averaged $90,000 per unit. Store rentals ranged from $5,000 to $20,000 a year, with an average payment of $8,000. Overhead costs were approximately 3% of gross store sales. Invested capital, per store, varied from $10,000 to $15,000. All shops were successful financially.

Eight of the eleven new shops had been established in cities within a 200-mile radius of Chicago—i.e., Gary, Indiana, and Peoria, Illinois. Perfection shops in all eight non-Chicago cities came into competition with retail outlets, such as drug and department stores which also sold Perfection packaged chocolates distributed by company wholesalers. This created a great deal of resentment on the part of the wholesalers, who felt their market was being usurped.

PRICE

Perfection chocolates had originally retailed at 65 cents a pound; by 1946, as has been previously stated, the retail price had been increased to 75 cents a pound or $1.45 for the 2 pound box. Retail prices were the same at both Perfection Chocolate Shops and retail stores supplied by company wholesalers. In 1947, Blakeston & Wilson sold Perfection chocolates to its wholesalers at 40 cents a pound and to Perfection shops at 42 cents a pound.

Manufacturing costs had increased 17 cents per pound between 1943 and 1946. Furthermore, prices of chocolate and other raw materials had continued to increase during the first quarter of 1947, and the possible removal of sugar rationing in October of 1947 was expected to raise the price of that important commodity.

Despite rising material costs, retail-price reductions were already appearing among some brands of packaged chocolates. One leading chain competitor of Perfection had reduced the price of its 2 pound box of candy from $1.55 to $1.50 in March of 1947. Mr. Sidwell Wilson did not plan to reduce the retail price of his candy to meet this competitive development. Any price reduction, he believed, would first have to be made to the wholesaler trade, since he was well acquainted with the extremely competitive aspects of wholesaling.

When material prices returned to normal, Blakeston & Wilson planned to use any savings resulting from lowered costs to improve the quality of Perfection chocolates. "Our chocolates, which we sold for 65 cents a pound in 1943, were of better quality than chocolates which we now sell for 75 cents a pound," Mr. Wilson stated. The company had been forced to reduce product quality, as had its competitors, to take care of increased raw-material prices.

ADVERTISING

"We spent over $100,000 in 1946 advertising Perfection chocolates," said Mr. Wilson. Two-thirds of this money was expended for radio advertisements, the remaining one-third for newspaper advertisements. Blakeston & Wilson financed but a small part of the Perfection advertising fund; most of the money had been supplied by the Retail Manage-agement Corporation with assistance from individual Perfection stores. Radio and newspaper advertisements were concentrated in the Chicago area and in cities where Perfection shops were located. These advertisements stressed the quality of Perfection chocolates but did not mention that Perfection candies were hand dipped; this was in conformity with industry advertising practices. By mutual agreement, candy manufacturers did not advertise whether their chocolates were hand dipped or machine dipped.

Advertising expenditures for Perfection chocolates, among packaged and bulk chocolate manufacturers, were second only to those of the Stephen F. Whitman & Son Company in Philadelphia. That company manufactured nationally advertised and distributed Sampler chocolates which retailed at $1.75 for a 20 ounce package. Mr. Sidwell Wilson said that expenditures for advertising in 1947 would be substantially higher than 1946 totals.

MANUFACTURING

The Blakeston & Wilson factory originally occupied the first three floors of a warehouse; the company had recently expanded into two floors of an adjoining building. Manufacturing operations and storage facilities were located on each floor so that raw materials would be in close proximity to the production activities in which they were used. All manufacturing departments were air-conditioned, and the plant was equipped with cold-storage facilities capable of holding 300,000 pounds of finished candy. Candy-making machinery was old but in good repair. In 1947 the plant was producing approximately 22,000 pounds of candy per day, five days a week. Capacity plant production was 30,000 pounds per day.

Mr. Sidwell Wilson believed that company manufacturing operations were efficient because (1) he personally owned and operated his business, which gave him a close check on all operations; (2) he had invented a continuous process production line which enabled him to hand-dip chocolates at a lower cost than other competitive hand-dip chocolate manufacturers; and (3) his labor force was more efficient and effective than employee groups in other companies.

Mr. Wilson did not believe that any company. could secure a significant advantage over its competitors, as far as raw-materials purchasing was concerned. Sugar and chocolate prices, he said, were normally set by the New York City and foreign exchanges, and the price for a specified type of product was identical to all large-scale purchasers. Sugar, the primary ingredient of candy, was purchased by most companies on a day-to-day basis. "The only way normally to secure bargain sugar prices would be to gamble on futures—we tried that once and lost." Manufacturers of medium-price candies, however, could and did make some savings on minor items by using substitute or average-quality fruit centers, cream, and butter. Perfection chocolates, contrary to this practice, were always made from the highest-grade ingredients obtainable.

Mr. Smith, production manager, was assisted in factory supervision by four foremen and two floor ladies. He believed this number was the minimum staff required. In fact, when one of these assistants was ill, Mr. Smith had to take over temporarily his or her duties. He received two weekly production reports, which were also available for Mr. Wilson's use. They listed production by department, the number of manufacturing employees, total hours worked, and indirect factory expenses. He believed, however, that his most effective control technique was close personal supervision over factory operations. Mr. Smith was completely responsible for all manufacturing activities; Mr. Wilson did not concern himself with production problems, unless some major change in policy was contemplated.

Hand-dipped chocolates were more expensive to produce than machine-dipped candies primarily because of substantially increased labor costs. Mr. Smith estimated that machine-dipping resulted in savings of from 4 to 5 cents a pound in labor and material costs over Blakeston & Wilson's hand-dipping process. "We can afford to hand-dip our chocolates only because of the savings effected by our low sales cost."

Mr. Sidwell Wilson, in 1937, had developed and patented his continuous production-line process for dipping, cooling, and packing varied selections of chocolates. This process, he believed, enabled Blakeston & Wilson to hand-dip chocolates for 3 cents less per pound than competing hand-dip chocolate manufacturers. He had installed four of these units in his factory in 1938 at a cost of $4,000 per unit. In 1947 two units were operating at capacity (7,500 pounds per unit a day); the other two units, because of material shortages, were operating at partial capacity. Mr. Wilson had attempted to sell the process to other manufacturers for $100,000 per unit, but only one sale had been made to a small Evanston, Illinois, chocolate manufacturer.

The company's labor force was composed of 200 employees, most of whom were women engaged in dipping and packing chocolates. Labor and management relations were excellent; the company had never been organized. Wages equaled those of competing firms in the Chicago area; in addition to their base pay, all employees who had been with the company more than five years (96) participated in a profit-sharing plan which company officials believed stimulated employee interest and productive efficiency.

Wages of employees had risen steadily since 1938. At that time dippers were paid 30 cents an hour; in 1947 they started at 87 cents an hour. In addition to base pay, dippers were eligible for a bonus of from 1 to 9 cents an hour if they approached or reached the maximum production rate (24 pieces a minute); in 1947 most dippers were earning the maximum bonus. Mr. Smith awarded the bonus to dippers by occasionally checking production operations. "The bonus is based on my judgment as to how well they are doing," he said, "not on time or motion studies." The bonus system, which had been in effect for a period of four years, had not been extended to other employees of the company.

Mr. Smith personally handled the limited amount of cost accounting work done on all manufacturing operations. He had established standard costs on materials and direct labor for producing 100 pound lots of each type of candy included in the Perfection selection. Standards for burden had not been established, he said, since these charges were fairly constant from year to year. Standard costs were occasionally checked against actual costs when Mr. Smith believed this necessary. Although many of the company's standard cost sheets were obsolete because of changes in materials prices, Mr. Smith did not believe revisions were necessary so long as the company secured a 28% gross manufacturing operating profit (exclusive of burden charges). Exhibit 5 lists standard cost information on a typical chocolate item manufactured both for bulk and package sale.

Exhibit 4

BLAKESTON & WILSON
Balance Sheets, 1938–46
(In Thousands)

	1938	1939	1940	1941	1942	1943	1944	1945	1946
Assets									
Current Assets:									
Cash in Bank and on Hand	$ 11	$ 10	$ 13	$ 8	$ 32	$161	$202	$134	$227
Accounts Receivable	21	24	33	26	54	73	60	61	26
Inventories at Cost or Market, Whichever Is Lower	9	21	24	90	44	36	56	62	118
Total Current Assets	$ 41	$ 55	$ 70	$124	$130	$270	$318	$257	$371
Cash Surrender Value of Life Insurance Policy	1	2	8	9	9	10	11	16	17
Total	$ 42	$ 57	$ 78	$133	$139	$280	$329	$273	$388
Postwar Refundable Portion of Estimated Excess Profits Tax	..	..	..	..	..	12	26	..	..
Fixed Assets	13	39	45	45	38	34	38	33	39
Deferred Charges	8	13	19	11	10	9	17	17	14
Total Assets	$ 63	$109	$142	$189	$187	$335	$410	$323	$441
Liabilities and Capital									
Current Liabilities:									
Note Payable at Bank	..	..	$ 7	$ 37	$ 7	$ 7	$ 6	..	..
Accounts Payable and Accrued Expenses	$ 15	$ 19	31	25	20	29	67	$ 41	$ 58
Reserve for Federal and State Taxes	3	5	5	10	21	139	200	133	160
Total Current Liabilities	$ 18	$ 24	$ 43	$ 72	$ 48	$175	$273	$174	$218
Postwar Refund of Estimated Federal Excess Profits Tax	..	..	..	..	..	$ 12	$ 26	..	..
Capital Stock:									
Preferred Stock:									
Authorized and Issued—500 Shares of $6 Cumulative without Par Value	$ 30*	$ 50	$ 50	$ 50	$ 50	$ 50	$ 50	$ 50	$ 50
Less: Held in Treasury	..	..	..	..	..	..	18	50	50	50
Common Stock:									
Authorized, Issued, and Outstanding 1,040 Shares without Par Value	..	..	..	..	..	..	104†	104	104
Total Capital Stock	$ 30	$ 50	$ 50	$ 50	$ 50	$ 32	$104	$104	$104
Earned Surplus:									
Balance, January 1	..	$ 15	$ 35	$ 49	$ 67	$ 89	$116	$ 7	$ 45
Add: Net Profit	$ 15	21	17	21	25	32	34	28	74
Postwar Refund of Excess Profits Taxes	..	..	..	..	..	..	..	26‡	..
Less: Dividends Paid	..	1	2	3	3	3	39	16	..
Amount Transferred to Capital Stock Account	..	..	..	..	..	..	104‡	..	..
Under Accrual of Prior Years' Taxes, etc.	..	..	1	..	..	..	..	..	..
Balance, December 31	$ 15	$ 35	$ 49	$ 67	$ 89	$116	$ 7	$ 45	$119
Total Liabilities and Capital	$ 63	$109	$142	$189	$187	$335	$410	$323	$441

* 300 shares of preferred issued and outstanding December 31, 1938.
† Stated value of $100 per share of common voted by board of directors.
‡ Treated as deferred income in prior years, transferred to earned surplus December 31, 1945.
Source: Company records.

CHAIN STORE CUSTOMERS

By April, 1947, increased sales of bulk and packaged chocolates were again being made to the variety chain with which Mr. Blakeston was associated. Mr. Wilson had not re-established sales relations with the retail grocery chain to which he had sold chocolates prior to World War II. That company was building its own large candy factory and was installing candy departments in all its retail outlets. "We don't want to sell to any customer who is in competition with us in the manufacture of candy," Mr. Wilson declared. He had not yet attempted to secure another large grocery chain outlet, since a shortage of raw

Exhibit 5

BLAKESTON & WILSON

Standard Costs for 100-Pound Mix
of Chocolate-Covered Cream Candy

Materials...$26.97
Direct labor..................................... 7.65
   Total...................................$34.62

Source: Company records.

Exhibit 6

BLAKESTON & WILSON

Income Statements, 1938–46 (In Thousands)

	1938		1939		1940	
	Amt.	% of Sales	Amt.	% of Sales	Amt.	% of Sales
Net sales..	$286	100.0%	$562	100.0%	$668	100.0
Cost of sales...	231	80.8	470	83.6	561	84.0
Gross profit on sales...............................	$ 55	19.2%	$ 92	16.4%	$107	16.0
Selling, general, and administrative expenses:						
Freight and cartage outward...........................	$ 10	3.6%	$ 22	3.9%	$ 29	4.5
Shipping wages and supplies...........................	3	1.0	11	2.0	15	2.2
Advertising, travel, entertainment, commissions, and other selling expenses......................................	6	2.1	11	2.0	13	1.9
Executive and office salaries...........................	12	4.2	18	3.2	19	2.8
Contributions to profit-sharing plan......................	..	..	..	..	..	..
Provision for state excise and federal capital stock tax.....	1	0.3	2	0.4	2	0.3
Miscellaneous..	5	1.7	3	0.5	9	1.3
Total expenses...................................	$ 37	12.9%	$ 67	12.0%	$ 87	13.0
Net profit before federal taxes on income..................	$ 18	6.3%	$ 25	4.4%	$ 20	3.0
Provision for estimated federal taxes on income and excess profits..........	3	1.0	4	0.7	3	0.4
Net profit carried to surplus.............................	$ 15	5.3%	$ 21	3.7%	$ 17	2.6

NOTE: Totals from 1943 through 1946 include sales made by Blakeston & Wilson to company-controlled Perfection shops.

materials still hampered production. Such an outlet would be necessary during normal times, he felt, to insure his plant of capacity operations during the entire year.

CONTROL

In conformity with Mr. Wilson's desire to keep administrative expenses to a minimum, only a few reports were prepared for his use. He received a monthly balance sheet and profit and loss statement from all corporations, as well as daily reports on Blakeston & Wilson production and sales made by individual Perfection Chocolate Shops.

Mr. Sidwell Wilson, in addition to the investigations made by Retail Management Corporation, inspected several Perfection shops on one day each week. "As far as store operations are concerned, our best indicator of trouble is when customers begin to complain—then we start action," he said.

Mr. Sidwell Wilson personally checked wholesaler relations on his visits to those concerns. "That gives me all the control I need over those operations. I believe this system will be effective as long as I am personally running the business; it may not prove effective under other operating conditions." He further believed that the widespread adver-

	1941 % of Sales	1942 Amt.	1942 % of Sales	1943 Amt.	1943 % of Sales	1944 Amt.	1944 % of Sales	1945 Amt.	1945 % of Sales	1946 Amt.	1946 % of Sales
$799	100.0%	$909	100.0%	$1,160	100.0%	$1,239	100.0%	$1,110	100.0%	$1,349	100.0%
663	83.0	762	83.8	877	75.6	906	73.1	867	78.1	1,041	77.2
$136	17.0%	$147	16.2%	$283	24.4%	$333	26.9%	$243	21.9%	$308	22.8%
$23	2.8%	$16	1.8%	$18	1.6%	$20	1.6%	$15	1.4%	$17	1.3%
22	2.8	21	2.3	22	1.9	24	1.9	25	2.3	27	2.0
20	2.5	11	1.2	17	1.5	21	1.7	34	3.0	23	1.7
26	3.2	40	4.5	40	3.3	40	3.3	45	4.0	50	3.7
..	..	..	..	..	..	19	1.5	21	1.9	27	2.0
2	0.3	3	0.3	8	0.7	11	0.9	5	0.5	8	0.6
14	1.8	13	1.4	15	1.3	14	1.1	20	1.8	22	1.6
$107	13.4%	$104	11.5%	$120	10.3%	$149	12.0%	$165	14.9%	$174	12.9%
$29	3.6%	$43	4.7%	$163	14.1%	$184	14.9%	$78	7.0%	$134	9.9%
8	1.0	18	2.0	131	11.3	150	12.1	50	4.5	60	4.4
$21	2.6%	$25	2.7%	$32	2.8%	$34	2.8%	$28	2.5%	$74	5.5%

Source: Company records.

tising campaign for Perfection chocolates would provide an incentive, both for his wholesalers to continue to carry the line and for the retailers supplied by these firms to hold to the advertised price.

EXECUTIVE ORGANIZATION

The executive organization of Blakeston & Wilson in April, 1947, was substantially the same as in 1938. An assistant treasurer had been engaged in 1946 to take charge of all detailed accounting work, with the exception of cost accounting records. Mr. Sidwell Wilson, fifty-six years of age, was still actively engaged in all company operations. "I can do anything from firing a boiler to selling packaged chocolates," he stated. He personally approved all major policy and operating decisions made for Blakeston & Wilson, Retail Management Corporation, or any of the seventeen Perfection Chocolate Shops.

At quarterly meetings of the board of directors, Mr. Wilson discussed general company problems with the board. All Perfection Chocolate Shops were operating at a profit, and Mr. Blakeston and his associates were convinced that the decision to enter the retail-sales field had been a wise one. All Blakeston & Wilson preferred stock had been retired by this time, and Mr. Wilson owned 52% of the outstanding common stock.

Mr. Smith, forty-five years of age, had been an accounting instructor before becoming associated with the company. The office staff of the company, excluding secretarial help, consisted of three women who handled all sales and production records, as well as payroll accounts. "Other companies of comparable size have large administrative organizations—up to twenty-five persons. By keeping a small stable customer list and using a minimum of expensive records, our administrative section can be kept to a minimum size," said Mr. Smith.

EXPANSION

Mr. Wilson was planning to expand his chain of retail shops. Four additional store leases had been signed, and before the end of 1947 the company planned to operate between twenty-five and thirty shops. "If I were a younger man, we would open 500." He believed that Perfection shops should expand immediately: (1) to get as many consumers as possible familiar with Perfection chocolates and (2) to become established in the retail candy business during 1947, a time when raw-material shortages prevented other companies from entering

Exhibit 7

BLAKESTON & WILSON

*Perfection Chocolate Shops (Combined),
Balance Sheet as of December 31, 1946*
(In Thousands)

Assets

Current Assets:		
Cash		$130
Inventories (at Cost)		18
Total Current Assets		$148
Fixed Assets		41
Deferred Charges:		
Improvement to Leased Premises	$ 56	
Unexpired Insurance Premiums	7	
Total Deferred Charges		63
Total Assets		$252

Liabilities and Capital

Current Liabilities:		
Accounts Payable		$ 32
Reserve for State and Federal Taxes		52
Total Current Liabilities		$ 84
Capital Stock and Surplus:		
Capital Stock:		
Preferred	$ 47	
Common	19	66
Earned Surplus:		
Balance, December 31, 1945	$ 20	
Net Profit, 1946	113	
	$133	
Less: Dividends Paid	31	
Balance, December 31, 1946		102
Total Liabilities and Capital		$252

Source: Company records.

this field. In 1947 about one-third of Blakeston & Wilson production was being sold through company-controlled stores, and Mr. Wilson wanted to increase substantially that amount.

Among the potential sites for new Perfection shops were Cleveland and Detroit. Retail candy shops, both locally owned and chain stores, were already in operation in these cities. Previous expansion had placed Perfection shops in direct competition with a seminational chain of retail candy stores. That company, incorporated in 1919, operated several hundred stores in the Middle West and along the East Coast which sold medium-price hand-dipped chocolates and salted nuts. Mr. Wilson believed that that company's sales volume averaged only $50,000 per store. "We know how to sell in volume at low costs."

Competition for Perfection chocolates sold by company wholesalers came from hundreds of locally and regionally promoted packaged chocolates, as well as from several brands of nationally distributed candies.

Mr. Wilson estimated that the productive capacity of the candy industry had expanded by 30% since 1939. In addition to the expansion of established companies, other firms were building entirely new candy plants. "Competition is going to be severe," he concluded. (See Exhibits 4, 6, and 7.)

NOTES ON THE CONFECTIONERY INDUSTRY

TYPES OF PRODUCERS

The confectionery industry may be divided into three types of producers: (1) manufacturer-wholesalers; (2) chocolate manufacturers; and (3) manufacturer-retailers.

Manufacturer-wholesalers (manufacturers who distribute their candies through wholesalers) are the predominant type of producer in the industry from the viewpoint of number of firms, volume, and value of output. These concerns, although they make the largest proportion of inexpensive candies, sell in every price class from penny goods to expensive boxed chocolates. While most manufacturer-wholesalers make a variety of goods with wide price differentials, some concentrate on one price line; in some cases the entire plant is designed to produce just one type of candy bar.

Manufacturer-wholesalers are divided into six basic types of producers: (1) general-line houses, which supply national or regional markets with a wide range of candies, such as penny goods, five- and ten-cent packages or pieces, and bulk goods; (2) bar-goods houses, which supply the national market with chocolate-covered candy bars; (3) specialty houses, which distribute either nationally or regionally one item or several types of variety candy (such as toy boats filled with candy); (4) package-goods houses, which distribute boxed and some bulk chocolates to a regional market; (5) bulk-goods houses; and (6) penny-goods houses.

Chocolate manufacturers (for example, Hershey, Baker, and Nestle), in addition to supplying the candy industry with chocolate items, such as coatings, syrups, and cocoa products, also manufacture molded chocolate bars. These products are sold both directly and through wholesale concerns.

Manufacturer-retailers (manufacturers who market the bulk of their output directly through their own stores) have the smallest volume among the three types of candy manufacturers. These manufacturers frequently build up reputations as specialists in making certain types of candy. Smaller manufacturer-retailers customarily make candy on the premises of their own store and sell it directly; larger companies have a factory and supply company-owned stores in a local or regional area.

PRODUCT

The candy market in the United States is dominated by the 5-cent candy bar. Shortly after the end of World War I, the first nationally advertised candy bar was introduced. Currently, there is a large number of nationally advertised bars on the market. In fact, more than one-half of all the candy sold in 1945 consisted of candy bars, 90% of which retailed for 5 cents. Packaged confectionery (primarily boxed chocolates) was the second largest selling item in 1945, the total making up about 20% of dollar sales. Bulk candy (approximately 15% of 1945 sales) and specialty candies (approximately 10% of 1945 sales) were the next largest selling items.[1]

INDUSTRY LOCATION AND SIZE

Candy manufacturing operations are geographically concentrated in the states of Illinois, New York, Pennsylvania, and Massachusetts, with Chicago the candy manufacturing center. In 1944 these four states produced, as measured by value, about 65% of the confectionery manufactured in this country.[2]

Sales by manufacturing concerns are likewise concentrated. In 1944, 87% of confectionery sales were made by 80 firms, each with more than a million dollar per year business.[3] Total industry manufacturing activities were carried on in 1,473 plants.

CHANNELS OF DISTRIBUTION

In the pre-war years the confectionery industry was making important changes in its methods of distribution. The chain store as a distributor of candy doubled in importance from 1927 to 1944. In 1927, 10 per cent of the candy distributed was marketed through chain stores, but by 1941 the proportion had risen to 21.4 per cent. Apparently this gain was at the expense of the independent retailer. The independent retailer's share of candy sales decreased from 27.5 per

[1] U.S. Department of Commerce, *19th Annual Report on Confectionery Sales and Distribution* (1945), p. 23.
[2] Edward T. Bullock, "Candy Takes Its Place at the Dinner Table," *Dun's Review,* July, 1946, p. 16.
[3] Fred Smith, "Sweetness and Light," *Advertising and Selling,* Vol. XXXIX, No. 2 (February, 1946).

cent in 1927 to 11.7 per cent in 1941. . . . Distribution through factory-owned stores has remained in the neighborhood of 9 per cent. . . .[4]

The candy wholesaler has been, and remains, the most important factor in the distribution of confectionery. The percentage of industry output which those wholesalers handled dropped from 61% (1937) to 40% (1942) and then rose to 48% (1945), following a marked reduction in military purchases of candy.[5]

SEASONALITY

Despite wartime scarcities of raw materials and the leveling influence of military demand, the candy industry never lost its characteristic seasonality.

The characteristic seasonal pattern of sales by the candy industry, shows that the highest activity is reached just before the Christmas holidays, with the market falling off in January. As the year progresses, there is a minor but well-defined rise in sales for Easter. In addition, the manufacturer-retailers experienced a pickup in sales for the February holidays, especially in the box trade for St. Valentine's Day. The bottom for all candy sales is reached in mid-summer, almost universally in July, with an upswing geared first to Thanksgiving and culminating in the Christmas trade.[6]

FLUCTUATIONS IN COSTS AND SALES VALUE

Confectionery material costs are subject to wide fluctuations. From 1927 to 1932 the average price of materials declined 50 per cent. By contrast, wholesale confectionery prices fell 40 per cent. In the recovery period to 1937, material costs rose 47 per cent and confectionery prices only 15 per cent. During the recession of 1937–1938, material costs again declined considerably more than the sales value of confectionery. The declines were 16 per cent and 7 per cent for materials and confectionery respectively. From 1938 to 1944 material costs and sales value have each risen 54 per cent.

If price history repeats itself, the next recession of any consequence will find material prices weaker than confectionery prices.

The demand for candy is but moderately affected by changes in general business conditions. In the severe depression of the early 1930's the quantity of candy consumed decreased only about 8 per cent.

Individual items, however, are subject to wide fluctuations. In 1933, for example, fancy package goods were down 70 per cent from the 1930 average. Bars other than chocolate declined 53 per cent. In the mild recession of 1937–1938, the only decline of magnitude was one of 20 per cent in plain package goods.[7]

---

[4] Bullock, *op. cit.,* p. 15.

[5] *Ibid.*

[6] Selina Caldor, "Seasonal Trends in the Candy Business," *Domestic Commerce,* Vol. XXXIV, No. 3 (March, 1946).

[7] Bullock, *op. cit.,* p. 16.

COMPETITION

The candy industry has always been characterized by intense competition. The situation in the industry during the 1920's was summarized, in 1927, by the Secretary of the National Confectioners Association as follows:

> The candy industry, representing a capital investment of approximately $300,-000,000 and annual sales aggregating $400,000,000, is beset with fears and doubts as to its future. . . . During the prewar period (1912–1917) . . . there was the keenest kind of competition and profits were things hoped for but seldom realized. . . . During the war period conditions were changed almost overnight from a buyers' to a sellers' market. . . . Manufacturers were able to dictate terms and conditions of sale. . . . What was the result? Plants were over-expanded. . . . I estimate that the potential capacity of the entire industry is anywhere from 25% to 35% more than is required to supply the demand . . . conditions tempted manufacturers to resort to practices which have developed situations that are decidedly detrimental to the industry. Free goods are given; secret rebates and special discounts are given to favored customers; over-extension of credits as to terms and quantity; special deals and concessions; rewards to customers' salesmen; and many others.[8]

During the depression years of the 1930's, competition in the industry continued to be severe; the average price per pound received by the manufacturer dropped from 23.2 cents per pound in 1927 to 13.9 cents in 1933. In addition to intense competition within the industry, external factors were limiting the confectionery market. Ice cream and soft-drink consumption had increased tremendously during this period, as did the consumption of cigarettes. The latter was aided to no small degree by increased sales to women smokers. Production (physical volume) increased 8% from 1929 to 1939, despite the fact that there were then 38% fewer plants and 22% less workers in the industry.[9]

A further factor currently affecting the competitive situation has been the rapid rise of chain grocery store candy sales.

> Grocery stores, food chains such as the A & P, and supermarkets are assuming increasing importance as distributors of confectionery. Grocery stores now sell a larger volume of candy than of coffee or butter.[10]

WORLD WAR II

The effect of World War II on the industry was reflected in three major developments: (1) rationing of basic raw materials used in candy manufacture; (2) a tremendous increase in industry sales, both

---

[8] *Confectioners Review,* August, 1927, p. 73.
[9] Bullock, *op. cit.,* p. 16.
[10] *Ibid.,* p. 18.

in terms of value and in pounds of candy manufactured; and (3) a distinct change in the types of candy manufactured.

Sugar rations for candy manufacturers were first set at 70% of the 1941 base use period; this quota was increased to 80% in July, 1942. The highest level of ration was reached from August, 1943, to December, 1944, when the sugar ration was 80% of the 1941 base, plus a 10% bonus. The lowest ration level was 50% for the last six months of 1945. In 1947 the ration was 75%.

Industry dollar sales rose from $308,000,000 in 1939 to peaks of $658,000,000 in 1944 and $620,000,000 in 1945. The gain resulted from both a higher output of candy and an increase in the price per pound. In 1939 the wholesale price of candy averaged 15 cents a pound; in 1946 it averaged 26.9 cents a pound. This price increase received by the manufacturer was primarily achieved by the producer diverting material from inexpensive lines to higher-priced boxed candies. From 1939 to 1944, production of plain and fancy packaged goods (primarily boxed chocolates) rose 30% and 310%, respectively.

EXPANSION

Sugar shortages during World War II had handicapped the expansion of established confectionery companies, as well as the development of new enterprises. In 1947, however, numerous companies were planning or were already in the process of plant expansion; for example, the Kraft Cheese Company, which had entered the caramel business before the war, planned erection of a $750,000 candy plant in Kendallville, Indiana. In addition to this new plant expansion, the manufacturing capacity of the industry had already been greatly increased by improved war-developed manufacturing processes.

Superior Separator Company

INTRODUCTION

In July, 1950, the board of directors of the Superior Separator Company, Hopkins, Minnesota, decided not to take advantage of an opportunity to purchase for $300,000 the name and fixed assets of a firm which manufactured construction equipment, a line of products not related to those produced by the company. The decision was motivated by a fear that the economic consequences of the outbreak of war in Korea might greatly increase the difficulties facing a management group attempting to operate two businesses concurrently. This action caused Charles F. Pierson, president, to consider fully the problems created by an over-all management policy designed to promote the maximum growth and development of the company. Mr. Pierson was concerned both with the direction and the rate of future expansion.

Superior manufactured seed- and grain-cleaning and grading machinery for country and terminal elevators and farm lifting, loading, and moving equipment (see Exhibit 1).

Net sales for the fiscal year ending October 31, 1949, were reported as $4,539,774 and net profit after taxes as $352,154. This marked the thirteenth consecutive year of profitable operation. In the 20 years of the company's existence, net worth had grown from an initial capitalization of $30,000 to $1,655,791, almost entirely through the reinvestment of earnings. (Balance sheets for selected years are shown in Exhibit 2; income statements for selected years, in Exhibit 3.)

COMPANY HISTORY, 1929–45

The Superior Separator Company was incorporated in November, 1929, to engage in the manufacture of grain-separators for country elevators. Carl C. Gray and Harry Johnson had developed an improved process for separating impurities from grain while employed by a Minneapolis manufacturer of grain-cleaning machinery. With the aim of securing financial backing for a new enterprise, the pair approached Harry C. Piper, partner in the Minneapolis investment banking house of Lane, Piper, and Jaffray. Mr. Piper and a few associates agreed to supply $15,000 in return for 5,000 shares of common stock, one-half of the amount issued. Mr. Gray and Mr. Johnson each received 2,500 shares as compensation for their inventive skills.

From 1929 until 1936 manufacturing operations were carried out in rented space in an old building in St. Paul. Mr. Johnson would design and build a machine, and Mr. Gray, the president, would go out to a grain elevator and sell it. In spite of a basic conflict in personalities and the prevailing adverse economic conditions, sales grew from $27,000 in 1930 to $126,000 in 1936; profits were earned in three of the first seven years.

The company purchased an old plant in southeast Minneapolis in 1936 and began to expand its line. Sales rose to a prewar peak of $306,000 in 1939 but declined to $232,000 in 1940. Afraid that maximum growth had been attained, Mr. Johnson sold his stock to the other stockholders but remained with the company as chief engineer.

Until 1939 all earnings were reinvested. In that year the first dividend, $10,000, was paid. (In the period 1940–49, $45,300, in total, was returned to stockholders.)

Late in 1939 a North Dakota farmer who was an acquaintance of Mr. Johnson came into the main office with an invention which he had previously offered to several large manufacturers of farm equipment without acceptance. The product was a high-lift hydraulic loader, designed to be affixed to any standard-size tractor to utilize its power to lift and stack hay.

Although the hydraulic loader bore little relation to grain-cleaning machinery, management believed that a large potential market existed for the farm implement and took an option to purchase the patent. Following a successful patent search, rights were purchased and ten experimental units were built and sold in 1940.

The Hydraulic Farmhand, as the new machine was called, met with an enthusiastic response from farmers, but Mr. Gray proceeded cautiously, and Superior built only 336 units in 1941. When war broke out in December, 1941, the War Production Board instituted controls restricting the annual production of a manufacturer of farm equipment to 125% of the company's 1940 output, and Superior was unable to produce the Farmhand in any quantity until 1944. In that year Farmhand sales exceeded grain-cleaner sales for the first time. (See Exhibit 4 for a comparison of the sales of the Farmhand Division and the Grain-Cleaner Division, 1940–49.)

With grain-cleaner production also limited by wartime controls,

Exhibit 1

SUPERIOR SEPARATOR COMPANY

Company Sales Brochure

"At last ... a farm implement maker that specializes in farm lifting, loading, and moving equipment"

Now farming's toughest chores are completely mechanized!

You've seen it coming for years . . . "Power Farming" . . . the mechanization of all the expensive, time-taking, back-breaking work involved in operating a farm. . . .

You've seen machines take over the labor and drudgery of seeding, cultivation, harvesting and other difficult jobs. . . .

NOW . . . thanks to the research and inventiveness of a specialized farm implement company . . . you're seeing a revolution in the last stronghold of old-fashioned farming methods . . . the laborious tasks involved in lifting, loading, hauling and moving of materials.

NOW . . . for the first time . . . one company makes efficient and thoroughly proved machines to perform almost *every* job of materials handling on your farm!

These FARMHAND machines, produced in a completely modern implement plant, are designed and built by *specialists* in materials handling tools. FARMHAND makes no other type of farm imple-

ment. All the skill and experience of FARMHAND'S master machinists and engineers is devoted solely to the problems of handling materials on the farm . . . lifting and loading materials for storage and transport . . . hauling materials in every kind of loose or bulky form . . . unloading materials in the easiest way . . . in the least possible time . . . with the utmost savings in money and manpower . . . with the greatest output of work of any implements per dollar invested.

The FARMHAND line includes well designed machines "tailored" to fit the requirements of nearly every type of farm in the country, large or small, engaged in the production of practically any kind of crop.

Look them over. See how these specialized lifting, loading, hauling and moving tools can save time and money for you. Then write for free literature on the machines that interest you . . . or see your nearest FARMHAND Dealer for a demonstration and all the facts about "Power Farming" the FARMHAND way.

Farmhand **Specialized machines for every farm lifting, loading, moving job**

made by Superior Separator Company, Hopkins, Minnesota

Exhibit 1—Continued

SUPERIOR SEPARATOR COMPANY

FARMHAND HIGH-REACH HYDRAULIC LOADER . . . America's No. 1 farm loader choice (according to impartial survey). 3,000 lb. lift . . . 21-foot reach . . . gentle "wrist-action" control for accurate, easy handling and placement of big loads.

A COMPLETE LINE OF ATTACHMENTS for performing mor of the year with the FARMHAND Hydraulic Loader. 1. Grappl from stacks, prevents them from blowing. 2. High-capacity Ma feed corn, etc. 4. High-capacity Hay Basket. 5. Push-Off for

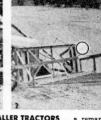

FARMHAND LOADER FOR SMALLER TRACTORS . . . a remark smaller tractors. Compactly built for low clearance. Easy to ge Power take-off shaft brought through pump for operating oth leveling . . . 16-foot reach . . . full 2,000 lb. lift. Four attachment Basket; 3. Push-Off for Hay Basket; 4. Sand and Gravel Plate.

FARMHAND "POWER-BOX" . . . revolutionary 4-ton capacity wagon box with tractor-powered unloading mechanism across full width of bed. Handles almost any kind of load—silage, corn, manure, etc. Precision engineered. Ball and roller bearings throughout.

MANURE SPREADER AND MIXER-FEEDER ATTACHMENTS . . . fit on the "Power-Box" . . . add new ease and speed to two of farming's toughest chores.

FARMHAND "90" permits full 90° turns tensible Tongue for front bolster . . . extr

Exhibit 1—Continued

SUPERIOR SEPARATOR COMPANY

The FARMHAND Hydraulic Loader fits more than 76 well-known tractor models and may be mounted or unmounted easily in a few minutes

than 50 farm jobs in every season Fork, ideal for taking hay or straw nure Fork. 3. Scoop for snow, silage, Hay Basket builds high stacks to 27 feet, folds flat against rear of Hay Basket when not in use. 6. Manure Fork Scoop attaches to fork for lifting sand, gravel, etc. 7. Heavy-duty Forage Fork for breaking frozen stacks and handling biggest, bulkiest loads, such as machinery, out buildings, feed bunks, etc. 8. Bulldozer Blade for earth moving, ground leveling, etc. 9. Rugged 8-foot V-Plow.

able performer especially designed for use on on and off. No cables or braces in your way. implements while loader is on tractor. Self-available: 1. Full Width Manure Fork; 2. Hay

FARMHAND DUMP-RAKE · · · doubles speed of ordinary dump rakes. Simple rope trip mechanism and steel clutch roll the rake a half-turn at a time without leaving unraked hay. Low-cost single-purpose machine.

FARMHAND POST HOLE DIGGER · · · a rugged, power-driven digger that fits easily on Farmhand Loader. Pull posts, carry new wire and new posts, with loader. A complete fencing outfit in one unit.

WAGON . . . the famous 5-ton capacity wagon that without backing, slipping or tilting. Quick-Hitch Extensible reach . . . fixed or rocking wide 72" construction . . . other great features.

FARMHAND 2½ TON WAGON . . . a lighter version of the FARMHAND "90" Wagon with all the special features, including 90° turns with full support under load.

FARMHAND SINGLE-AXLE TRAILER · · · ruggedly built for heavy loads. Takes any box. Adjustable height hitch and front support stand.

One of America's finest specialized farm equipment plants

PRECISION ENGINEERING and sound design make FARMHAND machines tops for efficiency, low-cost operation.

CAREFUL INSPECTION all along the line assures top quality, most dependable performance for you.

FINEST QUALITY MACHINING to exceptionally close tolerances goes into all precision parts and controls.

EXPERIENCED WELDERS are responsible for the sound, solid construction and exceptional strength of machines.

TYPICAL EXAMPLE of our complex manufacturing work is this CC16 Cylinder machine, product of our grain cleaner division.

IN THIS SHEET METAL SHOP are craft many of the FARMHAND machines and accessories that save work, time for you.

THE FARMHAND MAIN PLANT where 300 people work with precision equipment to make long lasting machines for handling materials on American farms. This large plant in Hopkins, Minnesota, contains more than 100,000 sq. ft. of factory, office and warehouse space. It is fitted with the most modern metal working tools, the finest of manufacturing facilities.

Exhibit 2

SUPERIOR SEPARATOR COMPANY

Comparative Balance Sheets for Selected Fiscal Years Ending December 31, 1930–48, and October 31, 1948–49, with Condition at June 30, 1950

(In Thousands)

Assets	Dec. 31, 1930†	Dec. 31, 1939†	Dec. 31, 1942	Dec. 31, 1944	Dec. 31, 1946	Dec. 31, 1947	Oct. 31, 1948	Oct. 31, 1949	Jun. 30, 1950
Current Assets:									
Cash	$ 1	$ 20	$ 78	$119	$ 96	$ 239	$ 85	$ 352	$ 5
Accounts Receivable	4	46	22	38	345	276	286	147	649
Inventory	2	29	47	103	492	658	1,224	1,042	1,440‡
Total Current Assets	$ 8	$ 95	$147	$260	$ 933	$1,173	$1,595	$1,541	$2,094
Fixed Assets:									
Patents and Patent License		...	$ 8	$ 5	$ 4	$ 2	$ 2	$ 5	$ 5
Miscellaneous Receivable		...	...	...	19	...	6	6	...
Prepaid Insurance and Deferred Charges		...	1	1	1	7	4	5	27
Investment in Subsidiaries		...	...	...	...	53	114	112	137§
Due from Subsidiaries		...	...	...	...	...	49	76	194‖
Plant and Equipment—Net		...	29	60	125	153	231	291	299
Total Fixed Assets		...	$ 38	$ 66	$ 149	$ 215	$ 406	$ 495	$ 662
Total Assets		$124	$185	$326	$1,082	$1,388	$2,001	$2,036	$2,756
Liabilities and Net Worth									
Current Liabilities:									
Accounts Payable		...	$ 6	$ 16	$ 174	$ 134	$ 216	$ 82	$ 162
Notes Payable		...	...	...	104	...	...	...	450
Accruals and Reserves		...	7	13	117	99	161	68	127
Advance on Orders		...	...	6	3	...	19	10	...
Reserves for Income Taxes		...	29	87	182	267	302	221	226
Total Current Liabilities		$ 37	$ 42	$122	$ 580	$ 500	$ 698	$ 381	$ 965
Common Stock	$30	$ 30	$ 30	$ 30	$ 30	$ 31	$ 31	$ 31	$ 31
Paid in Surplus		...	...	...	2	6	6	6	6
Earned Surplus	3*	57	113	174	470	851	1,266	1,618	1,754
Total Net Worth	$27	$ 87	$143	$204	$ 502	$ 888	$1,303	$1,655	$1,791
Total Liabilities and Net Worth		$124	$185	$326	$1.082	$1,388	$2,001	$2,036	$2,756

* Deficit.
† Complete statement not available.
‡ Raw material, $891,000; work in process and finished good., $598,000; inventory reserve, $57,000*; variance, $8,000.
§ Includes investment of $105,000 in and loan of $25,000 to the First Street Realty Company and $7,000 in the Superior Separator Company of Canada, Ltd.
‖ Accounts Receivable, the Superior Separator Company of Canada, Ltd.
Source: Company records.

Mr. Gray solicited subcontracts from several large manufacturers of war equipment. This production reached its peak in 1943 when war orders accounted for 41% of net sales, but total war production in the period 1940–45 amounted to only $221,000.

As raw materials again became available, the company placed primary emphasis on Farmhand sales. In anticipation of a period of rapid expansion, the board of directors attempted to strengthen the executive organization by bringing into the company in 1944 a group of men headed by Charles F. Pierson, son-in-law of Mr. Piper, the largest stockholder. Following a year as acting general manager, Mr. Pierson was named president to succeed Mr. Gray.

Exhibit 3

SUPERIOR SEPARATOR COMPANY

Comparative Profit or Loss Statements for Selected Fiscal Years
Ending December 31, 1930–47 and October 31, 1948–49

(In Thousands)

	1930	1939	1942	1944	1946	1947†	1948† (10 Mos.)	1949†	1950† (8 Mos.)
Net sales	$27	$306	$415	$681	$3,048	$5,068	$5,955	$4,539	$2,721
Cost of goods sold	16	166	279	481	2,296	3,962	4,716	3,374	1,989
Gross profit	$11	$140	$136	$200	$ 752	$1,106	$1,239	$1,165	$ 732
Administrative, general, and selling expenses	14	93	74	80	336	461	523	617	432
Operation profit	$ 3*	$ 47	$ 62	$120	$ 416	$ 645	$ 716	$ 548	$ 300
Additions-deductions and taxes	...	13	26	80	168	262	292	196	138
Net profit	$ 3*	$ 34	$ 36	$ 40	$ 248	$ 383	$ 424	$ 352	$ 162
Net sales	100.0%	100.0%	100.0%	100.0%	100.0%	100.0%	100.0%	100.0%	100.0%
Cost of goods sold	61.4	54.3	67.3	70.5	75.4	78.1	79.2	74.3	73.1
Gross profit	38.6	45.7	32.7	29.5	24.6	21.9	20.8	25.7	26.9
Administrative, general, and selling expenses	51.2	30.2	17.8	11.8	11.0	9.1	8.8	13.4	15.9
Operation profit	12.6*	15.5	14.9	17.7	13.6	12.8	12.0	12.3	11.0
Additions-deductions and taxes	...	4.2	6.4	11.8	5.5	5.2	4.9	4.3	5.1
Net profit	12.6%	11.3%	8.5%	5.9%	8.1%	7.6%	7.1%	8.0%	5.9%

* Loss.
† Subsidiaries excluded.
Source: Company records.

Exhibit 4

SUPERIOR SEPARATOR COMPANY

Sales by Divisions, 1940–49

(In Thousands)

	1940	1941	1942	1943	1944	1945	1946	1947	1948 (10 Mos.)	1949	1950 (8 Mos.)
Grain-Cleaner Division	$229	$241	$251	$144	$247	$ 412	$ 457	$ 822	$ 577	$ 612	$ 294
Farmhand Division	3	95	111	61	410	620	2,591	4,247	5,379	3,928	2,427
War Production	...	...	54	144	24	...	...	...	...	...	...
Total	$232	$336	$416	$349	$681	$1,032	$3,048	$5,069	$5,956	$4,540	$2,721
Grain-Cleaner Division	98.7%	71.8%	60.3%	41.2%	36.2%	40.0%	15.0%	16.2%	9.7%	13.5%	10.8%
Farmhand Division	1.3	28.2	26.7	17.5	60.3	60.0	85.0	83.8	90.3	86.5	89.2
War Production	...	...	13.0	41.3	3.5	...	...	...	...	...	...
Total	100.0%	100.0%	100.0%	100.0%	100.0%	100.0%	100.0%	100.0%	100.0%	100.0%	100.0%

Source: Company records.

COMPANY HISTORY, 1946–50

To provide more extensive production facilities, the company purchased an 11-acre industrial site in Hopkins, a suburb of Minneapolis, for $4,000, and constructed a modern one-story plant with nearly 40,000 square feet of floor space. Later additions increased this area to over 100,000 square feet. The total cost of the building and additions exceeded $600,000. The old building was sold, and the company moved to Hopkins in December, 1945.

When the new plant was constructed, a direct subsidiary, the First Street Realty Company, was incorporated to own the properties and lease them to the parent company. By such action mortgage indebtedness was removed from the balance sheet of the parent company and a line of credit of $150,000 was obtained from a Minneapolis bank. (By June, 1950, this line had been extended to $750,000.) The Superior Separator Company purchased 84% of the stock of the First Street Realty Company. Stockholders of Superior owned the remaining shares directly.

A second subsidiary, the Superior Separator Company of Canada, Ltd., wholly owned by the parent company, was established in 1947 with main offices in Winnipeg, Manitoba, to serve as sales agent for the company's products in Canada.

From 1945 through the first ten months of 1948 total net sales of the Superior Separator Company increased almost 600%. While sales of grain cleaners increased moderately, the Farmhand was principally responsible for the extent of growth. During this period the demand for farm equipment far exceeded the available supply, and all manufacturers were sorely pressed to fill dealers' orders. Because the farmer preferred to purchase haying machinery in the spring before the period of use, the productive capacity of the plant was particularly strained during the late winter months.

In an attempt to even out seasonal variation in shipments, the sales manager of the Farmhand Division had devised in 1947 a scheme to grant an additional 5% seasonal discount on all orders placed between November 1 and March 1. Shipments in November and December of 1948 and January and February of 1949 remained at a high level as dealers ordered in anticipation of a normal spring demand.

"However, for several reasons retail sales did not materialize in the spring of 1949 as expected," Mr. Pierson said. An unusually severe winter had delayed the haying season. The deferred demand for farm equipment resulting from nonavailability during the war had been largely satisfied. Net farm income, off slightly in 1948 from a 1947 peak, began to fall sharply. Increasing competition for the farmer's dollar was developing rapidly from all consumer goods.

When Farmhands did not move from dealers' floors, factory orders fell off considerably. Shipments in March, 1949, were down 35% from February, and April showed a further decline. Plant production planned on a normal seasonal sales curve began to build up finished-goods inventory in Hopkins. In the middle of March overtime was eliminated. On April 8, the second shift was dropped, all schedules were drastically reduced, and 108 plant and office employees were laid off. Forty-nine other employees accepted a wage cut and downgrading in preference to a layoff. Changes were not made soon enough, however, and the company found itself on April 30 in an overextended position with: (1) a heavy inventory of raw material and work in process, (2) practically no cash, (3) a $100,000 bank loan, and (4) 1,500 Farmhands in finished-goods inventory.

"We faced a major policy decision. We could cut back production still further and attempt to hold on until dealer inventories had worked down to a level where they would reorder, or we could attack the situation aggressively by revamping our entire organization, slashing costs to the bone, and modernizing and expanding our product line. We decided to gamble on a bold attack," said Mr. Pierson.

The sales manager of the Farmhand Division, who had not informed the president of the failure of retail sales to develop as anticipated because "he didn't want to worry him," was dismissed and Mr. Pierson assumed the added responsibility. Several sales territories were combined and the field salesforce was reduced one-third. The office staff was decreased further and the engineering staff cut in half.

The remaining members of the engineering department were charged with the responsibility of redesigning all machines then in production and adding several new ones to the line. With the department working around the clock, blueprints were drawn, experimental models were tested briefly and the first machines were delivered to dealers in late summer. Although dealer reaction was favorable, the season of heavy demand had passed and farmer acceptance could not be tested adequately in 1949.

Net sales for 1949 were 24% below the record figure of $5,955,891, achieved in the first ten months of 1948, but net profit after taxes was off only 17%. To Mr. Pierson the annual report indicated that the bold measures taken in the spring had been successful. By October "expenses had been cut, inventories reduced, the bank loan paid off, and an adequate cash balance accumulated."

Shipments through June, 1950, were almost $1 million below the comparable period in 1949. Reasons stated by the sales manager of the Farmhand Division were: (1) heavy floods in the Red River Valley and a late spring throughout the Midwest, (2) droughts in Kansas, and

(3) dealer reluctance to carry any machines in inventory. Sales in the month of June, 1950, were 54% greater than in the corresponding month in 1949. Mr. Pierson thought that this increase indicated that the season was merely late and that total 1950 sales would compare favorably with those of 1949 (see Exhibit 5). Net profit after taxes for the first eight months of 1950 was 5.9% of net sales, 2.1% lower than the figure for the year 1949.

Exhibit 5

SUPERIOR SEPARATOR COMPANY

Comparative Monthly Sales and Profit Figures for Fiscal Years
Ending October 31

(In Thousands)

	1949†				1950			
	SALES		PROFIT AFTER TAXES		SALES		PROFIT AFTER TAXES	
	Month	Total	Month	Total	Month	Total	Month	Total
November..........	$488	$ 488	$27	$ 27	$177	$ 177	$ 9*	$ 9*
December..........	526	1,014	41	68	210	387	5	4*
January...........	487	1,501	32	100	251	638	14	10
February..........	570	2,071	42	142	260	897	13	23
March............	377	2,448	4*	138	352	1,249	17	40
April.............	341	2,789	5	143	362	1,611	15	55
May..............	393	3,182	10	153	390	2,001	27	82
June.............	468	3,650	45	198	720	2,721	74	156
July.............	283	3,933	6	204				
August...........	285	4,218	10	214				
September.........	170	4,388	5*	209				
October..........	152	4,540	..‡	352				

* Loss.
† In 1949 a 5% seasonal discount was granted during the first four months.
‡ October profit figure unreliable because of year-end adjustment.
Source: Company records.

COMPANY PRODUCTS

The products manufactured by the company fell into two categories: grain-cleaning machinery and farm equipment. The Grain-Cleaner Division made a full line of cleaning, grading, scalping, and aspirating equipment for the processing of grains and seeds.

The Farmhand Division produced a selected line of materials-handling equipment for the farm. The principal product of the division was the Hydraulic Farmhand. The loader was built in two sizes, one for standard-size tractors and one for small-size ones. To increase the versatility of the loader, the company had designed a number of attachments for it. Among them were a hay basket, manure fork, grapple fork, forage fork, bulldozer blade, and snowplow.

Other farm implements manufactured were the Prairie Mulcher, a tractor-drawn rotary rake which spread straw into freshly plowed land to prevent erosion; the Power Box, a four-ton capacity wagon box with tractor-powered unloading mechanism for manure-spreading and automatic feeding of livestock; a two and one-half ton capacity wagon with a tongue permitting full 90 degree turns; a five-ton capacity wagon; a single-axle trailer; a tractor-drawn high-speed dump rake; a three-level forage unit; and a portable power pack to motivate the forage unit.

When the design for a new corn picker was shown to the engineering department in 1947, there was an executive difference of opinion as to whether or not rights should be purchased. Although the corn picker was considered to be a better machine than those then on the market, the board of directors decided that the cost of development work was too great for the company to bear and decided not to add the picker to the product line.

EXECUTIVE ORGANIZATION

After graduating from Yale University in 1934, Mr. Pierson was employed for four years by the Minneapolis-Honeywell Regulator Company, Minneapolis. He spent six months as a punch-press operator, one year in the dispatching crib, six months in the production-control department, one year as a correspondent in the sales department, and one year as a salesman assigned to the Detroit territory. "It was a four-year postgraduate course in manufacturing," said Mr. Pierson.

Desiring to return to Minneapolis following the death of his father in 1938, he accepted a position with Superior as assistant to the president, Mr. Gray. After handling various jobs in the production and sales departments, he became sales manager in 1940. In this capacity he soon encountered the same difficulty working with Mr. Johnson that Mr. Gray had experienced. Mr. Pierson remained with the company until he enlisted in the Navy in April, 1942. When he received a medical discharge in the spring of 1943, he went back to Minneapolis-Honeywell as an assistant production manager. On the condition that Mr. Johnson be dismissed, he returned to Superior in 1944 and brought a group of new men in with him to fill key positions.

None of these executives remained in 1950. Mr. Pierson said, "We faced a problem basic to many rapidly expanding companies. Executive growth did not keep pace with the growth of the company. When we hired a controller in 1945, we couldn't afford to pay more than $300 a month so we hired the best man we could get at that salary. As the company grew, the job got too big for him, and his health broke under the pressure. His retirement in 1948 saved us the unpleasantness of firing him." Several executives were dismissed.

"We have a team now," said Mr. Pierson, describing the executive organization in 1950. "Sure, we have our disagreements, but we get along pretty well." The following men were key executives in the organization:

John Randall, vice-president in charge of manufacturing, joined Minneapolis-Honeywell following graduation from Tuck Business School, Dartmouth College, in 1935. He was employed in the accounting and production departments and rose to the position of plant manager of the Minneapolis assembly plant. Before coming to Superior in December, 1947, he was sales manager of the Moduflow Division (residential home heating). In June, 1950, Mr. Randall was named general manager of the Grain-Cleaner Division. He remained responsible for all company production as well.

Bernard Carlson, chief engineer, was assistant chief engineer of the Moline plant of Deere & Company before coming to Superior in January, 1947. Following graduation from the University of Montana he spent seven years with the Allis-Chalmers Manufacturing Company and several with the army engineers. In 1950 he was thirty-eight years old.

D. L. Wahl, secretary and controller, graduated from the University of North Dakota and entered the accounting firm of Touche, Niven, Bailey, and Smart. After nine years he joined Minneapolis-Honeywell, where as head of the cost department he handled renegotiation and forward-pricing of government contracts. He came to Superior in June, 1948, as controller, and was named secretary two years later. He was forty-one years old in 1950.

Arthur W. Ostrander, sales manager of the Farmhand Division, worked for Superior for several summers during the late 1930's to help pay his expenses while attending Dartmouth College. In the summer of 1940 he traveled through Minnesota, North Dakota, and South Dakota enlisting dealers to handle the hydraulic loader. With this work as a background, he presented his master's thesis entitled "A Farm Market Analysis for the Hydraulic Farmhand" for graduation from Tuck Business School in 1941. He returned to Superior after graduation and remained until Farmhand production was restricted. From 1942 until 1945 he worked in the production-control department of the P. F.

Exhibit 6

SUPERIOR SEPARATOR COMPANY
Organization Chart—July, 1950

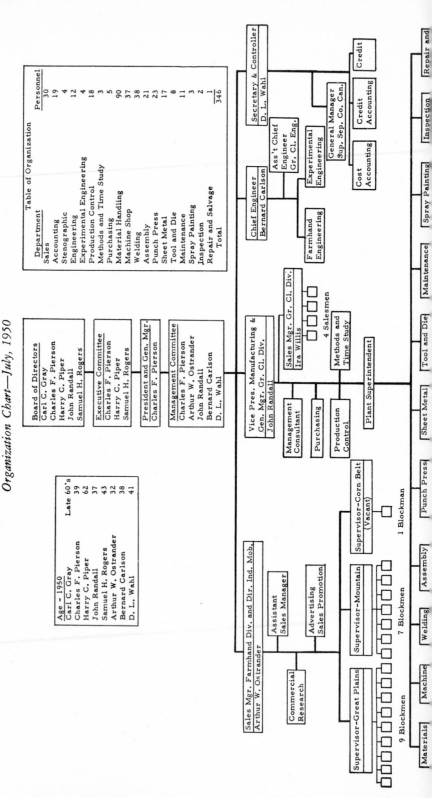

Table of Organization

Department	Personnel
Sales	30
Accounting	19
Stenographic	4
Engineering	12
Experimental Engineering	4
Production Control	18
Methods and Time Study	3
Purchasing	5
Material Handling	90
Machine Shop	37
Welding	38
Assembly	21
Punch Press	23
Sheet Metal	17
Tool and Die	8
Maintenance	11
Spray Painting	3
Inspection	2
Repair and Salvage	1
Total	346

Age – 1950	
Carl C. Gray	Late 60's
Charles F. Pierson	39
Harry C. Piper	62
John Randall	37
Samuel H. Rogers	43
Arthur W. Ostrander	32
Bernard Carlson	38
D. L. Wahl	41

Board of Directors
Carl C. Gray
Charles F. Pierson
Harry C. Piper
John Randall
Samuel H. Rogers

Executive Committee
Charles F. Pierson
Harry C. Piper
Samuel H. Rogers

President and Gen. Mgr.
Charles F. Pierson

Management Committee
Charles F. Pierson
Arthur W. Ostrander
John Randall
Bernard Carlson
D. L. Wahl

Chief Engineer
Bernard Carlson

Farmhand Engineering

Ass't Chief Engineer
Gr. Cl. Eng.

Experimental Engineering

Secretary & Controller
D. L. Wahl

General Manager
Sup. Sep. Co. Can.

Cost Accounting

Credit Accounting

Credit

Vice Pres., Manufacturing & Gen. Mgr. Gr. Cl. Div.
John Randall

Management Consultant

Purchasing

Production Control

Plant Superintendent

Sales Mgr. Gr. Cl. Div.
Ira Willis

4 Salesmen

Methods and Time Study

Sales Mgr. Farmhand Div. and Dir. Ind. Mob.
Arthur W. Ostrander

Assistant Sales Manager

Commercial Research

Advertising Sales Promotion

Supervisor-Great Plains

Supervisor-Mountain

Supervisor-Corn Belt
(Vacant)

9 Blockmen

7 Blockmen

1 Blockman

Materials | Machine | Welding | Assembly | Punch Press | Sheet Metal | Tool and Die | Maintenance | Spray Painting | Inspection | Credit | Repair and

Corbin Division of The American Hardware Corporation, New Britain, Connecticut. He then spent three years with Robert Heller and Associates, management consultants, and a year in the commercial research department of General Mills, Inc., before joining Superior in November, 1949. After submitting a report based on a two-month market analysis of the company's products, he was named sales manager of the Farmhand Division in January, 1950. In July, 1950, he was also named director of industrial mobilization.

These four executives, with Mr. Pierson, constituted a management committee which met formally at irregular intervals. Mr. Pierson usually ate lunch with these men, however, and saw them several times a day to discuss current developments.

GRAIN-CLEANER DIVISION

In the first eight months of the fiscal year 1950, grain-cleaner sales amounted to only 10.8% of total sales. Operations showed a net loss of $25,606, 8.9% of net sales (see Exhibit 7). What for ten years had been the only group of products manufactured was in 1950 a minor factor in the total operations of the company.

The rapid expansion of Farmhand sales in the postwar era had required an increasing amount of executive time. As a result the Grain-Cleaner Division was allowed to shift for itself. When he joined Superior to becomes sales manager of the Grain-Cleaner Division in 1947, Ira Willis became in effect acting general manager of the division as well. In February, 1949, he surveyed the market for grain-cleaners and reported that service was the basic factor in building sales. He discerned a definite feeling of animosity toward Superior because of poor service rendered during war years and up to and including 1948. To remedy the situation, he planned an aggressive program to contact all potential customers and convince them that Superior wanted their business.

These customers were scattered throughout the United States and Canada. In addition to the original customers—country and terminal elevators—the company sold machines to flour mills, feed plants, hybrid-corn houses, cereal plants, rice mills, seed houses, and malting plants. The four salesmen were stationed in Minnesota and North Dakota and sold direct to the user. To cover the remaining territories the company employed distributors located in principal cities throughout the country. There were few large companies in the grain-separator industry. Superior's greatest competition came from the Hart-Carter Company. Both had the reputation of producing quality machines using

Exhibit 7

SUPERIOR SEPARATOR COMPANY

Profit or Loss Statement for 8-Month Period Ending June 30, 1950, by Division

(In Thousands)

	Company		Farmhand Division		Grain-Cleaner Division	
Sales, less cash discount available	$2,776		$2,469		$307	
Deduct: returns and allowances	49		37		12	
	$2,727		$2,432		$295	
Cash discount available to customers	$ 121		$ 117		$ 4	
Cash discount allowed to customers	119*		115*		4*	
Out freight	...		2		1	
Truck rental	9*		9*		..	
Net sales	$2,721	100.0%	$2,428	100.0%	$294	100.0%
Cost of goods sold:						
At standard cost	$1,660	61.0%	$1,423	58.6%	$237	80.6%
Adjustment to standard cost	38*	...	....	...	38*	...
Variances:						
Labor	39	...	23	...	16	...
Burden	111	...	113	...	1	...
Material	165	...	163	...	1	...
Provision for inventory shrinkage	52	...	49	...	4	...
Total cost of sales	$1,989	73.1%	$1,771	72.9%	$219	74.5%
Gross profit	$ 732	26.9%	$ 657	27.1%	$ 75	25.5%
Selling expenses:						
Field expenses	$ 219	...	$ 158	...	$ 62	...
Home office	69	...	54	...	15	...
Total selling expenses	$ 288	10.6%	$ 212	8.7%	$ 77	26.2%
General and administrative expenses	86	3.2	75	3.1	10	3.4
Engineering	58	2.5	45	1.9	13	4.4
Total selling, general, and administrative expenses	$ 432	16.3%	$ 332	13.7%	$100	34.0%
Profit or loss from operations	$ 300	10.6%	$ 325	13.4%	$ 25*	8.5%*
Other charges	$ 9	...				
Net income before adjusted compensation and tax provision	$ 291	...				
Provision for adjusted compensation	17	...				
Net income before income taxes	$ 274	...				
Provision for income taxes	112	...				
Net profit for the period	$ 162	5.9%				

* Loss.

Source: Company records.

the separation-through-weight principle, although the operation of the competing machines was slightly different.

For some time Mr. Pierson had been concerned about the unprofitability of the Grain-Cleaner Division. He believed that the major reason why the division had not been making money lay in its pricing policy.

The line had been priced to produce a profit after granting salesmen 5% commissions. Distributors demanded 15%, however, and an increasing percentage of sales was being made through this channel.

To remedy the situation, the division raised its list prices 10–20% in August, 1950. Henceforth, the price range would be $310–$3,885. Mr. Pierson did not believe that the price increase would affect sales adversely. "Most purchasers probably won't even notice the change."

Another reason why the division had not been operating profitably, Mr. Pierson thought, was partly psychological. The division had long believed that it was necessary to separate physically the manufacture of grain-cleaners from the manufacture of farm implements. After the inventory crisis of 1949, in order to conserve cash management shelved a plan to build a separate building for the division. Mr. Pierson felt that, as a result of this decision, the personnel of the division were not exerting enough effort to make maximum use of present quarters.

Mr. Wahl believed that one reason for the unprofitable operation lay in the lack of information on costing. The company was not sure it knew its costs in the production of grain-cleaners, and this project was, therefore, a current assignment of the accounting department in June, 1950.

In that month Mr. Randall was appointed general manager of the Grain-Cleaner Division to pin responsibility. "Since 1940 we have been on the verge of 'getting grain cleaners straightened out' . . . ridiculous to continue this business unless it can be done at a profit," said Mr. Pierson.

FARMHAND DIVISION

Competitive Situation. The Department of Commerce estimated in March, 1949, that there were about 1,600 firms engaged in the manufacture of farm equipment. Of this number, 7 companies, led by the International Harvester Company and Deere & Company, produced approximately 65% of the total output of the industry. These large companies manufactured a long line of farm machinery. "However, since these firms concentrate on the manufacture of equipment used in the production and harvesting of the major field crops, they are not major producers of all types of agricultural equipment."[1] Many of the short-line concerns specialized in one item or in a certain type of equipment. The area in which Superior desired to compete was the specialized field of materials-handling.

---

[1] Department of Commerce, *Progress and Prospects in the Farm Equipment Industry,* March 31, 1949.

Direct competition for the Hydraulic Farmhand came not so much from other high-lift loaders as from other machines designed to put up hay. Indeed, salesmen ordered to report the appearance of competitive equipment in the field had revealed that only a few high-lift loaders produced by obscure small companies had been encountered. Usually a

Exhibit 8

SUPERIOR SEPARATOR COMPANY

Comparison of Performance of Superior with Performance of Six Long-Line Manufacturers, 1939–49

	Superior	Allis-Chalmers	J. I. Case	Deere	International Harvester	Minne-apolis-Moline	Oliver
NET SALES (1939 = 100)							
1949	1,481	472	819	515	428	547	530
1948	1,942*	442	741	441	445	544	541
1947	1,653	285	390	302	349	381	386
1946	972	126	184	207	227	237	266
1945	337	391	383	196	293	314	306
1944	222	511	366	244	301	319	227
1943	114	385	342	268	216	278	161
1942	136	264	242	190	172	222	149
1941	109	164	189	178	172	175	121
1940	76	117	111	120	129	122	100
1939	100	100	100	100	100	100	100
NET INCOME AS A PERCENTAGE OF NET SALES							
1949	8.0	5.3	10.3†	10.9†	6.7	8.6	6.1
1948	7.1	4.7	6.7	8.9	5.9	8.8	7.7
1947	7.6	2.6	6.1	6.5	6.5	9.2	5.5
1946	8.1	0.1	4.2	6.6	4.6	5.3	3.9
1945	4.7	2.4	3.9	6.3	3.9	2.5	2.9
1944	5.9	2.4	2.8	6.3	4.0	3.0	4.0
1943	12.0	2.8	3.4	6.2	5.6	4.1	5.7
1942	8.5	3.0	4.9	9.5	7.3	5.1	5.8
1941	6.5	4.7	8.3	11.4	8.4	8.8	7.2
1940	5.3	5.8	6.0	14.5	8.4	7.1	4.6
1939	11.3	3.3	1.7	10.9	3.8	0.4	2.3

* Ten months.
† Before reserve for inventories.
Source: Standard & Poor's *Industry Surveys*, "Machinery—Agricultural," February 23, 1950; company records.

machine would make a brief appearance and then would disappear as the company went into bankruptcy. Although rumors were constantly cropping up that several long-line companies were prepared to introduce a high-lift loader, not one had done so by mid-1950. Instead, the big companies concentrated on a low-lift manure loader, apparently in

the belief that there was a much larger potential market for this machine, particularly in the Corn Belt. The low-lift manure loader which
would lift material a height of about 9 feet sold for about $325, while a
high-lift hay loader which would lift material as high as 27 feet retailed
with the major attachments for almost $600. Thus the two machines
tended to reach a different market.

The two wagons were directly competitive with a great many other
farm wagons on the market after the war. According to Mr. Pierson,
the market was overcrowded when the products were introduced, but
the wagons were added to the line to complement the Power Box. There
was little direct competition for the fully equipped Power Box in its
range of about $900; again, the size of the market was the restricting
factor. The mixer-feeder attachment, for instance, was well received by
the large stockman, but the farmer with a small herd of cattle could not
see the economy of automatic feeding. If he needed a manure spreader,
he could buy a conventional one for about one-third the price of the
Power Box.

Competition for the dump rake came from two sources. The horse-
drawn dump rake was still being used widely in areas where it was the
custom to rake cut hay into small piles in the field to be picked up later
by a stacker, such as the Farmhand. Where a tractor-drawn hay loader
was used to elevate the hay into a wagon, the farmer preferred to use
a side-delivery rake which would produce a continuous windrow.[2]

The demands of World War II and international food shortages following the war stimulated a major increase in U.S. food production and
farm prices in the period 1940–48. Gross farm income rose from $11.0
billion to $35.1 billion, and net farm income (gross receipts less costs
of production) from $4.8 billion to $16.5 billion. Prices received by the
farmer increased 185% and prices paid by the farmer rose 159%.
While farm wages rose 242%, the average price of farm machinery
increased only 46%. Two factors, therefore, spurred mechanization of
the American farm: (1) necessity for the maximum production, and
(2) economy of substituting machines for men. In 1948 shipments of
all manufacturers of farm machinery were 250% greater than 1940
shipments, and 1948 shipments of manufacturers of haying machinery
were 665% larger than the 1940 figure (see Exhibit 9).

Net farm income began to decline in 1948 from its 1947 peak, and
the trend continued in 1949 and the first half of 1950. Nevertheless,

---

[2] "Windrow"—a row of hay raked up to dry.

Exhibit 9

SUPERIOR SEPARATOR COMPANY

Industry Statistics, 1940–50

(In Millions)

Year	Total Gross Farm Income	Total Net Farm Income	All Farm Equipment Manufacturers' Shipments	Manufacturers' Shipments Haying Machinery
1950...............	E $31,500	E $13,000	$	$...
1949...............	32,167	14,129	1,815	152
1948...............	35,071	16,526	1,734	153
1947...............	34,643	17,794	1,295	95
1946...............	29,255	15,017	850	60
1945...............	25,419	12,790	700	49
1944...............	24,159	12,126	617	45
1943...............	23,008	9,086	344	26
1942...............	18,551	6,412	659	34
1941...............	13,881	4,525	671	35
1940...............	11,009	4,783	498	20

E: Estimated.
Source: U.S. Department of Agriculture, Bureau of Agricultural Economics.
U.S. Department of Commerce, Bureau of the Census.

most observers predicted that net farm income in 1950 would be almost three times net farm income in 1940 and that the federal government would continue to support prices to prevent a substantial drop in farm income in the immediate future.

Sales. The company sold its line of farm equipment to approximately 900 retail dealers in 20 states in the Midwest and Far West, and about 100 dealers in western Canada. The company had tried to obtain the strongest established dealer in a community. Usually the dealer selected represented one of the major long-line manufacturers of farm machinery. Mr. Pierson estimated that in the 1945–50 expansion of from 300 to 1,000 dealers the company had been successful in securing the best or the next-to-best farm equipment dealer in nearly every locality. Approximately 40% were International Harvester Company dealers, 40% were Deere & Company dealers, and the remaining 20% represented miscellaneous manufacturers. Although a report of sales by dealers in 1949 was not available to Mr. Ostrander, he estimated that 50% of the dealers would do 80% of the business in 1950. Dealers were given a 20% margin.

Mr. Pierson hoped to work toward a system of independent Farmhand dealers handling the line exclusively. In July, 1948, the company opened a retail store at Moorhead, Minnesota, to determine whether a store handling only Farmhand equipment could be operated profitably.

After ten months operations showed a net loss of $1,305 with no allocation of general and administrative expenses of the home office, and the store was closed. The president felt that the number of items in the line would have to be increased materially to warrant a system of independent Farmhand dealers.

When the supply of farm equipment once again became plentiful in 1949 and the farmer reverted to his prewar habit of buying at the moment of greatest need, speed of delivery became of prime importance. Since the factory was located over 1,000 miles from many dealers, Mr. Pierson in May, 1949, took two steps to ease the situation:

1. Seven trucks were leased to supplement rail delivery with the dealer billed at the carload rate for shipment by rail. (The trucking operation was realizing a small profit in 1950.)

2. Eleven large dealers in the Mountain and Pacific states were secured to serve as warehouse distributors. In return for storing machines and parts on consignment, the distributor was paid by the dealer a handling charge of 60 cents per 100 pounds on machines and $2.00 each on mountings used to secure the Farmhand loader to various makes of tractors. The dealer in turn passed this charge on to the farmer. The distributor agreed to make the merchandise available to any dealer in his area.

As sales manager of the Farmhand Division, Mr. Ostrander supervised 3 territorial sales managers in the United States and the sales manager of the Canadian subsidiary. These men, in turn, oversaw 17 blockmen in the United States and 5 in Canada. (A block was defined as an area with an annual sales potential of $200,000.) The three territories in the United States—Mountain, Plains, and Corn Belt—were established as areas in which crops and methods of farming were largely similar. In 1950 there was no territorial manager for the Corn Belt. In 1949, 217 dealers in the Mountain territory accounted for 35% of total Farmhand sales, 381 in the Plains territory for 58%, and 315 in the Corn Belt for 7%.

Mr. Ostrander explained this poor performance in the Corn Belt territory: "The farmers' methods of putting up hay determine whether there's a market for a high-lift loader. In the Plains and Mountain territories the Farmhand does the best job of stacking hay in the field. In the Corn Belt you can drive for miles without seeing a hay stack. (See Exhibit 10.) Farmers put their hay up in barns and don't see the need for a high-lift loader. The farmer doesn't think about the 50 other materials-handling jobs the Farmhand will do until he buys the ma-

Exhibit 10

SUPERIOR SEPARATOR COMPANY

Hay: Percentage Stored in Stacks or Ricks at Haying Time, 1944

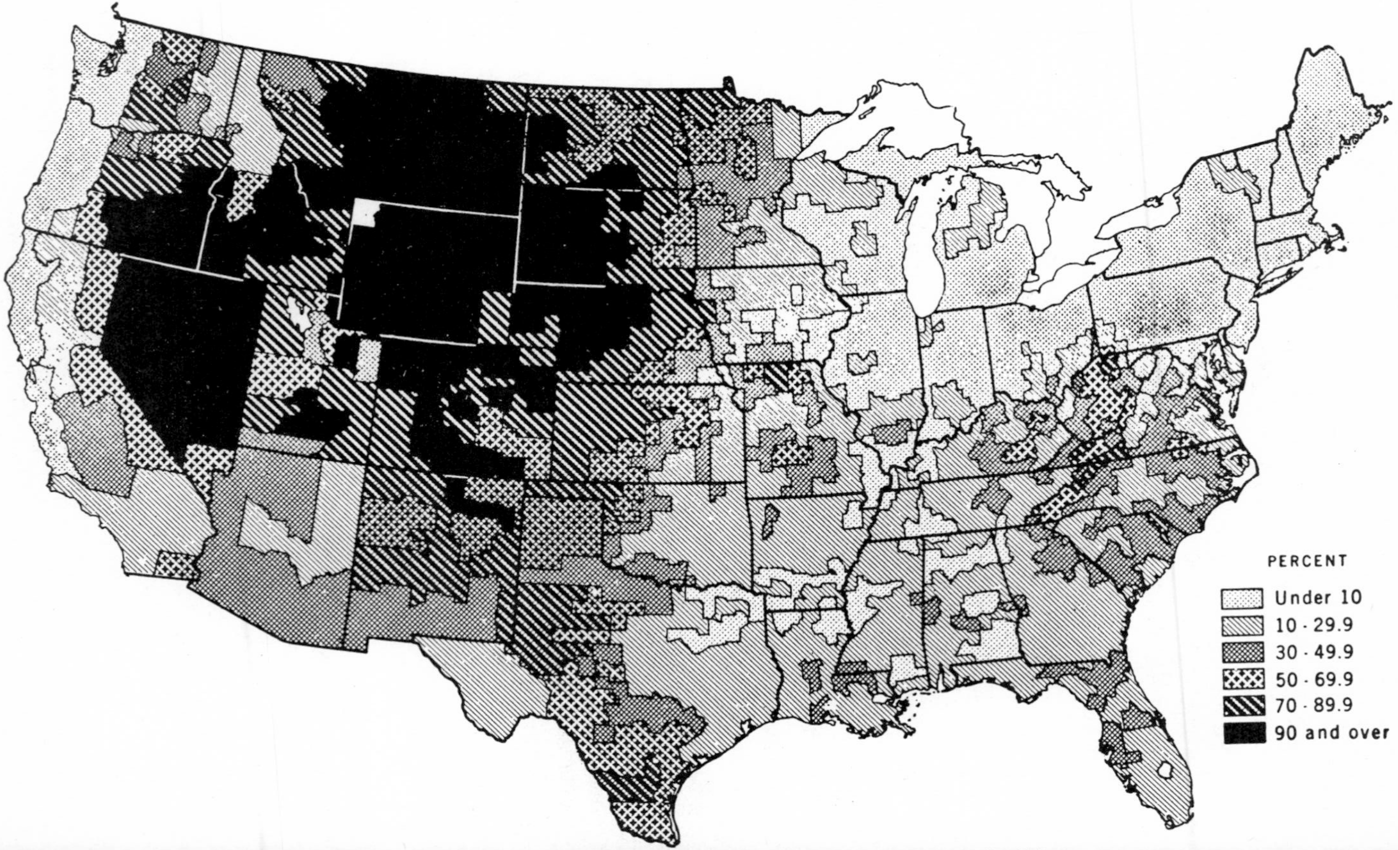

PERCENT

Under 10
10 - 29.9
30 - 49.9
50 - 69.9
70 - 89.9
90 and over

chine for its primary purpose. One of our biggest problems in marketing the Farmhand is to sell the Corn Belt farmer on the many uses of the machine. So far we haven't done it."

The company hoped that the addition of the Power Box, the five-ton wagon, the two and one-half ton wagon, the single-axle trailer, and the three-level forage unit would increase Farmhand sales in the Corn Belt by giving the dealer a longer line to demonstrate.

A blockman received a guaranteed monthly draw which varied from $250 to $350 depending upon his ability to meet monthly quotas and his over-all record. In addition each blockman was given a fixed amount, $50 a week, to cover expenses.

The volume required to cover the expense and draw for a blockman, based on $3\frac{1}{2}\%$ of net collections, determined the quota for each block. Once his quota was attained, the blockman received a $3\frac{1}{2}\%$ commission on all subsequent volume. Annual compensation varied from $5,500 for the salesman who did not make his quota to about $10,000 for the top salesman in the field. A weekly report on the status of sales-quota accomplishment was compiled and distributed to all blockmen and territorial managers. The July, 1950, report revealed that in the United States six blockmen had already attained their annual quota, six were ahead of where they should be at the $8\frac{1}{2}$-month mark, and five were below this point. No Canadian blockman had reached 40% of his 1950 quota.

Two Farmhand products presented particular marketing problems. The Prairie Mulcher was "either 20 years ahead of its time or 20 years behind," according to Mr. Ostrander. When the machine was introduced in 1947, farmers showed marked interest and dealers stocked heavily. But retail sales soon declined to almost nothing. Dealers were caught with unsalable machines and became wary of other new products introduced to the line. Consequently, little effort was being made by the sales department to push the mulcher.

Mechanical defects in the dump rake, introduced in 1949, were uncovered in the field, and the company in July, 1950, was in the process of recalling all machines to the factory for engineering changes.

Advertising and Sales Promotion. The company expended $167,-000 for advertising in 1949, about 3.7% of net sales. By far the greatest proportion of this amount was spent by the Farmhand Division around the basic theme "Designed by farmers . . . engineered for farmers. For every big lifting and loading job on your farm!" As a contribution to advertising expense the dealers were charged a fee of 1% of total bill-ings. For this charge they were supplied with newspaper mats and pro-motional material for mailing to prospects on a regular basis. There was some dealer criticism of this 1% charge since other manufacturers pro-vided direct-mail literature without charge and paid half of the cost of local newspaper advertising. The company believed, however, that the dealer would make better use of the mats and direct-mail folders if he were aware that he was paying a share of the cost.

The company backed up local advertising with page advertisements in regional farm papers. In the summer of 1950 this advertising em-phasized a contest offering $3,000 in prizes to 107 contestants who listed the largest number of farm jobs illustrated in a drawing as being done by hand which could be done better by a Hydraulic Farmhand. By July, 1950, over 80,000 entries had been received. At this rate it was estimated that the total response would reach 150,000 by the closing, September 30, 1950. The company employed the advertising agency of Batten, Barton, Durstine, and Osborn.

Sales-promotion efforts varied according to the season. In the summer exhibits were set up at state and county fairs. All Farmhand equipment was displayed, and the dealers and blockmen solicited inquiries from interested farmers. In the winter three films were made available to dealers to show to large gatherings with the central idea: "While tractor power has been the greatest single factor in mechanizing the American farm, it has not taken the back-break out of materials handling. The Farmhand line completes the mechanization of the farm." The block-men also held demonstrations in dealer towns.

Pricing. Although cost studies were made on a product before it was added to the Farmhand line, the price arrived at was generally the most accurate guess as to what the market would bear. Company officers often decided to price a basic machine low to stimulate the initial sale and to make high margins on attachments for it. Management had encountered difficulty with such a pricing policy because market information on a new machine was sketchy at best. The fear of overpricing a machine had led to underpricing several new products introduced in 1949. Once the price had been established, the sales manager was reluctant to raise it even though the higher price would have proven acceptable initially. Exhibit 11 reveals a cost and margin appraisal of selected items in the Farmhand line. Unit shipments for the eight-month period through June, 1950, are also included.

Exhibit 11

SUPERIOR SEPARATOR COMPANY

Summary of Profit Margin in Selected Farmhand Products February 15, 1950, and Shipments October 31, 1949—June 30, 1950

Description	Total Cost	Profit Margin	Net Price	Dealer Discount	List Price	Per Cent Margin	Shipments (Units) 8 Months through June 30, 1950
Basic machine—large loader	$194.11	$26.29	$220.40	$69.60	$290.00	12%	3,828
Main support standard angles	14.86	9.46	34.32	7.68	32.00	39	2,849
Torque tubes 178″ long	21.21	12.99	34.20	10.80	45.00	38	3,265
International W-9 mounting	22.49	13.23	35.72	11.28	47.00	37	.....
Hay basket	57.07	18.32	75.39	23.81	99.20	24	3,436
Manure fork	28.20	21.39	49.59	15.66	65.25	43	2,796
Gravel plate	4.62	3.17	7.79	2.46	10.25	41	2,659
Forage fork	34.49	19.47	53.96	17.04	71.00	36	851
Snow Scoop	43.35	48.61	91.96	29.04	121.00	53	490
Bulldozer blade	29.72	21.58	51.30	16.20	67.50	42	114
Basic machine—small loader	168.88	44.98	207.86	65.64	273.50	22	402
Hydraulic system	40.26	11.42	51.68	16.32	68.00	22	1,105
Basic Power Box	196.58	16.22	212.80	67.20	280.00	8	7†
Mixer-feeder attachment	262.03	22.97	285.00	90.00	375.00	8	44
Front and rear truck assembly:							
5-ton wagon	104.27	1.75	106.02	33.48	139.50	2	157
2½-ton wagon	92.43	3.89*	88.54	27.96	116.50	4*	141
Basic single-axle trailer	92.67	7.51*	85.16	26.89	112.05	9*	47
Dump rake	148.74	1.74	150.48	47.52	198.00	1	420

* Loss.
† 119 "complete" Power Boxes shipped.
Source: Company records.

RESEARCH AND DEVELOPMENT

Research and development were a combined responsibility of engineering and sales. The engineering department was constantly experimenting with new machines and new adaptations to present ones. The sales department tried to keep aware of equipment performance in the field and to measure the market for a machine before it was added to the line, but executives said they had often felt forced to introduce an implement before it was thoroughly tested or the market for it fully determined. The effect of such a policy was to require the farmer to do part of the testing job. Mr. Pierson believed that the higher rate of returns would be detrimental only if the reputation of the Farmhand name suffered.

Following the loss of an appeal to the Circuit Court of Appeals from a decision of the District Court against Superior in a suit brought against a small company for infringement of the patent on the Hydraulic Farmhand, Mr. Pierson had come to feel that the established brand name, "Farmhand," was more valuable than any patent in meeting competition.

In an attempt to gain closer co-ordination between sales and engineering in the summer of 1950, an engineer from the methods department was sent out into Wisconsin with the forage box to analyze farmer reaction and to suggest improvements, and a former commercial researcher for General Mills was brought into the sales department by Mr. Ostrander to perform permanent market analysis of the Farmhand line in the field.

PRODUCTION

The production of farm machinery was basically a fabricating and welding job which did not require close tolerances. Manufacture of certain parts, however, required close precision work. While many manufacturers of loaders purchased their hydraulic pumps, for instance, Superior manufactured its own. The only finished parts purchased were such items as ball bearings, chains, and tires.

The manufacture of grain-cleaners was a more complicated process, but still the operation principally involved the assembly of parts crafted in the sheet-metal shop.

The sharp seasonal nature of Farmhand sales presented a major problem to production control. The company had neither the space nor the financial resources to build up a large inventory of finished goods in the off season. As a result, the rate of production varied widely from season to season, depending on current demand. Grain-cleaner sales did not show the same seasonal variation, but the high cost per specialized machine and the limited market required almost a job-order operation. No more than 20 machines would be run through at a time, and very low finished stocks were maintained. There was some transfer of workers to grain-cleaner production when farm-equipment volume was at a low level, but the company had not yet been successful in developing a product which would level out yearly output. An increasing parts business was expected to help level off the cyclical variation in farm implement sales, but the seasonal variation was still a problem.

PURCHASING

The shortage of raw materials following the war made purchasing a serious problem area for most manufacturers. Steel, in particular, was in short supply, and most steel companies adopted a voluntary allocation system whereby a customer was entitled to purchase in proportion to his 1940 orders. For Superior, a company which had expanded 20 times over in the space of 10 years, such an allotment did not begin to satisfy its needs. The purchasing agent was forced to buy steel wherever he could obtain it. Even in early 1950 when the general situation had eased considerably he had been forced to pay a broker 11 cents a pound for sheet steel when the mill price on sheet steel was a little over 4 cents a pound.

LABOR RELATIONS

The company employed 160 to 240 factory workers, depending on the season. The contract between Superior and District 77 of the International Association of Machinists provided for a union shop and a check-off system for the deduction of union dues by the company. The wage scale was generally in line with surrounding manufacturing concerns. The 1950 contract provided for a minimum wage of $1.20 for a janitor to $1.88 for a tool and die maker. Joint wage review was to be held twice a year, in January and July.

In an attempt to promote a spirit of labor-management teamwork, Mr. Pierson in 1948 offered the union a profit-sharing plan and revealed production and financial records to the employees. The adjusted compensation proposal, offered to all employees whether union or nonunion, set a base rate profit of 7.5% after taxes for the investors. Above that, for each $\frac{1}{10}$ of 1% increase in profits, each worker was to receive an extra 1% of his gross earnings. Above 8%, the workers would receive 1% for every 1% increase in profits. The members of the union twice rejected the proposal before final acceptance. One year later both the union and the company praised the plan:

> As the company and the International Association of Machinists renewed the agreement last week, they announced that the plan had:
> 1. Eliminated layoffs in spite of seasonal nature of the firm's farm equipment and grain cleaner business.
> 2. Increased employees' pay by 5% of their annual gross earnings.
> 3. Established a basis for mutual understanding between employee and employer which removes many of the usual frictions in labor-management relations.[3]

Three months later the company was forced to lay off 108 men in the face of an inventory crisis, and labor-management relations deteriorated. When a review of wages was held in the summer of 1949 the union discarded the profit-sharing plan in favor of a flat 6 cents an hour increase in wages by a 74 to 61 vote. Office employees retained the plan, but because the highly profitable months of November and December, 1948, had been included in determining the 1948 bonus, no adjusted compensation was declared on 1949 profits.

In March, 1950, the union struck for a 25 cents an hour wage increase. The strike was settled within 48 hours on a 7 cents an hour raise across the board, but ill feelings lingered on both sides.

"You must expect that you're going to have occasional trouble with your labor force in any manufacturing operation," said Mr. Pierson. He credited the strike not so much to a desire for higher wages but to a dissatisfaction with management neglect of human relations problems created in the shop by the product redesign and expansion program of 1949. Another executive spoke of the strike and the high office turnover as due to the nature of the company. "We're an aggressive, hard-driving concern. Some people can't stand the pressure."

Superior did not have a personnel manager in June, 1950. "A personnel manager is no good unless he's top grade. Right now we can't afford such a man," said Mr. Pierson.

A labor-management committee of 40, under the leadership of Mr. Randall, met monthly to consider problems and to review the progress of the company. "It looks as if the office employees will get a bonus this year," said Mr. Pierson in July, 1950. "The reaction of the shop workers should be very interesting."

---

[3] *The Minneapolis Tribune,* January 3, 1949.

INTERNAL CONTROLS

The company used two standard cost systems. In one the standard was maintained unchanged throughout the year, in the other it was changed monthly. On each job, therefore, two variances were recorded for material, labor, and burden. In addition to detailed monthly financial statements, Mr. Pierson received from Mr. Wahl a daily management report which presented a rough balance sheet as of the day before and a profit and loss statement for the previous day and the month to date. Mr. Pierson also received weekly and monthly shipping reports and the weekly sales report by salesmen and territories.

FINANCE

In the spring of 1950 the company investigated the possibility of stimulating lagging sales by assisting Farmhand dealers financially. Mr. Pierson was aware that most long-line companies aided their dealers by several devices. The International Harvester Company and the Dearborn Motor Company had established credit companies for the purpose of financing dealer receivables. Other firms had worked out similar arrangements with sales-finance companies. Some companies offered floor-planning (extension of credit on inventory) to their dealers. Others shipped equipment on consignment. Almost all were returning to the prewar practice of seasonal dating whereby the dealer would be allowed as much as 130 days to 140 days to render payment.

The company felt that it did not have the financial resources to compete with the long-line companies, but it did take two steps to help its dealers:

1. On June 1, 1950, payment terms for all dealers entitled to receive shipments on open accounts were changed from 5%/10 days to 5% the tenth of the month following date of shipment. A month later management appraised the effect of this move and decided that the change in terms had not increased shipments significantly but that it had improved dealer relations.

2. Negotiations were conducted with a sales-finance company to offer all qualified dealers a factory-sponsored time payment plan covering the major items in the Farmhand line. Such a plan would have involved a 25% down payment, a 6% finance charge on the unpaid balance for 12 months' maturity, and assignment of the paper with recourse[4] on the

---

[4] "With recourse"—term used when endorser of negotiable instrument remains contingently liable to subsequent holders.

dealer. A questionnaire was sent to the dealer organization soliciting their opinion. While there was some feeling that such a plan might boost retail sales, most dealers stated that local banks were meeting their credit needs and the credit needs of the farmer in a satisfactory manner. There was an almost unanimous reaction against any plan with a recourse clause. As a result, negotiations were discontinued.

SUPERIOR SEPARATOR COMPANY OF CANADA, LTD.

Management had established the Canadian subsidiary in 1947 to serve as sales agent for the company's products in Canada. It had planned to begin manufacturing and assembling Farmhand machines there in 1949. About $50,000 was borrowed by the subsidiary from a Canadian bank with the parent company's guarantee, and subcontract negotiations were initiated with several Canadian firms. Difficulties arose, according to Mr. Pierson, largely as a result of the incompetence of the general manager, and plans for manufacturing were temporarily abandoned. In 1950 a new general manager was appointed, and the subsidiary commenced manufacturing operations in St. Boniface, Manitoba.

Sales of the Farmhand line in Canada were hampered by an 8% sales tax, and, until a change of tariff regulations occurred in February, 1950, by a 10% duty on all farm equipment suitable for nonfarm use. Since the Canadian subsidiary did not increase its prices, the devaluation of the Canadian dollar further restricted profitable operations. In 1949 on sales of $631,423 the subsidiary showed a net loss of $5,153.

BOARD OF DIRECTORS

The board of directors was composed of five men, two representatives from management and three outsiders. Management men were Mr. Pierson and Mr. Randall. The outside members of the board were Mr. Gray, the retired president; Mr. Piper, the principal stockholder; and Samuel H. Rogers, vice-president of the trust department of the Northwestern National Bank, Minneapolis.

Mr. Gray, in his late sixties in 1950, had moved from Minneapolis and did not take an active part in company affairs.

As senior partner in the investment banking house of Piper, Jaffray, and Hopwood, Mr. Piper had been asked to serve as a director of several prominent companies. In 1950, at the age of sixty-two, he was chairman of the board of Munsingwear, Inc., and a director of Pillsbury Mills, Inc., the Truax-Traer Coal Company, the Cream of Wheat Corporation, the Minneapolis-Moline Power Implement Company, the Diamond

Iron Works, Inc., the Vassar Company, and the Superior Separator Company.

Mr. Rogers represented the estate of James Vaughan, which owned the second largest block of stock. In addition to serving as a director of Superior, he was on the board of the Archer-Daniels-Midland Company, the Northwestern Terminal Company, the Home Gas Company, the Atlas Lumber Company, and three Canadian firms. Mr. Rogers was forty-three years old in 1950.

Together, Mr. Piper and Mr. Rogers held a controlling interest in the company. Officers of the company owned relatively few shares of stock. "One of our biggest problems," said Mr. Piper, "is to find a way for the young men who are running this company to share in its earnings. The present tax policy of the federal government makes it almost impossible for them to buy in."

"Management depends quite heavily on the board in the Superior Separator Company," said Mr. Rogers. Any expenditure over $10,000 had to be approved by the executive committee, consisting of Mr. Pierson, Mr. Piper, and Mr. Rogers. "I spend considerably more time in the capacity of a director of this company than I do for several other firms of which I am a director," said Mr. Rogers. Mr. Rogers had been largely responsible for the establishment of good bank relations in 1945. For several years he had been listed as a vice-president so that he could sign papers as an officer of the company. He had no other duties in this capacity.

Mr. Piper and Mr. Rogers conferred with senior executives frequently between monthly board meetings on a variety of executive problems. Mr. Rogers occasionally drove out to the plant and spent several hours with department heads. Mr. Piper often talked in his office with Mr. Pierson about company affairs over a morning cup of coffee.

Both Mr. Piper and Mr. Rogers believed that the future of the company lay in building a strong reputation as a manufacturer of materials-handling equipment for the farm. By producing a specialized line of products with limited demand, Superior, they felt, could avoid direct competition with the big concerns in the farm-machinery industry.

"There has never been a major clash between management and the board," said Mr. Piper.

FUTURE PLANS

In the summer of 1950 the company had been considering two major policy issues. A $200,000 program designed to improve existing plant facilities was rejected because, in the opinion of the board of directors, the anticipated savings in more efficient materials-handling were not adequate to warrant the investment. The purchase of the plant and equipment of a manufacturer of construction machinery was rejected because the board feared that there was an insufficient number of trained executives to control both operations and to meet the problems resulting from such a move.

"A little company gets to be a big one only by moving rapidly and aggressively," said Mr. Pierson. But the president was not sure just how fast it was safe to expand without unduly straining finances, facilities, and personnel, or in what direction this expansion would best take place. Should Superior try to increase sales of its present line of products by extending the Farmhand dealer organization geographically? Should it try to increase sales in present territories by adding new products to the line? If new products were to be added, should they be strictly materials-handling devices for the farm, or should management consider any product which appeared to offer a ready market? Should the company attempt to grow by purchasing other businesses? If so, should there be any product limitations in an absorption? These were questions executives were pondering. These were questions which Mr. Pierson felt were very important to the long-run future of the company.

One long-range goal of product development work was a self-propelled loader. Such a machine would combine the wagon, Power Box, and Hydraulic Farmhand with an integrated power unit. Mr. Pierson envisioned it as the answer to the materials-handling problem on the farm.

Provided the international situation did not necessitate production controls, Mr. Pierson still hoped to find a product which would level off the sharp seasonal variations in sales and make it possible to stabilize the volume of production throughout the year.

Should production controls be instituted, Mr. Pierson hoped to obtain a priority for the Farmhand line of equipment solely on the basis of their laborsaving features. The plant was surveyed by a representative of the War Department in the summer of 1949 to determine its ability to produce war material, and Mr. Pierson, Mr. Randall, and Mr. Ostrander were currently investigating in several quarters the possibility of securing government contracts. The engineering department was studying the possibility of the military application of the loader and Power Box as a self-propelled machine. Such a machine was perhaps five years away. A division of production with 65% of output destined for civilian use and 35% for military use was regarded by Mr. Pierson as a desirable ratio in the event of the establishment of economic controls.

PART VI

Day-to-Day Administrative Problems

Breitman & Company (A)

I. INTRODUCTION

"YOU OUGHT TO GET a case from my uncle, Judson Fischer, vice-president of Breitman & Company," a second-year student at the Harvard Business School suggested in early 1952 to Mr. John Williams, a case writer at the School. "The company is in New York and makes women's belts and handbags. It's a highly successful business, and its executives are wonderful people. Neither of the two partners who own the business, however, is much interested in management. Felix Breitman, the president, is primarily a designer, and there's no question that his skill there has a lot to do with the company's success. Jud, my uncle, has the title of vice-president, but he really is the one who runs most of the actual operations. He's primarily a salesman, though, not an administrator; and I suspect that if you look into the matter, you may well find that as the company has grown, there has been inadequate attention to production and to the use of control and cost information on the part of the two partners.

"I think you'd find them very receptive to giving you a case. For several years my uncle's lawyer, Irving Lasser, has been telling Jud that the company badly needs 'more and better administration,' and I suspect Jud would welcome an outsider's look at the situation, even if you don't give him any advice."

As an outgrowth of this conversation, the nephew made arrangements for Mr. Williams to see Mr. Fischer on Monday morning, March 15, 1952, about the possibility of a case on Breitman.

II. MR. WILLIAMS' FIRST DAY WITH THE COMPANY

Mr. Williams arrived at 10:35 A.M. on the appointed day for his first interview with Mr. Fischer in the company showroom and headquarters, on the sixth floor of a "loft"-type building, 31 East 32d Street, New York, New York. Mr. Fischer's "office" consisted of a desk and a couch in one corner of the colorfully decorated L-shaped showroom. After some discussion about how Mr. Fischer's nephew was doing at the Business School, Mr. Fischer turned to the question of the case.

We're very glad to have you study our operation. Irving Lasser—you know who he is?—thinks we don't know how to run this business, but we've been pretty successful. If this isn't going to take too much of my time, we'll be delighted to tell you anything you want to know. What is it you'd like to know about us?

WILLIAMS: Well, Mr. Fischer, before we start, I should explain that in letting us go ahead, you are in effect making a contribution to the Harvard Business School, without getting anything directly in return. Naturally, you will see whatever we write up, but I won't attempt to offer any direct advice.

FISCHER: Yes, I understand that, but we still think this will be of great value to us.

WILLIAMS: Well, at least to get started, I'd like to learn a little bit about your products, whatever figures you have to show how you've done sales- and profitwise, who the members of your executive staff are, and something generally about how you operate.

FISCHER: Well, to begin with, this is a young business—about 13 to 15 years old. I came in 10 or 11 years ago, and since then sales have jumped from $300,000 to over $5,000,000. Would you like some more figures? (*He pulls out some 5″ × 8″ catalogue cards.*) In 1948 we did $2,500,000; 1949, $3,200,-000; 1950, $4,000,000; 1951, $5,000,000. That last figure isn't quite accurate—let me get Miss Voss, the office manager, in here. (*He calls Miss Voss on the phone, asking her to come in.*) During the time I've been here, my interest in the business has increased from $25,000 to over $300,000, but we still don't really have enough capital.

Good morning, Miss Voss. This is Mr. Williams, who's going to make a study of Breitman & Company. (*The two exchange greetings.*) Miss Voss, the latest figure on 1951 is off by $100,000. Is that right?

MISS VOSS: Yes, Mr. Fischer.

FISCHER: How do I correct the monthly figures?

MISS VOSS: Well, I think the simplest way, since these are rough, would be to add $10,000 to each of 10 months. (*She corrects the card and remains seated in the office during the remainder of the interview.*)

FISCHER: To continue, let's start with the bag department, headed by Sidney Teplow. Would you like to know what he makes? He's our highest-priced executive, making $35,000, and does $2,000,000 worth of business in fabric bags. You'll want to visit our 14th Street factory, which he runs. He also controls five contractors, who make bags for us. Shall I give you the rest of the people who work for him?

WILLIAMS: Yes, please.

FISCHER: We've recently hired a designer who's making $10,000. There's also an assistant in buying—he's paid $10,000; the production manager, $10,000; and the man who ships handbags and handles raw materials, $7,000.

We also buy straw bags from Rostyn Brothers, one of our large contractors, run by three partners whom, incidentally, we were put in touch with by the millinery union. They operate on about $100,000 to $150,000 of capital.

Another part of our business is the Highline Corporation in Dandridge, Tennessee. Mr. Breitman and I own the stock of that, and I think now we were very foolish in opening it. We make there washable bags of scrap nylon and acetate. Our general manager there is paid $7,800 a year. Last year we sold $600,000 worth of handbags from Dandridge.

Now as to the belt business. Have you met Byron Steinmetz, our belt sales manager? (*Mr. Steinmetz is called on the telephone, comes in, is introduced to Mr. Williams, and leaves to return to a buyer with whom he has been working.*) We sold $2,750,000 worth of belts last year, which is a lot for this business. Our second competitor did only about a million dollars volume.

The secret of our success is Mr. Breitman, just an ordinary guy who happens to have a genius in this design field. Some people will tell you you can buy talent. I say "nuts!" The scarcest commodity in this business is talent.

You want to know something about our problems—I can very quickly tell you about our biggest problem—the one that has given my partner ulcers and makes me so nervous I have to take sleeping pills at night. This is a style business—we live on the special designs Mr. Breitman creates, and because our customers would like us to ship their orders yesterday, we have to maintain large inventories. The trouble is, that inventory could become worthless tomorrow—we couldn't even get 10 cents on the dollar on it—and we could be forced out of business tomorrow. As I told you, we're undercapitalized, and if we wake up tomorrow with a half-million dollars of worthless inventory, we'd be out of business. If you want something to worry about, tell us what to do about that.

Going back to Mr. Breitman and the belt business, one of our most successful lines—and one on which we have no competition—is the Breitweave line, a novelty fabric belt which Mr. Breitman designed. As a matter of fact, he worked with the yarn manufacturers to design a new yarn and worked out a new way of making braid. This originally started out as something primarily for the Southern market, but it's now a big thing in our summer line.

You might be interested in this "throwaway" which describes these belts. This, incidentally, is the only kind of advertising we do—to prepare these leaflets to be mailed out as enclosures by our customers. Last year we spent $50,000 on this kind of advertising. Regular fashion advertising is no good in this business—it just doesn't work in the belt business.

Is this the kind of thing that interests you?

WILLIAMS: Yes, certainly.

FISCHER: Well, to get back to the belt business. As I said, Byron Steinmetz is the sales manager of the belt department. We hired him from a competitive organization four years ago. Fred Apfel is our production man—you'll want to talk with him. He's paid $10,000. Our Breitweave belts are made in our factory on 25th Street, run by Mrs. Long, who is our oldest employee in point of service. You'll probably want to visit that factory. We sell roughly $600,000 a year in the Breitweave belt line. We also sell a line of metal belts, doing about

$250,000 a year, and leather belts—about the same. In addition to our own factory, we also have seven contractors who make belts for us. All our belts, though, are shipped from our stockrooms on this floor. You'll want to talk with Mr. Harry Block, who is responsible for shipping all our belts. Our bags, incidentally, all go out from the 14th Street factory.

You've met Miss Voss, our office manager. You'll probably also want to talk with our accountant, Mr. Morris Firth, and Mr. Irving Lasser, our attorney.

I should also mention that we have ten salesmen, all over the country, all on a commission basis. If you want to help us, you might tell us why our New York salesman hasn't been able to get our belts into ——— and ——— [New York City department stores].

Miss Voss, is there anything else you think Mr. Williams should know about?

MISS VOSS: Well, Mr. Fischer, I think Mr. Williams might be interested in knowing how important your own abilities are to Breitman & Company.

FISCHER (laughing): Oh, come now, Miss Voss!

MISS VOSS: I mean that sincerely, Mr. Fischer. (To Mr. Williams) Mr. Fischer is a marvelous person for this business. He knows the line, he has a sense of fashion, a sense of timing, and he knows the merchandise of the stores—all of which are very vital.

FISCHER (laughing): Well, that's all very flattering, Miss Voss, but I'm sure Mr. Williams knows an exaggeration when he sees it.

MISS VOSS: No, really, Mr. Fischer, I mean it.

FISCHER: Well, Mr. Williams, do you at this point have any questions?

Mr. Williams asked if he might restate what he had written down to be sure he had it correct. In the process he also learned that the company had another activity—French Lines, a one-man organization that made high-priced belts in very limited quantities; that Breitman's general line of merchandise was considered medium-priced; that the company in 1952 sold to over 5,000 accounts all over the United States, including department stores, specialty stores, and a variety of specialized retail outlets. He also learned that in addition to the people mentioned by Mr. Fischer originally, the executive group included Mr. Frank Rich, sales manager of the handbag department, who had been hired within the last six months; two girls who worked in the showroom; and Mickey, Simon, and Joe, three men in their twenties who performed "a variety of jobs." (See Exhibit 1.)

Mr. Fischer also indicated his belief that selling was the most important part of the business:

Anyone can manufacture belts and bags, and I don't even claim that our merchandise is necessarily any better quality than our competitors'. It's the job of selling that's most important. I'm no big-shot executive, and I don't know all there is to know about business or management, but I do know something about how to sell, which is one of the reasons we've been so successful.

On his first visit, Mr. Williams had a short interview with Mr. Breitman, who indicated he was quite busy getting ready for a trip to Japan:

We're delighted to have you work with us, and I think you'll enjoy your visits because we think we have a nice bunch of people working here. It may be that you'll come up with something in our methods to indicate that they aren't all they should be, and you may be very helpful by taking a look at them. Another question that we'd like the answer to is whether or not it's smart for us to keep on growing, or whether we have any choice in the matter.

I imagine you'll want to spend more time with Judson and with the rest of our people than you will with me, but don't hesitate to see me at any time you have any questions. I've learned, though, that the less I have to do with the business end of things, the better they work out.

On his first day Mr. Williams was served lunch at Mr. Fischer's desk together with Miss Voss and Mr. Fischer, with whom he discussed the possibility of looking over the company records. Miss Voss indicated that her office was primarily a record-keeping operation—that the company accountants compiled all the regular statements. She gave Mr. Williams a copy of the latest balance sheet but told him that any other financial records would have to be obtained from the accountants:

We don't have enough space to store any records here that we don't have to keep.

Mr. Fischer added that space was one of Breitman's major problems:

You'll see a lot of confusion here which results from the fact that we're too crowded. The difficulty is that this building is *the* location to have a showroom, and we can't get any more space here. We could move our belt stock room elsewhere, but I like to be able to have the merchandise right here to show customers. I think it really helps our business to have it here. You can take a buyer out back, and if she sees the merchandise there, she's more likely to place an order.

Mr. Williams learned from a brief visit with Mr. Apfel that, although the latter felt the company had no major problems facing it, he thought that Mr. Williams might be interested in taking a look at the way the company was organized:

I've been taking a course in organization and management at N.Y.U., and I know you ought to have better definitions of responsibilities than we have here. One of these days I'm going to have to have a showdown with the boss on this matter. I'm particularly referring to the way Mr. Fischer works with Harry Block and me. As a matter of fact, things are now a lot better than they were

Exhibit 1

BREITMAN & COMPANY

Company Personnel

32D STREET

Location	No. of People	Name	Title or Duties	Approx. Age
President's office....	1	*Felix Breitman*	*President, Treasurer*	50
Showroom.........	1	*Judson Fischer*	*Vice-President*	50
	1	*Byron Steinmetz*	*Belt Sales Manager*	45
	1	*Frank Rich*	*Bag Sales Manager*	45
	1	*	Assistant to Mr. Steinmetz- Advertising	35 ..
	1	*	Saleswoman	35
	12†	*	Salesmen	25–50
	1	*	Telephone Operator	..
Bookkeeping Department.......	1	*Muriel Voss*	*Office Manager*	30
	2	*	Stenographers	..
	20	*	Clerks, Bookkeepers	..
Order Department..	1	*Fred Apfel*	*Belt Production Manager*	35
	1	*Harry Block*	*Belt Shipping Manager*	45
	1	*Mickey*	*Order Processing*	25
	1	*	Account-Card Supervisor	..
	4	*	Account-Card Clerks	..
	2	*	Billers	..
Belt Storage Area...	1	*Joe*	*Assistant to Mr. Breitman*	25
	1	*Simon*	*Outside Calls, Misc. Duties*	25
	5	*	Order Pickers	..
	3	*	Lay-away Clerks	..
	1	*	Supervisor, Receiving Department	..
	25	*	Receiving Department Employees	..
	6	*	Shipping Clerks	..
	5	*	Miscellaneous Employees	..
Total at 32d Street..	99			

* Names given only for people mentioned by name in the case.
† Most salesmen usually traveling away from office.

when Harry first came in here. Mr. Fischer has a habit, though, of wanting something done right away—right now, for example, I'm preparing a report on our stocks of aluminum belts—and he's likely to ask the first person he can get ahold of to take care of it for him.

Mr. Williams spent much of his first day sitting in Mr. Fischer's office or waiting in the showroom while Mr. Fischer talked on the telephone, discussed problems with his people, or talked with customers. It seemed to Mr. Williams that many of the impressions he gained that day were relevant to his interest in the company, particularly if, in fact, Monday was a relatively slow day, as Mr. Fischer had indicated. Breitman & Company appeared a "beehive" of activity. After ten o'clock in

Exhibit 1—Continued

BREITMAN & COMPANY

Company Personnel

14TH STREET

Location	No. of People	Name	Title or Duties	Approx. Age
Office............	1	*Sidney Teplow*	*Bag Department Manager*	55
	1	*	Bag Production Manager	35
	1	*	Bag Designer	40
	3	*	Clerks	..
Factory..........	1	*	Factory Superintendent	30
	3	*	Cutters	..
	21	*	Pasters	..
	24	*	Sewing-Machine Operators	..
	13	*	Assemblers	..
	4	*	Inspectors	..
	1	*	Shipping and Receiving Superintendent	55
	2	*	Billers	..
	2	*	Receiving Clerks	..
	6	*	Shipping Clerks	..
Total at 14th Street.	83			

25TH STREET

Location	No. of People	Name	Title or Duties	Approx. Age
Factory..........	1	*Mrs. Long*	*Factory Superintendent*	30
	1	*	Cutter	..
	2	*	Crocheters	..
	16	*	Sewing-Machine Operators	..
	2	*	Tackers	..
	4	*	Trimmers	..
	9	*	Miscellaneous Factory Workers	..
	1	*	Clerk	..
Total at 25th Street.	36			

OTHERS MENTIONED IN CASE

Name	Position
Irving Lasser......................*Lawyer*
Morris Firth......................*Accountant*
Larry Goodman......................*Former Partner*
Jake Levy......................*Former Partner*

the morning the showroom nearly always contained at least half-a-dozen buyers, looking at sample bags and belts, and being waited on by someone from the Breitman organization. The call bell, controlled by the telephone operator, seemed to be in continual operation, necessitated by the fact that the people being called appeared to be away from their desks as much of the time as they were there. Mr. Williams observed that Mr. Fischer especially seemed to be engaged in a continuing stream of activity—talking to buyers, taking orders over the phone, reviewing orders as they came in, talking to his people about their particular problems, and checking up on orders.

At the end of his first day, Mr. Williams concluded that a study of Breitman & Company might well make an interesting case and that at least it would be worth his while to follow up the lead. At Mr. Fischer's suggestion, Mr. Williams also made arrangements to see the company's accountant, Mr. Morris Firth, before visiting the company again. Mr. Fischer also expressed interest in having Mr. Williams meet Mr. Lasser at an early date and promised to schedule such an interview whenever Mr. Williams was ready.

Following a visit with Mr. Firth during the last week in March, Mr. Williams made the definite decision to go ahead with a case. Over the next several months, therefore, he spent an aggregate of approximately 20 working days with various people in the Breitman organization. During much of this time he was unable to get the undivided attention of the people he wished to see, but this fact gave him the opportunity to watch what was going on. At the end of his stay with the company he felt he had become sufficiently "part of the scenery" so that he had a rough "feel for" how the Breitman organization worked.

III. INFORMATION OBTAINED FROM THE ACCOUNTANT

Mr. Williams' initial interview with Mr. Firth in the latter's office lasted a full day, and at Mr. Firth's suggestion, Mr. Williams returned again several weeks later to follow up the topics discussed during the first visit. Mr. Firth gave Mr. Williams the balance sheets, income statements, and ratio information shown in Exhibits 2–5. He also provided most of the data on the company history, summarized below, as well as a statement about the relationship between his accounting firm and the company. Mr. Firth also volunteered a number of comments about Breitman & Company's problems, which are summarized below.

Company History. Breitman & Company was established in 1937 by Mr. Felix Breitman and Mr. Jake Levy, both of whom made an initial investment of $4,000. When the firm started, it made only women's novelty fabric belts, which it sold to local department and retail stores, and the two partners constituted the entire management group. They personally designed the merchandise, sold it, supervised production and purchasing, and with the aid of a bookkeeper kept the records. As sales grew from $69,000 the first year to over $200,000 a year in 1940–41, Mr. Levy invited Mr. Fischer, then selling in the

Exhibit 2

BREITMAN & COMPANY

Comparative Balance Sheets, 1938–51
(Thousands of Dollars)

Assets	1938*	1939*	1940*	1941*	1942*	1943*	1944*	1945*	1946*	1947*	1948†	1949†	1950†	1951†
Cash	$0.6	$2.6	$7.4	$7.6	$10.2	$7.6	$24.7	$33.1	$47.7	$91.9	$22.1	$53.4	$141.6	$63.0
Notes and Accounts Receivable	8.7	16.4	30.4	43.1	122.9	91.4	96.1	174.3	226.1	236.0	224.2	287.4	336.8	595.5
Inventories	2.3	2.7	3.8	4.1	73.1	96.8	96.0	135.2	233.8	246.0	250.2	103.5	126.2	265.7
Merchandise at Contractors													168.4	231.1
Current Assets	$11.6	$21.7	$41.6	$54.8	$206.2	$195.8	$216.8	$342.6	$507.6	$573.9	$496.5	$444.3	$773.0	$1,155.3
Treasury Stock	$2.2	$2.6	$3.5	$6.6	$17.0	$17.9	$28.2	$52.0	$61.1	$64.1	$70.6	$65.0	$65.0	$65.0
Machinery and Equipment	0.1	0.1	0.3	0.7	1.0	2.7	1.6	12.7	7.5	7.1	13.0	70.8	75.2	80.6
Other Assets												33.3	31.4	39.5
Fixed Assets	$2.3	$2.7	$3.8	$7.3	$18.0	$20.6	$29.8	$64.7	$68.6	$71.2	$83.6	$169.1	$171.6	$185.1
Total Assets	$13.9	$24.4	$45.4	$62.1	$224.2	$216.4	$246.6	$407.3	$576.2	$645.1	$580.1	$613.4	$944.6	$1,340.4
Accounts Payable	$2.7	$5.5	$15.3	$20.7	$78.5	$75.6	$54.0	$71.7	$191.2	$121.3	$144.0	$130.8	$114.2	$209.2
Notes Payable			5.0	7.0	45.0		50.0	100.0	125.0	200.0	100.0	75.0	350.0	450.0
Accrued Expenses	1.2	0.9	3.0	3.9	12.3	25.8	6.0	29.6	26.4	60.7	57.6	65.9	85.5	171.6
Other Liabilities	5.6	5.0			13.5	3.2	4.6	5.6	18.1	30.4	56.9	45.8	39.9	104.5
Officers' Loans to Business	0.1			1.7		5.5								
Corporate Income Tax Liability		1.0	0.6					100.0	100.0	100.0				
Current Liabilities	$9.6	$12.4	$23.9	$33.3	$149.3	$110.1	$114.6	$306.9	$460.7	$512.4	$358.5	$317.5	$589.6	$935.3
Capital Stock—Common	$4.0	$7.4	$12.6	$12.6	$45.0	$66.1	$132.0	$100.4	$115.5	$115.2	$115.2	$115.2	$115.2	$115.2
Earned Surplus	0.3	4.6	8.9	16.2	29.9	40.2				17.5	106.4	180.7	239.8	289.9
Total Capital	$4.3	$12.0	$21.5	$28.8	$74.9	$106.3	$132.0	$100.4	$115.5	$132.7	$221.6	$295.9	$355.0	$405.1
Total Liabilities and Capital	$13.9	$24.4	$45.4	$62.1	$224.2	$216.4	$246.6	$407.3	$576.2	$645.1	$580.1	$613.4	$944.6	$1,340.4

* 1938–47, year ending April 30.
† 1948–51, year ending February 28 or 29.
Source: Records furnished by accountant.

Exhibit 3

BREITMAN & COMPANY*
Comparative Profit and Loss Statements, 1938–52
(Thousands of Dollars)

	1938†	1939†	1940†	1941†	1942†	1943†
Net Sales	$69.1	$100.6	$169.5	$239.3	$803.4	$870.2
Less Cost of Goods Sold	49.1	60.6	120.2	189.6	649.4	725.9
Gross Profit from Sales	$24.9	$ 40.2	$ 49.3	$ 49.7	$154.0	$144.3
Commissions—Handbag					29.1	29.9
Total Income	$24.9	$ 40.2	$ 49.3	$ 49.7	$183.1	$174.2

Deductions

	1938†	1939†	1940†	1941†	1942†	1943†
Compensation of Officers	$ 6.7	$ 16.2	$ 16.8	$ 23.0	$ 39.7	$ 31.8
Salaries and Wages	10.3	11.5	14.2	15.1	22.6	20.6
Rent	1.5	1.6	2.4	2.6	5.7	6.6
Repairs						
Bad Debts	0.1		0.3	0.2	0.2	0.2
Interest	1.2	0.1	0.1	§	0.9	0.1
Taxes (Other than Federal Income)	0.7	1.4	3.2	2.5	6.9	7.0
Contributions					0.4	1.3
Depreciation	0.2	0.3	0.4	0.5	2.1	2.7
Commissions					53.1	52.7
Traveling and Selling	0.6		2.4	2.5	8.9	7.7
Advertising and Promotion					2.2	2.8
Packing and Shipping—Freight and Cartage					3.1	2.4
Stationery and Postage	1.2				4.2	3.0
Legal and Professional	0.4	0.4	0.7	0.9	2.4	2.1
Insurance—Life					1.0	1.0
Other	0.2	0.7	0.5	0.5	1.1	1.9
Light and Power					1.2	1.0
Telephone and Telegraph	0.4	0.4	0.6	0.8	1.1	0.8
Credit and Association						0.7
Designing Expense and Sample Making						
Factory Expense					0.8	
California Office Expense						
Chicago Office Expense						
Sundry Expense	1.1	2.2	2.8	2.2	6.4	2.6
Health and Vacation Fund						
Belt and Bag Corrugated Boxes						
Auto Expense						
Hospitalization						
Total Deductions	$24.6	$ 34.8	$ 44.4	$ 40.8	$164.0	$149.0
Net Income	$ 0.3	$ 5.4	$ 4.9	$ 8.9	$ 19.1	$ 25.2
Federal Income and Excess Profits Tax	§	1.1	0.6	1.6	5.4	4.9
Net Income after Taxes	$ 0.3	$ 4.3	$ 4.3	$ 7.3	$ 13.7	$ 10.3
Surplus—Beginning of Year		$ 0.3	$ 4.6	$ 8.9	$ 16.2	$ 29.9
Surplus—End of Year	$ 0.3	$ 4.6	$ 8.9	$ 16.2	$ 29.9	$ 40.2

* Operated as corporation, April 30, 1937—November 30, 1942; as partnership, November 30, 1942—February 14, 1946; as corporation after February 14, 1946.
† Year ending April 30.
‡ Year ending February 28 or 29.
§ Less than $50.
‖ Includes partners' personal taxes on income.
Source: Records furnished by accountant.

Exhibit 3—Continued

BREITMAN & COMPANY

Comparative Profit and Loss Statements, 1938–52

(Thousands of Dollars)

1944†	1945†	1946†	1947†	1948‡	1949‡	1950‡	1951‡
$1,428.9	$1,440.1	$1,810.5	$2,394.9	$2,218.6	$2,508.9	$3,146.8	$4,194.5
1,020.7	1,075.6	1,291.8	1,733.2	1,404.5	1,627.2	2,195.2	2,989.0
$ 408.2	$ 364.5	$ 518.7	$ 661.7	$ 814.1	$ 881.7	$ 951.6	$1,205.5
$ 408.2	$ 364.5	$ 518.7	$ 661.7	$ 814.1	$ 881.7	$ 951.6	$1,205.5
$ 45.0	$ 45.0	$ 45.0	$ 61.6	$ 68.6	$ 81.6	$ 91.9	$ 106.1
56.4	94.9	100.4	159.7	164.2	201.9	216.6	282.3
12.1	18.8	17.5	20.3	20.7	20.8	29.7	29.6
			1.9	3.7	6.9	9.6	10.9
			2.2				
1.2	3.6	4.4	4.8	2.2	2.0	5.6	9.7
16.7	17.9	16.8	20.7	26.1	23.1	22.7	32.4
4.8	4.2	3.8	8.2	5.5	3.3	7.1	5.8
6.1	10.2	12.8	14.9	12.2	12.0	14.3	19.3
48.7	65.1	96.1	144.6	121.1	145.3	207.7	288.4
30.8	30.9	40.1	42.6	57.8	46.5	60.3	83.4
26.2	4.8	25.4	23.4	35.5	66.5	32.9	24.3
8.1	15.2	10.1	15.8	19.2	17.5	21.8	53.3
5.8	7.9	10.2	22.7	29.2	25.6	13.8	6.9
8.3	10.3	17.9	18.9	20.2	19.9	18.8	14.0
7.5	3.2		8.2	3.9	3.6	6.3	8.2
		8.2	13.5	9.5	12.3	9.2	13.3
2.1	4.8	6.4	5.3	5.4	5.3	4.8	4.7
1.5	2.4	3.0	4.1	5.3	5.4	5.9	7.8
2.5	1.9	2.2	2.2	2.9	4.6	3.5	4.0
	3.6	21.6	3.1	4.3	1.2	3.0	35.9
8.1	12.1	15.4	7.2	8.7	6.7	7.3	8.8
					1.4	1.9	2.9
			2.1				
5.5	9.1	9.5	16.4	12.5	9.8	9.5	9.3
		1.8		4.8	3.8	3.0	3.6
				24.8	32.5	43.6	43.9
					3.1	1.9	2.2
					2.1	1.9	2.2
$ 297.5	$ 366.1	$ 468.6	$ 624.4	$ 668.3	$ 764.7	$ 854.6	$1,113.1
$ 110.7	$ (1.6)	$ 50.1	$ 37.3	$ 145.8	$ 117.0	$ 97.0	$ 92.4
85.0‖	30.0‖	35.0‖	20.4	56.9	42.8	37.9	42.3
$ 25.7	$ (31.6)	$ 15.1	$ 16.9	$ 88.9	$ 74.3	$ 59.1	$ 50.1
$ 40.2	$ 132.0	$ 100.4	$ 0.6	$ 17.5	$ 106.4	$ 180.7	$ 239.8
$ 65.9	$ 100.4	$ 115.5	$ 17.5	$ 106.4	$ 180.7	$ 239.3	$ 289.9

Exhibit 4

BREITMAN & COMPANY

Accountant's Analysis of Income Statements
and Balance Sheets, 1938–51

	1938	1939	1940	1941	1942
Ratio of Current Assets to Current Liabilities	1.2 to 1	1.7 to 1	1.7 to 1	1.6 to 1	1.4 to 1
Average Capital Turnover in Relation to Sales:					
Capital Beginning of Year (in thousands of dollars)		$ 4.2	$ 12.0	$ 21.5	$ 28.8
Capital at End of Year (in thousands of dollars)	$ 4.2	$ 12.0	$ 21.5	$ 28.8	$ 74.9
Average Capital (in thousands of dollars)	$ 4.2	$ 8.1	$ 16.7	$ 25.2	$ 51.9
Average Capital Turnover in Relation to Sales	16	12½	10	9½	15½
Percentage of Net Profit (before Federal Taxes) to					
Average Capital	6.8%	66.0%	29.5%	35.7%	36.9%
Sales (in thousands of dollars)	$69.0	$100.6	$169.5	$239.4	$803.4
Percentage of Gross Profit to Sales	36.1%	39.9%	29.1%	20.8%	22.9%
Percentage of Net Income (before Federal Taxes) to					
Sales	0.4%	5.3%	2.9%	3.8%	2.5%
Inventory Turnover in Relation to Sales	30	40½	52	60½	20½
Inventory Turnover in Relation to Cost of Merchandise Sold	19½	24½	37	48	16½
Percentage of Officers' Salaries to Sales	9.8%	16.1%	9.9%	9.6%	4.9%
Percentage of Other Salaries to Sales	14.9%	11.4%	8.4%	2.2%	2.8%
Percentage of Commission Selling and Advertising Expenses to Sales	0.8%		1.4%	1.0%	8.0%
Percentage of Shipping, Packaging, Fitting Bags and Boxes to Sales					0.4%
Percentage of All Other Expenses to Sales	10.2%	7.1%	6.5%	4.2%	4.3%
Percentage of Total Expenses to Sales	35.7%	34.6%	26.2%	17.0%	20.4%

Source: Records furnished by accountant.

South for a nationally known men's clothing firm, to join Breitman & Company as partner and sales manager.

In 1941 the then three partners formed a separate corporation to sell women's handbags, but a year later merged it with Breitman & Company. They also started to distribute their belts and handbags through salesmen throughout the United States, most of whom also represented manufacturers of other noncompeting items (e.g., children's underwear, sweaters, luggage). Sales jumped from $293,000 in 1940–41 to $1,428,000 in 1944–45, and in 1945 the firm bought out the leather and fabric handbag business of Mr. Larry Goodman, making him a fourth partner. According to Mr. Firth, Mr. Goodman did not add to the firm the bag "know-how" that his other partners had expected of him, so he withdrew in 1946, selling his interest to the other three partners. A year later, in February, 1947, Mr. Levy suddenly withdrew from the firm after a dispute with Mr. Fischer. According to Mr. Firth, this dispute was almost entirely the result of Mr. Levy's desire to be "the complete boss." Mr. Levy received $65,000 from the corporation for his interest, and in 1952 he was the head of his own high-priced handbag business.

Exhibit 6, prepared by Mr. Williams from the balance sheets, shows the growth of the firm's financial position.

Exhibit 4—Continued

BREITMAN & COMPANY

*Accountant's Analysis of Income Statements
and Balance Sheets, 1938–51*

1943	1944	1945	1946	1947	1948	1949	1950	1951
1.8 to 1	1.9 to 1	1.1 to 1	1.1 to 1	1.1 to 1	1.4 to 1	1.4 to 1	1.3 to 1	1.2 to 1
$ 74.9	$ 106.3	$ 132.0	$ 100.4	$ 115.5	$ 132.7	$ 221.7	$ 295.9	$ 355.0
$106.3	$ 132.0	$ 100.4	$ 115.5	$ 132.7	$ 221.7	$ 295.9	$ 355.0	$ 405.2
$ 90.6	$ 119.1	$ 116.2	$ 107.9	$ 124.1	$ 177.2	$ 258.8	$ 325.4	$ 380.1
9½	12	12½	17	19½	12½	9½	9½	11
27.8%	93.0%	(1.4%)	46.4%	30.0%	82.3%	45.2%	29.8%	24.3%
$870.1	$1,428.8	$1,440.1	$1,810.5	$2,394.9	$2,218.6	$2,508.9	$3,146.8	$4,194.6
20.0%	28.6%	25.3%	28.6%	27.6%	36.7%	35.1%	30.2%	28.7%
3.0%	7.8%	(0.1%)	2.7%	1.5%	6.7%	4.6%	3.1%	2.2%
10¼	14⅝	12½	9½	10	9	14½	15⅝	10½
8½	10½	9½	7	7¼	5⅝	9½	11	7½
3.6%	3.1%	3.1%	2.5%	2.6%	3.1%	3.3%	2.9%	2.5%
2.4%	3.9%	6.6%	5.5%	6.6%	7.4%	8.0%	6.9%	6.8%
7.2%	7.4%	7.0%	8.9%	8.8%	9.5%	10.3%	9.6%	9.4%
0.3%	0.6%	1.1%	.6%	0.7%	2.0%	2.0%	2.1%	2.3%
3.5%	5.8%	7.6%	8.4%	7.4%	8.0%	6.9%	5.6%	5.5%
17.0%	20.8%	25.4%	25.9%	26.1%	30.0%	30.5%	27.1%	26.5%

The addition of executive personnel had more or less followed the growth of the firm's sales. Miss Voss had been taken on from Mr. Firth's accounting firm in 1945 to act "temporarily" as office manager and head bookkeeper. In 1952 she was still acting in that capacity. Mr. Fred Apfel was added at about the same time as belt production manager. Mr. Sidney Teplow was brought in to manage the bag department when Mr. Goodman left. The two sales managers, Mr. Byron Steinmetz (belts) and Mr. Frank Rich (bags), had been hired from competitive firms in 1949 and 1952 respectively. Besides the two officers, the executive group in 1952 included 16 people. Of this group 10 worked in the 32d Street office, 5, including Mr. Teplow, worked in the bag factory at 14th Street, and 1 was superintendent at the 25th Street belt factory.

Accounting Firm's Relations with Company. Mr. Firth's accounting firm, of which he was one of four partners, was retained by Breitman & Company in 1941. According to Mr. Firth, his firm performed the same services for Breitman & Company as it did for its other clients, which were mainly manufacturing concerns of about the same size as Breitman. Four times a year two junior accountants audited the Breitman books and also prepared quarterly and annual balance sheets and income statements as well as the company's tax returns. After each statement, Mr. Firth sat down with Mr. Fischer and Mr. Breitman, and occasionally some of the other Breitman people, to appraise the op-

Exhibit 5

BREITMAN & COMPANY

Sample Five-Month Income Statement in Form Used by Accountants
for Company Review
July 1—November 30, 1950

(Figures Rounded to Thousands by Case Writer)

	Total	Per Cent	Bag Department	Per Cent	Belt Department	Per Cent
Sales: Regular	$ 700.3		$669.5		$ 30.8	
Straw	17.2		17.2			
Job	555.9				555.9	
Metal	447.8				447.8	
Total Sales	$1,721.2		$686.7		$1,034.5	
Gross Profit: Regular	$ 206.4	29.5%	$187.9	28.1%	$ 18.5	60.2%
Straw	Loss					
Job	153.0	27.5%			153.0	27.5%
Metal	151.9	33.9%			151.9	33.9%
	$ 511.3	29.7%	$187.9	27.4%	$ 324.4	31.3%
Mark Downs	21.6	1.3%	8.2	1.2%	13.4	1.3%
	$ 489.7	28.4%	$179.7	26.2%	$ 310.0	30.0%
Commissions	124.4	7.2%	41.9	6.1%	82.5	8.0%
Profit after Mark Downs and Commissions	$ 365.3	21.2%	$137.8	20.1%	$ 227.5	22.0%
Expenses						
Direct: Manufacturing	$ 108.5	6.3%	$ 56.0	8.2%	$ 52.5	5.1%
Selling	20.8	1.2%	2.5	0.4%	18.3	1.8%
Shipping	37.2	2.2%	18.4	2.7%	18.8	1.8%
Total Direct Expenses	$ 166.5	9.7%	$ 76.9	11.3%	$ 89.6	8.7%‡
†Allocable: Manufacturing	$ 34.6					
Selling	65.3		$ 62.9		$ 95.3	
General Administration	58.3					
Total Allocable Expenses	$ 158.2	9.2%	$ 62.9	9.1%	$ 95.3	9.2%‡
‡Total Expenses	$ 324.7	18.9%	$139.8	20.4%	$ 184.9	17.9%
Net Profit	40.6	2.3%	($ 2.0)	(0.3%)	$ 42.6	4.1%

( ) Loss.
† Allocable Expenses distributed to various departments on basis of sales.
‡ Supporting schedules normally furnished to officers not included here. See Exhibit 3.
Source: Furnished case writer by Mr. Firth.

erating results and discuss items of cost which appeared out of line. Mr. Firth, together with Irving Lasser, the lawyer, also met once a year with vice-presidents of each of the two banks with which Breitman did business to establish lines of credit for the coming year. Bank practice required that loans not exceed the company's working capital, that the company maintain a deposit balance of at least 20% of loans outstanding, and that the composition and size of the inventories on hand play a major part in determining the size of loans. The company was also required to "stay out of the banks" for at least 30 days each year.

Exhibit 6

BREITMAN & COMPANY

*Case Writer's Analysis of Source and Application
of Invested Capital, 1938–51*

(Thousands of Dollars)

FISCAL PERIOD	SALES	INCREASES IN INVESTED CAPITAL FROM			TOTAL CAPITAL INCREASE	INVESTED CAPITAL INCREASES APPLIED TO INCREASES IN		
		Profits	Depreciation	Money Put in by Partners		Machinery and Equipment*	Other Assets	Net Working Capital
1938–39......	$ 100.6	$ 4.3	$ 0.3	$ 3.4	$ 8.0	$ 0.7	$ ...	$ 7.3
1939–40......	169.5	4.3	0.4	5.2	9.9	1.3	$ 0.2	8.4
1940-41......	239.3	7.3	0.5	...	7.8	3.6	0.4	3.8
1941-42......	803.4	13.7	2.1	32.4	48.2	12.5	0.3	35.4
1942–43......	870.2	10.3	2.7	21.1	34.1	3.6	1.7	28.8
1943-44......	1,428.9	25.7	6.1	...	31.8	16.4	(1.1)	16.5
1944–45......	1,440.1	(31.6)	10.2	...	(21.4)	34.0	11.1	(66.5)
1945–46......	1,810.5	15.1	12.8	...	27.9	21.9	(5.2)	11.2
1946–47......	2,394.9	16.9	14.9	0.3	32.1	17.9	(0.4)	14.6
1947–48......	2,218.6	88.9	12.2	...	101.1	18.7	5.9	76.5
1948–49......	2,508.9	74.3	12.0	(65.0)	21.3	12.2	20.3	(11.2)
1949–50......	3,146.8	59.1	14.3	...	73.4	18.7	(1.9)	56.6
1950–51......	4,194.5	50.1	19.3	...	69.4	24.7	8.1	36.6
Cumulative Total, 1938–51...		$338.4	$107.8	$ (2.6)	$ 443.6	$186.2	$ 39.4	$218.0

( ) Negative figure.
* Net increase based on book value of machinery and equipment.
Source: Compiled by Mr. Williams from company balance sheets.

The seasonal nature of the company's business was such that loans were usually repaid at the end of June. At various times in recent company history, Mr. Breitman and Mr. Fischer had lent as much as $100,000 of their own funds to the business, in addition to the money provided by the bank. According to Mr. Firth, the company's bank credit had always been unusually good. At the same time, Mr. Firth regarded it as his responsibility to see that Breitman & Company did not ask for too much credit. In 1951 he had persuaded Mr. Fischer to ask for $100,000 less than the latter had contemplated.

Mr. Firth said that it was Miss Voss's responsibility to see that sufficient funds were on hand to meet expenses (sometimes as high as $500,000 a month) and that she had done "an exceptional job" in "keeping on her toes" and handling her operation of the business efficiently. The accounting firm handled all credit inquiries about Breitman & Company.

Mr. Firth's Appraisal of the Company.   In talking about Breitman & Company, its history, and its way of doing business, Mr. Firth made frequent references to the company's unusual record of success and, by way of contrast, spoke of a number of other companies of the size of Breitman with less fortunate records:

Judson Fischer and Felix Breitman are wonderful people. They've been successful because they've been willing to work like dogs—because they have been able to work together in harmony and build up a wonderful spirit of co-operation in their organization. What, of course, is just as important is the fact that between them they've had the vision to stay ahead of the market in style trends.

In response to questions from Mr. Williams, Mr. Firth expressed skepticism as to the desirability for any more elaborate record-keeping, information, budgeting, or cost-control operations at Breitman & Company. He also indicated some concern about the continued operation of the business after the retirement of either of the partners, but doubted whether anything could at present be done about this problem. He also expressed doubt as to whether much could be done to improve Breitman's financial position, particularly since neither of the partners was a wealthy man. The company's financial strength, he felt, would put an automatic brake on future expansion:

You must remember that this is a highly risky business and a fast-moving business, and that it takes a lot of personal supervision to keep such a business alive. One bad season and Breitman & Company could be in serious trouble; two, and they'd be out of business. The kinds of things you teach your boys at the Harvard Business School about management are all very well, but they don't exactly fit this business.

IV. THE LAWYER'S VIEW OF THE COMPANY

Mr. Williams obtained another view of company operations from Mr. Lasser, whom he saw early in May. Mr. Williams had considerable difficulty in arranging an appointment with Mr. Lasser because of illness in the latter's family. Mr. Williams' one interview with Mr. Lasser took place at the home of Judson Fischer, where he and Mrs. Fischer entertained Mr. Lasser and Mr. Williams for dinner. From notes he took at the dinner table, Mr. Williams reconstructed the following transcript of what took place that evening.

LASSER: I'm delighted to have this opportunity to talk with you about Breitman & Company, particularly since it gives me another chance to preach to my good friend Judson, here, some things I've been trying to hammer into him for over two years now.

It won't take me very long to say what I have to say because my theme is pretty simple, and I don't pretend to be able to work out all the details. Besides, if you're from the Harvard Business School, you'll know what I'm talking about.

Perhaps I should begin by qualifying myself to talk about this. I, too, incidentally, am a graduate of Fair Harvard—the Law School. Our firm specializes in combining business and legal advice to manufacturing corporations; I myself am a director of several corporations, including the ———— Company, of which Mr. ————, a graduate of your Business School, is president. Our firm is retained by Breitman & Company to do all its legal work; and, in addition, this son-of-a-gun and I are very good friends. We think we've given pretty good advice so far.

There are four things I think this firm needs, and it needs help to get them: first, a critical look at its market acceptance and the reasons for its success; second, a modern, up-to-date control system with somebody to run it; third, some acceptance of the rudimentary concepts of good administration in its day-to-day operation; and fourth, a more diversified product line to protect it against a dip in the market and against being run by its salesmen, as is now the case.

Let me talk about each of these in turn. Market acceptance—you've been watching the company long enough to know something about how it operates. Have you seen anyone there who ever has had time to sit back and take a look at where this company ought to be getting its business from, find out where Breitman stands in relation to competition, and plan its marketing activities accordingly? You know what I mean.

My second point ought to be equally obvious, even after a quick look at the company. This firm badly needs some element of financial and cost control.

FISCHER: Are you saying that Miss Voss doesn't do a good job?

LASSER: She does a good job of seeing to it that she's all things to all people, and she probably does an efficient job as head bookkeeper; but in terms of providing management information, she doesn't do a thing. Why, do you realize that this company has no analyses of sales by products, profitability by product lines, or costs by operations?

FISCHER: We get all that from Mr. Firth.

LASSER: Well, if you do, you've never shown it to me. And as far as that goes, Mr. Firth is a good accountant, but he's highly conservative, and I'm not sure that he sees what I'm talking about.

And now for a point that I'm glad I can make with Judson here. I'm as fond of him and Felix as I can be of anybody, and in each of their lines they're both geniuses. Felix can come up with belt designs that are literally works of art, and Jud can smell what the market will buy in a way that's uncanny. But the point is, they're both lousy administrators. What they know about running an organization would fit on the head of a pin. Have you noticed the number of things Jud gets involved in? Have you ever seen him really delegate responsibility? Can you tell me who's responsible for what in that firm? Does either of these two know anything about training their people? Do you know who's responsible for production or purchasing?

FISCHER (*smiling*): He really thinks I'm a lousy boss, doesn't he?

LASSER: I know you are.

And now for the final point. Maybe, Mr. Williams, you can help me sell this to Jud here. As you know, this is a highly risky kind of business. You may not know that sales costs—salesmen's commissions—are a highly expensive item. And it's my contention that when Breitman & Company bargains with its salesmen, the salesmen have the upper hand. Clearest proof of that is the fact that in spite of what you pay them, they still aren't working full time for you. They're also selling other lines. And your name doesn't mean anything in the trade, so you need them more than they need you.

FISCHER: You're out of date on one point. We now only have two salesmen carrying other lines.

LASSER: Well, that doesn't invalidate my basic point. What I am proposing then is very simple. That in addition to belts and handbags, Breitman & Company carry what for want of a better name I call a "gift line"—scarves, handkerchiefs, umbrellas, leather goods—I'm not enough of an expert on these matters to say just what. My point is that by broadening the base of their products, the company will do several things: they will protect themselves against style trends in just one line; they can expand their volume without expanding their sales cost proportionately; and what is more important, they can afford to start advertising the Breitman name, to strengthen their position in the market.

Now notice one thing—I'm not suggesting they start to manufacture these items. I like to think that I've already done these guys some good by hammering at them hard enough to get them to take care of their present increased sales volume without expanding their production. And what I'm proposing doesn't contemplate their producing any of these things either.

Which, incidentally, is another point. The talent these guys possess is a design talent, a selling talent, not a manufacturing talent. Besides, you don't make money manufacturing in this business. I'm not even sure they need to do any manufacturing at all, although Judson here thinks differently.

FISCHER: You know what I think about that, Irving. If buyers get the idea you're just a jobber, they'll want to go directly to the manufacturer because they think they get a better buy that way.

LASSER: And you know what I think about the mentality of most buyers. With the appeal you have now, it doesn't make one bit of difference whether you make your merchandise or whether someone else does.

Well, Mr. Williams, I'm terribly sorry, but as I told you earlier, I have to leave now—but those are my essential ideas, and if you—or anyone else—can ever make Judson see them, you'll be doing him a favor.

FISCHER: Are you quite through, Irving?

LASSER: For the moment, yes.

FISCHER: Just so Mr. Williams doesn't get the wrong idea—you and I are old friends—but as I've said many times, you're really full of hot air, and on that idea of a gift line you're just plain nuts.

LASSER: Tell me why.

FISCHER: It just won't work. Besides, we've got enough problems on our hands without asking for more.[1]

V. BREITMAN, COMPETITORS, AND THE MARKET

Although in preparing his case Mr. Williams concentrated on the day-to-day activities of Breitman & Company, he thought that a picture of how business generally was done in the belt and bag industries emerged gradually from his study. Breitman, it appeared, was "typical" of belt and bag firms generally in a number of respects. Such companies usually had a rapid turnover of styles. They operated on a two-season-a-year basis with marked seasonal fluctuations in volume (see Exhibit 7). They themselves did little or no advertising and virtually no brand promotion. They sold directly to retail buyers from their own

Exhibit 7

BREITMAN & COMPANY

*Case Writer's Analysis of Seasonality
in Breitman and Department-Store Sales by Months, 1951*

| | MONTHLY SALES AS PER CENT OF YEAR'S TOTAL | | |
| | Breitman | | U.S. Department Stores |
	Handbags	Belts	Handbags and Small Leather Goods
January	10.9%	7.3%	5.0%
February	11.4	7.8	5.3
March	14.4	5.4	9.5
April	13.1	6.8	6.6
May	7.8	4.8	8.3
June	5.6	8.0	7.2
July	5.1	6.7	4.7
August	7.1	11.2	5.9
September	5.5	14.0	8.7
October	5.7	12.6	8.7
November	6.0	11.4	10.3
December	7.4	4.0	19.8
	100.0%	100.0%	100.0%

Source: Breitman figures computed from monthly figures furnished by accountant. Department store figures computed from Federal Reserve Board Index.

[1] At this point Mr. Lasser left for the evening, and Mr. Williams spent several hours with Mr. Fischer discussing the administration of Breitman & Company.

showrooms or through commission salesmen. They usually designed particular style items to fit an established price[2] rather than the reverse; that is, a typical price decision would be to decide whether a particular belt could be sold for $7.50 or $10.50 a dozen. Cash discounts to customers of 8% on belts and 3% on bags were allowed on payments within 10 days after the end of the month.

Most of the companies in the belt and handbag industries were located in or around New York City. They were, for the most part, closely held companies with relatively limited financial resources. Mr. Williams had learned of no publicly owned belt or handbag manufacturing companies. Executives with training and experience outside the garment or soft-goods industries were the exception, while the staffing of key jobs with the relatives of the owners was a common practice.

At the same time Breitman was unique, so far as Mr. Williams could determine, in being a relatively large company that sold both belts and nonleather handbags. A number of bag houses sold both leather and nonleather merchandise, although this was not a universal practice. ("We tried making leather bags when we had Larry Goodman in here and nearly lost our shirts," Mr. Fischer reported.) A number of lower priced belt houses sold directly to dress manufacturers, which Breitman & Company did not do.

Mr. Firth had reported that the belt and bag industry (like most fashion industries) was stratified into at least three layers: 1) those companies with well-known name designers, very high-priced "original" merchandise, and exclusive distribution; 2) those companies which employed their own designers, created some of their own styles, but also copied "originals" and sold medium-priced merchandise with wider distribution than the first group; and 3) those companies whose design activity consisted exclusively of copying higher priced designs and of competing on a low-price volume basis. Breitman & Company, Mr. Firth said, fitted in the second group.

Some of the questions that Mr. Williams believed were of importance in understanding Breitman's position in the market he had been unable to answer with any degree of completeness, since his study of the industry had been limited and had been confined to conversation with Breitman people and buyers in the showroom, and to a search of ma-

---

[2] Breitman sold its belts in 30 prices, ranging from $7.50 a dozen to $120 a dozen. These were typically sold at retail from $1 to $16 apiece, with the retailer's markup percentage varying according to the particular price. Breitman's bags sold at $35.65 or $57 a dozen, with the corresponding retail price usually $5.98 and $7.98.

terial in Baker Library of the Harvard Business School. How successful had the company, volumewise and profitwise, been in relation to competitors? The information shown in Exhibits 3 and 8–11 was his only

Exhibit 8

BREITMAN & COMPANY

Quarterly Sales by Products, 1949–52

(Thousands of Dollars)

Year	Handbags	Belts	Total
1949			
1st Quarter...............	$650.6	$283.4	$ 934.0
2nd Quarter...............	617.3	293.2	910.5
3rd Quarter...............	349.6	351.6	701.2
4th Quarter...............	366.3	330.8	697.1
Year.................	$1,983.8	$1,259.0	$3,242.8
1950			
1st Quarter...............	$614.8	$392.9	$1,007.7
2nd Quarter...............	706.8	358.5	1,065.3
3rd Quarter...............	382.3	600.8	983.1
4th Quarter...............	424.8	489.0	913.8
Year	$2,128.7	$1,841.2	$3,969.9
1951			
1st Quarter...............	$997.0	$563.0	$1,560.0
2nd Quarter...............	719.9	534.5	1,254.4
3rd Quarter...............	481.3	871.1	2,352.4
4th Quarter...............	520.0	765.0	1,285.0
Year.................	$2,718.2	$2,733.6	$5,451.8
1952			
1st Quarter...............	$728.6	$894.3	$1,622.9
April–May...............	561.8	817.9	1,379.7
Five Months............	$1,290.4	$1,712.2	$3,002.6

Source: 1949–51, Company accounts.

clue to that question. Exhibit 5 shows a loss in the handbag department for one period of operation. Mr. Fischer explained that while over the years the handbag operation had been profitable, it was never as profitable as the belt department. "One of the principal reasons for this," he explained, "is the highly competitive nature of the handbag industry in contrast to the belt industry. We just can't get as good a gross margin." How did the company's coverage of various segments of the market compare with that of competitors? Since neither Breitman & Company nor Mr. Williams had made any recent statistical analysis of Breitman account cards, the best clues Mr. Williams felt he had to answering that

Exhibit 9

BREITMAN & COMPANY

Comparative Rates of Growth—Company and U.S. Department-Store Sales, 1937–51

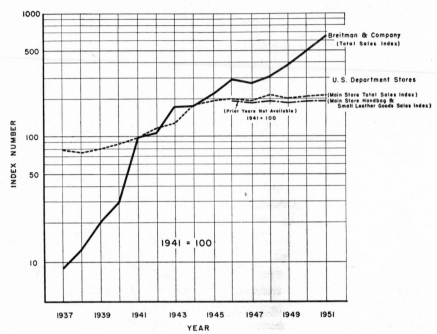

NOTE: Breitman year = fiscal year.

Sources: Breitman—Profit and Loss Statements; Department Stores—Federal Reserve Board Bulletins·

question lay in putting together an executive's statement that the company had 5,000 accounts, and that 75% of its business was with department stores with the information shown in Exhibit 12. Was it customary in the industry to subcontract production to the extent that Breitman & Company did? So far as Mr. Williams could learn, it was highly unusual. One buyer had reported that since buyers generally thought they could get better prices and better service by dealing directly with manufacturers, Breitman could subcontract to the extent that it did only because it was known as a manufacturer. How did Breitman's line compare with competitors' in number of items, style, quality, price? (See Exhibit 13.) Mr. Williams could only draw inferences from the rest of his data. He visited several department stores to see belts and bags displayed, but considered that he was incapable of making any qualitative judgments about Breitman merchandise in relation to competitors. One out-of-town department-store buyer with

Exhibit 10

BREITMAN & COMPANY

Industry Data on Handbags and Belts—1947

	Total	Establishments with an Average of							
		1–4 Employees	5–9 Employees	10–19 Employees	20–49 Employees	50–99 Employees	100–249 Employees	250–499 Employees	Over 500 Employees
Handbags and Purses:									
Number of establishments, 1947	734	176	139	140	163	70	43	3	
Number of proprietors and firm members	601								
Number of employees, average for year	20,301	431	963	1,925	5,120	4,809	6,056	997	
Units produced, in thousands:									
Leather	16,854								
Nonleather	37,488								
Value added by manufacture	$ 76,586	$2,025	$3,726	$8,165	$21,356	$16,794	$21,173	$3,347	
Net sales value, f.o.b. plant	$159,693*								
Leather	$ 74,306								
Nonleather	$ 75,991								
Belts:									
Number of establishments, 1947	396	91	94	99	75	26	8	2	1
Number of proprietors and firm members	361								
Number of employees, average for year	9,162	227	640	1,381	2,300	1,766	1,056	1,792	Withheld
Units produced, in thousands of dozens:									
Leather	6,464								
Nonleather	5,702								
Other, not specified									
Value added by manufacture	$ 38,037	$1,104	$2,824	$6,009	$ 9,009	$ 6,730	$ 4,625	$7,736	Withheld
Net sales value, f.o.b. plant	$ 60,117†								
Leather	$ 39,981								
Nonleather	$ 17,864								
Other, not specified	$ 2,272								

* Includes $4,396 value of other products manufactured by members of the handbag industry.
† Total value of all belts shipped by manufacturers classified in the belt industry and in other industries was $68,982.
Source: *U.S. Census of Manufactures, 1947.*

Exhibit 11

BREITMAN & COMPANY

Excerpts from WOMEN'S Wear Daily *on Handbag Industry*[3]

Manufacturers Operating at Profit Held Rarities in Industry

Because of the discriminatory features of the 20% excise tax and the reduction of duty rates, handbag manufacturing firms that operate at a profit have become rarities. Testimony to this effect will be delivered by Max Berkowitz, codirector of the National Authority for the Ladies' Handbag Industry, when he appears before the Senate Finance Committee. . . .

Mr. Berkowitz will point out that the handbag industry has shrunk from 800 firms doing a wholesale volume of 200 million dollars in 1946 to 500 firms doing 135 million in 1951.

—April 25, 1952, p. 32.

Tendency to Overproduce Is Held Bane of the Industry

What's wrong with the handbag industry? . . .

Critics point out that foremost among the industry's shortcomings is its tendency toward overproduction . . . hungry manufacturers quickly copy a successful item and the market is almost immediately glutted. . . .

It is too easy for a would-be manufacturer to go into the handbag business. . . . The industry attracts an excessive number of marginal producers [who are] prone to undersell in order to attract business. . . . When conditions are unfavorable . . . salesmen, production workers [and others] who may suddenly find themselves unemployed frequently form partnerships and go into the manufacturing business for themselves.

Another industry defect is an apparent indifference to the scientific production approach . . . not enough attention is paid to the accurate compilation of costs. . . .

Still another defect, which is less the fault of producers, but perhaps more basic, [is] the tendency to dress informally.

—May 2, 1952, p. 29.

whom Mr. Williams talked indicated that there were about four or five belt manufacturers and a half-dozen bag manufacturers whose lines most buyers tried, or at least examined, each season and that Breitman was included in both groups. Mr. Williams was of the opinion that there was much more he could have done to widen his understanding of the industry and Breitman's position in it.

VI. THE ORGANIZATION AT WORK

As Mr. Williams began to gain a mental picture of the internal workings of the company, he determined to concentrate on trying to see

---

[3] Reproduced by permission of the publisher.

Source: *U.S. Census of Business*, 1948.

Exhibit 12

BREITMAN & COMPANY

Selected Data on Retail Outlets Selling Handbags—1948

Type of Store	All Retail Stores This Type		Stores This Type Selling Handbags†				
	1948 Number (Thousands)	1948 Volume (Millions of Dollars)	1948 Number (Thousands)	1948 Handbag Volume (Millions of Dollars)	1948 Total Volume (As Per cent total Volume All Stores)	1948 Average Handbag Volume per Store (Thousands of Dollars)	1948 Average Total Volume per Store (Thousands of Dollars)
Women's ready-to-wear..........	30.7	$ 3,305	10.6	$101.0	63.0%	$ 9.6	$ 198
Department stores..............	2.6	10,645	2.3	98.0‡	96.5	42.1‡	4,380
Family clothing................	12.5	1,791	5.1	40.9	64.3	8.0	227
Women's shoes.................	3.2*	377	1.5*	25.1	74.5	17.1	192
Apparel, accessory, specialty....	7.7	328	1.5	21.3	30.8	13.7	66
Family shoes..................	13.2*	859	3.3*	16.3	45.4	5.0	119
Millinery.....................	5.7	109	1.9	7.8	41.4	4.2	24
Corsets and lingerie...........	2.7*	92	0.3*	1.2	17.4	3.8	49
Men's shoes...................	2.3*	198	0.1*	0.6	8.1	5.9	152
Dry goods, general merchandise..	29.7	2,824	18.3	NA	81.4	NA	126
Variety stores.................	20.2	2,507	14.7	NA	93.5	NA	159
General stores.................	21.6	1,233	10.9	NA	63.4	NA	71

NA Not available.

* Figures not exactly comparable with others in series.

† All figures except those for "Apparel, accessory, and specialty" and "Corsets and lingerie" based on reports from more than 90% of stores in each category. Forty per cent "Apparel, accessory, and specialty" reported breakdowns. Per cent of "Corset and lingerie" reporting not available.

‡ Includes small leather goods.

Exhibit 13

BREITMAN & COMPANY

Statistics on Product Line—Fall, 1952

Basic Type	Number of Styles	Number Carried Over from Spring Line	Approximate Number of Style-Color Combinations	Approximate Number of Style-Color-Size Combinations	Range of Manufacturers Price per Dozen
			BELTS		
Leather..........	109	76	400	2,000	$ 7.50–$ 60.00
Metal............	90	47	171	600	7.50– 96.00
French line.......	33	13	110	400	21.00– 120.00
Velvet...........	32	12	110	400	7.50– 66.00
Elastic..........	29	5	112	300	7.50– 72.00
Metallic leather...	21	17	47	107	7.20– 66.00
Suede...........	18	11	40	120	7.50– 60.00
Patent..........	14	10	25	100	7.25– 22.50
Reptile..........	13	4	35	120	7.50– 96.00
Satin............	5	0	5	20	10.50– 66.00
Calf staples.......	4	4	20	110	7.50– 16.50
Plastic alligator...	2	2	2	11	7.50– 10.50
Faille...........	2	1	9	54	7.50– 30.00
Total........	372	202	1,086	4,342	
			BAGS		
Faille...........	25	NA	75	*	$35.65
	15		45		57.00
Velvet..........	20	NA	60	*	35.65
	14		42		57.00
Novelty..........	14	NA	112	*	35.65
	15		120		57.00
Patent..........	11	NA	11	*	35.65
Evening..........	8	NA	80	*	35.65
Broadcloth.......	7	NA	21	*	57.00
Quilted..........	3	NA	3		35.65
Total........	132		569		

NA Not available.
* Not applicable.
Source: Tabulated by case writer from company listing of fall line.

whether he could understand what he believed to be five essential processes that were going on continually: (1) merchandising the line; (2) selling that line; (3) producing the merchandise; (4) keeping production and purchasing abreast of sales; and (5) processing orders. If he could fit the activities of people into these processes, he believed he would have a pretty good idea of how Breitman & Company worked on a day-to-day basis.

1. *Merchandising the Line.* For the most part, the belt and bag activities were carried out separately, although some of the same people were involved in each. The activities referred to as "merchandising the line" culminated in the decisions as to what styles (at what prices) would constitute Breitman's offering to the trade in both its fall and spring lines. The bulk of the activity involved in preparing a fall line was completed by late May, and the spring line by late November, although once a line had been established, particularly in the case of belts, additions or withdrawals were by no means uncommon.[4]

Within the belt line a limited number of styles, mostly leather, were known as "staples," or basic belts. These had been in the line for several years, and salesmen had been informed that the company would continue to carry enough inventory on these numbers at all times to permit shipments within 24 hours of receipt of orders.

SELECTING THE BELT LINE. Final selection of a season's full belt line took place in eight or ten 4–6-hour after-dinner meetings, usually attended by Mr. Breitman, Mr. Fischer, Byron Steinmetz, Fred Apfel, Harry Block, and any of the salesmen who happened to be available. Such selection appeared to Mr. Williams to be very much a group activity, involving the exchange of a great many opinions before a consensus was reached on which of the many samples examined by the group should constitute the line.

The following interchange from one such meeting, recorded by Mr. Williams in his notes, illustrates the type of discussion that took place in these meetings:

STEINMETZ: How do you like this number, Judson? It's very popular in Paris.

FISCHER: Haven't we already got enough wide contour belts? How much would we get for that?

APFEL: Mr. Fischer, I could give you that for $15. We'd get Leatherco to make it.

BLOCK: You'd never get $15 for that belt.

APFEL: Harry, we couldn't make a nickel on it if we sold it for less.

---

[4] Mr. Williams did not obtain any conclusive evidence as to the extent to which the line changed from season to season or within any particular season. According to Mr. Steinmetz, the belt sales manager, the company did not save records which would make such an analysis from season to season readily possible, although an analysis of changes in the spring, 1952, line could perhaps have been made from bulletins to salesmen. Mr. Steinmetz estimated that less than 25% of the belt line was ever carried for more than one season, with perhaps a higher carry-over in handbags. According to Mr. Williams' analysis of changes from the spring to fall line in 1952, 202 of the 372 numbers in the spring line remained in the fall line.

STEINMETZ: How about eliminating the pendant? That ought to save something.

BREITMAN: If you don't use the pendant here, maybe we could put it on the last number we looked at.

FISCHER (*smiling*): You don't like it when we throw away all your hard work, do you, Felix? (*To a salesman.*) What do you think, Abe?

ABE: For $15 I like it better than some we've already picked out.

BLOCK: How many sizes would we need in this one?

APFEL: This would be easy to make in 24 through 32, Harry. I could easily get it for $10.50 if we cut out the pendant, and show a nice profit.

STEINMETZ: Why don't we leave it in for now and come back to it?

FISCHER: All right, but I'm not sure I like it.

The samples from which selections were made were produced by the company's own belt factory or one of the contractors. Ideas for styles arose from a variety of sources; Mr. Breitman spent most of his time sketching belts or ornaments for them, and these provided the major source; salesmen, Mr. Fischer, or others of the executives brought in competitive merchandise they had seen in stores; and contractors and occasionally buyers made suggestions. In 1952 an important source of ideas developed from the several trips abroad made by various members of the organization: Byron Steinmetz made a trip to Europe looking for new belt styles in March, and Mr. Teplow planned a similar trip for the bag department during the summer. Mr. Breitman also made a six weeks' trip to Japan, during which he made arrangements with a number of Japanese manufacturers to produce novelty designs (both belt and bag) for the company, and in addition he brought back ideas for Breitman's own production.

As a season progressed, lines which did not "go" were dropped, and others added. Sometimes such decisions were made on a group basis, and sometimes they were arrived at as a result of suggestions initiated by Fred Apfel, Byron Steinmetz, a salesman, or one of the partners and approved by one of the partners.

"Merchandising" the handbag line was accomplished in much the same way, except that a number of decisions on the bag line were made by Mr. Teplow and his designer, sometimes, but not always, after discussing them with Mr. Breitman, Mr. Fischer, and Mr. Rich.

2. *The Selling Process.* Selling the Breitman line involved three essential relationships or activities, as Mr. Williams saw it: (1) The work done away from the showroom by salesmen in soliciting business from buyers; (2) the selling done in the 32d Street showroom, plus entertaining visiting buyers in New York; (3) the calls made by 32d

Street people on department-store resident buyers in New York City. In addition, the company prepared advertising material each season for the use of its customers.

THE SALES FORCE AND ITS FIELD ACTIVITIES.   Although Mr. Williams had met each of the salesmen at least once, his knowledge of their activities was limited to what Mr. Fischer and the two sales managers told him and to what the salesmen themselves reported about the jobs. Mr. Williams learned thus that salesmen received, with very few exceptions, 10% commissions on all sales made to their accounts, regardless of whether or not they personally made the sale. Most of them lived in their territories, except the men covering the New York, Philadelphia, and New England areas. Some of them had gross earnings larger than the salaries of the partners (see Exhibit 14). Mr. Williams understood that this was not at all uncommon in the soft-goods and style-merchandise industry. The group ranged in age from about twenty-five to forty-five, he judged, with three or four of the salesmen apparently under thirty.

Mr. Fischer said that salesmen usually tried to call on large department-store buyers at their offices but in many instances, in accordance with trade practice, set up their samples in a hotel room, where buyers came to inspect the merchandise. On one occasion Mr. Fischer remarked:

> Maybe you can tell me how you get the lead out of some of these salesmen, when making a good living these days is not too difficult. Actually most of our salesmen are first rate, but I don't know what you do about the few lazy ones.

Sales territories were assigned by Mr. Fischer, who said that the reason the territories were not divided on a strictly geographical basis was to take account of particular salesman-buyer relationships that had grown up. Mr. Fischer believed that having a salesman call on a store where he knew a particular buyer was more important than having a strict geographic division of territories.

Mr. Fischer indicated to Mr. Williams that Byron Steinmetz and Frank Rich were sales managers more in title than in fact:

> I guess at Harvard you'd say that was poor organizational practice, but I don't think you can just bring in two men and suddenly turn over to them something you've been doing for years. The salesmen know me, and I know them intimately. Besides, I sometimes wonder if either Byron or Frank knows what it takes to be a sales manager.

So far as Mr. Williams could tell, Byron's and Frank's principal sales-management functions consisted of preparing sales bulletins to the field,

Exhibit 14

BREITMAN & COMPANY

*Product Sales by Salesmen
and Salesmen's Commissions
July, 1950—June, 1952*

	July, 1950—June, 1951				July, 1951—June, 1952				Territory
	Belts	Bags	Total	Commission	Belts	Bags	Total	Commission	
House Sales	$ 145,340	$ 151,532	$ 296,872	$ 22,985	$ 198,193	$ 158,934	$ 357,127	$ 30,764	New York City area: 45 stores, 4 belts only
Salesman #2	145,666	110,389	256,055	3,322	258,518	101,027	359,545	5,387	New England, New York, and Pennsylvania: 8 states, 138 cities
Salesman #3	139,143	215,876	355,019	28,266	214,734	225,928	440,662	35,962	South Central: 3 states, 53 cities
Salesman #4	207,427	352,848	560,275	42,335	336,342	433,965	770,307	59,388	West and Southwest: 12 states, 3 foreign cities
Salesman #5	376,399	253,847	630,246	48,618	482,053	306,245	788,298	66,916	Central: 6 states, 241 cities
Salesman #6	211,996	266,562	478,558	38,366	299,379	333,989	633,368	51,543	South: 9 states
Salesman #7	99,696	219,829	319,525	25,602	197,162	284,795	481,957	38,343	Middle West: 10 states
Salesman #8	241,618	287,222	528,840	42,983	449,571	382,807	832,373	70,355	South: 4 states, 95 cities
Salesman #9 (1 month only: June, 1952)					2,410	1,710	4,120	360	
Salesman #10 (11 month totals: missing June, 1951, and June, 1952)	214,284	266,874	481,158	38,760	319,326	307,579	626,905	51,715	South: 4 states, Mexico
Salesman #11 (11 month totals: missing June, 1951, and June, 1952)	141,592	145,765	287,357	23,876	145,585	156,041	301,626	24,303	Six large cities, plus parts of New York City and Chicago
Salesman #12 (11 month totals: missing June, 1951, and June, 1952)	53,743	88,209	141,952	11,277	111,362	97,649	209,211	17,716	East Central: 4 states plus suburban New York City and Philadelphia
Salesman #13 (8 months: October, 1951, through May, 1952)					4,801	3,807	8,608	674	
Totals: (11 month totals: missing June, 1951, and June, 1952)	$1,790,238	$2,238,219	$4,028,557	$318,362	$2,786,938	$2,663,069	$5,450,007	$423,793	

Source: Mr. Fischer's desk records.

indicating changes in the line and numbers that were selling well, and reporting sales progress generally.

The particular individual whom a buyer saw in a customer organization varied from account to account. In the largest retail organizations the buying organization was a highly specialized activity. Many large department stores had at least one buyer who bought only handbags. A few stores with a separate bargain basement had two handbag buyers. Relatively few department stores had buyers responsible only for belts. That merchandise was often bought in large stores by individuals handling a variety of accessories—umbrellas, luggage, wallets, scarves, etc. —occasionally by the handbag buyer. In smaller stores the number of types of merchandise purchased by a buyer was greater—one buyer might, for example, be responsible for women's apparel and accessories as a group. In still smaller stores all buying might be done by the proprietor. To get some notion of the varying responsibilities of store buyers in a place like New York City, Mr. Williams put together the information in Exhibit 18.

During his visits Mr. Williams was told many times that good salesman-buyer contacts were the most important part of the business. One salesman described these contacts thus:

> Obviously, you've got to have the right merchandise, but if you can't get along with the buyers, you're through. Most of the time you're on a first-name basis with these people; you know about their private lives; you take them out to lunch or dinner; and in a lot of cases you spend a great deal of time with them, never even mentioning business. This week, for example, I took the belt buyer for ——— [a New York department store] to lunch—the third week running. We had a few drinks, I kidded her along—more like a date than a business conference—and as I dropped her off after lunch, she suggested I come in next Friday. Maybe she'll buy, maybe she won't, but it's all part of the game.

An important part of a salesman's job, Mr. Fischer reported, was seeing to it that stores did not overload with merchandise that would not sell:

> Twenty per cent of our customers are smart enough to know better than we do what will go, but the other eighty per cent don't. And it would be very poor business for us to overload a buyer with merchandise that she'd have to mark down—or try to return—at the end of the season.[5]

---

[5] Mr. Williams had never been able to get any exact information on customer returns, but had been assured by several people that this had never constituted a serious problem for Breitman & Company.

SHOWROOM SELLING ACTIVITIES. In terms of the demands on a number of people's time, waiting on customers in the showroom was the principal activity at 32d Street. This activity also contributed substantially, Mr. Williams believed, to the continued impression he had of the organization as an exceptionally busy place. Mr. Williams made only one brief visit to the showroom during "market season," the semiannual two-week period when all the salesmen came to New York, and the flow of out-of-town buyers into the showroom was occasionally so heavy that a line of buyers waited in front of the elevators in the first-floor lobby. At the same time, even during the so-called "slack season," Mr. Williams had never seen the showroom empty of buyers between ten in the morning and five at night, and it was not exceptional for a few buyers to be waiting in the lobby because the eight showroom tables were full.

During Mr. Williams' visits to the company, he observed that 11 members of the Breitman organization, in addition to whatever salesmen might be on hand, spent at least some part of their regular work week waiting on customers in the showroom. For the two girls who regularly worked there, this was apparently the only activity, except for such duties as putting samples back in their cases and, for one of them, working on preparation and distribution of advertising material. For Byron Steinmetz and Frank Rich, waiting on customers, Mr. Williams guessed, typically occupied at least one-half to two-thirds of most working days. Simon, Mickey, Fred Apfel, Harry Block, and Joe were called on as the occasion demanded, or as their immediate jobs permitted, more or less in that order. Mr. Williams estimated that each of them typically put in 10 to 15 hours a week in the showroom. Waiting on customers appeared to have "top priority." If any one of the showroom people already waiting on someone saw another customer unattended, he usually tried to locate someone else to come into the showroom.

Mr. Fischer himself also appeared to spend more than half of most working days either waiting on buyers or talking to them as someone else showed samples to the buyers. Mr. Breitman, on the other hand, usually came into the showroom briefly to greet someone he already knew or to meet a new customer if the salesperson working with that customer suggested it.

Mr. Fischer was acknowledged to be the best salesman in the house, and Mr. Williams could only sense—rather than describe—why this was so. Mr. Fischer appeared to have a very genuine warmth when he greeted people. He had an unusual capacity for remembering names and his previous conversations with customers, and he made only a limited number of references to himself. Mr. Williams had been told on a number of occasions by salesmen, the 32d Street group, and buyers that "Judson Fischer's personality is the most important asset this business has."

In addition to the showroom contacts with buyers, Mr. Fischer and the two sales managers spent most noon hours entertaining buyers at lunch, and it was not uncommon for Mr. Fischer to entertain buyers at home all the evenings in a week that he did not spend in the showroom.

CALLS ON RESIDENT BUYERS. Mr. Fischer and, starting in the spring of 1952, Simon, one of the young men in the 32d Street office, made calls about once a week on the larger "resident buyer" organizations in New York City. "Resident buyers" represented either a large department-store chain, like Federated Department Stores, or a group of independent department or other retail stores. The larger resident-buying offices had as many as from 50 to 75 buyers, specializing in various kinds of merchandise in the same way that the department-store buyers themselves did. A resident buyer had several functions: to keep the buyers of various department stores throughout the country informed on style trends; to select the source and type of merchandise to fill orders placed with them by the stores they represented; and to assist their affiliated stores in following up on merchandise deliveries. At least in the large stores, resident buyers were used as aids to the store buyers themselves; the store buyers typically maintained their own contacts with suppliers as well.

ADVERTISING. Breitman's advertising, Mr. Williams was told by Mr. Fischer, was limited to preparation of material for use by its customers because "people just won't decide they want a Breitman bag or belt and then go looking for it. It's the store name, rather than the manufacturer's name, that pulls in this business."

Breitman's principal advertising expense was for a semiannual "belt enclosure," a leaflet describing eight or ten items in a season's line and made available in quantity to the stores that bought from Breitman. These stores sent this leaflet, with monthly bills, to their customers. Breitman also provided customers with "mats" for newspaper ads, showing Breitman merchandise. In 1952 the company was having a 40-second film prepared on Breitman belts for use by department stores in local TV spot advertisements.

Mr. Steinmetz was responsible for working with artists and printers in preparing advertising material and was assisted in this work and in the mechanics of distributing the material by one of the showroom saleswomen. The final copy on enclosures was usually reviewed by the group which made decisions on belt merchandising.

3. *Production.* BELT OPERATION—THE 25TH STREET FACTORY. The 25th Street factory consisted of a 5,000-square-foot, third-floor loft, and numbered 43 production people supervised by Mrs. Long, whom Mr. Williams judged to be in her early thirties. In contrast to the 32d Street operation, and to some extent the 14th Street bag factory, the 25th Street factory appeared to have adequate room for its activities. On the day Mr. Williams visited the factory, it was making only Breitweave braided belts, but Mr. Williams understood that at other times of the year the factory also made other types of fabric belts. He observed seven different types of operations during his visit, done either by hand or by a variety of sewing or braiding machines: cutting, braiding, stitching, eyeletting, trimming, "tacking" (fastening buckles), and assembling (fastening ornaments, pasting leather strips, etc.). The supervisor appeared quite willing to explain her job:

This is really very simple, and I don't know what there is to explain. None of our operations is any different from what you'd find in any belt factory.

Mr. Apfel gives me cutting orders over the phone. I then write up cutting tickets, which stay with the belts until they are shipped. I also enter all cutting orders in a book. We ship to 32d Street once a day, and I write up shipping tickets for all shipments. On the basis of "feel," I order material over the phone from 14 different suppliers as we need it and find buyers for raw material that doesn't move. I'm not concerned with prices—that's Mr. Apfel's job. I discuss with him the places I buy from and send purchase requisitions up to 32d Street on everything I buy.

We can turn out 150 to 200 gross of belts here a week and can get most orders out in a couple of days after Mr. Apfel gives them to us. Every once in a while Mr. Breitman comes down and we figure out together how we'll make some new style.

I'm not concerned with prices or costs, except that, of course, it's up to me to see that waste is kept down and that we turn out good merchandise.

I guess you'd say we have a very happy place here, largely because my two bosses, Mr. Breitman and Mr. Fischer, are such wonderful people.

BAG OPERATION—THE 14TH STREET FACTORY. The 14th Street factory, equipped—according to the factory superintendent—to turn out 78 gross of bags in a 40- or 45-hour week, numbered approximately 65 employees who were engaged in four types of operations: cutting, pasting, sewing and assembling, and inspecting. "I don't know what there is to explain," the superintendent reported. "We get orders on what to make from the bag production manager, usually in three-gross lots; they go through the works, and it's my job to keep the factory going."

The 14th Street factory, in contrast to the belt factory, shipped its merchandise directly to customers and maintained its own shipping department, supervised by a Mr. Fox. The bag factory also sent out its own invoices, typed by a girl located in the shipping room.

THE DANDRIDGE, TENNESSEE, OPERATION.   While Mr. Williams was visiting Breitman, Mr. Fischer and Mr. Breitman decided to close the Tennessee operation. Frank Rich had made a visit to the Southern plant, and as a result of this trip an audit was made of that firm's books, which were, according to Miss Voss, "in terrible shape." Mr. Fischer reported: "We think actually we may have been cheated, and we're probably going to lose $100,000 in this before we're through. We were persuaded to make this mistake by a handbag competitor of ours—he put up half the funds involved."

Because the Dandridge company was personally owned by the partners, its profits—or losses—were not reflected in Breitman income statements. Its sales were reflected in Breitman's total sales figures, since it sold all its merchandise through Breitman & Company.

THE CONTRACTORS.   Mr. Williams had learned very little about the operations of the belt and bag manufacturers who did contract work for Breitman. He had at one point asked Miss Voss for a breakdown of the relative volume done by each of them. But when he was told that to furnish such data would involve running subtotals from the purchase register, he decided to withdraw his request. Exhibit 15 indicates the information on contractor and company manufacturing maintained in Mr. Fischer's desk records.

Mr. Williams had sat in on the negotiations with one belt manufacturer who began working with Breitman & Company in April and talked with another manufacturer who had made belts for Breitman for over a year. Both these men owned, and constituted the entire supervisory force of, their businesses; both had been recommended to Breitman by the garment workers' union representing Breitman workers. Both had been "in and out" of the business once before, one for reasons of health and the other because of voluntary liquidation.

4. *Keeping Production and Purchasing Abreast of Sales.*   The duties of co-ordinating belt production and purchasing with sales were performed entirely by Mr. Fred Apfel, who also was responsible for determining belt prices. Mr. Apfel worked closely with Mr. Fischer and Mr. Breitman. His counterpart in the bag department, except for differ-

Exhibit 15

BREITMAN & COMPANY

*Breakdown of Sales Showing Merchandise Manufactured by Company
and by Contractors, 1948–51*

(In Thousands)

	1948	1949	1950	1951
Belts:				
Company manufactured.	$ 748.4	$ 551.4	$ 581.7	$ 735.7
Job*.........................	373.4	354.2	761.6	1,354.6
Job—metal*..................	192.3	353.4	504.9	643.3
Total belts...............	$1,314.1	$1,259.0	$1,848.2	$2,733.6
Bags:				
Company manufactured........	$1,111.3	$1,237.9	$1,362.3	$1,954.4
Job—straw..................	80.4	741.5	729.6	736.8
Job—other..................		4.4	67.1	27.0
Total bags...............	$1,191.7	$1,983.8	$2,159.0	$2,718.2
Total sales.............	$2,505.8	$3,242.8	$4,007.2	$5,451.8

* Most of the contractors making metal belts were located in Rhode Island. Other contractors were, for the most part, in the New York City area.
Source: Mr. Fischer's desk records.

ences noted below, performed about the same duties as did Mr. Apfel.

BELT PRODUCTION SCHEDULING AND PURCHASING—MR. APFEL'S ACTIVITIES. "If you aren't an executive when you start this job, you sure are once you've been at it a while," Mr. Apfel reported. "I make more decisions a week about how to spend the bosses' money than I can count, and they've got to be right."

Mr. Williams observed that Mr. Apfel's activities, in addition to his participation in evening meetings, included deciding at what price each of the various belt items should be sold; deciding the amounts of the various styles to be produced, in what colors, and by whom; determining where various raw material items could be purchased; and in many cases placing orders, usually over the telephone, for shipments to contractors. In the process of deciding merchandise prices, Mr. Apfel also made frequent suggestions to Mr. Breitman about ways in which designs might be changed or new ones added to the line. Furthermore, Mr. Apfel in the late spring was handling all company contracts with a large mail-order house, which had ordered belts from Breitman for the first time that season. It was, moreover, not uncommon for Mr. Apfel to spend several hours in an afternoon working in the showroom.

Mr. Apfel made his price decisions[6] by using a table he had prepared, listing each of the various prices at which belts were sold and, for each price, the amount that should be spent on raw material and labor. This last amount he had calculated in each instance by deducting sales commission (10%), purchase discount (8%), a net profit figure (15%), and a "cost-of-doing-business" figure from the sales price. In making a particular price decision, he started with the price at which he believed a belt had to be sold, compared the appropriate balance for raw material and labor with his estimate of what a particular style would cost, and concluded that either the company could sell the particular belt at this starting price or that he must find ways to reduce the cost by minor modifications or review with Mr. Breitman or Mr. Fischer the basic decision to include the number in the line. His "raw material and labor" cost estimates were based on his own knowledge of what costs were, or on estimates he got over the phone from suppliers. His cost-of-business figure, he said, he reviewed approximately once a year with Mr. F. His net profit figure was a target from which he frequently varied.

Mr. Apfel's activities in purchasing and production scheduling were based on a running record of (1) orders placed on suppliers, (2) merchandise receipts, (3) orders received from customers, and (4) merchandise shipments. This information was recorded by individual style numbers in a loose-leaf notebook. Mr. Apfel himself kept this record up to date and based it on information he obtained periodically from the account-card desk. In addition to placing orders, he kept in frequent telephone contact (and had an occasional personal visit) with suppliers and contractors to follow up on his orders and to issue instructions to them. He also wrote up personally all purchase invoices involved in his activities.

Mr. Apfel also kept a record of monthly shipments by belt types (metal, leather, velvet, etc.) and used it as the basis for making initial purchase decisions at the beginning of a season. He said to Mr. Williams:

I always try to get Mr. Fischer's ideas before I commit the firm for any major amounts, but sometimes I just have to go ahead on my own. It works something

---

[6] Mr. Apfel's price decisions were, of course, an integral part of the merchandising process described earlier but are included here for convenience in describing his activities as a whole.

like this: At the beginning of a season I may decide we're going to sell at least $250,000 of aluminum belts, and I get Mr. Fischer or Mr. Breitman to let me go ahead with that much at the beginning of the season. Then after sales have come in for a month or so, I'll use my own judgment in placing more orders.

Mr. Apfel and Mr. Williams on several occasions had discussed the "frantic pace" that this job necessitated, particularly since Mr. Apfel's only assistance came from the girls at the account-card desk. On one such occasion, Mr. Apfel said:

> This is what it's like in this business, and, of course, there are a lot of compensations in working for people like Mr. Breitman and Mr. Fischer. At the same time I don't know if I can continue this way. You see, the difficulty with my job is that it would be very difficult to train anyone to assist me, particularly since so much of what I do is based on my feel for the business, my knowledge of the line and of customers, and my personal contacts with suppliers. They'll do things for me they won't do for anyone else because they know I'm fair.
>
> After this season is over, I hope to be able to turn some of my clerical work over to Olga [at the account-card desk] and that should straighten things out. Of course, it would be a lot easier if people weren't interrupting me all the time —and the boss is one of the biggest offenders on that score. He's always asking for information on how we stand on a particular number or a particular part of the line. And of course, there's the time in the showroom, but that helps keep me posted on what customers are buying.

BAG PRODUCTION SCHEDULING AND PURCHASING. From his single interview with the bag production manager, Mr. Williams understood that he had approximately the same responsibilities as Mr. Apfel, with such differences in day-to-day operations as resulted from the following circumstances: he worked directly under Mr. Teplow's supervision; he occupied an office located adjacent to the bag factory and shared only by three clerks who worked for him; he had to cope with only a relatively small number of styles in the bag line; and he did not deal at all with customers. These differences apparently resulted in his being subjected to few interruptions in his "normal" work, although the bag production manager was in frequent telephone contact with Mr. Fischer or salesmen about the status of orders.

5. *The Processing of Orders.* Mr. Williams devoted particular attention to understanding the detailed mechanics of the process of getting orders through the Breitman organization in view of: Mr. Breitman's initial comment to him about methods; the number of comments made to him about the difficulties in keeping up with this operation, particularly in the belt department; his own observation that Mr. Teplow discussed the system with Fred Apfel and Harry Block with

increasing frequency as he visited the company; and on several occasions Miss Voss's indicating to him that if space could be found, a mechanized operation would be highly desirable. Mr. Williams, in the course of his study, sat in on an evening conference when a young lawyer (Mr. Fischer's nephew) discussed with most of the executives of the company his views on the company's methods and procedures. The lawyer's two recommendations, made in general terms, were that the company should standardize its record forms in the belt and bag

Exhibit 16

BREITMAN & COMPANY

Steps Involved in Processing Orders

Steps	Performed by
STEPS COMMON TO BELT AND BAG ORDERS	
1 Mail orders opened...............................	Telephone operator
Orders taken in the showroom or by telephone............	Showroom sales person
2 Orders reviewed.....................................	Mr. Fischer
3 Orders coded..	Mickey
4 Credit checked......................................	Miss Voss or assistant
STEPS IN PROCESSING BELT ORDERS ONLY	
5 Orders entered on account cards.......................	Account-card clerk
6 Orders stapled to cardboard holders and placed in order bin..	Harry Block or order pickers
7a Orders picked.....................................	
7b Prices entered....................................	Harry Block or order pickers
7c (Back orders sent to lay-away bin).....................	
8 Invoice typed.......................................	Biller
9 Merchandise packed and shipped.......................	Shipper
10 Shipments entered on account cards....................	Account-card clerk
11 Orders placed in file................................	Account-card clerk
STEPS IN PROCESSING BELT BACK ORDERS	
7a Back orders entered in shortage book....................	Lay-away clerk
7b Incoming belt merchandise checked against shortage book...	Lay-away clerk
7c Back orders filled..................................	Lay-away clerk

operations and that immediate steps should be taken to mechanize some of the order processing and record-keeping operations. In Mr. Williams' opinion, the lawyer did not succeed in convincing Mr. Fischer or the group of the soundness of his recommendations, although Mr. Williams understood that the lawyer was to continue his study.

Exhibit 16 lists the steps involved in processing all belt orders, as well as the four steps common to both belt and bag orders. Each of these steps required the physical movement of orders from one part of the office to another, and orders were usually carried from point to point by the person who last handled them. That movement, according to Mr. Williams' observations, caused particular congestion in the area where Mr. Apfel, Mickey, the account-card clerks, and Harry Block had their desks. The processing of bag orders at 14th Street was essentially the same as the 32d Street belt process, except that no separate provision was made for handling back orders.[7] According to Mr. Teplow's production and purchasing assistant, such a system was unnecessary in the bag department because fewer styles were involved, back orders were less common, and it was considerably easier to follow through production such back orders as did arise.

According to Miss Voss, an average of 2,500 orders were processed each month. Some orders were taken in the showroom; some were received via the salesmen; and some directly from the customer. Although all orders were coded to show their source, no tabulation—to Mr. Williams' knowledge—was made of the relative volume of business which came in each way. Orders from outside the showroom came in by mail, telegraph, or telephone. As part of her normal routine the switchboard operator placed all telegraph and mail orders on Mr. Fischer's desk. Orders were taken over the telephone by either Mr. Fischer, the salesmen, or the showroom people.

Several salesmen and one or two others in the organization had indicated to Mr. Williams their belief that Mr. Fischer's insistence on seeing all orders was both a source and a symptom of one of Breitman & Company's chief problems—an overload on Mr. Fischer. Objections to this part of the system had also been raised directly to Mr. Fischer by members of his organization in Mr. Williams' presence. Mr. Fischer had replied to one of these objections by saying:

This doesn't really take much of my time, and it's a very important way for me to keep posted on what's going on. I can learn more about what's selling and who's buying from a quick look at orders than I ever could from a report. This is a fast-moving business, and I can't wait for a report. Besides, whom have we got to prepare it?

Orders were normally picked up by Mickey from Mr. Fischer or taken by whoever might pass Mr. Fischer's desk to Mickey, for a routine processing to indicate source of order and salesman's credit.

Mickey, a young man in his twenties, had joined Breitman & Company in 1950. He indicated to Mr. Williams that the order-coding part

---

[7] A back order is one which cannot be filled from merchandise in stock.

of his job involved no particular difficulties. This responsibility, however, was combined with the job of following up customer inquiries, "plus a few other things," and Mickey reported:

> I sometimes don't know whether I'm coming or going. Look, right now I'm three days behind in answering correspondence. I spend so much of my time walking around trying to find where the orders are that I can never catch up. Another problem is that I have to separate bag and belt orders. Our salesmen know enough to write them up separately, and so do many of our customers, but I have to copy off the bag orders if they're not separate.

Mickey, or a passer-by, carried orders to Miss Voss's office, where a credit check, in most cases routine, was made, and then the belt orders were returned to the account-card desk. After a clerk made a notation of the orders on the customer account cards, the orders were placed on Harry Block's desk.

HARRY BLOCK'S ACTIVITIES. "You know, Doc, you're from Harvard, and you probably know a lot about management, and you probably think getting orders out is simple and unimportant," Mr. Block said to Mr. Williams toward the end of Mr. Williams' stay. "Well, if you do, you're wrong. What we do here has as much to do with whether we stay in business as what the salesmen do, even if they do make more money—particularly if we foul up. I know something about the problems of this game, since I spent almost 20 years with Sears, Roebuck in their traffic department before coming here, and I set this system up."

Mr. Block and his group were also responsible for taking periodical physical inventories, an operation that usually took place over a week end. This group customarily was augmented by five or six other people from the executive group. Partly from his initial interviews with Mr. Block, partly from subsequent visits, Mr. Williams learned that Mr. Block worked with his four to six "order pickers" in taking the orders placed on his desk and stapling them on large cardboard cards together with an order sheet, and physically taking the merchandise off the shelves. This job of filling orders, Mr. Block explained, required a detailed knowledge of the "line" and of customers because in many cases it was necessary to make substitutions for what the customers ordered or to fill so-called "open orders" in which the customer left the particular merchandise to be shipped to the discretion of the manufacturer. He also explained that the job involved some judgment as to establishing priorities on orders:

> Our system has to be designed on the basis that we take care of orders as they come in, but at the same time we've got to give preference to big accounts.

The trouble is every salesman thinks his orders should be taken care of first, and I have to use my judgment. You can't please everyone, Doc.

Mr. Block also pointed out that a unique feature of the belt department, as contrasted to the bag department, was the so-called "lay-away system." If orders could not be filled, even by substitutions, they were carried to a lay-away area, where they were entered in a "back order" or "shortage" book and filed by date. When incoming merchandise was received, it was normally checked against the back-order book before being placed on the shelf, although Mr. Block explained that the need for giving priority to good customers meant that the system was not followed rigidly.

Like Mr. Apfel, Mr. Block was subject to a number of interruptions in his daily routine. He was frequently asked by salesmen, showroom people, or Mickey to assist them in locating unfilled orders. He also was asked by a variety of people when particular merchandise was expected; sometimes he referred such questions to Fred Apfel. He worked in the showroom as the occasion demanded, and took telephone calls from customers inquiring about their orders. Mr. Block indicated to Mr. Williams that a certain amount of the confusion that existed in his operation was the inevitable result of the very crowded situation in the back room and in the belt storage area:

The boss is reluctant to get our belt inventory out of this building, but we're going to have to do it.

With Mr. Fischer's approval, Mr. Block had placed an ad in the *New York Times* early in June, indicating an opening in a belt shipping department for a traffic executive. From the hundred-odd replies he received, he interviewed five and hired a man to work with him at $60 a week. "The guy left in a week," Mr. Block reported. "He seemed to have the notion that all executives sit with their feet up on the desk."

BELT RECEIVING.   An additional activity, related to the processing of orders and located adjacent to the belt storage shelves, was the belt receiving department. Here approximately 25 people, under the supervision of a man known to Mr. Williams only as "Smitty," checked all incoming belt merchandise, inspected it, and packed it in half-dozen or dozen lots in the boxes in which the merchandise was placed on the shelves. It was Mr. Williams' understanding that "Smitty" was responsible to Fred Apfel and Harry Block, although he observed Mr. Fischer and Mr. Breitman talking to "Smitty" about his operations on a number of occasions.

6. *Record-Keeping and the Process of Keeping Management Informed.* Exhibit 17 summarizes the data gathered by Mr. Williams on Breitman's record-keeping process. Mr. Fischer kept a set of 5" × 8" cards in his desk, on which Miss Voss entered monthly records of orders, shipments, and salesmen's sales and commissions, and the annual tabulation of sales going back to 1948. Mr. Fischer occasionally asked Mr. Block or Mr. Apfel for special reports in more detail on the status of particular numbers or types of merchandise in the line.

Although Mr. Williams did not go into the details of the bookkeeping operation, he was invited on half-a-dozen occasions to join Miss Voss for lunch at her desk and had talked with her on a number of other occasions. The bookkeeping operation, with the exception of Miss Voss's own activities, was almost entirely self-contained, and from Mr. Williams' general impressions of its day-to-day workings, he saw no need to investigate its activities in any detail. Miss Voss had indicated her belief that less crowded quarters would enable her to run a more efficient operation. She also expressed the hope that if more room were made available, she might be able to persuade Mr. Breitman to mechanize some of her operations:

We had an estimate from Remington Rand a year ago on a $25,000 installation which would speed up our billings considerably. Mr. Breitman wanted to know how quickly we could save that, and I had to tell him that we wouldn't realize any direct cash savings, so he turned it down.

Miss Voss indicated that one of her continuing headaches was not being able to maintain her help on the salaries she was permitted to pay. "In this business the money goes to the selling end. We don't pay either our office help or our production people competitive wages." Because of this fact, and because of her own college courses in personnel, she reported that she tried to take an interest in some of the personnel problems not only of her own people but also of the production people. "Last week I conducted what you'd call an exit interview with one of the boys out back who quit."

VII. MR. WILLIAMS' CONTACTS WITH MR. BREITMAN, MR. FISCHER, AND MR. TEPLOW

In view of Mr. Williams' interest in the over-all management problems of Breitman, he had been particularly interested in learning as much as he could about the two owners of the business, as well as about Mr. Teplow, whom several people in the organization had referred to

Exhibit 17

BREITMAN & COMPANY

*Analysis of Company Records and Reports**

BASIC RECORDS OF NORMAL BUSINESS TRANSACTIONS

Records	Number of Copies	Prepared by	Sent to	Use
Customer order....	1	Customers (mail orders) Breitman sales personnel	See Exhibit 16	Processing all orders
Customer invoice..	4	Biller	Customer as bill Customer as shipping ticket Completed order files Miss Voss	Establishing shipments made and accounts receivable
Purchase invoice...	2	Mr. Apfel Miss Voss Mrs. Long Bag Production Manager	Supplier† Miss Voss	Recording merchandise or material ordered
Supplier invoice....	1	Supplier Contractor	Receiving Departments Miss Voss	Checking incoming shipments Establishing accounts payable
Time cards........	1	Production employee	Miss Voss	Establishing payroll
Shipping receipts...	1	Post Office Railway Express	Clerk	Establishing shipments made
Cutting tickets....	1	Mrs. Long Bag Production Manager	Accompanies merchandise through factory—filed in production files	Getting merchandise produced in factory

* Does not include all records at 14th Street or 25th Street factories.
† Copy not always sent to supplier on telephone orders.
Source: Case writer's interviews with people involved.

INFORMATION ACCUMULATED BY ACCOUNTING DEPARTMENT
(MISS VOSS'S DEPARTMENT)

Ledger or File	Description
Purchase registers:......................... Handbags Handbag contractors Belts Expense	Chronological record of purchases and payments
Payroll register............................	Chronological record of payroll
Cash receipts and disbursements..............	Chronological record of other cash receipts and disbursements
Accounts receivable register.................	Customer accounts receivable cards

Exhibit 17—Continued

BREITMAN & COMPANY

Analysis of Company Records and Reports*

INFORMATION ACCUMULATED TO KEEP TRACK OF ORDERS AND SHIPMENTS

Record or File	Description	Maintained by	Use
Belt account cards...	5 × 8 cards, filed alphabetically by customer showing all belt orders and shipments made to customer	Account-card clerks— 32d Street	Permanent record of customer activity Follow-up on orders
Bag account cards...	Same for bags	Account-card clerk —14th Street	
Belt active-order file.	Orders awaiting processing, filed by date	Harry Block	Source of orders to be processed Follow-up of orders
Belt lay-away file...	Orders awaiting belt shipments, filed by date	Lay-away clerk	Processing back orders
Belt shortage book..	Chronological record of back orders, filled and unfilled		Follow-up of orders
Belt completed-order file.........	Completed orders, filed by customer	Account-card clerk	Permanent record
Bag active-order file.	Orders awaiting shipment, filed chronologically	Bag Department clerks	Order processing
Bag completed-order file.........	Completed orders, filed by customer		Permanent record

* Does not include all records at 14th Street or 25th Street factories.
† Copy not always sent to supplier on telephone orders.
Source: Case writer's interviews with people involved.

INFORMATION ACCUMULATED BY MR. APFEL FOR HIS OWN USE

Record	Description
Cost cards.............................	5 × 8 cards showing cost breakdowns on each style
Individual style sheets...................	8 × 11 sheets showing shipments, receipts, and orders placed for each style, broken down by size and color
Tabulation of monthly sales and shipments.	Cumulative monthly record of belts sold and shipped, under headings: metal, leather, other

Exhibit 17—Continued

BREITMAN & COMPANY

Analysis of Company Records and Reports*

REPORTS FOR MANAGEMENT USE		
(Prepared within the Organization)		
Tabulation	Prepared by	For
Daily belt shipments by basic types......... Daily belt orders by basic types............. }	Account-card clerks	{ Mr. Fischer { Mr. Apfel { Mr. Block
Monthly sales by salesmen...................	Miss Voss	Mr. Fischer
Monthly sales and shipments by types of bags and belts............................	Account-card clerks Miss Voss	Mr. Fischer
Annual sales by customers listed geographically (includes bags and belts).................	Whoever available	Mr. Fischer Salesmen
List of styles in the belt and handbag line......	Mr. Steinmetz's assistant	Salesmen Shipping depart-ments

(Prepared by Outside Accountants)		
	Frequency	Description
Balance sheet..	Four times a year	See Exhibit 2
Income statement....................................	" " "	See Exhibit 3
Ratio analysis.......................................	" " "	See Exhibit 4
Income tax form.....................................	Once a year	

* Does not include all records at 14th Street or 25th Street factories.
† Copy not always sent to supplier on telephone orders.
Source: Case writer's interviews with people involved.

as "a kind of informal general manager." By the end of his preliminary investigation, Mr. Williams had had much less opportunity to talk in detail with either Mr. Breitman or Mr. Teplow than he had with Mr. Fischer, and his picture of the former gentlemen's respective places in the organization was much less detailed.

Mr. Breitman, as both president and treasurer, talked frequently to Mr. Fischer about such matters as hiring of personnel, decisions on spending money, questions as to whether or not to add new lines (e.g., the novelty line Mr. Breitman brought back from Japan), and the volume of business being done. Otherwise, Mr. Breitman apparently devoted most of his time to his office or design room, working on new styles. (Joe, one of the younger men in the group, spent much of his time in acting as general assistant to Mr. Breitman.) "I've learned that the business gets along better if I keep out of most of the operating details," Mr. Breitman told Mr. Williams.

Mr. Teplow, general manager of the bag department, seldom discussed many of the day-to-day details of the handbag operations with either Mr. Fischer or Mr. Breitman, so far as Mr. Williams could learn. He did, however, review with Mr. Breitman and Mr. Fischer the items he proposed to include in the line as well as the results of his operation in terms of volume. Mr. Teplow had little day-to-day contact with Frank Rich, the bag sales manager, and had almost no contacts with customers. His system of follow-up in matters he regarded as requiring attention had been pointed out to Mr. Williams by others on several occasions. Mr. Teplow carried a sheaf of tablet paper in his coat pocket, on which he made notes of matters needing attention. "This gives him an unfailing memory," one person reported, "and if you haven't done what you said you would, look out." Mr. Teplow had answered freely any specific questions put to him by Mr. Williams, but had never volunteered much information about company problems.

Mr. Williams believed that his picture of Mr. Fischer's place in the organization was much more nearly complete, and Mr. Fischer had on several occasions talked at length about his views about the organization. Twice in his study Mr. Williams had spent a full day with Mr. Fischer, observing in detail his activities and listening to his conversations with others. Each day Mr. Fischer had kept up a pace of activity that made it perfectly clear why so many references had been made to his "busyness." In a single hour, for example, he might talk to half-a-dozen people in the organization about particular orders or particular problems, look at 20 or so orders, talk to a salesman on the long-distance phone, sign some checks, and say "Hello" to three or four buyers.

From numerous conversations Mr. Williams pieced together a number of Mr. Fischer's attitudes toward his own problems. "I know I'm too busy, but can you give me an easy answer on what to do about it? A great deal of my problem arises out of the fact that it's good business for the head of the firm to talk to buyers." Mr. Fischer reported on several occasions to Mr. Williams that once after he had turned over a customer to one of his sales managers, the customer had said: "What's the matter with Judson Fischer? Does he think he's a big shot?"

Mr. Fischer had offered the job as his assistant to a belt buyer for a large department store, but the buyer had turned down the job to enter his own business. Mr. Fischer indicated to Mr. Williams that he planned to offer the same job to one of his best salesmen:

But will you tell me what I do then? I'm no big shot—I'd go crazy cooped up in an office like Felix. I really enjoy what I'm doing now.

After Mr. Williams' interview with Mr. Lasser, Mr. Fischer had discussed some of Mr. Lasser's points with Mr. Williams:

> Irving talks about delegation, but let me talk about it. Do I tell Mr. Teplow how to do his job? Do I tell Miss Voss? The answer is, of course not. But what do you do when it's your business, and people don't always do what they're supposed to? I think I've got good people around me, but they slip up—let me give you a couple of examples. Last week I told Byron Steinmetz to get a belt rack for ———— [a Philadelphia department store]. Here a week later, he hasn't done it. And the week before last Fred Apfel and I were walking with a buyer past ———— [a department store], and she saw a belt she liked. I told Fred to get her one like it, and it still isn't done. Those may be details, but this business runs on details.
>
> Let me talk about another of Irving's points. He wants me to do some things now and spend some money while excess profits taxes are still in effect. The one thing he forgets is that it's my money. I've known what it's like not to have it, and I'm going to be careful spending it now that I have it.

On this same occasion Mr. Fischer talked about his attitude toward the absence of a board of directors (he and Mr. Breitman constituted the board) :

> Where am I going to get some people who understand my problems, who aren't going to try to act important? Irving Lasser is very smart and a good friend of mine, but he just doesn't understand our problems.

Mr. Fischer also expressed to Mr. Williams his "dream" that he might some day retire, but said he was uncertain as to how this could in fact be accomplished. (Mr. Fischer had no children, and Mr. Breitman's only daughter was in high school.)

. . . .

One of Mr. Williams' last visits to Breitman & Company took place on Monday, July 14, a day when Mr. Fischer had returned to work after a two weeks' minor illness. A description of this visit will be given in Breitman & Company (B).

Exhibit 18

BREITMAN & COMPANY

Selected Information on Belt and Handbag Buying in 36 New York City Department Stores

Size of Buying Group	Number of Stores	Number of Buyers Buying			Number of Belt or Handbag Buyers Who Also Buy					
		Handbags Only	Belts Only	Handbags and Belts	Jewelry	Leather Goods	Umbrellas	Neckwear	Gloves	Handkerchiefs
1–10 buyers	4	0	0	2	3	3	2	1	2	1
11–25 buyers	15	2	0	6	6	4	3	4	4	2
26–50 buyers	9	5	0	3	4	3	4	3	1	1
51–75 buyers	4	1	0	1	1	2	1	1	0	1
76–100 buyers	4	1	0	1	0	0	0	0	1	1
	36	9	0	13	14	12	10	10	7	6

Source: Compiled by case writer from trade sources.

Breitman & Company (B)

THE JULY 14TH CONFERENCE

AT THE REQUEST of Mickey, Simon, and Joe, an evening meeting was held on July 14th to take up some urgent problems which these three men wished aired. At eight o'clock, after the group[1] had eaten dinner together in the showroom, Mr. Fischer asked:

Well, what is it we're going to talk about tonight?[2]

JOE (*pulling out a sheet of paper on which he has written some notes*): Well, Mr. Fischer, we've been waiting for you to come back to get the answers to a lot of questions that have been bothering us. I've got a list of things here and if it's all right, I'd just like to go down some of them.

FISCHER: Sure!

JOE: The first thing that I think we probably ought to settle is about open orders.[3] We've got a problem there because they aren't filled when they first come in, and they go into the lay-away bins and we have no system for seeing that they get followed up.

FISCHER: That's a question of merchandise deliveries. Do we need to talk about that this evening?

JOE: Well, we can't just fluff it off. I think that's quite important.

APFEL: Mr. Fischer, this is a very important problem. Right now, a lot of our salesmen are writing open orders. Maybe as many as 10% of our orders come in that way. What happens is, when the boys go out to pick them in the "back," they can't find the merchandise, so they put the orders back in the lay-away bins. These orders don't appear in the shortage books, though, and there's no way of making sure they get filled.

---

[1] Present were: Mr. Fischer, Vice-President; Mr. Breitman, President; Mr. Teplow, Manager, Bag Department; Simon, resident-buyer calls, order processing; Joe, assistant to Mr. Breitman; Fred Apfel, Belt Production Manager; Frank Rich, Bag Sales Manager; Mickey, order-processing; and Mr. Williams.

[2] The transcript of this conference was dictated by Mr. Williams from notes he took during the conference.

[3] An "open order" is one on which the customer permits the manufacturer to ship whatever merchandise is available.

FISCHER: Is that your problem? I can solve that very simply. Why can't we just have Harry [Block, belt shipping manager] take all those orders aside and have him pick them and keep track of them?

APFEL: Mr. Fischer, Harry is a very busy man. He's already got too much to do. That isn't any answer.

FISCHER: Too bad Harry isn't here tonight. He ought to be here to discuss this. Well, what about Smitty [an order picker]? Could he do this?

BREITMAN: Smitty is working out nicely and doing a very fine job, but I don't think he knows enough yet to handle this kind of thing, and besides, we need him where he is.

APFEL: Mr. Fischer, I don't like to say this because I know Joey isn't going to like me to say it, but I think he's just the man to handle that. I think it might be a good idea if we got him to take care of it. He may not want to, but I think it's an important job, and it's to his interest and our interest that it be done.

FISCHER (*to Joe*): Do you want to?

JOE: Well, I'd like to talk to you about that and some other things later.

FISCHER: All right.

JOE: There's another matter here that I think I might bring up, which I think is related to this—and that is that we don't have any follow-up system on our orders.

FISCHER: Isn't that a little off the subject? We were talking about open orders.

JOE: No, not at all. That's very closely related to it.

SIMON: One of the reasons these open orders don't get taken care of is that we have no follow-up system at all on our orders.

FISCHER: Mickey, isn't that your job?

MICKEY: Well, I'm supposed to answer correspondence and inquiries about orders. To that extent it is my job, but I'm not supposed to follow up all orders; and, at that, I'm so busy now I can't keep up with the correspondence.

SIMON: Part of the problem is that we've never had any system, but it's gotten now completely out of hand because instead of taking orders in turn the way the system says we should, it's getting all messed up because everybody is making promises in taking care of "specials."[4]

FISCHER: Why, that's ridiculous. Do you mean to tell me that you're suggesting we shouldn't give special attention to our good customers?

---

[4] A "special" is an order handled out of sequence.

That's the way we built this business, and you're not suggesting we should be so foolish as to take care of the little stores ahead of our very best accounts, are you?

APFEL: Mr. Fischer, that's not the point. Of course we have to give special attention—have to have specials. We're so far behind now that even the promises on the specials don't do any good. Part of our problem is that we give customers a promise and then aren't able to keep it. And you've got to admit, Mr. Fischer, that you can never say "No" to anybody; even if somebody comes in who's only a small account, you still are going to make a promise to them.

SIMON: That's one of our big problems. We have a lot of people coming in here and you make promises, Mr. Fischer; Harry makes promises, the salesmen make promises, and when it's all done, none of those promises means anything. What makes it even worse is that a lot of our promises are to people who have never done any business with us before.

FISCHER: Do we have a lot of new accounts now?

BREITMAN: We really do, Judson.

SIMON: We opened up over a thousand in the last year. At the beginning of the season our cards were up to 4,000, and now they're up to 5,200.

RICH: A lot of people are coming in here to buy from us who have never bought anything from us before because of the shortage of cinches.[5]

FISCHER: There's one thing we can do something about. Simon, could you go through the [account] cards tomorrow and pick out all the orders that have been placed by people who've never dealt with us before?

APFEL: We can't pull out the cards because the girls will be working on them continually.

FISCHER: Well, then you can make a list.

RICH: One of the things you've got to be careful about is that some of the people who will appear on those cards as new accounts will actually be old bag accounts. You don't want to turn them down, do you?

FISCHER: Well, Simon, then when you get that list, you can check it with Sidney Teplow.

RICH: If you bring the list to me, I can tell you which of them are bag accounts.

---

[5] An elastic belt, for which a demand had arisen rapidly in the late spring of 1952.

FISCHER: But that still doesn't settle the basic problem about promises, does it?

APFEL: May I make a suggestion, Mr. Fischer? Right now I'm getting in about 30 gross of belts a day. That's 150 gross a week. You want to be able to make promises to your good customers. Supposing I were to take, say, 10% of those belts, which would be 15 gross a week, and set them aside, and you can promise them any way you see fit. Do you think that would be a good idea?

FISCHER: You mean you'd give me 15 gross of belts to promise any way I see fit? Gee, that would be wonderful.

BREITMAN: Do we need to set them aside?

SIMON: I don't think we should set them aside. Remember what happened last year when we had a lot of belts set aside for ———— [a salesman] and the other salesmen came in and took them all away from us. That, incidentally, is another problem. ———— [a salesman] was out back today picking out a lot of belts for his special customers.

FISCHER: After all, ———— is a good Breitman man, and I think he's probably entitled to get a little special treatment once in a while.

SIMON: Well, it isn't just ————. He's probably no worse than the rest, but the other salesmen will all come in here and want to do the same thing, and then we'll get all mixed up.

FISCHER: Well, then we don't need to put them aside. Is there anything wrong with Mr. Apfel's suggestion?

RICH: Is Mr. Breitman going to have the same, another 15 gross set aside for him?

BREITMAN: I wouldn't want to have that.

SIMON: What about Harry and all the salesmen?

APFEL: No, this is just for Mr. Fischer. If we do that, Mr. Fischer, you've got to limit yourself to that 15 gross, and if somebody else comes in, you've got to get tough with them. You've got to admit that you're soft, and if anybody comes in here and wants a promise, you'll give it to them.

FISCHER: Well, I just can't say "No" to a customer—you know that. We built this business by being agreeable to people, and I just don't think you ever say "No" to someone. You've got to play along with them. If you get tough with them, they'll get disgruntled and leave.

BREITMAN: Well, while you were gone, Judson, I got tough with some of these people and said "No" to them and made them like it.

FISCHER: Well, I think Fred's suggestion is a good one, but before we get too many more things, what about that open-order thing? Maybe we should cut out all open orders. How about this order which I have here in my pocket, which I wrote this afternoon? How is this as a way to write orders? (*Mr. Fischer pulls out an order in which he has listed all the style numbers, roughly 40 of them, which the customer wants in varying quantities to make up an order worth several thousand dollars.*) Is this perhaps a better way to do it?

BREITMAN: Well, I think open orders are a good idea, Judson. I don't think we ought to cut them out.

FISCHER: Well, then we have to have somebody to handle them, don't we? Could we perhaps hire somebody new?

TEPLOW: Well, it would have to be somebody who knows belts. You can't just take somebody off the street to do that.

FISCHER: Well, Simon, what about you? Would you like to go out back and handle them?

SIMON: If you're asking me if I *want* to, the answer is "No." There's more to this than simply the problem of open orders. People are running around there all the time not knowing what they're doing, everybody's trying to do everything. . . .

FISCHER (*interrupting*): Are you trying to tell me that you think that Harry Block is disorganized?

SIMON: Mr. Fischer, it isn't that I don't like Harry, and I know he works hard, and I know he's done a lot, but I think the answer to your question is, "Yes."

FISCHER: You mean, you don't want to work for Harry Block?

SIMON: It isn't that I don't like him.

FISCHER: You've never told me this before.

SIMON: You never asked me, and just now you did ask me, point-blank. My job is to do what I'm supposed to, not to go around and tell you about the faults of other people.

FISCHER: Gee, I wish Harry Block was here. You did try to get him, didn't you, Fred?

APFEL: Yes, and he had already left.

JOE: Coming back to this question of a follow-up system, Mickey's supposed to check on the orders, but right now there's just so much of that, he can't keep up with it. That results in the fact that everybody is going into the files, pulling out the cards to see what's happened to orders, and we're getting all mixed up. Three of the salesmen were out there this afternoon, for instance.

FISCHER: Well, that's one thing we can put a stop to. We just don't want to have any salesmen out back.

SIMON: Well, a lot of people have been calling Harry, too, to get orders. Right now when people call in here, they only want to talk to two people, either you, Mr. Fischer, or Harry Block. We could get rid of the entire rest of our sales force because they want to get a promise out of you, they know they can get it from you, and they've been getting it from Harry. Harry has been giving a lot of people promises and a lot of people special attention. A lot of customers have written in to say, in effect, that Harry was able to give them orders when nobody else could. Now he's finding that he can't continue that either; he's beginning to make a lot of enemies out of people he made promises to.

JOE: Well, another part of the problem is that when these orders get pulled out to be checked, they don't get put back, and so you have a lot of orders sitting around and nobody knows where they are.

FISCHER: Well, couldn't we take care of that by having somebody assigned simply to see to it that all the orders got put back in the files properly?

SIMON: We'd have to hire somebody new to do that. We haven't got anybody we can spare now.

FISCHER: Well, let's hire them.

SIMON: Well, I think that would help, but that wouldn't solve the problem.

(*At this point there was a discussion, primarily between Mr. Teplow, Fred Apfel, Mr. Breitman, and Frank Rich, as to whether or not a different system for handling orders would eliminate much of this difficulty. It was not clear to Mr. Williams exactly what was being proposed. After about five minutes of this discussion, Mr. Fischer resumed.*)

FISCHER: Well, it's getting late, and we're not going to change the system this season. I don't think there's any point in carrying this discussion on any further.

JOE: Well, whatever system we have, when a guy comes in for a sale, you still have to have a good system to tell him what you can give him.

FISCHER: Well, we've been talking about a lot of things here and we still haven't answered some of the questions we've brought up. What about this question of Mickey's load? Are you really overloaded, Mickey?

MICKEY: Well, I'm getting three or four hundred letters in here a day. Sally has been helping me, but I just can't possibly keep up with it.

FISCHER: How quickly are you answering telegrams?

MICKEY: Well, I try to get a letter out on them in about 48 hours.

FISCHER: How far behind are we on our promises?

MICKEY: Well, we've got some things that were promised for June 1, which still aren't shipped yet.

APFEL: Mr. Fischer, this is a tremendously difficult problem. We all know that Mickey's been working very hard to keep up. Probably we can't solve it completely, but I don't think. . . .

FISCHER: Well, there's no need to make a speech about it, is there? What do you have in mind?

APFEL: Well, the point is, Mr. Fischer, I don't think that when these letters come in, the customers want to know what we're going to do— I think they want goods. Maybe it isn't necessary to give them all the information that we're now giving them.

FISCHER: Well, what about that, Mickey?

(*At this point there was a discussion among Mickey, Fred Apfel, Mr. Fischer, and Mr. Teplow as to whether or not to give customers who had written in to check on orders complete information as to the status of those orders, and after three or four minutes of discussion it was agreed that such a procedure was, in fact, necessary and that Mickey should have an assistant. Discussion then turned to what to do to speed up shipments.*)

APFEL: Well, I'm going to spend tomorrow morning getting all the new people squared away on what they're supposed to do. Ninety per cent of our troubles come from improper training, and now that we've gotten some new people, if we can get people started on the right foot I think we can lick a lot of these things.

SIMON: Well, you may have some new people, but you still have a lot of the same old faces.

JOE: Our problem is that we have no organization out back.

SIMON: Our problem is that we have no organization, period.

FISCHER: Well, now you've said that before. Let's talk a little bit about that. Just what do you mean?

SIMON: Well, we have no organization. You've never broken down the duties that each of us is supposed to do.

MICKEY: Well, now in the Army you have tables of organization. You have a chart showing what each person is supposed to do. Everybody has an assignment of a responsibility. We don't have that here.

SIMON: You have no delegation of responsibility whatsoever. A lot of people are getting blamed for things they aren't even supposed to be responsible for.

FISCHER: Well, can't we do something about that right now? Suppose we took Mickey off his job and put Sally [one of the girls in the showroom] on that job and gave her some help and put Mickey out back and gave him some definite responsibility for, say, these open orders. Simon, you know what you're supposed to do. You're responsible for the locker stock.

SIMON: Yes, and I call on the resident buyers, take stock, work in the showroom, and help Mr. Breitman.

APFEL: Let's not forget that we're in this pickle now because of an unusual buying situation.

SIMON: You haven't got this situation because there's any emergency. You have this emergency because we've been in this type of situation for a long time.

APFEL: Mr. Fischer, supposing we did this. (*He takes out a pencil and a piece of paper and starts drawing an organization chart.*) Take out back. Now, we all recognize that Harry's got to be in charge. He's done a marvelous job under the circumstances, he's worked as hard as anybody possibly could work, and I think the thing is going to straighten itself out. But supposing now we gave him some help and some people with actually assigned duties. I still think that Joey ought to go back there. Supposing we made Joey responsible for all new orders and for the lay-away. Supposing we put Smitty [an order picker] in charge of shipping and receiving, and supposing that we took somebody else and put them in charge of, say ——— and ——— [mail-order houses]. I think perhaps he ought to report to me rather than to Harry. Suppose we have somebody else to follow up our old orders. Each of these people would have definite duties, definite responsibilities, but still all reporting to Harry Block.

FISCHER: Well, I don't think we ought to settle any of this without Harry Block's being here. After all, he's in charge out back, but I think I'd better call him in here tomorrow morning, and we'll talk about this. (*Turning to the case writer.*) Maybe what we need in here is an efficiency expert. Do you think we need an efficiency expert?

SIMON: That's just what we don't need, Mr. Fischer. The people who are working on this problem know what the answers to some of these problems are, but nobody ever asks them for their opinions. You've been having a survey in here every three months, but none of them has done any good. An outsider can't come in here and give us answers, but if you listen to us, we can work this thing out.

JOE: I'd like to bring up one more thing. As a result of a lot of things we've been talking about this evening, a lot of our salesmen are following the practice—when a customer doesn't get his shipment—of simply sending us in a whole new order. The result is that sometimes we know about that duplication and cancel the original order and sometimes we don't, and we ship out double shipments. Now in times like these when people will take anything they can get, that's fine, but if the business should ever fall off, we may find ourselves with a great many returns on our hands that we'll be stuck with.

RICH: Do you have good figures on your returns?

BREITMAN: Well, we tried keeping them for a while, but they didn't tell us very much, and we didn't think they were worth bothering with.

FISCHER: Well, it's getting late, and I want to have a talk with Mr. Teplow and Mr. Breitman before Mr. Teplow goes off to Europe, so maybe we ought to go back over what we settled this evening. Simon, first thing tomorrow morning you're going to go through the cards and pick out those accounts that have ordered from us for the first time. You'll check with Frank, and we'll pull all those orders out and set them aside.

RICH: Are you going to tell the salesmen and the showroom not to accept new accounts?

FISCHER: Yes, we'll put that into effect immediately. If somebody comes in here who hasn't bought from us before, we'll explain the situation to him and try to get him interested in buying from us next year but not take any of his orders this year.

SIMON: I'd like to make one more point, people, before we break up. I think this is very serious. We've talked a lot about this before, but we've never done anything, and I think it's about time we took some action.

FISCHER: Well, I'm going to get Harry in here and talk to him about this first thing tomorrow morning. What about this open-order thing? Simon, would you be willing to take over there for a couple of weeks just to help out?

SIMON: Well, yes, if you say so, Mr. Fischer, but I'm already behind on my locker stock work. I've been doing all that work at home at night, and I'm still far behind, and that plus calling on the buying offices, I just don't have time.

FISCHER: Well, maybe we could cut out the calls on the buying office.

SIMON: Well, I don't think that's a good idea, Mr. Fischer. Right now we're having a lot of trouble keeping them friendly as it is without problems on shipment, and if we don't pay any attention to them at all, the thing will get even worse.

BREITMAN: Well, I'd be glad to go over for the time being and pull those orders—just to get caught up.

TEPLOW: That's an awfully expensive way to pull orders.

FISCHER: Well, Joe, what about you? Felix, could we take Joe off the Japanese stuff for a while?

BREITMAN: Sure, we can get along without him for a while.

JOE: Well, of course that isn't all I'm doing right now, Mr. Fischer.

BREITMAN: I'll be glad to do it for a while, Judson. I think that's the answer. Well, it's getting late, and I think we'd better quit.

FISCHER: Sidney, when do you leave for Europe?

TEPLOW: Friday.

FISCHER: Well, I can see you tomorrow then.

(*As the group broke up, Mr. Breitman turned to Mr. Williams.*)

BREITMAN: This is all very well, but after all, we've been successful, and you can't argue with success.

FISCHER: Yeah, we could be very logically organized and get this place nicely set up, and we'd probably do about a half a million dollars' worth of business a year.

SIMON: I don't think so.

Wilton Oil Equipment Company (A)

"I KNOW this company has its problems," Mr. Bill Ellsworth, vice-president of the Wilton Oil Equipment Company, located in Wilton, New Jersey, told a visitor to the company in January, 1952. "I also know that I'm probably in the best position to do something about them The thing that concerns me is that I'm not at all sure where to begin or how to separate the things that we should do right away from the things on which we have a little more time.

"Even though we've been expanding more or less continuously over the last 15 years—and have always made money—I think we have reason to be concerned with our competitive situation. Tied in with that is the fact that I seriously question whether we can continue to sell through manufacturers' agents the way we always have. As I think you'll see, we have problems in the production area, and perhaps there I'm less in a position to evaluate our needs than with some of our other activities. We talk about the need for plant expansion—and if it were at all justified I'd like to see us build a new plant. That, of course, means more capital, and while I don't think there's any immediate urgency in our financial picture, we certainly haven't done any real financial planning. Our treasurer has just left, and that means that we've just put a new man in charge of all of our cost and financial work. I hope that the new man is up to making some real changes there, because we need them, but frankly I think it remains to be seen whether he has quite what it takes. Add to all this the fact that we're in a business where engineering is very important—and we have what I think is certainly a poorly managed engineering staff—and you really begin to wonder how we've managed to be as successful as we have been.

"What I'm saying, of course, is that it's clear we need more and better management; what I think is not clear is how we should go about getting it. Hire a general manager? Maybe, but Dad is still president, and I think he would not go along with that.

"For one thing, he's got his heart set on seeing me move into that spot. For another, I'm not sure we can offer a really first-rate man enough, either immediately or over the long run, to get the kind of

Exhibit 1

WILTON OIL EQUIPMENT COMPANY (A)

Operating Statements—Selected Years, 1938–51

(In Thousands)

	1938	1940	1941	1944	1945	1946	1947	1948	1949	1950	11 Months 1951
Gross Sales	$376.4	$617.8	$791.1	$1,032.8	$998.7	$1,306.5	$1,785.0	$2,033.5	$1,899.0	$2,087.6	$2,288.1
Less: Allowances and Discounts	92.6*	149.4*	190.4*	26.2	30.5	33.0	39.6	37.4	41.5	47.1	56.7
Net Sales	$283.8	$468.4	$600.7	$1,006.6	$968.2	$1,273.5	$1,745.4	$1,996.1	$1,857.5	$2,040.5	$2,231.4
Cost of Goods Sold	198.9	303.9	384.5	525.1	525.1	718.9	978.2	1,134.5	1,080.9	1,214.8	1,142.3
Gross Profit	$ 84.9	$164.5	$216.2	$ 481.5	$443.1	$ 554.6	$ 767.2	$ 861.6	$ 776.6	$ 825.7	$1,089.1
General Expense: Selling	NA	NA	$ 51.6	$ 283.8	$283.7	$ 368.4	$ 502.6	$ 573.4	$ 524.7	$ 566.4	$ 623.7
Administrative	NA	NA	109.6	110.4	112.3	101.5	129.2	132.6	128.9	134.0	151.7
Total	$ 83.5	$122.0	$161.2	$ 394.2	$396.0	$ 469.9	$ 631.8	$ 706.0	$ 653.6	$ 700.4	$ 775.4
Operating Profit	$ 1.4	$ 42.5	$ 55.0	$ 87.3	$ 47.1	$ 84.7	$ 135.4	$ 155.6	$ 123.0	$ 125.3	$ 313.7
Other Income	5.6	2.8	1.9	4.2	2.6	4.3	3.6	4.1	6.7	7.0	4.3
Other Expense	1.7	2.5	9.6	12.7	11.4	15.4	22.3	33.0	27.4	29.0	33.8
Net	$ 3.9	$ 0.3	($ 7.7)	($ 8.5)	($ 8.8)	($ 11.1)	($ 18.7)	($ 28.9)	($ 20.7)	($ 22.0)	($ 29.5)
Income before Taxes	5.3	42.8	47.3	78.8	38.3	73.6	116.7	126.7	102.3	103.3	284.2
Provision for Taxes	0.7	16.7	24.1	58.9	20.8	17.8	35.8	48.3	39.5	40.6	193.2
Net Profit	$ 4.6	$ 26.1	$ 23.2	$ 19.9	$ 17.5	$ 55.8	$ 80.9	$ 78.4	$ 62.8	$ 62.7	$ 91.0
Gross Sales	132.6%	131.9%	131.7%	102.6%	103.2%	102.6%	102.3%	101.9%	102.2%	102.3%	102.5%
Less: Allowances and Discounts	32.6*	31.9*	31.7*	2.6	3.2	2.6	2.3	1.9	2.2	2.3	2.5
Net Sales	100.0%	100.0%	100.0%	100.0%	100.0%	100.0%	100.0%	100.0%	100.0%	100.0%	100.0%
Cost of Goods Sold	70.1	64.9	64.0	52.2	54.2	56.5	56.0	56.8	58.2	59.5	51.2
Gross Profit	29.9%	35.1%	36.0%	47.8%	45.8%	43.5%	44.0%	43.2%	41.8%	40.5%	48.8%
Gen. Expense: Selling	NA	NA	8.6%	28.2%	29.3%	28.9%	28.8%	28.7%	28.3%	27.8%	28.0%
Administrative	NA	NA	18.2	11.0	11.6	8.0	7.4	6.7	6.9	6.5	10.8
Total	29.4%	26.0%	26.8%	39.2%	40.9%	36.9%	36.2%	35.4%	35.2%	34.3%	34.8%
Operating Profit	0.5%	9.1%	9.2%	8.6%	4.9%	6.6%	7.8%	7.8%	6.6%	6.2%	14.0%
Other Income	2.0%	0.6%	0.3%	0.4%	0.3%	0.3%	0.2%	0.2%	0.3%	0.3%	0.2%
Other Expense	0.6	0.5	1.6	1.2	1.2	1.2	1.3	1.7	1.4	1.4	1.5
Net	1.4%	0.1%	(1.3%)	(0.8%)	0.9%	0.9%	1.1%	1.5%	1.1%	1.1%	1.3%
Income before Taxes	1.9%	9.2%	7.9%	7.8%	4.0%	5.7%	6.7%	6.3%	5.5%	5.1%	12.7%
Provision for Taxes	0.3	3.6	4.0	5.8	2.2	1.4	2.1	2.4	2.1	2.0	8.7
Net Profit	1.6%	5.6%	3.9%	2.0%	1.8%	4.3%	4.6%	3.9%	3.4%	3.1%	4.0%

NA Not available.
* Includes agents' commissions.

Source: Compiled from Mr. David Ellsworth's book of accounts. Percentage figures computed by case writer.

Exhibit 2

WILTON OIL EQUIPMENT COMPANY (A)

Balance Sheets—Selected Years, 1936–51

(In Thousands)

Assets	1936	1938	1940	1941	1944	1945	1946	1947	1948	1949	1950	11 Months 1951
Cash	$ 10.7	$ 10.4	$ 21.9	$ 17.4	$ 52.1	$ 46.3	$ 50.2	$ 87.0	$ 118.0	$105.8	$ 66.9	$ 126.0
Accounts Receivable	56.7	55.7	85.5	100.5	108.6	108.1	212.7	259.1	200.2	163.5	288.5	271.2
Inventories	24.2	33.4	55.6	112.7	133.4	132.5	264.5	351.8	461.5	363.2	419.8	540.3*
Prepaid Expenses							12.5	26.5	30.8	29.5	36.7	33.9
Total Current Assets	$ 91.6	$ 99.5	$163.0	$230.6	$294.1	$286.9	$539.9	$724.4	$810.5	$662.0	$811.9	$ 971.4
Other Assets	$ 1.9	$ 2.2	$ 2.7	$ 4.0	$ 5.3	$ 18.1	$ 15.2	$ 17.7	$ 18.6	$ 19.5	$ 21.3	$ 21.4
Plant, Property and Equipment	$100.7	$ 95.5	$ 62.3	$ 68.7	$ 87.6	$ 98.8	$106.7	$185.8	$222.4	$221.0	$234.8	$ 262.1
Reserve	33.0	30.4	28.2	30.4	39.2	42.7	45.1	51.6	63.8	63.0	70.9	86.7
Net	$ 67.7	$ 65.1	$ 34.1	$ 38.3	$ 48.4	$ 56.1	$ 61.6	$134.2	$158.6	$158.0	$163.9	$ 175.4
Nonbusiness Real Estate			3.3	3.2	2.9	2.8	1.3	1.3	1.2			
Patents and Copyrights	1.7	2.7	3.6	3.1	4.6	4.9	4.8	4.9	5.6	5.0	6.2	5.7
Goodwill	41.5	41.5	41.5	41.5	41.5							
Organization Expense								1.8	1.7			
Deferred Charges	0.3	0.3					1.3	14.0	13.3	14.3	13.4	11.2
Total Assets	$204.7	$211.3	$248.2	$320.7	$396.8	$368.8	$624.1	$898.3	$1,009.5	$858.8	$1,016.7	$1,185.1
Liabilities												
Accounts Payable	$ 21.0	$ 21.8	$ 27.3	$ 24.7	$ 8.7	$ 36.4	$ 56.7	$ 81.9	$ 99.1	$ 47.0	$ 87.3	$ 36.8
Notes Payable Within One Year	4.9	4.3	0.1	22.4			89.3		34.4		33.2	5.0
Dividends Payable								11.2	2.6			
Provision for Taxes			16.7	24.1	58.9	20.8	33.5	38.4	86.0	39.5	40.6	201.3
Accruals	22.1	18.7	28.0	51.0	71.0	68.6	98.0	138.3	151.2	103.3	146.2	171.1
Total Current Liabilities	$ 48.0	$ 44.8	$ 72.1	$122.2	$138.6	$125.8	$277.5	$269.8	$373.3	$189.8	$307.3	$ 414.2
Notes Payable After One Year			54.1	90.0	90.0	90.0				3.3	5.0	2.6
Deferred Income					2.0				1.7	3.4	2.7	
Total	$ 48.0	$ 44.8	$126.2	$212.2	$230.6	$215.8	$277.5	$269.8	$375.0	$196.5	$315.0	$ 416.8
Preferred Stock	8.2	8.2		49.5	49.4	49.5	139.4	207.5	207.5	187.4	178.0	168.6
Common Stock	100.8	100.8	75.1	59.0	116.8	103.5	207.2	315.8	318.7	318.6	318.6	318.6
Surplus	47.7	57.5	46.9					105.2	108.3	156.3	205.1	281.1
Total Liabilities	$204.7	$211.3	$248.2	$320.7	$396.8	$368.8	$624.1	$898.3	$1,009.5	$858.8	$1,016.7	$1,185.1

* Inventory breakdown, November, 1951:

Raw Materials	45%
Work in Process	22
Manufactured Parts	26
Finished Goods	6
Consigned Merchandise	1
	100%

Source: Compiled by case writer from Mr. David Ellsworth's book of accounts.

person we'd need. And in my own mind, I feel an obligation to the people who are here and have helped build this company which I don't think an outsider would have much patience with.

"Besides, I see this situation as a real challenge—a ready-made opportunity I don't want to pass up. Dad, I think, would sell out the company if I didn't feel this way; he's had several good opportunities to do so, but unless I thought there was no other alternative, I'd never want us to do that."

Mr. Ellsworth was the son of the president and principal stockholder of the Wilton Oil Equipment Company, Mr. David Ellsworth. Bill, as the son was known in the company, was twenty-nine years old, a graduate of Rutgers University and of the Harvard Business School. He had served overseas with the air force for four years before doing graduate work, and after working for a year in a New York advertising agency, came into the Wilton company to replace the advertising manager who was retiring after 25 years of service.

THE COMPANY

Wilton Oil Equipment Company, in which the Ellsworth family owned the controlling interest, had been founded in 1910 as a supplier of specialty metal products to the oil industry. (See Exhibits 1 and 2.) Just before World War I the founder of the company developed a line of valves that had application in a number of industries and, after 1920, became the company's principal source of business. During the early twenties the company started to distribute its products through a group of manufacturers' agents who specialized in sales to construction engineers, chemical-process industries, oil refineries, and water-supply systems. At the same time, Wilton broadened its line to include pressure gauges, strainers, liquid-level indicators, and flowmeters. By 1925 sales had reached $100,000 a year and the company had built its own plant in Wilton, which it still occupied in 1952. The company added still other new products to its operation when in 1935 it acquired the assets of a small manufacturer of instruments and controls and started the manufacture and sale of equipment that could be used, in conjunction with its valves, for the automatic control of a wide variety of processes involving liquid flow. During World War II the company increased its sales volume but did not take on government or war orders for other than its normal products. Wilton, however, developed several new electronic amplifiers and control devices that lent themselves to sale with its regular products.

For an 11 months' period in 1951, valves, flowmeters, pressure gauges and associated equipment accounted for 20% of Wilton's sales (see Exhibit 3); control systems and panels, 29%; recorders and indicators, 6%; electronic equipment, 9%; and special instruments, 6%. The remaining 30% was made up of: repair parts, charts, and supplies (17%); resale of other manufacturers' equipment by Wilton in conjunction with its control equipment, for which Wilton received a 10% manufacturer's discount (12% of Wilton sales); and installation and service charges (1% of sales).

"You'd be amazed at the variety of products it takes to support our sales volume," Bill Ellsworth explained. "We've never counted them all, but since everything we make is tailored to customers' specifications as to size, material, finish, and performance, we probably make over 2,000 different kinds of items in a year.

"On valves alone we make 14 different types, including pressure-reducing valves, control valves operated either manually or electrically, vacuum-regulating, and so on. Each of those can vary in size from ⅛" to 12", and in rated pressure from ⅛ p.s.i. (pounds per square inch) to 3,000 p.s.i. Of course, we sell more of some of them than of others, but the possible variations on what a customer can want are tremendous.

"Probably the simplest of our product groups is our recorder and indicator line, essentially a means of either recording by pen on a chart or showing by deflection of a meter how something (pressure, flow, temperature, or what have you) varies with time. Even there, though, there's nothing really standard; a customer may want one pen or two; he may want a scale calibrated in ten units or a hundred.

"The most varied line is, of course, our line of control systems, or panels. Basically a control system is made up of a device to measure something (pressure, for example), and a device to translate that measurement either electrically or mechanically into a way of controlling something else, in our case usually a valve. Most of the time we mount such a system on a metal panel—which is why we use the term 'panel' or 'control system' interchangeably."

The company's line of special instruments consisted of a variety of devices for measuring, for example, temperature, thickness, or voltage. The instrument selling in largest volume in 1951 was a pyrometer, an electric resistance heat-measuring device developed during World War II.

Prices on company products (not including parts and supplies) var-

Exhibit 3

WILTON OIL EQUIPMENT COMPANY (A)

Sales Breakdowns by Product Lines—Selected Years, 1938–51

(In Thousands)

	1938	1940	1941	1944	1945	1946	1947	1948	1949	1950	11 Months 1951
Valves, flowmeters, pressure gauges, etc.	$ 86.2	$166.1	$254.8	$ 406.9	$324.4	$ 240.9	$ 295.3	$ 295.3	$ 279.0	$ 269.2	$ 450.9
Panels and control systems*	79.6	148.3	172.5	185.8	285.5	433.5	532.1	614.6	537.4	628.5	662.0
Recorders and indicators	63.3	90.1	111.8	90.0	93.2	110.5	130.3	136.6	119.2	97.8	125.2
Special instruments	33.4	29.1	32.4	95.2	69.1	65.7	102.8	108.7	81.2	108.3	142.6
Electronic equipment†	.....	.....	.....	.....	.....	.....	3.9	45.3	118.5	144.9	214.0
Parts, charts, and repairs	71.1	98.5	118.0	179.9	177.6	173.9	223.9	243.7	263.4	278.4	390.5
Installation	3.7	3.8	7.0	10.7	8.2	16.1	19.9	17.4	23.1	23.0	14.9
Jobbing‡	31.1	58.4	76.7	47.8	13.5	0.4	.....	.....	.....	.....	.....
Special equipment§	8.0	23.5	17.9	16.5	27.2	265.5	476.8	571.9	477.2	537.5	288.0
Total	$376.4	$617.8	$791.1	$1,032.8	$998.7	$1,306.5	$1,785.0	$2,033.5	$1,899.0	$2,087.6	$2,288.1

* Includes other equipment (e.g., valves, recorders, etc.) sold as part of complete systems, except for electronic equipment and special equipment purchased from other suppliers.
† Includes electronic equipment sold as part of panels and control systems.
‡ Includes war sales to government and prime contractors of parts and equipment not normally made by Wilton.
§ Includes major items (meters, instruments, etc.) purchased from other manufacturers for resale by Wilton.

Source: Compiled by case writer from Mr. David Ellsworth's book of accounts. "Sales," as defined in the company's accounts were "orders shipped."

ied from $15 for its cheapest valve upward to about $5,000 for a control system. The company in 1951 had sold one order to a major oil company for $150,000, but company officials indicated that none of its previous orders had been for as much as 50% of that amount.

COMPETITION

Wilton in 1952 was competing with a large number of companies. Approximately 550 companies were listed in *Thomas' Register of American Manufacturers* as manufacturers of valves and associated equipment, about 25% of which were listed as having over $1 million invested capital. Many of these companies specialized in valves for particular uses, such as air valves, high-pressure valves, corrosive-liquid valves, or plumbing and heating valves. Approximately the same number of companies made various types of electrical and electronic control equipment; these companies ranged in size from General Electric Company and Westinghouse to small one-man companies. According to one estimate,[1] sales of electronic control equipment and allied devices grew from about $15 million a year immediately before the war to ten times that amount in the years just after the war. Most of the larger companies were engaged only in part in the instrument field, while small companies typically made a very few specialized products. Companies which specialized primarily in instruments and offered a variety of such products included Brown Instrument Division of Minneapolis-Honeywell, the Foxboro Company, Taylor Instrument Company, and Leeds and Northrup. In addition, several dozen companies specialized in the sale of combustion control equipment for utility and industrial-power plants, including such organizations as the Bailey Meter Company (subsidiary of Babcock and Wilcox) and the Republic Flow Meter Company.

"Our competitive problem," Bill Ellsworth said, "is easy to see but hard to deal with. Basically we're a job-shop operation, competing, on the one hand, with small, low-cost, mass producers, particularly in the valve industry, who can underprice us every time and, on the other, with the 'giants' whose reputations, engineering skill, and product lines we can't match. Tied in with that, of course, is the fact that we sell through manufacturers' agents, who are a good outlet in the valve business but, with a few notable exceptions in our case, a very poor way to sell the rest of our products."

---

[1] "Present and Potential Applications of Electronic Devices in Industry," Research Department, McGraw-Hill Pub. Co., Inc., 1944.

ORGANIZATION

"One of the first things that will strike you about this company," Bill Ellsworth said, "is that we don't have an organization chart—and I wouldn't know how to draw one. Several of our people have proposed various charts to Dad, but he hasn't done anything about any of them. I'm not a slavish believer in their importance, but I wonder if we shouldn't spell out a little tighter formal organization.

"Dad is, of course, president. Fred Schmidt, who really helped Dad build up this company, is works manager, secretary, and treasurer. We have three vice-presidents: Steve Willman in sales administration; Joe Tilton in sales engineering; and myself as advertising manager. Fred, I suppose, would be shown on a chart as reporting directly to Dad, with the rest of us reporting to him.

"Our chief engineer, Phil Benton, is, in fact, responsible to everyone and no one, but actually the man who knows most about a number of phases of our engineering is Lew Jackson, head electrical engineer. We also have a chief project engineer, Jim Dill, who in theory reports to Steve but works more closely with Joe.

"We had an assistant treasurer who just left the company because we wouldn't match a better offer he had elsewhere. Since he left, the chief accountant had taken over his day-to-day responsibilities, and with Fred's blessing, Ray Marre, the accountant, is beginning to bring most of his problems to me.

"All the people I've mentioned are part of management, at least in the sense that they sit in on our weekly 'operating meeting' if they're here. Joe Tilton is usually out of town, and of late Dad hasn't been coming even when he is around. In addition, Al Danton, our production-control manager; Jack Schmidt, Fred's son and assistant; and Don Wolfe, our chief draftsman, sit in on that group. Al, incidentally, is leaving next month, although I'm the only one who knows it so far. What to do about Jack is another big problem; more about that later. Don sits in on the group because his responsibilities and his position in the organization are much more important than you might normally except of a chief draftsman."

The Wilton company in 1952 had a total of 169 employees, all of whom were employed in the Wilton plant (see Exhibit 4).

Mr. David Ellsworth had come with the company in 1921, five years after obtaining his bachelor's degree in mechanical engineering from

Exhibit 4

WILTON OIL EQUIPMENT COMPANY (A)

*Selected Data on the Company's 169 Officers and Employees**

Name	Title	Age	Formal Education	Years in Present Position	Years with Company
David Ellsworth....	*President*	57	B.S., Mechanical Engineering	28	30
Miss A.....	Secretary to President	49		25	25
Fred Schmidt......	*Works Manager, Secretary and Treasurer*	61	High School, Business College (1 yr.)	28	28
Jack Schmidt..	*Assistant to Works Manager*	29	B.S., Electrical Engineering	2	2
Al Danton....	*Production Control Manager*	36	High School, Night School (4 yrs.)	7	7
	Shop Employees (113)*				
Ray Marre........	*Chief Accountant*	26	High School, Night School (4 yrs.)	1 mo.	7
Mrs. B.....	Cashier	41		10	15
Mr. C.....	Bookkeeper	31		3	3
Mr. D.....	Credit Manager	30		1 mo.	3
	Clerks (6)				
Steve Willman....	*Vice-President (Sales Admin.)*	52	High School, Business College (1 yr.)	6	29
	Sales and Order Clerks (4) File Clerk Dictaphone Operators (2) Purchasing Clerk Receptionist-Telephone Operator				
Jim Dill......	*Chief Project Engineer*	42	B.S., Electrical Engineering	1	13
Mr. E.....	Sales Promotion Engineer	41	B.S., Electrical Engineering	1	14
	Project Engineers (5)				
Joe Tilton........	*Vice-President (Sales Engineering)*	52	High School, Elec. Eng. deg. I.C.S.	6	15
Bill Ellsworth.....	*Vice-President (Advertising)*	29	B.A., M.B.A. in Bus. Adm.	2	2
Miss F......	Secretary	22			
Mr. G.....	Photographer	21			
Phil Benton........	*Chief Engineer*	54	B.S., Mechanical Engineering	21	29
Lew Jackson...	*Head Electrical Engineer*	42	B.S., Electrical Engineering	4	16
	Engineering Employees (10)*				
Don Wolfe....	*Chief Draftsman*	39	3 yrs. college	18	20
	Draftsmen (7)				

* See Exhibit 7 for data on shop employees and Exhibit 8 for data on engineering employees.

Stevens Institute of Technology. Following three years with the A.E.F. in France and two years as a sales engineer with a large manufacturer of industrial machinery, he was hired as an assistant to the former president and owner of the Wilton company. When in 1923 that individual was forced to retire because of ill health, he sold the company to Mr. Ellsworth for $1,000 cash and Mr. Ellsworth's note for an additional $4,000. Shortly after purchasing the company, Mr. Ellsworth invited Mr. Fred Schmidt to take over supervision of the company's production activities. Mr. Schmidt at that time also purchased one-fifth of the company's common stock for $1,250. (This cash the company used to clear up a number of overdue accounts with its suppliers.)

Both Mr. Ellsworth and Mr. Schmidt described their working arrangement during the growth of the company as one in which Mr. Ellsworth devoted himself to working on the problems of selling and to establishing outlets, to envisioning new products that the company might make, and to interesting himself in design and production in a very general way. Mr. Schmidt, on the other hand, took the entire responsibility for deciding how products should be made, for determining costs, and for supervising most of the company's office routines and paper work. Mr. Ellsworth said in 1952 that he had always preferred to operate by coming up with ideas, by inspiring rather than closely directing his people, and by concerning himself as little as possible with the details of organization and operations. Bill described his father as a man who was "generous to a fault," who was "loved" by everyone who knew him, in and out of the company, and who disliked ever having to be harsh with people, but who could be "very rough" if he felt the occasion demanded it.

Mr. Schmidt was reared in Minnesota, and until joining the Army in 1917 had worked on his uncle's farm. After World War I he completed a year's course in business and, after another year as a bookkeeper for a New York manufacturer, went to work for a metal and machine shop in Wilton, where in five years he became the works manager. Bill said that Mr. Schmidt's capacity to solve almost any problem involving metal or machine work was legendary in the company. During World War II, for example, faced with difficulties in obtaining various sizes of copper tubing, Mr. Schmidt taught his employees how to use special dies to increase or reduce the diameter of the tubing the company had in stock.

Mr. Willman and Mr. Tilton were, according to Bill, considered by the organization to have equal responsibility in its management and were regarded as copartners in handling the company's sales operations. Mr. Willman started as the company's bookkeeper in 1923, following a year's training in a business school which he attended after graduation from high school. In the late twenties he became office manager, and shortly before World War II he was made responsible for keeping the company's sales records and handling home office contacts with distributors on day-to-day sales problems. He and Mr. Tilton were both given the newly created title of vice-president in 1945.

Mr. Tilton was hired in 1937 as a sales engineer and, after completing a correspondence course in electrical engineering in 1941, was assigned to the job of keeping in touch with company distributors and calling on customers and prospects with a view to the development of new uses for the company's products. In 1952 he continued in much the same capacity and spent most of his time traveling.

Bill described Mr. Willman and Mr. Tilton as an effective working team, whose loyalty to the company and willingness to work hard in its interest were exceptional. But he commented further: "Neither of them thus far has ever really seemed to want to grab the ball and run with it, however, and in their positions I wonder if I would either. Sometimes I wonder why they stay. Although they both are well paid—and get the same pay—I know they would like to have a chance to buy some of our stock and share in the company ownership. Dad, however, has not seen fit to offer them the opportunity, and, of course, neither of them has a great deal of money to put up."

Mr. Willman and Mr. Tilton were the only members of the organization who were located in what was referred to as the "front office," where Mr. David Ellsworth was located. Bill said he felt that there was some resentment over the fact that the two were considered to be closer to Mr. Ellsworth—both in their business and private lives—than were other members of "management." This resentment had recently taken the form of allegations to Bill by people in engineering, accounting, and production that "you get taken care of in this organization only if you work in sales."

Various company officials reported that Bill Ellsworth had done an exceptional job of moving into the organization and "establishing himself as a real part of management." Although early in 1952 his job as advertising manager required that the bulk of his time be spent in developing new advertising material and in working with the advertising agency, he was asked for advice on specific current operating problems by Mr. Willman, Mr. Schmidt, and Mr. Marre (the chief accountant). Furthermore, at Mr. Schmidt's suggestion, Bill had taken over responsibility for review of the company's salary schedules and hiring of new employees.

Because his father's health had required that he spend increasing amounts of time away from the plant, Bill in early 1952 also was presiding over the company's regular weekly operating meetings. In January, 1952, Mr. David Ellsworth had left for a four months' rest in California.

Although Bill had started as advertising manager in 1949, in the years when he was in high school and college he had held various summer jobs with the company. During these summers he had been a shop employee, bookkeeper, sales record clerk, assistant to the production-control manager, and assistant to the vice-president in charge of sales engineering. Several of the company officials reported that one of the chief reasons Bill had been able to "take hold" so quickly in the company was that he had had this experience and had handled himself so well in his "apprentice" jobs.

According to a statement by Mr. Schmidt, before it became clear that Bill was interested in ultimately succeeding his father, he (Schmidt) had grave doubts about whether the company offered much long-range promise for his son Jack. But Mr. Schmidt said he believed in 1952 that there was no question of Bill's being able to lead the company successfully.

Mr. Willman was equally enthusiastic in his praise of Bill; he said that the organization as a whole thought Bill had a rare capacity for coming up with new ideas, and at the same time for making full use of the ideas of those with whom he worked.

SALES

All the Wilton company's sales were made through 30 manufacturers' agents, located in principal cities throughout the United States. Twenty-two of these agents had represented the company for over 15 years; for the most part these were the agents doing the largest volume of Wilton business in 1952. The remaining agents had represented the company for varying periods of time; in the eight cities where these agents were located the company had changed representatives on the average of once every 5 years.

The company's agents all represented other manufacturers of non-competing complementary products, including a few valve manufacturers who specialized in types of valves not normally sold by Wilton. The six largest agents handled about the same types of products: engines, pumps, boilers, water-softening equipment, meters for measuring gas and liquid flow, gaskets, tubing, and the like. The product lines of the other agents followed various patterns: a few sold refinery-supply equipment; some specialized in boiler-plant equipment; several sold plumbing and heating supplies; and several sold a variety of steel products used in plant construction. Exhibit 5 gives selected data on the distributors.

Before 1950 the representatives were paid a 25% commission on all company products except parts and supplies, and 20% on the latter. When in August, 1950, the company announced an increase of approximately 20% on all its prices, it simultaneously decreased its commission rates on parts 5%. "Our commissions are still too high," Mr. Willman indicated, "and we believe they should probably be another 5% lower;

Exhibit 5

WILTON OIL EQUIPMENT COMPANY (A)

Selected Data on Company's Agents*

AGENT	SIZE OF CITY IN WHICH LOCATED†	SECTION OF the U.S. IN WHICH LOCATED	NUMBER OF COM- PANIES REPRE- SENTED	NUM- BER OF SALES- MEN	1947–51 TOTAL SALES		1951 SALES		
					Rank- ing of Agent	Per Cent of Total Wilton Sales	Rank- ing of Agent	Per Cent of Total Wilton Sales	Sales as Per Cent of Quota
A.........	Major	Middle Atlantic	11	15	1	15.3	1	15.4	126
B.........	Major	Midwestern	11	10	2	11.5	2	13.3	155
C.........	Major	Midwestern	8	9	3	8.2	3	9.1	130
D.........	Major	Midwestern	20	8	4	6.2	4	7.1	156
E.........	Major	Middle Atlantic	12	5	5	6.1	5	6.7	149
F.........	Large	Middle Atlantic	6	3	6	5.3	6	5.7	114
G.........	Medium	Midwestern	21	4	7	4.4	10	3.5	149
H.........	Large	Midwestern	11	5	8	4.3	9	3.7	111
I.........	Medium	Middle Atlantic	8	4	9	4.2	8	4.0	144
J.........	Large	Midwestern	6	2	10	3.8	7	4.4	149
K.........	Major	New England	14	12	11	3.8	13	2.5	79
L.........	Small	Southeastern	11	4	12	2.9	16	1.5	63
M.......	Major	Far Western	15	7	13	2.9	14	2.4	90
N.........	Large	Southeastern	13	3	14	2.5	11	2.7	97
O.........	Medium	Southeastern	15	3	15	2.2	18	1.4	68
P.........	Medium	Southeastern	12	4	16	2.2	15	1.9	82
Q.........	Large	Midwestern	9	1	17	1.8	17	1.5	136
R.........	Medium	Rocky Mountain	13	5	18	1.6	21	1.2	62
S.........	Medium	Southwestern	12	4	19	1.5	12	2.6	259
T.........	Medium	Far Western	6	6	20	1.5	27	0.5	53
U.........	Small	Southeastern	19	1	21	1.2	23	1.2	82
V.........	Small	Southwestern	15	5	22	1.2	22	1.2	134
W.......	Small	Midwestern	7	4	23	1.1	19	1.4	170
X.......	Medium	Southeastern	9	2	24	1.0	20	1.3	120
Y.........	Large	Midwestern	14	4	25	1.0	25	0.8	69
Z.........	Large	Southeastern	12	3	26	0.7	26	0.6	88
AA.......	Small	Southeastern	10	3	27	0.7	28	0.5	107
BB.......	Small	Southeastern	11	3	28	0.4	24	0.8	266
CC......	Small	Rocky Mountain	8	2	29	0.3	30	0.2	60
DD.......	Small	Southwestern	14	3	30	0.2	29	0.3	93
Totals			191‡	144		100.0%		100.0%	104%§

* All company *sales* department records based on reports of orders received by the company. Company *account-ing* records based on reports of orders shipped. Shipments were typically made from one to six months after receipt of orders.

† Size of cities per 1950 population as follows: Major: over 1 million; Large: 500,000–1,000,000; Medium: 250,000–500,000; Small: 100,000–250,000.

‡ Not a column total. Where a company is represented by two or more agents, it is counted only once.

§ Not a column total. Based on comparison of total company sales with total agents' quotas.

Source: Prepared by the case writer on basis of information available from Mr. Willman's records.

but management is reluctant to jeopardize our relations with our repre- sentatives by lowering them further, at least at present."

All the expense of Wilton's advertising and sales promotion literature was borne by the company. The company also billed all customers di- rectly, and did all the drafting and engineering work required in con- nection with any of its sales. Each representative was expected to main- tain a crew of installation and servicemen to handle all installation and repair work. In many cases, however, the company's own engineers went out from Wilton on major installation and repair jobs; in such cases the company billed the customer at a flat rate of $5 an hour for each man's time. The company's cost records had never been accumulated in such a way as to indicate whether the company made or lost money on its service operations. Bill Ellsworth indicated that one of his minor worries was whether or not the company's service and repair policies were adequate or even clear.

Although the division of responsibilities and "chain of command" in the company's internal sales organization had never been formally defined, both Mr. Willman and Mr. Tilton expressed the belief that there was no need for such definition, because, as Mr. Willman put it, "We're a small company, we know each other and get along well, and everyone does a little bit of everything." Mr. Tilton spent most of his time working with the company's representatives or seeing potential customers. Mr. Willman did very little traveling; he was responsible for all correspondence with customers and agents, maintaining the company's price list, handling and maintaining all sales records, and establishing sales quotas.

The company attempted to maintain its selling prices at "two-and-a-half times the cost at the shipping room door" (i.e., two-and-a-half times the "cost of goods sold") but in practice cut its prices below this figure whenever necessary to meet competition. The company's agents were authorized on "standard" items to quote a figure as much as 10% below list whenever they deemed it desirable; half this discount was charged against the company, and half against the agent.

Both Mr. Willman and Bill Ellsworth expressed dissatisfaction with the company's pricing policy. "Part of our problem" Mr. Willman said, "is that we don't have good enough cost figures to be sure just what our prices should be. Part of the problem is that the responsibility for pricing isn't—and can't be—assigned to just one person. If a customer or an agent wants a quote on a special job in a hurry, whoever is free at the time gets it for him, whether it's Dave Ellsworth, Joe Tilton, Jim Dill, or myself."

Mr. Willman maintained a large notebook in which he accumulated data monthly, on sales by product lines, sales by distributor, selling costs in dollars and as a percentage of sales, and a company sales index on valve sales which it furnished weekly to a trade association in return for an "industry index." Under a similar reciprocal arrangement the company furnished percentage data on its various monthly selling costs (commissions, advertising, sales promotion, and sales administrative overhead) to an instrument company trade association, and these data Wilton also could compare with the experience of other companies.

"Neither the weekly index nor the monthly sales percentages tell us too much," Mr. Willman said, "except as they show long-range trends. We're on the high side on our selling costs, and although our index on valves over the years hasn't shown us to be too far out of line with the industry generally, our index was relatively low compared with the industry in 1951."

Mr. Willman said he was concerned over the fact that he knew of no way to make a sales quota very effective. "Time after time, our good boys top their quotas, and the smaller agents are as low as 60% of quota. As a company, we typically hit it on the nose." Quotas were set annually by Mr. Willman to show the total dollar volume the company expected from each distributor for the coming year, and the annual quotas were divided by 12 to provide monthly quotas. Mr. Willman said he established the quota figures largely on the basis of agents' previous performances and his own estimate of "business conditions." The company had in 1948 hired a marketing consultant to study its quota system; the consultant had recommended the establishment of quotas based on area statistics of national income, business population, oil and chemical construction, and bank clearances. Mr. Willman had tried using such quotas for a year but did not feel that the figures finally arrived at were sufficiently different to be worth the effort or expense of preparing them.

Mr. Willman also reviewed each month's orders "to get a feel of how the business is going." He stated the belief that it might be helpful to analyze such orders in terms of order size, type of customer, sales by industry, and the like, but indicated he did not have the time or manpower to do so. "I can give management any kind of figures they want, but this organization is not 'figure conscious' so I've never done much with my records."

Mr. Willman had indicated to Bill Ellsworth his feeling that the company's most critical sales requirement was the determination of company objectives by management, and added that he felt the need for a willingness not to be bound by tradition in trying to grow. "We, for example, can try to become a manufacturer who sells a standard line of products to all kinds of industries—which is, I think, the 'production viewpoint' expressed by Fred Schmidt. That would require a gradual change in our selling. I think our future lies in doing better what we have done for years: specializing in the needs of a few industries, making what our customers want, and recognizing ourselves for what we are—a specialty-product, engineering-service type of organization. That of course might well mean a continual change in our products—and perhaps a new look at what we're making to see if we're making the right product line."

Bill expressed similar concern with the company's lack of over-all objectives, but more uncertainty as to what the objectives should be or how they should be defined. "I think perhaps our biggest problem in sales," he said, "is that we're being managed by our distributors instead of our managing ourselves and them. I think we should give serious consideration to setting up our own New York office as a first step in trying to decide where we want to go. That territory is nearby and has always been one of our richest markets. There are many arguments for moving in that general direction: one of them is that as it stands now we're tied to the markets reached by the distributor. Another is that the decisions to buy our stuff are typically made by engineers, and they would much rather deal with a sales engineer from the factory than an agent who represents six or eight companies and is much less of a specialized sales engineer. Most of our competitors, at least outside the valve field, have their own sales offices.

"When we had the marketing consultants in here after the war to study this problem, their recommendation in effect was: 'If you were starting from scratch, you certainly wouldn't try to set yourselves up the way you are. With what you've got, however, you should be extremely cautious in changing.'

"The trouble is that this problem is loaded with intangibles. There's no question that people like Nick Harriman in St. Louis, Al Sullivan in Chicago, and Fred Maybank in New York have had a lot to do with building up this business. Add to that the fact that Dad views his friendships with these people as an extremely important thing personally— and that he's the kind of person he is—and you begin to understand why we're so cautious about upsetting them.

"They, in effect, however, dictate our product and price policy. If they can sell something, we make it, even though maybe it's not really profitable over the long run.

"I see a need for our taking a good look at ourselves in terms of the markets we're after—and perhaps doing some market research. The organization as a whole, however, doesn't seem ready for that, and until I'm more in the driver's seat I don't think I could sell Dad on the need for such research. I have managed to sell the organization on the need for establishing a sales training program for our agents; the only problem is that they're now looking to me to take it over, and I'm not sure I should get involved in that."

ADVERTISING

Bill Ellsworth estimated that he was spending about 75% of his time in handling the company's advertising activities, although Mr. Willman and Mr. Schmidt were urging that he hire a successor in that post and had sold that idea to Mr. David Ellsworth. Both Mr. Willman and Mr. Schmidt indicated their belief that the company's advertising program had been better handled than it had ever been before. Bill had hired a new agency shortly after taking over the job and had, on the basis of several months' study, made several changes in the magazines in which the company advertised. He had changed over from advertisements with a primarily "institutional" approach to "specific-application" advertisements, which stressed the advantages and savings particular customers had found in using Wilton products. According to Bill, inquiries resulting from advertising had doubled between 1948 and 1950.

PRODUCTION

All Wilton's production operations were carried on in the company-owned plant (see Exhibit 6), which had been expanded by the addition of a partial third story and of several wings from the original floor space of 15,000 feet to about three times that amount. The "shop" was divided into about a dozen departments, each headed by a foreman. According to Mr. Schmidt, the only "real foreman" was the one heading the machine shop; he spent most of his time planning and supervising his shop's activities, whereas the other foremen were "working foremen," who were expected to spend the bulk of their time performing actual manufacturing operations.

In the foundry the company made most of its valve castings and a few miscellaneous parts for other products. The machine shop was equipped with approximately 25 lathes, presses, and other machine tools; this department handled the manufacture of all the company's tools and dies as well as the various machining operations necessary for the manufacture of company products. The welding and sheet-metal shop was located in a separate wing with the panel-assembly area; the former department was primarily concerned with welding large panel structures and fabricating chassis for electronic equipment and a number of small sheet-metal products for all departments. The panel-assembly group included assemblers and electricians, who were responsible for putting together and wiring panel equipment sold to customers as units.

Exhibit 6

WILTON OIL EQUIPMENT COMPANY (A)

Sketch of Company Plant Showing Department Locations

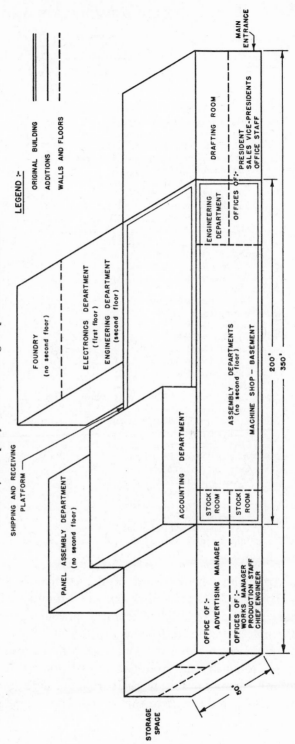

Exhibit 7

WILTON OIL EQUIPMENT COMPANY (A)

List of Shop Personnel

	Number of Employees
Works Manager (*Fred Schmidt*)...............................1	
Assistant Works Manager (*Jack Schmidt*).....................1	
Janitors and Maintenance Men...........................	5
Production-Control Manager (*Al Danton*)....................1	
Production Clerks.......................................	3
Cost Accountant...1	
Cost Clerks..	3
Foundry Foreman..1	
Foundry Workers.......................................	7
Machine-Shop Foreman..................................1	
Machinists...	25
Sheet-Metal Foreman....................................1	
Sheet-Metal Workers....................................	6
Welding Foreman.......................................1	
Welders..	3
General Painting Foreman...............................1	
Plating-Room Foreman..................................1	
Buffer and Polisher.....................................1	
Tool-Room Clerks......................................	2
Stock-Room Manager...................................1	
Stock and Inventory Clerks.............................	5
Ink-Room Foreman.....................................1	
Glass-Room Foreman....................................1	
Valve, Gauge, and Flowmeter Foreman....................1	
Assemblers...	6
Recorder and Indicator Foreman..........................1	
Assemblers...	5
Special-Instruments Foreman............................1	
Assemblers and Electricians.............................	5
Controller-Components Foreman..........................1	
Assemblers and Electricians.............................	4
Electronics Foreman....................................1	
Assemblers and Electricians.............................	7
Panel-Assembly Foreman................................1	
Assemblers and Electricians.............................	3
Shipping and Receiving Clerks...........................	4
	113

Approximately one-third of the company's productive employees worked in a large assembly room, divided into four departments for the final assembly of valves, recorders, pressure gauges, controllers, sub-assemblies, and miscellaneous instruments. Each of these four departments consisted of one or more work benches or assembly areas, including a "foreman" and from two to five workers. It was not uncommon for Mr. Schmidt to shift workers from one department to another as the work loads in the departments varied. The company's electronic department, located in a separate area, made all products and subassemblies involving the use of vacuum tubes.

The company's production operation also included a painting department, a plating department, a glass blower, an ink room, a stock room, and a receiving and shipping area, each headed by a "working foreman."

Typical production runs in the shop were small. On orders for finished products, a lot of 100 was considered large, and lots of 1 or 2 were not unusual. Similar lot sizes in production were common for the many small parts made for stock. The production-control manager estimated that the company maintained an inventory of upwards of 60,000 such parts and subassemblies. All production, except for parts, was for particular customer orders. The time between receipt of an order and shipment varied from one to six months.

All production records were maintained by the production-control manager, with the assistance of three clerks, and by the shop cost accountant, who had three cost clerks working with him. A log of all entered orders was kept by the production-control manager, who also was responsible for the job tickets and production schedules made up on all production runs. During a "typical" month in 1951, approximately 1,000 orders were processed for finished goods, and roughly five times that number of shop orders for parts and subassemblies. From time to time the production-control manager reviewed the maximum-minimum parts stock levels which the stock clerks kept, and made up purchase requests, which he forwarded to an order clerk. Mr. Danton followed up such requests to the extent of checking when material was not received on time. Whenever it became necessary to check with a supplier on why deliveries were not being received, Mr. Schmidt usually telephoned—or even occasionally went to see that supplier.

The company cost accountant maintained a card file showing labor, material, and overhead costs on every run of every part or product made by the shop. A standard shop overhead rate was established every six months by Mr. Schmidt and charged to a given job on the basis of the direct-labor hours involved. The cost accountant indicated his concern over the fact that because of extremely wide variations in the time taken in making a given product, he would very often "cost" a particular product at one rate one week and double or triple—or half—that rate several weeks later.

The accountant also maintained the company's ledger accounts on direct labor, indirect labor, materials purchased, work in process, inventories, manufacturing expense, and cost of goods sold. Once a month he furnished the chief accountant with a summary statement of the month's cost of goods sold. Occasionally he also furnished cost breakdowns in particular jobs to Mr. Schmidt, at the latter's request. "We are kept so busy just keeping our records up to date," he reported, "that we have very little time to furnish any reports to management other than the cost of goods sold. And besides, management doesn't seem to be very interested in such reports. We could, for example, give them a rough idea of the actual costs on every job, but no one has ever asked for such figures."

All the shop employees (including foremen) directly engaged in making or assembling the company's products were paid on an hourly basis; changes in rates of pay were made at the discretion of Mr. Schmidt. In 1950 Mr. David Ellsworth and Mr. Schmidt decided to hire a consulting firm to survey the company's manufacturing activities and recommend whether or not the company should adopt an incentive plan for paying shop employees. The report, according to Bill Ellsworth, was highly critical of the company's shop procedures, cost-accounting system, and organizational setup, and found that the "productivity" of Wilton's production workers was "definitely below average." The consultants had suggested that they be allowed to continue their work and make specific recommendations on a new cost system and an incentive plan, but Mr. Ellsworth stated that he had been insufficiently impressed with their first job to make this suggestion appear desirable. Nothing further was done about an incentive plan until August, 1951, at which time four of the foremen requested that Mr. Schmidt give all shop employees a 10% raise in pay. "Rather than do this," Mr. Schmidt reported, "I decided to establish a bonus system that would accomplish the same result. We now compare 'productivity' each month with that of the average productivity for 1950 and pay everyone a bonus based on performance. During December, for example, everyone got 19% above their base pay. Because our setup is so complicated, and because we have so many new workers, our bonus is actually based on the record of about 30 of our most experienced employees. No one in the shop knows that, however, so the effect is the same as if we did include everybody. Of course, if we ever got a union in here (which I hope I never live to see), that arrangement wouldn't stand up."

Mr. Schmidt said in early 1952 that he recognized the existence of a number of problems in the company's production operations, "many of which are probably caused by me. I know that our setup is too compli-

cated, that I do too much myself, that we ought to have more real foremen, that we probably need better costs, that we should have a purchasing department, and that I need to give Jack more responsibility. But
it's one thing to know those things and another to do something about
them. This shop is a game to me—I'll never retire, because I'd do what
I'm doing even if they didn't pay me, and it's not easy to change the
way you've operated for 30 years.

"I suppose that when Spike brings me a tough tool-making problem
I should let him work it out himself rather than doing as I did yesterday,
for example, spending most of the day helping him build a new die.
That's the way I built this organization, however, and I find it hard to
leave such problems to others. Take our purchasing: We ought to have
a purchasing department, but whom do we put in there? Chris, who
handles the actual ordering, can't write a letter worth a darn. Do we
let him handle it? Do we bring someone in from outside and make him
unhappy? That wouldn't be fair.

"I know we've got to do something about these things—and we will;
what I'm even more worried about are some things I can't do anything
about. Right now, for example, we're extremely short of space: we don't
have enough machine tool capacity; we're pressed for stock-room space;
even our assembly room is getting so crowded the men fall all over
themselves. Should we expand? I'm not too sure; we could turn out
three times the amount of stuff we're now making if our sales people
would sell what we're now making—rather than bringing in new products all the time. We've tied ourselves to a few types of customers, and
now make any damn' thing they want. I think we should turn our thinking around, and sell what we already know how to make, and maybe
take a look and see if we should drop a few things."

In January, 1952, Mr. Al Danton reported to Bill Ellsworth that he
was planning to leave the company and that he thought that Bill should
be the first to hear about it, because "you ought to know what I think
is going on."

According to Mr. Danton, "The Wilton production setup is best described as a 'surrey hitched to a jet engine.' We're in a modern, growing
business with an outdated production shop. When I was made production-control manager six years ago, the understanding was that I'd be
allowed to establish a real production-control system. But that just hasn't
worked out. I establish a production schedule and what happens: Fred
decides he wants some part ahead of the way I scheduled it, and my
schedule just goes by the board. Fred has said for years we don't have

real foremen, and yet every time I make a suggestion along that line he tells me he's read the same books on foremen I have. Right now if I want to establish a schedule on anything, I've got to sell at least six foremen on what I want—which is crazy in a setup like this. Another thing: Fred has no patience with paper work, and if Steve Willman asks him to get out something, he'll give it to shipping to send to a customer without so much as even a packing slip, and I'll spend half a day trying to straighten out our records.

"You've got to hand it to the old boy: If he says, 'jump,' the boys in the shop will jump (some of them have been here as long as he has)— and I've never yet seen him stumped on any kind of tough mechanical problem. But I doubt if he'll ever let anyone else working for him ever do any kind of job."

Mr. Jack Schmidt, son of the works manager, shared an office with his father, and described his job as being a "handy man for my Dad." He had started with the company in 1949 immediately after obtaining his B.S. in mechanical engineering from Rutgers University. In 1952 Jack was responsible for supervision of the company's janitors and maintenance men, as well as for seeing all salesmen who called at the company plant. He was authorized by his father to make purchases from these salesmen in amounts up to $25; decisions on larger purchases he referred to his father. Following the monthly determination of shop bonus rates, Jack also discussed with each foreman the productivity record of his department. "Dad tells me I should lay down the law to the foremen whose departments are behind, but I just can't operate that way, I guess. Mostly I just chat with them and try to find out why they've been ahead or behind. I guess ultimately I'm supposed to take over from Dad, and when I do I'll want to do things differently. I don't believe in being as tough with people as he is. I think I'd like to modernize this plant, too, bringing in new machines. I don't know anything about what it would cost, but I think we'd improve the morale of our people a lot if we had new machines."

Bill Ellsworth expressed his concern over whether or not Jack could ever handle the management of Wilton's production, and said he felt that Jack's position in the company constituted a major problem. "I know that things aren't going the way they should, and if Fred were a younger man, and if I didn't feel a great sense of obligation to him for the part he has played in building up this company, I might think of doing some things differently. In a sense the production problem has two parts: what to do now with Fred still very active, and how to deal with the problem of succession in the production organization.

"Fred is a wonderful guy, but some of the others (Steve Willman, in particular) are finding it increasingly difficult to come to any understanding with him on what to do about our problems. I myself don't have any trouble working with him, except that on such things as plant capacity and costs it's hard to pin him down to concrete statements you can examine on the basis of any evidence. We, for example, have an unwritten rule that we'll never buy anything we can make, and although Fred assures me that pays off, I'd like to see some figures sometime.

"I could live with our production problems if we had someone coming up under Fred, but I don't think we really do. For one thing, Jack has been given virtually no responsibility. For another, I think people in the company resent Jack in a way they don't appear to resent me. Until he appeared on the scene, Phil Benton [chief engineer] always used to take over the shop in Fred's absence, and I don't think the boys in the shop like that change. And Jack just doesn't seem to have the knack of handling people, although I don't think either he himself or Fred is aware that there's a problem there.

"Fred wants us to put Jack on the board of directors next month, and I think I'm going to get Dad to block that. Maybe the answer is to put Jack in Al Danton's job in production control when Al leaves, although I think the shop might really go to pieces then. Another possibility is to put Sid Martin in Al's job; Sid has headed our stock room for five years, is anxious to get ahead, and seems to get along well with Fred. I'd really like to bring in an outsider, but I doubt if he'd last very long, in view of what Al has told me."

ENGINEERING, SERVICE, AND DRAFTING ORGANIZATIONS

By early 1952, as the result of increasing need for engineering and drafting in handling panel orders, Wilton's engineering and drafting organization had expanded to the point where Mr. David Ellsworth had decided to build a new wing on the plant to house all engineering and drafting personnel. Of the company's nine engineers, three were classified as mechanical engineers, one as a metallurgist, and four as electrical or electronics engineers. In addition, the company maintained one engineer whom it classified as a full-time service engineer.

Mr. Phil Benton, a fifty-two-year-old mechanical engineer who had come with the company in 1923, had the dual title of chief engineer and

Exhibit 8

WILTON OIL EQUIPMENT COMPANY (A)

Selected Data on Engineering Department Personnel

Name	Title	Age	Formal Education	Years with Company
Phil Benton........	*Chief Engineer*	54	B.S., Mechanical Engineering	29
Lew Jackson......	Head Electrical Engineer	42	B.S., Electrical Engineering	16
Mr. A........	Electrical Engineer	27	B.S., Electrical Engineering	3
Mr. B........	Electrical Engineer	33	Three years of college	1
Mr. C........	Electronics Engineer	25	B.S., Electrical Engineering	2
Mr. D.......	Mechanical Engineer	35	B.S.,Mechanical Engineering	7
Mr. E........	Mechanical Engineer	29	Two years of college	6
Mr. F........	Metallurgical Engineer	31	B.S., Metallurgical Engineering	5
Mr. G.......	Service Engineer	61	High School	37
Mr. H.......	Machinist	47		12
Mr. I........	Mechanic	35		6
Miss J.......	Secretary	26		5

head mechanical engineer. Mr. Lew Jackson, thirty-nine, was head electrical and control engineer and, in addition, was responsible for supervision of the group of service engineers, headed up by a service supervisor, age sixty-one. According to Bill Ellsworth, Mr. Don Wolfe, chief draftsman, reported to Mr. Benton in theory, but as a matter of practice operated independently. Mr. Jim Dill, chief sales engineer, was considered by Bill to be part of the sales organization, although he and his project engineers worked closely with the engineering group. Mr. Dill's job was described by Bill as being one of liaison between the customer and the engineering organization. Mr. Dill had come to Wilton in 1939 after five years' experience with one of the company's representatives; he was one of five company employees (including Bill Ellsworth) who had ever worked for an agent.

"My chief problem in engineering," Bill said, "boils down to the fact that we have no management control of the organization. Phil is nominally the chief engineer, but has the title largely in recognition of his faithful service to the company over the years and his very real contribution, particularly in the twenties and thirties, to our valve designs. Phil is well liked, has a good mechanical sense, and is very useful in directing the work of our mechanical engineers and in helping Fred on shop mechanical problems. In addition, he's responsible for planning our plant layout or building changes. Lew is a real problem. He's brilliant, and knows it; there probably isn't a man in the country who knows more about the operations of oil refineries and chemical plants, and he can impress our customers as can no one else in the organization—when he wants to. He has had a lot of good ideas for improving our products, and can solve almost any technical problem, at least if it doesn't require too much 'theoretical' background.

"The only problem is that he is also very cordially detested by a number of people, in and out of the company, and has very clearly indicated by his attitude that he will tolerate direction from no one. He and Jim Dill get along all right, and he and Phil get along by keeping out of each other's way. I wouldn't give you two cents for what the rest of the organization thinks of him, and two of our distributors have told him they will throw him out bodily if he ever appears in their territory again.

"Much of our engineering program is directly determined by what he decides he'd like to work on. Very often if a customer has a problem that interests Lew, we take it on; if it doesn't, we don't. If Lew dreams up a new idea, he or one of his people go to work on it—without ever bothering to check with anyone in sales on whether there's a market for it, or to find out from Fred what it would cost to make. I'd have hit this one head-on long ago, but Dad feels we don't dare lose Lew. Last summer, for example, he decided he didn't have the people in electronics he wanted, so he hired a technician with no college training and offered him more money than any of the rest of our engineers are getting. Dad let that stick.

"I have tried to at least find out what's going on by asking him to sit in at lunch every Tuesday with Fred, Steve, Joe, Phil, and myself, and last November I got him to tell us what the engineering group was working on, and we talked about priorities. I was finally able to get down on paper a list of the 30 jobs that the engineers had in the mill as of November, half of which we agreed should have top priority, and 6 of which can be considered fill-in jobs. Of those 30 jobs, 6 involved taking the bugs out of products for which we already have orders. I tried to get Lew to go one step further and set up deadlines, but his response was that it can't be done.

"Maybe I'd feel better if I were sure that our group—including Lew —was really first-rate technically, but even that aspect worries me. One of the major oil companies gave us a contract three years ago to develop a special viscosity-measuring instrument, and according to Steve, it could have turned into something big. Last month, Lew persuaded Dad that the job couldn't be done; I'm not at all sure that Lew didn't just get tired of the project. As a matter of fact, along this same point it's interesting to note that the only fundamentally new thing we've successfully developed since the war, our pyrometer, was the work of an engineer who left last year because he couldn't get along with Lew. That same engineer, incidentally, designed most of our present electronic equipment."

In discussing the company's engineering activities, Mr. Jackson indicated that the pressure of keeping up with the specific requirements of each customer order prevented his group from spending much time on long-range development work. He spent a large amount of his time working with Mr. Dill in reviewing specifications on orders and customer proposals, and in advising the service supervisor on difficult installation and repair problems.

The company's service supervisor was described by Mr. Jackson as operating an "administrative clearing house" for such installation and service work as was done by company engineers. Service and installation work came intermittently and was handled by whichever engineer Mr. Jackson felt could be spared most readily. The service engineer maintained records of all jobs on which the company or its representatives actually installed equipment (as contrasted to providing valves or instruments to be installed by a customer) and handled the correspondence with distributors on service problems. He estimated that the work done by engineers in the field would keep one or possibly two men busy full time, but that it was impossible to schedule the load so that just one man could handle it.

"I don't think we can point with pride to our service setup," Bill Ellsworth said, "although somehow we manage, I think, to keep the customers satisfied. Some day I think we should really go whole hog and either have us do all servicing or require that our agents do it all. The agents, however, have a problem in getting good people, and we're not equipped to help them train their servicemen. Our products are too varied to make it worth our while to put out service manuals, although I think we should begin to think about developing manuals on some of our bigger lines.

"If all our operations were operated as efficiently as Don Wolfe runs our drafting room, we'd have reached the millennium," Bill Ellsworth continued. "Although it may look as though we have a large drafting department for our size of organization, our only problem there is that it isn't big enough. Because of the nature of our operations—or at least so we tell ourselves—we've always had to make a complete set of drawings to go with every job, and every job is different. That takes a lot of man-hours, and with bigger jobs moving in here from time to time, we sometimes get completely bottlenecked on drawings. We've had a standing order in with several employment agencies to hire anyone they send us who can read a blueprint and sharpen a pencil, but any kind of draftsman is as rare as a dodo right now." Of the seven draftsmen employed by the company, two were students as Rutgers University and worked for Wilton approximately 20 hours a week. The company had filed requests for additional draftsmen with three New York personnel agencies and ran monthly advertisements in several New York papers, but had been unable to secure additional drafting help since September, 1951.

A large proportion of the drafting department's time was taken in preparing drawings for large customer orders: these included mechanical drawings, circuit drawings, wiring diagrams, installation drawings, calibration sheets, and systems specifications. The chief draftsman indicated that a single job could easily occupy one draftsman's time for four to eight weeks. In addition the drafting organization made and kept up to date all drawings required by the shop for use in production or required by the engineers in development work.

ACCOUNTING

Mr. Ray Marre, chief accountant, was responsible for maintaining the company's books and supervising the work of the credit manager, cashier, and six clerks and bookkeepers reporting to him. Mr. Marre joined Wilton as a bookkeeper after graduation from high school in 1937, and had been made credit manager in 1946 after returning from a five-year period of service with the air force. When the treasurer left the company in January, 1952, Mr. Marre was made chief accountant. Bill Ellsworth said that Mr. Marre would be given the title of treasurer "if he proves he can do the kind of job we need in that spot." In 1952 Mr. Marre was continuing a night course in accounting at New York University and hoped to have a bachelor's degree by June, 1953.

Mr. Marre said that the company's bookkeeping and accounting records were quite simple in theory, "largely because management has never been interested in much figure detail." He prepared monthly income statements, balance sheets, and breakdowns of manufacturing, administrative, and selling expenses, which were bound in a loose-leaf book containing all such figures for a period three years back. A set of year-end cost figures included in the book for 1949–51 is shown as Exhibit 9; these, together with the income statements (Exhibit 1), balance sheets (Exhibit 2), and product breakdowns (Exhibit 3), were the only figures regularly seen by Mr. David Ellsworth or Bill Ellsworth, al-

Exhibit 9

WILTON OIL EQUIPMENT COMPANY (A)

Expense Breakdowns Contained in Mr. David Ellsworth's Book of Accounts

(In Thousands)

	1949	1950	(11 Mos.) 1951
Administrative Expense:			
Officers' salaries..	$ 45.5	$ 40.3	$ 54.9
Office salaries...	35.9	37.1	38.7
Telephone and telegraph................................	7.9	11.4	7.7
Stationery, supplies, and printing.........................	5.6	3.8	7.8
Postage..	3.3	3.3	3.2
Office expense..	3.8	3.8	3.8
Travel expense..	4.5	5.2	6.6
Entertainment..	1.6	1.1	1.7
Donations..	2.3	2.2	...
Business and trade magazines............................	0.3	0.2	0.4
Association and club memberships........................	3.2	3.2	4.2
Legal, auditing, consulting, and collection expense...........	6.3	9.0	9.0
Bank service charge.....................................	...	...	...
City, state, and county taxes.............................	1.7	2.9	3.1
Federal UCI..	0.3	0.2	0.3
Federal security tax.....................................	0.8	1.2	1.6
Property damage insurance...............................	0.3	0.4	0.3
Life insurance, employee group...........................	1.9	3.4	3.6
Life insurance, officers..................................	0.9	0.8	2.7
Directors' salaries......................................	0.1	0.1	0.1
Depreciation—Furniture and fixtures......................	2.1	2.2	2.2
Automobile..............................	0.7	1.1	0.9
Building................................	0.2	0.2	0.2
Organizational expense..................................	0.1	0.1	...
Total administrative expense..............................	$129.3	$133.2	$153.0
Advertising Expense:			
Salaries..	$ 5.7	$ 10.5	$ 13.2
Direct advertising.......................................	52.5	56.2	51.9
Travel and entertainment................................	0.8	1.9	2.6
Miscellaneous advertising................................	0.4	0.6	0.4
Photography..	...	0.4	0.5
Total advertising..	$ 59.4	$ 69.6	$ 68.6
Selling Expense:			
Salaries..	$ 37.8	$ 37.6	$ 38.8
Travel and entertainment................................	3.2	4.1	4.0
Miscellaneous..	8.4	6.5	6.2
Agents' commissions.....................................	373.2	399.1	433.7
Bad debts..	0.6	5.8	4.4
Packing and shipping wages..............................	10.5	9.5	10.2
Supplies and expense....................................	14.0	10.9	19.9
Royalties..	0.9	1.1	2.5
Drafting-room salaries...................................	2.2	3.2	2.8
Display and demonstration...............................	2.6	...	...
Special sales discounts...................................	...	...	8.5
Total selling expense....................................	$453.4	$477.8	$531.0

Exhibit 9—Continued

	1949	1950	(11 Mos.) 1951
Sales Promotion:			
Salaries..	$ 8.5	$ 10.3	$ 17.7
Travel and entertainment................................	3.0	3.9	5.1
Education and teaching sales representatives.................	...	4.6	...
Total Sales Promotion Expense...........................	$ 11.5	$ 18.8	$ 22.8
Total Selling and Administrative Expense................	$653.6	$700.4	$775.4
Manufacturing Expense:*			
Power and light..	$ 5.5	$ 5.6	$ 5.7
Heat...	2.6	2.9	3.5
Water and sewerage.......................................	1.1	1.0	1.1
Repairs—machinery and equipment.........................	1.8	2.3	2.5
Repairs—buildings.......................................	1.3	1.4	4.4
Truck supplies and expense................................	0.2	0.3	0.5
Freight express and cartage...............................	6.8	7.6	6.9
Property loss and damage insurance........................	2.4	3.1	2.7
No-charge replacements...................................	5.6	4.1	6.1
Indirect labor...	112.1	121.7	149.7
Indirect supplies and expense.............................	23.3	26.7	32.9
Small-tools expense......................................	4.1	5.3	6.5
Printing instruction tags.................................	4.2	4.7	4.9
Returnable containers....................................	0.3	...	...
Shortage and scrap expense................................	11.0	17.5	19.0
Cost and production salaries..............................	30.3	33.8	38.9
Cost and production supplies and expense....................	1.5	3.1	7.4
Paint, plate, and polish material...........................	5.0	4.9	9.5
City, county, and state taxes..............................	2.6	4.0	6.0
Federal UCI tax..	1.0	1.0	1.2
Federal OAB tax...	3.2	5.1	5.9
Drafting-room salaries....................................	20.1	22.3	23.2
Drafting-room supplies and expense.........................	1.3	2.1	1.4
Production engineering salaries............................	6.6	8.1	7.2
Production engineering salaries and expense..................	1.3	0.6	0.7
Miscellaneous engineering salaries.........................	22.3	29.2	19.7
Miscellaneous material and expense........................	18.7	29.1	17.8
Pattern expense..	0.2	0.3	0.1
Depreciation—Buildings...................................	1.8	1.8	1.8
Machinery and equipment.....................	7.1	7.5	7.1
Patterns and tools..........................	2.5	3.2	2.9
Truck.....................................	0.3	0.4	0.3
Patent amortization......................................	0.6	0.5	0.4
Patent Expense..	1.1	2.0	1.0
Total Manufacturing Expense............................	$309.8	$363.2	$398.9

* Includes overhead expenses only. At the request of the case writer, Mr. Marre furnished figures on direct labor expense, as follows:

	1949	1950	(11 Months) 1951
Direct labor....................................	$150.8	$200.1	$204.9

Source: Compiled by case writer from Mr. David Ellsworth's book of accounts.

though Bill had talked with Mr. Marre about obtaining further regular information from the company's accounts. Typically, the "books" of the company were seen only by Mr. David Ellsworth and Mr. Schmidt, although Bill had been permitted to review the company's statements since early 1951.

"I think that with Bill's help I can do a lot to improve our cost system," Mr. Marre said. "Right now we are so busy just trying to keep up with the basic accounts that I don't have time to do anything else, but ultimately I hope to be able to break out a lot of figures which we now have but which are just buried in our records."

COMPANY OWNERSHIP AND FINANCES

Bill Ellsworth expressed some concern with the company's financial position in January, 1952. "I don't think we have any immediate financial problems," he said, "particularly in view of the fact that our banker in New York has told us we can have up to $100,000 on short-term credit any time we want it. What worries me is that we do no financial planning, at least of the sort you reduce to paper. This year, for example, we have a $25,000 payment due on an employee trust fund, and we have to pay 70% of our income tax by July 1 under the new accelerated-payment plan. No one has figured out whether that means we will need to borrow. If we run short of cash later in the year, we'll borrow as we need the money.

"Dad thinks we should retire the preferred stock and perhaps have more capital in the business, and he was planning to borrow $100,000 on a ten-year note until he was advised that present voluntary credit restrictions made that impossible. Now he talks about selling debentures, because of the fact that interest is deductible on our taxes. He's perhaps more 'ownership-control' conscious that I am, and although we've talked about selling more common stock, he doesn't think that's wise."

Ownership of the company's 63,600 $5 par common stock shares was divided between the Ellsworth and Schmidt families on a four-fifths, one-fifth basis, with about 1,686 shares held by outsiders who had purchased shares of this convertible preferred stock in 1946. Mr. and Mrs. David Ellsworth owned one-fourth of the Ellsworth holdings; the remainder was divided equally among their four children. The Schmidt ownership was divided equally between father and son.

Bill Ellsworth had a brother and two married sisters. Both his brothers-in-law were doctors, and he considered it certain that they would never have any interest in the management of the company. His brother, in 1952, was a junior at college and, according to Bill, was developing "an antibusiness attitude," although Bill felt if he ever decided to work with Wilton he would be a valuable addition to the organization.

"One of my problems," Bill said, "is that there is some pressure from my brother and sisters for payment of dividends. They don't know anything about the business but feel that since I'm getting a fairly good salary they are entitled to something too—and of course I want to be fair with them. Dad and I have talked about the possibility of giving the plant to Ann and Louise (in return for their stock) and paying them rent so they'd have an income and we could restrict dividend payments. Then if Hal came into the company, at least everyone would have his share of the pie.

"Before leaving for California, Dad established a trust which gave me the authority to vote all the family's stock. I wasn't in on the arrangements so I don't know all the details."

In 1946 the company had sold privately approximately 2,000 shares of convertible $100 par, 5% preferred stock to about 150 outside stockholders. Mr. David Ellsworth had expressed his desire to retire this stock as quickly as possible. Dividends were paid quarterly on both preferred and common stock; dividends of 10 cents a share had been paid on the common stock in 1951.

According to Bill, the company's board was merely a legal formality, with its annual meetings devoted to ratifying management decisions on such matters as dividend payments, plant expansion, and changes in organizational title. The board consisted of Mr. David Ellsworth, Bill Ellsworth, Mr. Schmidt, the company lawyer, and the former company auditor, who was, in 1952, president of his own manufacturing company. "It's a rather interesting sidelight," Bill said, "to notice that our board's actions are considered so secret that Fred types up board minutes himself rather than trust them to a secretary."

BILL ELLSWORTH'S PLANS FOR THE FUTURE

"As you can see, I'm rather thoroughly dissatisfied with a lot of our operations, but I wouldn't want you to get the impression that I think the situation is hopeless.

"In some ways my own relationship with Dad is one of the most important elements in the situation. He's built this business, and done a wonderful job, and I feel a great sense of obligation to him and a great desire to do nothing which will hurt him. Our problem is that his way of operating and mine are so different. He can be happy living from day to day and doing only the planning that the immediate situation calls for; I feel the need for being more explicit about where we're going and what we're going to do. He operates on 'hunches'; I just don't have those hunches. He can direct and inspire our organization by being very much above and separate from the group (even Fred Schmidt calls him 'Mr. Ellsworth'); I'll need the help of others a great deal more.

"We've never talked about his plans for my taking over, but when he went off to California he told me I was in charge, and that I should feel free to do anything I wanted.

"He's by no means retired; except for the times he's out sick (which have been more frequent of late) he still takes charge of seeing and entertaining important customers when they're in town, and the trips he makes around the country to visit our distributors are still important to him. He still likes to get involved in a lot of little decisions, too. For example, last week Phil, Steve, and Fred and I spent quite a bit of time working out a new office layout for the girls in accounting and had it all set up by the week end. He came in here over the week end and left us a note on Monday suggesting a different way of making our layout. On that one, I just told the boys to leave it the way we had done it.

"I've talked to him a lot about the way I feel about things, and he's perfectly willing to listen to me on anything I have to say. The thing that makes it difficult is that I don't know what he thinks about our situation. I have a hunch he doesn't completely understand the urgency I feel about our problems, but I'm also beginning to feel that the time has come for me to try to start doing some things."

Wilton Oil Equipment Company (B)

FOLLOWING HIS DISCUSSION of the Wilton Oil Equipment Company's operations with a visitor to the company, Mr. Bill Ellsworth, vice-president and advertising manager, suggested that the visitor attend the company's regular Friday morning operating meeting.

"It's impossible to predict just what will come up, since we don't have a secretary or an agenda, but in the light of what I've told you it may be very interesting. This is an informal session and is an opportunity for anyone to bring up anything that's bothering him."

According to Bill Ellsworth, the weekly Friday meeting was an institution started by his father in 1940. "Originally it was designed to bring together people from sales, production, engineering, and finance to discuss their problems with Dad. That meant the group consisted of Dad, Fred Schmidt [works manager, secretary, and treasurer], Steve Willman [vice-president, sales administration], and Phil Benton [chief engineer]. As we've gotten a little bigger, we've kept inviting new people to sit in, until now practically everyone in the company—with the exception of Joe Tilton [vice-president, sales engineering] and Lew Jackson [head electrical engineer]—usually comes (see Exhibit 1). Joe, of course, is usually out of town, and Lew Jackson, although he's never been invited, says he thinks meetings are a terrible waste of time.

"Actually that attitude of his is in part the reason why I've tried to get two other groups of committees going since I've been here—the so-called "engineering council," which meets twice a month, and our Tuesday luncheon group, which has been going on for about three months and at which the company picks up the check. The engineering council represents an attempt on my part to get "Engineering" (and particularly Lew Jackson) to sit down with some of the rest of us and review periodically what we're doing in that area. The Tuesday luncheon group is also partly directed at Lew, although my general idea in setting up that group was to give people a chance to sound off about some longer-run ideas than we have time for in our operating meetings. Typically on Friday morning we deal with things that are 'hot' at the moment: bottlenecks, personnel problems, reports from the field and

661

Exhibit 1

WILTON OIL EQUIPMENT COMPANY (B)

Regular Attendance at Company Meetings

	Friday Meeting	Engineering Council	Tuesday Luncheon
David Ellsworth, President	†	†	†
Fred Schmidt, Works Manager	*	*	*
Jack Schmidt, Assistant to Works Manager	*	*	*
Al Danton, Production-Control Manager	*		
Ray Marre, Chief Accountant	*		
Steve Willman, Vice-President (Sales Administration)	*	*	*
Jim Dill, Chief Project Engineer	*		
Joe Tilton, Vice-President (Sales Engineering)		*	*
Bill Ellsworth, Vice-President (Advertising)	*	*	*
Phil Benton, Chief Engineer	*	*	*
Lew Jackson, Head Electrical Engineer		*	*
Don Wolfe, Chief Draftsman	*		

* Regular attendant.
† Mr. Ellsworth occasionally attended all of the meetings.
Source: Conversations with Bill Ellsworth.

so on. At the Tuesday affairs, I've tried to get the group to start thinking about such questions as, 'Where is the company going?' 'How do we get there?' 'What kind of planning do we need?' I've been surprised at the enthusiasm they've shown for these lunches.

"Dad, of course, is an ex-officio member of all the groups, but for the last several months he's rarely attended, even when he's here. That's meant that I've been running all these meetings since fall."

At the meeting held in Mr. David Ellsworth's office on January 18, 1952, all company officials who regularly attended the meeting (see Exhibit 1) were present except Mr. Wolfe (who arrived late) and Mr. David Ellsworth (who was in his office just before the meeting started but left for New York on a personal errand as the meeting opened). After a few preliminaries incident to introducing the visitor and setting up a company-owned tape recorder to record the meeting, Bill Ellsworth opened the meeting:

BILL ELLSWORTH (vice-president): Well, Ray, what have you got?

RAY MARRE (chief accountant): Well, backlog[1] as of the eleventh was $910,000 and compared with the end-of-the-year total, $872,106, so actually from the end of the year it was up $38,000. Now we had shipments[1] through the eleventh of $49,400. Our total product orders[1]

---

[1] *Backlog:* orders received but not yet shipped.
Unentered backlog: orders not yet released by sales department for production scheduling but recorded by sales department in "unentered backlog register."   *Cont.*

from the beginning of the month to that date were $79,000. So we had good product business so far this month.

FRED SCHMIDT (works manager): Well, that's very encouraging; we need it. Of course the shipments being short the first of the month— that's the usual thing.

RAY MARRE: Of course we were above normal on product orders received, too. You see, we're not halfway through the month yet, and normally if we run $175,000 in products that would be very good.

Exhibit 2

WILTON OIL EQUIPMENT COMPANY (B)

Sales Breakdowns by Product Lines, 1948–51

(In Thousands of Dollars)

	1948	1949	1950	11 Months 1951
Valves, flowmeters, pressure gauges, etc.	$ 295.3	$ 279.0	$ 269.2	$ 450.9
Panels and control systems*	614.6	537.4	628.5	662.0
Recorders and indicators	136.6	119.2	97.8	125.2
Special instruments	108.7	81.2	108.3	142.6
Electronics equipment†	45.3	118.5	144.9	214.0
Parts, charts, and repairs	243.7	263.4	278.4	390.5
Installation	17.4	23.1	23.0	14.9
Special equipment‡	511.9	477.2	537.5	288.0
Total Wilton sales	$2,033.5	$1,899.0	$2,087.6	$2,288.1

* Includes other equipment (e.g., valves, recorders, etc.) sold as part of complete systems, except for electronic equipment and special equipment purchased from other suppliers.
† Includes electronic equipment sold as part of panels and control systems.
‡ Includes major items (meters, instruments, etc.) purchased from other manufacturers for resale by Wilton.
Source: Compiled by case writer from Mr. David Ellsworth's book of accounts. For figures on earlier years, see Exhibit 3, p. 589, Wilton Oil Equipment Company (A).

FRED SCHMIDT: Well, of course, we were hoping that January would bring us up, because—well, one of the things I want to bring up is that it's getting to the point where we're getting in pretty bad shape in certain departments for work. Not enough loose stuff.

BILL ELLSWORTH: Loose stuff?

Entered backlog: orders released to the shop and recorded by production-control department in "entered backlog register."
Holding orders: unentered backlog held by sales department for extended period of time for definite reason (e.g., customer did not want delivery for six months).
Shipments: orders which have left factory. Record of shipments based on invoices sent by shipping department to accounting office.
Product orders: all orders for equipment (i.e., *not* parts of supplies) received during a given period regardless of when scheduled for production or shipment.

FRED SCHMIDT: Loose. Loose. The shop is working on panels.[2] Panels are moving through, but we're not building up enough shipments in the other departments because there isn't enough loose stuff.

PHIL BENTON (chief engineer): We're just not getting that kind of business. That kind of business isn't coming in any more.

RAY MARRE: Well, from the figures here, the unentered[3] total is way up; I mean the entered figure is down again from normal—the entered backlog is $385,000 and the unentered backlog is $525,000, so the bulk of it is unentered business right now. That's why we're not ready for. . . .

FRED SCHMIDT: I'm wondering if that seems to be big jobs. How about it?

JIM DILL (chief project engineer): Well, there are 15,000 Model ATL Control Valves, but they don't want those until the end of 1952, so there's no use of your making those up. They may as well stay in "holding orders" for a while. Of course there are a lot of control jobs that aren't entered, and I assume the main bulk of that business is control jobs.

FRED SCHMIDT: Well, I'm really very concerned because we're going to have to make some decisions here very definitely within the next week or so of what we're going to do. Whether we're going to continue on the hours that we're working at the present time, or—I hate like the dickens to cut the hours down, but unless some loose stuff comes out of the shop, we'll have to have shorter hours. We can't keep going at the pace we're going at the present time on the business that comes out into the shop.

STEVE WILLMAN (vice-president, sales administration): How many hours are you working, now, Fred?

FRED SCHMIDT: We're working 45 hours and every other Saturday. We could cut out that every other Saturday, but I hate to do it because with some of these other factories building up, there's such a shortage of men that we're likely to lose some, and I hate to take that chance. And, of course, it hurts the morale in the shop and everything else all the way down the line. And, of course, our production is way up. We're paying the men 19% this month.[4] That's 2% more than we've ever

---

[2] *Panel:* sheet-steel panel and associated equipment mounted on it. Usually not a control system, but a group or several groups of recording and indicating devices.

Control system: complete system, e.g., for the automatic control of flow. May or may not include one or more panels.

[3] See footnote 1, pp. 618–619.

[4] I.e., 19% bonus. See Wilton Oil Equipment Company (A), p. 604, for explanation of bonus system.

given them before. They're actually earning it. There isn't any question about it. December, which looked bad at the beginning, came way up, and we're going to have an exceptionally good January and even though we have $40,000 during the first 11 days that doesn't mean anything. I was talking to Joe [foreman of the electronics department] a little while ago, and he said, "They're sure pushing the big stuff in on us now," and I know electronics is going good. We ought to make around 25 units this month if everything goes all right. Even a few more, but it should be along that line. The thing that keeps the work up in January are the panels. They amount to something. They are going through in good shape. There are probably 15 or 16.

BILL ELLSWORTH: There is more business then. (*To Danton.*) Well, how are you?

AL DANTON (production-control manager): Well, it's just about what is has been.

FRED SCHMIDT: You see the work is—we haven't enough leeway now. We had eleven panels through in a row. Eleven of them in a row, two of them no wiring, and nine of them union wiring.[5] Nothing to do for our men. One of those jobs we're working on is a real complicated job with a lot of wiring.

JIM DILL: That's a problem you're going to have to live with, Fred. I don't know how you can get away with it.

FRED SCHMIDT: I know.

JIM DILL: I mean that's the way they come in, so that's the way you've got to work on them, so I know we'll have to.

FRED SCHMIDT: Here, let's put it this way. If we had a bigger back-log, more to choose from—I know our backlog is large, but it's large in dollars, not in panels that we're working on. As Ray said a while ago, our panel backlog went down to $375,000. That just isn't enough. If Al had had 30 or 40 of those jobs to choose from, he wouldn't have had to put 9 union jobs in the shop—he just didn't have enough to choose from.

BILL ELLSWORTH: Well, this year I've been keeping the same figures probably that Steve has, on unit sales of all these different products, be-cause we knew we changed our prices. [The dollar figures would be less significant.] And gee, it's just amazing that here our dollars come out ahead, and we're ahead in almost every category, but the unit sales—

---

[5] Many of Wilton's customers required that wiring on their equipment be done by union labor. Because Wilton was not unionized, wiring on such orders was done by two union electricians the company hired on a part-time basis. Customers were charged a 50% premium on "union jobs."

which is really your backlog, I mean it's the character of your backlog—well, valves are up 1951 over 1950, but recorders, panels, controllers, electronic equipment, special instruments are all down over 1950. So that's what's hitting you now, especially in the control systems.

FRED SCHMIDT: Well, Nick [foreman of the valve department] came to me yesterday and said, "Do you think you could arrange to send more ATL's [a type of valve] out here even if we had to work on stuff that isn't needed for the next five or six months?" Well, I didn't say anything. We're not holding up anything. We're sending everything out just as soon as it comes in.

BILL ELLSWORTH: I noticed that these ATL's were the ones that were up most in 1951. Is that that Consolidated Chemical order?

FRED SCHMIDT: Yes.

AL DANTON: Well, Consolidated had a large share of it, but there's still a lot more beside that.

FRED SCHMIDT: The ATL is the one that we need.

BILL ELLSWORTH: The thing that I was disappointed in was that electronics was down.

FRED SCHMIDT: Well, I can't quite figure that. You mean that the number of electronic units is less?

BILL ELLSWORTH: Well, this isn't shipments. This is unit orders received in 1950, and the unit orders received in 1951. I have 125 for 1950 and 103 in 1951—down 22.

AL DANTON: Well, I don't think that could be right, because we turned down a lot of jobs in 1951 that we took in 1952.

BILL ELLSWORTH: Yeh, our business—the number of people that wanted us to make them—is larger. That is, we have more orders than we took.

AL DANTON: Well, the ones we took in 1951 were more or less standard jobs, the ones that we could complete.

FRED SCHMIDT: We haven't got the rates [quantities in a period] that we actually shipped. Maybe—I'm inclined to think. . . .

STEVE WILLMAN: I have it. (*Making notes from a book on his desk.*) Here's something interesting that explains your statement that from the production standpoint you don't have enough units to work with. The last four months of 1950 gave us 99 panels and control systems (regardless of size) against 53 in the same four-month period in 1951—an average of 25 a month in 1950 for the last four months, and an average of 13 a month for the last four months of 1951. So that explains your production problem. The analysis, then, as to what business is being lost that creates this problem, shows it's on the small jobs.

FRED SCHMIDT: Dollarwise, you're probably ahead.

STEVE WILLMAN: Yes, we arc, but that does create an engineering and also a production problem.

FRED SCHMIDT: A serious production problem. I mean it used to be that we had a lot of orders and big backlogs, something to play with.

JIM DILL: What's actually happened is that these jobs are bigger and fewer. They're putting a bigger burden on the paper work and the engineering, and so forth, and less burden on the production. In other words, they're bigger jobs dollarwise, and it takes longer to get them under way, more work on drawings, and all that sort of stuff, and actually it don't take much longer for you to produce them in a plant than it does on the other.

AL DANTON: Well, now we can't pick up any loose ends the way we used to with the small panels. It takes us three or four days now to finish up one panel and there's nothing going through in the meantime. Now in the paint shop three days is all they take on any panel. So about every second panel you've got the whole day in the paint shop which is absolutely wasted.

FRED SCHMIDT: Well, that'll work out. That end will work out as soon as we get our new sandblaster.

JIM DILL: Well, I don't see yet why it's taking you any longer to produce one of those jobs, because you don't have any more equipment on the panel. Of course, you do have a lot more engineering and stuff to be worked out and so forth.

FRED SCHMIDT: Well, now, wait a minute! "You haven't got any more equipment on it." Of course you have! Of course you have more equipment on it.

JIM DILL: Well, I still don't think you yet understand my argument.

FRED SCHMIDT: Well, that's very definitely the case. I wish I had my records up here. They're down in my office. But I'm almost positive the number of meters and controllers[6] is keeping up or even a little ahead of the previous year. But the panels probably dropped off by about 30%. That's my impression. Now I may be wrong.

STEVE WILLMAN: It's more than 30% I believe. At least on the basis of that four-month period, if not for the year.

FRED SCHMIDT: What about the controllers?

---

[6] *Controller:* component part of a control system—a device for starting, stopping, and regulating motors, valves, cams, etc.

STEVE WILLMAN: I'm going to draw that off for the same period now. (*Turning to his record book.*)

JIM DILL: The reasoning behind that is that in previous years we got an awful lot of panels for just one installation.

FRED SCHMIDT: Yeh, but . . . .

JIM DILL: And we had typically four to six operations tied with them. Well now, we get one panel tied in with three or four process operations, so you have 12 or 15 systems on one panel, so naturally your volume of small equipment will hold up, and your number of panels will drop off.

FRED SCHMIDT: Well, that's why I say—we spend more time on the panels than on the—well, surely you don't think that we can make a panel for three process systems at the same time we make one for one process. It's a different thing.

JIM DILL: Well, I don't know how to explain myself. The dollar volume is still there, and you still need work in the shop.

FRED SCHMIDT: Sure.

JIM DILL: Whereas before the dollar volume wasn't there, but you had all the work you needed. I just don't know how to explain.

FRED SCHMIDT: You say the dollar volume is there. It isn't there right now. It's just the last few weeks. Our entered orders have dropped off from how much? $5,000? And when you turn out, say, 15 panel jobs instead of 10 panel jobs, there's more? The fewer jobs we have— we have to wait! We have to wait on engineering, and we have to wait on everybody else! We haven't got enough to do the real planning! That's it. That's what hurts! I don't know what the answer is. We'll have to come up with an answer as to what the sales are going to be so that we can know what we can expect and what's open, and what we can be working on!

JIM DILL: These jobs on control that we're getting now take more of my department's time, and it takes more of engineering's time and of Al's [production-control manager] time than it ever did before, and therefore it takes longer to get it to you than it did before.

FRED SCHMIDT: I know, I realize that.

JIM DILL: And therefore you don't get as many.

FRED SCHMIDT: I know.

JIM DILL: So what you should have is either a lot of loose equipment out there or a lot of full panels. Now the question is, do you want some of these panels? Do we want some of these United Machinery panels? I got one the other day. We've been losing most of them. We can get that business. All we have to do is cut the price a little.

BILL ELLSWORTH: Well, that brings up—I think we talked about it a couple of times before—should we set ourselves up special projects in the panel business? Say we're in the panel business, and we'll build anybody's panels regardless of whether we put anything on them or not.

FRED SCHMIDT: Well, we had that before, and the minute you start taking in panels like that people want them right away, and you have to put it ahead of your regular work and hold up the things you should be delivering. We can put through more panels. There's no question about it.

STEVE WILLMAN: This is rather interesting. We had 376 controllers through that four-month period of September, October, November, and December in 1950, and during the same period in 1951 we had only 301 controllers, which is about 75 controllers short and represents one-fifth by volume; and our prices went up about 20% on controllers, so the dollar sales would balance out, wouldn't they?

FRED SCHMIDT: Well, that may be your four months there, but . . . .

JIM DILL: Those four months in 1950 were the biggest backlog jump we had, on account of Korea.

STEVE WILLMAN: You have to go back over a longer period of time to catch the trend, I think.

FRED SCHMIDT: As I said, I haven't got my figures up here, so we can't go along together because I don't know where we are, but when I check through there, unless I'm very much mistaken, the controllers for the two years are practically on the same basis—practically the same number, within one or two, or very few. Yet the number of panels is way up. I'm sure that there's practically no difference in the number of controllers for the year.

BILL ELLSWORTH: Jim, at one time you were short a lot of engineering data on these jobs. Is that in the picture?

JIM DILL: Well, that's the reason a lot of these big jobs are being held up—because we don't have the data. Some of them they don't want until late in 1952. I'm playing around now with two that are a pretty good size. As a matter of fact on one of them they still haven't gotten the final approval on it yet.

BILL ELLSWORTH: Do you think you'll get it?

JIM DILL: No, because they haven't even sold all their new stock issue yet, and they won't sell all their stock until the end of 1952, and the other job is not too far away from being entered. Those deals take a lot of time. In the office we've been playing with one of them for a year now.

AL DANTON: I think I'd better go down and get my figures. It won't take but a minute. (*Leaving.*)

BILL ELLSWORTH: The thing that's difficult is, even if you have a signal—the flag that goes up that tells you something like this is happening—even if we knew four months ago that this was going to happen, what could you do if you did know that?

FRED SCHMIDT: Nothing much.

BILL ELLSWORTH: What could production do if they knew? You could spread the work over a longer period of time.

FRED SCHMIDT: I think the only thing we could have done then is do what we are going to have to do now—to work fewer hours.

BILL ELLSWORTH: From a sales standpoint, if you can see that you're losing a particular type of business—for example, if four months ago we'd known we needed this type of business, we could have gone out to our selling people and told them to go after this very heavily. The time factor is such that even if they'd started doing it right then, it wouldn't come until six months or a year later, would it? Six months would be early.

STEVE WILLMAN: No, because the markets aren't fluid. It's a very solid thing.

BILL ELLSWORTH: And it takes a long time of decision on a particular job.

STEVE WILLMAN: That's right. You don't go in and break up this market quickly as a new company in the field, or even as an old company which has decided it's going to try and penetrate more deeply a market that one of your competitors now has, because engineers just have a high inertia factor. They aren't subject to change. They don't respond to emotional appeal as much as your commodity market does. You can't change that. It takes a long time. It's a slow, steady process. They just don't respond to these emotional appeals.

FRED SCHMIDT: Steve, you come back from your meetings and tell us that the chemical-process field is going to be terrifically busy for the next five years, and everything is rosy! I got a slip from Joe Tilton [vice-president, sales engineering] the other day, an excerpt from a paper saying that the possibilities in this field were tremendous, and everything is going to get bigger and bigger and bigger, and we'll all have to expand, and damn it all, we're not expanding!

STEVE WILLMAN: Well, now we're caught between two stones as we said before and recognized before. The one stone on top is the competition we're getting from the larger companies who have a better-established engineering reputation and are better equipped to handle the bigger jobs; and the other one is the market, where price is important, particularly on valves, and there we're then pushed out by the low-cost, high-volume producers, who can underprice us every time. We've been under pressure from both ends. We've been squeezed in the middle, and we're going to have to find the answer to that. The figures and everything else prove that.

JIM DILL: So in order to get some more work for the shop why don't we push things like this CDL, the temperature controller, and this CRN, the pump controllers, and now we've got six orders from Vitamin Feeds for this mill controller. That's one that's supposed to develop into a lot of them, you know.

STEVE WILLMAN: Yeah, there's going to be several hundred of those. They are controllers for grinders in the animal-feed industry.

FRED SCHMIDT: There you go with your new products again, making up something new!

JIM DILL: It's not a matter of choice, Fred, that we can worry about. If we're going to lose the sequence business,[7] and some of our other business, it would appear to me that in order to get some more business we've got to push new items.

STEVE WILLMAN: Or with new designs of regular lines. One of them is this controller we mentioned, and we should go into that too, because the boys from New York [New York sales representatives] said they had applications for it.

FRED SCHMIDT: I was talking this morning to Lew [head electrical engineer] on this Vitamin Feeds thing. He was telling me how much he had had up in the engineering department and I said, "Let me have some of that downstairs." Our boys have the time to make some of that stuff. So we're going to bring some of those down. They've been developed now, so we can put them on the production basis.

BILL ELLSWORTH: I understand there were still problems on that mill-control job. When I was down there Maybank [the Kansas City agent] really poured it on me. He said, "Here you are pleading for more loose-equipment business, and I bring you this, and you drag your feet on it." I said that sounds very logical and I came back and talked to Lew [head electrical engineer] and Joe [vice-president, sales engineering]. As I understood it, Lew was a little leary about the number of different problems for each different installation. I know Vitamin Feeds

---

[7] *Sequence business:* orders for equipment to control electrically a sequence of operations (e.g., of a group of machine tools).

has their special engineering in Kansas City to cover all the country, and he was leary of each installation being made specifically and "goofed" around a little: you get into real service problems on it.

JIM DILL: Well, that's what he told me. He claimed in order to set it up right, he'd have to send somebody along to the factory, with each installation, but I understand he has made some modifications so that in time, as we progress with the ones we're making now, it may not be necessary.

BILL ELLSWORTH: Good.

STEVE WILLMAN: You see, there again I think it's a—well, Lew originally didn't want to get into that. That pressure to get into it came from the sales department. It came from Maybank against me personally. Maybank worked the old line-buck game, you know, and over a period of a few years after they tried one of them they finally got Lew into position again where he was put on a spot, and he couldn't say anything but "yes." He really didn't want to because he was so busy with other things. It was a matter of time, but now he's agreed to go along with it. He said there was an order for four a few minutes ago.

JIM DILL: Four and two.

STEVE WILLMAN: How does that work?

JIM DILL: You maintain the speed—the current on the motor constant, the speed on the motor constant, and therefore the speed of the grinder constant.

BILL ELLSWORTH: They really want them. I know they want them. Maybank is hot on them.

FRED SCHMIDT: Well, I haven't talked to them about that, but I think that's one of the items we could bring downstairs. If the changes aren't too great it would fit very nicely into our line.

STEVE WILLMAN: It should be pulled out of Lew's department, I think, because his men are better occupied in the company's interest when they are working on new things in the preliminary stages where they have bugs, and then they come out. Now, I can't see any reason for it to be kept up there in the engineering when it's ready to be manufactured, but that seems to be the tendency we're getting into. (*To Schmidt.*) Now is that a proper statement or isn't it?

FRED SCHMIDT: Maybe that's because we want to have more of what we have rather than boosting our sales by something new all the time.

BILL ELLSWORTH (*smiling*): Maybe you're controlling the rate of new ideas, Fred, by keeping those guys busy upstairs.

JIM DILL: Take that level control. We sold a lot of those. There are no bugs in it, are there, but I don't think that's ever come into the shop, has it?

FRED SCHMIDT: Now that level control was a new type of control, and it still needs a lot of engineering. That's why it's up there.

STEVE WILLMAN: Gee, if we're not getting enough business we better go out and do something.

FRED SCHMIDT: It's the same old story. Are we going to expand by selling the things we have or by making a lot of new things all the time but not dropping the old?

(SCHMIDT, WILLMAN, *and* DILL *all try to talk at once.*)

BILL ELLSWORTH: Now wait a minute here. Fred's contention is to sell more of what we have got. Correct?

FRED SCHMIDT: I can turn out 2,000 portable recorders in the same space as I can turn out 1,000 without taking any more space or needing any more people, but I can't turn out the equivalent in dollars on a new product unless I have an entirely new bench, floor space, stock room, inventories, and everything else. And that's where the rub is, you see. Here is the point. We're simply at the point where we can't stick more things in, new things all the time. It would be wonderful, but it just can't be done. We're reaching a saturation point down there in our manufacturing with this new stuff all the time.

JIM DILL: These level controllers we're talking about are made on the same benches as the stuff we've got out there. The only difference is you might need new drawings or something.

FRED SCHMIDT: It means drawings. It means new tools. It means new work into the stock room. It means new storage space. All the way down the line it's something new, you see. You don't realize it. I'm not really against it, but if we have to keep up our production by building new stuff all the time, why we're just in the wrong kind of business.

STEVE WILLMAN: But Fred, the industry has changed in that direction, which from a production man's standpoint is bad. I say that because the A——— Company was faced with the same thing when they started actively in this industry with sales promotion, with industry sales managers and everything, and then they no longer looked across the country at industries horizontally but they had to start pushing hell out of them vertically, and they developed all manner of special products and modifications for new applications until they set up a special engineering department separate from their standard engineering in order to handle them—the modifications and so forth. I don't think you can get away from that. I think it's something that the industry is cursed with, and it's going to get worse before it gets better.

FRED SCHMIDT: Please don't get me wrong. I'm not against change.

STEVE WILLMAN: Fred, it's something we're going to have to come up with a decision on.

FRED SCHMIDT: Don't get me wrong, I . . . .

PHIL BENTON: The B——— Company followed exactly the same line. They increased their products.

BILL ELLSWORTH: I think that one thing that might help do what Fred wants—and I think you're right too, Steve—I can't help but believe that if there were, say, one guy who spent most of his time doing nothing but figuring out new applications for . . . for flowmeters, for example, valves, recorders, special instruments, and the rest of our products—who did nothing but push, push, push, on one line—that was his only interest—that we might sell a lot more products that we know how to make here, and they would go through the plant without too much difficulty. You'd rather modify a panel, say, like the one that they put in this Highglo Wax plant, Fred, than put out an entirely new system of control, wouldn't you?

FRED SCHMIDT: Sure.

BILL ELLSWORTH: You'd rather make a modification of a product than an entirely new thing.

JIM DILL: Well, that's another thing we've never pushed.

FRED SCHMIDT: The only thing I want to put across is this. I'm not against making new stuff, not at all, but I want you—I want everybody—to realize you're at the point where you cannot go very much farther with new stuff and keep up the old at the same time, because we're limited in space. That's all there is to it. Now if the thing to do is to expand, well, O.K., let's expand, but we have to go into it with open eyes, and I think Bill's idea of—well, you're creating manufacturing problems constantly and I'm going to try to create sales problems making the things we have, and it's just a tossup between the two of us. That's what I'm after. I'm going to try to make you fellows produce more, and sell more in the lines that we have. That's how we make our money. We don't make it if we have to develop something new all the time. Have you ever realized how many dies we have down there?—punch-press dies—we have a measly little punch press. We have two now, but I mean one is in operation, and I think we have 450 or 500 punch-press dies down there! Every time you bring in a new product, that means new dies, and I'm beginning not to know where to put them any more! For such small items, our drill jigs are the same thing! We've got hundreds of them! We have hundreds of thousands of dollars tied up in drills, and in jigs, and in tools and equipment of that kind, and every time you make a little change and bring something new out it's a big investment! We have to get the money to make those things! That's the only thing I'm after! There's no other way out of it! Well, O.K., we'll make something new every day. That's all right, but you want to do it with open eyes. You want to know what we're doing. That's the only thing I want to bring out. That's why I talked with Bill Friday on the new job press. It means a new investment, a big investment, and I don't think it's justified at the present time, a new press for one item. We'll have to get away from this idea. I admit we built this business up on making everything for everybody. I think we'll have to get away from it. We just simply can't continue. Now I'm going to surprise some of you fellows at the next engineering council meeting. I've got something on the electronic recorder we want to talk over. From there I'm going in the other direction now for a very persuasive reason which I won't bring up now because I don't want to waste time, but I don't want to be stubborn about this thing. I just want you to realize what happens every time you come up with something new.

(AL DANTON, *production-control manager, returns to meeting followed by* DON WOLFE, *chief draftsman.*)

JIM DILL: Well, I think we all recognize the problem.

FRED SCHMIDT: If you can change your picture, and you can devise some way that will provide more of what we're making now and produce more orders for what we're doing, then that's what we should be doing.

BILL ELLSWORTH: Tell me, on this mill controller, the volume of which is getting bigger . . . .

FRED SCHMIDT: It's actually falling off.

AL DANTON: That wasn't because of any shortage of orders there or anything, but we just didn't get our potentiometer[8] in from Consolidated Electric last month.

FRED SCHMIDT: Are you short of orders?

AL DANTON: No, we're not short of orders, but we only got two potentiometers from Consolidated last month. I have here the over-all for 1950–1951 that we finished. Now that should go pretty close to

---

[8] A component purchased by Wilton for use in the manufacture of the mill controller.

sales. Now some of these that I got marked finished are finished when they leave the bench. That is, they may be held up for one thing or another after that, but on mill controllers it was definitely not that we couldn't produce from our own, but we didn't get the units in from Consolidated. We got two in right at the end of the month, and then we went out and didn't get any.

FRED SCHMIDT: Now tell me this, how many controllers—have you got the controllers—did we ship last week?

AL DANTON: No, I haven't got the controllers. I haven't figured it up yet. We've shipped more controllers this year. Most of them have gone on panel jobs, but I haven't figured that out yet. But we've certainly shipped more controllers by far than we have any other year.

FRED SCHMIDT: You've got the electronic controllers?

AL DANTON: No, I haven't got any totals on that. The only totals I have are on the instruments. Without going back and adding them up I could get them. I can have them for you in a few minutes if you want to see them.

STEVE WILLMAN: I think that we ought to pull off—if you want to study it over a period of years you should pull off two 5-year blocks.

JIM DILL: Steve, don't your sales records show that? I thought you had a complete record there. I don't know whether they've filled it in for 1951 yet, but . . . .

STEVE WILLMAN: We have all the figures to get anything we want. We could put sales in one column and shipments for that year in the next, and make them parallel, and study that over whatever period of years you want.

BILL ELLSWORTH: Shouldn't we also get—wouldn't it be a good thing if we got a quarterly report on the shipments of particular products and the sales that have been received during the same time, because the sales from that time are going to be the shipments for the following quarter? Correct? And if there is a discrepancy there, there is at least a signal. Again I'm wondering what we can do even if we know it. That's the thing that bothers me.

FRED SCHMIDT: Our backlog is—I'm watching the backlog. On the ATL for example, that hasn't gone bad.

AL DANTON: Our backlog of instruments is lower than it's been in many, many months.

JIM DILL: Are you talking about entered backlog?

AL DANTON: Yeah, that stuff going into the shop.

JIM DILL: Well, as I mentioned, I know we've got 15,000 ATL valves in holding orders.

AL DANTON: But we've only got 190 units out there in the back-log of ATL's now, and we've had 350 to 500 or 600 all last year.

JIM DILL: On the production backlog that is.

AL DANTON: Yeah, production backlog in the plant ready to work on.

BILL ELLSWORTH: Getting back to this mill controller, has that reached a volume where you can set up a department just knocking out those all the time?

FRED SCHMIDT: When we get set up it will fit into the electronic department very nicely, because if they're waiting for meters or some-thing like that they can shuffle off and make the parts on something like that. It only takes one or two men to put one of those through, you know, at least in final assembly in the shop, so it works in very nicely there. Of course, if we got a real volume we could set up a bench for it, but right now, the way it is set up right now it works in very nicely with the electronic equipment.

BILL ELLSWORTH: At this volume?

FRED SCHMIDT: Yes, if we get more.

BILL ELLSWORTH: If you doubled that volume would it be worth setting it up?

FRED SCHMIDT: Well, all you probably would have to do would be to put in one man for it. That would be very easy to control. Of course, if we get into quantity it's going to be a big problem again of storing all the parts.

BILL ELLSWORTH: I wonder if in an analysis of the mill controllers we've sold, there aren't a lot of the same models. I mean you could al-most make a gang of those knowing you'd sell them, couldn't you?

JIM DILL: We can't do that, Bill, because it takes various models depending on the kinds of applications you're going to be involved in.

FRED SCHMIDT: Well, it doesn't make much difference to us when we get them—if we make them today and ship them in three months, or make them today and ship them right away. We have our own parts. We stock them. That's all standard business all the way through—two or three different—that's the beauty of the thing. It's just one unit we make. No different models and so forth like we have in everything else.

BILL ELLSWORTH: Does anybody besides Vitamin Feeds use our mill controller?

JIM DILL: We've probably sold two or three to somebody else, but 95% are Vitamin Feeds.

FRED SCHMIDT: Well, isn't that an opportunity there? Somebody else besides Vitamin must have the same process?

BILL ELLSWORTH: Well, that's what I was thinking of. There's reason to believe that it can be used in the food field, and we're doing a story on that Vitamin installation, and a trade magazine is going to use it. I don't know.

JIM DILL: Well, I've had two or three inquiries in the last couple of months from grain people who had seen our controllers and are writing for information. I haven't seen any orders from that, but I don't think that the field in that type of business knows too much about it yet, because we haven't been too satisfied. We've made several changes. Even in this last one we've put in our own electronic relay which is replacing the Weston relay, and I think there's only been one of that made, so we don't know yet.

BILL ELLSWORTH: The only point is I can see the sales curve of this product going up, and I know that from the production standpoint it isn't a great problem, and it would be a nice thing if we could keep going up on that curve to make up for the other products that are declining.

FRED SCHMIDT: Well, of course, the control on that is over in Joe's department, while all the electronic equipment is in the electronic department.

JIM DILL: In the recent control job we just quoted we're offering that same type in a paper mill.

STEVE WILLMAN: Yeah, I think that's the first time that's been done, Jim, in that particular way.

JIM DILL: Maybe it's another field for us later.

FRED SCHMIDT: From the selling standpoint I don't—I'd just as soon kiss our sequence-control goodbye, because it's been nothing but a headache for Don, and for Jim, and for everybody else.

BILL ELLSWORTH: I'm glad you feel that way, Fred, because I'm afraid you're going to have to anyhow. From a manufacturing point of view we used to get out 13 or 14 a month and now we're getting out 10.

AL DANTON: He's interested in only the unit itself. He's forgetting about the effort required outside of his department to . . . .

FRED SCHMIDT: Well, actually we're not making a penny on it anyhow.

DON WOLFE (*chief draftsman*): What concerns me is that just a few months ago we were talking about the fact that we couldn't ask as much money as we're asking for it, and actually we should have more than we're getting for it now.

FRED SCHMIDT: Well, sure. The thing I can't understand is how competition gets away with what they are doing.

DON WOLFE: Well, it's possible they're not giving the service. That could be.

FRED SCHMIDT: But what the devil, they're selling when we don't.

DON WOLFE: If we could sell them as a unit and let somebody else worry about the installation it would be a swell item, then.

FRED SCHMIDT: Sure that would be. From the manufacturing it's O.K., but . . . .

STEVE WILLMAN: That's what these other people are doing. That's their approach to the problem. They recognize the field problem. They have selling discounts that are passed down to those different distributors. Like C——— for example: they're a fine example at C——— Engineering Service. They buy our unit and mount it in their own terminal box as a separate unit, but house it in that way, especially on the bigger jobs, but even on the smaller jobs, which was our field originally, they buy 1, and they buy 10, 15, at a time and stock them. I was up there and saw them. They do a good job. Now they get a special discount from a low price. Hell, we just can't touch it.

FRED SCHMIDT: There again you run into our method of selling.

STEVE WILLMAN: You cannot sell as we do. That's right. Nor can you manufacture as we do. We don't think in terms of mass production. We are in a specialty field. In our thinking and everything—you can see the way we handle things. Well, here's another trend. Joe, up in Boston, asked to see Fessenden, the head mechanical engineer at W——— and M——— [construction engineers] to show him the pictures of our new R7 flowmeter to get some of that business. This chap said to him, "It's all very interesting. I like the design," but now he says, "What is Wilton doing on miniature instruments?" So there you are. Now you're going to leapfrog ahead of something else and that's going to be completely special. You won't get into that bigger installation field until you get into the miniature.

FRED SCHMIDT: Well, of course, we thought we had the electric-transmission unit, but it isn't as easy as it looked on paper. Lew [head electrical engineer] seems to be running into trouble. It's going to be a long development job like everything else. You can't shake a thing like that out of a hat.

STEVE WILLMAN: No, it's always going to be that way. Take our balanced meter. We've had that now for 15 years, and our competitors know its weaknesses and they're slamming the hell out of it. Competitors slam the hell out of it, so what are you going to do? You've got to change over, so it means electronics. Well, Lew is working on that, and we hope to have that. Look what it does to the production drawings and everything else. It's the heart of most of our control systems.

FRED SCHMIDT: Well, of course, that's like everything else, we have to keep up on our products just like on the AS valve. We had to redesign that. That's something else again. That's progress. That you can't get away from. The only thing I regret about that is the cost.

STEVE WILLMAN: Fred, you had to do that. It was either that or go to a completely new concept.

FRED SCHMIDT: By the way, is anything being done on that new pyrometer catalogue?

BILL ELLSWORTH: The catalogue is coming out in another two weeks.

FRED SCHMIDT: Boy, we've got a beautiful setup on making that now. Even Lew is satisfied. I'd like to get some more things like that.

PHIL BENTON: What's that?

JIM DILL: The new pyrometer.

PHIL BENTON: Lew is satisfied? The miracle has happened.

STEVE WILLMAN: I hope we get as much business as Lew thought was in the bushes, because we've sure knocked that one around for a long time.

BILL ELLSWORTH: You think maybe it's too late now?

STEVE WILLMAN: Well, the G——— Company is becoming entrenched in there now.

FRED SCHMIDT: Every time I think of it I get hot under the collar. If we hadn't listened to our representatives that time and gone ahead with it, we could control the market now. Absolutely, we'd have a beautiful department there now.

BILL ELLSWORTH: Ray, how's your new man working out?

(*Following this question, the group discussed the performance of several members of the office staff, and then Bill Ellsworth adjourned the meeting.*)

As he left the meeting, Bill Ellsworth said: "You've probably witnessed a fairly typical session, although actually we got down to brass tacks a little more than we sometimes do. I come away from meetings like this one with the frustrated feeling that we've raised all the $64 questions and answered none of them."

Consolidated Drugs, Inc.

MR. RICHARD TRUCKS had been transferred to the Syracuse (New York) Division of Consolidated Drugs, Inc., in the first week of May, 1952. At this time he was appointed sales manager of the Syracuse wholesale drug division. Formerly he had been an assistant to the vice-president in charge of sales at the company's headquarters in New York.

At the month-end sales meeting on the last Friday of June, 1952, Mr. Asa Bush, a salesman in one of the division's rural territories, informed Mr. Trucks that he wished to retire at the end of July when he reached his sixty-fifth birthday. Mr. Trucks was surprised by Mr. Bush's announcement because he had been informed by the division manager, Mr. B. D. Burton, that Mr. Bush had requested and received a deferment of retirement until he reached his sixty-sixth birthday in July, 1953. The only explanation offered by Mr. Bush was that he had "changed his mind."

The retirement of Mr. Bush posed a problem for Mr. Trucks, in that he had to decide what to do about a successor to Mr. Bush's territory.

BACKGROUND OF THE SYRACUSE DIVISION

When Mr. Trucks became the divisional sales manager he was twenty-nine years old. He had joined Consolidated (as the firm was known in trade circles) as a sales trainee after his graduation from Stanford University in 1946. During the next two years he worked as a salesman. In the fall of 1948 the sales manager of the company made Mr. Trucks one of his assistants. In this capacity Mr. Trucks helped the sales manager to arrange special sales promotions for the lines of different manufacturers.

Mr. Trucks's predecessor, Mr. John K. Martin, had served as divisional sales manager for 15 years before his death in April. "J. K.," as Mr. Martin had been known, had worked as a salesman for the drug wholesale house that had been merged with Consolidated to become its Syracuse Division. Although Mr. Trucks had made Mr. Martin's acquaintance in the course of business, he had not known Mr. Martin well. The salesmen often expressed their admiration and affection for

681

Mr. Martin to the new sales manager. Several salesmen, in fact, made a point of telling Mr. Trucks that "Old J. K." knew every druggist in twelve counties by his first name. Mr. Martin had died of a heart attack while trout-fishing with the president of the Syracuse Pharmacists' Association. The Syracuse Division manager said that most of the druggists in town attended Mr. Martin's funeral.

The Syracuse Division of Consolidated was one of 25 wholesale drug houses in the United States owned by the firm. Each division acted as a functionally autonomous unit having its own warehouse, sales department, buying department, and accounting department. The divisional manager was responsible for the performance of the unit he managed. There were, however, line functions performed by the regional and national offices that pertained directly to the individual departments. A district sales manager, for instance, was associated with a regional office in Albany for the purpose of implementing marketing policies established by the central office in New York.

As a service wholesaler, the Syracuse Division sold to the retail drug trade a broad line of approximately 18,000 items. The line might well be described as consisting of everything sold through drugstores except fresh food, tobacco products, newspapers, and magazines. In the trading area of Syracuse, Consolidated competed with two other wholesalers; one of these carried substantially the same line of products; the other, a limited line of drug products.

The history of the Syracuse Division had been that of a profitable family-owned wholesale drug house before its merger with Consolidated in 1928. The division had operated profitably since that date with the exception of three years during the 1930's, although it had not shown a profit on sales equal to the average for the other wholesale drug divisions of Consolidated. Since 1945, the annual net sales of the division had risen each year. But since its competitors did not announce their sales figures, it was impossible to ascertain whether this increase in sales represented a change in the competitive situation or merely a general trend of business volume in the Syracuse trading area. Mr. Martin had been of the opinion that the increase had been at the expense of competitors. The district drug sales manager, however, maintained that, since the trend of increase was less than that of other divisions in the northern New York region, the Syracuse Division may have actually lost ground competitively. A new measuring technique for calculating the potential wholesale purchasing power of retail drugstores, which had been adopted shortly before Mr. Trucks's transfer, indicated that the share of the wholesale drug market controlled by the Syracuse Division was below the median and below the mean for Consolidated divisions.

Only a few of the employees working in 1952 for the Syracuse Division had also been employed by the predecessor company. Mr. Martin had been the only person in the executive echelon whose employment in the Syracuse Division antedated the merger. Most of the executives and salesmen currently active in the organization had come into the organization either between 1933 and 1941 or after the end of World War II. Two salesmen, however, Mr. Bush and Mr. John Jameson, had worked for the predecessor company before the merger.

Of those who were employed as executives or salesmen before World War II, only Mr. B. D. Burton, the division manager, had a college degree, which he had earned at a local Y.M.C.A. night school. All the young men employed since 1946 were university or pharmacy-college graduates. None of the younger men had been promoted when vacancies had occurred in the job of operations manager (who was in charge of the warehouse) and of merchandise manager (who supervised buying) in the Syracuse Division; however, two of the younger men had been promoted to similar positions in other divisions when vacancies had occurred.

THE SYRACUSE DIVISION SALES FORCE

From the time that Mr. Trucks took over Mr. Martin's duties he had devoted four days a week to the task of traveling through each sales territory with the salesmen who covered it. He had, however, made no changes in the practices or procedures of the sales force. The first occasion on which Mr. Trucks was required to make a decision of other than routine nature was when Mr. Bush asked to be retired.

When Mr. Trucks took charge of the Syracuse Division sales force, it consisted of nine salesmen and four trainees. Four of the salesmen, James Pepper, Michael Waller, Daniel Carmack, and Paul Smith, had joined the company under the sales training program for college graduates initiated in 1946. Concerning the other five salesmen, who had been with the company many years, Mr. Trucks was given the following information: Asa Bush and John Jameson were senior in terms of service to the others. John Dangler joined the company as a warehouse employee in 1928 when he was nineteen and became a salesman in 1933. Homer Babbidge came to Consolidated as a salesman in 1933 when the wholesale drug firm for which he had previously worked went out of business. In 1952 Mr. Babbidge, who was then forty-eight years old, had been a wholesale drug salesman for 28 years. Russell Means at the age of twenty-six came to Consolidated in 1938 after working as a missionary salesman for a manufacturer. Mr. Means served as an officer in the Army Medical Corps during the war and was discharged as a captain in hospital administration in 1945. He returned to Consolidated immediately after his discharge.

The four trainees had graduated from colleges the preceding June. When Mr. Trucks arrived in Syracuse, these men were in the last phase of their twelve months' training program. The trainees were spending much of their time traveling with the salesmen. Mr. Trucks, who now had the full responsibility for training these men, believed that Mr. Martin had hired four trainees to cover an anticipated turnover both among the salesmen and among the trainees themselves, as well as to implement the New York head office's policy of getting more intensive coverage of each market area. The trainees, he understood, expected to receive territory assignments either in the Syracuse Division or elsewhere on the completion of their training period.

Mr. Trucks had not seen very much of the salesmen. His acquaintance with them had been formed at the sales meetings and in traveling with them through their territories.

Mr. Trucks judged that Homer Babbidge was an easygoing, even-tempered person. He seemed to be very popular with the other salesmen and with his customers. Mr. Babbidge was proud of his two sons, one of whom was in high school and the other married, with a son named after Mr. Babbidge. Mr. Trucks thought that the salesman liked him, because Babbidge had commented to him several times that his suggestions had been very helpful.

Asa Bush had not, in Mr. Trucks's opinion, been particularly friendly. Mr. Trucks had observed that Bush was well liked because of his good humor and friendly manner with everyone; however, Mr. Trucks had noticed that on a number of occasions Bush had intimated that his age and experience should cause the sales manager to defer to his judgment. Mr. Bush and his wife lived in the town of Oswego.

On June 4, 1952, Mr. Trucks had traveled with Mr. Bush, and they visited five of Mr. Bush's accounts. On a routine form for sales managers' reports on field work with salesmen, copies of which were filed with the district sales manager and the New York sales manager, Mr. Trucks made the following comments about Mr. Bush:

Points Requiring Attention: Not using merchandising equipment; not following weekly sales plan. Pharmaceutical business going to competitors because of lack of interest. Too much time spent on idle chatter. Only shows druggist what "he thinks they will buy." Tends to sell easy items instead of profitable ones.

Steps Taken for Correction: Explained shortcomings and demonstrated how larger, more profitable orders could be obtained by following sales plan—did just that by getting the biggest order ever written for Carthage account.

Remarks: Old-time "personality." Should do terrific volume if trained on new merchandising techniques.

On a similar form made out by J. K. Martin on the basis of working with Mr. Bush on March 3, 1952, the following comments were made:

Points Requiring Attention: Not getting pharmaceutical business. Not following promotion plans.

Steps Taken for Correction: Told him about these things.

Remarks: Bush made this territory—can sell anything he sets his mind to—a real drummer—very popular with his customers.

Daniel Carmack, twenty-nine years old, was the oldest of the group of salesmen who had passed through the formal sales training program. Mr. Trucks considered him earnest and conscientious. He had increased his sales each year. Although Mr. Trucks did not regard Carmack as being the "salesman type," he noted that Carmack had been fairly successful in the use of the merchandising techniques that Mr. Trucks was seeking to implement.

John Dangler handled a number of the big accounts in downtown Syracuse. Mr. Trucks believed that Dangler was an excellent salesman who considered himself "very smooth." Mr. Trucks had been surprised at the affront Dangler had taken when he had offered a few suggestions about the improvement of Dangler's selling technique. Mr. and Mrs. Dangler were good friends of the Burtons. The Danglers were social friends of merchandise and operations managers and their wives. Mr. Trucks suspected that Dangler had expected to be Mr. Martin's successor.

John Jameson seemed to Mr. Trucks to be an earnest and conscientious salesman. He had been amiable, though not cordial, toward Mr. Trucks. Mr. Trucks's report on calls on ten accounts on June 5, 1952, with Mr. Jameson contained the following statements.

Points Requiring Attention: Rushing calls. Gets want book and tries to sell case lots on wanted items. Carries all merchandising equipment but doesn't use it.

Steps Taken for Correction: Suggested change in routing; longer, better-planned calls; conducted presentation demonstration.

Remarks: Hardworking, conscientious, good salesman, but needs to be brought up to date on merchandising methods.

Mr. Martin's comments on observations of Mr. Jameson on March 4, 1952, reported on the same form, were as follows:

Points Requiring Attention: Uses the want book on the basis of most sales. Not pushing promotions.
Steps Taken for Correction: Discussed shortcomings.
Remarks: Jameson really knows how to sell—visits every customer each week. Hard worker—very loyal—even pushes goods with very low commission.

On the day Mr. Trucks had traveled with Jameson, the latter suggested that Mr. Trucks have dinner at the Jamesons' home. Mr. Trucks accepted the invitation, but at the end of the day Jameson took him to a restaurant in Watertown, explaining that he did not want to inconvenience his wife because his two daughters were home from college on vacation.

Russell Means had caused Mr. Trucks considerable concern. Means complained about sales management procedures, commission rates, the "lousy service of the warehouse people," and other such matters at sales meetings. Mr. Trucks believed that most of the complaints were founded in fact, but concluded that the matters were usually trivial, since the other salesmen did not complain about them. Mr. Trucks mentioned his difficulties with Means to Mr. Burton. Mr. Burton's comment was that Means had been very friendly with Mr. Martin. Means seemed to be quite popular with his customers.

James Pepper was, in Mr. Trucks's opinion, the most ambitious, aggressive, and argumentative salesman in the Syracuse Division. He had been employed by the company since his graduation from the University of Rochester in 1948, first as a trainee and then as a salesman. Pepper had substantially increased the sales volume of the territory assigned to him. He had persuaded Mr. Martin to assign him six inactive hospital accounts in July, 1950. Within six months Pepper made sales to these accounts in excess of $36,000. The other salesmen considered him "cocky" and a "big spender." Mr. Trucks thought his attitude was one of independence. If Pepper agreed with a sales plan, he worked hard to achieve its objectives, but if he did not agree, he did not cooperate at all. Mr. Trucks thought that he had been very successful in working with Pepper.

Paul Smith, who was twenty-four years old, impressed Mr. Trucks as being unsure of himself. Smith seemed to be confused and overworked. Mr. Trucks attributed this difficulty to Smith's trying to serve too many accounts in too large an area. Smith was very interested in Mr. Trucks's suggestions on improvement in his work. Mr. Trucks believed that he would improve in time with proper help. Smith had raised his sales to the point where he was on commission instead of salary in March, 1952.

Michael Waller, twenty-five years of age, was the only salesman who worked on a salary. His sales volume was not sufficient to sustain an income of $325 a month, which was the company minimum for salesmen with more than one year's experience Waller was very apologetic about being on a salary. Mr. Trucks believed that Waller's determination to "make good" would be realized because of the latter's conscientiousness. When he had been assigned the territory two years before, it had consisted largely of uncontacted accounts. The volume of sales had tripled in the meantime. Mr. Trucks felt that Waller appreciated all the help he was given and that in time Waller would be an excellent salesman.

Both Bush and Jameson earned about $2\frac{1}{8}\%$ of sales in commissions. The other salesmen all earned about $2\frac{1}{4}\%$ of sales as commissions, except Pepper and Carmack who earned about $2\frac{3}{8}\%$. Mr. Trucks said that expense accounts amounted to about $\frac{3}{4}\%$ of sales for both city and country salesmen. The differences in percentage rates of commissions were explained by Mr. Trucks in terms of the differential commissions set by the company. Higher commission rates were given on items the company wished to "push," such as pharmaceuticals and calendar promotion items.

The trainees were something of an unknown quantity to Mr. Trucks. He had training conferences with them in which he had thought they had performed rather poorly. He believed that Mr. Martin had neglected the training of the new men. All four of them seemed to be good prospects and were eager to be assigned territories, as they informed Mr. Trucks as often as possible.

The turnover of the Syracuse Division sales force had been very low among the prewar salesmen. Six of the sales-training program men had left the division since 1947. Two of these men had been promoted to department heads in other divisions, whereas four had left to work for manufacturers. Because manufacturers valued salesmen with wholesaling experience and competing wholesalers did not have training programs for young men, there were many opportunities for a salesman who desired to leave.

SALES MANAGEMENT

Since Mr. Trucks had become sales manager, he had devoted considerable thought to the problem of improving the sales performance of the Syracuse Division. He had accepted a transfer to the new job at the urging of Mr. Cameron Crow, the vice-president in charge of sales. Mr. Trucks was one of a dozen young men whom Mr. Crow had brought into the New York office since the end of World War II to work as assistants to the top sales executives. None of the young assistants had remained in the New York office for more than three years, for Mr. Crow made a policy of offering the young men field assignments so that they could "show their stuff." Mr. Trucks believed that the sales performance of the Syracuse Division could be bettered by an improved plan of sales management. He knew that the share of the Syracuse market for wholesale purchases of retail drugstores[1] held by Consolidated was only 19.5% as against a 48% share for some of the other divisions in their respective markets.

Mr. Crow, for whom Mr. Trucks worked immediately before his transfer, had focused his staff's attention upon the qualitative aspects of sales policy. Mr. Trucks had assisted Mr. Crow in implementing merchandising plans intended to utilize the salesmen's selling efforts in such a way as to minimize the handling cost of sales and maximize the gross margin.

The company encouraged the salesmen to use a threefold plan for increasing profitability:

1) Sales of larger average value per line of the order were encouraged because the cost of processing and filling each line of an order was practically constant;

2) Sales of larger total value were encouraged because the delivery cost for orders having a total weight between 20 and 100 pounds was practically constant;

3) Because some manufacturers offered margins considerably larger than others, sales of products carrying higher margins were encouraged. Salesmen's commissions varied with the margins available to Consolidated on the products they sold.

The executives of the company also sought to increase the effectiveness of Consolidated promotions by setting up a sales calendar. The sales calendar co-ordinated the activities of all Consolidated divisions so that during a given calendar period every account would be solicited for the sale of particular items yielding satisfactory profits. The type of activity represented by the sales calendar required that the salesmen in

---

[1] The potential wholesale sales for retail drugstores were calculated by the New York office market-analysis section. This market estimate, called the P.W.P.P. (potential wholesale purchasing power) was calculated for each county by adjusting retail drugstore sales to an estimate of the purchases of goods from wholesalers.

each division follow a pattern in selling to every individual account. The sales manager was responsible for co-ordinating the activities of his own salesmen.

The matter of selling patterns was largely the responsibility of the division sales manager. Mr. Trucks believed that his predecessor had never really accepted the changes that had taken place in the merchandising policy of the New York office.

Mr. Trucks had inherited from his predecessor a system of sales-department records which had been carefully maintained. The national offices required each division to keep uniform sales and market-analysis records. During the period of Mr. Trucks's work in the New York office, he had developed a familiarity with the various uses for these records.

The basis of the sales and market-analysis record was the division trading area. The limits of the trading area were determined by the economics of selling costs, and the factors on which the costs were based were transportation costs of delivery and salesmen's traveling expenses. Mr. Trucks knew from his own experience that delineation of trading areas was influenced by tradition, geographic conditions, the number of salesmen, the number of calls a salesman could make, the estimated market potential, competition, and agreements with adjacent Consolidated divisions. The Syracuse Division was bordered by the trading areas of Consolidated divisions located in Rochester and Albany on the east, south, and west; to the north was the Canadian border. A map of this division is included here in Exhibit 1.

Within the divisional trading area the market was broken into sales territories. Exhibit 2 includes data on salesmen's territory assignments; Exhibit 3 shows the salesmen's territories by counties; Exhibit 4 indicates estimated potential sales and sales by counties for various classification of customers. During the time since his arrival, Mr. Trucks had formed the opinion that the present salesmen's territories had been established without careful regard for the number of stores in the area, the sales potential, or the amount of traveling involved. Although Mr. Trucks had not yet studied any one territory carefully, he suspected all his salesmen of skimming the cream from many of their accounts because they did not have adequate time to do a thorough selling job in each store.

Mr. Trucks had been able to observe the performance records of other divisional sales managers while he worked in New York. He knew that some sales managers had achieved substantial improvements over the past performances of their divisions.

Exhibit 1

CONSOLIDATED DRUGS, INC.

Syracuse Division Trading Area

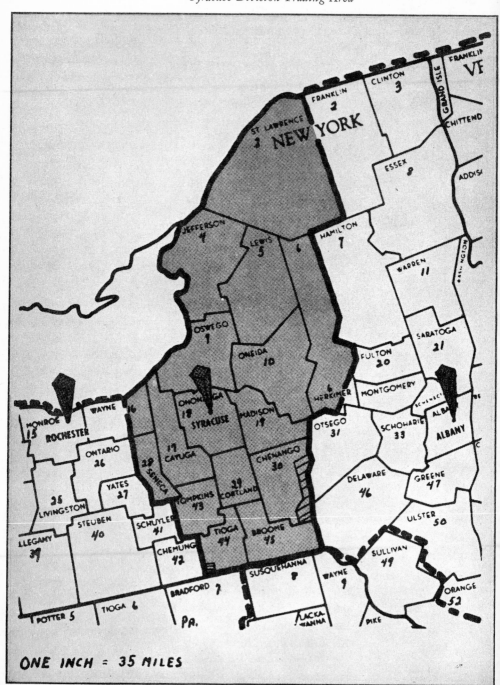

ONE INCH = 35 MILES

Exhibit 2

CONSOLIDATED DRUGS, INC.

Selected Data on Salesmen's Territory Assignments and Performance

Salesman	County	Sales, 1951*	Active Accounts	Estimated Potential†	Assigned Accounts‡
				(000)	
Babbidge	Chenango	$ 20,634	4	$ 189	15
	Tompkins	63,226	9	388	19
	Tioga	39,839	4	161	11
	Broome	122,968	22	1,807	45
	Total	246,667	39	2,545	90
Bush	Jefferson	81,162	16	371	20
	Lewis	28,798	8	87	11
	Oswego	148,073	25	517	37
	Total	258,033	49	965	68
Carmack	Onondaga	76,339	14	297	14
	Madison	86,950	12	417	19
	Cortland	46,005	6	146	11
	Total	209,294	32	860	44
Dangler	Onondaga	252,051	33	743	44
	Total	252,051	33	743	44
Jameson	St. Lawrence	136,058	25	364	32
	Jefferson	123,681	19	353	19
	Oswego	1,091	1	200	1
	Total	260,830	45	737	52
Means	Onondaga	244,642	29	1,009	48
	Total	244,642	29	1,009	48
Pepper	Onondaga	212,691	28	500	29
	Total	212,691	28	500	29
Smith	Herkimer	48,530	10	312	19
	Oneida	113,607	46	1,053	85
	Total	162,137	56	1,365	104
Waller	Wayne	22,675	4	103	5
	Cayuga	70,598	14	312	18
	Seneca	36,260	8	186	13
	Total	129,533	26	601	36
	Hospitals, Syracuse (Pepper)	$ 36,079			
	All others	$ 8,595			
	House accounts	$ 76,622			
	Total division sales	$2,197,174			

* This figure includes sales to chain and independent drugstores, and to miscellaneous accounts but does not include sales to hospitals.
† No potential is calculated for hospitals or miscellaneous sales. Where a county is divided among several salesmen, the potential-sales figure for each salesman is obtained by allocating the county potential in proportion to the *number* of drugstore accounts in that county assigned to that salesman.
‡ Includes hospitals and other recognized drug outlets in the territory.
Source: Company records.

SALES TERRITORIES OF BUSH AND JAMESON

The territory that Mr. Bush covered included accounts scattered through small towns in four counties of the rural area northeast of Syracuse (see Exhibit 5). Mr. Bush had originally developed the accounts in the four-county area for the predecessor company. At the time

Exhibit 3

CONSOLIDATED DRUGS, INC.

*Syracuse Division Salesmen's Territory Assignments,
by Counties*

Code Number	County	Salesmen
1............	St. Lawrence	Jameson
4............	Jefferson	Bush, Jameson
5............	Lewis	Bush
6............	Herkimer	Smith
9............	Oswego	Bush, Jameson
10............	Oneida	Smith
16............	Wayne	Waller
17............	Cayuga	Waller
18............	Onondaga	Means, Dangler, Pepper, Carmack
19............	Madison	Carmack
28............	Seneca	Waller
29............	Cortland	Carmack
30............	Chenango	Babbidge
43............	Tompkins	Babbidge
44............	Tioga	Babbidge
45............	Broome	Babbidge

he undertook this task the competing service wholesaler already had established a mail-order business with the rural druggists in this area. Mr. Bush had taken to the road in a Model-T Ford in 1922 to build up the sales in all four counties. He had been hired specifically for this job because he was a native of the area and an experienced "drummer."

Five years later Mr. John Jameson, a friend of Mr. Bush, became a division salesman, and, at the suggestion of Mr. Bush, covered other accounts in the same four-county area. Mr. Jameson had been a salesman for a proprietary medicine firm before he joined the wholesale drug house. He was seven years younger than Mr. Bush. Since that time Mr. Jameson had serviced a number of accounts in the four-county area. The list of accounts that each of these men handled appears in Exhibits 6 and 7. Mr. Trucks noticed that the incomes which Messrs. Bush and Jameson had received from commissions were very stable over the years.

A VISIT FROM MR. JAMESON

On the Wednesday morning following the June sales meeting, Mr. Trucks saw Mr. Jameson come in the front door of the Syracuse Division offices. Although the salesman passed within 30 feet of Mr. Trucks' desk he did not appear to notice the sales manager. Mr. Jameson walked through the office area to the partitioned space where Mr. Burton's

Exhibit 4

CONSOLIDATED DRUGS, INC.

Selected Data on Sales and Sales Potentials, by Counties

County	Code	Population	Per Cent	Sold	Inactive Accounts	Accounts Not Sold	Total	P.W.P.P. (in Thousands)	Per Cent Area P.W.P.P.	Sales (in Thousands)	Per Cent P.W.P.P.	Sold	Not Sold	Sales (in Thousands)	Sales (in Thousands)
				Chain and Independent Stores								Hospitals			Miscellaneous
St. Lawrence	1	99,400	7.0	19	2	5	26	$ 364	3.9	$ 107	29.4	2	4	$ 3	
Jefferson	4	86,700	6.1	26	8	...	34	724	7.8	201	27.8	2	2	2	
Lewis	5	22,800	1.6	8	...	1	8	87	0.0	29	33.1	...	1	...	
Herkimer	6	46,800	3.3	10	6	1	17	312	3.3	49	15.6	...	2	...	
Oswego	9	78,300	5.5	22	4	...	26	537	5.7	124	23.1	1	2	...	
Oneida	10	226,000	15.9	46	14	12	72	1,053	11.3	111	10.5	...	13	...	
Wayne	16	14,400	1.0	4	...	1	5	103	1.1	23	22.0	...	...	2	
Cayuga	17	71,100	5.0	12	4	...	16	312	3.3	56	17.9	2	...	2	
Onondaga	18	346,600	24.3	104	7	9	120	2,549	27.3	722	28.3	6	9	36	
Madison	19	47,000	3.3	12	2	3	17	417	4.5	87	20.9	...	2	...	
Seneca	28	29,700	2.1	6	1	3	10	186	2.0	28	15.1	2	1	2	
Cortland	29	37,700	2.6	6	2	1	9	146	1.6	46	31.5	...	2	...	
Chenango	30	39,900	2.8	4	2	6	12	189	2.0	21	10.9	...	3	...	
Tompkins	43	60,200	4.2	9	1	4	14	388	4.2	63	16.3	...	5	...	
Tioga	44	30,600	2.1	4	...	7	11	161	1.7	40	24.7	...	...	...	
Broome	45	187,800	13.2	22	2	13	37	1,807	19.4	115	6.3	...	8	...	
Total		1,425,000	100.0	314	55	65	434	$9,335	100.0						
Totals, 1951		......	...	...	...	...	...	......	...	$1,819	19.5	15	54	$45	$334
Totals, 1950		......	...	...	...	...	...	......	...	$1,659	18.6	...	...	$27	$ 256

Source: Company records.

Exhibit 5

CONSOLIDATED DRUGS, INC.

Counties Sold by Messrs. Bush and Jameson

Exhibit 6

CONSOLIDATED DRUGS, INC.

Accounts Sold by Asa Bush, by Counties, with 1951 Purchases

Jefferson County:

Adams Center, D*	$ 1,986
(Alexandria Bay, D	10,192)
(Alexandria Bay, D	8,764)
Bellville, D	1,165
(Carthage, D	33,903)
Chaumont, D	336
(Clayton, D	5,901)
(Clayton, D	9,113)
Deferiet, D	205
Dexter, D	6,481
Ellisburg, D	131
LaFargeville, D	290
Plessis, D	490
Redwood, M	60
Rodman, D	1,787
Sackets Harbor, D	358
County total	$81,162

Lewis County:

Beaver Falls, D*	$ 1,270
Croghan, D	8,199
Harrisville, D	6,172
Lowville, D	7,896
Lowville, D	1,438
Lyons Falls, D	2,008
Port Leyden, D	775
Turin, M	1,040
County total	$28,798

Oswego County:

Caloose, D*	$ 684
Central Square, D	743
Constantia, M	29
Cleveland, M	156
(Fulton, D	6,051)
(Fulton, D	9,817)
(Fulton, D	11,116)
(Fulton, D	15,396)
Hannibal, D	1,558
Hastings, M	1,539
Lacona, M	185
Mexico, D	6,371
Oswego, D	4,827
(Oswego, D	8,307)
(Oswego, D	9,641)
(Oswego, D	16,415)
(Oswego, D	17,593)
(Oswego, D	8,982)
Oswego, H	6
Parish, M	2,065
Phoenix, D	3,895
(Pulaski, D	3,501)
(Pulaski, D	11,636)
Sandy Creek, D	5,655
West Monroe, D	1,911
County total	$148,079

Territory total $258,039
Increase over 1950 . . . . 0.9%

*D: Independent Drugstore; C: Chain Drugstore; M: Miscellaneous Account; H: Hospital.
NOTE: Accounts in parentheses are those indicated by Mr. Jameson as the ones he wanted.
Source: Company records.

private office was located. Twenty minutes later Mr. Jameson emerged from the division manager's office and made his way to Mr. Trucks' desk.

"Hi there, young fellah!" he shouted as he approached.

"Howdy, Jack. Sit down and chat awhile," Mr. Trucks replied. "What got you out of bed so early?" he asked, knowing that the salesman must have risen at 6 o'clock to make the drive to Syracuse from his home in Watertown.

Mr. Jameson squeezed his bulky frame into the armchair next to the desk. "It's a shame Asa is retiring," he said. "I never thought he could stand to give it up. I never knew anyone who enjoyed selling as much

Exhibit 7

CONSOLIDATED DRUGS, INC.

Accounts Sold by John Jameson, by Counties, with 1951 Purchases

St. Lawrence County:

Canton, D*	$ 13,080
Edwards, D	672
Edwards, M	1,885
Gouverneur, D	226
Gouverneur, D	9,383
Gouverneur, C	16,519
Heuvelton, D	108
Massena, D	11,259
Massena, D	3,397
Massena, C	2,448
Massena, C	2,225
Massena, H	38
Madrid, D	1,432
Morristown, D	2,731
Norfolk, D	2,995
Norwood, D	3,139
Ogdensburg, D	8,090
Ogdensburg, D	22,555
Ogdensburg, D	7,203
Ogdensburg, D	3,380
Ogdensburg, M	149
Ogdensburg, H	2,653
Potsdam, D	15,444
Potsdam, C	7,371
Rensselaer Falls, D	367

Total county $138,749

Jefferson County:

Adams, C*	$ 1,049
Carthage, C	1,176
Evans Mills, D	1,229
Philadelphia, D	2,101
Watertown, D	16,782
Watertown, D	2,632
Watertown, D	4,889
Watertown, D	17,041
Watertown, D	10,262
Watertown, D	14,622
Watertown, D	21,249
Watertown, D	12,791
Watertown, D	5,388
Watertown, D	475
Watertown, D	6,282
Watertown, C	2,019
Watertown, C	3,318
Watertown, M	378
Watertown, H	70
Watertown, H	2,009

Total county $125,760

Oswego County:

Pulaski, C . . . .$ 1,091

Territory total $265,600
Increase over 1950 . . . . 11.6%

*D: Independent Drugstore; C: Chain Drugstore; M: Miscellaneous Account; H: Hospital.
Source: Company records.

as Asa—'cept, maybe me." Mr. Jameson continued praising Mr. Bush and telling anecdotes which illustrated his point until Mr. Trucks began to wonder whether Mr. Jameson thought that the sales manager was biased in some way against the retiring salesman. Mr. Trucks recalled that he had made some critical remarks about Mr. Bush to Mr. Burton, but he could not recall any discussion of Mr. Bush's shortcomings with Mr. Bush himself or any of the other salesmen. Mr. Jameson ended his remarks by saying, "Old J. K., God rest his soul, always said that Asa was the best damn' wholesale drug salesman he had ever known."

There was a brief silence as Mr. Trucks did not realize that Mr. Jameson was finished. Finally Mr. Trucks said, "You know, Jack, I think we ought to have a testimonial dinner for Asa at the July sales meeting."

Mr. Jameson made no comment on Mr. Trucks's suggestion; instead, he went on to say, "None of these green trainees will ever be able to take Asa's place. Those druggists up there are old-timers. They would resent being high-pressured by some kid blown up to twice his size with college degrees. No sir! You've got to sell 'em right in those country stores."

Mr. Trucks did not believe that Mr. Jameson's opinion about the adaptability of the younger, college-educated salesman was justified by the evidence available. He recalled that several of these men in country territories had done better on their May sales quotas than either Mr. Bush or Mr. Jameson. He was proud of his self-restraint when he commented, "Selling in a country territory is certainly different."

"That's right, Dick. I wanted to make sure you understood these things before I told you." Mr. Jameson was nervously massaging his double chin between his thumb and forefinger.

Mr. Trucks looked at him with a quizzical expression. "Told me what?"

"I have just been talking to Mr. Burton. Well, I was talking to him about an understanding between Asa and me. We always agreed that if anything should happen to the other, or he should retire, or something —well, we agreed that the one who remained should get to take over his choice of the other's accounts. We told J. K. about this and he said, 'Boys, what's O.K. by you is O.K. by me. You two developed that territory and you deserve to be rewarded for it.' Well, yes sir, that's the way it was."

Without pausing, Mr. Jameson went on, "I just told Mr. Burton about it. He said that he remembered talking about the whole thing with J. K. 'Yes,' he said, 'Tell Trucks about it,' he said, 'Tell Trucks about it.' Asa and I went over his accounts on Sunday. I went over his list of accounts with him and checked the ones that I want. Here is the list with the accounts all checked off.[2] I already know nearly all the proprietors. You'll see that—"

"Wait a minute, Jack! Wait a minute!" Mr. Trucks interrupted. "You've lost me completely. In the first place, if there is any assignment of accounts to be made I'll do it. It will be done on a basis that is fair to the salesmen concerned and profitable to the company. You know that."

"Dick, I'm only asking for what is fair." Mr. Jameson's face was flushed. Mr. Trucks noticed that the man he had always believed to be

---

[2] Mr. Jameson's selected accounts are the accounts in parentheses in Exhibit 6.

deliberately confident and self-possessed was now so agitated that it was difficult for him to speak. "I don't want my territory chopped up and handed to some green kid!"

Mr. Trucks noticed that everybody in the office was now watching Mr. Jameson. "Calm down, Jack," he whispered to the salesman, indicating with a nod of his head that others were watching.

"Don't talk to me that way, you young squirt!" replied Mr. Jameson. "I don't care. A man with 25 years' service deserves some consideration!"

"You're absolutely right, Jack. You're absolutely right." As Mr. Trucks repeated his words Mr. Jameson settled back in his chair. The typewriters started clattering again.

"Now, first of all, Jack," queried Mr. Trucks, as he tried to return the conversation to a friendly basis, "where did you get the idea that your territory was going to be 'chopped up'?"

"You said so yourself. You said it at the very first sales meeting when you made that speech about how you were going to boost sales in Syracuse." Mr. Jameson emphasized his words by pounding on the side of the desk with his masonic ring.

Mr. Trucks reflected for a moment. He recalled giving a talk at his first sales meeting at the end of May entitled, "How We Can Do A Better Job for Consolidated." The speech was a restatement of the merchandising policy of the New York office. He had mentioned that getting more profitable business would require that a larger percentage of the total purchases of each account would have to come to Consolidated; that attaining a larger share of the business from each store would require more selling time in each store; and that greater concentration on each account would necessitate reorganization of the sales territories. He realized that his future plans did entail reorganization of the territories; he had not anticipated, however, any such reaction as Mr. Jameson's.

Finally, Mr. Trucks said, "I do plan to make some territorial changes —not right away—at least not until I have looked things over pretty darn carefully. Of course, you understand that our first duty is to make greater profits for the company. Some of our territories would be a great deal more profitable if they were organized and handled in a different manner."

"What are you going to do about Asa's territory?" asked Mr. Jameson.

"Well, I just haven't had a chance to study the situation yet," he replied. "If I could make the territory more profitable by reorganizing it,

I guess that is what they would expect me to do." Since Mr. Trucks had not yet looked over the information about the territory, he was anxious not to commit himself to any course of action relating to it.

"What about the promises the company made to me about letting me choose the accounts I want?" the salesman asked.

"You don't mean the company's promise; you mean Mr. Martin's promise," Mr. Trucks corrected him.

"Well, if Mr. Martin wasn't 'the company' I don't see how you figure that you are!" Mr. Jameson's face resumed its flush.

"O.K., Jack. How about giving me a chance to look over the situation. You know that I want to do the right thing. Let me go over your list of the accounts you want. In a few days I can talk intelligently about the matter." Mr. Trucks felt that there was no point in carrying on the discussion.

"All right, Dick," said Mr. Jameson, rising. The two men walked toward the front entrance of the office. As they reached the top of the steps leading to the front door, Mr. Jameson turned to the sales manager and offered his hand, "Look, Dick. I'm sorry I got so mad. You just can't imagine what this means to me. I know you'll see it my way when you know the whole story." Mr. Jameson's voice sounded strained.

Mr. Trucks watched the older man leave. He felt embarrassed at the realization that Mr. Jameson's parting words had been overheard by several manufacturers' representatives standing nearby.

A CONVERSATION WITH THE DIVISION MANAGER

Mr. Trucks decided to talk at once to Mr. Burton about his conversation with Mr. Jameson. He walked over to Mr. Burton's office. He hesitated in the doorway; Mr. Burton looked up and then indicated with a gesture that Mr. Trucks was to take a seat.

The sales manager sat down. He waited for Mr. Burton to speak. Mr. Burton was occupied for the moment with the problem of unwrapping a cigar. Mr. Trucks opened the conversation by saying, "Jack Jameson just stopped by to speak to me."

"Yeah?" said Mr. Burton, removing bitten flakes of tobacco from the end of his tongue.

"He said something about getting some of Asa Bush's accounts when Asa retires," Mr. Trucks said in a deliberately questioning manner.

"Yeah."

The sales manager continued, "Well, this idea of his was based on a promise that he said J. K. had made."

"Yeah. He told me that, too."

"Did Martin make such a promise?" Mr. Trucks inquired.

"Hell, I don't know. It sounds like him." He tilted back in his swivel chair.

"What shall I do about it?"

"Don't ask me; you're the sales manager." Mr. Burton paused, holding his cigar away from his lips as if he were about to speak. Just as Mr. Trucks was about to say something Mr. Burton lurched forward to flick the ashes from his cigar into his ash tray. "Look here, Dick. I don't want any morale problems around here. You're the first of the 'wonder boys' to be put in charge of a department in this division. I don't want you to do anything to mess up the morale. We never had any morale problems when Martin was alive. We don't want anything like that in this division."

Mr. Trucks was momentarily bewildered. He knew by the way that Mr. Burton used the phrase "wonder boys" that he was referring to the college men who had been brought into the Syracuse Division since the war.

Mr. Burton went on, "Why the devil did you tell the men that you were going to reassign the sales territories without even telling me?"

"But you were there when I said it."

"Said what?"

"Well, at my first sales meeting, that one of the ways we were going to get more business was to reorganize the sales territory," Mr. Trucks replied.

"I certainly don't remember anything like that. Dick, you gave a good inspirational talk, but I sure can't remember anything about reassigning territories."

"Actually, I just mentioned the reorganization of territories in passing," the sales manager smiled.

"I'll be damned. That sort of thing is always happening. Here everybody is frothing at the mouth about something that they think we are going to do and we haven't the slightest idea why they think we're going to do it. You know, the real reason Asa Bush asked to be retired instead of staying on as he planned was probably this fear of having his territory reorganized. Both he and Jameson know that their pension on retirement is based on their earnings in the last five years of active employment. Now that I think of it, three or four of the other salesmen have stopped in during the last couple of weeks to tell me what a fine job they were doing. They probably had this territory reassignment bogey on their minds."

Mr. Burton's cigar was no longer burning. He began groping under the papers on his desk for a match.

Mr. Trucks took advantage of this pause in the conversation. "Mr. Burton, I think there are some real advantages to be won by an adjustment of the sales territories. I think—"

"You still think that after today?" the division manager asked in a sarcastic tone.

"Why, yes! The profit we make on sales to an individual account is related closely to delivery expense. The larger the total proportion of the account's business we get, the more profit we make because the delivery expense remains more or less constant."

"Look, Dick. You college men always have everything all figured out with slide rules, but sometimes that doesn't count. Morale is the important thing. The salesmen won't stand for having their territories changed. I know that you have four trainees that you'd like to put out on territories. You put them out on parts of the territories belonging to some of the more experienced men—bam! God knows how many of our good salesmen would be left. Now, I've never had any trouble with sales force morale since I've been manager of this division. Old Martin, bless his soul, never let me down. He wasn't any damn' Ph.D., but, by golly, he could handle men. Don't get off on the wrong foot with the boys, Dick. With the labor situation in the warehouse being what it is, I've just got too much on my mind. I don't want you to be creating more problems than I can handle. How 'bout it, boy!"

Mr. Burton ground out his half-smoked cigar, looking steadily at Mr. Trucks.

Mr. Trucks was upset because the division manager had imputed to him a lack of concern for morale problems. He had always thought of himself as being very considerate of the thoughts and feelings of others. He realized that at the moment his foremost desire was to get away from Mr. Burton.

Mr. Trucks rose from his chair saying, "Mr. Burton, you can count on me. I know you are right about this morale business."

"Atta boy," said the division manager. "It does us a lot of good to talk like this once in awhile. Now, you see if you can make peace with the salesmen. I want you to handle everything yourself."

"Well, thanks a lot," said the sales manager, as he backed out of the office door.

As he walked through the office after talking with Mr. Burton, he saw two manufacturers' representatives with whom he had appointments already seated near the receptionist's desk. His schedule of appointments that day did not permit him to do more than gather the material pertaining to the Jameson and Bush territories.

MR. TRUCKS GOES HOME

Mr. Trucks left the office shortly after five o'clock to drive to his home in a suburb of Syracuse. It was a particularly hot and humid day. Pre–Fourth-of-July traffic lengthened the drive by nearly twenty minutes. When he finally turned into his own driveway, he felt as though his skin were caked with grime and perspiration. He got out of the car and walked around the house to the terrace in the rear. Nancy, his wife, was sewing in a deck chair under the awning.

"Hello, Dick. You're late," she said, looking up with a smile.

"I know it. Even the traffic was bad today." He dropped his coat on a glass-topped table and sprawled out full length on the glider. "Honestly, I'm so exhausted and dirty that I am disgusted with myself."

"Bad day?"

"Awful. You just can't imagine how discouraging it is trying to get this job organized. You would think that it would be obvious to everybody that what ails the Syracuse Division is the organization of the sales force," said Mr. Trucks, arranging a pillow under his head.

"I didn't realize that you thought anything was wrong with the Syracuse Division."

"Well, what I mean is that we get only 20% of the potential wholesale business. If I could organize the salesforce my way—well, God knows, maybe we could get 40% of the business. That is what the New York office watches for. The sales manager who increases his division's share of the market gets the promotions when they come along. I knew Mr. Crow transferred me to this division because he knew these possibilities existed."

"I don't understand. Is Mr. Crow still your boss, or is Mr. Burton?" asked his wife.

"Nancy, it's terribly discouraging. Mr. Burton is my boss, but I'll never get anywhere with Consolidated unless Mr. Crow and the other people in New York promote me."

"Don't you like Mr. Burton?"

"I had a run-in with him today."

"You didn't!" she said crossly as she laid her sewing aside.

Mr. Trucks had not anticipated this reaction. He gazed up at the awning as if he had not noticed his wife's intent expression. "We didn't argue particularly. He just—well, he doesn't know too much about sales management. He put his foot down on my plans to reorganize the territories."

"I can't understand why you would go and get yourself into a fight with your boss when you haven't been here even two months. We should never have bought this house!"

"Honestly, honey, I didn't have any fight. Everything is O.K. He just —well, do you want me to be a divisional sales manager all my life?" She smiled and said nothing.

He continued, "I'm sorry you married such a grouch, but I just get plain mad when somebody calls me a 'wonder boy.' "

"You're tired," she said sympathetically. "Why don't you go up and take a shower while I feed the children. We can have a drink and then eat our dinner whenever we feel like it. It's only meat loaf anyway."

"That sounds wonderful," he said, raising himself from his prone position.

AN UNEXPECTED CALLER

Mr. Trucks had just stepped out of the shower when he heard his wife calling to him. "Dick, Jim Pepper is here to see you."

"Tell him I'll be down in just a minute. Give him a drink, Nancy."

As he dressed, Mr. Trucks wondered why the salesman had chosen the dinner hour to call. During the month since he had moved into his new home no salesman had ever dropped in uninvited.

When Mr. Trucks came downstairs, he found Mr. Pepper sitting on the living-room couch with a Tom Collins in his hand.

"Hello, Jim," said Mr. Trucks crossing the room with his right hand extended. "You look as if you had had a hot day. Why don't you take off your coat? If we go out to the terrace, you may get a chance to cool off."

"Thanks, Dick," the visitor said as he moved out to the terrace. "I'm sorry to come barging in this way, but I thought it was important."

"Well, what's on your mind?" said Mr. Trucks as he sat down.

Mr. Pepper started to speak but hesitated as Mrs. Trucks came out of the door with two glasses in her hand. She handed one glass to Mr. Trucks, then excused herself, saying, "I think I better see if the children are all right."

After she had disappeared into the house, Mr. Pepper said, "I heard about what happened at the office today, so I thought I'd come over to tell you that we stand 100% behind you."

Mr. Trucks was perplexed by Mr. Pepper's words. He realized that the incident to which the salesman referred was probably his meeting with Mr. Jameson. Mr. Trucks said, "I'm not sure what you mean, Jim."

"I heard that you and Jameson had it out this morning about changing the sales territories," Mr. Pepper replied.

Mr. Trucks smiled. Two thoughts entered his mind. He was amused at the proportions that the brief conversation of that morning had assumed in the minds of so many people; but, at the same time, he was curious as to how Mr. Pepper, who had presumably been in the field selling, had heard about the incident so soon. Without hesitation he asked, "Where did you hear about this, Jim?"

"Jack Dangler told me! He was down at the warehouse with Homer Babbidge when I stopped off to pick up a special narcotics order for a customer. They are all excited about this territory business. Dangler said Jameson came out to his house at lunch time and told him about it. Everybody figured that you were going to change the territories when you started traveling around with each of the boys, especially after what you said at your first sales meeting."

"Well, the reason I went on the road with each of the men, Jim," said Mr. Trucks, "was so that I could learn more about their selling problems and, at the same time, meet the customers."

Mr. Pepper smiled, "Sure, but when you started filling out a rating sheet on each account, I couldn't help thinking you had some reason for it."

Mr. Trucks realized that the salesman had spoken with irony in his voice, but he thought it was better to let the matter pass as if he had not noticed it. Since he was planning to use the information he had gathered for reorganization of the sales territories, he decided that he would be frank with Mr. Pepper in order to find out what the young salesman's reaction might be on the question of territorial changes. He said, "Jim, I've thought a lot about making some changes in the territories—"

Mr. Pepper interrupted him, "That's terrific. I'm sure glad to hear that. I don't like to speak ill of the dead, but old Martin really gave the trainees the short end of the stick when he put us on territories. He either gave a man a territory of uncontacted accounts so he beat his head against a stone wall until he finally quit, and that is just what happened to two guys who trained with me, or else he gave him a territory where somebody had to be replaced and where some of the best accounts had been handed over to one of the older salesmen. Well, I know for a fact that when I took over my territory from Rick Hunt, Jack Dangler and

Rusty Means got twelve of Hunt's best accounts. And, damn it, I got more sales out of what was left than Hunt ever did, but Dangler and Means' total sales didn't go up at all. It took me awhile, but, by golly, I had the laugh at every sales meeting when our monthly sales figures were announced."

"Is that right?" said Mr. Trucks.

"Damn' right! And I wasn't the only one. That's why those old duffers are so down on the four of us that have come with the division since the war. We've beaten them at their own game."

"Do you think that Waller and Carmack and Smith feel the same way?" asked Mr. Trucks.

"Think, hell! I know it! That's all we ever talk about. If you re-organize those territories and give us back the accounts that Martin took away, you'll see some real sales records. Take, for example, the Medical Arts Pharmacy out by Mercy Hospital. Jack Dangler got that one away from my territory and he calls there only once a week. If I could get that one back, I'd get in there three times a week and get five times as much business."

Mr. Trucks had to raise his hands in a gesture of protest. "Don't you have enough accounts already, Jim, to keep you busy?"

"Dick, I spend fifty hours a week on the road and I love it; but I know damn' well that if I put some of the time I spend in 'two-by-four' stores into some of those big juicy accounts like Medical Arts Pharmacy, I'd do even more business."

Mr. Trucks commented, "I'm not particularly anxious to argue the point now, but if you start putting your time into Medical Arts Pharmacy, what's going to happen to your sales to the 'two-by-four' stores?"

The salesman replied, "Those druggists all know me. They'd go right on buying."

Mr. Trucks did not agree with Mr. Pepper, and he thought that the salesman realized this.

After a moment of silence Mr. Pepper rose from his chair saying, "I'd better scoot home. My wife will be waiting for me with a rolling pin for being late so I'd better get out before your wife gets at me with a skillet." Mr. Pepper laughed heartily at his own joke.

The two men walked around the house to Mr. Pepper's car. As the salesman climbed into the car, he said, "Dick, don't forget what I said— Waller, Carmack, Smith, and I stand 100% behind you. You won't ever hear us talk about going over to a competitor!"

"Who's talking about that?" asked Mr. Trucks.

"Well," said Mr. Pepper as he started the motor and shifted into gear, "I don't want to tell tales out of school."

"Sure," Mr. Trucks said quickly. "I'm sorry I asked. So long, Jim. I'll see you soon."

Mr. Trucks watched the salesman back out of the driveway and drive away.

PART VII

The Business Leader
and Public Responsibility

Albert Manufacturing Company

THE ALBERT MANUFACTURING COMPANY was founded in 1938 to produce various machined and fabricated components for industrial users. Shortly after the start of World War II the company began to make mechanical and hydraulic assemblies for aircraft. This part of the business grew and in April, 1947, was set up as a separate division. To house operations the company leased a newly constructed plant in Wichita, Kansas, with 1.2 million square feet of floor space. By the end of 1954 sales of the Wichita Division were running at about $120 million annually. The division had approximately 1,200 employees.

Early in January, 1955, Mr. Henderson, works manager of the Wichita Division and a vice-president of the Albert Company, called Mr. Paul Bellows to his office. Bellows was purchasing agent for the division. Henderson told Bellows he had just received a telephone call from the manager of the local office of the Federal Bureau of Investigation. The manager informed him that an investigation then in progress by the FBI had brought to light information involving certain of the division's buyers. Henderson said he had arranged for the investigators to visit the division the following morning. He asked Bellows to receive them and to keep him informed as to developments.

The next day Mr. Arnold Rand and Mr. Peter Thomas, FBI agents, called on Bellows. Mr. Ralph Nance, assistant purchasing agent, was also at the meeting. After a brief exchange of pleasantries the following discussion took place:

BELLOWS: As you can well imagine Nance and I are very curious about this matter. We have not mentioned it to anyone but we have speculated between ourselves as to the nature of the thing. What's the story?

RAND: Well, I guess I ought to go back to last fall. We were conducting an investigation on placement of government contracts at the P. B. Blake Company on the north side of town. After several weeks and rather by accident, Pete Thomas was interviewing a witness who was a buyer in Blake's purchasing department. The fellow confessed to having accepted a $4,500 bribe from a local tool supplier. Later we

709

verified that he had received the money from the company he named. The supplier involved has gone on record that the money was a personal loan from their salesman and was to have been repaid. However, the buyer involved did not support this contention. The buyer turned state witness and gave us several other instances of similar occurrences, but they were not as serious—at least there wasn't as much money involved.

NANCE: Where is the tie-in with the Albert company?

RAND: This buyer has made a sworn statement that he knows three of your buyers have also been accepting expensive gifts and perhaps being bought off as he was. . . .

THOMAS: Bellows, this thing is nebulous as hell. We don't have much to go on, but there are enough basic implications that we think these three buyers of yours may well be tarred with the same brush.

RAND: I'd like to tell you about a fishing trip that our informant was on. He stated—and we have verified this—that he was one of 12 guests at an upstate fishing lodge over a three-day week end. The whole bunch were flown up to this lodge, spent the week end in substantial style and returned. All expenses were paid by the supplier. Now get this—your three buyers were there along with the chief tool designer and two manufacturing engineers from Albert. It was at this occasion that our informant states he learned of the arrangements, shall we say, between the supplier and your buyers.

BELLOWS: What can we do to get this thing off the ground? What can we do to help clear this thing up?

RAND: We would like to examine your records to see who placed orders with the specific company mentioned in the charge and two other companies also implicated. Then we think that sworn statements will be taken. After that if there are any concrete leads we will conduct an investigation outside the company to ascertain if the individuals have increased bank balances, are living beyond their means, and stuff like that. . . .

THOMAS: There is one thing that bothers us. We don't have jurisdiction.

BELLOWS: What do you mean jurisdiction?

THOMAS: At the P. B. Blake Company we could investigate because they held prime contracts from the government. You don't, and therefore we can't come in and do the same kind of thing.

BELLOWS: Could you if we asked you to?

THOMAS: That would take care of the matter completely.

BELLOWS: Well, that settles that. We are asking you now and will give you whatever you need in the way of an official request. Now then, when and how will you start the ball rolling?

RAND: In about three days if you can be ready for us. If possible, we would like to use a private office because of the secrecy necessary until we know where we are. We will also need personnel records, purchase order files, and a lot of other things.

BELLOWS: We will be ready for you. Let me say now I am more concerned than you are and want this cleaned up one way or the other as quickly as possible but with a minimum of disruption of the purchasing department. However, even if we have got to shake this department up hard, I will give you every support. Nance, get things organized to take care of this. Don't tell anyone what is going on until we decide the time is right . . . explain the presence of strangers by, well let them be headquarters auditors or something. Gentlemen, Ralph Nance will be your contact and will personally make all the necessary arrangements. Again, I want to assure you that you have our cooperation. Tell me, who are the vendors in question?

RAND: The Supreme Engineering Company is the firm specifically mentioned in the allegation. The other two are Superior Tool and Die, Inc., and Allied Tool Company.

NANCE: Thanks, you can be assured that things will be set up for you.

Mr. Bellows was especially concerned about this investigation because he had given special emphasis to a strict code of ethical conduct with suppliers since he had assumed his current assignment. The departmental policy was that no employee was to accept any gift or courtesy that he was not in a position to reciprocate. In a variety of ways Bellows had tried to get this standard of conduct understood and accepted by all those in the department. The topic was frequently discussed at weekly meetings with purchasing supervisors. All male employees of the department had attended a company school where one of the subjects discussed was the company policy on bribery. The issue had been discussed at the monthly dinner meetings held for male employees of the purchasing department. Bellows had authorized his buyers to make a fairly liberal use of expense accounts so that they could reciprocate in buying lunches, and so on, for suppliers' representatives and not feel under any obligation to them. He knew that some of the production and engineering employees had accepted Christmas gifts and entertainment from suppliers, but he had believed that his buyers had been completely honest in dealings with suppliers.

The Wichita Division was highly specialized in that it made only a limited line of small gear trains, landing gear assemblies, hydraulic pumps and actuators, and certain fabricated assemblies. The vast bulk of the more or less common components needed were obtained from subcontractors. In 1954 the purchasing department had paid slightly over $55 million to subcontractors, or about half of the total sales of the division.

Buyers for the division were divided into groups, each headed by a senior buyer. These groups were organized along product lines, each being responsible for purchasing items that fell within a broad classification. A service group typed purchase orders, maintained the files, expedited orders that were overdue, and performed other functions of a clerical or routine nature. The entire purchasing department employed 128 people.

The flow of work into the department was in the form of requisitions that specified the items required and the date they should be available. A requisition was first processed by a member of the service group, who entered it in a master log and then routed it to the proper buying group. The assistant buyer for the group upon receipt of a requisition determined what previous suppliers had furnished the item. Any specifications that applied were pulled out together with the blueprint of the part. Then invitations to quote were sent out to approved sources or, if there was only one source, the supplier's representatives were contacted for negotiation. After a supplier had been selected, the assistant buyer filled in on the requisition the supplier's name and the price per unit. Certain other details also were added, such as the storeroom that was to receive the goods, discount terms, shipping point, and so forth. The requisition then was passed on to the appropriate buyer.

In most of the groups the effective control in selection of suppliers was in the hands of the buyers. However, in all groups every requisition had to be signed by a senior buyer. At this stage it went back to the service group. The necessary number of copies were typed, hecto masters for receiving and accounting were prepared, the facsimile signature of the purchasing agent was applied, and copies were mailed to the vendor. The requisition had been transformed from a request to purchase into a contract with a supplier.

About a week after the FBI agents started their investigation, Nance and Thomas discussed progress made during the preliminary stage.

Thomas stated that he thought matters were progressing extremely slowly but that things should speed up in the near future. He and Rand had screened all the purchase orders placed by the division with the three suppliers in question during the past six months. All the orders had been for some type of tooling, primarily for tool repair work. All had been placed by the three buyers named in the original complaint.

Thomas gave Nance the following summary of the findings of the purchase order review:

1. All 1,976 purchase orders were initialed by the senior buyer for tools, Mr. Clinton Boles. The buyers that actually handled the orders and the distribution of orders among the suppliers in question were:

	Superior	Supreme	Allied	Total
Adolph Stimmer (assistant buyer)........622		257	48	927
John Lippen (buyer)................... 73		159	0	232
John Ruppert (assistant buyer).........280		531	6	817

2. While only 54 purchase orders were placed with Allied, the total dollar value of these orders was $86,409. The dollar value for Superior Tool and Die was $234,765 and for Supreme Engineering it was $303,040.

3. Among the orders were three, all placed with Supreme, which radically increased in price during the period of manufacture. The original quoted prices for these orders were $257.75, $1,166, and $2,500. The final prices on the orders, as authorized by change notices to the purchase orders, were $1,186.50, $3,775, and $4,996.[1]

Nance had intimate knowledge of tool buying and of the tool buying group. He at one time had been responsible for buying tools at the home plant of the Albert Company, and Stimmer then had been an assistant buyer reporting to him. Any tool supplier usually could build a new tool. Quotations of delivery and price could be readily obtained by furnishing the supplier with blueprints and specifications. Repair of tools was an entirely different matter. It was necessary for someone from the tool firm to inspect the tool requiring repair before submitting a quotation. Time was important because the tool generally was needed for production of a scheduled part. Therefore repair jobs were often placed on an advise price basis; that is, the supplier would take the tool and after completing his inspection at his plant would submit a price. The buyer then would judge whether or not this price was fair. If he

---

[1] During the manufacture of tools, design changes often become necessary or desirable. Such changes sometimes cause revisions in the delivered prices. Change notices also may tempt the supplier, particularly one who deliberately quoted under his costs to get an order, to demand an exorbitant price increase. This practice is frowned on by reputable tool vendors but is sometimes resorted to by marginal producers.

decided it was too high, he either negotiated a new price or moved the tool to another supplier.

The tool buying group, unlike the other buying groups, dealt in general with small firms. A relatively low capital investment was required to start a tool shop and there were many local tool makers that were highly specialized and extremely small, sometimes employing no more than four or five men. Adequate credit and other information was difficult to obtain for these small firms.

About two weeks after they began their investigation, Thomas and Rand told Nance they were going to interview, under oath, Stimmer, Lippen, Ruppert, and Boles. They further stated that they wanted to discuss the progress made to date with Bellows and Nance as soon as they had had time to weigh the statements of the men. Nance suggested they meet the following afternoon. Rand and Thomas agreed.

The next afternoon Rand, Thomas, Nance, and Bellows gathered in Bellows' office. Rand opened the meeting.

RAND: Guess you will be surprised to learn that we are ending the investigation.

BELLOWS: You're all through already?

RAND: That's right. We have been unable to uncover any concrete evidence. We must have proof and, while there is no lack of suspicious circumstances, we just can't pin down anything definite.

BELLOWS: You can't come out here, tear into everything, arouse considerable doubt in our minds, and then pull out. We want these men either nailed to the cross or exonerated—is this too much to ask?

NANCE: I thought you were making satisfactory progress.

THOMAS: Paul, you must realize we work for a boss too. He gave us almost five weeks to firm the investigation up. We just can't do it. There is a lot of smoke but no fire that we can find. So we want to give you everything we have and, if you come across some new evidence later on, we promise to give you all the help we can. That's all there is to it. We're sorry it turned out this way but. . . .

NANCE: Tell us what the score is now before we discuss this aspect further.

RAND: OK. First, Lippen is clean. He was recently transferred out of the tool group and actually was in the group only three weeks during the period of time the alleged offense took place. Both Stimmer and Ruppert absolutely deny the charge. They admit close knowledge of the suppliers but were rather evasive on the question of entertainment. Stimmer stated he was at the fishing party I mentioned to you earlier.

Ruppert says he doesn't associate with salesmen outside of the office.

THOMAS: I handled the outside investigation. We went over every phase of Stimmer's and Ruppert's personal affairs—bank accounts, recent large purchases, standard of living, and so forth. Both are clean insofar as concrete evidence is concerned, but there is considerable doubt in my mind as to whether these guys are on the level. Stimmer lives well but not too far over the level he could support on his income. Ruppert took a very expensive vacation last year—two weeks in Florida at a fancy hotel. I believe a supplier paid a large part of the bills while he was there, but again I have no proof.

RAND: I think you should also know that we have checked the suppliers very carefully too. I have tried to determine the expense account entries on the salesmen's reports turned into the companies. You realize that a company is in a box with the Internal Revenue if we catch it falsifying expenses. Again nothing conclusive, but, Paul, you should know that these companies all have substantial entries listing entertaining your people. I believe your name was even listed a few times.

BELLOWS: If you could check all of the 2,200 suppliers we do business with, I bet you will find my name quite often. Needless to say, I don't even know many of the salesmen, but a purchasing agent's name on the sales report for a lunch impresses the sales manager—and who is going to check to find the salesman is doing a little padding?

RAND: That is undoubtedly true, but there were still many of Albert's personnel on the statements. I was surprised that people outside of the purchasing department were mentioned freely. However, there was nothing to implicate Stimmer or Ruppert.

THOMAS: Well, what else can we say? We have a lot of suspicion that Stimmer and Ruppert are, at best, pretty close to these suppliers. Boles, of course, could be involved in this thing too. We didn't get around to checking his personal affairs as closely as the others, but I don't think he is completely out from under, from what little we have been able to determine.

BELLOWS: What do you say, Ralph?

NANCE: Well, I don't believe we can do much more. We have the information and can be on the lookout for future indications. It is regrettable that we can't run this thing into the ground, but there isn't anything we can do about it.

BELLOWS: Then I want to thank you gentlemen for your help so far and, if we do uncover anything, we will contact you.

Exhibit 1

THE ALBERT MANUFACTURING COMPANY—WICHITA DIVISION

Organization Chart—Purchasing Department

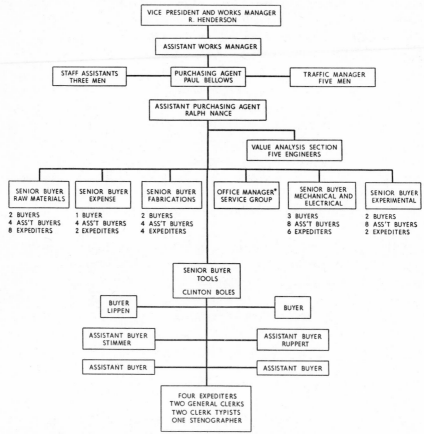

* Equal in classification to senior buyer. There were 18 women clerks, typists, and stenographers in the service group out of a total of 43 for the entire purchasing department.

THOMAS: Feel free to do that—even if we can't get out right away we can tell you what move you should make.

After Thomas and Rand had gone, Bellows and Nance talked over the situation. Nance expressed the following views.

NANCE: Paul, I'm not sure what I should do, but I'll tell you one thing: I don't want these guys in the tool group any longer. I've got to have a senior buyer that I can trust completely and buyers that are above reproach.

This whole mess is like shadow boxing. Just last November I rated Boles as ready for advancement and Stimmer and Ruppert certainly have always been considered as competent.

However, as I see it I have got to take action to make sure the situation is under control and guarantee this kind of thing doesn't happen again. Do you agree?

Skyway Electronics, Inc.

IN THE SUMMER OF 1958, Mr. Horace Jones of Jones, Evarts and Company was making an investigation of Skyway Electronics, Inc. Jones, Evarts was a small investment trust, and its officers were looking for an "up and coming" electronics firm in which to invest.

Mr. Jones met several Skyway officers, but talked chiefly with R. S. Huntley, the executive vice-president. Jones was attempting, among other things, to ascertain how the top executives of Skyway dealt with their officers and workers. It was a Jones, Evarts maxim that when one buys stock in a company one invests in its management's attitudes, traditions, and viewpoints as well as in the assets or liabilities more commonly taken into account.

Mr. Huntley and other Skyway executives answered all questions freely and frankly.

THE COMPANY AND ITS CHARACTERISTICS

Skyway Electronics had been established in 1945. It made a variety of unique electronic components developed through research and experimentation. These were protected by patents, some of which would expire between 1958 and 1962. The company also made some general-purpose components. Sales had risen from $100,000 in 1946 to about $26 million in 1957 (Exhibit 1). Production in 1958 was carried on at five locations: Ohio, Indiana, Pennsylvania, California, and Montreal. The Ohio facility was chiefly a pilot operation. The Indiana plant was a wholly owned subsidiary, the Cramden Company, acquired as a going concern in 1956.

Skyway was organized on a regional-division basis, each manufacturing unit having its own technical, sales, and manufacturing staffs. At headquarters, in Cleveland, the company maintained four supervisory groups, each under a vice-president—for marketing, technical direction, engineering services, and finance and control. A fifth vice-president was directly responsible for the performance of the five operating divisions (Exhibit 2).

The president of Skyway was Dr. Frank McLean, an electrical

engineer by training, who had risen through the technical departments of the company. His father, founder of the company, had retired from active management in 1953. Frank McLean concentrated on technical developments, while Mr. Huntley attended to organizational and managerial matters. Huntley had served Skyway since its inception.

The company enjoyed a largely unchallenged position for its specialized products, serving a variety of manufacturing customers. In

Exhibit 1

SKYWAY ELECTRONICS, INC.

Sales, Profits, and Gross Fixed Assets
Actual 1945 to 1957, Estimated 1958 to 1962

(Millions of Dollars)

Year	Sales	Pretax Profit (or Loss)	Profit as % of Sales	Annual Sales Increase	Gross Fixed Assets
1945........	$ ...	$ ...	..	...	$ ...
1946........	0.1	(0.1)	..	...	...
1947........	0.2	(0.3)	..	100%	...
1948........	0.4	(0.4)	..	100	0.2
1949........	0.9	(0.5)	..	125	1.0
1950........	2.1	(0.1)	..	135	1.3
1951........	5.4	0.5	9%	155	1.7
1952........	5.9	(0.9)	..	10	4.0
1953........	9.5	0.6	6	60	4.4
1954........	15.0	2.8	19	58	4.8
1955........	18.5	4.0	22	24	6.1
1956........	24.5	5.6	23	32	8.6
1957........	25.9	4.2	16	6	10.1
1958 (est.)...	30.0	6.4	21	16	12.0
1959 (est.)...	34.5	6.5	19	15	13.3
1960 (est.)...	40.0	6.8	17	15	15.1
1961 (est.)...	46.0	7.1	15	15	17.4
1962 (est.)...	52.0	7.4	14	15	19.4

1958, however, Mr. Huntley and Mr. McLean were concerned about the possibility of competitive developments. They considered technical obsolescence another threat from a long-range point of view. Profits had been highly satisfactory in the recent past (Exhibits 3 and 4).

The company sold its specialized components through a sales force of 145 men trained in all technical aspects and applications of the products. They sought new customers and called frequently on existing ones. Customers were exacting as to quality and delivery. Special machinery for production was required, and the work force needed a reasonable degree of skill and application to maintain satisfactory output.

Exhibit 2

SKYWAY ELECTRONICS, INC.

Organization Chart
June, 1958

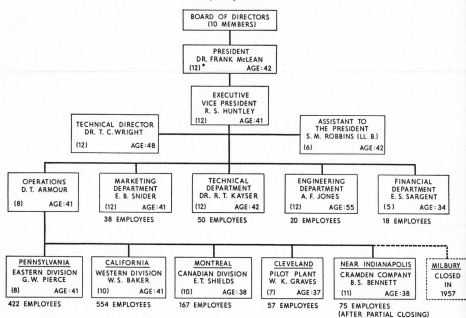

* Figures in parentheses denote years of service.

Exhibit 3

SKYWAY ELECTRONICS, INC.

Operating Statements, 1956, 1957, Nine Months 1958
(Thousands of Dollars)

	1956		1957		Nine Months 1958	
Net sales	$24,500	100%	$25,920	100%	$20,500	100%
Manufacturing cost of sales	13,700	56	14,300	55	11,050	54
Gross profit	$10,800	44%	$11,620	45%	$ 9,450	46%
Expenses:						
Selling	$ 3,150	13%	$ 4,990	19%	$3,400	17%
General and administrative	800	3	650	3	550	3
Research	1,200	5	1,310	5	1,000	5
Total	$ 5,150	21%	$ 6,950	27%	$ 4,950	25%
Net operating profit	$ 5,650	23%	$ 4,670	18%	$ 4,500	22%
Other income (expense)	(20)	..	(300)	1	(100)	0.5
Net profit before tax	$ 5,630	23%	$ 4,370	17%	$ 4,400	21%
Income taxes	2,900	12	2,150	8	2,300	11
Net profit	$ 2,730	11%	$ 2,220	9%	$ 2,100	10%

Exhibit 4

SKYWAY ELECTRONICS, INC.

Balance Sheets, December 31, 1956, 1957, and March 31, 1958

(Thousands of Dollars)

Assets

	1956	1957	1958
Current Assets:			
Cash	$ 1,600	$ 500	$ 700
Receivables—Net	3,100	3,800	3,100
Inventories	5,400	7,200	8,400
Other Current Assets	100	100	100
Total Current Assets	$10,200	$11,600	$12,300
Property and Equipment	$10,100	$12,000	$12,200
Reserves for Depreciation	2,500	3,100	3,300
Net Property and Equipment	$ 7,600	$ 8,900	$ 8,900
Deferred Charges	$ 100	$ 400	$ 400
Total Assets	$17,900	$20,900	$21,600

Liabilities

	1956	1957	1958
Current Liabilities:			
Notes and Accounts Payable	$ 800	$ 1,300	$ 1,100
Accrued Liabilities	200	500	400
Federal Income Tax	2,500	1,400	900
Total Current Liabilities	$ 3,500	$ 3,200	$ 2,400
Other Liabilities	$ 400	$ 400	$ 400
Long-Term Debt	1,000	2,100	3,500
Capital Stock (Common)	$ 8,000	$ 8,000	$ 8,000
Earned Surplus	5,000	7,200	7,300
Total Net Worth	$13,000	$15,200	$15,300
Total Liabilities	$17,900	$20,900	$21,600

Mr. Jones asked Mr. Huntley what problems the company had encountered in connection with the release, transfer, retraining, and moving of personnel during its growth.

Mr. Huntley began his answer by explaining that Skyway had an unwritten rule that any officer or supervisor who had been employed for 10 or more years would be kept on even though change in scope of company operations or other factors had reduced his usefulness. "If we have not found out in 10 years whether the person is any good, it was our mistake, and we are stuck with the problem," Mr. Huntley said. The company, he added, attempted to take the best possible care of all its employees.

Speaking of future problems of personnel transfers and promotions, Mr. Huntley observed that the company's management was young, the average age being not quite 42 years for the 14 top positions. He foresaw few vacancies to absorb lower management members or men freed by changes in operations. He expected a slower rate of growth in future years as patent protection diminished and competition increased (Exhibit 1).

Huntley and other Skyway officers then described in detail the company's treatment of employees under two sets of circumstances: (1) when a plant was closed; (2) when a company was purchased and operated as a subsidiary.

CLOSING A PLANT

When Skyway Electronics was established in 1945, initial efforts had been concentrated on product development and improvement. After suitable products had been designed, the original intent was to build a new plant in Cleveland near the research facilities, the pilot operations, and headquarters. The president, however, heard of an opportunity to purchase a vacated multistory factory building, formerly used for food processing, in Milbury, a Kentucky town of 30,000 people. The purchase price was attractive in comparison with the costs of erecting a new building. Furthermore, it was thought that labor union difficulties might delay construction in Cleveland. The purchase was made and operations were begun in 1946. By 1950 the building was being used practically to capacity, and it became apparent that a major period of expansion lay ahead. Plans were then made for a plant in California, which was completed in 1951. By 1953 the need for another plant in the East was obvious, and one was built in Pennsylvania. During this period, the needs of the Canadian market had been met by exports from the United States. In 1956, however, the company began construction of a plant in Montreal, chiefly to avoid the 20% import duty.

At the end of 1956, the Skyway executives believed the period of frantic company growth was ended and it was time to review operations. The three United States plants together provided excess capacity, as much as 50% at times. Thus, the question of closing the Milbury plant arose.

A study of operating records showed the Milbury plant to be about 15% lower in efficiency than the others. Moreover, wage rates were about 10% higher. The local labor union was strong. There were in the area about 8,000 workers. Of these, 6,500 were employed by a division of General Machinery Corporation. The assistant to the president of Skyway, Mr. Robbins, characterized the situtation as follows: "When our company was operating full swing in the early 1950's, it had scraped the bottom of the labor barrel. We were experimental then and needed more workers than we did when production became more routine. Because of a seniority clause in the union contract, however, most of these employees had to be kept on and this led to feather-bedding." Mr. Robbins thought the employees lacked motivation and the will to work, even though they were sufficiently skilled; workers in this plant had not been put on an incentive wage basis such as was used in the California plant. Further, Robbins said, it was common for them to live beyond their means, which led to garnishments and assignments of wages to local businesses.

The plant's location, moreover, was poor in relation to the company's major markets. Mr. Robbins pointed out that the decision to buy the plant had been made on the basis of expediency more than on considerations of location. In contrast, the new plants had been located after careul surveys of proximity to markets, local tax situations, available labor, and so on. In addition, the Milbury building was awkwardly constructed for the purposes of Skyway Electronics. The ground floor, especially, was poorly laid out and hampered manufacturing operations.

A report by the company's treasurer as of November 15, 1956, showed anticipated operating savings for 1957 from closing Milbury of $550,000 against a probable cost of shutdown of $200,000. A second estimate as of January 25, 1957, showed no net operating savings for 1957, but for 1958 and each year thereafter this estimate put net operating savings at $625,000. An estimate as of February 26, 1958 put future operating savings at $665,000 annually. Large capital savings also were expected (Exhibits 5 and 6).

The decision to shut down the Milbury plant was announced on March 8, 1957. Work stoppage was completed by June 1, with only a skeleton force remaining. The decision affected 251 workers.

According to Mr. Armour, operations vice-president, the contemplated move was kept secret until the March announcement because of the possibility of a charge by the union that the company was a "runaway employer." Mr. Huntley pointed out, however, that during the two years preceding the shutdown there had been several instances in which the inefficiencies of the operation had been called to the attention of the union and the workers. In one case, a study by a consulting firm had shown clearly that the plant's performance was substandard.

The company's relations with the union had not been cordial in the past, but neither had there been serious difficulties. In the early days of the operation a strike was called on an issue of technological unem-

Exhibit 5

SKYWAY ELECTRONICS, INC.

Memorandum on Closing Milbury
January 28, 1957

The following understanding of the situation in regard to closing the Milbury plant was reached in a meeting held January 25, 1957. This meeting was attended by Messrs. McLean, Huntley, Armour, and Sargent.

1. If we shut down Milbury in 1957, we will have to spend an additional $400,000 in the next five years (that is, through 1961) in the remaining factories in this country which would not otherwise be required.
2. Against this additional expenditure we have the following possible credits:
    a) Anything received for the sale of Milbury (book value $600,000).
    b) Reduction in working capital (estimated $100,000 for 1957, $300,000 estimated 1958–61).
    c) $135,000 ($150,000 less $15,000 duty) for miscellaneous equipment which would be shipped to Canada and which they otherwise have to buy.
    d) $50,000 production equipment which would not be needed if we close one U.S. factory.
    e) $70,000 reduction in capital needed for miscellaneous projects at Milbury.

Item (*c*) assumes that we go ahead with the Canadian plant and that the Milbury shutdown would be so timed that certain equipment could be transferred in time to take care of Canadian needs.

3. The savings which can reasonably be expected for a full year of operation with Milbury shutdown (starting in 1958) are as follows:
    a) $375,000 in lower manufacturing costs made up primarily of four items—lower labor rates, greater productivity, better flow, a greater divisor. We agree with the first three although we think there is a point beyond which the last point applies.
    b) $50,000 in reduced order and billing expenses. This is out of $125,000 contemplated for Milbury in 1957.
    c) $200,000 out of factory overhead expenses made up; $90,000 out of $500,000 of general overhead; $43,000 out of $105,000 for scheduling, production control, and so forth; $67,000 out of $107,000 for shipping and receiving. After sale of the Milbury property we can realize an additional $25,000 saving in building depreciation.

In 1957 the total operating savings are estimated at $200,000. This estimated saving will offset the estimated costs of $200,000 to be incurred in shutting down the plant and moving personnel and equipment.

We realize that a third plant gives a greater factor of safety and believe this is offset by the savings which accrue.

If sales in 1961 exceed the $46,000,000 presently estimated, a new plant will probably be needed, but we would be free to locate at the most desirable spot and build a properly laid out facility.

The mechanics of closing must be carefully planned.

Exhibit 6

SKYWAY ELECTRONICS, INC.

*Memorandum on Savings from Closing Milbury Plant
Dated February 26, 1958*

(Thousands of Dollars)

	For Year 1957			Annual 1958 and After
	November 15, 1956	January 25, 1957		February 26, 1958
1. *Capital Saving*	*Estimate*	*Estimate*	*Actual*	*Estimate*
a) Sale of building............$ 600		Undetermined	Undetermined	$503*
b) Working capital............. 100		$100	$358	358
c) Capital equipment for Canada plant............ 210		135	145	...
d) Other productive equipment.. 50		50	75	...
e) Reduced expenditures........ 72		70	69	...
f) Miscellaneous equipment..... ...		...	50	...
	$1,032	$355	$597	$861

	For Year 1957			Annual 1958 and After	
	November 15, 1956	January 25, 1957		January 25, 1957	February 26, 1958
2. *Expense Saving*	*Estimate*	*Estimate*	*Actual*	*Estimate*	*Estimate*
a) Manufacturing costs.....$300		...	$259	$375	$400
b) Order and billing....... 50		...	13	50	20
c) Factory overhead....... 200		...	238	200	300
Total savings.....$550		$200	$510	$625	$720
d) Less carrying costs (utilities, mainte- nance, depreciation, taxes, etc.)........ ...		...	84†	...	55‡
e) Net savings............. 550		200	426	625	665
f) Cost of shutdown....... 200		200	303	...	...
Saving before capital loss on building........$350		...	$123	$625	$665

* Less annual depreciation.
† $52,000 maintenance, and so on; $32,000 depreciation.
‡ Only as long as we own building.

ployment. The conflict was resolved by arbitration in two hours. During contract negotiations in 1955 there had been threat of a strike, and arbitration again was successful. Much time had been spent in 1955 in negotiations on the issue of termination pay. Mr. Armour believed this indicated the union leaders thought the plant would be closed sooner or later.

During the 1955 negotiations the union had asked for a pay raise of 17 cents an hour as against the company's offer of 8 to 10 cents. The local plant manager began negotiations on the basis that the company would rather take a strike than incur the extra wage expense. Both sides were firmly entrenched in their positions when the Skyway management suddenly realized, according to Mr. Armour, that forcing the strike issue could expose the company to charges of unfair practices if it subsequently closed the plant. Consequently, the plant manager was instructed to accept the union's demands. "We rigged the figures a little so it looked like they were getting 17 cents including fringe benefits, although it actually amounted to less," Mr. Armour explained. The union dropped its termination pay clause demand at this point.

When the decision to close the plant in 1957 was announced, there was great concern at headquarters that an unfair labor charge nevertheless might result. All correspondence with the union was sent to legal counsel for approval, and all statements to be made in discussions with worker representatives were rehearsed. To the great relief of the Skyway officers, the union made no charge. Mr. Armour commented that the local union agent, though often difficult to deal with, was a realistic man who understood the facts of business. "Once he was convinced we were honest about the economics of the shutdown, he came around and did not really have much of a basis for an unfair labor charge." Moreover, the attention of the union was directed primarily at the major employer in the community; Skyway was only a small factor in the labor situation. "The agent was not dependent upon our employees for his pay; he was mainly supported by dues coming from the General Machinery plant."

Of the 251 persons idled by the shutdown, 181 were hourly employees, 150 men and 31 women. The company's controller had worked out a termination pay arrangement which in essence amounted to what the union had asked for in 1955. Each employee was to be given one week's pay for each year of service.

In its preliminary estimates the company had expected the total cost of termination payments to be about $40,000. An additional $20,000 had been set aside for the cost of transferring to other locations 15 supervisory employees the company wished to keep. The actual costs of termination and transfer, however, were estimated at $113,000. There were several factors contributing to this increase, some of the more important of which are described in the following paragraphs.

Termination payments, mainly to hourly personnel, were higher than expected by $12,000 because of a larger than anticipated number of employees at the time of shutdown.

The moving expense of the 15 supervisory personnel amounted to

$25,000 rather than the estimated $20,000. Included in this amount was $7,500 spent by the company to help with real estate transactions. The shutdown at Milbury coincided with the withdrawal of two other minor employers from the community and with the first signs of the 1958 recession affecting the General Machinery plant. Consequently, those selling their homes faced a depressed market. The company helped five persons by paying taxes, insurance, and upkeep on their homes for several months. Also, it reimbursed several employees for capital losses and made some interest-free loans until mortgage financing could be arranged. This type of assistance was voluntary; company policy on the moving of personnel, which had been established prior to this specific instance, did not call for such help (Exhibit 7). "We wanted to keep these people," said Mr. Huntley. "Good people were hard to find in 1957."

Exhibit 7

SKYWAY ELECTRONICS, INC.

Subject: Moving Expenses (Policies in effect at time of Milbury shutdown).

The company will reimburse salaried employees for all direct expenses and for reasonable indirect expenses that they incur in moving to new job assignments.

Direct expenses include the cost of packing, transporting and storing household furnishings (and of insuring them while in transit and storage), and the one-way transportation fares of the employee and his family.

Reimbursement of indirect expenses is left to the judgment of the policy book holder concerned, who will determine their reasonableness (as to object and amount) in each case in the light of the following general guides:

We will *normally* pay, if circumstances justify:

1. Travel and living expenses of one or two trips by the employee and his wife to find housing in the new area.

2. Meals and lodging for the family for a reasonable time after it moves to the new area until housing is obtained and readied for occupancy. One month is considered a maximum "reasonable time," which shall not be exceeded without the approval of the president or vice-president.

3. Occasional week-end commuting expenses of an employee who does not move his family immediately to the new area because, for example, the reassignment was made on short notice, or there is illness in his family, or there are children who should finish the school term.

4. Incidental expenses of relocation, such as reinstallation of electric stoves and other heavy appliances, and refitting of rugs and draperies. Expenses of this type must be itemized with exactness and are particularly subject to screening as to reasonableness, both individually and in the aggregate. Normally, agreement as to type of expense and the approximate magnitude should be reached with employees in advance of moving.

Exhibit 7—Continued

In a case involving hardship or other unusual circumstances, subject to the approval of the president or vice-president in advance of any commitment being made to the employee, we may:

1. Pay the broker's fee in connection with the sale of a house.
2. Help an employee carry two houses (until the old one is sold) by making an interest-free loan secured by a second mortgage.
3. Pay the "closing" costs (i.e., the costs incidental to obtaining a new mortgage) when an employee is transferred to a new location within a few months of an earlier move.

We will normally not pay:

1. Any loss on the sale of a house.
2. Expenses of a second move in the new area.

The employee, with the approval of the Division or Department Manager or his designee, will select the mover in each case. An estimate should be obtained from the mover before the move. The mover will be instructed to bill the company for his services, and the company will pay the charges only after it has received a voucher showing that the employee has declared all the goods shipped to have been delivered in satisfactory condition. Any claims for loss or damage will be handled by the employee or by the company at his request, in which latter event the employee shall release the company from any liability for loss or damage resulting from the move.

Before the mover's services are engaged, the employee should understand that the mover's liability for loss or damage is limited to 30 cents per pound and excludes certain risks unless the employee obtains proper "all risk" insurance coverage (costing about $5 per $1,000 of declared value) through the mover or through his own insurance agent.

Immediately following a move, an employee should submit to his divisional headquarters (with a copy to the assistant general sales manager) a brief report as to his satisfaction with the move. These reports, which will include records of claims for damage—their nature and settlement—will build a file of experience that will be helpful in arranging future moves.

Moving expenses should be charged to the personnel procurement expense account (150).

The company incurred additional unforeseen costs of $36,000 because not all the 15 transferred persons could be immediately employed on tasks commensurate with their salaries. Mr. Adams, for example, had been an assistant superintendent at Milbury. He had served there 10 years, and his total time with the company was 12 years. Mr. Huntley said Mr. Adams was a man of unquestioned loyalty and some members of management thought very highly of him. Mr. Huntley did not, although he considered Adams capable in some ways. When Milbury was shut down Adams was transferred to California and put on a development project. Huntley commented that he had fitted well into his new position but was being paid more than he was worth. "I don't know what we will do with him once the project is finished," he said. "He is not as good as the other assistant superintendents who are being paid $5,500 against his $7,500." Huntley thought Adams' abilities were best utilized in the position of foreman, which he had orignally held.

Unanticipated termination expenses of $35,000 were incurred because of sick leaves taken by employees. Many of the employees of the plant asked for such leaves as soon as the decision to close became known. Mr. Huntley said most of them were "no more sick than any of us"; they took advantage of the company, he said, with the help of unscrupulous doctors in the community. Employees went on sick leaves for correction of conditions, such as hernias or hemorrhoids, that had existed for years without treatment. And there were treatments for what seemed to be imaginary conditions also. The opportunity to receive something for nothing led many of the workers, particularly the women, to arrange with their doctors for certificates of illness. In some cases medical payments, made through employers' insurance, continued for several months after the plant was shut down.

Mr. Huntley added:

This hurt our insurance rating as an employer, and the only way to prevent it would have been to ask the insurance agency to investigate the local doctors. The agency representatives became suspicious anyway when this rash of illnesses occurred, but we did not wish to press the issue because it would have meant very bad feeling for our company. As things were, the community at least did not hate us.

There were other ways in which the company assisted the employees to make the transition. The personnel manager of the plant, characterized by Mr. Huntley as a very able person, remained until the shutdown was completed. He and his staff assisted hourly employees who had several years of service with the company to find employment elsewhere. Furthermore, the company paid travel expenses for nine supervisors and other salaried personnel forced to seek employment with other firms. In some instances the company paid fares up to $250. In total, about $2,000 was spent for the purpose.

When the decision to close was announced, some of the workers immediately started to look for work in other areas. Under the rules of the termination agreement they would forfeit their separation pay if they left before the company released them. The company modified this policy. It released employees who found work on their own prior to their scheduled separation and gave everyone separation pay.

The impact on the community of the plant closing, together with the departure of other employers, was severe. Mr. Snider, the marketing vice-president, described Milbury as a dying town and in general not a very desirable place in which to live. He said white-collar employees in particular had considered the location the "Siberia" of the company, and all the people who had been transferred there originally were glad to leave.

Mr. Armour said he did not know what happened to all the employees the company left behind. About 30% of them had come from the rural surroundings of the town. He did not believe the large machinery company had hired many of them. Within a radius of about 50 miles there were several other large manufacturing and processing plants, and he supposed many of the workers had found jobs there. Four valuable employees with high technical abilities chose to leave the company. One elected to stay in the area because of family ties. The other three secured good positions with large firms elsewhere. Mr. Armour regretted their loss.

The company took losses on inventories of supplies originally worth thousands of dollars. Some in-process inventories were discovered which had been spoiled and apparently hidden by the foremen in charge.

Although various closing expenses were greater than expected, the company nevertheless had direct operating savings of $123,000 in 1957 as a result of the shutdown (Exhibit 6). Gross capital savings for 1957 were placed at $597,000 with no allowance for the value of the Milbury building.

This building, with a book value in 1957 of $600,000, stood empty for six months and then was leased on a short-term basis to the General Machinery Corporation. In the spring of 1958 it had not yet been sold. An independent appraiser set its market value at little more than $100,000 in view of the depressed state of the community. The company was hoping to sell to any reasonable bidder. The capital loss on the sale would be more than made up by the savings achieved through the consolidation of operations. And loss on sale of the building would be tax deductible.

The company's capital savings, including $145,000 from transfer of equipment to the new Canadian plant, were partially offset by expenditures at other plants called for by the Milbury closing. It had been anticipated that such expenditures would amount to $400,000 over a five-year period (Exhibits 5 and 6).

PURCHASING A COMPANY

Skyway Electronics acquired the Cramden Company in April, 1956, for $500,000 in Skyway stock and payment of Cramden's long-term indebtedness of $100,000. In addition, Skyway spent $200,000 for needed equipment and added $121,000 to working capital.

The two multistory buildings that housed operations were not included in the purchase agreement. These were leased from Mr. Cramden by Skyway for a five-year period at an annual cost of $23,000.

The Cramden Company manufactured electronic components. It had been founded and managed by a family trio: father, mother, and son. The Cramden family had built the enterprise around the inventive abilities of father and son and Mrs. Cramden's management ability. The company produced two distinct lines of components. One line, accounting for 60% of sales, consisted of specialty components for a market Skyway wished to enter. The other line consisted of general-purpose components. Total sales volume in 1957 was about $1 million. There were 90 hourly employees, a plant manager, and 13 salesmen.

Labor relations in the Cramden Company had been cordial throughout its history. The plant was not unionized. Mr. Robbins characterized management's past labor relationships as somewhat paternalistic.

The major purpose of the acquisition was to obtain the technical knowledge and the facilities for manufacturing Cramden's special components. By purchasing a going concern, Skyway hoped to gain time and to avoid many of the problems and costs involved in the alternative of setting up a research and development program of its own. The sales potential for the Cramden components appeared promising, as the total market was considered to be $100 million a year. Skyway hoped to capture about 10% of this market by 1960.

When Skyway took over the company the elder Mr. Cramden was retained as president; Mrs. Cramden became the treasurer; and the son, Elton Cramden, was named chief engineer. Huntley concluded fairly soon that the plant manager, Mr. Brown, was not doing a satisfactory job. He had been with Cramden for 15 years and was being paid $11,000 a year. Huntley told him the company could not keep him on as plant manager but could make him purchasing vice-president of the subsidiary at a salary of $7,500. Huntley reported that Mr. Brown gladly accepted the post, with the cut in pay, and had done adequate work.

After about a year of operations, the Skyway officers concluded, according to Mr. Huntley, that Mr. and Mrs. Cramden were not so efficient as had been hoped in managing the company as a subsidiary. Mr. Huntley went on to say that he and Mr. McLean decided to put pressure on the couple to retire from active management. Mr. Armour described Mr. Cramden as a born promoter and inventor, but a poor business manager. Mrs. Cramden, he said, was competent but was hampered by ill health and nervous tension. Elton Cramden was a very competent electrical engineer and inventor.

Mr. and Mrs. Cramden finally agreed to retire early in 1958. Elton was retained by Skyway to continue developing the Cramden special components.

Mr. Armour pointed out some of the difficulties encountered with Mr. Cramden. Cramden had found it very hard to adjust to the fact that his company now was part of a larger enterprise and he could no longer act independently. For instance, although Skyway officials informed Mr. Cramden they had decided the subsidiary was to concentrate efforts on further development of the specialty components, he gave much more time to some of the unprofitable standard items in which he had a personal interest. He managed to stay within his budgets, but the detailed spending did not correspond with the needs of the company. Furthermore, Cramden frequently argued with Armour and Huntley about the state of development of the products and about alternative manufacturing processes. His representations had led on several occasions to embarrassment with customers. Skyway management had relied on his word that certain components were ready for the market while in fact they had not fully cleared the development stage. "We made the mistake of listening and not looking," said Mr. Armour.

In view of these difficulties, and in consideration of the uncertain health of Mrs. Cramden, the Skyway officers felt that retirement for the Cramdens was a sound solution, especially since they were financially secure. As a face-saving gesture, Skyway retained Mr. Cramden in a consulting capacity. "This makes him feel important, and he does have quite a bit of know-how," Mr. Armour explained.

Conditions at Cramden, however, did not improve materially even after the Cramdens withdrew from active management. Serious quality problems were encountered with the specialty components on the one hand, and, on the other hand, the standard components met stiff price competition and were sold at a loss sufficient to make the entire operation unprofitable (Exhibit 8). A report dated May 8, 1958, pointed out that while operations at Cramden had shown a small profit in 1956,

Exhibit 8

SKYWAY ELECTRONICS, INC.

Operating Statements by Divisions,
1957

(Thousands of Dollars)

	Western	Milbury (Closed in 1957)	Eastern	Home	Canadian	Gramden	Total*
Net sales................	$13,250	$3,630	$9,890	$2,740	$2,510	$1,070	$25,920
Cost of sales...........	7,710	2,950	5,750	2,100	1,810	1,150	14,300
Gross profit...........	$ 5,540	$ 680	$4,140	$ 640	$ 700	$ (80)	$11,620
Expenses:							
Selling.............	$ 2,020	$ 460	$1,590	$ 160	$ 640	$ 120	$ 4,990
General and administrative........	290	80	160	50	40	30	650
Research............	560	120	220	280	90	40	1,310
	$ 2,870	$ 660	$1,970	$ 490	$ 770	$ 190	$ 6,950
Net operating profit (loss)..........	$ 2,670	$ 20	$2,170	$ 150	$ (70)	$ (270)	$ 4,670
Other income (expense).............	(60)	(10)	(40)	(180)	...	(10)	(300)
Net profit (loss) before tax.........	$ 2,610	$ 10	$2,130	$ (30)	$ (70)	$ (280)	$ 4,370
Income tax.............							$ 2,150
Net profit after tax....							$ 2,220

* Interdivisional sales amounting to $7,170 eliminated from total.

there was a loss in 1957 amounting to 26% of sales, and operations in the first quarter of 1958 showed an 8.6% loss. However, the report added that valuable know-how had been obtained and the desired diversification achieved.

In June, 1958, Skyway reached the decision to close down production of standard components at Cramden. The gross margin was generally much lower for standard components than for specialty items, 24% versus 43% in 1958. The specialty components showed a good potential, according to Mr. Huntley, although the quality problem was still present and competition could be expected to develop substitute products within the next five years. Huntley thought Skyway had not been sufficiently active to date in developing the market for the Cramden specialties.

The decision to discontinue production of Cramden standard components came after Skyway executives had weighed four alternatives:

Exhibit 9

SKYWAY ELECTRONICS, INC.

Cost of Alternative Ways of Dealing with Cramden Company
(Thousands of Dollars)

Type of Expense	Alternative 1 Close Down	Alternative 2 Close Down	Alternative 3 Close Partially to 1961	Alternative 4 Maintain as at Present to 1961
Immediate Expenses				
1. Cash Outlays:				
Termination—personnel	$ 25	$ 25	$ 15	$ ..
Transfer—personnel	10	10	5	..
Transfer—equipment	50	50	10	..
	$ 85	$ 85	$ 30	$ ..
2. Book write-offs:				
Equipment, building, inventory	100	180	50	..
3. Total immediate	$185	$265	$ 80	$ ..
Expenses in 1961				
(Termination of lease)				
1. Cash outlays:				
Termination—personnel	$ ..	$ ..	$ 5	$ 10
Transfer—personnel	..	..	5	10
Transfer—equipment	..	..	40	50
	$ ..	$ ..	$ 50	$ 70
2. Book write-offs:				
Equipment, inventory	..	..	10	50
3. Total 1961 expense	$ ..	$ ..	$ 60	$120
Grand total	$185	$265	$140	$120

1. Close the plant completely and transfer manufacture of specialty components to other locations. The payments for the remaining two and a half years of the leasehold agreement on the buildings would be the only continuing costs for the Cramden location under this plan.
2. Close the plant completely, moving specialty components manufacture. Settle the leasehold obligation by agreeing, in return for cancellation of the remaining lease payments of $23,000 per annum, to leave intact $112,000 in leasehold improvements, which included a sprinkler system and a freight elevator.
3. Continue production of specialty components, but not of general-purpose items, at Cramden for the remainder of the leasehold agreement. Keep overhead at a minimum.
4. Continue production of both lines at Cramden but cut administrative and sales expense to a minimum.

Exhibits 9 and 10 give a figure analysis of these alternatives. The third alternative was chosen partly because it required relatively low immediate cash outlay. Furthermore, it allowed for orderly liquidation of inventories and gradual reduction of specialty component production

Exhibit 10

SKYWAY ELECTRONICS, INC.

Operating Data under Alternative Plans for Cramden Company
Annual Estimate, 1958 to 1961
(Thousands of dollars)

	Alternative 1 Close Down	Alternative 2 Close Down	Alternative 3 Continue Specialties to 1961	Alternative 4 Maintain as at present to 1961
Sales:				
Special components	$550	$550	$550	$ 550
Standard components	...	...	...	600
Total	$550	$550	$550	$1,150
Cost of Sales:				
Special components	$275	$275	$275	$ 275
Standard components	...	...	...	460
	$275	$275	$275	$ 735
Gross margin	$275	$275	$275	$ 415
Leasehold expense (until 1961)	$ 65	$...	$ 68	$ 70
Factory expense:				
Special components	95	95	87	87
Standard components	..	..	..	93
Order and billing:				
Special components	15	15	15	15
Standard components	..	..	..	105
Total expense	$175	$110	$170	$ 370
Contribution	$100*	$165*	$105	$ 45

* Contribution would continue after 1961.

should expected competitive developments hurt the market outlook. Also, the effect on employees and the community would be less severe than under alternatives (1) and (2).

The company's decision meant that about half the 90 hourly employees and some of the 13 salaried salesmen would be laid off immediately. Mr. Huntley pointed out that there was a great deal of difference between the impact on the community in this case and in the case of Milbury. Although the Cramden plant, too, was in a community of only 30,000 people, it was very near Indianapolis. The Skyway officers thought the idled employees would not have extreme difficulty finding employment there.

Mr. Huntley said there was a possibility the plant would be kept open beyond the expiration of the lease, if it should appear there was use for it as a pilot operation and experimental shop. If it were closed, the company again would face the problem of personnel transfers. Huntley wished to transfer about five supervisors in case of a shutdown. He stated that Skyway also could not afford to lose all the other good employees who still were with Cramden. On the other hand, he was reluctant to resort again to organizational changes in other plants in order to accommodate more than five. "You cannot bust up the organization all the time." Huntley believed a final decision on the disposal of Cramden would come with adequate forewarning. He supposed the company would use the same termination agreements as were used at Milbury. There were, however, a few employees with 17 or 18 years of service who would be virtually unemployable anywhere else. Huntley did not know what the company would do in their cases if the plant were closed.

Belcamp Hardware Company, Inc.

IN 1950 THE GORDON family acquired virtually all the outstanding shares of stock of the Belcamp Hardware Company, Inc., of Louisville, Kentucky. This company was among the older and larger wholesale hardware distributors in Kentucky and Tennessee.

Together, Mr. Thomas Gordon and his two sons owned a little more than 94% of the stock outstanding: Thomas Gordon, aged 72 in 1950, held 164 shares, and Joseph Grodon, 45, and Charles Gordon, 40, each held 6,600 shares. Charles Gordon accepted the presidency of the company, but virtually complete responsibility for operations was given to Mr. Frank Robertson, a friend of the Gordons, who was persuaded to join the company as general manager.

Company net earnings declined sharply under Mr. Robertson's management, however, and by 1958 Charles Gordon was disillusioned as to Robertson's business judgment. The problem Gordon faced was what to do with the Belcamp Company. His own time, as well as that of his brother, was fully occupied by other family enterprises.

Company sales and earnings from 1942 through 1958 are summarized in Exhibit 1.

THE GORDON PURCHASE OF BELCAMP

Mr. Thomas Gordon had purchased 600 shares of Belcamp stock in 1934 from Mr. John Cole, then president of Belcamp. The two men were neighbors and close personal friends. Cole highly respected Gordon's business judgment and asked him to purchase the stock and serve on the Belcamp board of directors. At that time the largest single stockholder was a widow, Mrs. Fred Paine, whose husband had owned and managed the business before his death in 1912. She owned 4,800 shares. These she always voted in support of Mr. Cole's policies. Mr. Cole, after selling the 600 shares, owned 2,400. Mr. Thomas Kent, vice-president and treasurer of Belcamp, owned 1,200 shares. The remaining 5,164 shares outstanding were rather widely held by various Belcamp employees and Louisville businessmen.

When Thomas Gordon first invested in Belcamp, Mr. Cole closely

Exhibit 1

BELCAMP HARDWARE COMPANY, INC.

*Parent Company Sales and Consolidated Earnings
before Federal Income Tax*

Year	Sales Volume	Pretax Earnings or Loss
1942	$3,153,988	$115,750
1943	3,586,811	261,311
1944	3,398,858	203,340
1945	3,242,058	202,416
1946	5,509,142	409,499
1947	6,153,024	257,367
1948	5,489,823	363,614
1949	4,807,553	272,829
1950	5,092,155	256,183
1951	5,691,286	208,242
1952	6,946,265	166,213
1953	7,076,145	(36,219)
1954	5,714,067	39,794
1955	5,313,972	(61,219)
1956	5,966,467	115,637
1957	5,950,807	24,320
1958	5,780,328*	35,277*

* Preliminary figure.

supervised all company operations. Assisting him were three key individuals. Mr. Kent, who also was familiar with all phases of company operations, handled various duties assigned by Mr. Cole. Miss Carolyn Ashley, the assistant treasurer, was in charge of the company records. Mr. Harold Long served as sales manager. Cole and Kent were paid $50,000 a year. Long was paid $25,000 and Miss Ashley, $8,000. In addition, each received annual dividends through ownership of Belcamp stock. The total number of employees was approximately 170.

In February, 1950, Mr. Long suddenly died. At that time Mr. Cole was 71, Mr. Kent was 67, and Miss Ashley was 62. The purchasing agent, age 42, was made sales manager, but Cole and Kent assumed most of Long's former responsibilities.

In September, 1950, Mr. Cole, Mr. Kent, and Miss Ashley all decided to retire as soon as possible. Cole and Kent wished to sell their interest in Belcamp, and they ascertained that other stockholders with sufficient shares to make up a controlling interest also wanted to sell. As no open market existed for the stock, Cole began searching for possible buyers. One group of Louisville businessmen studied the situation but decided not to invest because no one was available to replace Cole and Kent in the company organization. A Chicago group of investors then indicated an interest and tentatively suggested, in October, 1950, a purchase price of $68 a share. This price was satisfactory to Cole, and he was confident the other stockholders would agree to any price he negotiated. The Chicago group asked to study the books in detail before making a definite offer. After this further study, these potential investors refused to pay $68. Although $50,000 "earnest money" had been deposited with Mr. Cole, the agreement stipulated that the money would be returned if the transaction failed to materialize for any reason.

The interested parties then began a series of price negotiations; prices of $63, $60, and $58 a share were suggested by Mr. Cole. Each time the Chicago group rejected the proposal, and, in November, 1950, Cole called off the negotiations.

At this point the Gordons offered to purchase 7,190 shares at $53. With the 600 shares they already held, this would give them 55% of shares outstanding. Mr. Cole accepted their offer.

The Gordons also owned and operated the Gordon Company, a building supply firm that earned after taxes $250,000 or more annually on sales exceeding $12 million and an investment of $3.2 million. Thomas Gordon was chairman of the board, Charles Gordon was president and manager of Louisville operations, and Joseph Gordon was vice-president and manager of the Nashville branch. Each of these officers received an annual salary in excess of $60,000, and each devoted at least 65 hours a week to this business. All three took great personal pleasure in their success in this highly competitive industry, in which single orders involved hundreds or thousands of dollars. In the hardware wholesale business, on the other hand, $65 was a big single transaction. The Gordons also owned majority interests in five other firms. They added Belcamp to their holdings only because they believed the company had a good chance of producing outstanding long-term capital gains. They did not intend to be active in its management.

Almost immediately after acquiring a controlling interest in Belcamp, the Gordons stopped payment of dividends to avoid increases in their personal income tax bases. Most of the minority stockholders, however, depended on the dividends as part of their livelihood. As these minority stockholders came to realize that dividend payments would not be resumed in the foreseeable future, they tried to sell their stock. Many of them asked the Gordon family to buy their holdings, since it seemed quite unlikely that any outsider would be interested in purchasing small blocks of stock in a company in which the management, with

55% of the stock, did not plan to pay dividends. Even though the Gordons did not wish to increase their holdings, they felt an obligation to purchase the stock. They tried to establish a price for each block of stock in light of such considerations as the price originally paid, contributions made by the seller to the company, and the needs of the seller. They ended by purchasing 87% of the minority holdings, or 5,574 shares, giving them ownership of 94% of all shares outstanding. Prices paid ranged between $25 and $50 a share and averaged $36. The Gordons, incidentally, were chagrined to discover that, after selling stock to them for $45 a share, the company's assistant treasurer immediately purchased the same number of shares from another party for $18 a share.

FINDING A GENERAL MANAGER

The Gordons did not anticipate any trouble in finding a good manager for Belcamp. Besides their investment in several local companies, each of the Gordons served as a director of at least one firm, and Charles and Thomas each served on the board of a local bank. Because of these varied interests, the Gordons knew or expected to meet several men seeking the type of opportunity offered at Belcamp. From among these candidates, one would be chosen for training under Cole and Kent, who had agreed to help develop a suitable replacement.

The Gordons interviewed a dozen men in December, 1950, before Charles Gordon mentioned the opportunity to Frank Robertson. Although not related, the Charles Gordons and the Robertsons had certain family ties. Charles' wife, Elizabeth, had a brother who was killed in World War II. The brother's widow, Kathleen, later married Mr. Robertson. Elizabeth and Kathleen had been close friends for many years, and the Robertsons and Charles Gordons were vacationing together in Florida at the time the opportunity with Belcamp was mentioned.

Mr. Robertson, whose father was the executive vice-president of a large oil company, was employed in Chicago as a district sales manager for another major oil firm. After graduation from college with a B minus average, Robertson worked for an oil well supply company and then for the oil firm where he was employed in 1950. Robertson, who was then 35 years of age, believed his advancement in this company had been quite satisfactory and thought his future progress seemed very promising. His salary in 1950 was $12,000 a year. After some preliminary investigation of Belcamp, however, Mr. Robertson said he definitely was interested in the job there.

Thomas and Joseph Gordon, after interviewing Robertson, agreed that he was a likeable individual who made an excellent appearance and had a good mind. Above all, the Gordons felt they could trust his integrity in handling their personal investment; consequently, they offered him the job.

Robertson deliberated about accepting the Gordon offer for approximately six months. During this time Charles Gordon was quite enthusiastic in his description of the potential opportunity offered by Belcamp. In June, 1951, Robertson accepted the offer at a salary of $9,000 a year. The Gordons also promised to sell Robertson some stock at a favorable price if things worked out, but the number of shares and price were not definitely set.

The Robertsons took up residence in Louisville. Thereafter they and the Charles Gordons were together socially at least once a week and often two or three times. Both families were boating enthusiasts, and they frequently got together for week-end boat trips, races, and regattas.

MR. ROBERTSON AT BELCAMP

A week after Robertson began working at Belcamp, Mr. Cole died suddenly, and within six months Mr. Kent was fatally stricken. Charles Gordon became president of the company, and Robertson became general manager and vice-president. As general manager, Robertson was completely responsible for the operation of the business. As a general rule, Gordon's approval was necessary only for decisions involving major policy changes or substantial investments. Gordon continued to devote most of his time to the Gordon Company.

In 1953, in an attempt to improve Belcamp's profits, Robertson undertook to modernize operations. Construction of a new building with 100,000 feet of warehouse space and 13,000 feet of office space was completed in 1954 at a cost of $700,000. The building was owned by the Corydon Company, a family investment trust company of the Gordons. Belcamp paid $73,000 annual rent plus taxes and insurance on the premises.

The new warehouse embodied the latest concepts in materials handling, and Robertson made several innovations that greatly simplified the work of the warehouse crew and cut in half the number of men needed. In addition, the new facility made it possible for the company to handle twice its current sales volume.

Robertson in 1955 supervised the installation of a modern IBM accounting system that incorporated several new ideas later reported in IBM company publications. The new system allowed further reductions in the warehouse crew, gave better control over the inventory level, speeded preparation of reports, and provided reports hitherto unobtainable. Furthermore, Robertson reduced the number of items carried in inventory from 30,000 to 18,000 without lessening the service given to retail accounts.

Nevertheless, company earnings did not improve. Exhibits 2 and 3 show the company's income statements and balance sheets, and Exhibit 4 presents a ratio analysis for selected items.

MR. ROBERTSON'S EVALUATION OF BELCAMP

Robertson believed that the moves he had made were necessary just to keep the company in business. He pointed out that during 1957 and 1958 major hardware distributors in Columbus, Kansas City, St. Louis, and Minneapolis had been forced to liquidate. Many factors were operating against the hardware wholesaler in Robertson's opinion. Average retail hardware store sales were no larger in 1957 than in 1947—$92,000 in each year, although during that period prices had increased by one third. Various types of competitors had cut into the wholesaler's unit volume: the supermarkets cut into houseware sales; the discount houses hurt electrical appliance sales; the lumber yards hit tool and building supply sales; and mail-order houses challenged the wholesaler across the board.

Furthermore, in the past few years many small operators had started distributorships operating out of their garages and car trunks. They, according to Robertson, performed all the separate jobs: purchasing, warehousing, promotion, sales, order layout, delivery, and billing. They gave personalized service to the retailers in their neighborhoods by delivering an item within an hour of receiving the order. Belcamp's quickest service in the outlying areas was four days.

In addition, manufacturers had started selling directly to some of Belcamp's large accounts, the ones most profitable to the company.

The increased number of distributors selling hardware items had cut down the time a retailer would give to a Belcamp salesman. An hour, according to Mr. Robertson, was the most that a salesmen could expect. For 55 minutes of the hour the dealer looked around his store, checking his inventory, and saying from time to time: "Give me one of these and three of those." This left the salesman with five minutes at most to devote to presenting new items. The company had 23 salesmen. They were paid on a straight commission basis and had no personal expense accounts.

Under Mr. Robertson's management, Belcamp had been trying to help the dealers by making them more promotion conscious, but these efforts had not had much success. Robertson believed that many persons operating hardware stores had no feel for retailing. Some had inherited their stores and knew no other business. Sometimes the local plumber or carpenter just backed into the business by buying in quantities in order to gain a discount. Some individuals opened hardware stores after failing in other lines.

Robertson believed also that the wholesaler had been caught in a price squeeze. The manufacturer had raised his prices, but the wholesaler couldn't raise prices to the dealer at will. Manufacturers customarily sent notices to dealers stating the prices paid by the wholesalers and the "fair prices" the wholesalers should charge.

At the same time, Belcamp's costs had increased tremendously. Delivery costs had risen from $\frac{1}{2}\%$ to $3\frac{1}{2}\%$ of sales. Labor costs had tripled. For many years the former owners had paid sweatshop wages, Robertson said. In 1947 a warehouseman was paid $26 for a 44-hour week; in 1958 he was paid $78 for the same time. The pay scales of all other employees had risen correspondingly. In 1947 the employees had no paid holidays; in 1958 they had $11\frac{1}{2}$ paid holidays. The employees deserved many of these increases, in Robertson's opinion, and he was not surprised that the Teamsters Union had organized Belcamp drivers and warehousemen in 1948. The fact was, however, that the workers of no other distributors in the area had been organized, and the pressures from the union increased Belcamp's headaches.

Mr. Robertson had found it difficult to obtain competent employees. He had brought a chief purchasing agent with him from his old company, and a friend of Charles Gordon had become controller in 1954. Both these men had been promised better rewards than the company so far had been able to provide. The company had picked up other employees from diverse sources, but staffing had been a problem.

In the judgment of Robertson, Belcamp's only hope lay in making some radical changes. He had concluded tentatively that the soundest step would be to open a chain of retail outlets and, in late 1958, was working on details of such a plan.

Exhibit 2

BELCAMP HARDWARE COMPANY, INC.

Balance Sheets, December 31, 1950–57

(Thousands of Dollars) *

Assets	1950	1951	1952	1953	1954	1955	1956	1957
Cash	$ 108	$ 130	$ 15	$ 94	$ 92	$ 71	$ 149	$ 69
Accounts Receivable (Net)	482	497	827	812	716	882	1,112	1,039
Tax Refund Claim	…	…	…	20	32	…	…	…
Inventory (Lower of Cost or Market)	837	972	1,326	1,038†	939	1,149	1,098	945
Prepaid Expenses	…	1	8	13	4	14	14	9
Total Current Assets	$1,427	$1,599	$2,175	$1,977	$1,783	$2,117	$2,373	$2,062
Facilities (Net)	12	22	25	22	86	93	84	81
U.S. Securities	100	…	…	…	…	…	…	…
Life Insurance (Cash Surrender Value)	37	36	37	38	38	…	…	…
Deferred Catalogue Costs	…	20	20	33	26	16	7	…
Total Assets	$1,576	$1,678	$2,273	$2,070	$1,934	$2,227	$2,464	$2,143
Liabilities and Net Worth								
Accounts Payable	$ 258	$ 237	$ 426	$ 185	$ 167	$ 321	$ 253	$ 221
Notes Payable	…	…	325	425	300	535	725	450
Accruals:								
Wages and Commissions	25	29	40	32	30	19	24	16
General Taxes	1	23	20	11	13	10	25	23
Other	…	8	17	9	16	1	8	9
Deferred Income	…	…	…	12	…	7	…	…
Reserve for Federal Income Tax	104	97	72	27	29	15	24	10
Reserve for Loss on Purchase Commitments	…	…	…	25†	…	…	…	…
Reserve for Loss on Lease	…	…	…	…	20‡	20	…	…
Total Liabilities	$ 388	$ 394	$ 900	$ 726	$ 574	$ 928	$1,059	$ 729

Capital Stock (18,500 Shares, Including 4,336 Shares in Treasury)	$ 283	$ 370	$ 370	$ 370	$ 370	$ 370	$ 370	$ 370
Earned Surplus:								
Beginning Balance	803	905	973	1,062	1,033	1,049	987	1,093
Add Net Income (Loss)	259	110	89	(29)	16	(62)	106	15
Increase in Life Insurance Value	3	..	..	..	..	..	..	..
Less:								
Tax Deduction	..	..	..	..	..	..	..	5
Reserve for Federal Income Tax	104	..	..	..	..	..	..	..
Dividends	57	14	..	..	..	..	..	..
Adjustment to Reflect Treasury Stock at Cost	..	28	..	..	..	..	..	..
Ending Balance	905	973	1,062	1,033	1,049	987	1,093	1,103
Less Treasury Stock (4,336 Shares at Cost)	..	59	59	59	59	59	59	59
Total Net Worth	$1,188	$1,284	$1,373	$1,344	$1,360	$1,298	$1,404	$1,414
Total Net Worth and Liabilities	$1,576	$1,678	$2,273	$2,070	$1,934	$2,227	$2,464	$2,143

* Detail will not necessarily add to totals because of rounding.
† Merchandise in discontinued lines has been valued at estimated realizable values. A reserve for loss on discontinued lines has been established in the amount of $25,000.
‡ At the close of 1954 the company moved its warehouse location. The company and the lessor of the former warehouse were in dispute concerning interpretation of the former lease which expired April 1, 1955. A reserve for possible loss on the lease was provided in the amount of $20,000.
§ Includes restoration of amount provided for loss on lease less charges of $2,000 incurred in terminating dispute with former lessor.

Exhibit 3

BELCAMP HARDWARE COMPANY, INC.

Income Statements, 1950–57

(Thousands of Dollars) *

	1950	1951	1952	1953	1954	1955	1956	1957
Net sales	$5,092	$5,691	$6,946	$7,076	$5,714	$5,314	$5,966	$5,951
Less cost of sales	3,917	4,509	5,647	5,805†	4,514	4,237	4,702	4,736
Gross profit	$1,176	$1,183	$1,299	$1,271	$1,200	$1,077	$1,265	$1,215
Operating expenses:								
Sales	786	NA	NA	362	296	254	288	295
Warehouse and delivery	...	NA	NA	402	369	370	345	337
General and administrative	127	NA	NA	356	339	368	339	380
Other	...	NA	NA	163	155	171	206	181
Total operating expenses	$ 913	$ 974	$1,144	$1,283	$1,159	$1,162	$1,178	$1,193
Net income (loss) from operations	263	208	156	(13)	42	(85)	87	22
Other income	1	...	11	...	...	24	29§	2
Other expense	(5)	...	...	(24)	(2)	...	...	...
Net income (loss) before federal income tax	259	208	166	(36)	40	(61)	116	24
Special charge	...	...	...	...	(47)‡	...	...	...
Provision for federal tax	...	98	77	...	23	1	10	9
Special credit for tax carry-back	...	...	...	7	...	...	...	...
Net income (loss)	...	$ 110	$ 89	$ (29)	$ 16	$ (62)	$ 106	$ 15

* Detail will not necessarily add to totals because of rounding.

† A reserve for loss on purchase commitments for discontinued appliance lines (which net sales approximated $1,113,000 in 1953) has been provided for in the amount of $25,000 and included in cost of sales.

‡ Includes $20,000 provision for possible loss on former lease incurred when company moved into a new warehouse facility. The company and former lessor are in dispute over the interpretation of the terms of the former lease.

§ The reserve for loss on lease in the amount of $20,000 which was provided for in 1954 was restored to income less charges of $2,000 incurred in 1956 in terminating dispute with former lessor.

Exhibit 4

BELCAMP HARDWARE COMPANY, INC.

Ratio Analyses

	1950	1951	1952	1953	1954	1955	1956	1957	Dun & Bradstreet 1957 Median Figures for Hardware Wholesalers
Sales	100.0%	100.0%	100.0%	100.0%	100.0%	100.0%	100.0%	100.0%	
Cost of sales	76.9	79.2	81.3	82.1	79.0	79.7	78.8	79.6	
Gross profit	23.1%	20.8%	18.7%	17.9%	21.0%	20.3%	21.2%	20.4%	
Operating expenses:									
Sales expenses	15.4%	NA	NA	5.1%	5.2%	4.8%	4.8%	4.9%	
Warehouse and delivery expenses		NA	NA	5.7	6.5	7.0	5.8	5.7	
General and administrative expenses	2.5	NA	NA	5.0	5.9	6.9	5.7	6.4	
Other operating expenses		NA	NA	2.3	2.7	3.2	3.5	3.0	
Total operating expenses	17.9%	17.1%	16.5%	18.1%	20.3%	21.9%	19.8%	20.0%	
Net income from operations	5.2%	3.7%	2.2%	(0.2)%	0.7%	(1.6)%	1.4%	0.4%	
Other income	0.0	..	0.2	(0.3)	(0.0)	0.5	0.5	0.0	
Other expenses	(0.1)	..	..	..	..	..	..	..	
Net profit (loss) before taxes	5.1%	3.7%	2.4%	(0.5)%	0.7%	(1.1)%	1.9%	0.4%	
Net profit (loss) after tax	3.0%	1.9%	1.3%	(0.4)%	0.3%	(1.2)%	1.8%	0.3%	1.5%
Net profit (loss) on tangible net worth	13.0%	8.6%	6.5%	(2.2)%	1.2%	(4.8)%	7.5%	1.1%	4.4%
Net profit (loss) on net working capital*	14.9%	9.1%	7.0%	(2.3)%	1.3%	(5.2)%	8.1%	1.1%	5.4%
Net sales to tangible net worth	4.3	4.4	5.1	5.3	4.2	4.1	4.2	4.2	3.0
Net sales to net working capital*	4.9	4.7	5.4	5.7	4.7	4.5	4.5	4.5	3.6
Net sales to inventory	6.1	5.9	5.2	6.8	6.1	4.6	5.4	6.3	4.1
Current assets to current debt*	3.7	4.1	2.4	2.7	3.1	2.3	2.2	2.8	3.9
Current debt* to inventory	46.4%	40.5%	67.9%	69.9%	61.1%	80.8%	96.4%	77.1%	40.5%
Inventory to net working capital*	80.6%	80.7%	104.0%	83.0%	77.7%	96.6%	83.6%	70.9%	83.9%
Debt to tangible net worth	32.7%	30.7%	65.5%	54.0%	42.2%	71.4%	75.4%	51.6%	54.2%
Fixed assets to tangible net worth	1.0%	1.7%	1.8%	1.6%	6.3%	7.2%	6.0%	5.7%	14.0%
Collection period (days outstanding)	34	31	43	41	45	60	67	63	33

* All outstanding debt including reserves on contingent losses is considered current debt by the Belcamp Hardware Company. Therefore, net working capital equals current assets less total liabilities.

MR. GORDON'S EVALUATION OF BELCAMP

Mr. Charles Gordon was convinced the company's profits were declining because of poor management. Although agreeing that the hardware wholesaling business was becoming more competitive, he pointed out that Belcamp's chief rival had continued to show through 1957 a profit in the neighborhood of $20,000 annually on a net worth of only $750,000.

Gordon believed that theoretically competition for hardware orders was based on three factors: service, terms, and "outs," or the ability to hold down the number of orders lost because the stock was unavailable. However, he thought profits also depended upon management's ability to obtain special discounts from suppliers. He thought Robertson, as general manager of one of the largest wholesale firms in the area, should "apply a little leverage on the prices charged by suppliers instead of paying the first price quoted." He believed that Robertson did not take advantage of this economic power, nor did he stock up on items offered at special prices by suppliers even though the Belcamp Company had tremendous warehouse facilities and adequate working capital.

Mr. Gordon made a five-page list of Robertson's errors. Some of what he considered the more costly mistakes were:

1. Publishing a bound catalogue at a cost of $40,000. Because of constant changes in the product line, the catalogue was out of date almost as soon as it was published. The mistake was corrected by adopting a loose-leaf catalogue, but the initial expenditure was almost completely wasted.

2. Adding several "lemons" to the Belcamp line which were very poor sellers and eventually were eliminated at losses ranging between $25,000 and $50,000.

3. Losing money during a part of his first year as general manager at the rate of $15,000 annually and not even knowing it until the end of the year because of an inadequate accounting system. Because of their intuitive familiarity with the business, Mr. Cole and Mr. Kent had not established a detailed accounting system. Robertson had not immediately recognized his need for a more formalized control system.

4. Failing to recruit a dynamic sales manager capable of stimulating the sales force to get increased business.

5. Refusing business from old established customers during the 1958 Christmas rush when the orders could have been handled by working the men overtime. When questioned by Mr. Gordon on this point, Robertson had replied that overtime premiums eliminated any profit margin, and he had thought Gordon did not approve of overtime. Gordon acknowledged that actually he had reprimanded Robertson for using overtime under conditions in which the men through laziness did not get their work done during the regular working

hours and that he had ruled that any further use of overtime must have his approval.

Gordon recognized that Robertson had made several contributions to improve the efficiency and service of the company and had worked day and night for seven days a week during the six months spent in moving to the new warehouse and installing the accounting system. However, he thought that Robertson lacked a certain quality of "sharpness." According to Gordon, this subtle quality separated a good, aggressive manager from one who was just average, and it could make a difference of thousands of dollars in profits.

Gordon was aware that Robertson was on the verge of presenting a plan for opening retail stores. Gordon's reaction to this was that a man who was unable to manage the business as it was certainly was in no position to manage a more complicated setup.

In view of the total situation, the Gordons were considering liquidating the business. They believed the inventory could be sold at no less than book value and they had been offered $900,000 for the warehouse. However, they felt some obligation to provide employment for the men and women who had worked for the company 15 to 20 years, underpaid during part of this time. As an alternative to liquidation, the Gordons also were considering selling their stock. Several individuals had indicated an interest in purchasing the firm.

By January, 1959, Robertson and Gordon held such varying opinions as to the business that they could no longer discuss the matter in front of their wives. Joseph Gordon repeatedly asked his brother: "When are you going to get enough guts to take some action?"

Exhibits 5, 6, and 7 give summary data on wholesale and retail operations in the hardware industry.

Exhibit 5

BELCAMP HARDWARE COMPANY, INC.

Operating Data—Hardware Wholesalers

Item	1948	1954
Establishments...	1,977	2,137
Sales (millions of dollars)................................	2,006	2,068*
Operating expenses (including payroll, as % of sales)........	15.6	18.3
Payroll, entire year (thousands of dollars)..................203,769		227,146
Paid employees (week ended nearest November 15)...........	59,330	54,245
Active proprietors of unincorporated (wholesale hardware) businesses, November................................	1,016	1,110

* "Cumulative sales for hardware wholesalers for the first 11 months in 1958 were $2,005 million." *Hardware Age*, January 29, 1959.
Source: *Statistical Abstract of the United States*, 1958.

Exhibit 6

BELCAMP HARDWARE COMPANY, INC.

Wholesale Price Index—Hardware
1947–49 = 100

1947.....................................	92.9
1950.....................................114.2	
1954.....................................139.3	
1955.....................................146.4	
1956.....................................155.9	
1957 (March).............................162.2	
1958 (March).............................168.9	

Source: *Statistical Abstract of the United States*, 1958.

Exhibit 7

BELCAMP HARDWARE COMPANY, INC.

Retail Store Sales—Hardware*
(In Millions)

1954....................................$2,702	
1955.................................... 2,788	
1956.................................... 2,893	
1957.................................... 2,737	
1958.................................... 2,653	

* Number of retail establishments was 34,009 in 1948, 34,859 in 1954, and 34,670 in 1958.
Source: *Statistical Abstract of the United States*, 1958 and 1961, and *Hardware Age*, February 26, 1959.

Better Foods, Inc.

BETTER FOODS, INC., a processor of a limited line of fine grocery specialties, was an old company with a good reputation. Its products were distributed nationally and sales volume had grown steadily, reaching a peak of almost $50 million in 1958. In 1959, however, a large and aggressive competitor had cut deeply into the market for a Better Foods specialty on which the company relied heavily for volume. As a result, at the insistence of a group of large stockholders, a new president, Mr. Harold Williams, and two other executives had been brought in about the middle of 1959. The company up to then had been conservatively operated, had paid dividends regularly, and its financial position was thoroughly sound; nevertheless these dissatisfied stockholders wanted a more dynamic management.

By increasing advertising and by adding a few products, the new management had built back some of the sales volume by the end of 1959. The company still had unused capacity, however, and had not fully regained its 1958 sales level. Mr. Williams continued to search for ideas as to new products with large volume potentials.

The startling success of Metrecal, a dietary product for weight control introduced by Mead Johnson & Company late in 1959, suggested to Mr. Williams that perhaps the development of a similar product would meet his company's need. He discussed this possibility with several of the stockholders responsible for bringing him to Better Foods. They were enthusiastic and recommended immediate developmental steps. At this time, early in July, 1960, Metrecal had only minor competition, from a few private-label and local brands which had been introduced as Metrecal's success became evident.

By the middle of July, 1960, Better Foods' chemists and other food experts had developed a formula for a product they were convinced would be essentially indistinguishable from Metrecal in taste or appearance and equal to it in nutrition, with identical caloric content. As there were no secret ingredients in Metrecal, it was fairly simple to imitate. The product, provisionally named "Bettrecal," could be pro-

751

duced in the company's unused capacity, and its production would present no significant difficulties.

The existing sales organization was thought to be adequate to obtain distribution, which would be chiefly through the company's usual channels. These were, of course, the grocery trade. However, it was believed the company could also develop some volume in drugstores, which it would hope to do through drug wholesalers and drug chains. (Metrecal in mid-1960 was sold only in drugstores.)

The Wall Street Journal of January 15, 1960, had carried the following news story about Metrecal:

> Seekers after slimness can drink their way to weight loss, a drug company promises. The diet: Four drinks a day, no food at all.
>
> The drink is a bland, vanilla-like beverage made by dissolving a powder called Metrecal in water. [The following month two additional flavors were offered—chocolate and butterscotch.] Four glasses a day provide a hunger-satisfying 900-calorie-a-day diet that can lead to the loss of about a half-pound a day, according to Mead Johnson & Co., which developed the new diet product.
>
> A day's supply of Metrecal retails at $1.59, the company said.
>
> The company, which has just introduced Metrecal, reports studies at Good Samaritan Hospital, Phoenix, Ariz., show that 97 out of 100 people who took the new diet drink—and ate no food—lost an average of one-half pound a day.
>
> Metrecal, a non-drug product that does not require a doctor's prescription, contains all of man's essential nutrients . . . the company claims. . . . An average nondieting person consumes 2,500 to 3,500 calories [a day].

When first introduced, Metrecal had been advertised to the medical profession only, through medical journals, direct-mail pieces, and samples. It was, in fact, not until June, 1960, that Mead Johnson began advertising Metrecal to the public through the mass media. Even without consumer advertising, sales volume had soared. Trade sources estimated that Metrecal sales were at an annual rate of $10 million in July.

An indication of the demand for weight reducers was given by Secretary Flemming in some remarks quoted in *The New York Times* of September 3, 1959.

> Secretary Arthur S. Flemming today [September 2, 1959] listed by name and maker twenty-seven products and devices that he said had been fraudently "foisted on the public as weight reducers."
>
> The head of the Department of Health, Education, and Welfare called the reducing schemes "probably the most lucrative medical frauds today." He quoted an American Medical Association estimate that the public was spending $100,-000,000 a year on the fraudulent weight reducers.

The tone of the Mead Johnson Metrecal advertisements in mass media was dignified and emphasized the importance of the physician in weight control and the "medical evidence of effectiveness."

Typical paragraphs from advertisements of Metrecal were:

In September of 1959, Mead Johnson & Company introduced a new product to the medical profession under the brand name Metrecal. It was developed to provide physicians with a new technique for use in judicious weight reduction of overweight patients.

What does Metrecal do?

Overweight persons are able to lose weight through the use of Metrecal simply because they take in fewer calories than are required to maintain weight. In this manner they lose weight naturally, without resorting to fad diets, complex schedules, or artificial appetite depressants. And users of Metrecal are remarkably free from hunger—the appetite is satisfied normally.

What Metrecal cannot do

Metrecal is not a miracle cure for overweight. It cannot provide the will power required for weight reduction. It has to be used properly. It is imperative that the person who desires to lose weight stay on the diet of Metrecal. This is not difficult since little, if any, hunger occurs after a day or two.

Medical evidence of effectiveness

Extensive clinical studies, conducted under medical supervision, have shown an average weight loss by Metrecal users of approximately one-half pound per day for periods up to six weeks. Some lose even more.

Most patients in the studies report little, if any, hunger. Many report that they feel better than before. Almost all find it relatively easy to continue on Metrecal.

What is in Metrecal?

One-half pound of Metrecal powder mixed with water (a frequently specified day's supply) provides 900 calories or energy units, 70 grams protein, 110 grams carbohydrate, 20 grams fat and all essential vitamins and minerals in quantities that meet or exceed minimum daily requirements established by the Food and Drug Administration. Metrecal is available in all drugstores.

In the interim report of Mead Johnson & Company for the six months ended June 30, 1960, the president stated:

Sales for the first half of 1960 reached a new all-time high of $47,931,149, an increase of $15,062,815 or 45.8% over the same period of 1959.

New products introduced during the past 12 months were primarily responsible for the favorable sales performance. These products are:

Vasodilan, a myo-vascular relaxant; *Enfamil,* an infant formula patterned after human milk; *Metrecal,* dietary for weight control; *Cytoxin,* a new palliative agent for the treatment of certain types of cancer; and *Tacaryl,* a new anti-allergic drug.

Net after-tax profit was $5,092,815 which, after provision for preferred dividends, was equal to $2.78 for each share of outstanding common stock compared to $1.58 for the first six months of last year, an increase of 76%.

The company's statement of Consolidated Profit and Loss for the six-month period showed "Cost of products sold" of $17,006,137 and "Marketing, research, and administrative expenses" of $16,345,156.

The closing price for Mead Johnson's common stock on the American Stock Exchange had risen from $66 a share early in January, 1960, to $103 in mid-July. As early as March 26, 1960, *Business Week* had reported: "Another drug stock getting a ride from a rumor is Mead Johnson, which shot up from 70 to 79 this week on the American Stock Exchange. The story is that its ethical drug, Metrecal, offers painless dieting."

Mr. Williams was convinced that the success or failure of Better Foods in marketing its own version of Metrecal would turn largely upon the extent and nature of its advertising and promotional program, including the selection of name, packaging, and basic appeals.

Then, within rather wide limits, the company had a choice as to price. Would it be effective to underprice Metrecal, as other competitors had done? Or would a slightly higher price add prestige and encourage sales?

One of Mr. Williams' colleagues had suggested "Bettrecal" be concentrated so enough water could be added to allow the dieter six servings a day with no more nourishment than was provided by four servings of Metrecal. Would the customer be pleased to be able to have these additional servings? Or would the customer feel he or she was "cheating," or fear that the more greatly diluted product might not be so effective?

Mr. Williams believed these and other decisions should be made as rapidly as possible, in order to get ahead of additional competition which he was convinced was likely to appear in both the drug industry and the food industry. He was apprehensive, however, that the agency which customarily prepared the company's advertising, hitherto of a sober and traditional nature emphasizing chiefly prestige and quality, was not equipped to give the best possible advice and help in promoting a product like "Bettrecal."

While Mr. Williams was at about this nebulous stage in his planning, he was visited by Mr. C. A. Anderson, head of a motivation research firm with a reputation for success in launching new products. Mr. Anderson said he had learned from Mr. Carlton, one of the stockholders of Better Foods, of the company's intention to enter the dietary market, and he suggested his firm could be of help.

MOTIVATION RESEARCH

Professor Lawrence C. Lockley, College of Business Administration, University of Santa Clara, made a study of motivation research at the request of the National Industrial Conference Board. In his report he said the use of the term "motivation research" was misleading: "What is really being referred to by the term is the use of psychiatric and psychological techniques to obtain a better understanding of why people respond as they do to products, advertisements and various other marketing situations."[1]

The underlying theory, Professor Lockley explained, was that people often were ignorant of their own motivations or compelled to rationalize their behavior. It therefore was necessary, if the true explanations were to be known, to use techniques which served to uncover unconscious or preconscious attitudes rather than to rely on simple questioning procedures. People, in short, were thought to be motivated in large measure by emotional rather than rational factors, by hidden anxieties, aggressions, desires.

The techniques used in motivation research in marketing, Professor Lockley wrote, "are borrowed from clinical psychology and psychiatry, and have been modified for application to marketing problems. Their value depends almost entirely upon the skill with which they are used and upon the competence of the person who interprets the results."

On its editorial page November 16, 1960, *The New York Times* commented on the growth and use of motivation research:

> After World War II, American business was faced with the huge task of finding customers to absorb the vastly increased productive capacity of the country. The response was development of what became known as motivational research—the attempt to get at the "why" of consumer behavior by depth interviews, sentence-completion tests and the other technical paraphernalia of clinical psychology, psychoanalysis and sociology. Out of early M.R. studies came many promotional and marketing coups, such as that of the black eye-patch that turned an obscure shirt into a whirlwind seller. . . .
>
> In the last few years a new muckraking literature has devoted itself, among other things, to demolishing the claims of "the hidden persuaders," who are

---

[1] *The Use of Motivation Research in Marketing,* National Industrial Conference Board, Inc., Studies in Business Policy, No. 97, 1960.

seen as an insidious force preying on the public's fears and anxieties. But the National Industrial Conference Board, a nonprofit business group, recently issued a study saying that while motivational research is hardly a universal panacea for business, it is, when properly used with more conventional methods, a useful tool for management. It found particular merit in M.R. as a source of hunches and new ideas and also stressed its value in pre-testing advertising, the equivalent of the technique known on Broadway of "trying out shows on the road."

Far from the battlefield, meanwhile, undaunted motivational researchers peer into every nook and cranny of American life, turning up findings that often result in major corporate about-faces. Philip Morris, for example, recently changed the package of one of its filter brands when investigation showed that the package was favored by women as against men, whereas men smokers outnumber women by two to one. Social Research, Inc., conducted a study for a staid Wall Street brokerage house that brought on a complete change in its advertising and public relations and resulted in opening a street-level board room on Park Avenue.

The following brief description of techniques used in motivation research in marketing are based on the Conference Board study by Professor Lockley.

Picture Story Test. Pictures of people performing some action, such as taking a prepared cake mix from a supermarket shelf, are used. Persons shown a picture are asked to make up a story about it, and from their stories the investigator deduces their attitudes. A respondent may begin her story, for example: "This is a working woman . . . ," thus perhaps indicating that only a woman pressed for time is justified in using a prepared product. Similarly, paired pictures, showing competing products, may be the subject of "stories."

Sentence Completion Test. "A woman who uses a prepared cake mix is _____."

Word Association Test. "Its success depends on rapidity of reaction to each word for which an association is asked. . . . In the almost hypnotic effect of responding to word after word, the 'censor' that keeps us from probing our own preconscious and unconscious minds may be 'lulled' long enough to allow significant association to be offered."

The Depth Interview. In clinical psychology and psychiatry the depth interview represents a "distinct method of probing the unconscious mind." ". . . Hours of talking, probing, and trained listening to uncover every incident that may have a bearing on a present emotional state are routine." In marketing research the term is more loosely used to cover almost any type of interview other than the conventional fixed-answer questionnaire. "It is a special type of interviewing in which there is less rigidity of structure than in ordinary interviewing, more probing of the respondent, and a more complete record of his responses obtained."

Mr. Anderson in talking with the president of Better Foods, Inc., said the advertiser who relied on facts, logic, or common sense ran the risk not only of missing the strongest appeal for his product, but also of alienating potential customers. He cited the case of a client, a manufacturer of machine-knit neckties. In its advertising this client had emphasized that the ties were as soft and fine "as though knit by your own grandmother." Sales results were very poor. Motivation research had quickly revealed that the image of a female relative in conjunction with neckties was repellent to most men and so, to a lesser degree, was the suggestion of made-in-the-home clothes. A change to a theme of envy on the part of the tie owner's peers, always pictured as somewhat less virile and successful than the owner, brought a startling increase in sales.

With a diet product, necessarily involving sensitive areas of overweight and personal appearance, selection of an advertising theme and a product image was a particularly delicate matter, Mr. Anderson said. He also thought that for the new product to make substantial inroads in the market for Metrecal, imitation of the Mead Johnson advertising copy would not be effective.

He pointed out, further, that when competing products were essentially alike it was futile to emphasize their physical properties in advertising. What was needed, he said, was to find a superior emotional appeal; it was here that the techniques of motivation research were particularly effective.

Mr. Anderson said his firm was in a position to have sound answers to Mr. Williams' promotional and pricing problems within a few weeks. He and his associates were highly experienced in the use of motivation research techniques and in obtaining the co-operation of consumers selected for interviews on an appropriate sampling basis. He offered to submit a detailed plan, with cost figures, for Mr. Williams' consideration within a few days.

Mr. Williams asked Mr. Anderson whether he could make a rough estimate as to probable promotional costs. Mr. Anderson said he figured Mead Johnson's promotional expenses for Metrecal were then running at an annual rate of about $3 million and he understood the company shortly intended to take extensive time on TV for Metrecal promotion, probably reaching a total annual promotional expenditure of around $5 million; he thought Better Foods would have to expect to spend at least half a million dollars on promotion of its product in the first six months. (The company was financially able to spend this sum, or even more, if that were deemed wise.)

Mr. Anderson went on to say that overweight was so serious a health problem to Americans he felt promotion of sound products to help them reduce was truly a public service. The U.S. Department of Public Health, he pointed out, estimated the number of overweight people in the country at 30 to 40 million and most physicians agreed that such persons were unusually prone to many serious diseases.

Mr. Williams pointed out that some prominent physicians objected to any dieting not based on the development of proper, permanent eating habits. They believed that persons following stringent, temporary diets usually regained weight rapidly between diet periods, and it was rapid, repeated shifts in weight that were particularly harmful. Also he had heard, Mr. Williams said, one doctor declare that a prolonged liquid diet, if substituted for conventional eating habits, could lead to emotional and psychological disturbances because of people's strong cultural ties with chewing, with variety in food textures, and with the habit of spending considerable time at a meal, usually in the company of other people.

Mr. Anderson gave it as his view that Mead Johnson obviously had received full co-operation from a large proportion of the medical profession. The pressure on doctors from patients for suggestions as to simple, agreeable diets, he alleged, must be tremendous and no doubt many harried physicians were delighted to have a harmless, palatable, and effective product to recommend. Most overweight people, he believed, did not take kindly to the suggestion that they merely eat smaller and fewer servings of a balanced variety of foods, though this probably was the sensible course of action in most cases.

Mr. Williams did not commit his company to a course of action at this July, 1960, interview. After talking with his fellow officers, however, he was inclined to favor the introduction of "Bettrecal" and the employment of the Anderson firm to advise as to advertising and sales promotion for this product. The decision, they agreed, should be made very shortly; otherwise an important "time advantage" might be lost.

Lead and Zinc Quotas

On Tuesday, September 23, 1958, President Eisenhower established quotas limiting imports of lead and zinc. The quota for each exporting country was set at 80% of its average annual exports to the United States during the period 1953–57.

Members of the United States Tariff Commission, after investigation, had agreed that the domestic lead and zinc industry had been seriously injured by competition from foreign imports. Many leaders in the industry had testified before the commission as to the damage caused by imports. *Forbes* magazine reported that one company president had said: "Importers have flooded the country. The whole question is: Does this country want a lead or zinc industry of its own?" Another company president had testified: "The cause of this critical injury to an important United States industry is the lack of adequate protection against foreign imports of lead and zinc." He went on to say that what the industry needed was "a degree of protection aimed at improving the lead-zinc price structure to 17 cents and 14.5 cents."[1] At the time, lead was quoted domestically at 10.87 cents per pound, and zinc was quoted at 10 cents.

Nor were lead and zinc producers and their employees the only ones claiming injury. Other business groups dependent upon lead and zinc operations also were affected. In a small lead and zinc mining community, for example, the shutdown of the local mine wrought economic hardships upon the entire town. Grocers, hardware dealers, filling station operators, bankers, and the many other groups whose business depended upon mining operations and payrolls suffered from the decline in fortune of the lead and zinc producers.

Officials and other citizens of countries adversely affected by the quotas immediately protested against President Eisenhower's action. *The New York Times* of September 24, 1958, reported the following comments, for example:

---

[1] *Forbes,* January 1, 1958.

Mexico: Filiberto Ruvalcaba, secretary general of the Pan American Federation of Mine Workers, said the quota set for Mexico would be "disastrous" to Mexico's economy. "Such a step by President Eisenhower makes a mockery of the good-neighbor policy," he charged.

Peru: The morning paper *El Comercio* said: "It is inconceivable that President Eisenhower for internal political reasons should have authorized a hard blow at the economy of friendly countries, especially Peru."

Australia: The Acting Minister for Trade, Athol Gordon Townley announced tonight that Australia would officially protest the quotas. The Minister for National Development, Senator William Henry Spooner, told the Senate that the cuts were of "tremendous consequence" and could have a serious effect on the the Australian economy.

Canada: The Canadian press reported that Canada planned a sharp protest against United States import restrictions. John R. Bradfield, president of Noranda Mines, Ltd., said United States smelters had long "been dependent on exports of our concentrate, and we have maintained these supplies despite opportunities for higher prices in other markets."

One United States company, American Smelting & Refining, also objected to the quotas. *The New York Times* reported a spokesman for the company as saying that the company would have to shut down two smelters that depended on foreign ores.

The imposition of import quotas on lead and zinc was *only one* of a series of steps taken by the United States Government in an effort to help the domestic industry and assure domestic supplies of these critical raw materials. Other steps included changes in tariff rates and introduction of a stock-piling program.

Exhibit 1 shows the effect the quotas were expected to have upon United States imports of lead and zinc.

THE UNITED STATES LEAD AND ZINC INDUSTRY

The United States primary lead and zinc industry could be broadly viewed as a series of production operations beginning with the discovery and mining of ores and terminating with the output of metals. The usual operations for producing the metals were prospecting, mining, milling, smelting, and refining; ores destined for the chemical and paint industries, unlike ores for other purposes, were diverted for end-use manufacturing immediately after the milling stage. The ores of lead and zinc usually were found interlocked in complex deposits, and, consequently, lead and zinc production was often considered as one industry. At the smelting operation, however, a sharp division of techniques and facilities existed between lead production and zinc production.

An increasing quantity of the lead and zinc metal used in the United

Exhibit 1

LEAD AND ZINC QUOTAS

U.S. Average Monthly Imports before and after
Quota Restrictions, by Countries of Origin
(In Short Tons of Metals or Metal Content of Ores)

COUNTRY	MONTHLY AVERAGE IMPORTS JANUARY TO JUNE, 1958	FORECAST OF MONTHLY AVERAGE IMPORTS UNDER QUOTA RESTRICTIONS	% CHANGE
	Lead	Lead	
Canada	4,891	4,890	− 0%
Mexico	11,283	6,147	−46
Peru	10,561	4,840	−54
Bolivia	1,240	840	−32
Americas	27,975	16,717	−40%
Australia	10,589	5,627	−47
Yugoslavia	3,486	2,627	−25
Union of South Africa	4,344	2,480	−43
Others	6,721	2,107	−69
Non-Americas	25,140	12,841	−49%
Total	53,115	29,558	−44%
	Zinc	Zinc	
Canada	19,648	17,387	−12%
Mexico	17,048	12,800	−25
Peru	10,484	6,480	−28
Americas	47,180	36,667	−22%
Belgium	2,933	1,253	−57
Belgian Congo	2,049	907	−56
Italy	490	600	+22
Others	5,485	3,987	−27
Non-Americas	10,957	6,747	−38%
Total	58,137	43,414	−25%

Source: *E&MJ Metal and Mineral Markets*, September 25, 1958.

States was being produced from materials other than ores. These secondary materials (scrap, dross, metal dust, skimmings, and so on) entered the production sequence at the smelters. Usually the same smelter did not produce both metal from ores and metal from the secondary materials.

Lead. The United States lead industry had been traced back to a Virginia mine opened in 1621. By 1881 the United States had surpassed Spain and Great Britain to become the world's leading producer of lead. United States mine output reached its maximum in the late 1920's, declined sharply in the early 1930's, and then recovered during World War II. Since then, with the exception of an increase during the Korean conflict, lead mine production in the United States had tended to decline.

Between 1952 and 1957, seven commodities or groups of commodities accounted for almost 85% of the total lead consumed in the United States: storage batteries, 31%; tetraethyl lead for gasoline, 14%; cable covering, 12%; lead pigments, 11%; solder, 7%; lead pipes, traps, bends, and sheets, 5%; calking lead, 5%; and all other uses, 15%. In later years plastics and other metals had been substituted for lead to some extent as a cable covering and in paint alloys and foil sheets. Lead recovered from scrapped batteries accounted for a high proportion of the lead used in battery manufacture.

Zinc. The United States zinc industry began in the first half of the nineteenth century. The industry continued to grow, and in 1909 the United States became the world's leading producer by surpassing Germany, Belgium, and Great Britain. As in the lead industry, the zenith of United States mine output came in the late 1920's and was followed by an almost catastrophic production decline in the 1930's. Production increased during the war years, but except for the period of the Korean action mine output declined between 1946 and 1958.

In the period from 1952 to 1957, zinc consumption in the United States was divided by uses as follows: for galvanizing iron and steel, 32%; for zinc-based alloys used in die casting, especially for automobile parts, 26%; in brass and bronze products, 23% (during World War II this use had accounted for more than 50% of consumption); chemical compounds, 12%; rolled zinc products, 4%; and miscellaneous uses 3%. There had been no appreciable development of suitable substitutes for zinc in the above uses.

Exhibit 2 presents a summary for lead and zinc of United States and world mine output, smelter production, and consumption.

Lead and Zinc Ore Deposits. Lead and zinc did not occur free in nature; generally they were found in ores that were complex aggregates of minerals, one or more of which contained the desired metal in economically producible amount. The most commonly exploited lead mineral was galena, or lead sulfide, and the most commonly exploited zinc mineral was sphalerite, or zinc sulfide. Deposits of galena unmixed with other minerals occasionally were found, but usually zinc, silver, gold, iron, or a combination of these, was present. Sphalerite almost always occurred in association with galena.

Lead and zinc ores were found in many countries of the world and

Exhibit 2

LEAD AND ZINC QUOTAS

U.S. and World Mine Production, Smelter Production, and Consumption

	UNITED STATES			WORLD*			RATIO OF U.S. TO WORLD		
	Mine Output† 1,000 Short Tons	Smelter Output‡ 1,000 Short Tons	Consumption§ 1,000 Short Tons	Mine Output† 1,000 Short Tons	Smelter Output‡ 1,000 Short Tons	Consumption 1,000 Short Tons	Mine Output† %	Smelter Output‡ %	Consumption %
Lead									
1937–38 (average)	418	416	476	1,902	1,865	1,846	22.0	22.3	25.8
1948	390	400	745	1,571	1,504	1,578	24.8	26.6	47.2
1950	431	505	885	1,850	1,810	1,922	23.3	27.9	46.0
1952	390	472	782	2,030	1,990	1,762	19.2	23.7	44.4
1953	343	468	784	2,090	2,060	1,940	16.4	22.7	40.4
1954	325	487	764	2,230	2,190	2,137	14.6	22.2	35.8
1955	338	479	810	2,370	2,220	2,260	14.3	21.6	35.8
1956	353	542	743	2,420	2,380	2,208	14.6	22.8	33.6
Zinc									
1937–38 (average)	572	502	514	1,936	1,758	1,730	29.5	28.6	29.7
1948	630	788	818	2,048	1,881	1,896	30.8	41.9	43.1
1950	623	843	967	2,370	2,170	2,189	26.3	38.8	44.2
1952	666	904	853	2,850	2,460	2,165	23.4	36.7	39.4
1953	547	916	986	2,940	2,600	2,354	18.6	35.2	41.9
1954	473	802	886	2,930	2,700	2,567	16.1	29.7	34.5
1955	515	964	1,120	3,180	2,970	2,927	16.2	32.5	38.3
1956	542	984	988	3,330	3,110	2,800	16.3	31.6	35.3

* Partly estimated.
† Recoverable metal content of ores produced.
‡ Primary metal produced.
§ Primary metal consumed, but not including purchase for U.S. Government stock piles.

Source: U.S. Tariff Commission, *Lead and Zinc*, Report to the President on Escape-Clause Investigation No. 65, Washington, D.C., April, 1958.

also in many of the states of the United States. Total estimated world reserves of lead in measured classifications exceeded 40 million tons in 1958. Between 80% and 90% of this amount was believed to be recoverable with processes then available. Estimated distribution of ore reserves by locations was: 12.5 million tons in Australia; 10 million tons in North America (Canada, 6.5 million tons; United States, 2.5 million tons; Mexico, 1 million tons); 10 million tons in Europe and the USSR; 3.5 millions tons in Africa; 2.5 million tons in South America; and 2 million tons in Asia (excluding deposits in the USSR). Zinc reserves in measured classifications were estimated at almost 70 million tons: North America, 25 million (Canada, 15 million tons; United States, 7.5 million tons; Mexico, 2 million tons); Europe, 21 million; Australia, 11 million; South America, 6 million; and Africa and Asia, about 6 million tons.

The discovery of new ore deposits suitable for economic production with existing processes had become increasingly difficult. The legendary prospector with pick and pack mule had yielded to highly trained teams of men employing advanced geophysical and geochemical techniques. Exploration costs had increased greatly.

Mining. Open-pit methods seldom could be used in lead and zinc mining. Most of the ores recovered in the United States had been taken from underground mines, and operations had penetrated to ever greater depths in the earth's crust as the more easily removed ores were used. One mine was known to have 52,000 feet of tunnels branching from a shaft that was sunk 3,200 feet. Power equipment had become more and more important in opening the underground slopes from which the ore was taken. Improvements in lighting at working faces, in ventilation and air-conditioning systems, and in pumping equipment had made it possible to drive shafts to deeper and deeper levels.

The output of mines was measured by the amount of recoverable metal in the ore lifted. In 1956 a total of 353,000 tons of recoverable lead and 542,000 tons of recoverable zinc were produced in the United States at 544 lead and zinc mines and as a by-product of 152 additional mines. In 1952 a total of 390,000 tons of recoverable lead and 666,-000 tons of recoverable zinc had been taken from 912 lead and zinc mines and from other mines primarily producing other mineral ores.

Additional data about United States production, by states and by size of mines, are given in Exhibits 3, 4, and 5. The number of persons employed, the hours worked, and average wages are given in Exhibit 6. World mine output of lead and zinc is given in Exhibits 7 and 8.

Exhibit 3

LEAD AND ZINC QUOTAS

Lead: Mine Output in the United States, by States
(In Short Tons of Recoverable Lead)

	Average 1925–29	Average 1937–39	1948	1950	1952	1954	1955	1956	1957*
Eastern states:									
Wisconsin	1,746	600	861	532	2,000	1,265†	1,948	2,582	2,030
Illinois	552	223	3,695	2,729	4,262	3,232	4,544	3,832	2,840
Kentucky	135	92	216	66	60	80	...	228	...
Tennessee	250	...	...	113	18	...	...	5	...
New York	...	6,573	1,231	1,484	1,120	1,187	1,037	1,608	1,186
Virginia	2,357‡	...	4,703	3,254	3,792	4,324§	2,999§	3,045	3,244§
West Central states:									
Arkansas	38	16	22	9	4				
Kansas	26,121	14,981	8,386	9,487	5,916	4,033	5,498	7,635	4,300
Missouri	202,240	145,313	102,288	134,626	129,245	125,250	125,412	123,783	125,000
Oklahoma	58,306	26,188	16,918	20,724	15,137	14,204	14,126	12,350	6,500
Western states:									
Alaska	982	918	329	149	...	...	1‖	1‖	...
Arizona	9,743	11,232	29,899	26,383	16,520	8,385	9,817	11,999	12,500
California	2,070	736	9,110	15,831	11,199	2,671	8,265	9,296	3,640
Colorado	30,112	9,154	25,143	27,007	30,066	17,823	15,805	19,856	21,000
Idaho	141,610	95,623	88,544	100,025	73,719	69,302	64,163	64,321	70,225
Montana	18,871	14,613	18,411	19,617	21,279	14,820	17,028	18,642	13,328
Nevada	9,807	6,087	9,777	9,408	6,790	3,041	3,291	6,384	5,800
New Mexico	6,730	5,618	7,653	4,150	7,021	887	3,296	6,042	5,350
Oregon	6	49	7	17	1	5	3	5	7
South Dakota	21	...	16	...	2	...	...	...	...
Texas	213	321	170	129	56	...	...	...	...
Utah	149,509	74,250	55,950	44,753	50,210	44,972	50,452	49,555	44,200
Washington	1,323	3,611	7,147	10,334	11,744	9,938	10,340	11,657	12,342
Total	662,742	416,198†	390,476	430,827	390,161	325,419	338,025	352,826	333,492

* Preliminary.
† Includes small quantity from Iowa.
‡ Average for 1925–27.
§ Includes small quantity from North Carolina.
‖ Based on smelter receipts.

Source: U.S. Tariff Commission, *Lead and Zinc*, Report to the President on Escape-Clause Investigation No. 65, Washington, D.C., April, 1958.

Exhibit 4

LEAD AND ZINC QUOTAS

Zinc: Mine Output in the United States, by States

(In Short Tons of Recoverable Zinc)

	Average 1925–29	Average 1937–39	1948	1950	1952	1954	1955	1956	1957*
Eastern states:									
Wisconsin	23,055	4,972	7,864	5,722	20,588	15,534	18,326	23,890	22,130
Illinois	1,174	111	12,980	26,982	18,816	14,427	21,700	24,039	22,110
Kentucky	644	500	639	731	3,280	458		417	
Tennessee	22,446†	39,147	29,524	35,326	38,020	30,326	40,216	46,023	56,467
New Jersey	93,839	91,988	76,332	55,029	59,190	37,416	11,643	4,667	12,409
New York	7,091	32,867	34,566	38,321	32,636	53,199	53,016	59,111	64,883
Virginia	5,629‡	16,935	15,882	12,396	13,409	16,738	18,329	19,196	18,878
West Central states:									
Arkansas	71	172	31	8	26				
Kansas	114,323	74,098	35,577	27,176	25,482	19,110	27,611	28,665	15,800
Missouri	16,708	15,307	6,463	8,189	13,986	5,210	4,476	4,380	3,000
Oklahoma	226,968	129,667	43,821	46,739	54,916	43,171	41,543	27,515	14,300
Western states:									
Alaska			22	6					
Arizona	2,628	5,850	54,478	60,480	47,143	21,461	22,684	25,580	33,300
California	3,999	9	5,325	7,551	9,419	1,415	6,836	8,049	2,980
Colorado	32,868	3,543	45,164	45,776	53,203	35,150	35,350	40,246	46,200
Idaho	29,128	48,592	86,267	87,890	74,317	61,528	53,314	49,561	58,642
Montana	72,519	27,604	59,095	67,678	82,185	60,952	68,588	70,520	49,790
Nevada	5,570	9,803	20,288	21,606	15,357	1,035	2,670	7,488	5,000
New Mexico	23,352	27,173	41,502	29,263	50,975	6	15,277	35,010	30,900
Oregon		8	29	21	1				
South Dakota					3				
Texas									
Utah	44,386	38,728	41,490	31,678	32,947	34,031	43,556	42,374	40,200
Washington	574	8,550	12,638	14,807	20,102	22,304	29,536	25,609	23,139
Total	726,972	575,624	629,977	623,375	666,001	473,471	514,671	542,340	520,128

* Preliminary.
† Includes Virginia in 1928–29.
‡ Average for 1925–27. Data for 1928–29 included with Tennessee.

Source: U.S. Tariff Commission, *Lead and Zinc*, Report to the President on Escape-Clause Investigation No. 65, Washington, D.C., April 1958.

Exhibit 5

LEAD AND ZINC QUOTAS

U.S. Mine Output, by Size of Mine*

Size of Mine (In Terms of Short Tons of Recoverable Lead and Zinc Produced during Year)	Mines		Output of Recoverable Metal	
	Number	% of Total	Short Tons	% of Total
	1954			
0– 499	524	81.3	26,394	3.3
500– 999	31	4.8	20,053	2.5
1,000–1,999	30	4.7	46,005	5.8
2,000–2,999 . . . . :	11	1.7	28,135	3.5
3,000–3,999	8	1.2	27,073	3.4
4,000–4,999	8	1.2	35,022	4.4
5,000 and over	33	5.1	616,208	77.1
	643	100.0	798,890	100.0
	1956			
0– 499	557	80.0	27,248	3.0
500– 999	27	3.9	18,750	2.1
1,000–1,999	29	4.2	41,984	4.7
2,000–2,999	24	3.4	61,544	6.9
3,000–3,999	13	1.9	46,607	5.2
4,000–4,999	9	1.3	41,901	4.7
5,000 and over	37	5.3	657,132	73.4
	696	100.0	895,166	100.0

* This analysis includes all mines in the United States that produced any recoverable lead or zinc, regardless of their industry classification; hence, some production is included from mines producing ores valued chiefly for their content of metals other than lead and zinc.

Source: U.S. Tariff Commission, *Lead and Zinc*, Report to the President on Escape-Clause Investigation No. 65, Washington, D.C., April, 1958.

The grade of lead and zinc bearing ores produced by the countries supplying the bulk of United States imports generally was of a much higher quality than most of the domestic ores. The average lead content of ores mined abroad in 1956 was more than double that of the ores mined in the United States, and the average zinc content of foreign ores was almost double that of United States ores.

United States lead and zinc mines had been faced with increasing costs for labor, supplies, and transportation. Labor wages, which accounted for 50% of total mining costs, had risen from an hourly average of $1.95 in 1952 to $2.27 during January–October, 1957. Nor could costs be completely eliminated by the temporary shutting down of a mine. The cost of mine maintenance and upkeep to prevent serious damage and safeguard investment would continue. The Tariff Commission reported that maintenance costs such as those for pumping and

Exhibit 6

LEAD AND ZINC QUOTAS

Lead and Zinc Mining and Milling: Employment and Wages in the United States

STATE OR AREA	AVERAGE EMPLOYMENT*		WAGES PAID TO PRODUCTION WORKERS (IN THOUSANDS)		TOTAL PRODUCTION MAN-HOURS		AVERAGE PRODUCTION WAGE PER HOUR	
	1956	1957†	1956	1957†	1956	1957†	1956	1957†
Eastern states............	2,450	2,842	$ 8,252	$ 7,926	4,174	3,863	$1.98	$2.05
West Central states......	4,552	4,054	16,679	12,285	7,790	5,528	2.14	2.22
Western states...........	9,706	8,540	41,664	30,321	18,387	12,846	2.27	2.36
Arizona.................	558	542	2,366	2,024	1,093	902	2.16	2.25
California..............	322	153	1,378	565	591	234	2.33	2.42
Colorado...............	1,495	1,401	5,862	4,751	2,703	2,029	2.17	2.34
Idaho..................	2,484	2,458	11,473	9,863	4,636	3,854	2.48	2.56
Montana................	1,976	1,567	8,797	4,821	3,996	2,217	2.20	2.18
Nevada.................	200	177	861	643	336	244	2.56	2.62
New Mexico.............	622	513	2,233	1,451	1,158	723	1.93	2.01
Utah...................	1,691	1,404	6,871	4,753	3,142	2,090	2.19	2.27
Washington.............	358	327	1,823	1,450	732	553	2.49	2.62
United States..........	16,708	15,436	$66,595	$50,532	30,351	22,237	$2.19	$2.27

* Total persons on payroll including proprietors and supervisory workers. Other data in table refer to production and closely related workers. Data by state or area for production and related workers alone were not available, but the U.S. total for such workers was 14,458 in 1956 and 13,132 in 1957.
† 1957 figures computed for January to October data only.

Source: U.S. Tariff Commission. *Lead and Zinc*, Report to the President on Escape-Clause Investigation No. 65, Washington, D.C., April, 1958.

Exhibit 7

LEAD AND ZINC QUOTAS

Lead: World Mine Output, by Countries or Regions

(In Thousands of Short Tons of Recoverable Lead)

Country or Region	Average 1937–39	1948	1950	1952	1954	1955	1956
Australia................	298.7	243.0	245.1	260.7	319.0	331.5	333.7
North America:							
United States..........	416.1	390.5	430.8	390.2	325.4	338.0	352.8
Canada................	235.7	167.2	165.7	168.8	218.5	202.8	189.0
Mexico................	264.5	213.1	262.4	271.2	238.8	232.4	220.0
W. Europe:							
Yugoslavia............	82.2	69.3	94.8	87.0	92.7	99.3	96.3
W. Germany..........	100.3*	24.6	51.1	56.5	74.2	74.3	72.1
Spain†................	34.1	29.8	43.3	46.7	61.0	69.0	66.8
Italy.................	45.1	33.5	44.2	44.2	47.4	56.1	53.2
Sweden...............	9.8	26.0	25.0	22.7	32.7	35.5	36.1
France................	5.2	8.4	13.7	13.6	12.3	9.9	9.3
Other................	33.8	8.6	16.8	23.0	24.4	27.6	28.1
E. Europe and USSR......	103.3	101.4	161.4	216.6	269.9	299.0	335.0
Africa..................	63.5	101.6	131.1	202.0	231.8	265.8	270.1
Central and S. America:							
Peru.................	53.7	53.5	68.5	105.6	121.3	130.9	133.5
Argentina............	24.6	24.0	21.4	21.0	32.0	26.5	31.7
Bolivia†..............	16.7	28.2	34.4	33.1	20.1	21.1	22.7
Other†...............	1.1	7.1	11.7	12.7	10.6	15.0	20.3
Rest of world:							
China†...............	...	...	1.3	2.2	11.0	13.2	16.5
Japan................	14.2	7.4	12.0	19.3	25.2	28.9	32.5
All others............	122.7	33.4	15.3	32.9	61.7	93.2	100.3
Total†............	1,925.3	1,570.6	1,850.0	2,030.0	2,230.0	2,370.0	2,420.0

* Includes East Germany and Austria.
† Data partly or completely estimated.

Source: U.S. Tariff Commission, *Lead and Zinc*, Report to the President on Escape-Clause Investigation No. 65, Washington, D.C., April, 1958.

retimbering a shut-down mine were frequently the only alternative to what would amount to permanent closure of the mine; unless maintenance was continued, costs of restoring a mine closed for some time would be prohibitive.

Milling. Located close to the United States mining centers were 109 mills which crushed and ground ores to liberate the valuable mineral particles. The desired particles were then separated by gravity, flotation, or some combination process into ore concentrates. The particular combination of ore dressing equipment which was used depended upon the quantities and kinds of ore minerals present, their value, the gangue content, and particle size. During the ore concentration process some metallic content was lost. Ore dressing practices in use in 1958 resulted

Exhibit 8

LEAD AND ZINC QUOTAS

Zinc: World Mine Output, by Countries or Regions
(In Thousands of Short Tons of Recoverable Zinc)

Country or Region	Average 1937–39	1948	1950	1952	1954	1955	1956
Australia	239.1	213.3	221.8	221.0	283.0	287.4	311.3
North America:							
United States	575.5	630.0	623.4	666.0	473.5	514.7	542.3
Canada	261.1	277.4	313.2	371.8	376.5	433.4	419.4
Mexico	169.4	197.3	246.4	250.6	246.4	297.0	274.4
W. Europe:							
Italy	106.0	80.8	95.9	124.5	129.7	131.9	134.9
W. Germany	200.3*	31.9	79.8	89.0	103.9	101.6	101.8
Spain†	46.3	51.8	71.0	95.0	97.0	102.0	96.0
Yugoslavia	46.1	42.8	42.0	52.7	63.1	65.8	63.4
Sweden	38.4	39.1	40.9	42.4	64.4	64.8	72.8
Greece	8.8	1.5	3.5	8.0	7.9	13.5	22.3
Other†	18.7	16.4	23.4	31.4	29.1	30.6	30.0
E. Europe and USSR†	2.6	220.1	239.3	331.7	392.0	462.3	532.0
Africa†	35.1	99.3	141.7	215.8	229.8	220.2	264.9
Central and S. America:							
Peru	19.9	65.6	97.0	140.9	174.8	183.1	167.4
Argentina	15.3	13.4	14.0	17.0	22.0	23.3	26.1
Bolivia†	11.0	23.3	21.6	39.3	22.4	23.5	18.8
Guatemala	...	...	0.4	9.0	4.4	10.4	12.0
Chili	...	...	0.1	3.7	1.7	3.2	3.3
Rest of world:							
Japan	58.0	36.5	57.5	96.4	120.6	119.8	135.2
All others†	93.4	7.6	37.1	43.8	87.8	91.5	101.2
Total†	1,945.0	2,048.1	2,370.0	2,850.0	2,930.0	3,180.0	3,329.5

* Includes East Germany.
† Data partly or completely estimated.
Source: U.S. Tariff Commission, *Lead and Zinc*, Report to the President on Escape-Clause Investigation No. 65, Washington, D.C., April, 1958.

in recovery of approximately 85% to 90% of lead and zinc minerals from the sulfide deposits. Some authorities believed that at least some of the loss could be eliminated with advances in milling practices.

Smelting and Refining. The ore concentrates were shipped to mammoth plants or smelters which released the metals from the concentrates by various chemical and physical processes and then formed them into pigs, slabs, blocks, or bars. Smelting and refining were large-scale operations. They required heavy capital investments and, to be profitable, large and continuous supplies of raw materials. Lead concentrates were smelted or refined in 13 plants in 11 states, and zinc concentrates were processed in 18 plants located in 8 states. Not only were lead and zinc concentrates processed at different smelters, but within this breakdown each smelter specialized in particular types of lead or zinc concentrates. The various concentrates required use of different fuels and operating processes. Consequently, some smelters specialized in domestic ores, while others specialized in foreign ores.

Lead was removed from concentrates almost exclusively by smelting in blast furnaces. The concentrates usually were roasted to remove sulfur before being fed into the blast furnaces. There they were mixed with coke and fluxing materials such as silica and lime. Air was blown through the heated charge, burning the coke to carbon monoxide and carbon dioxide and producing a temperature of approximately $1400°$ centigrade. The lead compounds thus were reduced to lead bullion, which settled in the crucible of the furnace. If the original concentrates contained very few impurities, the smelting process could be simplified by using open hearths instead of blast furnaces. In 1958 one lead smelter in the United States was of the open hearth type, and the rest used blast furnaces.

The slag from the blast furnace process for lead recovery often contained considerable quantities of zinc and unrecovered lead. These slag residues were re-treated in slag fuming furnaces to recover the zinc and remaining lead. The recovered zinc residues usually were shipped to zinc smelters for further refining. The lead bullion produced in the blast and slag furnaces was further processed at lead refineries to remove remaining precious metals and metallic impurities.

The lead refining process was extremely complex and varied according to the types of materials that were in the bullion. To remove copper, the bullion was heated to a temperature just above the melting point of lead. Copper, which had a higher melting point, rose to the surface and was skimmed off. By applying additional heat, surface oxidation of some additional minerals could be effected. Arsenic and antimony were among the minerals skimmed off in this process. Silver and gold were removed by adding metallic zinc to the molten bullion. The silver and gold united with the zinc and so could be removed from the mixture.

In the zinc smelting process, the zinc sulfide was first roasted to remove sulfur. The roasted concentrate was then either refined by electrodeposition or distillation in either vertical or horizontal retort plants heated either electrothermically or by fuel.

When the zinc concentrate was to be processed in a retort, the retort was first charged with solid carbon fuels and fluxing materials and then heated to release zinc vapor and hot reducing carbon monoxide. The vapors from the retort passed into condensers of various types where the zinc was collected as liquid metal. If the zinc residues collected in this manner still contained unwanted metals, they usually were shipped to smelters specializing in removal of the metals in question.

When the zinc was to be refined by electrodeposition, the roasted concentrates were first leached with sulfuric acid. Copper, cadmium, cobalt, and iron then were removed by a variety of processes. The solution then was passed to tank houses where the zinc was electrodeposited on cathodes of high-grade aluminum. If the residues contained other valuable minerals, especially silver or gold, they usually were shipped to smelters specializing in the processing of these minerals.

U.S. and world smelter output of lead and zinc were given in Exhibit 2. Employment at United States smelters and wages paid are given in Exhibit 9.

Marketing. The output of the smelters was classified into various grades. Among grades of lead were: Common, 99.73% pure; Desilverized, 99.85% pure; Acid Copper, 99.90% pure; Chemical, 99.90% pure; and Corroding, 99.94% pure. The United States market price usually was quoted for Common lead on the New York market. Higher grades sold at premiums over the base price. The world base price usually was quoted on the London market.

Zinc normally was marketed in six standard grades: Prime Western, 98.32% zinc; Selected, 98.75% zinc; Brass Special, 99% zinc; Intermediate, 99.5% zinc; High Grade, 99.9% zinc, and Special High Grade, 99.99% zinc. East St. Louis traditionally had been the price basing point for zinc in the United States, and the standard quotation had been for Prime Western zinc. Other grades brought premiums ranging from 0.10 cents to 1.75 cents per pound. The two grades with the highest premiums usually were sold on a delivered-price basis rather than f.o.b. East St. Louis. World prices were based on London quotations.

Prices of both lead and zinc were typically very unstable and reacted sharply to short-term market influences. Changes in market prices usually affected mine prices inasmuch as the rate per ton charged by custom smelters to process ore concentrates was more or less fixed. On some drops in market prices, however, even the smelters were forced to reduce their rates. Exhibit 10 gives some price comparisons for various years.

In addition to market grades, lead and zinc metals were distinguished by brand names. The 1958 *Metal Statistics Year Book* listed 32 brands of lead and 60 brands of zinc.

Exhibit 9

LEAD AND ZINC QUOTAS

Lead and Zinc Smelting and Refining: Employment and Wages in the United States

YEAR	Average Number* of All Employees at Primary Smelters Using		Production and Related Workers at Primary Smelters†		Wages Paid	
	Domestic Materials	Imported Materials	Average* Number	Man-Hours Worked	Total	Per Man-Hour
Lead						
1952	3,577	1,180	3,885	NA	NA	NA
1953 (January–October)	3,320	1,255	3,684	NA	NA	NA
1956	3,572	1,281	3,939	8,128,324	$18,007,255	$2.22
1957 (January–October)	3,541	1,281	3,884	6,507,287	14,940,614	2.30
Zinc						
1952	10,365	2,767	11,135	NA	NA	NA
1953 (January–October)	10,165	2,807	11,026	NA	NA	NA
1956	6,358	5,833	10,092	20,674,797	$46,124,658	$2.23
1957 (January–October)	6,271	6,018	10,034	16,602,198	38,363,756	2.31

* Based on the average number on the payroll on the payday nearest the 15th of each month.
† Companies reporting to the Tariff Commission were told to report as production and related workers those workers engaged directly in production and other employees engaged in maintenance, repairs, shipping, power plant, and record keeping, and to exclude officers, supervisors above foreman level, salesmen, and technical employees.
NA = not available.

Source: U.S. Tariff Commission, *Lead and Zinc*, Report to the President on Escape-Clause Investigation No. 65, Washington, D.C., April, 1958.

Exhibit 10

LEAD AND ZINC QUOTAS

Average Monthly Lead and Zinc Prices

(In Cents per Pound)

Month	Lead		Zinc	
	New York	London	East St. Louis	London
June, 1948	17.500	NA	12.000	NA
December, 1948	21.500	NA	17.500	NA
June, 1949	12.000	NA	9.548	NA
December, 1949	12.000	NA	9.753	NA
June, 1950	11.808	NA	14.647	NA
December, 1950	17.000	NA	17.500	NA
June, 1951	17.000	NA	17.500	NA
December, 1951	19.000	NA	19.500	NA
June, 1952	15.257	NA	15.740	NA
December, 1952	14.125	NA	12.500	NA
June, 1953	13.413	11.085	11.000	8.856
December, 1953	13.500	11.299	10.000	9.288
June, 1954	14.106	12.182	10.960	9.990
December, 1954	15.000	13.027	11.500	10.340
June, 1955	15.000	12.852	12.232	11.425
December, 1955	15.558	14.168	13.000	12.305
June, 1956	16.000	14.153	13.500	11.751
December, 1956	16.000	14.460	13.500	12.671
June, 1957	14.320	11.461	10.860	9.288
December, 1957	13.000	9.152	10.000	7.849
June, 1958	11.224	9.160	10.000	8.029
September, 1958	10.872	8.815	10.000	8.134
October, 1958	12.642	9.255	10.838	8.806
November, 1958	13.000*	9.196	11.367*	9.422

* The December 30, 1958—January 2, 1959, calendar week average price for lead was 13.000, New York, and for zinc, 11.500, East St. Louis.

Source: U.S. Tariff Commission, *Lead and Zinc,* Report to the President on Escape-Clause Investigation No. 65, Washington, D.C., April, 1958; *E & MJ Metal and Mineral Markets.*

World consumption of lead and zinc, by countries, is given in Exhibits 11 and 12.

Industry Organization. The United States Tariff Commission reported that in 1956 the 10 companies, including their subsidiaries, that were the largest producers of newly mined lead accounted for 81%

Exhibit 11

LEAD AND ZINC QUOTAS

World Consumption of Primary Lead, by Countries

(In Thousands of Short Tons)

Country	Average 1937–38	1948	1950	1952	1954	1955	1956
Australia.................	27.5	42.2	54.9	37.5	53.3	56.5	46.8
North America:							
United States............	475.7	745.2	885.2	781.9	763.5	809.9	742.9
Canada.................	24.7	59.5	54.7	53.4	67.9	69.4	68.0
Mexico.................	...	8.1	10.6	10.9	12.8	19.8	29.6
W. Europe:							
United Kingdom.........	405.4	210.5	183.0	115.8	215.1	237.5	193.0
W. Germany............	265.6*	54.1	110.8	125.8	195.3	220.5	195.9
France.................	106.6	76.0	65.1	108.3	108.7	110.7	125.1
Italy...................	56.4	13.5	48.1	46.8	55.8	62.0	56.2
Belgium................	44.1	45.3	55.6	42.8	49.5	50.3	53.8
All other†.............	110.0	94.4	133.8	106.4	161.6	152.4	166.0
E. Europe and USSR†.....	137.7	121.8	170.5	220.0	280.0	306.7	342.1
Africa†.................	6.6	5.5	10.0	16.5	17.0	20.0	20.0
Central and S. America:							
Argentina‡.............	...	38.0	38.6	30.9	28.7	27.6	22.0
Brazil‡................	...	6.0	21.8	11.0	29.2	15.0	10.9
Rest of world:							
Japan..................	104.9	23.3	27.1	20.9	51.6	48.9	79.1
India..................	8.8	10.1	17.1	5.7	14.7	15.6	20.6
All other†.............	72.2	24.4	35.5	27.0	32.0	37.3	36.1
Total.............	1,846.2	1,577.9	1,922.4	1,761.6	2,136.7	2,260.1	2,208.1

* Includes data for East Germany.
† Partly or completely estimated.
‡ Included in "all other" category in 1937–38.

Source: U.S. Tariff Commission, *Lead and Zinc*, Report to the President on Escape-Clause Investigation No. 65, Washington, D.C., April, 1958.

of the total United States mine output of lead, and the 10 largest zinc producing companies accounted for 74% of total United States mine output of zinc. Seven of the companies in these two groups were the same, and in 1956 these seven accounted for 74% of the lead, 61% of the zinc, and 66% of the combined lead and zinc mined in the United States.

According to the Tariff Commission, concentration of control was even more pronounced in primary smelting and refining of lead and zinc than in the mining and milling of these metals. The 13 primary lead smelters in the United States were controlled by six companies, and five of these six, together with seven other companies, controlled the 18 primary zinc smelters. Most primary smelting companies also

Exhibit 12

LEAD AND ZINC QUOTAS

World Consumption of Primary Zinc, by Countries

(In Thousands of Short Tons)

Country	Average 1937–38	1948	1950	1952	1954	1955	1956
Australia.................	32.8	45.9	52.4	56.8	70.7	81.5	79.3
North America:							
United States...........	513.6	817.7	967.1	852.8	886.3	1,119.8	988.1
Canada................	16.8	46.9	54.4	51.6	45.8	66.7	59.2
Mexico................	...	5.2	10.5	9.9	12.5	13.8	15.6
W. Europe:							
United Kingdom........	244.3	250.0	265.3	191.4	269.2	281.5	253.6
Germany...............	287.2*	55.3	130.1	146.4	232.2	241.6	228.
France................	99.8	101.5	105.2	135.5	138.3	139.4	135.4
Belgium...............	111.3	85.6	66.6	73.3	98.4	99.2	99.3
Italy..................	39.7	23.0	36.9	56.5	58.6	62.1	60.
Other.................	62.0	111.7	109.9	112.7	143.5	134.2	133.7
E. Europe and USSR†.....	159.6	223.0	242.0	315.0	392.5	447.0	495.0
Africa†................	3.9	13.8	16.6	14.0	15.0	20.0	20.0
Central and S. America:...							
Brazil‡................	...	5.5	11.6	10.9	23.3	15.4	21.3
Argentina‡............	...	12.0	13.8	13.8	16.5	22.0	19.8
Rest of world:							
Japan.................	102.3	47.2	56.8	74.7	112.9	119.3	126.3
India.................	25.3	31.7	27.6	26.8	28.6	38.8	39.8
All other.............	31.9	20.0	22.0	23.0	22.5	25.0	25.5
Total.............	1,730.5	1,896.0	2,188.8	2,165.1	2,566.8	2,927.3	2,800.5

* Includes data for East Germany.
† Data partly or completely estimated.
‡ Data included in "all other" category in 1937–38.

Source: U.S. Tariff Commission, *Lead and Zinc*, Report to the President on Escape-Clause Investigation No. 65, Washington, D.C., April, 1958.

controlled mine sources of materials, but many in addition did contract work for other mining companies. In 1956, 10 of the companies that controlled primary lead and zinc smelting and refining in the United States produced 75% of the country's mine output of lead and 72% of the mine output of zinc.

Exhibit 13 presents some selected information about representative companies in the lead and zinc industry. (Some data in Exhibit 13 were taken from Standard and Poor's *Industry Guide* and do not agree fully with the figures just cited from the report of the Tariff Commission.)

Smelters refining secondary sources of lead and zinc also played an important part in the lead and zinc industry. There were 275 secondary lead smelters and 12 secondary zinc smelters in the United States in 1957.

Exhibit 13

LEAD AND ZINC QUOTAS

Selected Facts on Some Representative Companies in the Lead and Zinc Industry

COMPANY	ZINC		LEAD		
	1956 Mine Output*	Smelter Capacity† (12/31/56)	1956 Mine Output*	Smelter Capacity‡ (12/31/56)	Refinery Capacity§ (12/31/56)
American Smelting & Refining Co.	43,534	158,400	16,760	1,092,000‖	476,000
American Metal Co.	......	87,600	......	......	......
American Zinc, Lead Smelting Co.	NA	151,800	......	......	......
Anaconda Co.	46,504	251,500	18,735	300,000	......
Bunker Hill Co.	24,010	57,800	38,641	300,000	......
Combined Metals	7,155	......	4,406	......	......
Day Mines, Inc.	1,441	.....	3,499	......	......
Eagle Picher Co.	67,274	50,000	18,204	......‖	10,000
Matthison & Hegler Zinc Co.	......	72,850	......	......	......
National Zinc Co.	......	41,600	......	......	......
New Jersey Zinc Co.	NA	70,100	......	......	......
Resurection Mining Co.	1,981	......	......	......	......
St. Joseph Lead Co.	61,446	165,000	108,319	......‖	120,000
U.S. Smelting, Refining, & Mining Co.	31,551	......	48,881	250,000	112,000
United Park City Mines Co.	8,041	......	5,921	......	......
U.S. Steel Co.	......	54,750	......	......	......
Total	292,937	1,161,400	263,366	1,942,000‖	718,000
Total U.S. output	542,340		352,826		
% by companies listed	54.01%		74.64%		

* In short tons of recoverable metal.
† Estimated short tons of slab zinc.
‡ Nominal estimates by proprietors. Roasting and smeltering capacity may limit full use of smelter, which may reduce full use of some of the above capacities to 80% of those shown. Smelter rated according to charge which includes ore and flux, but not fuel.
§ Tons of refined lead.
‖ Does not include some capacity for smelting, which is done in refining plant.
Source: Standard and Poor's *Industry Guide* (Nonferrous Metals); and U.S. Tariff Commission, *Lead and Zinc*, Report to the President on Escape-Clause Investigation No. 65, Washington, D.C., April, 1958.

TARIFFS AND OTHER GOVERNMENT MEASURES AFFECTING THE LEAD AND ZINC INDUSTRY

Tariffs on lead and zinc had been in effect in the United States for many years. The 1958 tariff structure was based on the Tariff Act of 1930. Under this act the maximum allowable tariff levy on lead and zinc ore imports was 1.8 cents per pound of metal content. The actual 1930 levy was 1.5 cents per pound of metal content. Tariffs on other unmanufactured lead and zinc products ranged around this rate.

In 1939 for zinc and 1943 for lead the rates of duty had been reduced from the 1930 level, pursuant to trade agreements. During World War II, greatly increased imports of lead and zinc had entered the United States duty free as purchases of the government. Import duties on lead had been suspended completely from June 20, 1948, to June 30, 1949. Between 1949 and 1950 sales fell off, producers' stocks increased, and prices declined, but demand strengthened and prices sharply increased following the start of hostilities in Korea.

On June 6, 1951, the United States again reduced the tariff on both lead and zinc in accordance with the multilateral General Agreement on Tariffs and Trade (GATT). The new rate on lead was 0.75 cents per pound of lead content, and the rate on zinc ores was 0.6 cents per pound of zinc content.

In 1952, the United States government anticipated increasing shortages of lead and zinc, and tariffs on these materials were suspended completely between February 12, 1952, and the summer of that year. The GATT rates were re-established at that time and were still in effect when the president's import quotas were introduced.

In July, 1953, the Senate Finance Committee and the House Ways and Means Committee had passed resolutions requiring the Tariff Commission to investigate the condition of the United States lead and zinc industry. These resolutions were passed in accordance with the Trade Agreements Extension Act of 1951. That act provided that the Tariff Commission, upon the request of the president, upon resolution of either house of Congress, upon resolution of either the Senate Committee on Finance or the House Committee on Ways and Means, upon its own motion, or upon application by any interested party, should promptly conduct an investigation to determine whether any product on which a trade agreement concession had been granted was, as a result, in whole or in part, of the duty or other customs treatment reflecting such concessions, being imported into the United States in such increased quantities, either actual or relative, as to cause or threaten serious injury to the domestic industry producing like or competitive products. The act required that the commission hold a hearing if at any time it found evidence of serious injury or threat of serious injury.

Should the commission find, as a result of its investigation, the existence or threat of serious injury as a result of increased imports due in whole or in part to the customs treatment reflecting the concession, it must, according to the law, recommend to the president, to the extent and for the time necessary to prevent or remedy such injury, the withdrawal or modification of the concession in whole or in part or the establishment of an import quota.

A safeguarding clause, commonly known as the standard escape clause, was included in most of the trade agreements that had been negotiated by the United States under the Trade Agreements Act. The standard escape clause provided in essence that either party to an agreement could withdraw or modify any concession made therein if the article on which the concession was granted entered in such increased quantities as to cause or threaten serious injury to the domestic industry producing like or directly competitive articles. The Trade Agreements Act of 1951 made it mandatory for an escape clause to be included in all trade agreements concluded by the United States thereafter and, as soon as practicable, in all trade agreements then in force.

In 1954 the Tariff Commission reported to the president that its members unanimously recommended that duty concessions on lead and zinc ores be modified for an indefinite period to prevent "serious injury to the domestic industry." The president had not followed this recommendation but, instead, had instituted a stock-piling program which continued for zinc until March, 1958, and for lead until June, 1958. Government data on resource stock pile were not released to the public.

In April, 1958, the Tariff Commission completed another study of the lead and zinc industry and again unanimously found that imports of lead and zinc were such as to cause serious injury to United States producers. The three Republican members of the commission recommended that the tariff rate be raised to the maximum permitted under the Tariff Act of 1930 and that import quotas be imposed for an indefinite time. The three Democratic members recommended duty increase for an indefinite time to the rate originally imposed by the Tariff Act of 1930.

On April 15, 1958, *The New York Times* reported:

Senators from the lead and zinc states—New Mexico, Arizona, Colorado, Idaho, Utah, Montana and to a lesser extent Wyoming—have served notice on the Administration that they will not vote for the reciprocal trade agreements program unless the lead and zinc mines are given relief in one form or another.

This informal "mining bloc," most of whose members have previously favored the reciprocal trade agreements program, is working closely with the Senate "textile bloc" and "oil bloc," both of which also want protection against foreign competition.

On August 22, 1958, the House of Representatives killed a bill previously passed by the Senate requiring price supports for lead and zinc. The votes on this bill in House and Senate, by state and party, are given in Exhibits 14 and 15.

Exhibit 14

LEAD AND ZINC QUOTAS

House Vote on 1958 Metals Subsidy Bill

STATE	VOTING YES OR PAIRED FOR		VOTING NO OR PAIRED AGAINST		NOT VOTING	
	Republican	Democrat	Republican	Democrat	Republican	Democrat
Alabama	.	4	.	5	.	.
Arizona	1	1	.	.	.	.
Arkansas	.	4	.	2	.	.
California	6	11	11	1	.	1
Colorado	2	2	.	.	.	.
Connecticut	1	.	5	.	.	.
Delaware	.	.	.	.	1	.
Florida	.	.	1	7	.	.
Georgia	.	2	.	7	.	1
Idaho	.	1	.	.	1	.
Illinois	2	10	9	1	1	.
Indiana	1	1	7	1	1	.
Iowa	1	1	4	.	2	.
Kansas	4	1	.	.	1	.
Kentucky	.	5	2	1	.	.
Louisiana	.	5	.	1	.	1
Maine	.	1	.	.	2	.
Maryland	.	2	3	2	.	.
Massachusetts	3	.	4	4	.	3
Michigan	2	4	9	2	1	.
Minnesota	1	4	3	1	.	.
Mississippi	.	1	.	5	.	.
Missouri	.	7	1	2	.	1
Montana	.	2	.	.	.	.
Nebraska	2	.	1	.	1	.
Nevada	.	1	.	.	.	.
New Hampshire	1	.	1	.	.	.
New Jersey	5	5	4	.	.	.
New Mexico	.	1	.	.	.	.
New York	3	10	18	5	5	2
North Carolina	.	3	1	6	.	2
North Dakota	2	.	.	.	.	.
Ohio	2	1	9	5	6	.
Oklahoma	1	5	.	.	.	.
Oregon	.	2	1	1	.	.
Pennsylvania	4	11	12	2	1	.
Rhode Island	.	.	.	2	.	.
South Carolina	.	1	.	5	.	.
South Dakota	1	.	.	1	.	.
Tennessee	2	5	.	1	.	1
Texas	.	12	1	5	.	3
Utah	2	.	.	.	.	.
Vermont	.	.	.	.	1	.
Virginia	.	1	2	7	.	.
Washington	3	1	3	.	.	.
West Virginia	.	1	2	3	.	.
Wisconsin	1	.	5	3	.	.
Wyoming	1	.	.	.	.	.
Totals	54	129	119	88	24	15

Exhibit 15

LEAD AND ZINC QUOTAS

Senate Vote on 1958 Metals Subsidy Bill

STATE	VOTING YES OR PAIRED FOR		VOTING NO OR PAIRED AGAINST		NOT VOTING	
	Republican	Democrat	Republican	Democrat	Republican	Democrat
Alabama	.	2	.	.	.	.
Arizona	1	1	.	.	.	.
Arkansas	.	2	.	.	.	.
California	2	.	.	.	.	.
Colorado	1	1	.	.	.	.
Connecticut	.	.	2	.	.	.
Delaware	.	1	1	.	.	.
Florida	.	1	.	.	.	1
Georgia	.	1	.	.	.	1
Idaho	1	1	.	.	.	.
Illinois	1	.	.	1	.	.
Indiana	1	.	1	.	.	.
Iowa	2	.	.	.	.	.
Kansas	2	.	.	.	.	.
Kentucky	2	.	.	.	.	.
Louisiana	.	1	.	1	.	.
Maine	1	.	1	.	.	.
Maryland	2	.	.	.	.	.
Massachusetts	.	1	1	.	.	.
Michigan	1	1	.	.	.	.
Minnesota	1	.	.	.	.	1
Mississippi	.	2	.	.	.	.
Missouri	.	2	.	.	.	.
Montana	.	2	.	.	.	.
Nebraska	2	.	.	.	.	.
Nevada	1	1	.	.	.	.
New Hampshire	.	.	2	.	.	.
New Jersey	2	.	.	.	.	.
New Mexico	.	1	.	.	.	1
New York	2	.	.	.	.	.
North Carolina	.	2	.	.	.	.
North Dakota	2	.	.	.	.	.
Ohio	1	.	.	1	.	.
Oklahoma	.	1	.	.	.	1
Oregon	.	2	.	.	.	.
Pennsylvania	.	1	1	.	.	.
Rhode Island	.	2	.	.	.	.
South Carolina	.	2	.	.	.	.
South Dakota	1	.	.	.	1	.
Tennessee	.	2	.	.	.	.
Texas	.	1	.	.	.	1
Utah	2	.	.	.	.	.
Vermont	1	.	.	.	1	.
Virginia	.	.	.	2	.	.
Washington	.	.	.	.	.	2
West Virginia	2	.	.	.	.	.
Wisconsin	1	1	.	.	.	.
Wyoming	1	1	.	.	.	.
Totals	36	36	9	5	2	8

On September 23, the president imposed the import quota restrictions on lead and zinc. The president said he acted because the Congress failed to pass his proposal for a subsidy plan for the ailing industry. *The New York Times* reported that in the background was strong pressure in favor of the quotas from several Republican senators who were facing tough election fights at that time.

Compensation of Corporation
Officers and Directors

INTRODUCTION

High-salaried executives in many companies are under suspicion by their stockholders for feathering their own nests too liberally.

It's a minor rebellion against the many schemes for extra pay that company officials urge for themselves . . . stock options, big pensions, compensation deferred until after retirement, other forms of incentives. Usually the companies tell stockholders that such schemes are necessary to get and keep top quality executives . . . that it's cheap at the price. But stockholders are starting to wonder whether things have gone too far, whether their own holdings are being diluted, and whether top executives aren't a trifle "grabby". . . at the expense of company AND stockholders.

Bethlehem Steel is fighting a stockholder suit on these grounds. And stockholders are questioning officials of *Gen. Motors, U.S. Steel, Standard Oil of N.J.* Keep your eye on this, for it's likely to spread.[1]

The New York Times in June, 1959, had reported with reference to the stockholders' suit against Bethlehem Steel:

Stockholders of the Bethlehem Steel Corporation at a special meeting in Wilmington, Del., on July 28, will be asked to approve a new incentive plan for the compensation of the company's executive staff.

The immediate effect of the plan, if approved, would be to cut the total compensation for the company's twenty top officers by $1,200,000 during the second half of 1959.

. . . .

The new compensation plan was agreed to by directors of the company as a result of litigation brought about two years ago in the Court of Chancery in Delaware, by minority stockholders who asserted that Bethlehem paid its executives excessive compensation.[2]

In an article in the *Harvard Business Review* of January–February, 1959, Professor Selekman pointed out certain dangers to the business community inherent in the very large remuneration received by some

---

[1] *The Kiplinger Washington Letter,* Saturday, September 5, 1959.

[2] *The New York Times,* June 17, 1959, p. 49.

business executives. These payments, he said, add to the "illusion of omnipotence" and may boomerang in times of business declines. The quotation which follows is from Mr. Selekman's article:

I have mentioned several ways in which business leaders have created—often unwittingly—an illusion of omnipotence. There is still another way that needs to be considered. It is, in fact, so symptomatic of the general problem we are discussing, and poses such an important moral issue, that I shall single it out for special attention.

I refer to the prevailing standards of executive compensation. Given the technical limitations of management under the present state of the art of administration, can the high emoluments now paid to corporate executives be justified? Whether the president of a corporation is entitled, by virtue of profits, total sales, or some other test, to the compensation agreed on between him and the board of directors is not the question. If the man responsible for the creation of wealth for stockholders is worthy of substantial payment in their eyes— if the matter could be considered a private, domestic one within the four walls of the corporation—then any salary might be justified.

But business now operates in a goldfish bowl, and in reality takes on more and more the characteristics of a public trust. The larger the corporation, the more is this the case. Moreover, because of ethical affirmations which businessmen have been articulating in recent years, and because of the pledge to direct business activities toward moral goals, materialistic standards alone can no longer be applied. If they are, and if business exacts remuneration completely out of all scale with that paid to other groups that are concerned with the public good, then management is in a perilous condition of being suspect.

.   .   .   .

. . . compensation of the dimensions now in practice conveys the image of supermen. A man worth $200,000 a year or more must, in the eyes of the man on the street, be a genius who has it in his power to control economic factors so as to avoid recessions, unemployment, and so forth. Accordingly, when things do not go right, when men have to be laid off, put on part time, or told that the wage they ask for is too high, they simply disbelieve what they hear or become cynical.[3]

Mr. William T. Gossett, vice-president and general counsel of the Ford Motor Company, speaking in 1957 of the responsibilities of business corporations, remarked:

If we conclude then that the law is a delayed reflection—so to speak—of social ideas and mores, the effort to safeguard corporate freedom requires constant attention to the whole environment and ideological climate of the enterprise. We are concerned more than ever here with what goes on in the minds

---

[3] Benjamin M. Selekman, "Sin Bravely: The Danger of Perfectionism," *Harvard Business Review*, Graduate School of Business Administration, Harvard University, January–February, 1959 (Vol. 37, No. 1), p. 116.

of people—of some uneasiness that they may feel as a result of the conduct of the corporation.

.   .   .   .

For our purpose, we need only to observe that as a practical matter, Americans do constantly exercise with organized effectiveness what they consider to be their "rights." And among these are their "right" to know the details of the way in which the management of today's corporation conducts its affairs and their "right" to impose corrective measures on policies and actions that they disapprove. The age-old cry that "there ought to be a law" will always be heard in America.[4]

The following statement appeared as part of a full-page advertisement placed by the United Steelworkers of America in various newspapers on August 10, 1959.

How the Chief Executive of One of the Major Steel Companies Benefits Personally, while Steelworkers' Families Suffer the Hardships of a Shutdown

Stock options awarded to themselves at the expense of the stockholders are the means steel executives use to siphon off the great wealth of the Steel Industry for their personal fortunes.

Take the example of Mr. X, an executive of one of the Steel companies. Every time the market price of his company's stock rises just 1 point he becomes richer by another $32,000. In the last few months his company's stock has risen about 15 points which gives him a profit of about $480,000. If this same man exercised all his stock options and sold the stock in his company he would make a gross profit of over $2,500,000 and a Take Home Pay of over $2,000,000 after taxes . . . *for which he risks not one penny.*

This is in addition to his salary, pension, apartments, clubs, airplanes, railroad cars and unlimited expenses he may use for personal luxuries plus any special bonus deals, or post employment benefit he may have. *And 19 of the top 22 Steel Companies* have stock option plans similar to the one above. Little wonder that these executives want to "hold the line" on wages. Their personal profits and stock equities will rise even further.

Their arrogance, greed, and desire for personal gain would make old-time "steel barons" blush with envy.

Steel profits are at an all time high. Executive Stock Options are at an all time high. Executive Salaries are at an all time high. Cost-of-Living is at an all time high.

Yet, Steelworkers regular wages have increased but 1 penny in the last 13 months.[5]

---

[4] "Corporate Citizenship," Reprinted from Volume II, *The John Randolph Tucker Lectures,* 1953–1956 (Lexington, Va.: Washington and Lee University, 1957), p. 185.

[5] Advertisement placed widely in newspapers by United Steelworkers of America.

PART I: SOME LEGAL COMPLAINTS OF THE 1930'S

Complaints as to the level of executive compensation are not new. They reached a high point in the early 1930's when many people felt they had good cause to question the competence of business management.

In an article in the *Harvard Law Review,* March, 1941, Mr. George T. Washington described and documented some of the legal cases of the 1930's involving executive compensation. The information which follows was taken from Mr. Washington's article, either quoted directly or paraphrased.[6]

Until after World War I, earnings of corporate executives were not as a rule conspicuously high. "Taussig and Barker found that in the decade from 1904 to 1914 the largest manufacturing companies, those having capital over $1,500,000, paid average yearly salaries of $9,958 to their ranking executives. The corporate manager, as such, simply had no place in the upper income levels."

However: "By 1928 the executives of some of our largest companies were receiving compensation as high as $1,000,000 or $1,500,000 annually."

Cash bonuses to top executives were a feature of the compensation plans of many companies, and bonus payments typically were not made public. Bethlehem Steel was one such company. "In 1930, litigation over a proposed merger brought to light many facts about the executives' rewards. It appeared, for instance, that bonuses had totaled $36,493,688 since 1911, that the average annual bonus paid Eugene Grace since 1918 was $814,993, and that in 1929 he had received total compensation of $1,635,754."

In 1931 four of Bethlehem's stockholders brought suit seeking a return of bonuses paid and an injunction against further payments. The suit was withdrawn when the company adopted a bonus plan satisfactory to the complaining stockholders.

Distribution of stock and payment of bonuses to executives of the American Tobacco Company were attacked in suits brought by a stockholder in 1931. The plaintiff lost both cases in the Circuit Court of Appeals. However, in a dissenting opinion, one judge stated: ". . . a bonus of $840,000 to an officer when added to a salary of $168,000, . . . is presumptively so much beyond fair compensation for services

---

[6] George T. Washington, "The Corporation Executive's Living Wage," *Harvard Law Review,* Harvard Law Review Association, Vol. LIV, No. 5 (March, 1941), p. 734 ff.

as to make a prima facie showing that the corporation is giving away money, and a by-law which sanctions this is prima facie unreasonable, and hence unlawful."

The cases were appealed to the Supreme Court and finally were terminated by a consent order. The order provided for retention of the bonus system, but restricted the amounts to be paid in the future. It also provided for the return of the officers' allotments under the "employees stock subscription plan."

At about this time a suit was brought against certain directors and officers of the National City Bank, of New York City, and the National City Company, an affiliated investment house, by several stockholders seeking restitution of sums paid to executives. Among other things, it had come to light that Mr. Charles E. Mitchell, the principal executive officer, had received awards under executive compensation plans of $1,156,230 in 1927, $1,417,150 in 1928, and $1,375,535 in 1929. "Apparently, these sums were in addition to a fixed salary."

The trial began on March 22, 1934. Mr. Mitchell took the stand. "The plan," he said, "had a marked effect on the morale of the Bank's organization," adding: "Unless the man of energy and perhaps ability can see within the organization for which he is working a point that he can possibly reach that has great material benefit attached to it, I say unless he can see that, that his work is going to be less effective, that his endeavor is going to be somewhat dulled. . . . That the entire organization was spurred to endeavor by a general knowledge that pervaded the institution that I was receiving a very substantial compensation. . . ."

However, Mr. Mitchell also testified that "neither his fellow officers nor the employees knew the amounts he was receiving, and that the officers were in ignorance of the payments made by the Bank to each other."

This National City Bank case was finally settled by payment by the defendants of costs and restitution to the corporate treasury of $1,200,-000. The decision was based on technical matters of computation of payments and did not disapprove the payment plan in itself.

The resentment felt against business managers during the depression years led in the 1930's to various restrictions and requirements for disclosure. "Mr. Pecora, counsel to the U.S. Senate Committee on Banking and Currency, in conducting his investigations, brought out into daylight the amounts paid to many leading executives during the prosperous years. Congress ordered the Federal Trade Commission to take a census of corporate salaries. In the securities legislation of 1933 and 1934, and the revenue acts of 1934, 1936, and 1938, Congress laid down strict requirements as to the reporting of compensation paid to executives of large companies. Air Mail and ocean mail contracts for a time were denied to companies paying more than $17,500 to their chief executives. Rates of taxation on large incomes were substantially raised, though there was no special discrimination against corporation managers."

PART II: EXECUTIVE COMPENSATION PLANS—THE FORD MOTOR COMPANY

In 1956, the Institute for Business Planning, Inc., published a report called *Executive Pay Plans*. The following material (through page 797) which deals chiefly with the compensation program of the Ford Motor Company is quoted, with permission, directly from that report. (Several footnote comments are included from a memorandum of November 9, 1959, prepared by Mr. Robert A. Taub, supervisor of Supplemental Compensation Section, Ford Motor Company, who kindly reviewed this case while it was in the process of preparation.)

Executive Pay Plans[7]

Today, a new class of "payroll millionaires" is being created. It consists of well over 100,000 Americans who are developing a new kind of estate.

.   .   .   .

The Trend to Multiple Forms of Executive Compensation. A continuing survey of the proxy statements put out by companies listed on the organized stock exchanges shows these companies steadily adding new compensation elements for their executives. Very, very few companies now pay their executives in cash salary only. There are usually at least four—and frequently more—types of compensation. Four elements—cash salary, either an incentive bonus or stock options, pension rights and group insurance—have become almost a minimum.

A sound executive compensation program for a company is increasingly made up of these components:

1. A basic salary rate for the job.
2. An incentive feature, usually a bonus geared to profits, to sales or to some other measure of performance.
3. Deferred or retirement elements—participation in a pension, profit sharing or thrift plan, or a deferred compensation contract with a single executive.
4. Family protection elements—group insurance, death benefits under a deferred pension, profit sharing or thrift plan, or under a deferred compensation contract with the individual executive.

---

[7] William G. Casey (of the New York Bar), *Executive Pay Plans,* Institute for Business Planning, Inc., New York, N.Y., 1956, pp. 1–20.

5. Health elements—insurance covering the payment of hospital, medical and surgical bills, catastrophe insurance, sick pay and disability income, regular medical examinations.
6. Ownership element—stock options or participation in stock purchase plans.
7. Supplementary benefits—scholarship funds for children, company car, expense arrangements which assure that the executive will not be meeting company expenses, vacation facilities, etc.

These compensation elements may be combined. For example, an incentive bonus may be credited during working years but not paid out until retirement. Moreover, all or part of the payout may be in company stock. Thus a single plan will have the elements of incentive, ownership and deferment.[8]

.   .   .   .

What's behind the Trend.   Today's executive is blocked from getting capital for himself and from providing adequate security for his family. High tax rates on current salary and bonus payments make it difficult to keep up the scale of living required by an executive job. Little or nothing is left for savings. Inflation eats up present take-home pay and past savings.

Additional salary is largely consumed in higher taxes. As a result, companies have developed pay plans, which, in effect, accomplish through the company the accumulation of capital which the executive can't accomplish for himself.

Holding Executives.   Some companies have distributors who make more than their president. Many a vice president handles nation-wide responsibilities, with the knowledge that he could net more income and build up more security for his family by taking on a distributorship in Hartford, Connecticut or Topeka, Kansas. For example:

An energetic man sets up a sales agency with $20,000 investment which is good for a net of $50,000 a year. He takes $25,000 a year in salary, which leaves him $18,656 after taxes. The tax on the $25,000 of corporate income, after all deductions, is $7,500. That leaves $17,500 in the corporate treasury. This figure is reduced by 25% capital gain tax, to reflect the fact that a dollar in the corporate treasury isn't worth as much as a dollar in the owner's pocket. After application of all taxes—individual, corporate and capital gain tax—the owner is left with $31,781 for the year.

Suppose he drew $25,000 in salary in an executive position in somebody else's company. He'd have to get an additional $26,000 in investment income to come out as well. To get that from an investment paying 6% would take capital of $435,000. By operating his own small company, our man does as well with a $20,000 investment.

This example was forwarded to us by a correspondent who figures that the owner gets $5,800 [of additional] annual tax free income by charging off auto expenses and depreciation, entertainment, club dues, etc. If we set that much

---

[8] From the Taub memorandum: "a substantial portion of the benefits listed are available to all salaried employees as well as the executive group. In two instances (retirement and profit sharing plans), a broad participation base is required in order to qualify for beneficial tax treatment."

extra value on expense allowances from one's own business, our man would have to invest $750,000 in a 6% investment to match the $20,000 he put into his sales agency.

Don't hold us too strictly on these figures. The broad comparison is very close to reality—and does tell us why so many corporate executives are hunting for low capital enterprises into which they can put some or all of their time and talent.

It also tells us why companies are working so hard on pay plans which will offer enough capital prospects and inflation protection to hold executives against this kind of competition.

Cost of Family Security. The liability of a company to underwrite an executive's take home pay can be reduced if the company can provide adequate family security in a manner which avoids or postpones the impact of the high personal tax rates which hit the executive. Thus, the cost of an executive to the company may be minimized by group insurance protection which is deductible to the company and not taxable to the executive, or by a split-dollar insurance plan which can give the executive protection approximating personally carried insurance for fewer out-of-pocket dollars and also save him income tax on the difference.

Pension plans and deferred pay plans also provide the necessary security standard with a smaller number of dollars. Roughly, we have these measures:

1. Money put into a *qualified pension plan* will provide two thirds more retirement income than the same amount paid as salary and saved in an annuity contract.

2. The same money applied to a *deferred pay contract* within the company will provide ⅓ more retirement take home pay than savings out of current salary.

.   .   .   .

Attracting Executive Talent. It has become very much more difficult to obtain experienced executives who may be required for expansion or replacement purposes. High taxes and pensions have made executive talent very much less fluid and available. An experienced executive who has found his niche in a company in which he has invested a number of years is likely to be reluctant to take the risk of starting all over again in another organization. . . . For example, one company lost its chief executive by death. It was necessary to get a man experienced in the industry. A logical successor was discovered. In negotiating with him, it was discovered that for ten years he had been accumulating benefits under a pension scheme. Now at age 50, he is still 15 years away from retirement benefits of $1,500 per month. But if he leaves the company, he will lose the benefit of $75,000 of cash value which has been accumulated for him under his company's plan.

He would have to receive more than $150,000 in salary before he would have after taxes an equivalent of the amount which had been accumulated for him in a company's pension fund.

.   .   .   .

Cost of Specific Salary and Take Home. Even though the executive keeps less and less of current salary income, the salary is important as a measure of value and prestige for the job. Also executives with family responsibilities must take home definite amounts even when the tax rates go up.

Therefore companies must increasingly think in terms of the salary needed to give an executive a specific take home pay.

The net cost of salary will vary with the tax rate. Here's what the specific take home amounts (for a married executive using the standard deduction) cost a corporation.

Executive Take Home	Salary Required	Cost to Company at 52% Tax Rate
10,000	12,200	5,856
15,000	19,289	9,259
25,000	36,588	17,562
50,000	107,986	51,833
75,000	269,839	129,523
100,000	529,412	254,118

.   .   .   .

THE FORD PACKAGE OF EXECUTIVE COMPENSATION PLANS

"When a new management team under Henry Ford II undertook the reorganization of Ford Motor Company, it found itself short of everything but determination. It faced a post-war market with rundown plants, obsolete products, almost no financial control, an inadequate engineering staff, and just enough cash to meet daily needs." From speech by Ernest R. Breech, Chairman of the Board of Ford Motor Company, at the 25th National Business Conference of the Harvard Business School Association.

The measure of Ford Motor Company's recovery in the last 10 years is highlighted by two significant figures—$8,100,000 net loss in 1946 . . . $437,000,-000 net profit (after taxes) in 1955, the highest in the 53-year history of the company. To effect this dramatic and phenomenal comeback, President Henry Ford II, in 1946, had to recruit a brand new Executive Management Team.

To attract the executive talent that it needed, to hold on to them, and to stimulate them to supreme efforts in getting the company back on the track of economic recovery, Ford offered its new Executive Management Team the following package of compensation rewards.

.   .   .   .

Ford's Contract with Breech. Ford's chief executive and next in command to President Henry Ford II—Ernest R. Breech—was employed in 1946 on a year-to-year basis. He was then about 49 years old. The contract calls for a basic salary of $150,000 a year, in addition to bonuses or other compensation that the company may award. The contract further provides:

1. If Mr. Breech's employment is terminated before he reaches age 65 for any reason other than retirement, he (or his designee if he should die) is to get $50,000 a year until he reaches age 65 and $25,000 a year for the next 10 years. These payments are all conditioned on his refraining from "certain acts of competition as defined in the contract."

2. If Mr. Breech remains with the company until age 60 (February 24, 1957), he may retire or be retired by the company at any time. In either event, he is to get $25,000 a year for the rest of his life.

Mr. Breech's present base salary is $185,000 a year.

Under the Supplemental Compensation Plan in effect for 1954, a total of $239,500 was awarded to Mr. Breech as additional compensation, of which $136,500 was paid to him in 1955 and the balance of $103,500 is to be paid to him in January 1956 (if earned out), or added to his "contingent termination credits."[9] To date, Mr. Breech has a total of $925,000 in accumulated contingent termination credits. These credits will be paid to him in five equal installments after he leaves the company, if he "earns them out" by refraining from certain acts of competition with the company and by making himself available to consult with the company. If he dies, his estate gets the payments. Nor is this all!

Under the Stock Option Plan in effect in 1953, Mr. Breech was granted options for 90,000 shares of the new Ford Common Stock at $21 per share. On the basis of the $64.50 price at which the Ford Stock was sold to the public, Mr. Breech has a potential profit of $3,915,000 [before taxes] on the shares optioned to him.

As a ground floor participant in the Dearborn "deal" which Ford engineered for six of its key executives, Mr. Breech was given a 22.4% low-cost stock interest in Dearborn Motors Corporation. The details of the Dearborn transaction are spelled out below. What is noteworthy is that this Dearborn deal has enabled Mr. Breech to build up a capital fund in the neighborhood of $4,000,000 and probably more, upon which he will have to pay only a maximum 25% capital gains tax, or just an estate tax (but no income tax), if he holds on to the Dearborn stock until death.

Supplemental Compensation Plan. As the keystone of the reorganized management program, Mr. Breech stated, "we set up an incentive system based on supplemental compensation, and we made it clear that rewards would be commensurate with performance."

In essence, the Supplemental Compensation Plan provides for a sharing of company's profits with executives and salaried employees who contribute to the company's success, according to a predetermined formula, with a deferred payout in four (4) annual installments.

As revised in the 1955 Plan, the profit-sharing formula sets higher profit goals before the executives can get any share thereof in the form of supplemental compensation. There are two aspects to the formula:

1. In the first place, there is a "floor" set on profits, so that if the company's profits in any year sink below the "floor" level, no part of the company's profits is set aside for distribution to the executives. Thus, under the 1955 Plan, the executives do not get any supplemental compensation [from current earnings], if the company's consolidated net income (after taxes), in any year, falls *below* 6% of the capital employed in the business. (Under the Old Plan, the "floor" limitation was 5%.)

2. Only when the company's profits get above the 6% "floor" limitation do the executives come in for a share thereof. That share is determined by a special

---

[9] From the Taub memorandum: "Mr. Breech's 1954 award of supplemental compensation was $272,000; $136,000 paid in 1955, $103,500 paid in 1956, and $32,500 added to contingent termination credits."

formula which is designed to first provide a fair return to stockholders on their investment as well as an accumulation of profits for the company's future expansion and capital needs. Under the 1955 Plan, the company is committed to set aside each year in a Supplemental Compensation Reserve 6% (as compared with 7% under the Old Plan) of part of the company's annual net profits, computed as follows:

a) Consolidated Net Income of the company (*before* deducting U.S. income and excess profits taxes, provision for supplemental compensation, and interest on long-term debt)..XXXX

b) Less 10% of capital employed in the business which is defined in the Plan to include total capital and debt with certain adjustments. (Under the Old Plan, 8% was deducted).. **X**

c) Balance of profits on which Supplemental Compensation is calculated......... **XXX**

Individual awards of supplemental compensation to executives and other salaried employees participating in the Plan are determined each year by special committees designated by the Board.[10] Unawarded amounts in any year are carried forward in the Reserve and are available for award in future years.

The Supplemental Compensation awards are payable in four (4) equal annual installments. Thus, payment of the 1956 awards will be spread over the years 1957, 1958, 1959 and 1960. Payments of the three installments after the first will be made only if the employee "earns them out" by continuing in the employment of the company (or upon termination of such employment for reasons other than death), by refraining from certain acts of competition with the company, and by making himself available for consultative services. These "earning out" conditions are designed to foreclose any attempt to tax the employee on the deferred installments of supplemental compensation, in the year that the award was made, under the doctrine of constructive receipt.

Stock Option Plans. Under the Stock Option Plan introduced by Ford in 1953, 107 key employees, collectively, stand to make a total profit of close to $94,000,000 on the basis of the 15-to-1 reclassification of the old Ford Class A Common Stock and the $64.50 market price at which the new Ford Common Stock, as reclassified, was sold to the public.

These 107 key employees were given options in 1953 to purchase Ford Common Stock at the equivalent of $21 per share for the new, reclassified shares. They already own 647,100 of the new shares through exercise of their options in 1955, and since they also have unexercised options to buy at the same price an additional 1,513,500 shares in the next three years, this gives them a total of 2,160,600 shares subject to present and future stock ownership. Assuming that the Ford stock maintains the $64.50 price at which it was issued to the public, there is a spread of $43.50 on each of the optioned shares. On the total of 2,160,600 shares allocated to the 107 key employees, they thus have a potential gain of $93,986,100.

The top Ford executives have potential gains on the shares optioned to them running into millions of dollars. Mr. Breech has a potential gain of $3,915,000

---

[10] From the Taub memorandum: "Members of the committees determining the awards were not themselves eligible for such awards."

on the 90,000 shares allotted to him. Messrs. Crusoe, Gossett and Harder have gains of $3,262,500 each on the 75,000 shares allotted to each of them. Messrs. Bugas, Davis, Duffy and Yntema have gains of $2,610,000 each on the 60,000 shares allotted to each of them.

In fact, Financial Vice President Yntema has already converted part of his potential gain into cash. On August 31, 1955, he sold back to Ford Motor Company 1,000 shares of the Old Class A Common Stock (equivalent to 15,000 shares of the new, reclassified Common) at a price of $902.50 per share for the Old Common (equivalent to $60⅙ per share for the New Common), for which he received a total of $902,500. Since the shares cost him $315,000 his realized gain amounted to $587,500. And he only has to pay a long-term capital gain tax at a minimum rate of 25% on this gain, which would amount to $146,875. This transaction alone has enhanced Mr. Yntema's personal fortune and estate to the extent of $440,625, and he still can look forward to a potential gain of $1,957,500 on the remaining 45,000 new shares optioned to him, as yet unsold.

Both the original Stock Option Plan adopted in 1953 as well as the new Stock Option Plan put into effect in 1956 were set up as an incentive to encourage stock ownership by certain key officers and other permanent employees of the company, to provide them with a proprietary interest in the company's success, and to induce them to remain in the employ of the company. The options granted are designed to qualify as restricted stock options under the provisions of the Internal Revenue Code.

Under the 1953 Plan, the option price was fixed at $315 per share for the Old Class A Common (equivalent to $21 per share for the new, reclassified Common). The price represented the market value of the stock on January 30, 1953 (the date when the first options were granted), as established by the higher of two independent appraisals. The options are exercisable in four (4) installments: 30% in 1955, 25% in 1956, 25% in 1957, and 20% in 1958. All unexercised option rights expire in 1963. Payment for the optioned shares may be made in installments.

Under the new 1956 Plan, up to 900,000 shares of the new common stock may be granted to officers or other salaried employees at any time prior to January 5, 1961. The Board of Directors has already authorized the granting of options for 446,250 such shares at $64.50 per share (the price at which the shares were offered and sold to the public). Any additional shares optioned later on will be priced at the fair market value of such shares as of the date when the option is granted. No individual may be granted an option for more than 90,000 shares, including the shares optioned to him under the old 1953 Plan. Each option may be exercised over a period of eight years, beginning with the third year after the year in which it is granted. All unexercised options terminate 10 years from the date on which the option is granted. Payments for the shares purchased may be made in installments.

The stock option agreements under both the 1953 and 1956 Plans provide that all rights to purchase shares cease to accrue upon the death or termination of employment of the optionee and that any accrual rights not then exercised must be exercised within a limited period of time. As consideration for each option granted, the employee agrees to remain in the employ of the company for a period of two years from the date on which the option is granted.

Since the options granted qualify as restricted stock options and the option price is fixed at fair market value as of the date of grant, each executive or employee receiving such option is not subject to any tax upon receipt or exercise of the option. Furthermore, upon sale or disposal of the optioned stock, the entire gain realized thereon will be taxable at the maximum 25% tax rate applicable to long-term capital gains.

The Dearborn Deal. The Dearborn "deal" is a spectacular example of the aggressive and challenging methods employed by Ford to attract, hold and incentivate the new Executive Management Team that it needed to start the company back on its uphill road of recovery. To give the members of the new Management Team additional straight salaries and bonuses was not enough. Since they were already in high income positions, any additional cash compensation paid to them would be subject to top-bracket tax rates, and the tax collector would get the greater part of it. What the executives needed was not additional heavily taxed remuneration but attractive capital building opportunities, which would permit them to build up a sizeable personal estate, without tax, for themselves and their families, or to cash in on the enhanced capital values at favorable capital gain tax rates. Here's how Ford provided this capital-building opportunity for its top executives.

Ford set up a subsidiary—Dearborn Motors Corporation—to handle the distribution, sale and financing of Ford tractors, farm implements and related parts and accessories. As a new enterprise, the Dearborn stock necessarily had a low, speculative value at the beginning. However, its future growth value had a tremendously high potential because of the large volume of business that Ford could direct its way.

Ford gave 6 of its key executives, collectively, a 67% stock interest in the Dearborn venture. Mr. Breech got a 22.4% interest; Mr. Davis, a 13.4% interest; Mr. Harder, a 11.2% interest; and Messrs. Bugas, Crusoe and Gossett, a 6.7% interest each.

On July 31, 1953, Ford purchased substantially all of Dearborn's assets (other than cash and assets of Dearborn's subsidiary engaged in the financing business) for a total consideration of $16.8 million, of which $13.8 million was paid in cash and $3 million in Dearborn liabilities assumed by Ford, which can also be considered as the equivalent of cash. This establishes a *minimum* cash value of $15.69 a share for the Dearborn stock, over and above the cash and other assets retained by Dearborn, which were not transferred to Ford; Dearborn has not been liquidated. Its subsidiary, Dearborn Motors Credit Corporation, has continued to handle a substantial part of the business of financing the purchase of Ford tractors and farm implements, at wholesale and retail.

Here's how the Dearborn deal has paid off the six top Ford executives: Collectively, their 67% stock interest in Dearborn is worth at least $11.3 million (based on the minimum cash value of $15.69 a share that Ford paid for the Dearborn assets) and, in all likelihood, it is worth considerably more. Mr. Breech's stock interest in Dearborn today represents a built up capital value of at least $3.8 million; Mr. Davis, $2.3 million; Mr. Harder, $1.9 million; and

Messrs. Bugas, Crusoe and Gossett have each built up for themselves and their families a capital fund of at least $1.1 million.[11] If they sell their Dearborn stock, or Dearborn is eventually liquidated, they will only have to pay a 25% capital gains tax on the profit realized. If they hold on to the stock until death, an estate tax will be due on their holdings but the income tax will be entirely avoided.

Savings and Stock Investment Plan. For junior executives and other salaried employees, Ford has instituted a Savings and Stock Investment Program, which is expected to become effective early in 1956, subject to Treasury and Labor Department rulings.

Under the Plan, the 47,000 salaried employees of Ford will be permitted to contribute up to 10% of base salary, subject to maximum individual contributions of $2,000 per year. The company will contribute 50% of the employee's contribution. Participation by employees granted stock options is limited by special rules.[12]

Provision is made for progressive vesting on the part of the participating employees in the company contributions. Vesting starts at the beginning of the third year and becomes 100% vested at the end of the fifth year following the year of contribution.

All contributions are to be held by a Trustee, who will invest the company contributions entirely in Ford common stock. The employees' contributions will be invested 50% in Ford common stock and 50% in U.S. bonds. However, under certain conditions, employees may elect to have all their contributions invested in Ford common stock.

The Plan has a unique guaranty provision. Ford guarantees to each employee the return of an amount equal to the employee's contributions plus interest for a period of five years after the year in which such contribution is made. This guaranty applies only if the employee's contribution is invested half in Ford stock and half in U.S. bonds. If the employee's contribution is invested solely in Ford stock, the guaranty is limited to the amount that the company would be required to pay, if the employee's contribution had been invested 50% in Ford stock and 50% in U.S. bonds.

On the basis of the current salaried payroll, it is estimated that if all eligible employees participate to the maximum extent permissible under the Plan, the company's annual contributions will be in the neighborhood of $14,000,000.

A tax-exempt Savings Plan such as Ford's confers important tax advantages on the participating employees. The employee does not have to pay any current

---

[11] From the Taub memorandum: "The computation of a value per share of $15.69 is approximately correct as a measure of Ford's cost in buying Dearborn Motors; however, it is not correct to use this value as the amount paid to shareholders. The amount paid to shareholders was equal to total consideration ($16.8 million) less assumed liabilities ($3 million), or $13.56 per share. As a result, the worth of the stock interest of the six named Ford executives is overstated by about $1.5 million in total and in amounts ranging from $.5 million to $.2 million for the named individuals."

[12] From the Taub memorandum: "Since this article was written, the Savings and Stock Investment Plan has been changed to remove the $2,000 limit on contributions and action has been taken to permit stock optionees (except those who were members of the Board of Directors at the time that the savings plan was adopted) to participate. This plan was never intended to be limited to 'junior' executives."

income tax on the contributions made on his behalf by the company, nor on the dividend and interest income accumulated by the Trust, exempt from tax, for his account. These benefits become taxable to the employee only when actually received by him or made available to him. If Ford stock is distributed to the employee under the Plan after it has appreciated in value, he may not have to pay any tax on the rise in value until he has sold or disposed of the stock. And, under certain conditions, he may get the benefit of the favorable tax rate applicable to long-term capital gains.[13]

Exhibits 1 through 4 provide further information about the Ford Motor Company and payments under its executive compensation plans.

---

[13] This concludes the quotation from Casey, *Executive Pay Plans, op. cit.*

Exhibit 1

COMPENSATION OF CORPORATION OFFICERS AND DIRECTORS

Ford Motor Company—Stock Options for Directors and Officers

The table below sets forth information with respect to the exercise during the period January 1, 1957, through March 14, 1958, of options to purchase common stock at $21 per share by certain of the officers named in Exhibit 2 under "Remuneration of Directors and Officers" and by all officers and directors as a group. All of such options were granted in 1953 pursuant to the company's 1953 Stock Option Plan, and originally provided for the purchase of shares of old Class A common stock of the company at $315 per share, which represented the higher of two appraisals of the fair market value of such shares made by two independent appraisers as of January 30, 1953, the date on which the first of such options were granted. In the reclassification of the capital stock of the company in January, 1956, each of such shares of old Class A common stock was changed and reclassified into 15 shares of common stock and, in accordance with the plan, the option price adjusted to $21 per share.

NAME OF INDIVIDUAL OR IDENTITY OF GROUP	DATE OR PERIOD OF PURCHASE	NUMBER OF SHARES PURCHASED	MARKET PRICE OF COMMON STOCK ON NEW YORK STOCK EXCHANGE AT DATE OR PERIOD OF PURCHASE	
			Low	High
Ernest R. Breech..........	Jan. 30, 1957	22,500	$55.75	$56.875
John S. Bugas............	Jan. 30, 1957	15,000	55.75	56.875
Lewis D. Crusoe..........	Feb. 4, 1957	18,750	57.125	57.75
Irving A. Duffy...........	Jan. 30, 1957	15,000	55.75	56.875
William T. Gossett.......	Jan. 31, 1957	18,750	56.875	57.50
Delmar S. Harder.........	Mar. 8, 1957	18,750	56.75	57.25
	Jan. 30, 1958	15,000	40.75	40.875
Robert S. McNamara......	Jan. 30, 1957	7,500	55.75	56.875
	Jan. 30, 1958	6,000	40.75	40.875
Theodore O. Yntema......	Jan. 30, 1957	9,000	55.75	56.875
Directors and officers as a group (including those named above)...	Jan. 1–Mar. 31, 1957	195,750	54.125	59.625
	Apr. 1–June 30, 1957	1,125	54.125	58.50
	July 1–Sept. 30, 1957	....	49.875	58.625
	Oct. 1–Dec. 31, 1957	....	35.875	50.50
	Jan. 1–Mar. 14, 1958	51,600	37.375	41.625

No option to purchase securities was granted or extended by the company during the period covered by the above table. [On October 8, 1958, options were granted for 265,500 shares of common at $47 7/16 per share. As of December 31, 1958, options were outstanding for 121,252 shares of stock under the 1953 Plan, at $21 per share; under the 1955 Plan (with option prices of $47 7/16, $58 1/8, and $66 per share, depending on date of award), there were options outstanding for 756,750 shares. Annual report 1958.]

Source: Notice of annual meeting of stockholders, May 22, 1958.

Exhibit 2

COMPENSATION OF CORPORATION OFFICERS AND DIRECTORS

Ford Motor Company

Information is set forth in the first three columns below with respect to the remuneration for 1957 (consisting of salaries, fees, and supplemental compensation) of each director whose direct aggregate remuneration on an accrual basis exceeded $30,000 (including the three highest paid officers of the company) and all directors and officers as a group. Certain related information is set forth in the last three columns.

Names and Capacities in Which Remuneration Was Received*	Salaries and Fees for 1957†	Supplemental Compensation Awarded for 1957, Payable in Four Annual Installments If Earned Out‡	Net Compensation Received in 1957, after Deduction of Estimated Personal Income Taxes§	Estimated Annual Retirement Benefits Beginning at Age 65 If Employed until Then‖	Total Estimated Contributions by Employees toward Retirement Benefits‖
Ernest R. Breech,¶ chairman of the board of directors	$ 185,000	$ 185,000	$89,365	$ 418	$ ......
John S. Bugas, vice-president of industrial relations and group vice-president	115,000	120,000	71,378	49,668	116,973
Lewis D. Crusoe, executive vice-president of car and truck Divisions; director	66,242	......	74,540	297‖	......
Irving A. Duffy, group vice-president	115,000	100,000	71,791	546	......
Benson Ford, vice-president and chairman of the dealer policy board	120,000	100,000	71,928	74,935	177,208
Henry Ford II, president	185,000	185,000	89,365	1,134	......
William C. Ford, vice-president of product planning and styling	65,625	70,000	53,534	48,581	117,834
William T. Gossett, vice-president and general counsel	125,000	145,000	78,315	41,105	97,767
Delmar S. Harder, executive vice-president of basic manufacturing divisions	150,000	165,000	83,565	16,618	35,417
Robert S. McNamara, group vice-president	97,500	150,000	69,453	56,096	135,452
Theodore O. Yntema, vice-president of finance	115,000	120,000	71,928	29,163	69,727
Directors and officers as a group (including those named above)	2,853,610	2,676,000			

* Where the title of an officer was changed during 1957, the table shows the latest title during that year. Lewis D. Crusoe retired from the position of executive vice-president of Car and Truck Divisions in May, 1957.
† Directors' fees paid (in Canadian currency) by Ford Motor Company of Canada, Limited, to Ernest R. Breech ($1,000), John S. Bugas ($250), Henry Ford II ($1,000), and Delmar S. Harder ($750) are not included.

‡ One-fourth of the supplemental compensation in this column was paid in March, 1958. One-fourth is payable on January 10 in each of the years 1959, 1960, and 1961, provided such installments are earned out by fulfilling the conditions set fourth in the Supplemental Compensation Plan of the company. Under a former Supplemental Compensation Plan of the company, which was terminated in 1955 except as to awards already made, certain amounts were withheld, in the company's interest, from supplemental compensation awards to certain officers and employees for the years 1947 to 1954, inclusive. Under the plan, these amounts are payable as "contingent termination credits" in five equal annual installments to the recipients after the termination of their employment, if they earn them out by fulfilling certain conditions as set forth in such plan. The amounts of the annual installments so payable after termination of employment with respect to contingent termination credits accumulated for all years prior to 1955 are as follows: Ernest R. Breech, $185,000; John S. Bugas, $95,000; Lewis D. Crusoe, $144,500; Irving A. Duffy, $85,000; Benson Ford, $96,000; Henry Ford II, $185,000; William C. Ford, $28,500; William T. Gossett, $125,000; Delmar S. Harder, $150,000; Robert S. McNamara, $24,500; Theodore O. Yntema, $90,500; and directors and officers as a group, $1,613,500.

§ Since personal income taxes generally are computed upon a cash receipts basis, the figures in this column include, in addition to salary, supplemental compensation actually received from the company during 1957 pursuant to awards for prior years, but do not include any part of any supplemental compensation awarded for 1957. Estimated federal income taxes have been computed at 1957 rates upon the assumption that the taxpayer is married and files a joint return, without giving effect to dependency exemptions, allowable deductions or any income other than such remuneration.

|| The amounts listed for each individual, other than Lewis D. Crusoe, are based on the assumption that he will remain in the employ of the company until normal retirement (age 65), that the company's General Retirement Plan will continue in its present form, and that his salary will continue at the present level. Ernest R. Breech, Lewis D. Crusoe, Irving A. Duffy, and Henry Ford II, have elected not to participate in the contributory portion of the Retirement Plan. The amounts listed for the other individuals are based on the assumption that they will continue to make contributions under the plan until normal retirement. Contributions by employees under the plan are at the rate of 5% of base salary in excess of $300 per month, provided that the contributions shall not exceed $416.67 in any month. The company pays the balance of the cost of the contributory portion, and the entire cost of the noncontributory portion, of the plan. Lewis D. Crusoe retired during 1957 and will be entitled to an annual noncontributory benefit of $297 beginning at age 65.

¶ The company has a contract with Ernest R. Breech (effective July 1, 1946) under which he is employed on a year-to-year basis. The contract calls for a basic miniumm compensation of $150,000 per year in addition to such bonus or other payment as the company may award. The contract further provides that (a) if his employment is terminated prior to his attainment of age 65 (February 24, 1962) for any reason other than retirement, the company will make payment to him (or his designee if he should die) of $50,000 per year until the 65th anniversary of his birth and thereafter $25,000 per year until the 10th anniversary of such termination, all provided that he refrains from certain acts of competition as defined in the contract, and (b) by virtue of having remained with the company until age 60, he may now retire, or be retired by the company, at any time, in which event he will receive from the company $25,000 per year for the remainder of his life.

Source: Notice of annual meeting of stockholders, May 22, 1958.

Exhibit 3

COMPENSATION OF CORPORATION OFFICERS AND DIRECTORS

Ford Motor Company and Consolidated Subsidiaries—
Net Sales and Net Income

Year	Net Sales	Net Income
1946	$ 894,500,000	$ (8,100,000 loss)
1947	1,501,700,000	62,700,000
1953	4,211,300,000	165,800,000
1954	4,062,300,000	227,800,000
1955	5,594,000,000	437,000,000
1956	4,647,000,000	236,600,000
1957	5,771,300,000	282,800,000
1958	4,130,300,000	95,700,000

Source: Annual reports.

Exhibit 4

COMPENSATION OF CORPORATION OFFICERS AND DIRECTORS

Ford Motor Company Directors as of March 1, 1958, and Shares
of Ford Stock Held

Name	Position	Shares Held*
Harold Boeschenstein	Director	500 common
Ernest R. Breech	Director and officer	61,000 common
John S. Bugas	Director and officer	42,625 common
Paul C. Cabot	Director	1,000 common
Lewis D. Crusoe	Director (retired officer)	50,000 common
Donald K. David	Director	500 common
Irving A. Duffy	Director and officer	37,700 common
Benson Ford	Director and officer	981,891 class B†
Henry Ford II	Director and officer	909,470 class B† / 72,250 common
William C. Ford	Director and officer	979,453 class B†
William T. Gossett	Director and officer	42,800 common
Delmar S. Harder	Director and officer	74,100 common
Robert S. McNamara	Director and officer	24,250 common
Sidney Weinberg	Director	1,500 common
Theodore O. Yntema	Director and officer	24,750 common

* Shares of Ford Motor Company only; certain directors held stock also in Ford foreign subsidiaries. Total shares of Ford Motor Company common stock outstanding December 31, 1958, numbered 54,761,843.
† All shares of class B stock (nonvoting) were held by members of the Ford family.
Source: Notice of annual meeting of stockholders, May 22, 1958.

PART III: SELECTED DATA FOR GENERAL MOTORS CORPORATION, CHRYSLER CORPORATION, AND AMERICAN MOTORS CORPORATION

In the notice of the annual meeting of stockholders of General Motors Corporation, May 23, 1958, the company's bonus plan and the stock option plan adopted in 1957 were described as follows:

At the 1957 annual meeting the stockholders approved the adoption of an incentive program consisting of the long-established General Motors Bonus Plan, with certain modifications, and a new General Motors Stock Option Plan. Participation of employees, including directors and officers, in this incentive program with respect to the year 1957 is described below.

Bonus Plan. For the year 1957, the Bonus and Salary Committee of the Corporation determined that the minimum salary rate for bonus eligibility for employees in the United States should be $685 a month. As determined by the Bonus and Salary Committee, bonus awards related to 1957 were granted to 13,260 employees, including directors and officers, of the Corporation and its subsidiaries, including a few special awards made to employees receiving less than the eligible salary rate. These awards, including those to directors and officers, aggregated $72,656,159 and were comprised of 904,014 shares of General Motors $1⅔ par value common stock and $35,501,183 in cash.

The bonus shown in the preceding table [see Exhibit 6] is payable in five equal annual installments. Each installment of awards to executives who have not been granted stock options is payable partly in cash and partly in common stock of General Motors Corporation, with the cash and stock portions of the individual awards varying with the sizes of the awards. The stock was valued for award purposes at $41.10 per share. This award value represents the average value, as determined by the independent public accountants in accordance with the provisions of the Bonus Plan, at which all unawarded common stock in the special treasury stock account designated for purposes of the Bonus Plan and the Stock Option Plan was carried at December 30, 1957. The first installment of bonus awards related to 1957 was delivered on March 25, 1958, on which date the closing sales price of common stock of General Motors Corporation on the New York Stock Exchange was $35.50 per share. The remaining four installments of all such bonus awards will be delivered in January 1959, 1960, 1961, and 1962 if earned out in accordance with the provisions of the Bonus Plan. Undelivered bonus in stock and in cash will be retained by the Corporation until it is earned out and delivered, the stock to be held in the treasury with no right to vote. On dividend payment dates after March 31, 1958, the Corporation will pay an amount equal to the value of the dividends that would have been paid on such stock had it been delivered. The Bonus Plan provides that a beneficiary who leaves the service of the Corporation shall, under certain conditions, lose any right to earn out his unearned bonus. No part or amount of bonus delivered to such directors and officers during 1957 under award related to years prior thereto is included in the above tabulation [Exhibit 6] for the year 1957.

Stock Option Plan. Under the General Motors Stock Option Plan options to purchase an aggregate of 369,861 shares of General Motors Corporation $1⅔ par value common stock were granted on March 18, 1958 to 255 executives, including directors and officers, of the corporation and its subsidiaries, as determined by the Bonus and Salary Committee. The option price is $35.25 per share, equal to the average of the highest and lowest sales prices of such common stock on the New York Stock Exchange on the date the options were granted. These options included options to purchase 120,567 shares granted to 32 directors and officers of the corporation, including options to purchase the following shares granted to: Frederic G. Donner, 6,843 shares; Louis C. Goad, 5,928 shares; John F. Gordon, 5,289 shares; Carl H. Kindl, 4,377 shares; Roger M. Kyes, 2,463 shares; Cyrus R. Osborn, 5,109 shares; George Russell,

Exhibit 5

COMPENSATION OF CORPORATION OFFICERS
AND DIRECTORS

*General Motors Corporation and Consolidated
Subsidiaries—Net Sales and Net Income*

Year	Net Sales	Net Income*
1946	$ 1,962,502,000	87,526,000
1947	3,815,159,000	287,991,000
1953	10,027,985,000	598,119,000
1954	9,823,526,000	805,974,000
1955	12,443,277,000	1,189,477,000
1956	10,796,443,000	847,396,000
1957	10,989,813,000	843,592,000
1958	9,521,966,000	633,628,000

*After provision for bonus and stock option plans. (Stock option plan adopted in 1957.)

Source: Annual reports.

4,560 shares; Sherrod E. Skinner, 5,289 shares; and Charles G. Stradella, 4,104 shares.

Each option will be exercisable only after the executive has completed 18 months of employment following the date it was granted and will be exercisable thereafter in whole or in part at any time or from time to time prior to its termination. Each option will terminate 10 years after the date it was granted or earlier in the event of the executive's termination of employment. No option is assignable or transferable during the lifetime of the executive. All shares purchased upon the exercise of any option must be paid for in full at the time of purchase.

Under the Stock Option Plan, there was conditionally credited to each of the executives, including directors and officers, granted a stock option in 1958 a Contingent Credit equal to one-third of the amount of his bonus award related to 1957. Such Contingent Credits are in the form of 123,287 shares of General Motors Corporation common stock, this number of shares having been determined by dividing the amount of Contingent Credits, or $5,067,096, by $41.10 which is the value of stock for purposes of bonus awards related to 1957. The bonus awards related to 1957 plus the Contingent Credits of executives granted

Exhibit 6

COMPENSATION OF CORPORATION OFFICERS AND DIRECTORS

General Motors Corporation—Remuneration of Directors and Officers, 1957

Name and Title (a)	Salaries and Fees for 1957 $	Bonus Related to 1957 Payable in Five Annual Installments If Earned Out in Accordance with Bonus Plan		
		Payable in Shares of General Motors $1 ⅔ Par Value Common Stock with an Award Value of $41.10 per Share		Payable in Cash $
		Number of Shares	Award Value $	
Directors granted stock options in 1958 (b):				
Frederic G. Donner (executive vice-president)......................	161,250	....	.....	281,250
Louis C. Goad (executive vice-president)......................	146,100	....	.....	243,750
John F. Gordon (vice-president)......	121,200	....	.....	217,500
Carl H. Kindl (vice-president)........	111,100	....	.....	180,000
Roger M. Kyes (vice-president)......	110,500	....	.....	101,250
Cyrus R. Osborn (vice-president).....	110,900	....	.....	210,000
George Russell (vice-president).......	101,325	....	.....	187,500
Sherrod E. Skinner (vice-president)...	121,100	....	.....	217,500
Charles G. Stradella (president of General Motors Acceptance Corporation).....................	101,350	....	.....	168,750
Other directors:				
Albert Bradley (chairman)...........	120,367	....	.....	......
Harlow H. Curtice (c) (president)....	201,100	1,514	62,225	357,775
Thomas H. Keating (c) (vice-president)...........................	146,200	1,259	51,745	263,255
Charles F. Kettering (research consultant)........................	36,100	....	.....	......
Ivan L. Wiles (vice-president)........	145,900	1,040	42,744	182,256
60 directors and officers as a group (including the 14 directors shown above) (b) (d)...................	4,100,977	6,038	248,162	6,179,338

a) Listed by name is each director whose aggregate compensation from the corporation and its subsidiaries exceeded $30,000; the list includes the three highest paid officers.

b) The bonus of each executive employed by the corporation, or its subsidiaries who was granted a stock option in 1958, including executives who are directors and officers of the corporation, is payable wholly in cash. The aggregate amount of bonus awarded to such executives was equal to 75% of the amount of bonus which, in the opinion of the bonus and salary committee, would have been awarded to them if they had not been granted stock options.

c) Harlow H. Curtice and Thomas H. Keating were not eligible to participate in the stock option plan in 1958, pursuant to the policy of the bonus and salary committee that options should not be granted in a given year to executives who on March 31 of such year are within 18 months of their automatic retirement dates.

d) Under a contract, the details of which were reported in the proxy statement for the annual meeting of stockholders in 1956, Harley J. Earl. vice-president in charge of styling staff, will receive a salary at the rate of $130,000 a year until his retirement on December 1, 1958 (or earlier retirement with the consent of the corporation) and, following retirement, will receive "post-retirement" payments of $50,000 a year for five years and of $75,000 a year for an additional 10 years. In case his death occurs after retirement, any unpaid "post-retirement" payments will be paid to his legal representatives. Mr. Earl has agreed that after retirement he will be available to the corporation for certain consultative services and will not engage in competitive activities. Payments under the contract will be in addition to any bonus, pension, or other benefits to which Mr. Earl may become entitled under any employee benefit plan.

Source: Notice of annual meeting of stockholders, May 23, 1958.

stock options in 1958, both of which are charged to the reserve maintained for the purposes of the Bonus Plan and the Stock Option Plan, are equivalent in the aggregate to the amount that, in the opinion of the Bonus and Salary Committee, would have been awarded as bonus to such executives if they had not been granted such stock options. Each option is for three times the number of shares in the executive's Contingent Credit. The shares of common stock in the Contingent Credits of the 32 directors and officers granted stock options were 40,189, including the following shares in the Contingent Credits of: Frederic G. Donner, 2,281 shares; Louis C. Goad, 1,976 shares; John F. Gordon, 1,763 shares; Carl H. Kindl, 1,459 shares; Roger M. Kyes, 821 shares; Cyrus R. Osborn, 1,703 shares; George Russell, 1,520 shares; Sherrod E. Skinner, 1,763 shares; and Charles G. Stradella, 1,368 shares.

Upon the exercise of an option in whole or in part the related Contingent Credit will be reduced in the same proportion as the option is exercised, with the amount of such reduction being credited to income of the corporation. Upon the termination of an option which has not been exercised in full, the shares of stock corresponding to the balance of the related Contingent Credit will be delivered to the executive in five equal annual installments provided that certain conditions prescribed in the Stock Option Plan are satisfied. On dividend payment dates after March 31, 1958, the corporation will pay each executive, with respect to any undelivered shares of stock in his Contingent Credit, an amount equal to the value of the dividends which the executive would have received thereon if such stock had been delivered.[14]

Exhibit 6 shows salaries paid and bonuses awarded in 1957 to directors and officers of General Motors.

General Motors also had a contributory and a noncontributory retirement plan. Under the noncontributory plan, retirement benefits

Exhibit 7

COMPENSATION OF CORPORATION OFFICERS
AND DIRECTORS

*Chrysler Corporation and Consolidated Subsidiaries—
Net Sales and Net Income*

Year	Net Sales	Net Income
1946	$ 870,000,000	$ 26,889,000
1947	1,567,933,000	89,187,000
1953	3,347,864,000	74,788,000
1954	2,071,598,000	18,517,000
1955	3,466,222,000	100,063,000
1956	2,676,334,000	19,953,000
1957	3,564,983,000	119,952,000
1958	2,165,382,000	(33,825,000 loss)

Source: Annual reports.

[14] Notice of annual meeting of stockholders, May 23, 1958.

varied with salaries received and years worked. Executives, for example, with average annual salaries of $150,000 during the 10 years preceding retirement would receive on retirement should they have worked 30 years for the company $25,000 annually. An employee whose average salary had been $10,000 would receive $1,800 annually on retirement after 30 years of service. Benefits under this plan for persons with monthly salaries of more than $375 were conditional upon their participation in the company's contributory retirement program.

Exhibit 8

COMPENSATION OF CORPORATION OFFICERS
AND DIRECTORS

*Chrysler Corporation—Remuneration of the Four
Highest Paid Officers, 1957*

Officer	Salary	Additional Compensation*
L. L. Colbert, president...............	$250,900	$238,000
E. C. Row, vice-president............	130,600	153,400
James Zeder, vice-president...........	135,350	47,600
W. C. Newberg, vice-president........	110,450	124,300

* Awards under incentive compensation plan, payable in five equal annual installments if earned out.

Source: *Business Week*, McGraw-Hill Publishing Co., Inc., May 24, 1958, p. 87.

Exhibit 9

COMPENSATION OF CORPORATION OFFICERS
AND DIRECTORS

*American Motors Corporation and Consolidated
Subsidiaries*—
Net Sales and Net Income*

Year	Net Sales	Net Income
1955..................	$441,100,000	$ (6,900,000 loss)
1956..................	408,400,000	(19,700,000 loss)
1957..................	366,392,000	(11,833,000 loss)
1958..................	470,349,000	26,085,134

* Nash-Kelvinator and Hudson Motor merged in May, 1954, to form American Motors Corporation.

Source: Annual reports.

Exhibit 10

COMPENSATION OF CORPORATION OFFICERS AND DIRECTORS

American Motors Corporation—Remuneration of the Three Highest Paid Officers, 1957

Officer	Position	Aggregate Remuneration*	Estimated Annual Benefits upon Retirement
George W. Romney	Chairman of the board, president, general manager and director........	$101,446	$14,040
Roy D. Chapin, Jr.	Executive vice-president and general manager of Automotive Division, and director...............	66,057	14,040
Bernard A. Chapman	Executive vice-president and general manager of Appliance Division, and director....................	67,884	14,040
All directors and officers as a group..		$924,228	

* There was in effect during fiscal 1957 a plan authorizing the provisional accrual of an executive bonus plan based on operating improvements. The amount accrued for the benefit of the 275 officers and employees participating in the plan was $759,784, being equivalent to approximately 3¾% of the reduction in net operating loss in 1957 as contrasted with 1956. Since the bonus fund "can be paid only out of 50% of the operating profit earned in any year or years in the period ending September 30, 1961, no payment has been made as yet." *Directors* were not eligible under the plan.

Source: Notice of annual meeting of stockholders, February 5, 1958.

PART IV: ADDITIONAL INFORMATION ON COMPENSATION OF EXECUTIVES IN BUSINESS, GOVERNMENT, AND OTHER OCCUPATIONS

Exhibit 11

COMPENSATION OF CORPORATION OFFICERS AND DIRECTORS

Selected Incomes before and after Federal Taxes— Gross Income Required to Provide Specified Amounts of Net Income

Gross Income	Federal Income and Social Security Taxes*	Net Income
$ 10,000.....................	$ 1,397	$ 8,603
15,000.....................	2,504	12,496
25,000.....................	5,355	19,645
50,000.....................	15,770	34,230
100,000.....................	42,751	57,249
200,000.....................	105,444	94,556
500,000.....................	326,844	173,156

* Federal taxes were computed for a married couple with two children. No allowance was made for other taxes.

Sources: Treasury Department; The Conference Board. From National Industrial Conference Board, Inc., *Compensation of Top Executives*, Conference Board Reports, Studies in Labor Statistics, No. 17, 1956.

Exhibit 12

COMPENSATION OF CORPORATION OFFICERS AND DIRECTORS

Remuneration of the Ten Highest Paid U.S. Business Executives in 1956 and Their Remuneration in 1957

EXECUTIVE*	1956			1957†	
	Salary	Additional Compensation	Total	Salary	Additional Compensation
Eugene G. Grace, chairman, Bethlehem Steel..............	$150,000	$659,011	$809,011	$150,000	$469,036
Harlow H. Curtice, president, General Motors..............	201,100	494,000‡	695,100	201,100	357,775
Arthur B. Homer, president, Bethlehem Steel..............	120,000	549,176	669,176	120,000	503,336
Crawford H. Greenewalt, president, E. I. du Pont................	190,886	410,000	600,886	197,942	123,000§
Frederic G. Donner, executive vice-president, General Motors	157,625	420,000‡	577,625	161,250	281,250
Louis C. Goad, executive vice-president, General Motors.....	146,100	375,000	521,100	146,100	243,750
Robert E. McMath, vice-president, Bethlehem Steel..............	75,000	439,340	514,340	75,000	407,082
J. W. Schwab, president, United Merchant & Manufacturers (textiles)....................	100,300	286,288	386,588	100,320	269,138
Morse G. Dial, president, Union Carbide & Carbon............	300,000	83,386	383,386	300,000	......
Ernest R. Breech, chairman, Ford Motor.....................	185,000	185,000	370,000	185,000	185,000

* *Business Week* listed also 12 other executives with reported total individual compensation in 1956 of more than $300,000. The *Business Week* survey represented a "cross section of larger publicly owned corporations."
† "This year, *Business Week* is not consolidating totals. Supplementary compensation plans vary widely. In some, additional awards are immediate cash payments; others must be earned out over a period of years on a contingent basis; in still others, payment is deferred until retirement. As a result, totals do not always mean the same thing."
‡ In stock.
§ Plus 2,514 "dividend units."
Source: *Business Week*, May 25, 1957, p. 116 ff., and *Business Week*, May 24, 1958, p. 86 ff.

Exhibit 13

COMPENSATION OF CORPORATION OFFICERS AND DIRECTORS

Business Executives Receiving the Highest Remuneration by Specified Industrial Categories Not Represented in Exhibit 12 (1957)

Industry and Executive Position	Salary	Additional Compensation
Agricultural Machinery		
International Harvester, chairman	$203,675	......
Aircraft Manufacturing and Components		
United Aircraft Corp., chairman	196,540	......
Cigarettes		
Liggett & Myers, president	70,000	197,235
Communications		
American Telephone & Telegraph, president	187,850	......
Containers		
American Can Co., president	208,600	......
Distillers		
National Distillers & Chemical Corp., president	203,019	2,341 shares*
Electrical Equipment and Appliance		
General Electric Co., president	264,973	1,863 shares†
Food Products		
General Foods Corp., chairman	130,000	22,000
Mail Order Houses		
Sears, Roebuck & Co., president	133,200	1,400
Nonferrous Metals		
National Lead Co., president	242,500	36,375
Office Machinery and Equipment		
International Business Machines, president	151,260	131,325
Oil Companies		
Standard Oil (N.J.), chairman	250,000	26,854
Paper Products		
International Paper Co., chairman	200,000	......
Radio and Television		
Columbia Broadcasting, chairman	299,807	35,584
Retail Chains		
F. W. Woolworth Co., chairman and president	209,907‡	......
Tire and Rubber Companies		
Goodyear Tire & Rubber, president	187,300	1,166 shares§
Toilet Preparations		
Colgate Palmolive Co., chairman and president	150,000	150,000‖
Transportation		
N.Y. Central R.R., president	132,046¶	......
Utilities		
Commonwealth Edison (Ill.), chairman	120,000	......

* Common stock, under company's extra compensation plan.
† Common stock, valued at 56⅜ a share, payable after retirement.
‡ Includes a share in profits.
§ Valued at $79.50 a share, deferred contingent remuneration set aside for 1957.
‖ Payable in five annual installments if earned out.
¶ Includes first installment of bonus award made January, 1957, payable over five-year period.

Source: *Business Week*, May 24, 1958, p. 86 ff. (In connection with its compensation surveys, *Business Week* pointed out: "The figures are compiled by *Business Week* from individual company statements submitted to the Securities & Exchange Commission. They represent a cross section of larger publicly owned companies, but necessarily do not include all executives at comparable salary levels. Nor do they include individual entrepreneurs, or executives of closely held companies. . . . Amounts given represent only those paid them as executives, and are not intended to indicate any individual's total income.")

Exhibit 14

COMPENSATION OF CORPORATION OFFICERS
AND DIRECTORS

*Distribution of Highest Paid Executives in
644 Manufacturing Companies by Amount
of Total Compensation, 1957**

Total Compensation†	Number of Executives
$200,000 and over	39
175,000–$199,999	21
150,000– 174,999	28
125,000– 149,999	59
100,000– 124,999	106
75,000– 99,999	133
50,000– 74,999	189
30,000– 49,999	62
Under 30,000	7
Total	644

* The 644 manufacturing companies covered in this survey represented 12 manufacturing industries. They constituted more than three-quarters of the 838 companies in these industries with securities listed with the New York Stock Exchange and/or the American Stock Exchange. Of the 644 companies, 175 had annual sales of more than $299 million and 469 had annual sales of less than that amount, 325 having sales in the range of $50 million to $199 million.

† Includes current bonus and incentive awards to be paid either in cash or stock; payments to be deferred until after the employees' retirement are excluded.

Source: National Industrial Conference Board, Inc., *Compensation of Top Executives*, Conference Board Reports, Studies in Personnel Policy, No. 173, 1959.

Exhibit 15

COMPENSATION OF CORPORATION OFFICERS AND DIRECTORS

*Distribution of Second Highest Paid and Third Highest Paid Executives in 644
U.S. Manufacturing Companies by Amount of Total Compensation, 1957**

Total Compensation	Number of Executives	
	Second Highest Paid	Third Highest Paid
$125,000 and over	68	24
100,000–$124,999	31	38
90,000– 99,999	29	19
80,000– 89,999	38	27
70,000– 79,999	62	43
60,000– 69,999	94	63
50,000– 59,999	92	100
40,000– 49,999	101	111
30,000– 39,999	89	133
Under 30,000	40	86
Total	644	644

* See footnotes and source, Exhibit 14.

Exhibit 16

Compensation of Selected U.S. Public Officials, 1958*

Office	Salary	Other Compensation
President of the United States.......	$100,000	$50,000 for expenses of official duties. 40,000 (nontaxable) for travel and official entertainment. 25,000 Annual pension for life; $10,000 for widow.
Vice-president....................	35,000	10,000 for expenses.
Cabinet members.................	25,000	. . . . .
Chief Justice of the United States....	35,500	. . . . .
Associate justices.................	35,000	. . . . .
Senators, United States............	22,500	. . . . .
Representatives, United States......	22,500	. . . . .
Speaker of the House.............	35,000	10,000 for expenses.
State governors (three highest paid):		
New York........................	50,000	. . . . .
California.......................	40,000	. . . . .
Pennsylvania.....................	35,000	. . . . .
Mayor of New York City...........	40,000	. . . . .
Military: General of the Army (5 star)....... Fleet-admiral....................	} 12,261.60	2,052 Quarters allowance if dependents. 574.56 Subsistence allowance. 5,000 (nontaxable) personal money allowance.
Chief of staff, USA................	22,500	Quarters and subsistence allowances as above. 4,000 (nontaxable) personal money allowance.

* All compensation taxable except as indicated.

Source: *The World Almanac and Book of Facts* (Published by the New York World-Telegram and the Sun); *U.S. Army Register,* 1 January 1959, and *Register of Commissioned and Warrant Officers of the U.S. Navy and Marine Corps,* 1 January 1957.

Exhibit 17

U.S. Labor Union Officials—Compensation of the Three Highest Paid and Selected Others, 1956

Union*	Membership	Official	Salary	Other Pay	Years in Office
Railway clerks..............	293,500	George Harrison	$60,000	$4,719	29
Operating engineers.........	200,000	W. E. Maloney	55,000	5,000	17
Teamsters...................	1,231,000	Dave Beck	50,000	9,194	5
Mineworkers................	Not reported	John L. Lewis	50,000	....	37
Steelworkers...............	1,194,000	David McDonald	50,000	....	4
Garment workers............	440,650	David Dubinsky	23,400	....	25
Musicians..................	248,078	James C. Petrillo	23,000	....	17
Auto workers...............	1,239,000	Walter Reuther	22,000	....	11

* Of 146 unions reporting salaries, two-thirds paid their top officials less than $20,000 per year and 50 paid less than $12,000.

Source: *Business Week*, McGraw-Hill Publishing Company, Inc., July 6, 1957, pp. 46-48. From data read into the Congressional Record by Senator Styles Bridges.

Exhibit 18

Presidents of 650 U.S. Universities and Colleges by Salaries Received 1957–58

Salary Range	Number of Presidents
$45,000–$45,999 (highest)...................	1 (nonpublic university)
36,000– 36,999..........................	2 (state universities)
30,000– 35,999..........................	7
25,000– 28,999..........................	19
Less than $25,000*.........................	621

* The median salary of the 650 presidents for whom information was obtained was $12,407; in many instances living quarters were provided.

Source: Higher Education Series Research Report 1958–R1. *Salaries Paid and Salary Practices in Universities, Colleges, and Junior Colleges, 1957–1958*, Research Division, National Education Association of the United States, Washington, D.C., May, 1958, pp. 30, 34.

Exhibit 19

Professional Engineers—Earnings by Grade, 1956*

Grade*	Number Responding	Median	Average Earnings Upper Decile
1............................	30	....	....
2............................	129	$ 5,870	$ 8,510
3............................	652	6,490	8,750
4............................	740	7,530	10,620
5............................	862	8,810	13,230
6............................	570	11,080	20,900
7............................	633	14,140	28,220
8............................	808	20,480	49,450

* Based on a survey of members of the National Society of Professional Engineers. For purposes of the survey, the engineers were classified in eight grades according to the responsibilities of their positions. Those in Grade 8 supervised and directed "with final administrative authority a large engineering or research organization comprising major divisions." Typical titles of men in this grade were "chief engineer; director of research; dean of school of engineering."

Source: National Society of Professional Engineers, *Professional Engineers' Income and Salary Survey 1956*, p. 18.